Anglo-Norman Castles

Anglo-Norman Castles

EDITED BY
Robert Liddiard

THE BOYDELL PRESS

First published 2003
The Boydell Press, Woodbridge

ISBN 0 85115 904 4

The Boydell Press is an imprint of Boydell & Brewer Ltd
PO Box 9, Woodbridge, Suffolk IP12 3DF, UK
and of Boydell & Brewer Inc.
PO Box 41026, Rochester, NY 14604–4126, USA
website: www.boydell.co.uk

A catalogue record for this book is available
from the British Library

Library of Congress Cataloging-in-Publication Data
Anglo-Norman castles / edited by Robert Liddiard
p. cm.
Includes bibliographical references and index.
ISBN 0–85115–904–4 (alk. paper)
1. Castles – Great Britain. 2. Great Britain – Social life and customs – 1066–1485. 3. Great Britain – History – Norman period, 1066–1154. I. Liddiard, Robert.
GT3550 A55 2002
728.8'1'0941 – dc21 2002014688

This publication is printed on acid-free paper

Printed in Great Britain by
St Edmundsbury Press Ltd, Bury St Edmunds, Suffolk

Contents

List of illustrations

Acknowledgements

The original source details for the articles in this volume are listed below, alphabetically by author. The editor and the publishers are grateful to all authors, institutions and journals for permission to reprint the materials for which they hold copyright. Every effort has been made to trace the copyright holders; we apologise for any omission in this regard, and will be pleased to add any necessary acknowledgement in subsequent editions.

J. Blair, 'Hall and Chamber: English Domestic Planning 1000–1250', *Manorial Domestic Buildings in England and Northern France*, ed. G. Meirion-Jones and M. Jones, Society of Antiquaries Occasional Papers 15 (London, 1993), pp. 1–21. By permission of the Society of Antiquaries of London.

R. A. Brown, 'Royal Castle Building in England 1154–1216', *English Historical Review* lxx (1955), pp. 353–98. By permission of Oxford University Press.

L. Butler, 'The Origins of the Honour of Richmond and its Castles', *Château-Gaillard* xvi (1992), pp. 69–80.

M. Chibnall, 'Orderic Vitalis on Castles', *Studies in Medieval History Presented to R. Allen Brown*, ed. C. Harper-Bill, C. J. Holdsworth and J. L. Nelson (Woodbridge, 1989), pp. 43–56.

C. Coulson, 'The Castles of the Anarchy', © Charles Coulson 1994. Reprinted from *The Anarchy of King Stephen's Reign*, edited by E. King (Oxford, 1994), pp. 67–92. By permission of Oxford University Press.

C. Coulson, 'Fortress Policy in Capetian Tradition and Angevin Practice: Aspects of the Conquest of Normandy by Philip II', *Anglo-Norman Studies* vi (1983), pp. 13–38.

C. Coulson, 'The Impact of Bouvines upon the Fortress Policy of Philip Augustus', *Studies in Medieval History Presented to R. Allen Brown*, ed. C. Harper-Bill, C. J. Holdsworth, and J. L. Nelson (Woodbridge, 1989), pp. 71–80.

P. Dixon and P. Marshall, 'The Great Tower at Hedingham Castle: A Reassessment', *Fortress* xviii (1993), pp. 16–23.

R. Eales, 'Castles and Politics in England, 1215–1224', *Thirteenth Century England* ii (Woodbridge, 1989), pp. 23–42.

R. Eales, 'Royal Power and Castles in Norman England', *Medieval Knighthood* iii, ed. C. Harper-Bill and R. Harvey (Woodbridge, 1990), pp. 49–78.

T. A. Heslop, 'Orford Castle: Nostalgia and Sophisticated Living', *Architectural History* xxxiv (1991), pp. 36–58. By permission of the Society of Architectural Historians.

R. Higham, 'Timber Castles: A Reassessment', *Fortress* i (1989), pp. 50–60.

J. R. Kenyon, 'Fluctuating Frontiers: Normanno-Welsh Castle Warfare *c.*1075 to 1240', *Château-Gaillard* xvii (1996), pp. 119–26.

T. McNeill, 'Hibernia Pactata et Castellata', *Château-Gaillard* xiv (1990), pp. 261–75.

S. Painter, 'Castle-Guard', *American Historical Review* xl (1934–5), pp. 450–9.

D. Renn (with an appendix by D. Parsons), 'Burhgeat and Gonfanon: Two Sidelights from the Bayeux Tapestry', *Anglo-Norman Studies* xvi (1994), pp. 177–86.

G. S. Simpson and B. Webster, 'Charter Evidence and the Distribution of Mottes in Scotland', *Essays on the Nobility of Medieval Scotland*, ed. K. J. Stringer (Edinburgh, 1985), pp. 1–24. By permission of John Donald Publishing.

F. Suppe, 'Castle Guard and the Castlery of Clun', *Haskins Society Journal* i (1989), pp. 123–34. By permission of Hambledon Press and the Haskins Society.

A. Williams, 'A Bell-House and a Burh-Geat: Lordly Residences in England Before the Conquest', *Medieval Knighthood* iv, ed. C. Harper-Bill and R. Harvey (Woodbridge, 1992), pp. 221–40.

Abbreviations

Anderson, *Early Sources*	*Early Sources of Scottish History 500–1286*, ed. A. O. Anderson, Edinburgh 1922
Anderson, *Scottish Annals*	*Scottish Annals from English Chroniclers 500 to 1286*, ed. A. O. Anderson, London 1908
Ann. Mon.	*Annales Monastici*, ed. H. R. Luard, 5 vols, RS XXXVI, London 1864–69
ANS	*Anglo-Norman Studies*
Antiq. Journ.	*The Antiquaries Journal* (Society of Antiquaries of London)
Archaeol. Cantiana	*Archaeologia Cantiana*
Arch. Journ.	*The Archaeological Journal*
ASC	*Anglo-Saxon Chronicle*, ed. D. Whitelock, D. C. Douglas and S. Tucker, London 1961
BAA	British Archaeological Association
Barrow, *Era*	G. W. S. Barrow, *The Anglo-Norman Era in Scottish History*, Oxford 1980
Barrow, *Kingdom*	G. W. S. Barrow, *The Kingdom of the Scots*, London 1973
Battle	*Proceedings of the Battle Conference* (*Anglo-Norman Studies*)
Book of Fees	*Liber Feodorum. The Book of Fees Commonly Called Testa de Neville*, 3 vols, London 1920–31
BA	British Academy
Brit. Archaeol. Assoc.	British Archaeological Association
Brit. Archaeol. Rep. Brit. Ser.	British Archaeological Reports, British Series
BSAN	*Bulletin de la Société des Antiquaires de Normandie*
Bull of Barnet and District Local Hist. Soc.	*Bulletin of the Barnet and District Local Historical Society*
Cal. Charter Rolls	*Calendar of Charter Rolls*, London 1903 etc.
Cal. Docs France	*Calendar of Documents Preserved in France . . .* i, 918–1216, ed. J. H. Round, HMSO, 1899
Carmen	*The Carmen de Hastingae Proelio of Guy of Amiens*, ed. C. Morton and H. Munz, OMT, 1972
CBA	Council for British Archaeology
CChR	*Calendar of Charter Rolls*, London 1903 etc.
CDS	*Calendar of Documents Relating to Scotland*, ed. J. Bain, Edinburgh 1881–8

Cowan (Easson)	D. E. Easson, *Medieval Religious Houses: Scotland*, 2nd edn, I. B. Cowan, London 1976
Chron. Maj.	*Matthaei Parisiensis, Monachi Sancti Albani, Chronica Majora*, ed. H. R. Luard, 7 vols, RS LVII 1872–83
Chrons. Stephen, Henry etc.	*Chronicles and Memorials of the Reigns of Stephen, Henry II, and Richard I*, ed. R. Howlett, 4 vols, RS LXXXII, London 1884–90
Coventry	*Memoriale Fratris Walteri de Coventria*, ed. W. Stubbs, 2 vols, RS LVIII, London 1872–3
CPR	*Calendar of Patent Rolls*, London 1901 etc
CR	*Calendar of Close Rolls*, London 1902 etc
Davis, *Stephen*	R. H. C. Davis, *King Stephen 1135–1154*, 3rd edn, London 1990
DBM	*Documents of the Baronial Movement of Reform and Rebellion, 1258–1267*, selected R. F. Treharne, ed. I. J. Sanders, Oxford 1973
Dialogus	*De Necessariis Observantiis Scaccarii Dialogus qui vulgo dictur Dialogus de Scaccario*, ed. C. Johnson, London 1950
Diceto	*Radulphi de Diceto Opera Historica. The Historical Works of Master Ralph de Diceto, Dean of London*, ed. W. Stubbs, 2 vols, RS LXVIII, London 1876
Docts. Illustr. of English History	*Documents Illustrative of English History in the Thirteenth and Fourteenth Centuries*, ed. H. Cole, Record Commission, London 1844
Dryb. Lib	*Liber S. Marie de Dryburgh*, ed. J. Spottiswoode, Edinburgh 1847
Duncan, *Scotland*	A. A. M. Duncan, *Scotland: The Making of the Kingdom*, Edinburgh 1975
EHR	*English Historical Review*
Faroux	*Recueil des acts des ducs de Normandie (911–1066)*, ed. M. Faroux, Mémoires de la Société des Antiquaires de Normandie xxxvi, 1961
FW	*Florentii Wigornensis Monachi Chronicon ex Chronicis*, ed. B. Thorpe, 2 vols, 1848–9
GC	*Gervase of Canterbury: Historical Works*, ed. W. Stubbs, 2 vols, RS LXXIII, 1879–80
GDB	Great Domesday Book
GEC	*Complete Peerage of England, Scotland, Ireland, Great Britain and the United Kingdom, Extant, Extinct or Dormant*, ed. G. E. Cockayne, new edn, V. Gibbs *et al.*, 13 vols in 14, London 1910–59
Gesta	*Gesta Regis Henrici Secundi*, ed. W. Stubbs, 2 vols, RS XLIX, London 1867
Gesta Guillelmi	William of Poitiers, *Gesta Guillelmi . . .*, ed. R. Foreville, Paris 1952

Glasgow Reg.	*Registrum Episcopatus Glasguensis*, ed. C. Inns, Edinburgh 1843
GS	*Gesta Stephani*, ed. K. R. Potter and R. H. C. Davis, OMT, Oxford 1976
Haskins, *Norman Institutions*	C. H. Haskins, *Norman Institutions*, Cambridge, Mass 1925
HH	Henry of Huntingdon, *Historica Anglorum*, ed. T. Arnold, RS LXXIV, London 1870
HMSO	Her Majesty's Stationary Office
Holm Cultram Reg.	*The Records and Register of Holm Cultram*, ed. F. Grainger and W. G. Collingwood, Cumberland and Westmoreland Antiquarian and Archaeological Society Record Series, 1929
Hovedon [*Howden*]	*Chronica Magistri Rogeri de Houedene*, ed. W. Stubbs, 4 vols, RS LI, London 1868–1871
J. Chester Archaeol. Soc.	*Journal of the Chester Archaeological Society*
Journ. BAA	*Journal of the British Archaeological Association*
Journ. British Studies	*Journal of British Studies*
JMH	*Journal of Medieval History*
Kent Archeol. Soc.	*Kent Archaeological Society*
Lawire, *Charters*	*Early Scottish Charters prior to 1153*, ed. A. C. Lawrie, Glasgow 1905
LDB	Little Domesday Book
Lind. Cart.	*Chartulary of the Abbey of Lindores*, ed. J. Dowden, SHS 1903
Mag. Rot. Scacc. Norm.	*Magni Rotuli Scaccariae Normanniae*, ed. T. Stapleton, 2 vols, London 1840–44
Med. Arch.	*Medieval Archaeology*
Melrose Liber	*Liber Sancte Marie de Melros*, ed. C. Inns, Edinburgh 1837
MGH	*Monumenta Germaniae Historica*
MGH SS	*Monumenta Germaniae Historica, Scriptores*
Monasticon	W. Dugdale, *Monasticon Anglicanum*, ed. J. Caley, H. Ellis, and B. Bandinel, 8 vols, London, 1817–30
Moray Reg.	*Registrum Episcopatus Moraviensis*, ed. C. Inns, Edinburgh 1837
NMT	Nelson Medieval Texts
Occ. Paper	Occasional Paper
OMT	Oxford Medieval Texts
Orderic/OV	Orderic Vitalis, *Historia Ecclesiastica*, ed. M. Chibnall, OMT, 1969–80
Paris, CM	*Matthaei Parisiensis, Monachi Sancti Albani, Chronica Majora*, ed. H. R. Luard, 7 vols, RS, LVII, London 1872–83
PBA	*Proceedings of the British Academy*
PR	Pipe Roll (as published by Pipe Roll Society)

Proc.	Proceedings
Proc. Brit. Acad.	*Proceedings of the British Academy*
Proc. Soc. Antiq. London	*Proceedings of the Society of Antiquaries of London*
Proc. Cambridge Antiq. Aoc.	*Proceedings of the Cambridge Antiquarian Association*
Proc. Suffolk. Arch. Inst.	*Proceedings of the Suffolk Institute of Archaeology*
PRO	Public Record Office
PSAS	*Proceedings of the Society of Antiquaries of Scotland*
RBE	*Red Book of the Exchequer*, ed. H. Hall, 3 vols, Record Commission, London 1896
RCHM(E)	Royal Commission on Ancient and Historic Monuments (England)
RCAHMS	Royal Commission on the Ancient and Historical Monuments of Scotland
RCAHMW	Royal Commission on the Ancient and Historic Monuments of Wales
Rec. Com.	Record Commission
Rec. Soc.	Record Society
Red Book of the Exchequer	*Red Book of the Exchequer*, ed. H. Hall, 3 vols, Record Commission, London 1896
Regesta	*Regesta Regum Anglo-Normannorum*, i, ed. H. W. C. Davis, Oxford 1913; ii, ed. C. Johnson, H. A. Cronne, Oxford 1956; iii, ed. H. A. Cronne, R. H. C. Davis, Oxford 1968
Religious Houses	D. Knowles and N. Hadcock, *Medieval Religious Houses: England and Wales*, 2nd edn, London 1971
Renn, *Norman Castles*	D. F. Renn, *Norman Castles in Britain*, 2nd edn, London 1973
RLC	*Rotuli Litterarum Clausarum in Turri Londinensi Asservati*, ed. T. D. Hardy, 2 vols, Record Commission London, 1833–44
RLP	*Rotuli Litterarum Patentium in Turri Londinensi Asservati*, ed. T. D. Hardy, Record Commission, London 1835
Rot. hundredorum.	*Rotuli Hundredorum*, ed. W. Illingworth and J. Caley, 2 vols, Record Commission, London 1812–18
Rot. Prest	*Rotuli de Liberate ac de Misis et Praestits*, ed. T. D. Hardy, Record Commission, London 1844
Rotuli de Liberate etc.	*Rotuli de Liberate ac de Misis et Praestits*, ed. T. D. Hardy, Record Commission, London 1844
Rotuli de oblatis et finibus	*Rotuli de Oblatis et Finibus in Turri Londinensi Asservanti*, ed. T. D. Hardy, Record Commission, London 1835
Round, *Geoffrey*	J. H. Round, *Geoffrey de Mandeville*, London 1892
Roy. Arch. Inst.	Royal Archaeological Institute

Royal Letters	*Royal and Other Historical Letters Illustrative of the Reign of Henry III*, ed. W. W. Shirley, RS, 1862–6
RRAN	*Regesta Regum Anglo-Normannorum*, i, ed. H. W. C. Davis, Oxford 1913; ii, ed. C. Johnson, H. A. Cronne, Oxford 1956; iii, ed. H. A. Cronne, R. H. C. Davis, Oxford 1968
RRS	*Regesta Regum Scottorum*, ed. G. W. S. Barrow *et al.*, i (1153–65), 1960; ii (1165–1214), 1971; vi (1329–71), 1982
RS	Rolls Series
RT	Robert of Torigny, *Chronicle*, in *Chronicles and Memorials of the Reigns of Stephen, Henry II, and Richard I*, ed. R. Howlett, 4 vols, RS LXXXII, London 1884–90
Scottish Arch. Forum	Scottish Archaeological Forum
Ser.	Series
SD	*Symeon of Durham: Historical Works*, ed. T. Arnold, 2 vols, RS, London 1882–5
SHS	Scottish History Society
Soc.	Society
Soc. Antiq. London Res. Rep.	Society of Antiquaries Research Report
SRO	Scottish Record Office
St Andrews Liber	*Liber Cartarum Prioratus Sancti Andree in Scotia*, ed. T. Thomson, Edinburgh 1841
Stenton, *First Century*	Sir Frank Stenton, *The First Century of English Feudalism 1066–1166*, 2nd edn, Oxford 1961
Surrey Archaeol. Soc. Research Vol.	Surrey Archaeological Society Research Volume
Trans.	Transactions
TDGAS	*Transactions of the Dumfriesshire and Galloway Natural History and Antiquarian Society*
TRHS	*Transactions of the Royal Historical Society*
VCH	Victoria County History
WM *HN*	William of Malmesbury. *Historia Novella*, ed. K. R. Potter, NMT 1955
WN	William of Newburgh, *Historia rerum Anglicarum*, in *Chronicles and Memorials of the Reigns of Stephen, Henry II, and Richard I*, ed. R. Howlett, 4 vols, RS, London 1884–90
Yorks. Arch. and Topog. Journ.	*Yorkshire Archaeological and Topographical Association Journal*

Introduction

In the introduction to his 1992 volume *Anglo-Norman Warfare*, Matthew Strickland commented that 'a collection of articles on the organisation and conduct of war in eleventh and twelfth-century England and Normandy needs little justification'.[1] The same can be said of a collection of articles on Anglo-Norman castles. Alongside the great cathedrals, the castles of the eleventh and twelfth centuries are one of the most potent symbols of the Anglo-Norman world to have come down to us. Their remains are an eloquent testimony to the achievements of a particularly ambitious and culturally self-aware warrior aristocracy which dominated Western Europe for nearly two centuries. Since the nineteenth century, historians have chosen to place the castle at the centre of their interpretations of Anglo-Norman society. There is little doubt that this interest simply reflects that of contemporaries. For Orderic Vitalis, castles were a major feature in the English defeat following 1066; for William of Newburgh royal castles were 'the bones of the kingdom'; the great Angevin fortress at Dover was, in the words of Matthew Paris, 'the key of England'. Be they grand projects forced through at breathtaking speed like Richard I's Château-Gaillard, or a modest motte and bailey occupied for only a few generations, the impact of castles was felt throughout all levels of Anglo-Norman society.[2]

The origins of the castle (at least in the form most familiar to us) have been sought in the later ninth and tenth centuries in the disintegration of Carolingian authority in Western Frankia and the corresponding development of specific social ties of lordship and tenure, a process traditionally labelled by historians as the rise of 'feudalism'.[3] The appearance from the early tenth century of the

1 M. Strickland, *Anglo-Norman Warfare* (Woodbridge, 1922), p. ix. It should be stated from the start that the core of articles reprinted here have been taken from a list originally compiled by Dr Matthew Strickland. I would like to thank him for his generosity since the project passed to me and for his courteous advice in the preparation of this volume. Both he and Charles Coulson commented on a draft of this introduction and offered many helpful suggestions. John Kenyon provided bibliographical help at a late stage. Needless to say, all errors of fact, interpretation and editorial practice are entirely my own responsibility. The preparation of this introduction has proved particularly difficult coming as it does after the major historiographical review by Charles Coulson, 'Cultural Realities and Reappraisals in English Castle-Study', *Journal of Medieval History* xxii (1996), pp. 171–207. There is inevitably some overlap of material but an attempt has been made to keep this to a minimum.

2 See recent surveys by T. McNeill, *Castles* (London, 1992); M. W. Thompson, *The Rise of the Castle* (Cambridge, 1991); N. J. G. Pounds, *The Medieval Castle: A Social and Political History* (Cambridge, 1990), also D. J. C. King, *The Castle in England and Wales: an Interpretative History* (London, 1988); C. Platt, *The Castle in Medieval England and Wales* (London, 1982); R. Allen Brown, *English Castles*, 3rd edn (London, 1976).

3 F. L. Ganshof, *Qu'est-ce que la Féodalité?* (Bruxelles, 1944), trans. P. Grierson, *Feudalism* (London, 1952); M. Bloch, *La Société Féodale* (London, 1944), trans. L. A. Manyon, *Feudal Society* (London, 1961); Jean-Pierre Poly and Eric Bournazel, *La Mutation Féodale, Xe–XIIe Siècles* (Paris, 1980), trans. Caroline Higgitt, *The Feudal Transformation* (New York, 1991); but see also C. Coulson, *Castles in Medieval Society* I (Oxford), forthcoming.

fortified residences of individual lords and the emergence from the early eleventh of the fully developed 'great tower' were triumphant expressions of a new social order.[4] In the subsequent two centuries architectural expertise in both secular and ecclesiastical spheres produced in the Anglo-Norman realm a number of buildings that in both size and complexity of design superseded any comparable structure in Western Europe.[5]

Castles were one particular form of noble castellated architecture, a genre that also included monastic buildings, churches, town walls, halls and chamber blocks.[6] Within this broad range of building types it was the particular combination of residence, administrative centre and fortification that set the castle apart (albeit not exclusively) from other dwellings of the Anglo-Norman aristocracy. Traditionally the great masonry castles of the eleventh and twelfth centuries have attracted the most attention from scholars, but the results of excavation at sites such as Hen Domen, Goltho and South Mimms have demonstrated the diversity and complexity of those constructed from earth and timber.[7] Equally, Cathcart King's massively detailed *Castellarium Anglicanum* has made it impossible to ignore the baronial and sub-baronial castles that are in many respects more typical of noble dwellings than their royal counterparts.[8] Yet one theme that was common to structures as varied as the great tower at Loches and those of earth and timber situated at the centre of minor baronies was their association with seigneurial power. Castles were the residences of the *pugnatores* who ruled medieval society and in the splendour of their design they were above all intended to enhance the dignity of aristocracy. Nothing highlights this more than the contemporary term often used for the great tower, *donjon*, deriving from the Latin *dominarium*, equating the noble dwelling with 'lordship'.[9]

The classic conjunction of castle, town and monastery neatly encapsulates the self-expression of those who fought, worked and prayed in the Anglo-Norman world.[10] It was via a network of chiefly urban fortresses that royal, ducal or comital authority in the localities was given tangible focus.[11] The elaborate sophistication of buildings such as the White Tower in London not only conspicuously demonstrated the wealth of the king or duke but their

4 The 'great tower' (of which early examples in north-west France include Mayenne, Doué-la-Fontaine, Langeais and 'fully developed' types at Loches, Montbazon, Ivry-la-Bataille) were innovative in as much as they united in a single structure those elements traditionally found in the Carolingian palace. For earlier examples in the Languedoc: B. Bachrach, 'Early Medieval Fortifications in the "West" of France: A Revised Technical Vocabulary', *Technology and Culture* xvi (1974), pp. 531–69.

5 E. Fernie, *The Architecture of Norman England* (Oxford, 2000), pp. 299–303.

6 For general discussions of architecture in this period see A. Clapham, *Romanesque Architecture in Western Europe* (Oxford, 1936); R. Stalley, *Early Medieval Architecture* (Oxford, 1999) and now Fernie, *Architecture*, above.

7 The most comprehensive review of earth and timber castles is to be found in R. Higham and P. Barker, *Timber Castles* (London, 1992).

8 D. J. C. Cathcart King, *Castellarium Anglicanum* (New York, 1983).

9 Fernie, *Architecture*, p. 52.

10 J. Le-Patourel, *The Norman Empire* (Oxford, 1976), pp. 317–18; M. W. Thompson, 'Associated Monasteries and Castles in the Middle Ages: a Tentative List', *Archaeological Journal* cxliii (1986), pp. 305–21; M. Beresford, *New Towns of the Middle Ages* (London, 1967).

11 H. M. Colvin, R. Allen Brown, H. Colvin and A. J. Taylor, *The History of the King's Works*, *The Middle Ages*, 2 vols. (London, 1963); B. English, 'Towns, Mottes and Ringworks of the Conquest', *The Medieval Military Revolution*, ed. A. Ayton and J. Price (London, 1995), pp. 43–62.

complex iconography was that of a specific architectural vocabulary of power. Colchester was deliberately placed on the site of the former Claudian temple in part to evoke images of legitimate authority, while the architectural embellishment of Norwich carried allusions to the buildings of classical antiquity.[12] It was castles such as these that provided a suitable setting for set piece social occasions such as the royal crown wearing, when the authority usually latent in the building was made real to the political community of the realm. It was their role as repositories for documents and treasure; as gaols; as venues for the shire court; and as centres of shrieval administration that made the custody of royal castles an attractive prize in peace but also ensured they were often the focus of baronial rebellion.[13]

Baronial castles were primarily aristocratic dwellings, with an estate staff usually resident and inhabited by the lord and his mobile household on either a temporary basis or more permanently, depending on circumstance.[14] As feudal *capita* castles were frequently the place where the honorial court, one of the most important tenurial innovations of the Norman Conquest, was held.[15] At those manorial centres where castle-building took place, it was at the residence that dues and renders were owed and accounted for, where legal transactions could take place and where the lord's justice was obtained.[16] If monarchs used their castles as the venue for scenes of regal authority then the baronial castle too played a role in displaying seigneurial power. The aristocrats of the Conquest years signalled their authority by appearing at the castle gate, whereas a later generation seemingly preferred their visitors to negotiate an intimidating processional route before being allowed access to the lordly presence.[17] As a physical expression of lordly rights and jurisdiction it is unsurprising that the castles of the Anglo-Norman aristocracy were a sign of a lord's general position and, *in extremis*, provided ultimate place of refuge in time of war.[18]

The construction of castles was not simply the preserve of the secular nobility. Bishop Gundulf, master of works at the White Tower and later instructed to re-build the castle at Rochester, illustrates the role of ecclesiastics as

12 E. Impey and G. Parnell, *The Tower of London: The Official Illustrated History* (London, 2000); P. J. Drury, 'Aspects of the Origins and Development of Colchester Castle', *Archaeological Journal* cxxxix (1982), pp. 302–419; P. J. Drury *et al.*, 'The Temple of Claudius at Colchester Reconsidered', *Britannia* xv (1984), pp. 7–50; T. A. Heslop, *Norwich Castle Keep: Romanesque Architecture and Social Context* (Norwich, 1994), esp. pp. 33–7.

13 Pounds, *Medieval Castle*, pp. 96–101.

14 F. M. Stenton, *The First Century of English Feudalism* (Oxford, 1954), chapter 6.

15 M. Chibnall, *Anglo-Norman England* (Oxford, 1986), chapter 6.

16 See for example the charter at Castle Acre in Norfolk witnessed '*In baelo ante portam castelli apud Acram*', B.L. MS Harley (Castle Acre cartulary) 2110, f.5v.

17 See Dixon and Marshall, in this volume.

18 For a recent discussion of the relationship between warfare and lordly rights see J. France, *Western Warfare in the Age of the Crusades 1000–1300* (London, 1999). For more general discussions of the castle in war see B. Bachrach, 'Medieval Siege Warfare – a Reconnaissance', *Journal of Military History* lviii (1994), pp. 119–33; J. Bradbury, *The Medieval Siege* (Woodbridge, 1992); I. A. Corfis and M. Wolfe, eds, *The Medieval City Under Siege* (Woodbridge, 1995); S. Morillo, *Warfare Under the Anglo-Norman Kings, 1066–1135* (Woodbridge, 1994); M. Prestwich, *Armies and Warfare in the Middle Ages: the English Experience* (New Haven, 1996).

castle-builders and designers.[19] It was another prelate, Archbishop William of Corbeil, who was responsible for the present *egregia turris* at Rochester and this must be placed alongside other episcopal enterprises such as those of Roger of Salisbury who, 'wishing to be thought of as a great builder', raised castles at Sarum, Devizes and Malmesbury, or Henry of Blois, at Taunton, Farnham, Downton, Merdon, Bishops' Waltham and Wolvesey.[20] The political role of the episcopate ensured that their castles also assumed national significance. King Stephen's arrest of the bishops in 1139 and the seizure of their castles was viewed in both England and Normandy as a major political event of the reign. The twinning of episcopal castles with cathedrals provides a valuable reminder that the architectural distinction between the two was never as clear cut as has been supposed, vividly demonstrated by Bishop Remigius' castellated and machicolated display at Lincoln, which was later incorporated into the cathedral itself.[21] As residences, administrative centres and symbols of authority, the castles of the episcopate performed a similar role to those of their secular counterparts. In terms of their projections of power they provide valuable reminders that the symbolic meaning of crenellation was equally resonant in ecclesiastical as well as secular circles.

The political importance of castles was inseparable from their social and economic aspects. It was often by reference to castle-building that chroniclers marked out the social advancement of particular individuals. It was through the 'well-fortified castle of ashlar blocks' at Montreuil that the royal administrator Richard Basset 'made of show of superiority to all his fellow countrymen'.[22] What impressed contemporaries about such structures was not any intrinsic defensibility, but the magnificence of individual buildings. In the famous description of Arnold II's tower at Ardres by the local priest Lambert, it is the number of rooms and the complexity of the design that drew attention and admiration.[23] The individuality of design revealed by excavation of both earth and timber and masonry castles is explicable in part by the desire to overawe social peers and inferiors. With their towns, markets and fairs castles were often nodal points in the medieval economy and served as centres of aristocratic production and consumption.[24] The parks, lakes, forests and chases that surrounded their walls provided places of recreation and leisure where nobles could take their

[19] M. Ruud, 'Monks in the World: The Case of Gundulf of Rochester', *Anglo-Norman Studies* xi (1988), pp. 245–60.

[20] K. R. Potter (trans.) and E. King (ed.), *William of Malmesbury, Historia Novella* (Oxford, 1998), p. 24; R. A. Stalley, 'A Twelfth Century Patron of Architecture: A Study of Buildings Erected by Roger Bishop of Salisbury', *Journal of the British Archaeological Association* 3rd Series xxxiv (1971), pp. 62–83; J. N. Hare, 'Bishop's Waltham Palace, Hampshire: William of Wykeham, Henry Beaufort and the Transformation of a Medieval Episcopal Palace', *Archaeological Journal* cxlv (1988), pp. 222–54.

[21] D. Stocker and A. Vince, 'The Early Norman Castle at Lincoln and a Re-evaluation of the Original West Tower of Lincoln Cathedral', *Medieval Archaeology* xli (1997), pp. 223–33; R. D. H. Gem, 'Lincoln Minster: ecclesia pulchra, ecclesia fortis', *Medieval Art and Architecture at Lincoln Cathedral* (British Archaeological Association Conference Transactions for 1982), pp. 9–28.

[22] M. Chibnall, ed., *The Ecclesiastical History of Orderic Vitalis*, vi, p. 468.

[23] Brown, *English Castles*, p. 36; Higham and Barker, *Timber Castles*, pp. 115–16.

[24] D. Austin, 'Barnard Castle, Co Durham', *Château-Gaillard* ix–x (1982), pp. 293–300; C. Dyer, *Standards of Living in the Later Middle Ages*, revised edn (1998), Chapter 3. esp. pp. 80–83.

ease, entertain guests, and exercise their passion for hunting.[25] It was no doubt within the bounds of their 'designed landscapes' that social relationships among the aristocracy were forged and reinforced.[26] In the Arthurian literature of Chrétien de Troyes and the great romances of the twelfth century, castles appear precisely in these terms: as magnificent edifices that provide a backdrop to courtly drama and embody the very essence of nobility.[27] It is hardly surprising then that the image of the castle provided a powerful ecclesiastical metaphor. In a sermon of Ailred of Rievaulx it was the image of the castle that represented the hierarchy of virtue with the strongest and finest structure, the *magna turris*, symbolising charity, the highest virtue.[28]

Although castles were emblematic of aristocratic status they often impinged directly on the lives and interests of the artisan classes and peasantry.[29] It was from these social groups that the workers, masons, cutters, carpenters, diggers and labourers who turned the speculative designs into physical reality were recruited or pressed into service. While many must have benefited from the massive building projects of the Anglo-Norman aristocracy there were also those who bore the financial cost or tenurial burden. To judge from the *Anglo-Saxon Chronicle*, the obligation to build and maintain earthworks, *operationes castellorum*, was deeply resented; readily explicable when considered against the estimates of the labour needed to raise earthworks.[30] It was at the castle-gate where estate renders were delivered and where tenants witnessed their lord's *dominatio*. As a visible sign of lordship, castles were differently, but no less, significant to the Anglo-Norman peasantry as to the aristocracy.

Given that castles were so multifarious in form, performed such a variety of functions, and had such a profound effect on Anglo-Norman society, it is perhaps unfortunate that the role of the castle in war has had a disproportionate place in the historiographical literature. For many decades castles were confined to the category 'military architecture', an artificial creation of the nineteenth century that effectively cut the study of castles off from that of churches, cathedrals and more mainstream developments in the study of medieval elite culture. The development of *real* castles (defined as *seriously fortified* buildings) was explained teleologically as an evolutionary struggle between attacker and defender in which the buildings themselves became increasingly militarily

25 For entertainment of guests see S. Landsberg, *The Medieval Garden* (London, 1995), chapter 1.

26 For a review of recent research see C. Taylor, 'Medieval Ornamental Landscapes', *Landscapes* i (2000), pp. 38–55; P. Everson, G. Brown and D. Stocker, 'The Castle Earthworks and Landscape Context', *Ludgershall Castle, Excavations by P. Addyman 1964–72*, ed. P. Ellis (Wiltshire Archaeological and Natural History Society Monograph Series ii 2000), pp. 97–119; R. Liddiard, 'Castle Rising, Norfolk: A Landscape of Lordship?', *Anglo-Norman Studies* xxii (2000), pp. 169–86; J. Cummins, *The Hawk and the Hound. The Art of Medieval Hunting* (London, 1988). For a rare discussion of gender in connection with castles see R. Gilchrist, *Gender and Archaeology: Contesting the Past* (London, 1999), chapter 6.

27 W. Van Emden, 'The Castles in Some Works of Medieval French Literature', *The Medieval Castle: Romance and Reality*, ed. K. Reyerson and F. Powe (Dubuque, 1984), pp. 1–26.

28 Thompson, *Rise*, p. 181.

29 C. Coulson, *Castles in Medieval Society* (Oxford) forthcoming.

30 D. Whitelock, D. Douglas and S. Tucker, eds, *The Anglo-Saxon Chronicle* (London, 1961), pp. 145, 164; Pounds, *Medieval*, pp. 18–19; McNeill, *Castles*, pp. 42, 45.

complex. It was only with the demise of 'feudalism' that real castles went into slow, but inexorable, 'decline'.[31]

The origins of this interpretative framework and the reasons why it proved so tenacious are complex. The *anarchie féodale* school of the nineteenth century ensured that in French historical writing the castle was perhaps always going to become a symbol of the military threat posed to public order by the 'robber baron'.[32] Within the English historical tradition it was J. H. Round and Ella Armitage who, following the *Anglo-Saxon Chronicle*, placed castles firmly as a 'Norman import' and established their role as a tool of English subjugation.[33] For Freeman this too was acceptable since it provided an explanation for the successful Norman settlement and saved the honour of the freeborn Englishman who could not possibly hope to resist in the face of such a foreign innovation.[34] Thus the castle's image as the fortification of a brutal age was set in place and attempts to understand and define its role and function became bound by the straitjacket of military architecture.[35]

The military orthodoxy that developed within castle studies embodied a whole series of tensions and inconsistencies that detailed work on individual buildings, fortress customs, and royal attitude to baronial building has shown to be apparent. The typology of great towers from a square to rounded design, traditionally held to be a tactical response to the danger of mining, is far from agreeing with the known chronology: cylindrical *donjons* and their variants such as those at Houdan and Etampts in France and New Buckenham in England appear in the 1130s and 1140s yet Henry II chose square designs at, among other places, Scarborough, Newcastle and Dover long after this date. The supposed progression of 'military' castles of the Conquest slowly giving way to more 'residential' structures was turned on its head by excavations at Castle Acre that seemed to show the opposite, and the clear defensive weakness of several early 'proto-keeps' is clearly at odds with the military imperative nor-

31 This was the basic assumption behind much of the literature of the late nineteenth and twentieth centuries: G. T. Clark, *Medieval Military Architecture* (London, 1884); E. Armitage, *Early Norman Castles of the British Isles* (London, 1912); A. H. Thompson, *Military Architecture in England during the Middle Ages* (Oxford, 1912); W. H. St J. Hope, 'English Fortresses and Castles of the Tenth and Eleventh Centuries', *Archaeological Journal* xlviii (1903), pp. 72–90; E. D'Auvergne, *The English Castles* (London, 1907); C. Oman, *Castles* (London, 1926); H. Braun, *The English Castle* (London, 1936); S. Toy, *The Castles of Great Britain* (London, 1953); B. St J. O'Neil, *Castles* (London, 1954); S. Toy, *A History of Fortification from 3000 BC to 1700 AD* (London, 1955); R. A. Brown, *English Medieval Castles* (London, 1954); King, *Castle*; R. A. Brown *Castles from the Air* (Cambridge, 1989); for reinterpretations of the later medieval period see P. Dixon and B. Lott, 'The Courtyard and the Tower: Contexts and Symbols in the Development of Late Medieval Great Houses', *Journal of the British Archaeological Association* cxlvi (1993), pp. 93–101; C. Coulson, 'Fourteenth-Century Castles: Apotheosis or Decline?', *Fourteenth Century England* 1, ed. N. Saul (Woodbridge, 2000), pp. 133–51.

32 For the origins of military determinism see M. W. Thompson, 'The Military Interpretation of Castles', *Archaeological Journal* cli (1994), pp. 439–45; C. Coulson, 'Freedom To Crenellate by Licence – an Historiographical Revision', *Nottingham Medieval Studies* xxxviii (1994), pp. 86–137.

33 J. H. Round, 'The Castles of the Conquest', *Archaeologia* lviii (1912), pp. 144–59; E. S. Armitage, *The Early Norman Castles of the British Isles* (London, 1912) and Williams in this volume.

34 E. A. Freeman, *The History of the Norman Conquest of England*, vols 1–6 (London, 1876–1879), especially comments vol. 5, pp. 646–7.

35 For a discussion of how 'military architecture' came to dominate castle studies see J. Goodall, 'When an Englishman's Castle was his House', *Country Life* (April 1998), pp. 68–71.

mally ascribed to the Conquest period.[36] That baronial castles appear to become more 'military' as the twelfth and thirteenth centuries advance sits uneasily with the view that this period witnessed an apogee in the ability of monarchs to restrict and control castle-building.

The last decades of the twentieth century saw a reaction to this military deterministic approach, principally focussed on the later medieval period, but increasingly applied to the eleventh and twelfth centuries.[37] Essentially, the shift has involved a move away from a 'functional' explanation for fortifications to an interpretation based on the 'symbolic' connotations inherent in military architecture. That the Anglo-Norman elite chose to project their power through their residences has always been self-evident; the debate turns on whether the martial style they frequently chose was a response to military necessity or reflected the aesthetic ambition of a warrior aristocracy whose *raison d'être* was inextricably linked with war.

Warfare was so central to notions of aristocratic identity that it permeated every aspect of elite culture.[38] Next to the known ambition and belligerent competitiveness of the Anglo-Norman political elite the architectural vocabulary of many noble dwellings is readily explicable. Within the constraints and opportunities provided by a warrior aristocratic culture the desire to build in a martial fashion is much more likely to be a result of the need to project a suitable image both to rivals and supporters than to be a reaction to military insecurity. Viewing castles as aristocratic residences built in a martial style is to place them back into the dynamic of the aristocratic culture that was responsible for their construction and allows valuable comparisons with churches, cathedrals and monastic buildings.[39]

One of the problems for scholars has been to reconcile the castle's clear residential function with its occasional military significance – a difficulty apparent in long descriptions and qualifications over definitions.[40] In fact there is no tension between interpreting castle architecture in symbolic terms and recognising that, in extreme circumstances, they could become important military buildings. A valuable point that has been made, but perhaps is easily overlooked, is that 'display' is no less 'functional'.[41] Within a society where warfare was pri-

36 J. G. Coad and A. D. F. Streeton, 'Excavations at Castle Acre Castle, Norfolk, 1972–1977', *Archaeological Journal* cxxxix (1982), pp. 138–301; J. G. Coad and A. D. F. Streeton and R. Warmington, 'Excavations at Castle Acre Castle, Norfolk, 1975–1982: The Bridges, Lime Kilns, and Eastern Gatehouse', *Archaeological Journal* cxliv (1987), pp. 256–307; M. W. Thompson, 'Keep or Country House', *Fortress* xii (1992), pp. 13–22; M. W. Thompson, 'A Suggested Dual Origin for Keeps', *Fortress* xv (1992), pp. 3–15.

37 D. Stocker, 'The Shadow of the General's Armchair', *Archaeological Journal* cxlix (1992), pp. 415–420; C. Coulson, 'Structural Symbolism in Medieval Castle Architecture', *Journal of the British Archaeological Association* cxxxii (1979), pp. 73–90; *idem*, 'Hierarchism in Conventual Crenellation: an Essay in the Sociology and Metaphysics of Medieval Fortification', *Medieval Archaeology* xxvi (1982), pp. 69–100.

38 Strickland, *Anglo-Norman Warfare*, pp. ix–xii.

39 J. Goodall, 'The Key to England', *Country Life* 18 (March 1999), pp. 45–47; *idem*, 'In the Powerhouse of Kent', *Country Life* (25 March 1999), pp. 110–13.

40 See Brown, *English Castles*, pp. 14–24; King, *Castle*, pp. 1–2.

41 Coulson, 'Cultural Reappraisals', p. 186 also at p. 173, 'the lordly mansion put out the same message of power, but it was more emphatically military after 1066; fortification was always dual purpose'.

marily a noble activity and was regulated by an aristocratic ethos, what was 'functional' was far removed from modern notions of military utility.[42] The symbolism and vocabulary of architecture are usually indicative of a distinct agenda on the part of its builder. Quite why Roger Bigod re-built Framlingham in a particularly belligerent martial style; why his rival William D'Albini II at Rising chose to imitate the royal castle of Norwich, and why Henry II at Dover chose to build a great tower that echoed those of his grandfather are perhaps more important, and more interesting, questions than whether or not they were ever primarily intended to be defended in war.[43]

Yet this is not to deny that castles were sometimes of crucial importance in the practice of warfare in the Anglo-Norman period.[44] Yet even here, there is a good deal of room for caution. Recent studies have shown that castles were often only of minor military importance, even in frontier areas that were exposed to invasion such as the English/Scottish border.[45] The future priorities for the study of the Anglo-Norman castles' role in war probably lie in reconstructing and analysing the precise political reasons why an individual castle at a particular time became the focus for military operations, an approach fruitfully adopted for the later medieval period.[46] Within the broader context of the political meaning of architecture, more qualitative insights into the nature of Anglo-Norman castles will reveal themselves.[47]

42 To describe medieval warfare as 'aristocratic' is not, of course, to deny the importance of non-noble combatants or non-combatants to the practices of warfare, see Strickland, *War and Chivalry: The Conduct and Perception of Warfare in England and Normandy 1066–1217* (Cambridge, 1996), chapter 10; C. T. Allmand, *The Hundred Years War* (Cambridge, 1989), chapter 3.

43 Of some interest here are current reinterpretations of the great tower at Dover. The strategic location of the site has focussed interest on the military aspects of the castle, yet the potential weaknesses in the design of the great tower have proved problematic, Brown suggesting that it was 'a conventional battleship in an atomic age'. The great tower is currently the subject of a detailed survey by English Heritage that has revealed much new evidence concerning the building's construction. At the Castle Studies Group Conference 'The Origin and Purpose of the Donjon' (Sept. 2001) the results of ongoing work strongly suggested that the great tower was not primarily a defensible building. See *Castle Studies Group Newsletter* 15 (2001–2002), pp. 27–29 and K. Booth and P. Roberts, 'Recording the Keep, Dover Castle', *Château-Gaillard* xix (2000), pp. 21–23; also D. F. Renn, 'The Avranches Traverse at Dover Castle', *Archaeologia Cantiana* lxxxiv (1969), pp. 79–92. At Framlingham, a 'modern' military design did little to prevent the castle being taken during the siege of 1216: D. F. Renn, 'Defending Framlingham Castle', *Proceedings of the Suffolk Institute of Archaeology* xxxiii (1973), pp. 58–67; R. Allen Brown, 'Framlingham Castle and Bigod 1154–1216', *Proceedings of the Suffolk Institute of Archaeology* xxv (1951), pp. 127–48.

44 For a major survey of warfare in the period see M. Strickland, *Warfare and Chivalry.*

45 M. Strickland, 'Securing the North: Invasion and the Strategy of Defence in Twelfth-Century Anglo-Scottish Warfare', *Anglo-Norman Warfare*, ed. M. Strickland (Woodbridge, 1992), pp. 208–29, also Eales, this volume.

46 For the role of castles in the fourteenth century see M. C. Prestwich, 'English Castles in the Reign of Edward II', *Journal of Medieval History* viii (1982), pp. 159–78; also comments by Robert Higham directing attention at the 'level' of violence ever expected to be encountered by builders as a way forward, *Castle Studies Group Newsletter* xii (1998–9), pp. 47–50.

47 Perhaps best illustrated by recent discussions of Richard I's Château-Gaillard. Explaining some alarming military defects becomes unnecessary when it is considered as a visible statement of Angevin intent to reassert lordship over lost territories. The provision for the reception of high-status guests in the *donjon*'s probable throne room underlines its political purpose: the name 'saucy castle' needs little refinement. J. Gillingham, *Richard I* (New Haven and London, 1999), pp. 301–5; D. Pitte, 'Château-Gaillard, dans la Défense de la Normandie Orientale 1196–1204', *Anglo-Norman Studies* xxiv (2002).

At the time of writing castle studies are in a state of flux. An old orthodoxy has been seriously questioned and now is a time of new issues and agendas. 'Peaceable Power' is beginning to replace Norman 'Militarism'.[48] The papers presented here have been chosen partly to reflect this time of change, but also to recognise the importance of certain seminal articles that have defined the study of Anglo-Norman castles and led us to where we are today.[49] All the contributions are, needless to say, of their own time and reflect particular interests and questions. Although the focus is primarily historical rather than archaeological or architectural, an attempt has been made to demonstrate the diversity of approaches to the study of the Anglo-Norman castle. Each piece has a particular contribution to make. The material chosen for inclusion naturally reflects the editor's interests and personal bias. Others would undoubtedly have chosen differently. I am acutely aware that some major aspects of study, such as the depiction of the castle in literature and the landscape context of castles, are not represented here, but these areas are currently the focus of much new research, have still only been examined systematically for the later medieval period, and are therefore outside the specific remit of this volume.[50] Were this project to be undertaken in ten years time the articles for inclusion would probably reflect a whole new set of questions and concerns. This is surely a reflection of an academic subject in very good health.

The origins of the castle in continental Europe have proved a less contentious issue than its development in England.[51] While it now seems clear that both the motte and the great tower were brought to England in 1066, there is still much ambiguity over the precise differences between baronial and sub-baronial aristocratic dwellings in both England and Normandy before 1066.[52] In the debate over origins of castles in Britain, Old English residences have usually figured somewhat tangentially: worthy of study only in so much as they were the precursors to something more important. In the first article presented here, Ann

48 C. Coulson, 'Peaceable Power in Norman Castles', *Anglo-Norman Studies* xxiii (2001), pp. 69–95.

49 For reasons of space it has proved impossible to reproduce the seminal article by J. Yver, 'Les Châteaux-forts en Normandie jusqu'au Milieu de XIIe Siècle', *Bulletin de la Société des Antiquaires de Normandie* liii (1955–6), pp. 28–115.

50 Sandy Heslop and Olga Grlic at the University of East Anglia are currently working on a major project on the depiction of Anglo-Norman castles within Romance literature. For the insights to be gained from analysis of castle landscapes see note 26, above.

51 R. Allen Brown, 'A Historian's Approach to the Origins of the Castle in England', *Archaeological Journal* cxxvi (1969), pp. 131–48; *idem*, 'The Norman Conquest and the Genesis of English Castles', *Château-Gaillard* iii (1969), pp. 1–14; B. K. Davison, 'The Origins of the Castle in England', *Archaeological Journal* cxxiv (1967), pp. 202–11; A. D. Saunders, ed., *Five Castle Excavations: Reports on the Institute's Research Project into the Origins of the Castle in England* (London, 1978).

52 There is particular ambiguity concerning the nature of ringworks, an earthwork form found in both England and Normandy prior to the Conquest. See D. J. C. King and L. Alcock, 'Ringworks of England and Wales', *Château-Gaillard* iii (1969), pp. 90–127; B. K. Davison, 'Early Earthwork Castles: A New Model', *Château-Gaillard* iii (1969), pp. 37–47; for a recent analysis supporting a number of Davison's conclusions see English, 'Towns, Mottes and Ring-works of the Conquest', note 11, above. In the future more useful comparisons may be made with the Scandinavian impact on western European fortifications. See the excellent survey of Continental material in Higham and Barker, *Timber Castles*, chapter 3; also, E. Roesdahl, 'The Danish Geometrical Viking Fortresses and their Context', *Anglo-Norman Studies* ix (1986), pp. 209–26.

Williams examines the nature of seigneurial fortification in Anglo-Saxon England on pre-Conquest terms, without unnecessary reference to the debate over origins. The word frequently used to describe fortifications in pre-Conquest England was *burh*: a term that referred both to the large defensive works raised by Alfred the Great and his successors in their struggle against the Vikings, and the predominately rural residences of the Old English nobility, such as those excavated at Goltho in Lincolnshire and Sulgrave in Northamptonshire.[53] Alfred's works have generally attracted more attention and here Williams offers a more detailed picture of the private aristocratic residences of English lords. Such *burhs* normally consisted of a wooden hall with outbuildings, themselves surrounded by a ditched and fenced enclosure. Some significance seems to have been attached to the entrance (*burhgeat*), which often appears to have taken the form of a tower, and which probably served as a marker of thegnly rank. Such buildings were only one part of a wider manorial complex and were often found at the head of estates and served as the focus for estate dues and renders. Just as much as post-Conquest castles, English thegnly *burhs* functioned as centres of lordship – a fact with considerable implications for the debate over castle origins. This said, contemporaries were convinced that in some respects castles were innovative and Williams concludes that it was the role of the castle as a fortified administrative centre that may have set it apart from the English thegnly *burh*. The distinction between public government and the private jurisdiction of the hall that existed on the eve of the Conquest became blurred after 1066, when Norman lords dispensed public justice at their seigneurial seats, a situation apparently rare in Anglo-Saxon England.

Pursuing the question of continuity over the Conquest years, the possibility that some architectural features of Norman castles may have been influenced by the English *burhgeat* or models of lordly expression is the implication of Derek Renn's article on eleventh-century towers. Renn examines the depiction of the *burhgeat* in the Bayeux Tapestry and relates their large upper openings to throne balconies. Significantly, this *burhgeat* idea may also be found in several early castle gateways such as Exeter and Richmond. The implication of this for the function of these structures is clear: 'such galleries weakened the passive defensive capacity of a gatehouse, and must have been designed for display'. Renn suggests the analogy of the balcony of Buckingham Palace; clearly a long way from Norman lords resisting the active or passive hostility of the native English from fortifications designed to subjugate a native population.[54] The conclusions

53 M. Beresford, 'Goltho Manor, Lincolnshire: the Buildings and their Surrounding Defences, c.850–1150', *Anglo-Norman Studies* iv (1981), pp. 13–36; see however the re-dating of the site, P. Everson, 'What's in a Name? Goltho, "Goltho" and Bullington', *Lincolnshire History and Archaeology* xxiii (1988), pp. 92–99.

54 This idea is often been implicit in the discussion of the Norman settlement, but for explicit equation see King, *Castle*, p. 6: 'Peasants in revolt play an important part in some sorts of history; but in England they were not generally dangerous except at two periods: the years after the Norman Conquest, when the new lords appeared as upstart and tyrant foreigners . . . and their lords found the shelter of a castle opportune' – the other period was after the Peasants' Revolt. The picture of Normans sheltering in their castles occupying their newly won territory in military style is not the situation described in the most recent detailed survey of the years 1066–86: A. Williams, *The English and the Norman Conquest* (Woodbridge, 1995).

of Williams and Renn point up the trend of examining elements of continuity across the Conquest years, rather than seeing the year 1066 as a cataclysmic break with the past. The idea that the upsurge of castle-building following 1066 represented a widespread replacement of existing late Saxon *capita*, akin to the re-building of parish churches, is certainly the implication from topographical evidence, the results of excavation at sites such as Goltho and Sulgrave and analysis of the Norman land settlement.[55] It remains to be seen how widespread and regionally diverse such practices may have been, but the study of castles has a potentially important role in assessing the 'military' character of the Norman settlement.

If historians and archaeologists are beginning to examine how perceptions of power were articulated through castle-building and now place increasing importance on pre-Conquest antecedents for siting and some architectural forms, there is little doubt that the scale of castle building after 1066 was unprecedented and that this had important implications for the relationship between royal power and that of the aristocracy. In his 'Royal Power and Castles in Norman England' Richard Eales revisits several old debates and provides fresh insights into a number of problematic issues surrounding castle-building after the Conquest. Significantly, he outlines an explanatory model for the process of castle construction during the period of Norman settlement. Eales stresses the highly unusual circumstances of the Conquest, resulting in a wave of castle-building that penetrated relatively far down the social scale and endowed relatively large numbers of lords with customary rights in virtue of their fortresses. Ironically, this may have meant that Norman kings had less control over the fortifications of their vassals in England than they had in Normandy. Reviewing the evidence for numbers of castles in the period 1066–1100, he suggests that the demands of the Conquest led to a peak of around 500–600 'active' castle sites around 1100 followed by a decline over the twelfth century. The impetus behind castle construction in the wake of 1066 was the need of greater lords not only to legitimise succession by building but also to provide support for the imposition of castle works by their immediate followers. A secured Norman settlement meant that lords were increasingly less likely to encourage their tenants to raise castles or to demand labour services. Organic social and economic changes would have aided a decline in overall numbers: as families died out or slipped down the social scale this would have led to the abandonment of many sites. It is circumstances such as these that account for many of the undocumented motte and bailey and ringwork castles scattered across the countryside.

Whilst Eales establishes rough estimates of actual numbers of castles in the eleventh and twelfth centuries and provides an explanatory framework for

55 R. Morris, *Churches in the Landscape* (London, 1989); V. Horsman, 'Eynsford Castle: a Reinterpretation of its Early History in the Light of Recent Excavations', *Archaeologia Cantiana* cv (1988), pp. 39–58 and note 52, above. For historical context of the Norman settlement see J. Green, *The Aristocracy of Norman England* (Cambridge, 1997) chapter 2 and Williams, *English*, Chapters 1–2. The tenurial effects of 1066 remain a matter of dispute, R. Fleming, *Kings and Lords in Conquest England* (Cambridge, 1991).

changing numbers, Lawrence Butler, in a case study of the Honour of Richmond, examines the social, geographical and tenurial factors that shaped castle-building at a local level. Analysis of individual tenants and the manorial descents of their holdings reveals detailed information on potential castle-builders that can be related to the observable pattern of sites on the ground. Chronologically, several periods of building across the Honour can be identified: an initial phase where the Norman settlement was secured; a period of consolidation by principal tenants; and a lesser phase associated with the Anarchy and occasional major building projects. Importantly, an investigation of the tenants themselves allows Butler to isolate the level at which castle-building by knightly families became viable. In twelfth-century Yorkshire 2½ knights' fees was the crucial threshold below which building was not seemingly possible. The strength of this type of analysis is its ability to provide a direct historic context for a particular castle that can then be related to wider frameworks of political and social geography. The problem of providing such a context for ostensibly undateable sites is one that is common to all regional studies of Anglo-Norman castle-building.[56] While it is impossible to reach conclusions for all castles within a particular area, analyses such as this can help separate those that are likely to have had a longer life span or a more important social role from those that otherwise have no known history.

In a volume where many of the contributors bemoan the lack of excavation at given sites, Robert Higham summarises the very real contribution made to castle studies from the discipline of archaeology. He concentrates on earth and timber castles, often seen as the poor relation of their masonry counterparts. Higham points out that, far from being ephemeral structures, many had a long life span and also that stone castles frequently retained earth and timber defences well into the later medieval period. If Richard Eales has outlined in the clearest way yet the rapid upsurge in castle-building following 1066, Robert Higham offers a reminder that castles of earth and timber probably constituted the majority of sites during the eleventh and twelfth centuries. This analysis also highlights the fact that for too long castle-studies have suffered from a concentration on stylistic change at a relatively small number of masonry structures. Throughout the Anglo-Norman period and beyond earth and timber castles remained an integral part of the medieval landscape.

In terms of approaches to the medieval castle Higham discusses two major techniques: excavation and field survey. Excavation can recover in fascinating detail the day to day fabric of medieval life at castle sites and reveal the development of buildings and defences.[57] Field survey, both on the ground and from the air, helps to define the characteristics of a site and to relate a castle to its wider hinterland. In addition to advances there are also problems. Field survey often records a site in its final form, leaving the chronological development of complex earthworks uncertain whilst partial excavation will often miss vital evi-

56 Even when excavation is undertaken the problems of dating are considerable, see R. A. Higham, 'Dating in Medieval Archaeology: Problems and Possibilities', *Problems and Case Studies in Archaeological Dating*, ed. B. Orme (Exeter, 1982), pp. 83–107.

57 See also J. R. Kenyon, *Medieval Fortifications* (Leicester, 1990).

dence and total excavation is time-consuming and expensive – and so consequently rare. Nonetheless, the tremendous value of archaeology to castle studies is amply demonstrated by the recently published final report of excavations at Hen Domen, Montgomery.[58] Here the complex development of the site and many phases of re-building are revealed in astonishing detail. When considered in the light of Eales' conclusions on numbers of 'active' sites in the post-Conquest period, Hen Domen reveals the potentially vast amount of information to be gained from excavation.

The benefit of combining archaeological and historical evidence is illustrated by Simpson and Webster's analysis of mottes in Scotland. Scottish mottes show considerable variation in distribution with the majority having no documentary record. The exceptions are those situated along the Tweed valley, that can be identified with named royal sites. Within Annandale and Nithsdale the majority of mottes appear to be the dwellings of individual barons whilst in Galloway there are virtually no documentary references to castles but a large cluster of mottes. The latter is best explained by the settlement of Anglo-Norman families in the area, a policy encouraged by the kings of Scotland in an attempt to bring the district more firmly under their control. This suggests a determined effort on the part of the Scottish royal house to extend their control over this area, a process only obliquely referred to in documents.

This use of the castle has long been seen as one of the principal means by which the Norman Conquest of England and subsequent expansion into Wales and Ireland were achieved.[59] In 'Fluctuating Frontiers' John Kenyon examines the role of the castle in warfare on the English-Welsh border in the eleventh and twelfth centuries. Welsh chronicles provide a wealth of information on the nature of siege warfare in a border area where the likelihood of attack appears to have been substantially greater than elsewhere. It is from here that we gain details of individual sieges and campaigns and valuable insights into the physical realities of storming fortifications in the Anglo-Norman period. Yet even here, the relative ease with which some castles were taken cautions against seeing their role as a tool of conquest too literally. The idea that castles played a key role in subjugating a hostile population has a long history, best exemplified by Gerald of Wales who produced a blue-print of how castles should be used to establish English rule in Ireland and pacify its native inhabitants. In 'Hibernia Pacta et Castellata' Tom McNeill evaluates the extent to which Gerald's commentary on the role of castles reflected the reality of the Norman settlement. Perhaps surprisingly, McNeill finds little evidence that Gerald's analysis found expression in castle-building in twelfth-century Ireland. The purpose of early castles in Ireland was not that of military defence, but rather to provide a suitable setting for newly established lords, an observation applying particularly to the relatively few masonry castles. Concentrations of principally motte and

58 R. Higham and P. Barker, *Hen Domen Mongomery: A Final Report* (Exeter, 2000).

59 For castles built as part of a military strategic network designed to hold territory see J. H. Beeler, *Warfare in England 1066–1189* (New York, 1966), chapter 2; see also B. Bachrach, 'The Angevin Strategy of Castle-Building in the reign of Fulk Nerra, 987–1040', *American Historical Review* lxxxviii (1983), pp. 533–60.

bailey castles are to be found in frontier areas where they were probably intended to prevent or resist external raiding. Gerald's advice that castles should be used to suppress the native population seems to have been ignored. Primary castle-building was a symbol of a triumphant seizure of land and it was only later that external threats necessitated the construction of secondary fortifications on the periphery of established territories.

If there has been much progress on issues such as assessing numbers of castles in the Anglo-Norman period and on the form that these sites took, then the same is true for royal castle-building and the problems surrounding what control existed over baronial fortifications in the eleventh and twelfth centuries.[60] Several of the articles presented here deal with the difficult questions that centre on royal attitudes to baronial castle-building, in particular the supposed prerogative of 'licensing' new fortifications and the right of a feudal superior to temporarily enter the castles of his vassals in time of need or 'rendability'.

In his seminal article 'Royal Castle Building in England 1154–1216', R. Allen Brown examines the extent and nature of castle construction in England under the Angevin kings. By utilizing the records of central government (chiefly the Pipe Rolls) he is able to build up a remarkable picture of royal expenditure on castles over the period. This took the form of a 'large-scale and practically continuous building programme' both of new fortifications and the modification of existing sites. What still resonates from his figures is the sheer cost of castle construction and maintenance during the twelfth century. The thousands of pounds spent on castles such as Dover, Newcastle and Scarborough are testimony to the remarkable importance and significance that rulers attached to their buildings. Unsurprisingly, there is a close relationship between the royal itinerary and the programme of building. The pattern of royal spending was not uniform; rather there were bursts of activity at times of instability and in areas of political disturbance. This strong political dynamic leads to the conclusion that royal castle-building represented the 'latent military power of a strong centralized government'. The statistical data collected by Brown was later to lead him to suggest that there was a distinct 'Angevin castle policy' under which, by a careful strategy of building and forfeiture, the ratio of royal to baronial castles was altered to enhance royal power over that of the aristocracy.[61]

Brown's conclusions stimulated questions concerning the exact mechanisms by which Norman and Angevin rulers had the right to place restrictions on, or simply control, the construction of baronial castles in their territories: a concept with a long pedigree in castle-studies. In the world of 'anarchie féodale' it was seemingly axiomatic that the baronial castle was a threat to public order that could only be curbed by strong monarchic authority.[62] A whole generation of scholars saw in later medieval 'licenses to crenellate' a restrictive system of royal sanctioning of baronial fortresses and applied this retrospectively to the

60 The importance attached to this issue is best exemplified by Stenton who stated that rights over castles 'raise in concrete form the whole question of the relations between the Anglo-Norman baronage and the king': Stenton, *First Century*, p. 197.

61 R. Allen Brown, 'A List of Castles, 1154–1216', *English Historical Review* lxxiv (1959), pp. 249–80.

62 For a major historiographical treatment see Coulson, 'Freedom To Crenellate by Licence', note 32 above.

eleventh and twelfth centuries. Upon this issue hang many other questions, in particular the problem of defining so called 'adulterine' fortifications.[63]

In his 'Castles of the Anarchy' Charles Coulson examines castle-building during the reign of King Stephen, traditionally seen as the period when royal rights over 'licensing' fortifications were usurped, resulting in 'adulterine' castles prejudicial to public order springing up across the kingdom.[64] Coulson presents a subtler picture, distinguishing between those castles already in existence in 1135, those that could have been expected to have been built during the reign, and those that were indeed raised for military purposes during organised campaigning or which impinged upon existing tenurial rights. In contrast to the impression given by (usually pro-Angevin) chroniclers, there were remarkably few of the latter – a finding that questions the extent to which they alone could be seen as instruments of disorder.

Coulson raises serious objections to the traditional interpretation of 'illegal' building during the reign. The equation of *adulterinus* with 'unlicensed' is in itself highly problematic; the term itself is rare and may be due to Abbot Suger or to Orderic Vitalis.[65] The only near-contemporary definition comes from the third issue of Magna Carta (1217), which explicitly refers to fortifications raised during the previous civil war, a description that equates remarkably well with those structures singled out for attention following other periods of general armed hostilities during the eleventh and twelfth centuries. While there is no doubt that evidence such as the Norman *Consuetudines et Justicie* of 1091 and the *Leges Henrici Primi* do appear to detail royal or ducal rights over fortifications, Coulson sees them as more the product of rulers upholding the Carolingian tradition of royal sponsoring of 'public' fortification rather than evidence for licensing.[66] Equally, isolated sources from Stephen's reign that do appear to detail royal 'control' over actual building are interpreted as guarantees of possession sought by the recipient – the natural response of the baronage to the insecurities of the reign. Both Coulson and Eales stress the fact that there is no conclusive evidence for any royal prerogative or defined policy concerning either royal 'licensing' or control over baronial castles prior to 1135, leaving flawed the idea that Stephen presided over a diminution in central control over castle-building.[67] Henry II's campaign of demolition following his accession to

63 King, *Castle*, chapter 3. S. Painter, 'English Castles in the Early Middle Ages: their Number, Location and Legal Position', reprinted in *Feudalism and Liberty*, ed. F. Cazel (Baltimore, 1961), chapter 11; C. W. Hollister, *The Military Organization of Norman England* (Oxford, 1965); J. C. Holt, 'Politics and Property in Early Medieval England', *Past and Present* lvii (1972), pp. 25–27; C. Coulson, 'The Sanctioning of Fortresses in France: "Feudal Anarchy" or Seignorial Amity?', *Nottingham Medieval Studies* xlii (1998), pp. 38–104.

64 H. A. Cronne, *The Reign of Stephen, 1135–1154, Anarchy in England* (London, 1970); J. Bradbury, *Stephen and Mathilda* (Stroud, 1996).

65 See also Coulson, 'Hierarchism', p. 96.

66 C. H. Haskins, *Norman Institutions* (Harvard, 1918), pp. 277–84; trans R. Allen Brown, *The Origins of English Feudalism* (London, 1973), p. 146; L. J. Downer, ed., *Leges Henrici Primi* (Oxford, 1972), pp. 108, 116, 323–24. See also D. Bates, *Normandy before 1066* (Harlow, 1982), pp. 162–63

67 Although it does seem that kings could use the 'illegal' construction of a castle as a pretext for moving against an enemy. One of the charges levelled by Henry I against Robert of Bellême was that he had built a castle without his permission at Bridgenorth: T. Jones, ed., *Brut Y Tywysogyon* (Cardiff, 1952), p. 23.

the throne is best seen as a programme against enemies rather than a reinstatement of a royal policy over licensing of fortifications that dated back to the Norman period. Castle-building during the Anarchy was a symptom of insecurity, rather than the cause.

Nonetheless, there is no mistaking the fact that Angevin kings did show a keen interest in acquiring or regaining custody of castles throughout their realm. Richard Eales in 'Castles and Politics in England, 1215–1224' examines the relationship between castles and political power during the civil war of John's reign and the minority of Henry III. As Brown has shown, King John began his reign in possession of more castles than his potential opponents but this was no guarantee of victory. In reality the situation was far more complex and many castles simply proved to be either a liability or militarily irrelevant to the outcome. Of far greater importance to the survival of royal government over the period 1215-17 was the loyalty of sufficient members of the aristocracy. Successful royal policy turned on the ability to appoint as castellans men who would prove to be loyal servants to the crown but who would also not alienate those in the locality upon whom the king relied for political support. While control over castles did translate into political power through various agencies, this was not simply a matter of straightforward military potential. For a magnate, custody of a royal castle represented security of position, and (particularly when combined with a shievalty) provided a platform for wider participation in politics. This was particularly the case during periods of civil war when royal castellans wielded wide powers over territories centred on their castles. After hostilities had ceased the Crown's ability to place loyal men as castellans around the country was a powerful symbol of royal recovery. When control of major castles was anchored to central government through loyal servants, royal power in the localities became a reality. Conversely, the danger during the minority of Henry III was to allow the alienation of royal offices to men who were outside the control of government. In the case of Ranulf Earl of Chester, it was his concentration of lands and political loyalties that made his possession of individual castles a potential threat.[68] Overall, the events of the early thirteenth century highlight continuity from the Norman period. Royal rights over castles were still evolving, and there is little indication that down to the mid-thirteenth century royal intervention in baronial castles proved a major bone of contention between crown and nobility: rather there is much evidence of co-operation.

On a similar theme, in two closely linked articles Coulson examines how notions of public authority in France affected the royal attitude to nobles' fortifications. The idea that fortifications were public works whose construction was the preserve of royal authority did not substantially survive the disintegration of the Carolingian Empire. In practice, those lords who filled the power vacuum left by the collapse of central authority were able to appropriate rights over fortification for themselves. While the legacy of royal power was bequeathed to Capetian monarchs and may in theory have appeared substantial, in reality they

68 Perhaps the classic case of a disaffected castellan is that of Falkes de Bréauté who 'with foolish bravery and stubborn probity' held Bedford castle against the king for eight weeks: D. A. Carpenter, *The Minority of Henry III* (London, 1990), pp. 360–370.

had lost the ability to regulate building and simply kept up the appearance of regalian 'control' over fortifications. With little to lose, monarchs continued to endorse fortification and claim that all such buildings, no matter how they were held, were public works at the king's disposal. This at least allowed the opportunity to facilitate the exercise of their lordship and improved their chance defending rights or claims in disputes with possible opponents. While sub-Carolingian doctrines over fortifications were an inheritance common to both the Capetians and Angevins, Coulson argues that it was Philip Augustus who broke with the tradition of claiming complete royal control as such over fortifications and chose instead to re-negotiate royal rights on the basis of customs that had developed between lords and their direct vassals.

New fortress rights chiefly concerned 'rendability': the right of a lord to temporarily enter the castles of his vassals in time of need, different from 'pledging' which carried connotations of suspicion or disloyalty.[69] Rendability was essentially a method of reconciling potential conflicts of interest between lord and vassal over fortifications. By agreeing to hand over use of a castle to the lord in time of need, the vassal was acknowledging his superior's lordship. It also served to guarantee the vassal's right of ownership, with no hint of bad faith or implication of insecurity of tenure. This policy is best illustrated by the case of towns, where Philip Augustus carefully endowed municipal authorities with control of 'royal' privileges, particularly over revenues and powers of fortifying. This ensured their loyalty and provided the king with a potential military advantage, namely the right of the royal army to use them during campaigning. This readjustment in fortress-tenure may appear to neatly reconcile the interest of lord and vassal but it was clearly a legalistic cloak whereby Philip bolstered his position in his war against the Angevins. In the aftermath of the decisive battle of Bouvines his strengthened negotiating position saw a slightly closer approximation between Carolingian theory and Capetian practice.

Whilst historians have always taken a strong interest in the degree of royal control over castle-building and on customary rights over fortifications they have also placed emphasis on the mechanisms by which they were staffed. Initially this was in part influenced by the perceived role of the castle in the Norman settlement – if they were instruments of Conquest there must have been a strong feudal mechanism to ensure adequate garrisons. The practice of castle-guard (the obligation of a vassal to spend part of the year at his lord's castle) has therefore been seen as an important aspect of military tenure in the Anglo-Norman period.[70]

In another seminal piece, Sidney Painter significantly alters Round's conclusion that the widespread evidence for money payments in lieu of actual castle-guard service was a result of commuting obligations at the rate of pay

69 C. L. H. Coulson, 'Rendability and Castellation in Medieval France', *Château-Gaillard* vi (1973), pp. 59–67; R. W. Kaeuper, *War, Justice and Public Order: England and France in the Later Middle Ages* (Oxford, 1988).

70 J. H. Round, 'Castle Guard', *Archaeological Journal* lix (1902), pp. 144–59; *idem*, 'The Staff of a Castle in the Twelfth Century', *English Historical Review* xxxv (1920), pp. 90–7; C. W. Hollister, *The Military Organization of Norman England* (Oxford, 1965); for garrisons see J. Moore, 'Anglo-Norman Garrisons', *Anglo-Norman Studies* xxii (2000), pp. 205–60.

needed to hire a substitute. This could not in fact be the case, as the payment was not enough to hire a substitute for the required period of duty. He suggests instead that tenants owing castle-guard refused to commute their services at the prevailing rates of pay. Rates of commutation were the result of individual bargains struck between lord and vassal. Many tenants still chose to serve in person but generally the more onerous the obligations, the more likely tenants were to pay instead of serving. Commutation was thus designed to pay for a small garrison in time of peace and still provide for a larger one in time of war.

In the face of considerable variation in practice, specific case studies provide the clearest means of elucidating the precise obligations at individual sites. In 'Castle Guard and the Castlery of Clun' Frederick C. Suppe examines the origin and function of castle-guard obligations at the important baronial castle of Clun in Shropshire. Working back from 1272, when there is definite evidence for the castlery, he demonstrates that the initial establishment of the constituent elements of the castle-guard arrangements probably took place during the reign of Henry I and were then subject to considerable alteration over the course of the twelfth century. As was suggested by Painter, many of the arrangements in the thirteenth century were probably in fact the result of individual negotiations between the lords of individual fiefs in the castlery and their sub-tenants. More significantly, Suppe shows that the overwhelming majority of tenants who owed castle-guard were only obliged to serve when it was militarily necessary. At least as far as Clun is concerned, castle-guard retained its military role, even if the garrison raised needed to be augmented by paid troops.[71]

Suppe's analysis does cast some doubt on Painter's general idea that the castle-guard system was always designed to provide permanent garrisons, even in time of peace. It also highlights the dangers of relying too heavily on the monetary valuations of castle-guard as evidence for actual commutation of service: at Clun the recording of a monetary value was made even though the system was physically operational. He concludes that more work is needed on specific examples before any general comments concerning castle-guard can be made. Yet, if a similar complexity is found elsewhere, then it suggests that there is more to the origins and operation of castle-guard than general theories have suggested.

Of course any discussion of Anglo-Norman castles cannot move far from the physical nature of the buildings themselves. Many of the issues surrounding the nature of the Anglo-Norman castle are encapsulated in the study of perhaps their most quintessential feature – the great tower – which has been the focus of much recent attention and revision.[72] This is particularly the case for Orford

[71] See also F. Suppe, 'The Garrisoning of Oswestry, a Baronial Castle on the Welsh Marches', *The Medieval Castle: Romance and Reality*, ed. K. Reyerson and F. Powe (Dubuque, 1984), pp. 63–78; *idem*, *Military Institutions on the Welsh Marches: Shropshire, 1066–1300* (Woodbridge, 1994); and now F. Suppe, 'The Persistence of Castle-Guard in the Welsh Marches and Wales: Suggestions for a Research Agenda and Methodology', in R. P. Abels and B. S. Bachrach (eds), *The Normans and their Adversaries at War* (Woodbridge, 2001), pp. 201–21.

[72] P. Dixon, 'The Donjon of Knaresborough: the Castle as Theatre', *Château-Gaillard* xiv (1990), pp. 121–39; *idem*, 'Design in Castle Building: The Controlling of Access to the Lord', *Château-Gaillard* xviii (1998), pp. 47–56; see also P. Dixon and P. Marshall, 'The Great Tower in the Twelfth Century: The Case of Norham Castle', *Archaeological Journal* cl (1993), pp. 410–32.

castle in Suffolk, a site that has long been seen as marking an important position in the history of Western fortification. The polygonal design of Henry II's tower has traditionally been interpreted as an innovative military response to the inherent weakness of the Anglo-Norman square keep, the corners of which were vulnerable to mining, picking and boring.

Sandy Heslop approaches the castle from the perspective of the art historian. He notes how the rigid distinction between 'secular' and 'ecclesiastical' architecture has impoverished the study of castles: encouraging the study of their military function, while leaving their architectural aspects relatively neglected. As Heslop explains, the traditional interpretation of the building has several problems. The clasping towers in fact multiply the number of square corners on the building, clearly a major error if a military role for the building was envisaged. This is compounded by several blind spots around the keep, enabling any intruder to work at the foot of the wall unscathed. Moreover, the internal arrangement of rooms and lofty stairways meant that scant regard was given to preventing any assailant moving around the building. Unsurprisingly, Heslop concludes that the keep 'was not primarily devised with military requirements in mind' and was ill designed to meet a serious attack.

If the form of the keep at Orford contradicted defensive capability, it certainly ensured that it was imbued with considerable cultural meaning. The geometrical principles behind its construction were also found in ecclesiastical buildings, a lesson that the aesthetic metaphors traditionally only applied to churches and cathedrals were also present in castles. Although there are practical considerations that explain the form of the building, Heslop also notes that much is only explicable by reference to 'complexity for the sake of its cleverness' – a telling comment on Orford's meaning. The vocabulary of the building is expressed through classically inspired door heads and windows, with the whole ensemble, Heslop suggests, intended to invoke images of an eastern tradition of palace building with associations of imperial kingship and spiritual authority. In the 1160s, with Henry II embroiled in his struggle with Thomas Becket, such imagery for a royal castle must have been particularly potent. There is much subtlety in Heslop's argument. While arguing that the study of castles should be integrated with that of ecclesiastical buildings he also stresses the cultural and social parameters that produce differences in architectural response.

Philip Dixon and Pamela Marshall in their analysis of the tower of Castle Hedingham in Essex throw light on the social relationships which found expression in the great towers of Anglo-Norman castles. They suggest a radically new interpretation of the well-known *donjon*, raised *c.*1140 by Aubrey de Vere after his elevation to the Earldom of Oxford. In a similar manner to Orford, the building exhibits some curious anomalies if it is simply a defensive or, indeed, a residential structure. Rejecting the idea of an original fourth storey, the internal arrangement of the building appears to have consisted of a basement, with a lower and upper hall. The puzzling absence of kitchen, sleeping accommodation or oratory leads to the conclusion that the great tower at Hedingham was primarily a ceremonial building with an internal hierarchy of rooms. An elaborately contrived approach to the lord's upper hall took the visitor along a set route resulting in a stage-managed and intimidating approach to the lord himself. Such analyses have long been used to elucidate the social function and perception of space in other medieval buildings and will no doubt prove to be fruitful in the future. The projection of lordly power through orchestrated, even theatrical, ceremony is clearly a long way from the necessities of siege warfare.[73]

Although great towers remain one of the most enigmatic monuments to the lifestyle of the Anglo-Norman aristocracy it must be remembered that castles were simply one form of aristocratic dwelling, and many Anglo-Norman lords inhabited houses of lesser status. In 'Hall and Chamber: English Domestic Planning 1000–1250' John Blair significantly alters the long-standing argument propounded by Margaret Wood and Patrick Faulkner that the chief component of the twelfth-century manor house was a first floor hall raised over a basement. On the basis of upstanding remains, excavations and documentary evidence, Blair argues that those structures hitherto defined as first floor halls are in fact detached chamber blocks originally accompanied by free-standing ground floor halls that have since been lost. While it is possible to find halls at first floor level in some Norman castles, the typical arrangement of aristocratic dwellings in the Anglo-Norman period was that of a detached hall and chamber. The late twelfth century saw the beginning of the developed 'services' end at the lower end of the hall with chambers above, and by the beginning of the thirteenth century the chamber was increasingly being attached to the upper end of the hall with the resulting structure becoming the typical plan for the later medieval English manor house. The study of such buildings serves to place the study of castles into a broader context.[74] In particular, Thompson's comment that the castle can be seen as either the 'culmination' or a 'temporary aberration' of the hall culture and of the aristocratic dwelling has the potential to tell us much about what was distinctive about Anglo-Norman high-status domestic arrangements.[75]

The thread that links all the individual pieces reproduced here is the tremendous value that contemporaries attached to all kinds of castles during the Anglo-Norman period. This theme comes across most vividly in the work of the great historians of the Anglo-Norman world. In her 'Orderic Vitalis on Castles' Marjorie Chibnall examines how one such individual viewed the castles of the twelfth century. Despite his life in the cloister Orderic was well-informed about the secular aristocracy and his narrative is almost unrivalled in its picture of how castles functioned in peace and war. It is from him that we hear such details as the heated arrows fired at the shingle roof of the castle at Brionne, and of Robert

73 M. Girouard, *Life in the English Country House* (New Haven, 1978); *idem*, *Life in the French Country House* (London, 2000); R. Tittler, *Architecture and Power: The Town Hall and the English Urban Community c.1500–1640* (Oxford, 1991); P. A. Faulkner, 'Domestic Planning from the Twelfth to the Fourteenth Centuries', *Archaeological Journal* cxiv (1958), pp. 150–183; *idem*, 'Castle Planning in the Fourteenth Century', *Archaeological Journal* cxx (1963), pp. 215–35.

74 E. Impey, 'The Seigneurial Residence in Normandy, 1125–1225: an Anglo-Norman Tradition?', *Medieval Archaeology* 43 (1999), pp. 45–73; for possible English influences on halls in Normandy. M. W. Thompson, *The Medieval Hall: the Basis of Secular Domestic Life 600–1600* (Aldershot, 1995); P. W. Dixon, 'Towerhouses', *Archaeological Journal* cxxxvi (1979), pp. 240–52; for the later medieval period see Philip Dixon, '*Mota, Aula et Turris*: the Manor-Houses of the Anglo-Scottish Border', *Manorial Domestic Buildings in England and Northern France*, ed. G. Meirion-Jones and M. Jones, Society of Antiquaries Occasional Papers vol. 15 (London, 1993), pp. 22–48.

75 Thompson, *Rise*, p. 12.

of Bellême rushing into the undefended Saint-Ceneri to find pots of meat still cooking over fires. What emerges from Orderic's narrative is how ownership of castles was a visible statement of changing relationships among the aristocracy. Unsurprisingly, this was tied to the use made of the castle in war where Orderic emphasises both offensive and defensive capabilities. Orderic is of great value when he relates the protocol of siege warfare. Thus we hear of truces, negotiated agreements and pacts made between besieger and besieged. Although the literary influences on his work do not permit any technical analysis of his terminology with the aim of identifying individual types of fortifications, his work is a reminder that in some respects contemporaries saw castles in a similar manner to modern historians: as buildings that influenced many aspects of Anglo-Norman society.

1

A Bell-house and a Burh-geat: Lordly Residences in England before the Norman Conquest

Ann Williams

I was recently conducting a tutorial with a student who had been asked whether or not William the Conqueror had introduced feudalism into England. The student maintained that he had, supporting his argument by the absence of feudal vocabulary in Old English. Knights, he declared, were unknown in England and in English before the Norman Conquest. When I remarked that the word 'knight' itself was Old English, he was, to use the vulgar parlance, gobsmacked. I don't say that his conclusion was thereby wrong (or indeed right) but introduce the anecdote simply to justify a paper on pre-Conquest England as suitable fare for a Knights Conference.*

I must make it clear at the outset that this is not a paper on the origin of English castles. The word 'castle', unlike the word 'knight', is not Old English. It first appears in an English context in the *Anglo-Saxon Chronicle* for 1051, when '*þa welisce menn gewroht aenne castel on Herefordscire*'.[1] In its Old English setting, the foreign word *castel* stands out, not least, alas, because it is now the one most familiar to modem ears. There were several native words which the chronicler could have used to describe a fortification – *burh*, *geweorc*, *herebeorg*, Old English had even borrowed, in the form *ceaster*, the Latin word *castrum* from which 'castle' itself is derived. The chronicler chose none of them. What King Edward's Normans had constructed was something new, to be described in the tongue of the *welisce menn* (foreigners) who built it.

The castles of the newcomers were seen by contemporaries as different from the residences of the native nobility. Leaving aside for the moment the question of where the differences lay, it should be remarked that there is a singular unanimity of opinion among modern historians on what English lordly residences were like. This opinion is epitomized in the description of Dorothy Whitelock, written in 1952:

* I should like to thank Professor H.R. Loyn, Dr David Roffe and Dr Stephen Church for reading and commenting upon a draft of this paper. Thanks are also due to the members of the Strawberry Hill Conference, especially Dr Richard Eales, Dr Jane Martindale and Mr Matthew Bennett, for much helpful criticism and advice. I have thus been saved from many errors. Those which remain are entirely mine.

1 *Two of the Saxon Chronicles Parallel*, ed. John Earle and Charles Plummer, Oxford 1892, i, 173–4 (compare p. 175 for the *castel* of Dover). See also p. 217, where the 'feudal terminology' of the Salisbury Oath is rendered in Old English without recourse to French or Latin.

> . . . they were commonly built of wood, and in the early days consisted of a single-storied great hall, used for meals, entertainment and all the main daily business, and as sleeping-quarters for the retainers at night, with smaller, detached buildings, called 'bowers', for the bedrooms of the owner, his family and guests. The whole was surrounded by an earthwork and a stockade, and was known as a *burh*, that is, a fortified residence.[2]

It is unfortunate that the word *burh* inevitably conjures up images of an urban settlement. Its development into Modern English 'borough' stems from the fact that most (though not all) of the fortifications built by King Alfred and his successors were, or became, towns. The primary meaning of *burh* is, however, simply a fortified or defended place; its root is the verb *beorgan*, 'to protect'. In the formation of place-names, *burh* and its derivatives, *byrh* and *byrig*, are applied to a variety of defensive structures: prehistoric earthworks, Roman camps, Anglo-Saxon fortifications, castles, fortified houses and manors, market-towns and suburbs.[3] Only the context will determine the meaning intended in any given case. Concentration on the *burh* as walled town has obscured the *burh* as fortified house, yet it continued in use (at least in place-name formation) in this latter sense well after the Norman Conquest. Nobury, in Inkberrow, Worcs., means 'the new borough' and probably refers to a new manor-house built there in 1235.[4] Such work as exists on the *burh* as fortified house has tended to concentrate on its influence, or lack of influence, on the development of the English castle.[5] What is missing is a survey of English lordly residences for their own sake, rather than as the prelude to something else.

This paper is an attempt to redress the balance. It is based on what material I have been able to find, and is in no sense the fruit of any exhaustive (or even systematic) research. I have in the process strayed far out of my field and apologize in advance for my lack of skill in linguistic and archaeological sources. To compensate for these shortcomings, I have tried to confine my enquiries to the tenth and eleventh centuries, and to concentrate on examples of unambiguously aristocratic, as opposed to royal and ecclesiastical, residences, other than for purposes of comparison.

My first *burh* does, however, date from the pre-Alfredian period. It occurs in

2 Dorothy Whitelock, *The Beginnings of English Society*, Harmondsworth 1952, 88; cf. H.R. Loyn, *Anglo-Saxon England and the Norman Conquest*, London 1962, 220; Nicholas Brooks, 'The development of military obligation in eighth- and ninth-century England', *England before the Conquest*, ed. Kathleen Hughes and Peter Clemoes, Cambridge 1971 (henceforth Brooks, 'Development of military obligation'), 83; Kathryn Hume, 'The concept of the hall in Old English poetry', *Anglo-Saxon England* iii, 1974, 64; P.H. Sawyer, *From Roman Britain to Norman England*, London 1978, 155–6; Eric Fernie, *The Architecture of the Anglo-Saxons*, London 1983 (henceforth Fernie, *Architecture*), 29.

3 A.H. Smyth, *English Place-name Elements*, Cambridge 1956 (henceforth Smyth, *Place-name Elements*), i, 58–62.

4 Margaret Gelling, *Signposts to the Past*, London 1978, 143.

5 The debate is exemplified in R. Allen Brown, 'An historian's approach to the origins of the castle in England', *Archaeological Journal* cxxvi, 1969 (1970) (henceforth Brown, 'Origins of the castle'), 131–8.

a memorandum from the archives of the church of Worcester.[6] In 822 or 823, King Ceolwulf I of Mercia asked the bishop and community of Worcester to give him the estate (*þaet lond*) at Bromsgrove, Worcs. The memorandum is not easy to interpret, but it seems that Bromsgrove was held of the church by the thegn Wulfheard of Inkberrow. The bishop therefore summoned Wulfheard, and asked him to relinquish his interest in Bromsgrove. Wulfheard agreed, on condition that the bishop would compensate him with some other estate (*swelce londare*), 'where he could live honourably and have his dwelling (*wic*) in the *burh* during his life'. *Burh* in this context clearly means the manor-house, to which the estate (*land*) was appurtenant. It emerges from the memorandum that what Wulfheard was after was Inkberrow itself. This estate had been bequeathed to the church of Worcester by Wulfheard's kinsmen, and had been the subject of an earlier dispute between the bishop and Wulfheard. It had ended (as was usual in such cases) in compromise; Wulfheard was to hold the estate for life, with reversion to the church. Now Wulfheard was trying to bargain his interest in Bromsgrove for outright possession of Inkberrow, but he was unsuccessful. From the present viewpoint the interest lies in the description of the residence which Wulfheard considered suitable to his status; a matter quite separate from what kind of structure actually existed at Inkberrow in the ninth century.

The description of Wulfheard's ideal residence can be contrasted with the highly undesirable dwelling in the Old English poem, *The Wife's Lament*. Like the Worcester memorandum, the poem is not easy to interpret, but it seems that the speaker is a lady who has been driven from her home and forced to live in a cave or barrow, under an oak-tree, in a woodland grove. To the modern reader comfortably ensconced by the fire it sounds romantic and charming, but the poem's heroine comes from a harder world, and complains bitterly:

> '. . . *burgtunas brerum beweaxne, wic wynna leas.*'
>
> 'The *burhtunas* are overgrown with briars, and the dwelling (*wic*) is joyless.'[7]

The word *burhtun* is often found as a place-name, in the forms Burton, Bourton and Broughton. Its meaning is 'fort settlement' and it has been interpreted in various ways.[8] In this particular case, it seems that the meaning 'defensible house' is intended: the wife is comparing the tangled undergrowth around her miserable hole in the ground with the well-kept hedges surrounding the manor-house where she used to live.

6 P.H. Sawyer, *Anglo-Saxon Charters: an annotated list and bibliography*, London 1968 (henceforth S.), no. 1432, printed in A.J. Robertson, *Anglo-Saxon Charters*, Cambridge 1956 (henceforth Robertson, *Charters*) no. 4. For Wulfheard's previous claims on Inkberrow, see S. 1430. There had been a minster at Inkberrow, founded in the seventh century (S. 53).

7 Bruce Mitchell and Fred C. Robinson, *A Guide to Old English*, Oxford 1964, 248–51 (lines 31–2); *burgtun* is glossed 'protecting hedge' (p. 294).

8 Smyth, *Place-name Elements*, 62; Matthias T. Löfvenberg, *Studies on Middle English Local Surnames*, Lund 1942 (henceforth Löfvenberg, *Middle English Local Surnames*), 29. Margaret Gelling has argued that the pre-Alfredian *burh-tunas* were 'a system of defence posts', notably on the borders of Mercia and Wales ('The place-name Burton and variants', *Weapons and Warfare in Anglo-Saxon England*, ed. Sonia Chadwick-Hawkes, Oxford 1989, 145 ff); compare the 'defensible houses' in Herefordshire discussed below.

It is to such *burhs* that the Laws of Alfred refer, in the clause concerned with *burh-bryce*, the crime of breaking into a fortified residence.[9] The fines are graded according to the status of the *burh's* owner; the king, the archbishops, the bishops and ealdormen, the men with a 1200*s* wergild, and the men with a 600*s* wergild. The clause makes it clear that a nobleman's house is intended, for it ends with the fine for *ceorles edorbryce*, breaking through the fence surrounding the residence of a ceorl. A famous and spectactular example of *burh-bryce* occured in 786, when the ætheling Cyneheard surprised and killed King Cynewulf of Wessex in the royal *burh* of Meretun (possibly Martin, Dorset), where the king was visiting his mistress.[10]

A later estate similar to that specified by Wulfheard is described in a writ of Edward the Confessor, issued between 1042 and 1046.[11] The king confirmed to Westminster Abbey an estate in Essex, given to the abbey by Azur Swart (the Black) and his wife Aelfgyth. It consisted of the *burh* of Wennington, with 4 hides of land belonging to it, the church and the churchsoke, and the land called 'At the Lea'; this last tenement probably lay in the neighbouring vill of Aveley, whose name (Aelfgyth's *leah*) preserves that of Azur's wife, Aelfgyth. This estate can be compared with another at Burwell (*burh*-spring) in Cambridgeshire, which the thegn Aelfgar gave to Ramsey Abbey towards the end of the tenth century.[12] It consisted of his house and court (perhaps the enclosure within which the house stood), along with 3 hides, 40 acres and a virgate of land, and the church of Burwell, of which Aelfgar was patron. Both Azur and Aelfgar were of thegnly rank, though perhaps not of the highest status. Azur Swart was remembered at Westminster as the donor of land at Leyton as well as Wennington, and is probably the father of Swein Swart, who in 1066 held land in Leyton, Upminster and Aveley amounting to 12½ hides.[13] Aelfgar was probably in the service of the lay patron of Ramsey Abbey, Ealdorman Aethelwine of East Anglia (d.992); he is described as *aldermanni familiaris et a secretis*.

9 Alfred 40, repeating and refining Ine 45; see F.L. Attenborough, *The Laws of the Earliest English Kings*, Cambridge 1922 (henceforth Attenborough, *Laws*), 83.

10 ASC sub anno 757. The description of Meretun mentions the bur (bower, private room) in which the king was being entertained by his lady-friend, while his hearthtroop was elsewhere (presumably in the hall); and the gates of the *burh* which the aetheling's men locked against the royal host, and around which the fighting took place.

11 S. 1117, printed and discussed in F.E. Harmer, *Anglo-Saxon Writs*, Manchester 1952, no. 73, pp. 492–3, 556.

12 *Chronicon Abbatiae Rameseiensis*, ed. W. Dunn Macrae, RS 83, 1886, 51; C.R. Hart, *Early Charters of Eastern England*, Leicester 1966 (henceforth Hart, *Charters of Eastern England*), 238. For the use of *curia*, in the sense of enclosure, see the case of Shalford discussed below. The customs of Oxford (below) speak of breaking into a man's *domus vel curia*.

13 For Swein Swart, see *LDB* fos 78v, 91. He is not distinguished by his bye-name in the entry for Aveley (*LDB* fo 84v) and Swein is, of course, a common name but his tenure of Leyton, associated with Azur Swart, suggests he is the Swein who held Aveley, which preserves the name of Azur Swart's wife. A Swein Swart, described as Earl's Edwin's man, held Lamport, Bucks (*GDB* fo. 147v). Sons could 'inherit' their father's bye-name; see Aethelmaer the Fat, son of Aethelwold the Fat and Esbeam Bigga, son of Aethelric Bigga (Robertson, *Charters*, 387, 436); and Aelfgar Meaw, son of Aethelweard Meaw (Ann Williams, 'An introduction to the Gloucestershire Domesday', *The Gloucestershire Domesday*, ed. Ann Williams and R.W.H. Erskine, London 1989, 22). In the last case, the bye-name seems not to have descended to the third generation; Aelfgar Meow's son, Beorhtric, is nowhere called Beorhtric Meaw. For a possibly inherited toponymic, see Siward and Sired of Chilham, below.

Wennington and Burwell come close to the ideal thegnly residence described in the eleventh-century tract *Geþyncðo* (the so-called 'promotion law'). It occurs in the passage relating how a ceorl may thrive to thegnhood:[14]

> And if a ceorl prospered so that he had fully five hides of his own land (*agenes landes*), [church and kitchen], bell [house] and *burh-geat*, seat and special office in the king's hall, then was he thenceforward entitled to the rank of a thegn.

The passage has been much discussed and doubts have been expressed whether it should be taken as a literal description of eleventh-century reality, rather than a nostalgic image of the mythical 'good old days'.[15] Given, however, that it comes from the pen of Archbishop Wulfstan of York (1002–23), whose deep knowledge of English law and custom is reflected in his drafting of the later law-codes of Aethelred II and those of Cnut, it would be unwise to dismiss the description as moonshine. The ideal residence of the tract is reflected not only in Wennington and Burwell, but in the twelfth-century estate of the Cockfield family, described in the appendix to Jocelin of Brakelond's Chronicle, and consisting of 'the large messuage (in Bury St Edmunds) where the manor-house of Adam (I) of Cockfield formerly stood, with its wooden belfry 140 feet high'.[16] Adam I of Cockfield lived in the time of King Stephen, and was of English descent; his father bore the Old English name of Leofmaer.

Part of the unwillingness to accept *Geþyncðo* at face-value stems, I think, from the equation of *ceorl* with 'peasant'. This is, to my mind, misleading. In the late Old English period, the category *ceorl*, like the category *thegn*, covered men of widely differing status; it included all 200*s* men, as opposed to the 1200*s* men who made up the thegnly class. The term *ceorl* would describe the *geneat* Byrhtwold who fought beside his lord, Ealdorman Byrhtnoth, at the battle of Maldon in 991; or the *cnihtas*, Sexi and Leofwine, whom their lord sent to the archbishop of Canterbury, Eadsige (1038–50), to ask for a renewal of his lease on Halton, Bucks. Such men might hold land, and owe service, including agricultural service, in respect of it, as did the radmen and radknights of Domesday Book; but they are rather more than semi-servile peasants. They are best described as non-noble free men, who might, by the favour of their lords, advance their fortunes and aquire thegnly status. Indeed the line between such men and the lesser thegns is not easily drawn in practice.[17] It is men of this type, surely, that *Geþyncðo* has in mind.

The marks of thegnly status in *Geþyncðo* are four: land, church, *burh-geat*

14 F. Liebermann, *Die Gesetze der Angelsachsen*, Halle 1903–16 (henceforth Liebermann), i, 456; translated in Dorothy Whitelock, *English Historical Documents*, i, *c.*500–1042, 1955 (henceforth *EHD*), 431–2. The words in square brackets are found only in the *Textus Roffensis* version.

15 Brown, 'Origins of the castle', 141; F.M. Stenton defended the reality behind *Geþynðo*'s image ('The thriving of the Anglo-Saxon ceorl', *Preparatory to Anglo-Saxon England*, ed. D.M. Stenton, Oxford 1970 (henceforth Stenton, 'Thriving of the ceorl'), 383–93).

16 Jocelin of Brakelond, *Chronicle of the Abbey of Bury St Edmunds*, ed. Diana Greenaway and Jane Sayers, Oxford 1989, 123.

17 D.E. Scragg, *The Battle of Maldon*, Manchester 1981, 67, 108; Robertson, *Charters*, 174–5; Ann Williams, 'An introduction to the Worcestershire Domesday', *The Worcestershire Domesday*, ed. Ann Williams and R.W.H. Erskine, London 1988, 6–7.

and royal service. The last stipulation shows that the status intended is that of a king's thegn, rather than the median thegn who serves a lord other than the king. This may also be the implication of the statement that the ceorl's five hides must be his own land, if *agenes landes* here means not demesne, but land held by charter, for such land (bookland) was the characteristic mark of a king's thegn.[18] The *burh-geat* (the gate of the *burh*) presumably stands for the whole manor-house. It is used in the same sense in the tenth- or eleventh-century tract on the king's personal peace, known as *Be Griðe* or *Pax*. In this tract the extent of the king's peace is defined as follows:[19]

> Thus far shall be the king's *grið*, from his *burh-geat* where he is dwelling, on its four sides; 3 miles, 3 furlongs, 3 acres' breadth, 9 feet, 9 palms, 9 barley-corns.

Here the *burh-geat* presumably means the king's royal residence.[20] King Edmund, in his code regulating the blood-feud, lays down the penalties for attacking those who have sought refuge in a church or in his *burh*, here meaning not the fortified towns established by his father and grandfather, but the royal residences or king's *tunas* ('Kingstons'), whose role in articulating the royal administration has been described by Professor Sawyer.[21] Like *burhtun*, the word *burh-geat* occurs as a place-name, in the forms Burgate, Boreat and Buckhatch. The precise nature of the *burh* in such places needs to be established by the individual context, but some of the 'Burgates' may represent defensible manor-houses.[22]

The use of the word *burh-geat* to indicate the manor-house or residence suggests that the gate-house was the most prominent feature of the defences; a parallel appears in the Bayeux Tapestry, which represents Norman castles by their most obvious feature, their mottes. A gate implies a fence or hedge, and the enclosures were probably ditched as well. A *burh*-ditch occurs among the boundary-marks of an estate at Upper Winchendon, Bucks., in a charter of 1004, and topographical examination of the area suggests that the ditch of the estate's manor-house is intended.[23] The construction of such works was a duty laid on the peasants of the estate. The survey of Tidenham, Gloucs. (a manor belonging to Bath Abbey), which was made about 1050, prescribes that each

18 Stenton interpreted *agenes landes* as demesne ('Thriving of the ceorl', 389) but see the arguments of Richard Abels, *Lordship and Military Obligation in Anglo-Saxon England*, London 1988, 141.

19 Liebermann, i, 390. The clause is repeated in the *Leges Henrici Primi*, ed. L.J. Downer, Oxford 1972, 120–1, where *burh-geat* is Latinized as porter. For a discussion of *grið*, see H.M. Chadwick, *Studies on Anglo-Saxon Institutions*, Cambridge 1905, 115; N.D. Humard, 'The Anglo-Norman franchises', *EHR* lxiv, 1949, 303–5.

20 Maitland believed that the *burh-geats* of both *Geþyncðo* and *Be Grið* referred to the gates of fortified towns, but so far as *Geþyncðo* is concerned, he was using a faulty text; see W.R. Stevenson, 'Burh-geat-setl', *EHR* xii, 1897, 489–92, who showed that a manorial *burh* was intended.

21 II Edmund 2, see A.J. Robertson, *Laws of the Kings of England from Edmund to Henry I*, Cambridge 1925 (henceforth Robertson, *Laws*), 8–9; P.H. Sawyer, 'The royal *tun* in pre-Conquest England', *Ideal and Reality in Frankish and Anglo-Saxon Society*, ed. Patrick Wormald, Donald Bullough and Roger Collins, Oxford 1983, 273–99.

22 Smyth, *Place-name Elements*, 62; Löfvenberg, *Middle English Local Surnames*, 28.

23 Margaret Gelling, *Early Charters of the Thames Valley*, Leicester 1979 (henceforth Gelling, *Charters of the Thames Valley*), 181–4.

gebur (or villan) should 'fence and dig one pole of the *burh*-hedge: *tyne & dicie i gyrde burhheges*'.[24] A similar obligation, 'to build and fence the *burh*: *bythan & burh hegegian*', appears in the eleventh-century tract on the *Rights and Ranks of the People* (*Rectitudines Singularum Personarum*), though here the burden fell not upon the *geburas*, but on the higher-ranking free men, the *geneatas*.[25] The duties of the good reeve included 'to make good the hedges' (*hegan godian*) of the *burh*.[26] A *burh*-hedge may not sound a very impressive structure, but the same word is used in a tenth-century boundary-clause to describe the walls of the royal city of Winchester, to whose upkeep 2,400 hides were assigned by the *Burghal Hidage*.[27]

Such services resemble royal rights to labour on the king's works, and indeed, where bookland is concerned, derive from those rights.[28] When land was booked, that is granted by a royal diploma or land-book, the public obligations due from it were remitted, with the exception of military service, geld, and some judicial rights. In practice this meant that the holders of bookland could intercept for their own benefit the services formerly due to the king. Tenure by book, once the preserve of the church, was by the eighth century extended to lay landowners, and by the tenth century was the characteristic tenure of the king's thegns. They discharged their service, which was primarily military, directly to the king; thus Tewkesbury, Gloucs., held in King Edward's reign by the rich nobleman, Beorhtric son of Aelfgar, was 'quit of all royal service and geld except the service of the lord himself whose manor it was'.[29] All other services were appropriated by Tewkesbury's lord, Beorhtric.

The services due from the estate were rendered to the hall (*heall, aula*) and the court (*curia*), the public part of the manor, which defined the identity of the land attached to it. Thus Thurstan son of Wine in his will (1043–1045) defined his two manors at Shouldham, Norfolk, as 'the estate at the north hall' and 'the estate at the middle hall' respectively, and when Ringulf of Oby, Norfolk, forfeited his land for rebellion after the Norman Conquest, his *terra et aula* were taken into the hands of the king's officials.[30] It is this aspect of the manor, its function as the collecting-point of seigneurial dues and services, that interested the Domesday commissioners. In Domesday Book the presence of a hall is one of the criteria used to identify a manor; indeed places without halls are called manors only in exceptional circumstances. A manor which lost its hall lost also its manorial status; at Irish Hill, Berks., Hugolin the steersman 'transferred the hall and other houses' to another manor, of which Irish Hill, once a manor in its own right, became a dependency.[31] In some cases the hall may be a notional

24 S. 1555, printed in Robertson, *Charters*, 204–7.

25 Liebermann, i, 445.

26 Liebermann, i, 454–5, translation in *Anglo-Saxon Prose*, ed. Michael Swanton, London 1975, 26. For similar services in the post-Conquest period, see David Austin, ed., *Boldon Book: Northumberland and Durham*, Chichester 1982, 36–7.

27 S. 1560.

28 Brooks, 'Development of military obligation', 71, gives examples of the services remitted.

29 *GDB* fo. 163v.

30 Dorothy Whitelock, *Anglo-Saxon Wills*, Cambridge 1930, 81; F.M. Stenton, 'St Benet of Holme and the Norman Conquest', *EHR* xxxvii, 1922, 227.

31 R. Welldon Finn, *An Introduction to Domesday Book*, 1963, 50–1; *GDB* fo 63.

concept rather than a physical building, as at Eaton, Notts., which was assessed at only 6½ bovates but held, before the conquest, by no less than 10 thegns, each of whom had his hall.[32] In such cases the 'hall' may only indicate the rights to a separate share in the profits of the estate. Conversely the entry for Shalford, Surrey, may indicate a joint-tenure, for the manor there was held before the conquest by two brothers, each of whom had his own house (*domus*) 'but nevertheless dwelt within one court (*curia*)'.[33] A single manor held in common seems to be implied.

It is at the time of Domesday that the variety of manorial estates can be most clearly seen. Some manors were co-terminous with the townships in which they lay, but some vills were divided between several manors or parts of manors, while some manors extended into several separate vills. The latter have been given many modern names, multiple-estates, composite estates, and the like. They did not necessarily consist of a contiguous block of territory; often their component parts were widely scattered. Tewkesbury, Gloucs., held before 1066 by Beorhtric son of Aelfgar, is a particularly well-defined example. It had been 'destroyed and dismembered' at some point between the Conquest and 1086, and its description in Domesday is in the past tense, probably deriving from a pre-Conquest or at least pre-Domesday survey.[34] It was assessed at 95 hides, with another 5 hides in the manor of Oxenton, which, despite having its own hall, was part of Tewkesbury. The chief vill was Tewkesbury itself, where Beorhtric's hall and court were situated, and to this was attached 45 hides of land in seven vills, inhabited by the peasants who owed service to the hall. These holdings would have been described elsewhere as berewicks of Tewkesbury. A further 30 hides in four vills were held by tenants, probably on some form of leasehold tenure, and 20 hides in seven vills belonged to the church of Tewkesbury, an old minster situated at Stanway. Tewkesbury was a large estate and growing larger, for to the original 95 hides had been added another 32¼ hides in six vills, whose holders 'had submitted themselves and their lands into the power of Beorhtric'.

It is at the focal points of such great estates that we might expect to find the fortified houses of the Old English aristocracy. Only physical examination of likely sites will reveal their presence. For example, Edwin, earl of Mercia, had a hall at Laughton-en-le-Morthen, Yorks. (WR) on the eve of the Conquest.[35] The parish church of Laughton, dedicated to All Saints, has pre-Conquest fabric, possibly the remains of a *porticus*, at its west end. Given the relationship observed elsewhere between churches and seigneurial residences, it has been suggested that Edwin's hall may have lain on the site of the later motte and bailey castle, constructed to the west of All Saints.[36] Only archaeological exca-

32 *GDB* fo 284v.

33 *GDB* fo. 35v.

34 *GDB* fo. 163–163v.

35 *GDB* fo. 319. Laughton-en-le-Morthen, held by Roger de Bully in 1086, was an estate of 18 carucates, including a berewick in Throapham, to which was attached 36 carucates of sokeland in seven vills; compare the estates of Barton upon Humber and Earl's Barton, discussed below, pp. 35–6.

36 R.K. Morris, *Churches in the Landscape*, London 1989 (henceforth Morris, *Churches*), 258–9.

vation could confirm this suggestion and it is to the archaeological evidence for aristocratic *burhs* that we must now turn.

Attenborough remarked, in 1922, that 'stones or earth can hardly have been used; otherwise such residences would frequently be traceable now'.[37] Since then matters have changed considerably. The dramatic discoveries at Goltho, Lincs., have shown what a pre-Conquest aristocratic *burh* was like.[38] Occupation layers from early Saxon to late medieval revealed the successive stages in the development of the site, which was abandoned towards the end of the middle ages. By the late ninth or early tenth century, a large hall (80 feet by 20) and its subsidiary buildings lay within a banked enclosure, surrounded by a ditch up to 7 feet deep and 18 feet wide. This *burh* went through successive rebuildings, and in the eleventh century occupied an area some 325 feet by 270, surrounded by a rampart still standing up to 5 feet high when excavated and a ditch up to 6 feet deep. After 1066, a motte and bailey castle was erected over the former *burh*.

Although no site has, as yet, produced the same volume of detailed material as Goltho, it is unlikely to be unique. A similar complex was excavated at Sulgrave, Northants. Here in the early eleventh century a large hall (80 feet long) and its outbuildings were associated with a contemporary bank and ditch. To the east stood a church, whose west door was aligned on the same axis as the hall, suggesting that the two buildings were associated. The hall of Sulgrave must have been an imposing structure:

> This great house, of five square bays with an open, cobbled porch at one end, seems to anticipate the traditional medieval arrangement, having a service-end, separated by a screen and cross-passage from the hall proper, with its central hearth and benches. There was an L-shaped chamber-block at the other end, perhaps over-sailing the hall. Near the porch-end, on the axis of the hall, was a detached timber building, perhaps a kitchen. There was a free-standing stone building set to one side of the hall, later incorporated into the post-Conquest defences to serve as a gateway.[39]

Sulgrave's chamber-block may have been two-storied. On the Bayeux Tapestry, Earl Harold is shown feasting in the upper room of his hall at Bosham, which was reached by an outside staircase.[40] Doubts have been expressed whether the Tapestry is representing an English building, rather than reflecting continental

Morris covers in detail many of the subjects touched upon in the present paper, and my debt to his work will be obvious.

37 Attenborough, *Laws*, 190.

38 Guy Beresford, 'Goltho manor, Lincolnshire: the buildings and their surroundings', *Anglo-Norman Studies* iv, Woodbridge 1982, 13–36; *Goltho: the development of an early medieval manor*, 1987. Paul Everson ('What's in a name? Goltho, "Goltho" and Bullington', *Lincolnshire History and Archaeology* xxiii, 1988, 93–9) argues for a revision of Beresford's dating of the successive stages at Goltho.

39 P.V. Addyman, 'The Anglo-Saxon house: a new review', *Anglo-Saxon England* i, 1972, 297; for the excavations, see B.K. Davison, 'Excavations at Sulgrave, Northamptonshire', *Archaeological Journal* cxxxiv, 1977, 105–14.

40 D.M. Wilson, ed., *The Bayeux Tapestry*, London 1985 (henceforth *Bayeux Tapestry*), plates 3 and 4; Fernie, *Architecture*, 22.

models, but some English halls had upper rooms. There was a spectacular accident at the royal residence of Calne, Wilts., in 978, when 'the leading councillors of England fell down from an upper story (*of anre upfloran*), all except the holy archbishop Dunstan, who alone remained standing on a beam'.[41] If the designer of the Tapestry really could distinguish between the details of English and Norman hair-styles and armour, he could perhaps tell the difference between English and continental building traditions.[42]

The excavations at Goltho are not only important in themselves, but show the possibilities of sites as yet unexplored. They also demonstrate the necessity for full and detailed excavation. A site which bears more than a passing resemblance to that at Goltho was recently destroyed to make way for a playing-field. It consisted of a group of earthworks in a field called Very (previously Berry) Croft, in the village of Hillesley, Gloucs.[43] The main mound was surrounded by a ditch, with a causewayed entrance; two smaller ditched mounds were associated with it, and a low bank to the south may have been the outer bank of a bailey. Three periods of building were identified in the rescue dig, the earliest associated with what may have been a timber hall. There was some indication that the site, classed as 'Saxo-Norman', had been in use before the construction of the earthworks, but no details were available. Whether the earliest defences were pre- or post-Conquest could not be determined, and no conclusions could be drawn about the nature or function of the earthworks.

Both Goltho and Sulgrave continued in use after the Conquest and were re-modelled by their later lords.[44] It is quite possible that the more heavily-defended castles of the post-Conquest period may overlie other pre-Conquest lordly residences. This hypothesis sheds some light on the nature of the two 'defensible houses' recorded in the Herefordshire folios of Domesday Book. One *domus defensabilis* lay at Eardisley, a manor situated 'in the midst of a certain wood', and the other at nearby Ailey, where there was 'a large wood used for hunting'.[45] Both manors were close to the borders of Wales, an area whose inhabitants were doubtless more conscious than most of the need for security. Indeed a castle was later built at Eardisley, when it became the caput of

41 ASC sub anno 978. The same word, *upflor*, is used for the vantage-point from which the Norman archers (*cnihtas*) shot at the English monks in the infamous massacre in the church at Glastonbury (*ASC* 'E', sub anno 1083).

42 Nicholas Brooks and H.E. Walker, 'The authority and interpretation of the Bayeux Tapestry', *Anglo-Norman Studies* i, 1979, 19–20; but see also Ian Peirce, 'Arms, armour and warfare in the eleventh century', *Anglo-Norman Studies* x, 1988, 238.

43 Bruce Williams, 'Excavations of a medieval earthwork complex at Hillesley, Hawkesbury, Avon', *Transactions of the Bristol and Gloucestershire Archaeological Society* cv, 1987, 147–63. The 1086 tenant was Bernard, probably Bernard Pauncevolt, holding of Turstin fitzRolf; the 1066 tenant was a thegn with the ubiquitous name of Aelfric (*GDB* fo. 169v).

44 Goltho itself does not appear in Domesday Book. It lay in Bullington, a vill divided in 1066 between the holdings of Lambi or Lambakarl (*GDB* fos 349v, 351) and those of Aelfric (*GDB* fos 340v, 354, cf. 3750, whose family's lands had passed to the bishop of Durham. It was probably on Aelfric's manor that the manor-house of Goltho lay (Steven Basset, 'Beyond the edge of excavation: the topographical context of Goltho', *Studies in Medieval History presented to R.H.C. Davis*, ed. Henry Mayr-Harting and R.I. Moore, London 1985, 24). Sulgrave belonged to Giles fitz Ansculf in 1086; its pre-Conquest holder is not recorded (*GDB* fo. 227).

45 *GDB* fos 184v, 187; Frank and Caroline Thorn, *Domesday Book: Herefordshire*, Chichester 1983, entry 10, 42 note.

the Baskerville fee. In 1086, Eardisley was held by Robert (de Baskerville) of Roger de Lacy, and Ailey by Gilbert fitz Turold, as the gift of his former lord, William fitz Osbern, earl of Hereford.

It has been suggested that these two defensible houses, lying as they do in 'the long gap between Wigmore and Clifford castles', were part of the string of defences built by the Normans against the Welsh. The suggestion is an attractive one but does not explain the unusual terminology used to describe them.[46] Clearly they were not castles, not even little castles, like the *castellulum* at Sharpness, Gloucs.[47] Were they pre-Conquest aristocratic *burhs*?

It is true that in neither case does Domesday say or imply that the *domus defensabilis* was in existence before 1066. When we look, however, at the pre-Conquest tenants of Eardisley and Ailey, the possibilities are interesting. Eardisley belonged to Eadwig *cild*, an important local landowner, whose estates were the main source for Roger de Lacy's fee in Herefordshire; Eadwig's manor of Weobley became the *caput* of that fee, and the site of its castle. Eadwig's manor did not take up the whole vill of Eardisley; part of it was in the hands of a still greater lord, Harold Godwineson, who was *inter alia* earl of Herefordshire.[48] It was Earl Harold who held Ailey before the Conquest. Harold's responsibility for the defence of the Welsh borders might well provide a context for the construction of particularly strongly defended residences in exposed and outlying places, given especially the presence of actual castles in the region before 1066.

Identification of the vestigial defences of pre-Conquest *burhs* is problematic, but another indication of their presence has been longer lasting. The church of the manor may survive, even when the hall and its outbuildings, and the surrounding defences, vanish or are subsumed into a later structure. Churches formed part of the seigneurial estates at both Wennington and Burwell, quoted above; the church was an integral part of the thegnly estate described in *Geþyncðo*. In the only surviving pictorial representation of an English manor, that of Bosham on the Bayeux Tapestry, the lord's hall stands adjacent to the church.[49] The connection between church and manor-house has been very fully explored by R.K. Morris, who has drawn attention to 'the frequency with which parish churches are found next to buildings or monuments of lordly status'.[50]

The relationship between churches and the lords on whose lands they were established long pre-dates the Conquest. Such 'estate-churches', though relatively rare in the period before Alfred, become more and more common in the tenth and eleventh centuries, with the break-up of ancient estates (usually royal)

46 See *Domesday Book: Herefordshire* (see previous note), Introductory Notes, 4. No other *domus defensabilis* appears in Domesday, but compare the entry of Eardington, Shrops., to which were attached a *nova domus*, and a *burgum* called Quatford; there was later a Norman castle at Quatford, eventually transferred to Bridgnorth (Frank and Caroline Thorn, *Domesday Book: Shropshire*, Chichester 1986, entry 4, 1, 32 and note; *GDB* fo. 254).

47 *GDB* fo. 163.

48 For Earl Harold's land in Eardisley, see *GDB* fos 181, 187.

49 *Bayeux Tapestry*, plates 3–4. Like Tewkesbury, Bosham was an estate divided between a lay lord, Earl Godwine, and the canons of Bosham.

50 Morris, *Churches*, 248.

as their component vills were booked to the king's thegns. It can sometimes be shown that the discrete estates formed in this way bore the names of the thegns to whom they were granted. Woolstone, Berks. (*Wulfric's tun*) was once part of the great estate of *Aescesbyrig* (the *burh* in this name refers to the Iron Age hillfort known as Uffington Castle). Woolstone acquired its name after it was given to Wulfric by successive grants of the kings Edmund and Eadred in the middle of the tenth century.[51] On such estates the king's thegns built their residences, sometimes encouraging or compelling their dependent peasants to settle around the manor-house, and re-organizing the layout of their tenements in the surrounding fields. Thus nucleated villages might be created out of previously scattered settlements and farmsteads. The estate churches were built to serve such 'new' villages, or, in places where such agglomeration did not occur, the needs of the lord and his family. This process, operating throughout the tenth, eleventh and twelfth centuries, gave rise to the parochial structure of the later middle ages.[52]

Already by the reign of Edgar (959–75) it had become necessary to regulate the relationship between such estate-churches and the old minsters on which the earlier parochial structure had been based. The main bones of contention were payment of tithes, and burial-rights, for which soul-soot (mortuary dues) could be charged. Edgar's Second Code, promulgated between 959 and 963, allowed 'the thegn who on his bookland has a church and a graveyard' to pay one-third of his demesne tithes to that church, the remainder going to the old minster in whose *parochia* the estate lay. If the thegnly church had no graveyard, the full tithe was to go to the minster, and the thegn could 'pay what he chooses to his priest from the [remaining] nine parts'.[53]

As we have seen, *Geþyncðo* envisaged that a church would form part of the ideal thegnly residence. Its use of the word 'bell-house' (the tower or loft in which the bell was hung) for such a church may not be merely symbolic. The word 'belfry' (from Middle English *berefrey*) has the root-meaning of a secure or defended place, like the 'wooden belfrey 140 feet high' which belonged to Adam of Cockfield (see above). The first element, *bel-*, *bere-*, is derived from the same verb *beorgan* ('to protect') which lies at the root of *burh*. Thus a church, tower associated with a defensive wall or hedge could itself form part of the defences of the lord's *burh*.[54] This is particularly true of turriform churches, which consisted of tower-naves with porches and small chancels attached.

One of the largest and most elaborate tower-churches still remaining is St

51 S. 503 (dated 944), 575. If the date, 958, of S. 575 is correct, it cannot be a charter of Eadred, who died in 955; either it is a charter of his successor, Eadwig, or, more likely, the date is wrong (see Gelling, *Charters of the Thames Valley*, 36, 49, 53).

52 John Blair, ed., *Minsters and Parish Churches: the Local Church in Transition, 950–1200*, Oxford 1988, 1–19; Alan Everitt, *Continuity and Colonization: the Evolution of Kentish Settlement*, Leicester 1986, 198–205.

53 II Edgar 2, see Robertson, *Laws*, 20–1.

54 Morris, *Churches*, 255; cf. pp. 250–5 for examples of churches used in a military context. Morris notes the frequent addition of towers to pre-existing local churches in the eleventh and twelfth centuries, and suggests that this 'might be explained as a result of the adoption by local lords of a status symbol which had its beginnings at a higher social level'.

Peter's, Barton upon Humber, Lincs. Archaeological and topographical examination of the site has revealed several stages in its development.[55] In the period before 900, the settlement was enclosed with a bank and ditch; the area within the bank was sub-circular in shape, with an average diameter of 820 feet, and covered twelve acres. By the tenth century, there was a graveyard to the west of the settlement, and presumably a church, though none has yet been found. When the tower-church was built, between 970 and 1030, the ditch was in-filled, 'leaving no significant physical boundary between the hall and the church'. The late Saxon and medieval manorial complex lay within the area defined by the bank and ditch.

The site at Barton upon Humber bears a strong resemblance to that at Earl's Barton, Northants. Here also is a pre-Conquest tower-church, dedicated to All Saints, and dating from the same period as St Peter's, Barton upon Humber.[56] It stands on the end of a spur of land, which falls away upon three sides; on the fourth side, to the north, the neck of the spur is cut across by a ditch, which cups a large mound lying partly within the present churchyard. Neither ditch nor mound have been investigated, and their dates are unknown.[57]

In the reign of Edward the Confessor, both Barton upon Humber and Earl's Barton were centres of large estates, held by rich and powerful king's thegns. At Barton upon Humber there were in 1066, besides the church and its priest, two mills, a market and a ferry which produced £4 a year. To Barton were attached lands in Horkstow and South Ferriby (where there was another ferry). The estate, assessed at just under 20 carucates of land, belonged to Ulf Fenman, whose extensive lands, the bulk of which lay in Lincolnshire, passed after the Conquest to Gilbert de Ghent.[58] Earl's Barton (whose church is not recorded in Domesday) was the *caput* of a group of vills including Great Doddington, Wilby, Mears Ashby and (probably) Ecton, a total of 20 hides of land. It was held by Bondi the staller, with sake and soke, that is, as bookland, and by 1086 had passed to Countess Judith. Most of Bondi's estate, however, amounting to 110 hides in six shires, had gone to Henry de Ferrers.[59] Bondi's title implies that

55 Warwick Rodwell and Kirsty Rodwell, 'St Peters Church, Barton upon Humber: excavation and structural survey, 1978–81', *Antiq. Journ.* lxii, 1982, 283–315, especially 308–9; see also Morris, *Churches*, 153.

56 The church is dated by the Taylors to the late tenth century (H.M. and J. Taylor, *Anglo-Saxon Architecture*, Cambridge 1965, i, 222); Fernie prefers a date in the early eleventh century, perhaps *c.*1030 (Fernie, *Architecture*, 143–4, 161, 178).

57 *Historical Monuments in the County of Northampton*, Royal Commission on Historical Monuments, London 1979, ii, 39–40; see also Morris, *Churches*, 253–5.

58 *GDB* fo. 354v. Ulf Fenman's land in Lincolnshire amounted to over 200 carucates of land; his other estates lay in Cambridgeshire and Huntingdonshire (22½ hides), Nottinghamshire and Derbyshire (25½ carucates), and Yorkshire (at least one carucate and perhaps more): see *GDB* fos 197, 197v, 207, 277v, 280v, 290v, 298v, 354v, 355, 355v, 364v, 369v, 373v, 376v, 377. In Nottinghamshire, Derbyshire, Yorkshire and Lincolnshire, he was one of those who held full jurisdiction and in Cambridgeshire he is called a king's thegn (see Olof von Feilitzen, *Pre-Conquest Personal Names of Domesday Book*, Uppsala 1937, 400–1).

59 *GDB* fo. 228. For the Earl's Barton estate, see David Hall, 'The late Saxon countryside: villages and their fields', *Anglo-Saxon Settlements*, ed. Della Hooke, Oxford 1989 (henceforth Hall, 'Late Saxon countryside'), 104–6. Bondi held about 110 hides of land in Berkshire, Buckinghamshire, Essex, Gloucestershire, Northamptonshire and Oxfordshire (*GDB* fos 60, 151, 157v, 166v, 225, 228, 228v; *LDB* fo. 57). His title implies a position in the royal administration; in Oxfordshire he had charge of a

he held office in the royal administration and Ulf Fenman was one of the leading thegns of the Danelaw. It is tempting to see in Barton upon Humber and Earl's Barton the *burhs* of these two prominent pre-Conquest magnates.

Nor do Barton upon Humber and Earl's Barton stand alone. Another 'estate-church' with a graveyard has been excavated at Raunds, Northants. An extensive dig on the site of the medieval manor of Furnells, in the north of the present village, revealed occupation levels going back to the settlement period. From the seventh century onwards, a series of timber halls occupied the site, each with associated outbuildings. About 900, a small stone church was built to the east of the hall, and by about 930, this church had acquired a chancel and a cemetery. It was by then surrounded by a ditch, which linked with the ditch of the hall-complex.[60]

The whole village of Raunds has been subjected to intensive archaeological and topographical investigation over the last few years.[61] By the middle of the eleventh century, there were several distinct holdings within the vill. The major manor, associated with the Furnells site, was held by Burgraed, a thegn with a considerable estate in Northamptonshire, Buckinghamshire and Bedfordshire, where he and his sons, Edwin, Ulf and Wulfsige, had land assessed at over 160 hides. Burgraed was a benefactor of Peterborough Abbey, and had some connection with the abbey of St Albans. I have argued elsewhere that his family was of sufficient importance to provide a wife for Edward the Confessor's nephew, Ralph, and that this marriage was the prelude to Ralph's appointment as Earl of the East Midlands in 1050.[62]

It was Earl Ralph's wife, Gytha, who held the second major tenement in Raunds. Her land there was attached, as sokeland, to her manor of Higham Ferrers.[63] It can be identified as the later manor of Burystead situated just to the north of the parish church and facing Furnells across the valley in which the village of Raunds lies. Excavation is still in progress around Burystead, and it is not yet clear whether a pre-Conquest manor-house underlies the later structure, or whether the tenement only acquired manorial status, and therefore a hall, in the twelfth century.[64] The name Burystead means 'the site of a *burh*', but may be a post-Conquest formation, referring to the twelfth-century hall.[65]

wood attached to the royal manor of Bampton (*GDB* fo. 154v) and he was probably reeve of the royal manor at Luton, Beds (*GDB* fo. 2180). He witnessed several royal charters in the 1060s (S. 1033–4, 1036, 1042) and two private transactions (S. 1235 and S. 1426, in Bedfordshire and Gloucestershire respectively).

60 Brian Dix, 'The Raunds area project: second interim report', *Northamptonshire Archaeology* xxi, 1986–87, 18–19; W.J. Blair, 'Local churches in Domesday Book and beyond', *Domesday Studies*, ed. J.C. Holt, Woodbridge 1987, 268.

61 Graham Cadman and Glenn Foard, 'Raunds: manorial and village origins', *Studies in Late Anglo-Saxon Settlement*, ed. Margaret Faull, Oxford 1984, 81–100; Glenn Foard and T. Pearson, 'The Raunds area project: first interim report', *Northamptonshire Archaeology* xx, 1985, 3–21; Hall, 'Late Saxon countryside', 106–7, 111–13 and see note 60 above.

62 *GDB* fo. 220v; see Ann Williams, 'The king's nephew: the family and career of Ralph, earl of Hereford', *Studies in Medieval History presented to R. Allen Brown*, ed. Christopher Harper-Bill, Christopher Holdsworth and Janet L. Nelson, Woodbridge 1989, 327–43.

63 *GDB* fo. 225v.

64 See note 60 above (first reference).

65 Smyth, *Place-name Elements*, 62; Karl-Inge Sandred, *English Place-names in -stead*, Uppsala 1963, 58.

Even if Gytha, like her kinsman Burgraed, had a manor-house in Raunds, it is another matter how often she was to be found there. The rich king's thegns held numerous manors and probably visited them in turn as occasion arose, just as the king and his court journeyed around the royal demesnes. Some traces of these aristocratic itineraries can be found in Domesday Book. At Eardisland, Herefordshire, which belonged to the earl of Mercia, the reeve 'had the custom . . . that on the arrival of his lady at the manor, he would present her with 18 *orae* of pence, so that she would be well-disposed'.[66] Earl Godwine had to buy his wife Gytha an estate at Woodchester, Gloucs., to live off while she stayed at Berkeley, whose produce she refused to consume, because of the destruction of its abbey.[67] Traces of favoured residences also appear from time to time. Aethelwine, ealdorman of East Anglia from 962 to 992 'had his hall and kept his court' at Upwood, Hunts.[68] Earl Godwine and his sons seem to have favoured Bosham, perhaps because its harbour was a convenient place to keep their ships in case of emergency.[69] Tovi the Proud, who held land both in Somerset and in Essex, chose to celebrate his wedding-feast in 1042 at Lambeth; it was on this occasion that King Harthacnut collapsed 'as he stood at his drink', and died soon afterwards.[70]

A few noblemen in the late Old English period were occasionally distinguished by the names of estates which belonged to them. Surnames are rare in pre-Conquest England, and toponymics very rare, so their use is of some interest. It has been said that 'an Anglo-Saxon toponymic will usually lead to a village', whereas a Norman toponymic leads to 'a lordship or castle'.[71] This I find somewhat misleading. The toponymics applied, albeit sporadically and rarely, to English thegns, do not indicate mere residence in a rural community, but the lords who owned the estates of which those communities were composed. Sired of Chilham did not simply live in the village of Chilham, Kent. He held the manor of Chilham *de rege Edwardo*, as one of the king's thegns who had full rights of jurisdiction in West Kent.[72] It may even have been his patrimony, if (as seems possible) he is related to Siward of (*aet*) Chilham, a member of the shire-court of Kent in the reign of Cnut.[73] Aristocratic *burhs*, no less than Norman castles, functioned as centres of lordship, to which dues and services were rendered.

That such places should be defensible is not surprising, given the conditions prevalent in the tenth and eleventh centuries. The struggle of the West Saxon kings against the Viking rulers of York was both bitter and prolonged. Though it ended with the incorporation of the north into the West Saxon hegemony,

66 *GDB* fo. 179v.

67 *GDB* fo. 164.

68 Hart, *Charters of Eastern England*, 231.

69 Ann Williams, 'Land and power in the eleventh century: the estates of Harold Godwineson', *Anglo-Norman Studies* iii, 1980, 185.

70 *ASC* sub anno 1042.

71 J.C. Holt, *'What's in a Name?' Family Nomenclature and the Norman Conquest*, The Stenton Lecture 1981, Reading 1982, 10.

72 *GDB* fos 1, 10.

73 Robertson, *Charters*, 170, 372, 419.

raiding from Scotland, Wales and the Norse colonies in Ireland did not cease. As late as the year 1000, Aethelred II was ravaging Cumberland and the Isle of Man to prevent incursions from Ireland. Raids from Scandinavia recommenced in 980, and the later part of Aethelred's reign saw the devastating campaigns which led to the Danish Conquest. Even in the reign of Edward the Confessor, the south-east was raided by a fleet from Scandinavia, and the assessment of Fareham, Hants, was reduced from 30 hides to 20, 'on account of the Vikings, because it is on the sea'.[74] The prevalence of war and violence might be expected to encourage the building of stronger defences around the halls of the English noble. Such defences, however, were not primarily military in character or function. The *burhs* which figure so largely in the wars of the early tenth century, and again, to a lesser extent, in Aethelred II's time, were not defensible manor-houses, but the urban and quasi-urban fortifications built by Alfred and his successors. Fortification for specifically military purposes may have been a royal prerogative. Nowhere is private fortification actually forbidden, but the statement of William of Malmesbury that King Athelstan, when he took York in 927, demolished the *castrum* of the Viking kings 'so that there might be no place for disloyalty to shelter in', is suggestive.[75] The *castrum* cannot refer to the walls of York, and presumably means a smaller fortification within the city, perhaps on the site of the Viking palace in the area known as King's Court.[76] It might be objected that William of Malmesbury is attributing to Athelstan actions more appropriate to the twelfth century than to the tenth, but such internal strongholds are not unknown. Traces of a ditched enclosure were found under the site of Stamford Castle.[77] At York itself, the area of Marygate, around St Olave's Church, was once known as *Earlesburgh*, which suggests a fortified residence belonging to the earls of Northumbria; it was Earl Siward (before 1035–1055) who founded the church of St Olave.[78]

The defences of the *burh* in its manorial sense seem to be directed not against external enemies, but against neighbours. Successive West Saxon kings legislated against private violence, beginning with Alfred, who laid down the circumstances in which a man can besiege his enemy's house.[79] In the second code of Edmund (940–6) the crime of *hamsocn*, assault on a man in his own house, makes its first appearance. The penalty was forfeiture of the offender's property, 'and it shall be for the king to decide whether his life shall be preserved'.[80] *Hamsocn* was one of the pleas of the crown, whose judgement was reserved to

74 *ASC* sub anno 1048; *GDB* fo. 40v.

75 *Willelmi Malmesberiensis Monachi de Gestis Regum Anglorum*, ed. William Stubbs, RS 90, 1887 (henceforth *GR*) i, 197.

76 For the Viking palace see R.A. Hall, ed., *Viking-age York and the North*, Council for British Archaeology Research Report xxvii, London 1978, 34.

77 Christine Mahoney and David Roffe, 'Stamford: the development of an Anglo-Scandinavian borough', *Anglo-Norman Studies* v, 1983, 203–4.

78 Alfred P. Smyth, *Scandinavian York and Dublin*, ii, Dublin 1979, 235; *ASC* sub anno 1055.

79 Alfred 42, see Attenborough, *Laws*, 82–5.

80 II Edmund 6, see Robertson, *Laws*, 10–11. Cf. Rebecca V. Coleman, 'Domestic peace and public order in Anglo-Saxon law', *The Anglo-Saxons: Synthesis and Achievement*, ed. J. Douglas Woods and David A.E. Pelteret, Waterloo (Ontario) 1985, 49–61. It was *hamsocn* that Eustace of Boulogne and his men committed at Dover in 1051 (*ASC* 'E', sub anno 1051).

the king. The *Institutes of London*, which date from Aethelred II's reign, decree that anyone slain while committing *hamsocn* 'shall lie in an unhonoured grave' and the customs of Oxford, preserved in Domesday Book, distinguish between *hamsocn* which results in injury to the householder and his family, and that which results in death; in the latter case, the offender's 'body and all his substance shall be in the king's power, except for his wife's dowry'.[81] Yet private violence was not rare, and was often abetted by those officials charged with its control. In the 990s, the widow of Wulfbald of Bourne 'went, along with her son, and slew Wulfbald's cousin, Eadmaer the king's thegn, with his 15 companions, on the estate of Bourne'.[82] At about the same time, three brothers in Oxfordshire, whose servant had stolen a bridle, were involved in a fight with the bridle's owners, in which two of them were killed, but the royal reeves of Oxford and Buckingham allowed the thieves Christian burial.[83] A particularly flagrant example of *hamsocn* on the part of a royal officer occurred in 1002, when Earldorman Leofsige slew the king's high-reeve, Aefic, 'in his own house, without warning' and was exiled. When Leofsige's sister Aethelflaed attempted to help him, thereby committing *flymenafyrmth*, the crime of harbouring fugitives, she lost her property.[84]

It is in this context that the fortified houses of the English nobles should be seen. More serious acts of defiance, against the king himself, took a different form. It was the private fleet, not the private *burh*, which was used in such cases. When, in 1009, the South Saxon thegn, Wulfnoth *cild*, was 'accused to the king', he took twenty ships from the fleet and went raiding along the Sussex coast. In like manner the staller, Osgod Clapa, when he was exiled in 1046, collected his fleet at Bruges, and three years later ravaged around the Naze in Essex. In 1051, to quote the most famous example, Earl Godwine gathered his men at Beverstone, a member of his manor of Berkeley, Gloucs., but when things came to the crunch, it was not to any manor-house that he turned, but to his fleet, lying in the harbour at Bosham.[85] It never seems to have occurred to a disgruntled nobleman to retire to his *burh* and fortify it against attack.[86] The bishops, abbots and lay noblemen who travelled the roads of Europe on their own or the king's business must have seen the castles rising, but they never felt tempted to build them on their own account.

This leads us to consideration of the difference, clear to eleventh-century commentators, between a castle and a private *burh*. On the continent, a distinction between castles and other fortifications and defences was as old as the ninth century. In the Edict of Pitres, 864, Charles the Bald ordered the destruction of

81 IV Aethelred II, 4, see Robertson, *Laws*, 74–5. The Oxford customs, see *GDB* fo. 154v.

82 S. 877, printed Robertson, *Charters*, 128–31.

83 S. 883, translated *EHD* i, 526–27.

84 *ASC* sub anno 1002, S. 926; see F.M. Stenton, *Latin Charters of the Anglo-Saxon Period*, Oxford 1955, 76–80.

85 *ASC* sub anno 1009, 1046, 1049, 1051.

86 An apparent exception is the occupation of Wimbome and Christchurch by the rebellious aetheling, Aethelwold, in 901 (ASC sub anno 901). Both may have been 'urban' *burhs* however; Christchurch appears in the almost contemporary *Burghal Hidage*, and Wimborne had burgesses by 1066. For Wimborne, see also John Blair, 'Minster churches in the landscape', *Anglo-Saxon Settlements*, ed. Della Hooke, Oxford 1989, 41–4.

all *castella et firmitates et haias* built without royal permission, because 'the villagers (vicini) and those dwelling round about suffer many depredations and impositions from them'.[87] The comments of Jean Dunbabin on this passage seem relevant to the English as well as the Frankish situation:[88]

> . . . whether the large number of simple defended towers in which individual families lived ought to be considered castles at all and whether they posed any threat to public order must be doubted. . . . It is only the . . . castle, *the fortified administrative centre* (my italics), which is at issue.

Fortified administrative centres are precisely what aristocratic burns were not. The public administration of the English kingdom was based upon the shire, the hundred and the vill, not on the manors of even the greatest lords. Even in those cases where whole hundreds had come into lay or (more usually) ecclesiastical hands, the king's officers could not be denied entry. However powerful the earls and king's thegns, or for that matter, the bishops and abbots might be, they were not allowed to slip through this net. The *burh* was the centre of its estate, and the men of that estate were justiciable, in lesser matters, in its court; the lord of the burn answered to the shire and hundred. The lord's *burh* remained a private house.

To quote the words of Allen Brown, 'there was no room, no occasion, no power–vacuum at the centre to promote the growth of local and feudal territorial power'.[89] It was the king's business to provide for the defence of the realm, and even in the darkest days of King Aethelred's reign, when 'one shire would not help the next', the local magnates did not take matters into their own hands.[90] The outrage against the Norman castle in Herefordshire was directed precisely against its encroachment on royal and comital power; it intruded into Earl Swein's district (*folgoð*) and its castellans 'inflicted every possible injury and insult on the *king's men* (my italics) in those parts.'[91] The language of the entry in the *Anglo-Saxon Chronicle* is strikingly similar to that in the Edict of Pitres, quoted above. The king was the unity of his folk, the guarantor of law and justice, the source of patronage and power. It did not occur to anyone to question this situation; the English, as William of Poitiers was to remark, 'were accustomed to serve a king and wished only for a king to be their lord'.[92] In such circumstances it is not surprising that no castles arose on the estates of the Old English nobility. They preferred, as William of Malmesbury unkindly remarked, 'to consume their whole substance in mean and despicable dwellings' than to live frugally 'in noble and splendid mansions'.[93] After all, an Englishman's house is his castle.

87 MGH *Legum*, i, 499. See also the similar distinction between *castelli* and *fortitudines* in cap. 4 of the *Consuetudines et Justicie* of 1091 (C.H. Haskins, *Norman Institutions*, New York and London 1913, 1960, 281ff).
88 Jean Dunbabin, *France in the Making, 843–1180*, Oxford 1985, 41.
89 Brown, 'Origins of the castle', 139.
90 *ASC* sub anno 1010.
91 *ASC* B' sub anno 1051.
92 R. Allen Brown, *The Norman Conquest*, London 1984, 37.
93 *GR* ii 305.

2

Royal Power and Castles in Norman England*

Richard Eales

All the great historians of Norman England, from J. H. Round to Allen Brown, have given a central place to the castle in their pictures of Anglo-Norman feudal society, including the evolving role and status of knights within that society. To some, it may appear that there is little more to be said. In 1969, for example, Allen Brown wrote, with perhaps a little calculated overstatement, that 'it sometimes seems . . . almost every question one may raise about castles has already been raised, and answered, often definitively answered', by Mrs Ella Armitage in her book *The Early Norman Castles of the British Isles*, published in 1912.[1] This, however, can hardly be the case as long as Norman England itself is still subject to reassessment and reinterpretation. The construction and use of castles in this period is not a discrete subject which can be satisfactorily resolved in isolation. It is intimately bound up with other changes of all kinds: perceived military threats and opportunities, within England and on its borders; fluctuations in incomes and resources at different social levels; the legal enforcement of lordship and its economic base; the symbolic assertion of social and political status; as well as the degree of control exerted over local affairs by kings and their officials. The study of all these general problems helps to throw light on the development of the castle, and *vice versa*. To take merely one example: the painstaking research required to unravel tenurial geography over the Anglo-Norman period still has a long way to go, but it must inevitably help to associate feudal *capita* and the economic centres of lordships with active castle sites, even if many of the identifications can never be made with certainty. The present paper is a much more general undertaking. It aims to survey the findings of Norman castle studies in several key areas, and to draw out their implications for political history, and especially for the effectiveness of royal territorial power.[2]

* I should like to thank Charles Coulson and Bruce Webster for reading drafts of this paper; also John Gillingham and Ann Williams for helpful comments and information supplied after the Strawberry Hill meeting. A longer-term debt felt by many is to Allen Brown, whose pioneering work did so much to set a standard for the historical treatment of this subject which is hard to follow.

1 Ella S. Armitage, *Early Norman Castles of the British Isles*, London 1912 (*henceforth* Armitage). R. A. Brown, 'An Historian's Approach to the Origins of the Castle in England', *Archaeological Journal* cxxvi, 1969, 131–48, quotation at 134.

2 This means that certain aspects of the subject are not discussed in detail here, though the author is aware of their importance, including especially castle-guard services and their equivalents. See n. 64 below.

I

It is no accident that Allen Brown's verdict, quoted above, comes from a paper on 'the origins of the castle in England'. Mrs Armitage's main aim in her book was to set this particular question to rights. Her achievement was to demonstrate to most people's subsequent satisfaction that the castle, defined as the seriously fortified residence of a lord and his household – give or take the qualifications over terms inevitable in any such definition – was introduced into England by the Normans. Furthermore, the characteristic and predominant, though not universal, form of the early castle, the 'motte and bailey' plan consisting of an artificial mound crowned with defences and a fortified enclosure attached to it, was in all cases a Norman importation. Nineteenth-century identifications of mottes with Anglo-Saxon *burhs* or Roman burial mounds were comprehensively swept away.[3] So marked was the arrival of the new phenomenon with the Normans that the only mottes for which there now seems to be probable pre-conquest evidence are the handful built by Norman colonists in the reign of Edward the Confessor, like Ewias Harold and Richard's Castle in Herefordshire. The new architectural form arrived with an admixture of new technology, both in building and in the mounted warfare techniques practised by military households of knights, together with the social organisation needed to support them. Mrs Armitage's conclusions thus fit into a specific historiographical context: they form the architectural equivalent of J. H. Round's thesis about the introduction of knight service into England, developed in the 1890s.[4] Both historians postulated a sudden departure in all essentials from what had gone before, and hence tended to underwrite a cataclysmic view of the Norman Conquest.

Cataclysmic views of the Norman Conquest have never, of course, commanded general assent, but for many years Mrs Armitage's arguments have seemed much less debatable or in need of modification than J. H. Round's. Naturally, though, her views were not restated with such force in 1969 because the peace of ages had closed over them, but because they were just then being queried, in several important respects. Archaeologists had begun to emphasize the fact that a significant proportion of early Norman castles in England did not possess mottes, but were simple ditched and banked enclosures, now christened 'ring-works'.[5] This in itself was not new, but in 1966 Brian Davison combined it with the then less well-known observation that there is an embarrassing lack of clear evidence for mottes in Normandy itself before 1066, to suggest that the characteristic motte and bailey design was not necessarily brought to England from Normandy.[6] It may rather have evolved in the course of the conquest

3 Armitage, 1–79.

4 J. H. Round, 'The Introduction of Knight Service into England', in *Feudal England*, London 1895, 182–257 in 1964 edn. Originally published *EHR* vi, 1891, 417–43, 625–45; vii, 1892, 11–24.

5 D. J. C. King and L. Alcock, 'Ringworks of England and Wales', in *Château-Gaillard* iii, *European Castle Studies*, ed. A. J. Taylor, 1969 (*henceforth* King and Alcock, 'Ringworks'), 90–127, with references to earlier literature.

6 B. K. Davison, 'Early Earthwork Castles: a new model', in *Château-Gaillard* iii, *European Castle Studies*, ed. A. J. Taylor, 1969, 37–47.

process, among the Normans and their continental allies, who could pool experiences of fortification over much of northern Europe. His hypothesis took some support from the observations of D. J. C. King and L. Alcock, who pointed out that Norman ring-works were commonest in the southern counties first exposed to settlement after 1066 – though the distinction is not a sharp one – hence that mottes may have become more common as settlement progressed.[7] Then in 1967, in a paper designed to launch the Royal Archaeological Institute's research project into the origins of the castle in England, Davison advanced the further suggestion that if many of the castles built by the Normans after 1066 were simple ring-works, then such a basic form of defence can hardly have been unknown to their Saxon predecessors.[8] Size of enclosures is a crucial variable in this. The Saxons were, of course, familiar with defensive earthworks, and indeed stone walls, but the most characteristic fortifications of late Saxon England, the network of *burhs* constructed by Alfred and his successors, were places of mass refuge, ancestors of the Normans' planted towns rather than their castles. Davison very reasonably queried whether it could be assumed that private and seigneurial fortification was unknown before 1066, at least without further investigation. The excavation of some promising late Saxon sites was accordingly set down as one of the aims of the Royal Institute project. Rather more ambitiously, in advance of the evidence, he called for 'a complete rethinking of our ideas concerning the place of private fortification in the late Saxon state'.[9]

Twenty years on, it can only be concluded, provisionally, that the archaeological findings have thrown little new light on the question of origins. The work of the Royal Institute project published over the years, most substantially in 1977 as *Five Castle Excavations*, has underlined just how difficult it is to test general historical theories by investigating a few selected sites.[10] The thorough excavation of substantial earthworks is not easy. Even the most modern archaeologist equipped with the latest scientific techniques may be unlucky in his finds, and have nothing on which to base a reasonably precise date, or simply pick the wrong site for an investigation which, because it is so expensive and time-consuming, cannot easily be repeated elsewhere.[11] At Sulgrave in Northamptonshire Brian Davison failed to identify serious defences around the stone and timber pre-conquest buildings; the existing substantial ring-work is Norman.[12] Only from Goltho in Lincolnshire, so far, is there unambiguous evidence of a pre-conquest lordly residence with considerable earthwork defences, first constructed before 900, and passing through two further phases of rebuilding before the intrusion of a 'considerably stronger' Norman motte and bailey castle in the

7 King and Alcock, 'Ringworks', 102–106.

8 B. K. Davison, 'The Origins of the Castle in England: The Institute's research project', *Archaeological Journal* cxxiv, 1967 (*henceforth* Davison, 'Origins'), 202–11.

9 Davison, 'Origins', 207.

10 *Five Castle Excavations*, Royal Archaeological Institute 1978, first published *Archaeological Journal* cxxxiv, 1977, 1–156.

11 For a survey of recent methods, see L. Alcock, 'Castle-studies and the archaeological sciences: some possibilities and problems', in *Castles in Wales and the Marches: Essays in honour of D. J. Cathcart King*, ed. J. R. Kenyon and R. Avent, Cardiff 1987, 5–22.

12 B. K. Davison, 'Excavations at Sulgrave, Northamptonshire, 1960–76: an interim report', in *Five Castle Excavations*, Royal Archaeological Institute, London 1978, 105–14.

late eleventh century.[13] Attempts to investigate the very earliest Norman sites in England have encountered similar difficulties. Excavations at Richard's Castle in 1962–64, for instance, discovered a great deal about the later history of the castle, but nothing about its likely origins in the Confessor's reign.[14]

The door is not yet closed on the possibility of private fortification in late Saxon England, despite the problems in demonstrating its existence. The word *burh* has an early generic meaning of 'enclosure', but is usually identified in the tenth and eleventh centuries with the fortified boroughs, or towns, of the Wessex kings. Yet, at the same time as it became the characteristic term for these elaborately defended centres, it also continued down to the end of the Saxon period to be applied to manorial enclosures. The *burh-geat*, or burh gate, identified in the early eleventh-century tract *Of People's Ranks and Laws* as one of the distinguishing marks of thegnhood, must have had some physical reality as well as being a symbol of lordly jurisdiction.[15] If late Saxon England was thickly sown with seigneurially significant sites which were even lightly defended – and this has yet to be proved – then it would be a fact of some significance, with implications for the local power taken over by incoming Norman lords after 1066. Norman castles were symbols of seigneurial authority too. To assert *a priori* that any pre-conquest structures were not castles, and therefore can be ruled out of the subject altogether, is to pursue definition at the expense of explanation. Yet the archaeological fuel to power a 'complete re-thinking' of the subject will take many years to accumulate, if indeed it can be obtained at all.

On the other hand, it is as clear as ever that the building of Norman castles in England after 1066 was something fundamentally new; entirely so in scale and largely so in form. The main consequence of modern excavation on castle sites since the 1950s has been to emphasize the sheer range and variety of Norman construction, with mottes added to earlier banked enclosures, as at Castle Neroche in Somerset, mottes built to contain the foundations of towers which were to surmount them, as at Farnham in Surrey and South Mimms in Middlesex, and in general successive phases of redesign and adaptation on almost every site occupied for any length of time.[16] Techniques were adapted to local conditions of topography and surface geology, to make use of whatever materials were available. It must be remembered too that while the Normans built many ring-works, there survive from this period, according to the most

13 G. Beresford, 'Goltho manor, Lincolnshire: the buildings and their surrounding defences *c.*850–1150', *Anglo-Norman Studies* iv, 1981, 13–36.

14 P. E. Curnow and M. W. Thompson, 'Excavations at Richard's Castle, Herefordshire, 1962–4', *Journal of the British Archaeological Association* xxxii, 1969, 104–27.

15 For general discussion see Armitage, 11–30 and R. A. Brown, *English Castles*, 3rd edn, London 1976 (*henceforth* Brown, *English Castles*), 44–49; for *burh* as manorial enclosure A. J. Robertson, *Anglo-Saxon Charters*, 2nd edn, Cambridge 1956, no. 109 at 204–207, and F. E. Harmer, *Anglo-Saxon Writs*, Manchester 1952, no. 73 at 339–40; for the *burh-geat* Davison, 'Origins', 204. Brown is wilfully misleading at 49, when he writes 'there is a difference between one's garden fence or wall and the walls of Caernarvon castle'. The difference in question is between Saxon and Norman enclosures of the mid-eleventh century.

16 For general accounts of findings, see Brown, *English Castles*, 52–65; D. J. C. King, *The Castle in England and Wales: an Interpretative History*, London 1988 (*henceforth* King, *Interpretative History*), 42–61.

recent counts, between three and four castles with mottes for every one without. The characteristic Norman castle thus was a new visual feature in the landscape, which helps to explain the use of the alien local-word *castel* to describe it in the Anglo-Saxon Chronicle 'E' version for 1051.[17] Surveying and aerial photography, as well as excavation, have shown that many Norman castles, like Pleshey in Essex, overlie earlier field boundaries and were apparently new, even as seigneurial centres, built to serve the new lordships created by the conquest.[18] In urban centres too, Norman castles, with their characteristics of small area and defence by height, were obvious intrusions into the Saxon *burhs*, or surviving Roman forts, which contained them. A plan or an aerial photograph of Tamworth, Wallingford, Lydford, Portchester, Pevensey, or many others, makes this point very clearly.[19]

Nothing produced by modern research therefore denies the accuracy of the much-quoted assessment made by the early twelfth-century chronicler Orderic Vitalis: 'the fortifications called castles by the Normans (*Galli*) were scarcely known in the English provinces, and so the English – in spite of their courage and love of fighting – could put up only a weak defence to their enemies'.[20] It seems to be the case, though, that Normandy as well as England experienced a dramatic surge in castle construction between 1066 and the time that Orderic wrote his judgement on the conquest of England, about 1125. Even now, it remains very difficult to say anything with much confidence about pre-1066 Norman castles, and that is especially true of mottes. No early motte can be dated with the same accuracy as the large ring-work of Le Plessis-Grimoult, fortified in the 1040s and known to have been abandoned after the unsuccessful revolt of 1047.[21] Recent excavation has tended to transfer accepted pre-1066 sites to the late eleventh or twelfth centuries, and David Bates recently concluded, on the basis of work done in the Pays de Caux, that 'castle-building in pre-1066 Normandy was restricted to a small élite'.[22] It remains, though, almost inconceivable that mottes were unknown in Normandy at this time, even if they were still few in number. There are at least a few motte sites elsewhere in northern France which have reasonably secure early dates, and the line of dissemination through Normandy, Flanders and Brittany to England cannot seriously be questioned.

17 King and Alcock, 'Ringworks', 96–106; D. J. C. King, 'The field archaeology of mottes', *Château-Gaillard* v, *Etudes de Castellologie médiévale*, Caen 1972 (*henceforth* King, 'Mottes'), 102; and for a more recent discussion C. J. Spurgeon, 'Mottes and castle-ringworks in Wales', in *Castles in Wales and the Marches*, 23–49. *The Anglo-Saxon Chronicle*, ed. D. Whitelock, 1961, 119 (for 1051), 125 (for further use of the term under 1052).

18 On Pleshey see Brown, *English Castles*, 51, 54 (with aerial photograph).

19 C. A. Ralegh Radford, 'The Pre-Conquest Boroughs of England, ninth to eleventh centuries', *PBA* lxiv, 1978, 131–53, contains many such illustrations.

20 *OV* ii, 218. See also M. Chibnall, 'Orderic Vitalis on castles', in *Studies in Medieval History presented to R. Allen Brown*, ed. C. Harper-Bill, C. Holdsworth and J. L. Nelson, Woodbridge 1989 (henceforth *Studies for R. A. B.*), 43–56.

21 E. Zadora-Rio, 'L'enceinte fortifiée du Plessis-Grimoult, résidence seigneuriale du XIe siècle', *Château-Gaillard* v, *Études de Castellologie médiévale*, Caen 1972, 227–39.

22 D. Bates, *Normandy Before 1066*, London 1982 (*henceforth* Bates), 115. Compare Brown, English *Castles*, 25–39; J. Yver, 'Les châteaux forts en Normandie jusqu'au milieu de XIe siècle', *Bulletin de la Société des Antiquaires de Normandie* liii, 1955–56, 28–63.

The debate launched in the 1960s about the origins of the castle in England did not turn out to be one of those set-piece historical controversies – it has been too one-sided for that – but it has opened many new approaches and lines of research. Perhaps what is most needed now is to move the debate on from the origins to the uses of castles in the Norman period.

II

The sheer scale of castle building in Norman England is crucial, so it is useful to review the various estimates which have been made of the numbers of castles between 1066 and 1200. No such estimates can usefully aspire to precision, and they will always be incomplete. If based on documentary sources, they are rendered selective by the partial survival of the sources, especially for the 'first century of English feudalism' after 1066. There is also the problem of the fluctuation and interchangeable use of castle terms: *castrum, castellum, oppidum* and so on.[23] In the main this is only a secondary issue for the enumeration of Norman castles, as almost every site referred to in documents by any of these terms qualifies as a castle on archaeological grounds too, unless it cannot be located or has been completely destroyed. But it is salutary to bear in mind that contemporary vocabulary was fluid, and affords no easy answer to modern worries over what was or was not a castle. The problems of archaeological research have already been referred to. Ring-works cannot easily be assigned a Norman date on the evidence of surface morphology alone. Mottes appear less problematic, and in the main they are, but hidden among the current listings are broad flat 'mottes' only a metre or two above the surrounding land surface that may well turn out to have been wrongly identified. Whatever definitions and methodologies be adopted, there will always be marginal cases.[24] Yet all these doubts and reservations should not obscure the progress in recent work towards more reliable approximate figures.

For the early period before 1100, documentary sources provide only a starting point, and irreducible minimum numbers. Domesday Book mentions about fifty castles in 1086, but the references are incidental and unsystematic. In Kent, for instance, Canterbury castle is mentioned only in connection with an exchange of houses between the King and the abbot of St Augustine's Abbey; Rochester castle only under Aylesford manor, where the bishop of Rochester was compensated for the land which had gone to form the castle site. The *leuga* or jurisdictional area around Tonbridge castle is referred to, but not the castle itself.[25] Other possible or certain sites, like Dover, do not appear; and elsewhere too, Domesday Book fails to mention some castles built by William I in his

23 The 'Index Verborum' in *OV* i, 244–386, is a valuable guide to use of vocabulary in one major source. See also M. Chibnall, 'Orderic Vitalis on castles', in *Studies for R. A. B.*, 53–54; Armitage, 383–84. Attempts to suggest that these terms could be used consistently, as by B. S. Bachrach, 'Early medieval fortifications in the west of France; a revised technical vocabulary', *Technology and Culture* xvi, 1975, 531–69, are not entirely convincing.

24 King, 'Mottes', 101–12, discusses the classification of sites by height.

25 H. Ellis, *A General Introduction to Domesday Book*, 1833, i, 211–24; H. C. Darby, *Domesday*

major campaigns, like Pevensey and Exeter. By taking the narrative sources and all other available records into account Mrs Armitage added names like these, and increased her list of known pre-1100 castles in England to eighty-four. A few additions have been proposed by more recent scholars, but not many, and it is difficult to push the total much above ninety, with another ten or so in Wales, which Armitage did not attempt to include in her list.[26] Norman historians, however, have always been convinced that the number of castles built before 1100 was very much greater than this. In 1932 Sir Frank Stenton accepted that the great majority of motte and bailey castles were undocumented, and referred to 'the scores of earthworks in the heart of England which we now know to represent castles built between the battle of Hastings and the death of King Stephen'.[27] He declined, however, in the current state of knowledge, to venture any numerical estimates. Sidney Painter in 1935 followed a similar approach, but was typically more prepared to press it to an intelligent conjecture: that the maximum number of English castles active at any one time was probably 500 to 600, and should be placed around the year 1100.[28] All such assessments rest on two linked arguments. The first is the certainty, from archaeological survey, that high figures can be established for castle sites over the 'Norman-Angevin' period as a whole – 1066 to *c.*1200 – even if archaeology alone cannot date many of them more precisely. The second is the overwhelming probability, on general historical grounds, that most of these castles were built in the early part of the period: before 1100, and in southern or midland England at least probably before 1075 or 1080.

Lists of castles identified by archaeological survey were originally obtained by combining the county studies carried out under the auspices of the Victoria County History and the Royal Commission on Historical Monuments since the early years of the century, though new work has been added in the last thirty years.[29] John Beeler, in his pioneering 'list of castles in England and Wales, 1052–1189', published in 1966, gives 910 names, 784 English and 126 Welsh. But for most of them no evidence or descriptions are cited, and the claim that he had included all 'castles considered by specialists to have been built before (1189)' is hardly enlightening.[30] Derek Renn's study and gazetteer *Norman Castles in Britain*, first published in 1968, covers the period down to 1216, but yields a smaller list of sites: 491 English and 121 Welsh, making a total of 612. Renn gives descriptions of these castles, but is nowhere very forthcoming about

England, Cambridge 1977, 313–17. For Kent, *Domesday Book, vol. 1 Kent*, ed. P. Morgan, Chichester 1983, C–1, 1–2, 2–4.

26 Armitage, 94–250 and table at 396–99. The list in J. Beeler, *Warfare in England 1066–1189*, Ithaca 1966 (*henceforth* Beeler, *Warfare*), Appendix B at 427–38 gives 93 in England and 11 in Wales; King, 'Mottes', gives 94 English castles, with some differences from Beeler.

27 F. M. Stenton, *The First Century of English Feudalism 1066–1166*, Oxford 1932, 2nd edn, 1961 (*henceforth* Stenton, *First Century*), 192–217, quotation at 199.

28 S. Painter, 'English castles in the early middle ages: their number, location and legal position', *Speculum* x, 1935, 321–32, reprinted in *Feudalism and Liberty*, Baltimore 1961 (*henceforth* Painter), 125–43, figure given at 127.

29 D. J. C. King, *Castellarium Anglicanum*, 2 vols, New York 1983 (*henceforth* King, *Castellarium*), i, xi–xiv discusses the history of the subject.

30 Beeler, *Warfare*, Appendix A, 397–426, quotation at 397. Totals are calculated by me.

his criteria for selection, or more specifically for omission, of candidate sites listed by other writers.[31] Larger numbers have been restated in the recent work of D. J. C. King. In 1969 King and L. Alcock gave a total of 1,062 known castles from eleventh- and twelfth-century England and Wales: 723 mottes, 198 ring-works, and 141 others such as stone buildings, though only the ring-works were named and described. Of these 770 are English, 292 Welsh.[32] King's full materials, with supporting descriptions and references, were published in *Castellarium Anglicanum* in 1983. He does not give separate listings for 'early' castles in this book, though the implied figure is evidently rather higher than the 1969 one.[33] All such figures, though, must remain to some degree provisional, because future research may add names or remove them from the list; and approximate, because there will always be marginal cases. It might be best to imitate demographic historians and seek to define a range of plausible estimates. In the light of King's work, this might be set as between 950 and 1150 for pre-1200 English and Welsh castles, with the balance of probability lying in the upper part of the range.[34] The maximum number of sites in active use at any one time is, of course, quite another matter. If that number was two-thirds or less of the total over the whole century and a half, as is not improbable, then we return to a figure much closer to Sidney Painter's guess of 500 or 600 castles.

The other half of Painter's thesis, that the peak number of castles was reached around the year 1100, can only be confirmed in terms of probabilities. But there is firmer ground in the period after 1154, with the survival of the pipe rolls from the 1150s and the chancery rolls from the end of the century. Allen Brown exploited these records to construct his 'List of Castles 1154–1216' published in 1959. It contains about 270 castles in both 1154 and 1214; a total of 327 over the whole sixty-year period. Since the pipe rolls, for instance, include not just royal castles but baronial castles even temporarily in the king's hands, it is likely that his list – in contrast to document-based lists for earlier periods – contains, as Brown claimed, 'a high proportion of active sites'.[35] The large numbers of undocumented castles known only from survey must accordingly be assigned to an earlier period, with the implication not only that they were built before 1154, but that they had ceased to be in active use by that date, or soon afterwards.

31 D. Renn, *Norman Castles in Britain*, London and New York 1968, 2nd edn, 1973 used here, 'County guide to castles' at 358–69, discrepant in a few cases with the main gazetteer. Totals are calculated by me, counting Monmouth as part of England, as in Beeler, *Warfare*.

32 King and Alcock, 'Ringworks', 98; increased to 741 mottes and 205 ringworks in King, 'Mottes', 102. I have again counted Monmouth with England in the English and Welsh figures.

33 King, *Castellarium*, addition of county totals gives a figure of 1,944 castles of all kinds (1,528 English, 399 Welsh, 17 on islands) compared with 1,580 in King and Alcock, 'Ringworks'. But many of the additional sites are later ones. Northumberland alone accounts for over 100 of the new sites, mostly late medieval tower houses.

34 If this figure turns out to be seriously wrong, it is likely to be as an underestimate. But there is no warrant for some of the exaggerated figures still circulating in textbooks, e.g. F. Barlow, *The Feudal Kingdom of England 1042–1216*, 4th edn, London 1988, 87: 'by 1100 some five or six thousand castles had risen in England'.

35 R. A. Brown, 'A List of Castles, 1154–1216', *EHR* lxxiv, 1959 (*henceforth* Brown, 'List'), 249–80, quotation at 259. Elsewhere Brown, *English Castles*, 215, and 'The Castles of the Conquest', in *Domesday Studies*, Woodbridge 1987, 69, suggests that the documented figure 'may well be incomplete by at least 12 per cent' and proposes a corrected guess of 400 sites in this period.

Documents can be misleading on this point: a phrase like '*castellum firmare*' could mean to build a castle, or rebuild it, or just stock and prepare it for war – in some later sources this meaning is demonstrable.[36] In general it seems reasonable to draw the corollary from archaeological evidence that castles occupied over long periods were repeatedly refurbished and rebuilt, to argue that sites not so treated were in use only for short periods. Even longer occupation could be discontinuous.

All this is very relevant to the question of what happened to castles in Stephen's reign. The Anglo-Saxon Chronicle, 'E' version, gives a famous description of anarchy at the local level: 'every powerful man built his castles and held them against (the king) and they filled the country full of castles. They oppressed the wretched people of the country severely with castle-building. When the castles were built, they filled them with devils and wicked men.'[37] But despite the familiarity of this translation, it is far from clear that a large number of new castles were built in response to the conflicts of 1138–1153. The civil war was intermittent and occasional in all except a very few areas. Not many places were exposed to repeated attacks like Wallingford, which is surrounded by a number of siege works from this period.[38] Narrative sources also describe the construction of some improvised castles, like the conversion of Bampton church tower near Oxford into a miniature fortress by supporters of Matilda in 1141, referred to in the *Gesta Stephani*. Such expedients were unlikely to have provided anything more than temporary refuges; Bampton was stormed within a few months by Stephen's forces.[39] F. M. Stenton pointed out that 'the castles which determined the general course of the war, with hardly a single prominent exception, were castles which are known to have been in existence before the troubles began'.[40] Even for minor strongholds, men, whether loyal adherents of one of the claimants to the throne or freebooting anarchists, are likely to have taken over and refurbished existing sites, rather than building afresh. D. J. C. King estimated that, of 110 castles first mentioned in Stephen's reign, only 'some twenty-seven are recorded as *having been built* at that time', and even that figure might be queried because of the ambiguous terminology employed.[41] The chronicle sources provide much better evidence for the occupation and use of castles during the civil war, and for their relative desertion and disuse after 1153, than for a renewed spate of castle building in Stephen's reign. Even when new sites do appear in this period, they should not necessarily be set down as part of a general reaction to anarchy. Tenurial changes and the rise of new families, like monastic foundations, continued under Stephen as they had under Henry I, and demanded architectural expression. William d'Aubigny's works at Castle Rising and New Buckenham in Norfolk during the 1140s might be

36 Stenton, *First Century*, 204–205.

37 *ASC*, 199.

38 King, *Castellarium* i, 13; ii, 566–67 brings together the evidence on Wallingford.

39 *Gesta Stephani*, ed. K. R. Potter, 2nd edn, Oxford, OMT 1976, 138–140.

40 Stenton, *First Century*, 202.

41 King, *Castellarium* i, pp. xxxi–xxxii. The figure of 110 is almost the same as in Beeler, *Warfare*, 430–34.

regarded as falling into this category.[42] It must remain uncertain to what extent events in Stephen's reign led to an interruption, or even a temporary reversal, of the decline in the numbers of English castles which is otherwise a general trend of the twelfth century. But only a small proportion of the very large numbers of undated Norman sites are likely to have been constructed after 1135. Most of them were already in existence when Stephen came to the throne.[43]

The argument from probability thus leads back to the late eleventh century, the primary phase of Norman settlement in England, as the period in which the great majority of pre-1200 castles were founded. Almost without exception the hundred or so documented eleventh-century sites were major fortresses, sooner or later to be substantially rebuilt in stone. The royal *burhs* and other urban centres were the first to be controlled by castles, a process which can be followed in the narratives of William I's campaigns by William of Poitiers and Orderic Vitalis.[44] Other major castles must have been built at the honorial centres of new great estates, as they were formed. But, on grounds of military needs, it cannot have been long before chains of defensible outposts – minor castles in the hands of subtenants and the honorial baronage – began to take shape around and between the major centres. The corollary of Orderic's statement, that the Normans believed their conquest of England had been facilitated by the lack of native castles, was that they should secure their new position by castle building that was as rapid and extensive as possible. The threats of native resistance and foreign invasion, which the Normans were trying to provide against, were at their height in the decade after 1066. Already in 1067, while King William returned to Normandy to celebrate and procure reinforcements, 'Bishop Odo and Earl William (fitz Osbern) stayed behind and built castles far and wide throughout the country, and distressed the wretched folk', according to the Anglo-Saxon Chronicle, 'D' Version.[45] The text implies that there was already a dense scattering of castles in the southern counties, even at this early date. As for the distress, a great deal of native labour must have been called on for castle building in these years. When more than simple coercion was involved, it must have been done by extending the Anglo-Saxon service of *burh-bot*, the general obligation to maintain town defences, which helps to explain the anxiety of churches, especially new Norman foundations, to obtain freedom from such burdens for themselves and their tenants. Exemptions of this kind make up much the most common references to castles in pre-1100 royal charters. One of the earliest was granted to Battle Abbey in 1070 or 1071.[46]

It may now be possible to describe a notional graph which would give a more

42 King, *Castellarium* ii, 306, 308.

43 R. Higham, 'Early castles in Devon, 1068–1201', *Château-Gaillard* ix–x, *Etudes de Castellologie médiévale*, Caen 1982, 101–16, includes an interesting attempt to distinguish the pre-1100 and 1135–54 building phases from analysis of local settlement. This sort of work constitutes a promising line of enquiry.

44 Orderic's narrative from late 1067 to early 1071, *OV* ii, 208–58, is based on the now-lost final section of William of Poitiers. This includes his judgement on the lack of Anglo-Saxon castles, quoted above.

45 *ASC*, 145.

46 *The History of the King's Works*, i–ii, *The Middle Ages*, ed. R. A. Brown, H. M. Colvin, A. J. Taylor, London 1963, i, 24–25. For the Battle charter, see *Regesta Regum Anglo-Normannorum, i, 1066–1100*, ed. H. W. C. Davis, Oxford 1913, no. 58 at 15–16.

dynamic impression of the numbers of castles in England between 1066 and 1200. The total rose dramatically from almost nothing to a near peak figure of more, perhaps much more, than 500 in the decade after 1066. It then remained at that level, or even increased gradually, for twenty or thirty years. After 1100, however, numbers began to fall and fell steadily through the twelfth century, except for a brief reversal in Stephen's reign, so reaching the much lower figures recorded in the more secure documentation of the Angevin royal administration after the 1150s. The greatest difficulty in turning this general trend into absolute figures at any point in the process lies in the rate of turnover. The population of 'live' castles was influenced by the death rate as well as the birth rate. The onward progress of new castle building can be traced as it followed the advance of Norman settlement and colonisation: at its height in the north of England in the 1080s and 1090s, continuing unabated on the Welsh marches down into the twelfth century, resumed in Ireland from the 1170s. But even early on in the period, when the total number of castles was still increasing, some early-fortified sites in the south and midlands of England may already have been passing out of use. This phenomenon is much harder to identify, either in documents or in the archaeological record, than periods of construction and occupation. The process of attrition: permanent giving way to temporary residence, decay and dereliction setting in, more rapidly on sites which had few or no masonry buildings, passing beyond the point at which reconstruction was worth while, is almost by definition silent, though the pipe rolls do remind us just how much routine maintenance castles required.[47] Similar difficulties were also experienced in the better-documented thirteenth century: royal records contain quite a number of surveys full of laments about urgently needed repairs, often not carried out.[48]

It is important to recognise that an explanation for the numerical decline of castles in twelfth-century England is likely to be complex, if only because the functions of castles were so multifarious. In warfare they could fulfil an aggressive purpose, by laying claim to new territory, or a defensive one, by retaining lands exposed to attack. They also served as centres of jurisdiction and local government, and as centres for the exploitation of economic resources. Any or all of these practical purposes might be facilitated by the fact that the castle was also a potent symbol of its lord's status and authority. In no medieval aristocratic society were castles confined to the role of border defence. It follows that expansion of Norman colonisation in the north and on the Welsh marches in the second generation after the conquest was not in itself sufficient reason for a decline in the number of castles in the interior of the kingdom. What other explanations can be advanced? The one most frequently alleged – or assumed – by modern historians, that of royal disciplinary action and administrative control, will be discussed more fully below. It is, though, only one possible candidate, and the evidence for it is not immediately forthcoming. Allen Brown's

47 R. A. Brown, 'Royal Castle-Building in England, 1154–1216', *EHR* lxx, 1955, 354–98; Beeler, *Warfare*, 186–88, 439–46, analyse the pipe roll figures.

48 See *The History of the King's Works* i, 114–15; M. W. Thompson, *The Decline of the Castle*, Cambridge 1987, 12–15.

list for the period 1154–1214 contains the names of about thirty castles destroyed by royal command: a figure which falls far short of the postulated reduction in numbers since before 1154.[49] Narrative sources yield more dramatic totals, the classic example being the Norman chronicler Robert of Torigni, who claimed that 1,115 '*castella noviter facta*' were destroyed after the peace settlement of 1153. This figure is no more credible as a measure of destruction in the 1150s than as a measure of construction in the 1140s, though it is sometimes cited by modern historians without an appropriate health warning.[50] But, along with other chronicle sources, it might be taken as evidence of a general impression among contemporaries that English castles were falling out of use in some numbers after 1154, just as they had been brought – or brought back – into use in the preceding period. Such evidence, drawn from the reign of Henry I, as well as those of Henry II and his sons, might serve to substantiate a modified thesis of royal influence. The mere threat of intervention might deter castle builders, or more generally, the achievement of relatively peaceful conditions might make castle building – or maintenance – less necessary.[51] As a partial explanation this can hardly be denied, but it is no more than that. Castles were not built just to ensure personal security, and the partial eclipse of one of their functions could not have rendered them redundant, though it may have led to architectural changes within them.

This leads on to a second line of argument: that technological changes in warfare and in building, especially the progressive switch to stone construction, confined castle ownership to a narrower group among the aristocracy, and concentrated resources on fewer sites. The sheer slowness of stone building may also have made it, in some cases, harder to avoid the unwelcome attentions of the king, or powerful neighbours.[52] This too must be accepted as a partial explanation, but should not be pushed too far. The change from timber to stone was hardly clear-cut. Stone halls and towers had been among the characteristic castle forms from the very beginning in France and in England, though constituting only a small minority of early sites, and many English castles continued to have 'mixed' defences right down to the end of the twelfth century. Nor is it true that timber and earthwork castles had no value at this date; as late as 1225 King Henry III ordered that all the mottes in the Vale of Montgomery should be put into a state of active defence against the Welsh.[53]

All the considerations advanced so far can only be evaluated against the general background of social and economic change in the twelfth century. It is hard to escape the conclusion that economic pressures played a large part in determining whether early castle sites were sustained in permanent defence – very rare at any time – permanent occupation, permanent repair, or at all.

49 Brown, 'List', figure given at 257.

50 As by W. L. Warren, *Henry II*, London 1973, 39. Text of Torigni in *Chronicles of the Reigns of Stephen, Henry II and Richard I*, ed. R. Howlett, iv, RS 1890, 177, 183. King, *Castellarium* i, p. xxxi defends the value of the passage, if not the actual figure.

51 As expressed by Painter, 127.

52 See D. Renn, *Norman Castles in Britain*, 12–26, for an outline account of building times and their implications.

53 *Rotuli Litterarum Clausarum ii*, 1224–1227, ed. T. D. Hardy, 1844, 42.

Equally, there were social pressures for more elaborate lifestyles and new forms of seigneurial display. Timber and stone castles could contain quite elaborate towers and residences, but many of the lesser castles of Norman England can have offered only fairly rudimentary accommodation, so were liable to be abandoned for something more comfortable, if the alternative of full-scale reconstruction was ruled out on grounds of cost. The overriding economic need of Norman lords at all levels was to provision and sustain their households. Beyond that, there were competing priorities for their resources: investment in land, in political patronage, in family alliances, in conspicuous display, in endowment of the church, as well as in fortification.[54] These pressures alone must have determined many lesser lords to abandon the maintenance of a castle. For others, the additional considerations of changes in military conditions or in royal law enforcement may have proved decisive. It is not necessary to postulate a general economic crisis among the lesser nobility in twelfth-century England to explain this re-ordering of priorities, or to call in witness economic historians whose conclusions might bolster such a view. A figure of 500 or more castles in the hands of men below the major tenants-in-chief in the early Norman period would, after all, take us well down into the ranks of lesser lords in Domesday England. These were men who could hardly sustain seigneurial pretensions from their own landed resources without direct aid and patronage from their lords. Such assistance for subtenants' castles was unlikely to be forthcoming after the initial phase of Norman settlement, except in disputed border areas or exceptional episodes.

Norman England was a society of tremendous flux in individual and family fortunes. New castles were always being built and rebuilt as old ones fell out of use. The little motte and bailey castle built over the Saxon enclosure at Goltho, for instance, was substantially extended after 1150, when its lord Simon fitz William greatly increased his wealth and power by marriage to an heiress.[55] But the aggregate trends of development seem clear enough: the rise and fall of the castle in numerical terms between 1066 and *c.*1200. There also seems strong evidence to suggest that the decline which took place after the early Norman settlement was caused by largely autonomous social and political changes, and is not to be explained simply as the consequence of royal policies.

III

A secondary issue of some importance is the strategic siting of castles in Norman England. Modern historians have produced various theories about this, which might profitably be reassessed. The most enthusiastic advocate of a grand national plan imposed by William I and his successors was John Beeler, in his article 'Castles and strategy in Norman and early Angevin England', published

54 For a review of these issues over a longer period see C. Dyer, *Standards of Living in the Later Middle Ages: Social Change in England 1200–1520*, Cambridge 1989, 27–108.

55 See above n. 13.

in 1956.[56] Dividing England into regional zones and counting the sites within each, he drew attention to significant numbers of castles forming what he claimed were planned defences in depth around both London and Coventry – Coventry according to this theory was England's second major 'communications centre'. The whole argument rests very heavily on extrapolating significance from national distribution maps, and the general assumption that a military commander like William I must have intended an overall scheme of national defence. Subsequent historians have generally been unconvinced. C. W. Hollister, who is more sympathetic to these views than most, believed that Norman kings did have the power to license – or forbid – new castles, so that they possessed the practical means to implement a grand scheme of defences. He argued, though, that William I and his successors lacked the detailed geographical knowledge to design one and were unlikely to have 'actually selected the locations' of baronial castles in accordance with one.[57] In general, Sidney Painter's view that castle planning and the needs of national defence after 1066 were achieved by a coincidence of interests between king and aristocracy rather than detailed direction from above has been accepted: 'the safety of the realm required that it be studded with castles which lay more thickly in the more exposed regions. The interests of the barons guaranteed that this end would be achieved.'[58] It is easy to see some of the ways in which this worked in practice. The uncontroversial fact that castles tend to be placed on roads and rivers, near towns and strategic crossing places, needs no elaborate explanation. In the process of conquest and settlement, castle lords naturally built fortresses at centres best placed to control their new lands, and the greatest concentrations of wealth within them. In the whole European history of castles there was a recurrent tension between the needs of local defence – perhaps best served by an isolated site – and the strategic need of usefulness – being placed near to valuable assets, often at the cost of natural strength. The chronicler Bruno of Magdeburg wrote of the German King Henry IV that in the 1060s and 1070s 'he sought out high hills, fortified by nature, in uninhabited places, and built castles there'.[59] Such examples can be found in England, like Peak castle in Derbyshire, but they are not typical. The balance of interests after the Norman Conquest tended the other way, towards securing the major centres, though a sort of compromise could sometimes be achieved, enhancing defensibility without retreating too far, as at Corfe in Dorset.

But in rejecting most of John Beeler's theories, it is necessary to guard against going too far the other way. It would evidently be absurd to argue that William I was indifferent as to where his companions and their followers built their castles. A random distribution of castles is only likely to have followed a random distribution of lands. On the contrary, it is clear from Domesday Book

56 J. Beeler, 'Castles and strategy in Norman and Early Angevin England', *Speculum* xxxi, 1956, 581–601.

57 C. W. Hollister, *The Military Organization of Norman England*, Oxford 1965 (*henceforth* Hollister, *Military Organisation*), 161–65, quotation at 163.

58 Painter, 128–34, quotation at 134.

59 *Bruno, De bello saxonico liber*, ed. H. E. Lohmann, *MGH* 1937, 22; cited in R. Bartlett, 'Technique militaire et pouvoir politique, 900–1300', *Annales* xli, 1986, 1142 and n. 33.

and other sources that the Conqueror overrode existing tenurial patterns, even alienating royal lands in some cases, to create consolidated blocks of subinfeudated territory where he felt this was strategically necessary. In the first phase of conquest and settlement castles were constructed along the line of march of Norman armies. Already in 1066 they were built on the personal orders of Duke William at Pevensey, Hastings and Dover, fortresses in London and Winchester following after his Christmas day coronation. When William returned to Normandy in March 1067, a team of military commanders headed by Odo of Bayeux and William fitz Osbern were left in charge of the occupied lands in the southern counties. It has already been argued that they must have built more castles almost at once, with or without direct royal commands.[60] But the second phase of settlement could not be long delayed. On his return to England in December 1067, or at the latest by early 1068, William made land grants to create a series of consolidated lordships: one in the Isle of Wight and others along the coast of Sussex and Kent. In many cases, this amounted to giving those who had temporarily controlled an area more permanent possession of it, or part of it. On this basis, Hugh de Montfort was granted lands around Dover, William de Warenne the lordship of Lewes. There were exceptions: Humphrey of Tilleul returned to Normandy in 1068 and so lost Hastings, which he had held since the original landing in 1066; while Roger of Montgomery, who came to England for the first time with the king in 1067, was given Chichester and Arundel.[61]

The association of these lordships with the siting of castles is apparent. F. M. Stenton pointed out that relatively compact holdings of this kind were frequently called 'castleries' (*castellariae*) in early Norman sources, and can all be described as 'a well-defined district within which the whole arrangement of tenancies was primarily designed for the maintenance of the castle'.[62] By the end of William I's reign they can be found all over England; some at least, like Dudley and Tutbury in the midlands, far removed from anything resembling a border when Domesday Book was compiled. Usually the term was applied to lordships like the Sussex 'rapes': substantial territories, but medium-sized when compared with the total holdings of the greatest tenants-in-chief. There was, however, no semantic reason why it could not be applied to much bigger lordships too, like the '*castellatus*' of Richmond, which appears in the Yorkshire Domesday, containing 199 manors.[63] Even in the conquest of England, opportunities to create new consolidated power blocs on this scale were few. The claims of pre-conquest holders and Norman first-comers could not always be overridden so dramatically. Even the castleries that were created were only relatively concentrated, with at least some of their manors and possessions intermingled

60 Above pp. 50–51.

61 J. F. A. Mason, *William the First and the Sussex Rapes*, London, Hastings Historical Association 1966. Mason also demonstrates that there were planned readjustments of these lordships after 1070. On Humphrey and Roger, see *OV* ii, 210 and n. 1, 220 and n. 1.

62 Stenton, *First Century*, 194–96, quotations at 194. See also J. Le Patourel, *The Norman Empire*, Oxford 1976, 303–18; M. Chibnall, *Anglo-Norman England 1066–1166*, Oxford 1986, 11–15.

63 Stenton, *First Century*, 194–95, *Domesday Book, vol. 30: Yorkshire*, ed. M. L. Faull and M. Stinson, 2 vols, Chichester 1986, ii, SN Ct.A 45.

with those of others. Lords of castleries generally also held substantial lands widely scattered elsewhere, often in other parts of the country. In some areas of England compact or exclusive lordships seem never to have been set up, and all substantial estates were fragmented, shaped as much as anything by the form of the pre-conquest holdings which had been dismantled or assembled to bring them into existence. But the many castleries which did exist are clear evidence of royal strategic planning. Even in cases where new entities of this kind were not set up, it would be unwise to assume it was because the possibility was not even considered. The evidence as a whole suggests that William I's government, despite all the emergencies with which it had to deal, on both sides of the Channel, was capable of supervising very closely the initial process by which new baronial lordships were created. Lands were granted, either with castles already on them, or in the expectation that castles would be built by the recipient. With this process too, the king is likely to have been concerned, though the extent of his intervention in individual cases remains a matter for speculation.

But the limits of royal strategic planning show up clearly on consideration of the third stage in the consolidation of Norman settlement, following the two initial steps of military occupation and grant to tenant-in-chief. The new lord would have to take stock of his commitments, allocate his military resources, and at some point decide how far to enfeoff his followers on their own lands. It has never been supposed that kings intervened closely in this latter process, which completed the formation of the castlery as Stenton described it, with its 'whole arrangement of tenancies' designed in relation to the central castle. Later records of castle-guard services can throw light on it, though unfortunately details are known for only a handful of baronial castles.[64] In many respects, the creation of both sub-tenancies and lesser castles must have mirrored the dealings between king and superior lord. The greater the size of the original estate, especially if it had several geographically separated honorial centres, the greater the need of its lord to multiply the numbers of his castles, and leave them in the hands of trusted retainers. Among the grievances of the English in 1067, according to Orderic Vitalis, was the oppressive greed of 'the petty lords (*praefecti minores*) who had custody of the castles'.[65] Some at least of these arrangements must have been turned into permanent grants, just as a number of royal castles were alienated from the crown to those who had once been their custodians. Other sub-tenants must have received lands and built their own castles, though hardly without their lord's consent and probably – especially in the early period of tenuous Norman control – with his active encouragement. It is, though, almost inconceivably unlikely that William I and his officials were able to monitor and regulate this proliferation, which boosted the number of fortified sites in King William's England to levels unknown in Duke William's

64 See the lists given by S. Painter, 'Castle-guard', in *Feudalism and Liberty*, Baltimore 1961, 144–56; and King, *Interpretative History*, 15–19. For most castles there are only passing references to guard service. The fewer well-documented cases have served as the basis for a debate on commutation terms. See especially Hollister, *Military Organisation*, 138–61; T. K. Keefe, *Feudal Assessments and the Political Community under Henry II and His Sons*, Berkeley 1983, 37–40, 76–79.

65 *OV* ii, 202.

Normandy, where castles were still 'restricted to a small élite' in 1066.[66] Occasional royal intervention was possible at any level, where the king's itinerary or a complaint to his court brought him within range; close and continuous supervision was not.

The interlinked processes of estate formation and castle building continued to repeat themselves as Norman colonisation extended across England from south to north. Already in 1067 William fitz Osbern was given the earldom of Hereford, and by 1071, the year in which the fall of Edwin of Mercia finally opened up all of the midlands for Norman exploitation, Roger of Montgomery had acquired Shrewsbury and Hugh of Avranches Chester. It has usually been assumed that these three great border earldoms were equivalent in status and organisation; within each the earl took over whatever land had previously belonged to the king, and held a virtual monopoly of overlordship, except for some ecclesiastical estates. Hugh of Avranches, for instance, was given the castle of Chester, which a royal army had founded in 1070.[67] His county of Chester forms a classic example of the determination of local settlement and castle building at the level of the great lordship, a process which it has already been argued was a general one. The earl's *curia* would have provided a natural forum for such arrangements. At this level, too, inferences may reasonably be drawn from distribution maps. The chain of motte and bailey castles along the river Dee in Cheshire must have been built in the early 1070s, before the rapid Norman territorial expansion into north Wales which followed in the next twenty years, though the castles may have been augmented after 1094, when a great Welsh revolt pushed the border back almost to its starting point.[68] Recently, Christopher Lewis has convincingly argued that the earldom of Hereford, largely because of its earlier foundation, was structured differently from those of Chester and Shrewsbury.[69] William fitz Osbern's landed power in Herefordshire had to co-exist with that of several other groups, notably pre-conquest Norman settlers and other Normans independently enfeoffed by the Conqueror after 1066. His local pre-eminence was based at least in part on his high standing with the king, which was not inherited by his son Roger of Breteuil, whose frustrations drove him into unsuccessful rebellion in 1075. It may be that William I's concern was to maintain some degree of balance of power in Herefordshire in 1067, or to conciliate local loyalties. Certainly in 1075 he welcomed the opportunity presented by the revolt to put through an elaborate new deal, retaining some of the castles built by fitz Osbern and his son in his own hands, while granting out others to augment the power of rising families, like the Mortimers at Wigmore. The contrast with his treatment of Cheshire and Shropshire in 1071, where local dispositions were subcontracted almost

66 Above p. 45 and n. 22.

67 *OV* ii, 236; also 260–62 and iii, 216, for a famous description of Hugh's extravagant life style.

68 See J. Tait's introduction and map in *The Domesday Survey of Cheshire*, Chetham Society 2nd series lxxv, 1916; J. Tait, 'Flintshire in Domesday Book', *Flintshire Historical Society Publications* xi, 1925, 1–37; J. Le Patourel, *The Norman Empire*, Oxford 1976, 312–14.

69 C. Lewis, 'The Norman Settlement of Herefordshire under William I', *Anglo-Norman Studies* vii, 1984, 195–213; challenging the established view of W. E. Wightman, 'The palatine earldom of William fitz Osbern in Gloucestershire and Worcestershire, 1066–1071', *EHR* lxxvii, 1962, 6–17.

entirely to the new earls, is intriguing. Such changes show that the boundary between William I's concern for the planning of new great estates and his unwillingness – or inability – to regulate subinfeudation and castle building within them was a flexible one. It varied from case to case, depending on the political importance of what was at stake and the king's estimate of the political loyalties involved.

In the 1080s and 1090s Norman settlement was pushed forward in the north of England. Again the familiar stages reappear: first, the establishment of major castles under royal direction, notably at Newcastle in 1080 and Carlisle in 1092; second, the carefully-calculated construction of new lordships and distribution of them to trustworthy families; third, the completion of tenurial settlement and its defensive dispositions at local level. The degree of strategic planning in the construction of castleries at Tickhill, Pontefract, Richmond, Holderness and elsewhere is evident, though the king also took pains to retain sufficient lands in his own hands and even, around Carlisle, to populate them.[70] Similar conclusions can be drawn from the elaborate repackaging of the northern estates forfeited by Robert de Mowbray on his rebellion in 1095. Many of them were used by King Henry I to form a new endowment for Nigel d'Aubigny after 1106.[71] Henry I was, of course, a virtuoso in the manipulation of patronage and inheritances to secure men's loyalties, though by his time the process was usually one of transferring estates and castles, rather than defining and building them. The great exception was on the expanding frontier of south and mid-Wales, where Norman advance was halted only after the accession of Stephen in 1135. Between 1100 and 1135, according to John Beeler, just twenty-six new documented castles can be added to the list for England, but twenty-one for Wales, surely only a very small proportion of those actually built.[72] In border areas, the conditions of primary settlement persisted into the twelfth century and beyond. Castles, small local ones as well as major baronial centres, continued to be built and rebuilt because they literally paid for themselves; enabling their lords to hold territory and raise incomes which otherwise would have slipped out of their control. Distribution maps of castles on the Welsh march testify to this by their sheer density of sites, only to be interpreted as the result of repeated desertion and new building, rather than defence in depth by hundreds of simultaneously-occupied outposts. Henry I's especial concern was to establish royal centres in the forefront of the advance, notably at Carmarthen castle, and in Pembroke, which fell into his hands after the rebellion of the Montgomery family in 1102.[73] The same upheaval brought him the forfeited earldom of Shrewsbury, which he broke up, retaining Shrewsbury castle for the crown.[74]

70 *ASC*, 169, for Carlisle. See also W. E. Wightman, *The Lacy Family in England and Normandy, 1066–1194*, Oxford 1966, 17–86; W. E. Kapelle, *The Norman Conquest of the North: the Region and its Transformation 1000–1135*, London 1979.

71 See D. E. Greenway's introduction to *Charters of the Honour of Mowbray 1107–1191*, British Academy Records of Social and Economic History, n.s. 1, 1972.

72 Beeler, *Warfare*, 429–30, 437. The sources for Wales are naturally less full.

73 R. R. Davies, 'Henry I and Wales', in *Studies in Medieval History presented to R. H. C. Davis*, ed. H. Mayr-Harting and R. I. Moore, London 1985, 132–47.

74 J. F. A. Mason, 'Roger de Montgomery and His Sons, 1067–1102', *TRHS* 5th series xiii, 1963, 1–28; C. W. Hollister, 'The Campaign of 1102 against Robert of Bellême', in *Studies for R. A. B.*, 193–202.

Such very great territorial power blocs were now liable to be perceived by kings as more dangerous than useful, a conclusion anticipated by William I's treatment of Herefordshire in 1075.

William I took great pains to ensure that English lands were granted to his Norman followers only on his terms and to preserve the reality of royal overlordship. His successors continued in that tradition. Nevertheless the pressures of the conquest process led to a proliferation and distribution of castles in England, extending a long way down the hierarchy of noble society, which had taken shape very largely outside direct royal control. This too was inherited by the Conqueror's sons in 1087 and 1100, and could not easily be changed.

IV

Comparisons with France are helpful in drawing conclusions about the operation of royal power over castles in Norman England. It has already been suggested that the dynamic of change in England was an exceptional one. Numbers of castles rose very rapidly in the late eleventh century, with a consequent devolution of control over them. In the twelfth century numbers fell back for a variety of reasons, and the territorial distribution of sites shifted to some degree. It is debatable whether the fall returned England to a state of 'normality' by French standards, after the exceptional militarization of the post-conquest period, or whether England was left – after 1154 at least – with an unusually small number of castles by comparison with the continent. This depends largely on which region of France is taken for comparison, as they differed considerably. But generally in France the construction of castles and lordship over them was diffused more gradually over a longer period than in England, both in geographical terms and downwards in society from greater to lesser nobility. This diffusion was accompanied by the progressive definition of castle customs, by which French kings and lords claimed a variety of rights over fortification in their territories.[75] They can be grouped under two headings: licensing the creation of new castles and 'rendability' – the obligation of a vassal to surrender his castles temporarily to his lord in case of need. They vary in form from province to province, and particularly between the lands north and south of the Loire. As with other early feudal customs, there is considerable scope for debate on the strength of the thread linking them back to Carolingian traditions of public power. Pre-twelfth-century evidence, though it exists, is very thin.[76] But certain general features of the customs stand out, and can be documented in great detail from *c.*1200 or a

75 C. L. H. Coulson, 'Readability and castellation in medieval France', *Château-Gaillard* vi, *Etudes de Castellologie médiévale*, Caen 1973, 59–67; C. L. H. Coulson, 'Seigneurial Fortresses in France in Relation to Public Policy, *c.*864–*c.*1483', unpublished Ph.D. Thesis, University of London 1972. R. W. Kaueper, *War, Justice and Public Order: England and France in the Later Middy Ages*, Oxford 1988, 211–25, is a rather preliminary attempt to compare English and French customs over a longer period.

76 C. L. H. Coulson, 'Fortresses and social responsibility in late Carolingian France', *Zeitschrift für Archäologie des Mittelalter*s iv, 1976, 29–36.

little before. First, they operated at all tenurial levels between those who had the status to fortify – there was no royal monopoly of jurisdiction. Second, the licence to fortify was seemingly almost invariably sought as a 'courtesy' – that is, it was not as a rule refused to an applicant of appropriate status who was not trespassing on someone else's rights. To receive such a grant was in effect an acknowledgement of lordship; the grantor could then bring the resultant castle under his jurisdiction, as expressed in the claim to rendability. Taken at face value, these customs had a sort of rationale in balancing the interests of lords and vassals in a mutually satisfactory way. In practice, they often served as a kind of legalistic thicket through which political operators manoeuvred to gain their ends, while paying lip service to the rules. King Philip Augustus proved himself a master of these tactics in the latter part of his reign.[77]

The contrast with England is clear. English historians, almost without exception, have seen the right to license new fortifications in the Anglo-Norman realm as a royal monopoly, admitting only a few exceptions like the Welsh marcher lordships and the later 'palatine' counties of Cheshire and Durham, whose lords had special privileges.[78] Unlike their French counterparts, English kings had no reason to press grants on their vassals or encourage applications, in order to establish claims over castles, for if they possessed a monopoly there could be no other lords in the market. French kings and lords naturally sometimes banned the construction of unwelcome castles, or denied them their protection. But English kings, it has been supposed, did this systematically, setting up a mechanism of restrictive control which became an integral part of their authority. F. M. Stenton's formulation is typical: 'the Norman Kings insisted that no castle should be built without their licence'.[79] Historians of later periods too, considering the rather different 'licences to crenellate' of the thirteenth, fourteenth and fifteenth centuries, tend to assume they are seeing something which is uncontroversially accepted as dating back to the early Norman period.[80] On this model, any castle built without royal authorization was illegal, or 'adulterine', and so subject to demolition. Such terms are applied above all to Stephen's reign, as by W. L. Warren, who wrote that 'the decay of the royal power to control castle building led to the erection of many unlicensed castles'. Allen Brown referred to Henry II's reign as beginning 'with the demolition of the "adulterine", or unlicensed, castles of the Anarchy'.[81] The point at issue here is not just whether there were in fact a lot of castles occupied in Stephen's reign, and demolished or abandoned after 1153–54, but whether there was an established system of rules and customs by which kings could control castles and castle building in normal times. On further reflection, doubts about the way this

77 C. Coulson, 'Fortress-Policy in Capetian Tradition and Angevin Practice: aspects of the conquest of Normandy by Philip II', *Anglo-Norman Studies* vi, 1983, 13–38; C. L. H. Coulson, 'The impact of Bouvines on the Fortress-policy of Philip Augustus', *Studies for R. A. B.*, 71–80. See also J. Baldwin, *The Government of Philip Augustus*, Berkeley 1986, 294–303.

78 See e.g. King, *Interpretative History*, 20–22, for a statement of these 'exceptions'.

79 Stenton, *First Century*, 207.

80 E.g. R. Stacey, *Politics, Policy and Finance under Henry III*, 1216–1245, Oxford 1987, 14: 'the king's long-established right to license all crenellations in England, whether private or royal'.

81 W. L. Warren, *Henry II*, London 1973, 39; Brown, 'List', 250.

is supposed to have worked begin to multiply. Did kings always deal directly with castle builders, ignoring the rights of intermediate lords? Were all castles 'adulterine' if their builders had not taken the initiative in seeking out the king and receiving his specific approval? It has already been argued that William I would have encountered great – probably insuperable – practical problems in exercising such supervision during the initial Norman settlement in England. What is the evidence that he or his successors actually attempted to do so?

The crucial early text is the *Consuetudines et Justicie*, a statement of ducal rights and customs in Normandy drawn up for the Conqueror's sons in 1091. It includes the provision that 'no one in Normandy might dig a fosse in the open country of more than one shovel's throw in depth, not set there more than one line of palisading, and that without battlements or alures. And no one might make a fortification on a rock or in an island, and no one might raise a castle in Normandy, and no one in Normandy might withhold the strength of his castle from the lord of Normandy, if he wished to take it into his own hand.'[82] This seems unambiguous both for control over building and for rendability. It only remains to add the general assumption, well expressed in Sidney Painter's words, 'it is unlikely that the Conqueror claimed less authority over the castles of England than over those in Normandy', to conclude that such powers were asserted in England too.[83] Yet it is dangerous to read statements of law and custom from this period out of their immediate context. The *Consuetudines* claimed to describe the customs of William the Conqueror's time. During his long rule over the duchy, William certainly did much to strengthen his power over its castles; in some cases he demolished the fortresses of those he did not trust, in others he imposed ducal garrisons upon them.[84] As with other aspects of government, his aim was to make good the losses suffered in the disorders of his minority. It seems that there was indeed an increase in aristocratic castle building in the 1030s and 1040s, though it was very limited in comparison with post-conquest England. But modern research suggests that the real proliferation of baronial castles in Normandy took place in the twenty years after the Conqueror's death, during the ineffective rule of his son Robert Curthose, and at a time when many Norman barons could draw on personal experience of the settlement in England. Already in 1057, when William's death was known, men like Robert of Bellême and William count of Évreux seized the opportunity to expel ducal troops from their castles.[85] The 1091 *Consuetudines* were compiled in the midst of the subsequent conflict. Accordingly, despite their all-embracing phraseology, there is much to be said for the view that the castle provisions in the text were really aimed at recent and temporary fortresses set up in the succession war between William's sons. They describe a jurisdictional state of

82 Text in C. H. Haskins, *Norman Institutions*, Cambridge, Mass. 1918, 277–84; translation of relevant clause in R. A. Brown, *Origins of English Feudalism*, London 1973, 146.

83 Painter, 140.

84 See above p. 45 and nn, 21–22. There are clear examples in *Guillaume de Poitiers. Histoire de Guillaume le Conquérant*, ed. R. Foreville, Paris 1952, 20, 54, See Bates, 113–15, 165–66.

85 *OV* iv, 112–14.

affairs which was actually ceasing to apply in Normandy, temporarily at least, at the very time they were written down.[86]

Even if the *Consuetudines* represent a literal and accurate account of the powers William I had exercised over castles in Normandy, which must be at least to some extent doubtful, this does not mean that such powers were simply transferred to England. After 1066 castles were built – and had to be built – in England on a scale unknown in Normandy, and with great practical pressures to leave decisions over the construction and siting of many of them to the higher aristocracy. It seems inescapable that this process created precedents which would have tended to be consolidated into customary rights. The heirs of the first generation of Norman colonists inherited not merely their castles, but surely, in their own eyes at least, presumptive rights to fortify on those sites. From the king's point of view this meant that once the Norman occupation of England was secure there were already so many established castles that insistence on the licensing of all new sites would have been of marginal advantage, even if feasible. Of course, Norman and Angevin kings intervened in individual cases on almost any pretext, if not by their sheer arbitrary power. One of Robert of Bellême's offences in 1102 was that he had 'established' Bridgnorth castle 'against the command of the king', according to the Welsh 'Chronicle of the Princes'.[87] But such cases do not prove the existence of established rules. It has always seemed plausible to historians to suppose that the 1091 Norman custom applied also in England because of the general assumption that William I possessed more centralized authority as King of England than as Duke of Normandy. In the particular case of the alleged power to license new castles, it may be that what happened was the exact opposite.

It remains to consider the possibility that later kings may have attempted to introduce stricter controls over castle building in England retrospectively. In the passage already quoted Sidney Painter conceded that in practice William I could hardly have authorized every castle built in his reign, but 'by the time of Henry I the danger of a Saxon uprising had passed, and the country was supplied with a large number of fortresses. The king could then begin to enforce his right to control new constructions.'[88] The main evidence that he might have done so consists of two references in the early twelfth-century legal collection the *Leges Henrici Primi*. Among a list of 'jurisdictional rights which the King of England has in his hands solely and over all men' appears '*castellatio trium scannorum*', implausibly translated by the most recent editor of the text as 'fortifications consisting of three walls' but more likely a reference to the three-fold defences of ditch, bank and palisade. A later passage lists '*castellatio sine licentia*' among offences which bring a man into the king's mercy.[89] The meaning is undeniable, though as a statement of English law it had no official status. But

[86] Bates, 162–66, takes a rather higher view of the 1091 *Consuetudines* and their Carolingian precedents, while acknowledging the contemporary lapse in ducal authority.

[87] *Brut y Tywysogyon. Red Book of Hergest Version*, ed. T. Jones, Cardiff 1955, 42; *Brut y Tywysogyon: Peniarth Ms. 20 Version*, ed. T. Jones, Cardiff 1952, 23. Above n. 74.

[88] Painter, 140.

[89] *Leges Henrici Primi*, ed. L. J. Downer, Oxford 1972, 108, 116, 323–24. No recent work on this text seems to provide any real clue to the derivation of these passages.

this source stands very much in isolation. Generally one searches royal charters of the twelfth century in vain for licences to construct castles, or anything approaching them. The grants made to Geoffrey de Mandeville by Stephen and the Empress Matilda in 1141, alienating great swathes of royal power at the height of a dynastic civil war, including rights over castles with the rest, can hardly be taken to 'prove conclusively that a specific licence from the crown was required for castle building', as Painter claimed.[90] Even more exceptional was the grant by the future Henry II to Robert fitz Harding in 1153 of land at Berkeley with authority to build a castle there.[91] This was one of a series of deals which Duke Henry, fresh from France and making his first serious intervention in English politics, was striking to smooth his way to the throne; clearly it is not worth much as evidence for English customary law. Because they have assumed that a 'licensing system' existed, many historians have tended to describe almost any royal grant concerning a castle as a 'licence'. This has produced a mixed bag of instances, including such royal acts as Henry I's grant of the custody of Rochester castle to Archbishop William of Corbeil in 1127, and Stephen's concession to Earl Ranulf of Chester, in the middle of a general charter of privileges issued probably in 1146, that he could continue to hold a tower in Lincoln castle.[92] Another example is a grant by Stephen confirming Henry de Lacy in the possession of two castles. W. E. Wightman argued that this 'was in effect a licence' and that its issue shows Stephen's government was still functioning sufficiently well for licences to be sought, even from outlying parts of the country. A whole administrative system is conjured up, almost from thin air.[93] What is really striking about these examples is how few they are, and how far they fall short of proving the existence of an acknowledged system of royal control.

Another dubious point is the equation of 'adulterine' with 'unlicensed' when applied to twelfth-century castles. The term was given a precise definition in a slightly later source, the second reissue of Magna Carta in 1217. According to this, '*castra adulterina*' were 'those built or rebuilt since the beginning of the war between the lord John our father and his barons of England'.[94] Subsequent enforcement makes it clear that this was in fact the rule applied – castles built in

90 Painter, 141. *Regesta Regum Anglo-Normannorum iii*, *1135–1154*, ed. H. A. Cronne and R. H. C. Davis, Oxford 1968, nos. 274, 276, at 99–103.

91 *Ibid*., no 309, at 117. This is the third of the three charters given in Davis and Cronne's subject index under 'castles, licence to fortify'. It is also one of a group of 'pretended originals', probably written after 1172–73. See *ibid*., 369 and *Acta of Henry II and Richard I*, ed. J. C. Holt and R. Mortimer, List and Index Society special series xxi, London 1986, 74–75. The text could alternatively mean that Henry promised to build the castle himself.

92 On Rochester: *Regesta Regum Anglo-Normannorum, ii, 1100–1135*, ed. C. Johnson and H. A. Cronne, Oxford 1956, no. 1475 at 203; I. W. Rowlands, 'King John, Stephen Langton and Rochester Castle, 1213–15', *Studies for R. A. B*., 268–69. For the Chester grant, *Regesta Regum Anglo-Normannorum, iii*, no. 178 at 64–65; translation in H. A. Cronne, *The Reign of Stephen*, London 1970, 78–79. The text is based on a late abstract, made in 1325.

93 W. E. Wightman, *The Lacy Family in England and Normandy, 1066–1194*, Oxford 1966, 78–79, 244–45. The source is again late; a summary compiled for a catalogue of charters at Pontefract in 1322.

94 Text in J. C. Holt, *Magna Carta*, Cambridge 1965, 357. See R. Eales, 'Castles and Politics in England, 1215–1224', in *Thirteenth-Century England* ii, ed. P. R. Coss and S. D. Lloyd, Woodbridge 1988 (*henceforth* Eales), 39–40.

time of war established no presumptive rights for the future. Issues raised by building in time of peace were not discussed. It has been observed that the term 'adulterine' was rarely applied to the castles of Stephen's reign by contemporaries[95] – it has proved much more popular with modern historians – but when it was used the presumption must be that it bore a meaning very similar to that given in 1217.

A more substantial issue is the possible importation of Norman-French customs of rendability to England in the eleventh or twelfth century. For a long time English historians neglected this possibility. Castle licences were seen everywhere, but legal obligations to render castles nowhere, even though both appear in the 1091 Norman customs. Royal actions which might seem to fit the description of rendability, like Stephen's occupation of the castles of Bishop Roger of Salisbury and his relatives in 1139, were treated in narrative terms as exercises of arbitrary power.[96] More recently, however, the subject has been reassessed. I. W. Rowlands drew attention to the debate in a church council at Winchester, which followed the surrender of the bishops' castles. According to William of Malmesbury, Hugh archbishop of Rouen argued there that, 'as it is a time of suspicion, all the chief men ought to hand over the keys of their fortifications to the disposal of the king, whose duty it is to fight for the peace of all'.[97] Yet the passage is subject to different interpretations, as clerical ideas of the public good may not have been synonomous with secular custom, and Hugh qualified his remarks with the perhaps significant phrase 'in accordance with the custom of other peoples (*secundum morem aliarum gentium*)'. A more striking example occurred in 1176, when Henry II, at the height of his power after crushing the baronial revolt of 1173–74, used the occasion of a council at Windsor to promulgate new decrees for the reimposition of order. According to the chroniclers Roger Howden and Ralph of Diss, the king seized all the castles of England into his own hands, and even placed his own custodians in them.[98] No record evidence supports the view that such a general dispossession actually took place; politically, it would hardly have been practicable. The incident can, however, be interpreted as an assertion in principle of a royal right to resume control of fortresses, or rendability. In practice, it served as a cover for the process by which Henry struck selectively at his enemies and those whom he suspected, with the demolition of at least twenty baronial castles after 1174 and the confiscation of others. The 1176 Assize of Northampton included an instruction to the justices to see that these orders were actually carried out.[99] The exact nature of the demand made by Henry II in 1176 must remain unclear. But

95 King, *Castellarium* i, p. xxxi. He, however, suggests as the reason for this that 'the great majority of them must have been licensed'.

96 E.g. R. H. C. Davis, *King Stephen*, London 1967, 31–35; E. J. Kealey, *Roger of Salisbury*, Berkeley 1972, 173–89.

97 I. W. Rowlands, 'King John, Stephen Langton and Rochester Castle', *Studies for R. A. B.*, 277–78; *Historia Novella*, ed. K. R. Potter, London NMT 1955, 32–33.

98 Brown, 'List', 253, gives the relevant extracts from the sources. See also King, *Castellarium*, i, p. xxiv.

99 Figures taken from Brown, 'List'. Assize of Northampton cap. 8, see W. Stubbs, *Select Charters*, 9th edn, 1913, 180.

if he intended it to serve as a precedent, rather than just to meet immediate political needs, it cannot have had much effect. There is no evidence that rendability was enforced as a general royal right in subsequent English law.[100]

The practical effects of Angevin policy were another matter. Better documentation after 1154 leaves no doubt that the Angevin kings had formidable success in disciplining castle lords and strengthening their own territorial position. Allen Brown, in his classic account of this process, argues that 'it seems justifiable to speak of an Angevin castle policy, consciously directed to the augmentation of royal power, chiefly at the expense of the baronage'; or expressed statistically '225 baronial and 49 royal castles in 1154, a ratio of nearly 5 to 1; 179 baronial and 93 royal castles in December 1214, a ratio of just under 2 to 1'.[101] This looks like an impressive achievement, though it had its limitations. The dividing line between royal and baronial castles was often a blurred one, especially in a crisis. More castles in royal hands meant finding more custodians, some of whom proved disloyal in the conflict of 1215–16. The mere accumulation of fortresses may not in the end have been sufficient compensation for the grievances aroused by the dispossession of their former holders. In all these respects, Henry II broadly extended his power while keeping just within the tolerance limits of aristocratic society; John went decisively beyond them and suffered the consequences.[102] But whatever the final estimate of its success, Angevin castle policy worked in a selective and opportunistic way, rather than by seeking to define and implement customary rules.

The contrast between England and France remains significant, despite underlying political similarities. In France there were well-developed castle customs, expressed in the twelfth century through characteristic legal formulae in charters and other documents. Not everyone was law-abiding, but the customary law served as a background to the process of political aggrandisement, and conditioned the way it was pursued. In Norman and Angevin England there remained always something of a legal vacuum so far as castles were concerned. Whatever notions of right and obligation there were, specific to castles, they were not elaborated or written down in standard forms.[103] Into this vacuum, as the Channel was evidently no barrier to the passage of political ideas in the twelfth century, kings especially might draw such elements of French custom as might serve their interests at any time. Henry II's claim in 1176 looks like one such attempt, which happens to be recorded in detail in chronicle sources. There were no doubt others, both by kings and at the level of the great lordships, as long as cross-channel estates existed. It is quite unnecessary, and actually mis-

100 On this point, King, *Interpretative History*, 25: 'This duty of rendability was enforced in England as a general rule of law, for the benefit of the King . . . being established by Henry II at the Council of Windsor, 1176', states the exact opposite of the truth with great precision.

101 Brown, 'List', 256–57.

102 Eales, 23–43, considers these issues in the light of what happened in the decade after 1215.

103 Painter, 139, comments that 'one would expect to find' that castle customs feature prominently in legal collections, but 'the subject was almost entirely neglected'. J. C. Holt, 'Politics and Property in Early Medieval England', *Past and Present* lvii, 1972, 25–27, defends the existence of general licensing and 'a prerogative right of seizure', citing the Norman customs of 1091, but the narrative examples he gives prove only (episodes of) practical royal success.

leading, to try and fit all examples of this kind into a continuous insular tradition, extending back to William the Conqueror. But the evidence as a whole indicates that such borrowings never took root in English law, any more than they are all traceable back to the Norman customs of 1091. For most purposes the piecemeal policies towards castles employed by Norman and Angevin kings served their needs well enough. Rulers were not obliged to pursue a universal claim to castle licensing or rendability as a matter of principle, and the evidence suggests they did not. This is true even if we look forward to the more bureaucratic and better documented royal government of the thirteenth century, and the appearance of 'licences to crenellate' in the chancery rolls after 1200.[104] The inheritance of Norman England – of rights derived from long possession of castles rather than from any formal system of royal authorization – was not easily cancelled or eroded.

That inheritance was shaped above all in the late eleventh century: the exceptional generation of post-conquest settlement, when the customs and institutions of Norman feudal society were adapted – or distorted – to serve the needs of colonisation. Accordingly, castles and knights were to be found in much greater numbers in late eleventh-century England than in late eleventh-century Normandy, and in much greater numbers too than in twelfth-century England. There must have been many lords of castles in England in 1080 or 1100 whose sons and grandsons were not lords of castles, just as there were many knights whose descendants did not maintain their status.[105] Cumulatively this had qualitative as well as quantitative effects: the knight and the castle were not quite the same thing in 1200 as they had been in 1100. It has already been argued that the cutting edge of change in most of this was economic, though royal policies also played their part, and the whole process was conditioned by political needs and expectations at every stage. The view, most clearly expressed by C. W. Hollister, that baronial castles away from borders served no useful purpose to the crown after William I's reign, so that 'the natural response of the royal government was an anti-castle policy such as was followed by Henry II, and perhaps also Henry I', is far too simple.[106] It was not possible to retain the political system planted on England after 1066, including aristocratic allegiance to the king and acceptance of his rule, while discarding an integral element of that system – the baronial castle – deeply linked as it was with assertions of both power and status. The extent to which royal power, even in the Angevin period, could be sustained by a combination of bureaucracy, mercenary troops and the king's own castles has often been exaggerated. Henry II survived in 1173–74 largely because of a favourable balance of power among the aristocracy, while the events of 1215–17

104 Eales, 40–43. Only ten 'licences' are recorded 1200–1215, six more 1216–1231, and none at all 1232–1251. No sort of standard form appears until the second half of the century. C. H. Coulson is preparing an edition of the enrolled licences which will throw light on these issues.

105 S. Harvey, 'The Knight and the Knight's Fee in England', *Past and Present* xlix, 1970, 3–43; R. A. Brown, 'The Status of the Norman Knight', in *War and Government in the Middle Ages: Essays in honour of J. O. Prestwich*, ed. J. Gillingham and J. C. Holt, Woodbridge 1984, 18–34. The dynamic changes around the conquest provide a possible means of reconciling these divergent views.

106 Hollister, *Military Organization*, 165–66, though Stenton, *First Century*, 194: 'The baronial castle had become an anachronism' (by 1200) takes a similar view, if not about the 'first century' itself.

clearly showed the dangers to which royal government was exposed by the loss of loyalty. The role of castles in the development of royal power was substantial, but it can only be assessed in relation to the surrounding pattern of political, social and economic forces.

3

Burhgeat and Gonfanon: Two Sidelights from the Bayeux Tapestry

Derek Renn

A scene embroidered two-thirds of the way along the Bayeux Tapestry brings together my two otherwise diverse subjects.[1] A figure wearing a conical helmet, coat of mail and sword holds a lance which bears a flag with streaming tails; he is about to take the reins of a ready-saddled horse from a groom. The armed figure is usually identified as William, duke of Normandy. Just to his left is a building of at least two and probably three storeys beside a turret with a large wide-open door, drawn as if William had just emerged from it.[2] I believe that the artist intended to represent something other than a church and prayer before battle and so I propose to look at all the representations of towers in the Tapestry (except those on mottes) and to compare them with those contemporary buildings with large upper openings which have survived in England.[3]

My second theme is the flags of the Tapestry. An analysis suggests that most of them were drawn to indicate movement; and that three of the four war banners mentioned by the chroniclers can be identified at two different stages of the battle.

I am grateful to Matthew Bennett, Claud Blair, John Blair, Marjorie Chibnall, Dione Clementi, John Cowdrey, Brian Durham, Sandy Heslop, Christopher Lewis, David Parsons, Ian Peirce, John Weaver and Ann Williams for advice and argument, even if not always followed.

1 Citations of the Bayeux Tapestry throughout will be BT followed by three numbers giving respectively (a) the scene number written on the backing linen and used on the *dépliant* sold at Bayeux, (b) the plate number in *The Bayeux Tapestry*, a comprehensive survey, ed. Sir F.M. Stenton *et al.*, revised and enlarged edition, London 1965, and (c) the plate number in *The Bayeux Tapestry; The Complete Tapestry in Colour*, ed. Sir D.M. Wilson, London 1985. Roman numerals on pages 78 to 85 refer to the gonfanons listed in Appendix 2 (page 89).

2 BT 48, 53, 51. The Tapestry shows William frequently (but not exclusively) on a large black horse in Brittany, in Normandy and at Hastings (sic). The dramatic crash of an enormous black stallion during the subsequent battle may be coupled with the preceding picture of such a horse being axed and the following picture of the unhorsing of a rider by a soldier on foot grabbing the girthband, as the incidents described in the *Gesta Guillelmi*, 196–8 and the *Carmen*, xxv, xxvii, 32–4, 93, 96, 97.

3 *Med. Arch*. xiv, 1970, 224–5, reviewing *Château-Gaillard III: European Castle Studies: Conference at Battle, Sussex, 19–24 September 1966*, ed. A.J. Taylor, Chichester 1969, with reference to A.J. Taylor, 'Evidence for a pre-Conquest Origin for the Chapels in Hastings and Pevensey Castles', 144–51. For towers on mottes in the Bayeux Tapestry, see Arnold Taylor, 'Belrem', *ANS* xiv, 1992, 1–23.

The Burhgeat

In the scene representing Harold's return from Normandy, his landfall is watched by a group of men in and on a very curious building.[4] The main structure is four storeys high: the topmost has been missed by most commentators on the Tapestry because its three round-topped openings (the central one slightly larger than the others) do not stand out from the chequer-work on black-and-white photographs. Below this storey is another from which a face looks out through a tall round-headed frame. More faces peer out through three shorter round-topped openings in the storey below and finally at the bottom is the largest round-headed opening of all, reached up three steps. Level with the second storey of the tower is a platform on which stands a figure looking (like all the others) at the approaching ship. One hand shields his eyes either from the sun or from bad news. The platform is supported at one end by the tower and by a central column with moulded base and capital. At the other end is another pillar, with three small steps (or another moulded base?) at its foot and a dragon-head finial at the top. The wavy lines under the ship run on in front of the platform but slope away from the right-hand part of the tower and may indicate a pier or jetty standing at the seaside. The curving lines might indicate a wooden tower and platform, although the diagonal chequer-work of the top and ground storeys is used to denote masonry elsewhere in the Tapestry.

At the very beginning of the Tapestry is a comparable structure attached to a hall.[5] This also has a ground-floor round-headed doorway up three steps and a top floor with three windows, the central one higher than the others, both groups surrounded by chequerwork. But this tower has flanking turrets, the gateway is ornamented with capitals and bases to the jambs and there is only one intermediate storey, with a three-cusped ceiling, and the Tapestry indicates that it is some distance from the coast: Harold rides some distance both before embarking and after disembarking.

After that return, attached turrets can be seen in the succeeding 'debriefing', 'deathbed' and 'Halley's Comet' scenes.[6] Freestanding turrets flank the 'Harold/William conversation + Aelfgyva' scene and also follow the building of Hastings Castle.[7] The 'open and shut' pair may signify gatetowers, and the other may be the turret at Hastings represented again in the next scene.

One other three-storey tower with an attached turret is shown here, namely that from which Duke William emerges to mount his horse before riding to battle.[8] To Arnold Taylor's identification of this structure with the central elements of the church now within Hastings Castle,[9] I then added the idea that the embroidery might be meant to indicate a lord's seat in an upper room (rather

4 BT 24, 30, 27.
5 BT 1, 1, 1.
6 BT 25, 31/2, 28/9; BT 27, 33, 30; BT 32, 35, 32.
7 BT 14/5, 18/9, 16/17; BT 45/6, 51 and detail, 50. E.F. Freeman, 'The identity of Aelfgyva', *Annales de Normandie* xli, 1991, 117–34.
8 BT 48, 53, 51.
9 Note 3.

than an apse), with an upper doorway opening into space. Perhaps this links with the previous scene in which William sits high alongside Hastings Castle and a turret.[10] The castle was erected within an Early Iron Age hillfort which had probably become the site of the tenth-century *burh*; therefore the pre-Conquest tower might have had a secular origin.[11] Three steps from ground level into both sides of the tower as well as into both turrets are shown, just like those into the buildings previously described, and the large central opening of the top floor may be a doorway opening into space. Finally, attention may be drawn to the curious building whose oddly-tiled roof is being set on fire just before William sets out from Hastings.[12] Its upper storey has a large central doorway opening into space.

Where was the four-storey tower? Harold's landfall is unknown. Bosham, whence he set out, is a possibility and the church tower there has a monumental east arch and three upper storeys with small windows. But the drawing is very different from that of the Bosham church shown earlier in the Tapestry.[13] This tower is not topped off with a cross, as other buildings are in the embroidery, to indicate a religious use; indeed it has a very lived-in look with large openings at three levels.

Just across the harbour from Bosham at Warblington church is the upper part of a small tower with round-topped openings above roof level to north, south and west which are big enough to stand up in (Figure 1).[14] The foundations of two secular stone towers of eleventh-century date have been excavated overlooking harbours near Bosham. Building S18 at Portchester Castle was originally associated with a large timber hall before being rebuilt as a tower 6m. each way with two rows of posts inside.[15] Itself associated with late Saxon burials, it was demolished about 1100. At Church Norton (Selsey), there were tower foundations about 9m. each way, with a smaller and slighter stone-based building alongside. Pottery evidence indicated a Saxo-Norman date.[16] Neither of these latter towers was clearly ecclesiastical in purpose; the building of churches nearby (but not on the same site) after the towers had been demolished suggests a change of use. A stone secular building 6m. square in Tanner Street, Winchester, was incorporated later into the nave of St Mary's church.[17] At Chilham and Eynsford castles in Kent, multi-storey buildings (10m. or so each way) have been found below Norman work.[18]

10 BT 46, 51, 50.

11 P.A. Barker and K.J. Barton, 'Excavations at Hastings Castle 1968', *Arch. Journ.* cxxxiv, 1977, 80–100 especially 83.

12 BT 47, 52. 50.

13 BT 3, 3, 3.

14 E.A. Fisher, *The Greater Anglo-Saxon churches: an Architectural-Historical Study*, London 1962, Plates 277 and 278. Figures 1 to 15 are diagrammatic and only intended to show the size and positions of large upper openings, overlaid on to one elevation for economy.

15 B.W. Cunliffe, *Excavations at Portchester Castle Vol. 11: Saxon*, Report xxxii of the Research Committee of the Society of Antiquaries of London, London 1976, 49–52, 60.

16 F.G. Aldsworth and E.D. Garnett, 'Excavations on "The Mound", Church Norton, Selsey in 1911 and 1965', *Sussex Archaeological Collections* 119, 1981, 217–220.

17 M. Biddle, 'Excavations at Winchester 1971: Tenth and Final Interim Report, Part II', *Antiqs. Journ.* lv, 1975, 295–337 especially 308–13.

18 A.W. Clapham, 'An Early Hall at Chilham Castle', *Antiqs. Journ.* viii, 1928, 350–3; V. Horsman,

Oxford has two four-storey towers connected only later with a church. St George's Tower (in the castle) is wrongly oriented and the plans made before the rebuilding of the early Norman crypt show no congruence with the tower. Apart from a restored east arch and narrow west window the only openings are four round-headed doorways in the parapet (Figure 2). Standing on the bank of the Thames beside the Saxon east-west street, St George's Tower might be associated with the first west gate of the town. The motte (which presumably dates from the foundation of the castle in 1071 and carried a tower at least from the thirteenth century) effectively neutralized St George's Tower by blocking its view over Oxford.[19]

David Parsons has suggested that the church tower of St Michael at the Northgate was originally a pedestrian gate-tower into the city, a *burhgeat* or secular tower. A large tall blocked doorway exists at first floor level in the south wall; the west window here has been altered at least twice, and there is another large doorway higher up in the north wall, all below two tiers of belfry openings with central balusters (Figure 3).[20]

In his magisterial survey of Anglo-Saxon buildings, Harold Taylor has referred to the use of church towers for the storage of valuables, the display of relics from galleries and also for private use by the founder and his family.[21] As well as St Michael, Oxford, four or five other Anglo-Saxon church towers appear both in Taylor's table of towers with upper doorways opening into space and also in a list of turriform naves compiled by David Parsons, which may have been of secular origin.[22]

Brian Davison has drawn attention to the defensive earthworks around Earl's Barton church.[23] There are no less than six – possibly seven – upper doorways opening into space from this tower, with its all-over decoration of narrow pilaster strips (Figure 4). Another such decorated Saxon tower is at Barnack with not only a similar upper doorway into space but also internal masonry which Baldwin Brown interpreted as a 'seat of judgment' on the west side, which was formerly accompanied by ranges of oak benches round three sides of the tower (Figure 5).[24] A third church tower with elaborate decoration is St Peter's,

'Eynsford castle – a reinterpretation of its early History in the light of recent Excavations', *Archaeologia Cantiana* cv, 1988, 39–58.

19 E. King, *Vestiges of Oxford Castle*, London 1796; Royal Commission on Historic Monuments, England, *Inventory of . . . City of Oxford*, London 1939, 156–8; T.G. Hassall, 'Excavations at Oxford castle, 1965–73', *Oxoniensia* xli, 1976, 232–308 especially Fig. 2, 252–4 and J. Cooper, 'The Church of St George in the Castle', 306–8.

20 B. Durham *et al.*, 'Oxford's Northern Defences: Archaeological Studies 1971–1982', *Oxoniensia* xlviii, 1983, 13–40 especially 14–18, 33–5; Council for British Archaeology Churches Committee *Newsletter* 22, 1985; T.G. Hassall, *Oxford, the Buried City*, Oxford 1987, 22–3. I am grateful to Brian Durham for showing me the draft of his forthcoming monograph, and to David Parsons for providing Appendix I in elaboration of his side of the argument.

21 H.M. Taylor, *Anglo-Saxon Architecture* iii, Cambridge 1978, 826–7, 887–94.

22 M. Audouy, B. Dix and D. Parsons, 'The Tower of All Saint's Church, Earl's Barton, Northamptonshire: its construction and context', *Arch. Journ.* 152, 1995, 73–94.

23 B.K. Davison, 'The Origins of the Castle in England', *Arch. Journ.* cxxiv, 1967, 202–11 especially 208–10.

24 H.S. Syers, 'The building of Barnack Church', *Reports and Papers of the Associated Architectural Societies* xxiii, 1895–96, 143–51 extended as 'Barnack Church', *Journ. BAA* second series 5, 1899, 13–28.

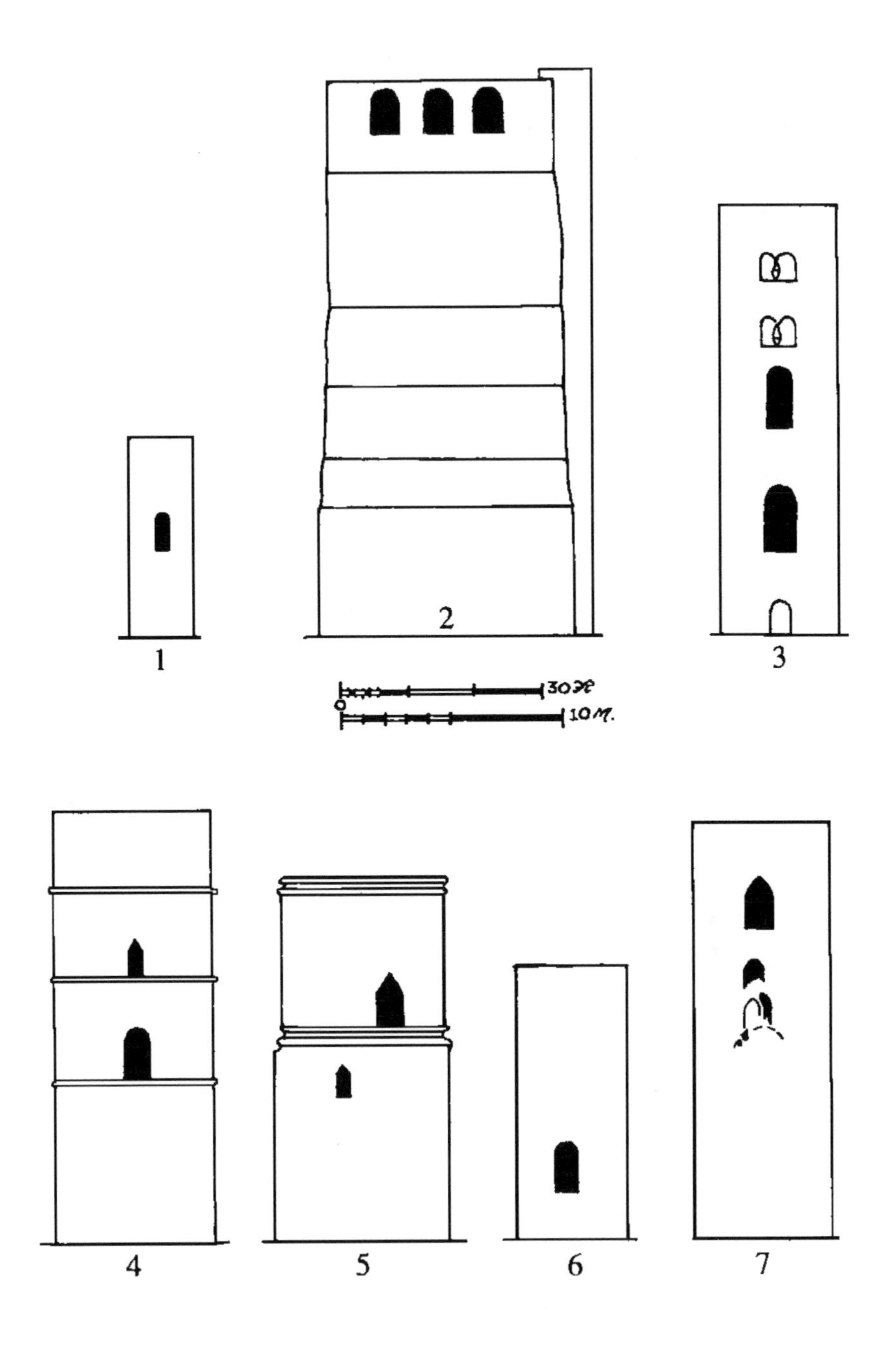

(1) Warblington (Hants); (2) St George in the Castle (Oxford); (3) St Michael at the Northgate (Oxford); (4) Earl's Barton (Northants); (5) Barnack (Northants); (6) Wickham (Berks); (7) Guildford (Surrey)

Figures 1–7

Barton-on-Humber, but there the upper doorways were intended from the first to open into the east and west annexes, and the evidence for a previous tower there is slender.[25] But the church stands immediately outside a Middle Saxon enclosure which was levelled in the Late Saxon period when a large square mortared foundation was built on the line of the bank just east of the church, together with an oven and three wells. It might be the base of a secular tower, connected with the adjoining manorial site. A formerly freestanding Saxon tower at Wickham (Berks) has two blocked doorways about 3m. up, with no lower openings (Figure 6).[26] At St Mary's church, Guildford the central tower has four narrow flint pilasters on each face, cut into by early Norman and later arches.[27] There are traces of external arcading and the size of the upper openings to east and west (each at two levels) are commensurate with doorways opening into space (Figure 7).

Elaborate ornament and large upper doorways are unusual in pre-Conquest towers. Such towers draw the eye, particularly to their upper openings, and may be called 'towers of display'. An abbey like Jumièges had an obvious need for display but (apart from Deerhurst) the other churches with upper openings into space seem to have been manorial in origin, and the towers may involve the secular arm and its needs as well as the Church's. A church must have a ground-floor entrance somewhere, but this could be blocked in an emergency, and a stone tower might not be a death-trap, since stout timber takes a long time to burn through.

The definition and function of the *burhgeat* mentioned in Wulfstan's 'Of People's Ranks and Laws' have provoked much debate, but a consensus view would be 'entrance to a protected enclosure'.[28] The accompanying *bellhus/an* may

[25] W. and K. Rodwell, 'St Peter's Church, Barton-on-Humber: Excavations and Structural study 1978–81', *Antiq. Journ.* lxii, 1982, 283–315 but cf. H.M. Taylor, 'Old St Peter's Church, Barton-on-Humber', *Arch. Journ.* cxxxi, 1974, 369–73. Sir David Wilson, 'Defence in the Viking Age; private defence', in *Problems in Social and Economic Archaeology*, ed. G. de G. Sieveking *et al.*, London 1976, 443–4 suggested the stone church towers of Barton-on-Humber, Earl's Barton and Barnack as integral fortifications. See also G. Baldwin Brown, *The Arts in Early England II: Anglo-Saxon Architecture*, second edition, London 1925, especially 273–94, 330–2 and J.T. Micklethwaite, 'Something about Saxon church building', *Arch. Journ.* liii, 1896, 293–351 especially 335 and *Arch. Journ.* lv, 1898, 340–9.

[26] Fisher (note 14 above), 386; H.M. and J. Taylor, *Anglo-Saxon Architecture* II, Cambridge 1965, 660–2.

[27] J.H. Parker, 'The church of St Mary Guildford', *Arch. Journ.* xxix, 1872, 170–80; F.W. Holling, 'Early foundations of St Mary's church, Guildford', *Surrey Archaeological Collections* lxiv, 1967, 165–8.

[28] F.W. Maitland, *Township and Borough*, Cambridge 1898, 489–92; *Domesday Book and Beyond*, Cambridge 1987 reprint, 184, 190 (as a seat of justice); F.M. Stenton, 'The Thriving of the Anglo-Saxon Ceorl', expanded version of a 1958 lecture printed in *Preparatory to Anglo-Saxon England: Being the collected papers of Frank Merry Stenton*, ed. D.M. Stenton, Oxford 1970 (as a fortified dwelling); Davison, 'Origins' (note 23 above) especially 204; B.K. Davison, 'Sulgrave', *Current Archaeology* 2, 1969, 19–22 (but the thinwalled building turned out not to be turriform, see B.K. Davison, 'Excavations at Sulgrave Northamptonshire, 1960–76', *Arch. Journ.* cxxxiv, 1977, 105–14). R. Allen Brown, 'An Historian's approach to the origins of the Castle in England', *Arch. Journ.* cxxvi, 1969, 131–46 (with Davison's reply 146–8), reiterated in *Origins of English Feudalism* (Historical Problems: Studies and Documents 19), London and New York 1973, 80–2, 145 and *English Castles*, third edition, London 1976, 46–9 (town or manor gate); H.R. Loyn, 'Towns in Anglo-Saxon England: the evidence and some possible lines of enquiry', in *England before the Conquest: studies in primary sources presented to Dorothy Whitelock*, ed. P. Clemoes, Cambridge 1971,

derive from the Germanic words for peace and protection and not necessarily require a bell.[29] David Parsons has suggested to me that some early towers fulfilled several of the requirements for a ceorl's promotion: the gate, the chapel and the belfry might be all in one building. So I have appropriated the term '*burhgeat*' in this paper to mean a free-standing building of at least two storeys, the upper with large openings, whose architectural detail suggests a date no later than the twelfth century. Its purpose might be either secular or religious, or a joint corporate venture with compatible objectives. An open gallery or a large upper doorway can only have been for display (of people or of relics) and not for defence, particularly if the openings go down to the floor level. Shooting slits need breast-high defence and only a small opening for missiles; the cross-shaped openings in the embrasures at Earl's Barton would be impossible to shoot through. Even if the Tapestry designer was not showing actual buildings but using conventional symbols, the symbols should have been recognisable by those who saw the Tapestry when new.

St Leonard's Tower at West Malling (Kent) can perhaps therefore be seen as an early Norman essay at a *burhgeat*, its two surviving upper floors having large openings into space on all four sides, external arcading and no groundfloor entrance (Figure 8).[30] The nearby early Norman church tower originally had an east annexe of similar width and length, giving a unitary plan.[31] A clear example of this plan in use can be seen in the upper floor of the church tower of Brook (Kent) where the altar recess is flanked by large openings (which seem to have originally gone down to floor level) clearly visible from the nave and lit by the tower windows, an 'ecclesiastical theatre', probably due to prior Ernulf of Christ Church, Canterbury (1093–1107).[32] Richard Gem has drawn attention to the military and domestic architectural features of another unitary church at Shipley (Sussex), Templar work of c.1140. The openings in each face of the top storey of the tower are very large – 3m. high and lm. wide.[33]

115–28 especially 119–20 (fortified centre); Ann Williams, 'A Bell-house and a Burh-geat: Lordly Residences in England before the Norman Conquest', *Medieval Knighthood* iv, ed. C. Harper-Bill and R. Harvey, 1992, 221–40, especially the reference to Adam of Cockfield's manorhouse in Bury St Edmunds with its 140 foot high timber belfry. The whole catalogue of requirements (. . . *burgrete*) is later used in the pretended original Berkeley charter from duke Henry to Robert fitzHarding of early 1153 (*Regesta* iii, no. 309). The Irish round towers (from 950 A.D. onward) were usually called *cloicthech* (bellhouse): M. Hare and A. Hamlin, 'The study of early church architecture in Ireland; an Anglo-Saxon viewpoint', in *The Anglo-Saxon Church . . . in honour of H.M. Taylor*, ed. L.A.S. Butler and R.K. Morris, CBA Research Report 60, London 1986, 131–45.

29 R. Morris, *Churches in the Landscape*, London 1988, 255.

30 Unpublished notes by H. Sands in the library of the Society of Antiquaries of London correcting inter alia G.T. Clark, 'St Leonard's Tower, West Malling', *The Builder* xxxix, 1880, 640–2. U.T. Holmes, 'The Houses of the Bayeux Tapestry', *Speculum* iii, 1959, 179–83, plate V reproduces a carving from Moissac of a tall building with a large arch to the ground floor, two major round-topped openings above and two oculi to the second floor below a ridged roof.

31 J. Newman, *West Kent and the Weald*, Buildings of England 29, ed. N. Pevsner, Harmondsworth 1969, 375; G.M. Liven in A.W. Lawson and G.W. Stockley, *A History of the parish church of St Mary the Virgin, West Malling, Kent*, West Malling 1904.

32 S.E. Rigold, 'The demesne of Christ Church at Brook', *Arch. Journ.* cxxvi, 1969, 270–2.

33 R.D.H. Gem, 'An Early church of the Knights Templars at Shipley, Sussex', *ANS* vi, 1983, 238–46. Gem has separately argued that the original west front of Lincoln Minster had a fortified aspect and intent: R.D.H. Gem, 'Lincoln cathedral: Ecclesia Pulchra, Ecclesia Fortis', in *Medieval Art and Architecture at Lincoln Cathedral*, ed. T.A. Heslop with V.A. Sekules, BAA Conference Transactions

Several eleventh-century castle gatehouses carry on this *burhgeat* idea. Probably the first in England is that at Exeter, 7m. square with three floors over the gatepassage.[34] The first floor is blind, but those above have triangular-headed openings – doors and windows – leading to platforms both inside and outside over the forearch (Figure 9). The West Gate at Lincoln castle as rebuilt seems to have been openbacked above the gatepassage with a doorway to the platform in front (Figure 10).[35] The inner gatehouse at Ludlow (Salop) originally had four large openings at first-floor level and two loops to the next higher floor (Figure 11). The masonry suggests that originally only the facade was built, with flanking vaulted chambers.[36] At Richmond castle, the simple doorway was converted into a square gatehouse and by the early twelfth century the upper floor had been added, with three tall openings (the central one with a plain tympanum) on the outside looking over the town, cut straight through the wall (Figure 12).[37] Over 1m. wide and 2m. high, they cannot have been meant for defence. On the staircase leading up from this floor is another opening which gave access to a wooden gallery on the inside of the castle. The second phase of the tower of Bramber Castle formerly had at least two openings one metre wide and two to three metres high above the wide arch of the gatepassage (Figure 13).[38] Another opening survives leading to a dogleg passage in a side wall; fallen masonry fragments suggest that part of the front wall had a gallery as well.

The main gatehouses to the episcopal castles of Newark and Sherborne probably date from the 1130s. At Newark, three former windows can be traced over the gatepassage, with two more one storey higher and positioned between them (Figure 14).[39] The north-west gate to Sherborne castle has an opening 2m. each way in each of the four walls at first floor level, three of them being outside the curtain wall (Figure 15).[40]

The gatehouses of the castles of the Angevin kings after 1154 lack large upper 'display' openings as do the surviving ones of Henry de Blois which all seem to date from after his return from exile in 1159.[41]

for 1982, Leeds 1986, 9–28. The only apparent defensive feature – the skied machicolations over the side recesses – could have been simply for liturgical use.

34 S.R. Blaylock, 'Exeter Castle Gatehouse; architectural survey', *Exeter Archaeology* 1984–85, 18–24.

35 E. King, 'Observations on antient castles', *Archaeologia* vi, 1782, 261–6.

36 D.F. Renn, ' "Chastel de Dynan": the first phases of Ludlow', in *Castles in Wales and the Marches: Essays in honour of D.J.C. King*, ed. J.R. Kenyon and R. Avent, Cardiff 1987, 55–73. The decorated gatehouse at Tickhill (Yorks) appears to have traces of gallery windows over the entrance arch, and may date from Roger de Bush's time: M. Chibnall, 'Robert of Belleme and the castle of Tickhill', *Droit Privé et Institutions Régionales: Études offertes à Jean Yver*, Paris 1976, 151–6.

37 G.T. Clark, 'Richmond Castle', *Yorkshire Archaeological Journal* ix, 1886, 33–54. I cannot find any evidence for the earlier tower shown on the folding plan in Sir Charles Peers, *Richmond Castle, Yorkshire*, London 1953.

38 K.J. Barton and E.W. Holden, 'Excavations at Bramber Castle, Sussex, 1966–67', *Arch. Journ.* cxxxiv, 1977, 11–79 especially 15, 16, 30, 37.

39 H.S. Braun, 'Newark Castle', *Transactions of the Thoroton Society* xxxix, 1935, 53–91.

40 Royal Commission on Historic Monuments, England, *Inventory . . . Dorset I: West*, London 1952, 64–6, folding plan and plate 90.

41 M. Biddle, *Wolvesey: the old bishops' palace, Winchester*, London 1986; M.W. Thompson, 'Recent excavations in the keep of Farnham castle, Surrey', *Med. Arch.* iv, 1960, 81–94 and *Farnham Castle, Surrey*, London 1961; J.N. Hare, 'Bishops Waltham Palace, Hampshire . . .', *Arch. Journ.* cxlv, 1988, 222–54 especially 225–6.

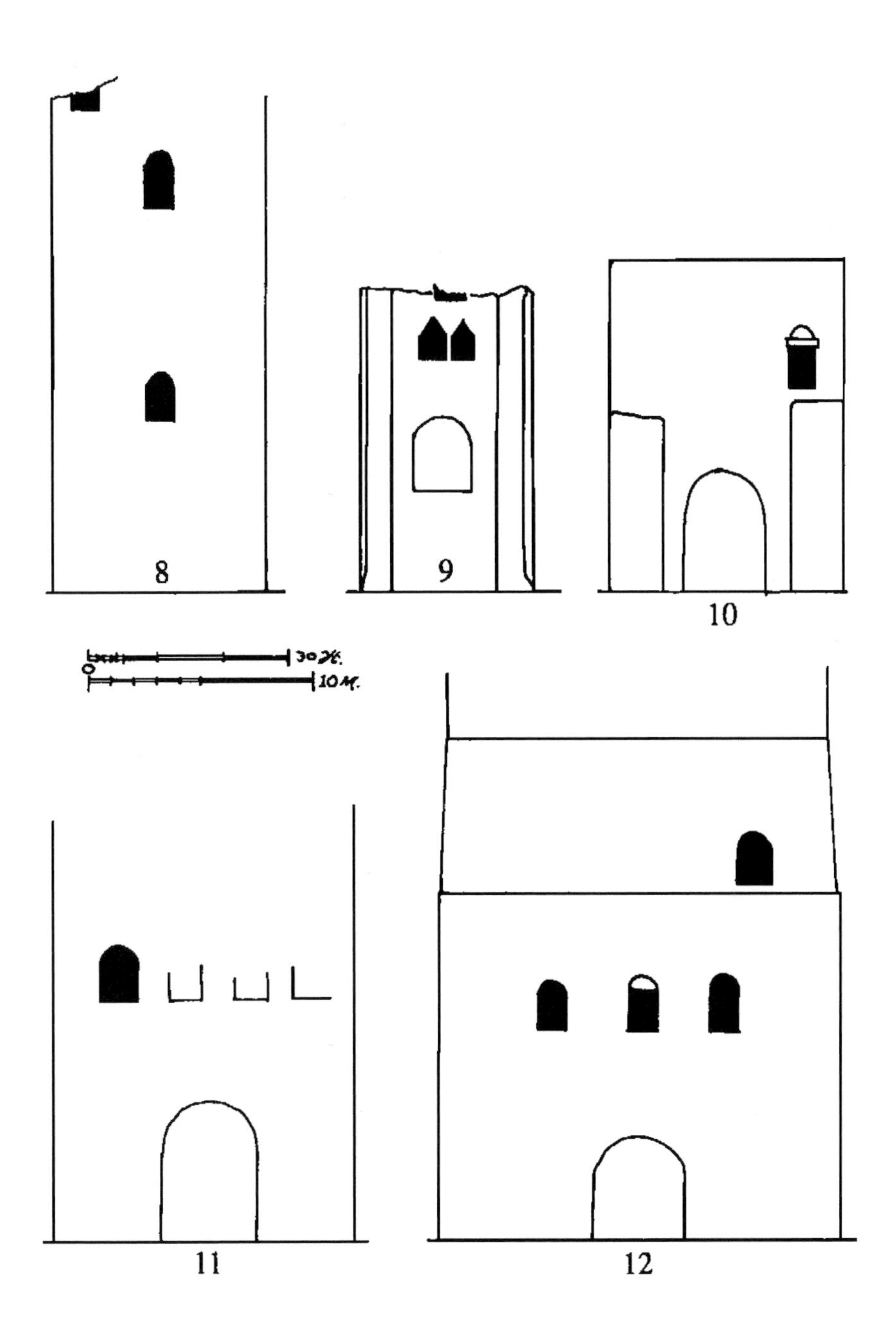

(8) St Leonard, West Malling (Kent); (9) Exeter Castle (Devon); (10) West gate Lincoln Castle; (11) Inner gate, Ludlow Castle (Salop); (12) Richmond Castle (North Yorks)

Figures 8–12

A late medieval carved oriel bracket at New Buckenham (Norfolk) represents a timber castle, with a large stone gateway having two-storey turrets and rooms flanking the main arch, with another row of three doorways one above, all twelve openings having round heads.[42]

Such galleries weakened the passive defensive capability of a gatehouse, and must have been designed for display, analogous to today's box at the theatre, the balcony of Buckingham Palace or the declaration of an election result. Although features designed to give the occupier a dramatic context can be found in later castle architecture (for example the approach to the audience chamber and its setting at the Wakefield Tower, London, Knaresborough and Warkworth, or the heraldic panels over the entrance at Bodiam, Herstmonceux, Hylton, Kirby Muxloe or Warkworth), this concept of public exhibition does not seem to have outlasted the middle of the twelfth century in England.[43] Whether motivated by considerations of comfort or safety, later medieval magnates preferred not to demonstrate their *dominatio* by displaying themselves from a staged setting over the castle gate.

The Gonfanon

Thirty-seven flags are embroidered on the Tapestry, including the two 'plastic' (cut-out) wyverns which Brooks and Walker identified as one and the same Saxon standard which, with its white-bearded bearer, his sword still sheathed, is shown falling before a horse which treads on the wyvern.[44] The standing figure carries a conical shield and holds the wyvern on a stout spike-topped pole (XXXI), whereas the unprotected toppling figure has dropped a thin 45 staff carrying the wyvern (XXXII).[45]

Although the figures are technically wyverns (with two feet) they presumably represent the dragon of Wessex. Is it simply coincidence that St Vigor of Bayeux was a dragon-slayer?[46] Nearly two hundred years later, King Henry III ordered a dragon standard with jewelled eyes and a simulated flickering tongue.[47] Such flags were valuable trophies: King Henry I paid 20 silver marks for the standard of King Louis after the battle of Brémule.[48]

Brooks' and Walker's identification of the same standard being shown twice

42 P.A. Barker and R.A. Higham, *Timber Castles*, London 1992, 161–4.

43 P.E. Curnow, 'The Wakefield Tower, Tower of London', in *Ancient Monuments and their Interpretatio n: essays presented to A.J. Taylor*, ed. M.R. Apted *et al.*, Chichester 1977, 155–89 especially 163–71 and pl. XID; P. Dixon, 'The donjon of Knaresborough: the castle as theatre', *Château-Gaillard* xiv, 1988, 12–39; B.K. Davison on Warkworth, Oxford symposium on recent work on medieval castles, 9 October 1982. Heraldic panels are usually only treated in the guidebook on sale at the castle, but special mention should be made of B.M. Morley, 'Hylton Castle', *Arch. Journ.* cxxxiii, 1976, 118–34.

44 N.P. Brooks and H.E. Walker, 'The Authority and Interpretation of the Bayeux Tapestry', *ANS* i, 1978, 1–34. H.E.J. Cowdrey suggested that it was dropped by one man and picked up by another: 'Towards an interpretation of the Bayeux Tapestry', *ANS* x, 1987, 59–60.

45 The Roman figures in brackets refer to the numbering of Appendix 2, page 198.

46 D. Bernstein, *The Mystery of the Bayeux Tapestry*, London 1986, 31.

47 *Calendar of Close Rolls, 1242–47*, London 1916, 201.

48 Orderic vi, 240/1; see 242/3 for the cognizances thrown away and changed in 1119.

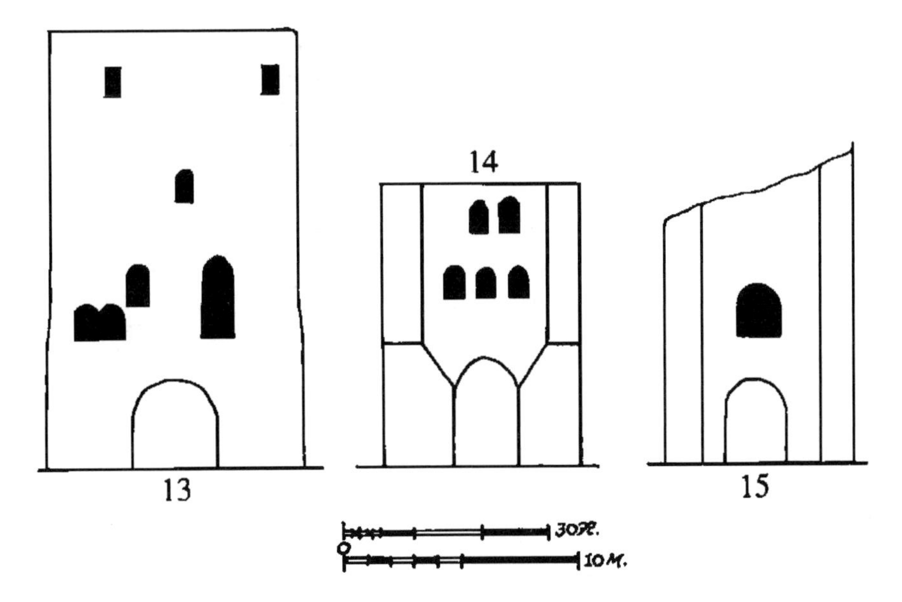

(13) Bramber Castle (Sussex); (14) Newark (Notts); (15) Sherborne (Dorset)

Figures 13–15

(albeit with slight differences) led me to look at the rest of the flags to see if others were duplicated to identify an individual (or a group) as they moved through the narrative. The flags (like any of the details of the text and drawings) may have been altered from those of the original Tapestry story, but there does seem to be an underlying unity.

The remaining thirty-five flags have the fly (that is, the side of the flag furthest from the support or hoist) in the form of three or more narrow strips usually tapering to points (tails). Five of them are masthead pennants, three-tailed without a field between hoist and fly. Four occur on the ships of the invasion fleet, and one on the English ship carrying the news of Harold's coronation to Normandy.[49] I can see no special significance in these pennants, English and Norman alike, and therefore exclude them from further study here. We are now down to thirty flags (plus the two 'plastic' wyverns mentioned above) which are all carried just below the head (either a blade or a barbed point) of

49 Appendix 2, M. Repair work may conceal another on the English ship earlier under way carrying Harold to Ponthieu (BT 5, 5, 6), but it is more likely that this was intended to be a masthead cap (truck) like that embroidered on the ship (probably the same one) about to anchor. The largest ship of the invasion fleet (BT 38, 43 and detail, 42) has a large square object at the masthead, quartered and topped by a cross. Usually this is identified with Poitiers' signal lantern, but it might be William's symbol: C. Erdmann, *Die Entstehung ties Kreuzzugsgedankens*, Stuttgart 1935, trans. by M.W. Baldwin and W. Goffart as *The Origin of the Idea of Crusade*, Princeton 1977, 198; T.A. Heslop, *'Image and Authority': English seals of the 11th and 12th centuries*, chapter 2 (forthcoming). But to be a flag it should have either been offset from the mast or given tails/pennants like the others.

either a thin staff (embroidered as a single row of stitches) or a stout pole (two parallel rows of stitches with contrasting colour between). Only a minority of the lances shown carry flags, and consequently I see them (as Allen Brown did) as marking out the leader of an army or at least of a fighting unit (*conroi*). A long flag with a split fly is usually called a gonfanon (meaning a war flag) more properly hung from a cross staff.[50] Here I shall use the term 'gonfanon' to mean not only a flag with split tails but also the lance to which it is attached.[51] Many such flags are held upright, gripped at shoulder height. Riders usually hold the gonfanon in their right hand, butting it into their stirrup, managing the reins and their shield in the left hand. Those on foot hold the gonfanon in their left hand whilst gesturing with the right. There are exceptions: where Harold is given arms by William (VIII) and in the heat of battle, where 'Eustace' transfers the gonfanon (XXX) to his left hand and stirrup to point out William, and also where the dragon standardbearer (XXXII) uses his left hand to hold his shield. Sometimes a rider holds his gonfanon in front of him, either at an angle or almost horizontal (e.g. II, V).[52] Usually the lance is held at the point of balance, but there are instances (e.g. IX) where it appears to be held near the butt.

At the beginning of the Tapestry, none of the figures is in full military array: Guy of Ponthieu and his men have shields and weapons, but it is not until William's expeditionary force reaches Mont St Michel that the first two figures in chain mail and helmets appear in the throng, the first man bearing a lance with a flag (1). After the crossing of the Couesnon and the attack on Dol, everyone is in armour. The Norman *Consuetudines* required war to be announced by the wearing of the hauberk (*lorica*), the carrying of the flag (*vexillum*) and the

50 Erdmann, 42 distinguishes the war banner, with a flag attached to a staff, from the holy banner, with its flag hung from a transverse bar. Dione Clementi suggested to me that the flag was first attached to a lance as an improvised signal. The earliest gonfanon carried by a tenant-in chief comes in the Otto-Evangeliar (983–1002): H. Schnitzler, *Rheinische Schatskammer* i, 1957, Koln 1957, tafel 102, p. 30. If the free end was split in two, this could indicate the tenant-in-chief of an imperial tenant-in-chief. For the Lombard and Norman gonfanons in southern Italy, J. Deer, *Papsstum and Normannen*, Koln 1972, 23 and D. Clementi, 'Stepping-stones in the making of the Regno', *Bullettino dell' Istituto Storico per il Medievo* 90, Roma 1982/3, cap. II. Wace (*Roman* iii.6, 405/6 cited by M. Bennett, 'Wace and Warfare', *ANS* xi, 1988, 46) distinguished between the gonfanons of the barons and the pennants of the knights.

51 J.F. Verbruggen, 'La tactique militaire des armdes des chevaliers', *Revue du Nord* xxix, 1947. A. Ailes, 'The Knight, Heraldry and Armour: The Role of Recognition and the Origins of Heraldry', in *Medieval Knighthood*, ed. C. Harper-Bill and R. Harvey, iv, Woodbridge 1992, 14, notes 56, 57. For the significance of the left hand, see Cowdrey, 'Interpretation' (note 44 above), 57–9.

52 The lances are not technically couched. Using the arm as well as the hand to support the lance's weight is only commonsense, and the blow might be delivered using the momentum imparted by the forward movement of the horse. Couching was designed to weld man, horse and lance together to unhorse a mounted opponent, and the Normans had no such opposition here. They were moving uphill, and consequently the lanceheads were held higher than was usual to attack men on foot. Once the target has been struck, if the lance remains unbroken, the holder risks a broken arm or a fall unless he lets go or pulls it out instantly. If William was armed with the stump of a lance at the end of the day (*Gesta Guillelmi* 202), this does not prove he had been using a couched lance. For the literature on couching see in particular, R. Buttin, 'La lance et l'arrêt de cuirasse', *Archaeologia* xcix, 1965, 77–178 especially 80–2, D. Nicolle, 'The impact of the European couched lance on Muslim military tactics', *Journal of the Arms and Armour Society* x, 1980, 6–40 and J. Flori, 'Encore l'usage de la lance . . .', *Cahiers de civilisation médiévale* xxxi, 1988, 213–40.

sounding of the horn (*cornu*).[53] Here we have the first two elements; the latter two will be seen later during the seaborne invasion.

Is the standardbearer William himself? The infulae at the nape of the neck are shown elsewhere on representations of the duke in the Tapestry, where he gives arms to Harold (VIII) and also when he sets out from Hastings (XVII).[54] This first flag is sewn very delicately. The hoist has three spaced bands wrapped round the staff, the field (between hoist and fly) carries a thin upright (red) cross between vertical bands and the fly has three long pointed tails. The cross on the field of the gonfanon does not reappear in the Tapestry until the army reaches Hastings (XIV), when it appears in a very different form (see below). Although this cross appears in Montfaucon's engraving (but with expanding equal arms), it might be an eleventh-century change to link the two events, the beginning of hostile action after the invasion of Brittany and of England.[55]

The red cross makes an Englishman think of St George, who had appeared to support Roger de Hauteville at the battle of Cerami in 1063 with 'a white banner bearing a wondrous cross'. Almost certainly this appearance is commemorated by the remarkable tympanum over the south door of St George's church at Fordington (Dorset) where the saint carries a large gonfanon on a launcegay, with a lengthwise plain cross and three tapering tails.[57] He is triumphing over three tumbled figures with conical shields to the obvious relief of two praying mailed figures with kite-shaped shields. The style is very close indeed to that of the Tapestry. This St George's church was in existence by 1091, and so this tympanum may have predated the appearance of the saint (together with Demetrius and Mercurius) leading a heavenly host with white banners (no mention of crosses) in support of the crusaders at Antioch in 1098.[58]

Can this gonfanon be the papal banner given to the duke of Normandy?[59] Here, at the start of the Breton campaign of 1064 it would be an anachronism, since Harold was then supporting William and Edward the Confessor was still alive.

After trying several classifications, I found two groups of approximately equal size and have attempted to distinguish individual flags within each group.

53 C.H. Haskins, '*Consuetudines et Justicie* of William the Conqueror', *EHR* xxiii, 1908, 502–8, expanded in *Norman Institutions*, New York and London 1918, reprinted 1960, Appendix D section 4.

54 C. Stothard, 'Some observations on the Bayeux Tapestry', *Archaeologia* xix, 1820, 184–91; I. Peirce, 'Arms, Armour and Warfare in the Eleventh Century', *ANS* x, 1987, 241 note 22; Cowdrey, 'Interpretation' (note 44 above), 60.

55 Dam B. de Montfaucon, *Les Monuments de la Monarchie Francaise I*, Paris 1729, plates XXXV–XLIX; *II*, Paris 1730, Plates I–IX.

56 Erdmann (note 49 above), 135 citing Geoffrey Malaterra, *RIC 2*, II, 33, 141.

57 S. Alford, 'Romanesque Architectural Sculpture in Dorset: a Select Catalogue and Commentary', *Proceedings of the Dorset Natural History and Archaeological Society* 106, 1984, 1–22 especially 1–5. The dragon does not appear until the twelfth century: Erdmann (note 49 above), 278.

58 Orderic v, 112/5.

59 The gift of a papal banner is mentioned by William of Poitiers (*Gesta Guillelmi* 153, 184), and Orderic ii, 142/3 but C. Morton argues that it did not arrive before 1070 at the earliest: 'Pope Alexander II and the Norman Conquest', *Latomus* xxiv, 1965, 362–82. Several papal banners were awarded in 1063/4: Erdmann (note 49 above) 154, 185–9 explains the distinction between a feudal investiture and a holy war symbol.

Some inconsistencies remain, as so often with an attempt to explain the details of the Bayeux Tapestry.

The thirty gonfanons may be divided between the seventeen which have a border round all four sides of the field, and the thirteen which are simply striped, or rolled up so that it is uncertain whether they have a border or not. I will call the latter 'simple' and the former 'bordered' gonfanons. In the Tapestry there are several cases where a gonfanon of one type held erect is followed by another sloped forward and finally one held horizontally. I suggest that this indicates the same group (*conroi*) moving through the scenes of action.

If we first consider the Breton campaign, then a 'simple' gonfanon is held upright at Mont St Michel (I), sloped forward as Rennes is passed (II) and finally held horizontally to receive the keys of Dinan (VI). This last scene also has four 'bordered' gonfanons. Two (III, IV) stand upright, with very long staves embroidered right across the lower border of the Tapestry. They have shields leaning against them, perhaps belonging to the mailclad pair of attackers with a flaming torch in each hand who seem to be getting in each other's way. The other two 'bordered' gonfanons are held horizontally, one (V) by Conan in both hands and carrying the keys on its point, the other (VII) by one of the recipient's riding companions. If the 'bordered' gonfanon bearers were meant to be distinguished from the 'simple' ones, this runs counter to the explanation of them being William's men besieging Dinan. Other explanations are

a separate *conroi* (with a 'bordered' gonfanon) threatens to fire Dinan and takes the keys to hand over to the superior leader who has a 'simple' gonfanon or

Conan is the holder of the 'bordered' gonfanon; he takes Dinan by threats, surrenders and finally makes off or

a muddle by the artist or embroiderer, which could be resolved by reversing the gonfanons offering and receiving the keys. Montfaucon shows the recipient's gonfanon (VI) differenced with a central disk, which might support this explanation.

The next scene shows Harold receiving a gonfanon (VIII) from William which has two disks inside the border and four tails, just possibly captured (Breton) arms made to look more important. We do not see this gonfanon again for certain, which is only to be expected: Harold would be unlikely to flaunt signs of his new vassalage on his return to England.

We now move on to the embarkation of the invasion fleet. The leading figure wears a mantle and carries a partly-furled gonfanon (IX), perhaps indicating that the war would begin at the English shore and not in Normandy. Something of the same idea can be seen today in the casing of military colours. The sloping staff is being held at its lower end, probably so that it can be seen by the whole army.

On the great ship of the fleet, the hornblowing figure on the sternpost slopes his small 'simple' gonfanon (X) towards England. On landing, two figures with rolled-up gonfanons (XI, XII) on poles across their horses' necks gallop up to a more leisurely rider who holds his 'simple' gonfanon (XIII) erect. Next a mounted scout has planted his 'simple' gonfanon (XIV) on the hill but points (double-jointedly) to it from the saddle.

Staying with the 'simple' gonfanons, three are successively held erect (XXI), then forward (XXII) and then horizontal (XXIII) as William orders the advance. This action is then repeated with 'simple' gonfanons (XXIV, XXV, XXVI) differenced with three disks on the field, ending just as the Norman horses reach the massed English foot. Finally a 'simple' upright gonfanon (XXVII) can be seen between the first two Englishmen, and crossed by a broad-bladed axe. Since none of the English can spare a hand from spear and shield for either axe or gonfanon (it is remarkable that the first Englishman here is also a greybeard, indicating a veteran) the latter gonfanon must be Norman insignia.

My interpretation is that the first *conroi* to disembark goes scouting, rallying on the hill. When battle begins, their gonfanon is lowered for action and then after engagement, raised to rally. Another *conroi* then follows them into action.

We now turn to the 'bordered' gonfanons. Two figures oversee two stages of the building of Hastings castle: first, the collection of the labourers (XIV) and then the halfbuilt structure (XV). The cross now reappears; a fat one on the first upright gonfanon may be then shown 'reversed' as the four disks embroidered on the second. Both figures are wearing mantles like William as he gets news of Harold, seated and holding a stout pole displaying a gonfanon (XVI) with a fat cross and four tails. He then stands outside the Hastings *burhgeat* grasping an erect gonfanon (XVII) charged with a single disk.

As the advance quickens to a gallop, there are two 'bordered' gonfanons on poles borne like the rolled-up pair carried by the first men galloping off the boat earlier: the first (XVIII) has five tails and a quatrefoil charge, the other (XIX) is semi-elliptical, with a charge which has been described as a bird or a chalice and nine short flamelike tails.

At the far right of the massed English infantry stands yet another bearded man, with both hands grasping a gonfanon (XXVIII) charged with a central disk and five tails. On his left he is protected by an axeman, to his right are four spearmen with shields, the furthest away providing breast-high protection by poking his spear between the second and third shields.

A fallen triangular gonfanon (XXIX), with four tasselled indented streamers, appears before the deaths of Harold's brothers. Worsaae identified this 150 years ago as the *danbrog*, the Viking warflag to be seen associated with the raven on the coins of Anlaf Cuaran, ruler of Northumbria 941–44. The bird on the nine-fringed flag shown earlier (XIX) could be a raven and so might be intended to represent the same flag.[60]

'Eustace' holds an elaborate gonfanon (XXX), charged with a cross with four small disks in the quarters and another four in a strip before the fly and points to William who pushes back his helmet. This flag is another candidate for the vexillum given by pope Alexander II to William. '*[E] . . . cius*' is suspect, not

60 G.J. French, 'On the banners of the Bayeux Tapestry and the earliest heraldic charges', *Journ. BAA* 13, 1857, 113–30 especially 129; *Encomium Emmae Reginae*, ed. A. Campbell, Royal Historical Society Camden third series lxxii, 1949, 96–7; Ailes (note 51 above), 8 note 34; *Coinage in Tenth-century England from Edward the Elder to Edgar's reform*, ed. C.E. Blunt *et al.*, Oxford for the British Academy 1989, chapter 14, especially 221–2.

least because the standardbearer is elsewhere named as Thurstan fitz Rou.[61] If Eustace's name was interposed in the Tapestry for political reasons, the damage to the border may have been later censorship.

This gonfanon is the one clear case in the Tapestry of a cross formy with expanded ends which we find in later pictures, e.g. on crusaders' helmets and on their gonfanons at the battles of the First Crusade at Ascalon, Dorylaeum, Nicaea and Antioch on the glass formerly in a window at St Denis.[62] There Robert of Flanders' banner also had four disks between the limbs of the cross formy. This glass must have dated from the middle of the twelfth century at earliest, and so cannot be used as contemporary evidence for the gonfanons of the First Crusade. But the cross formy with disks design appears on the reverse die of William's coinage, both as duke of Normandy before 1066 and also on his English coins after 1080. It does not appear on the lance flags carried on the royal counterseals before 1100, however, which are simple separate streamers, without a field.[63] Neither William I nor Rufus wished to acknowledge papal authority after 1066. The cross was simply Christian (and used as a *signa* for attestations); the flag, if originally papal, acquired a wider use in and after the First Crusade. We might expect a more explicit emblem of St Peter, but the earliest image of a papal banner – the mosaic in the Lateran Tribune of the banner given by Leo III to Charlemagne – is of a three-tailed gonfanon sprinkled with tiny stars and six disks coloured like archery targets.[64]

The gonfanon with a plain cross occurs several times in the Scylitzes manuscript (1057 × 1081) borne by the Byzantine forces (as supporters of Christ) against the Muslims.[65] The similar standard here may be a Christian banner, appearing first (I, perhaps as an anachronistic 'papal amendment') at the start of the Breton campaign, three times at Hastings *ceastra* (XIV, XV and XVI with four 'tails'), once (XVIII with 5 'tails') during the advance and finally in elaborate detail (XXX) at the crucial point of the battle. This may be pushing symbolism too far, and the cross emblem may simply identify William at various points of the narrative where he is not otherwise obvious.

This leaves two 'bordered' flags to be accounted for; one (XVII) with three tails and a central disk held by William before setting off from Hastings and another (XXIX) with five tails and a central disk held by the unarmed (but mail-clad and protected) man on the right of the English line. Both flags appear to be heavily oversewn, and the disks may be the result of bad repairs. The first might have been intended as a cross but crowded out by the expanded border. A

61 M. Bennett, 'Poetry as History? The Roman de Rou of Wace as a source for the Norman Conquest', *ANS* v, 1982, 33 n. 68; Freeman, 'Identity' (note 7 above), 134; Erdmann (note 49 above), 197–9.

62 BN Ms Fr15634 (i) engraved in Montfaucon (note 55 above), i, Paris 1729, plates l–liv and reproduced in R. Allen Brown, *The Normans*, Woodbridge 1984, 118–19, 126–8.

63 A.B. and A. Wyon, *The Great Seals of England*, London 1887 especially plate 2. Dr Heslop tells me that the swallowtailed second seal of William II is a forgery. Ailes, 15 n. 58.

64 D.L. Galbreath, *A Treatise on Ecclesiastical Heraldry, part 1: Papal Heraldry*, Cambridge 1930, 1; Erdmann (note 49 above), 185.

65 A.B. Hoffmeyer, 'Military Equipment in the Byzantine Manuscript of Scylitzes in the Biblioteca Nacional in Madrid', *Gladius* v, Granada 1966, especially figures 19, 28, 34.

similar explanation for the other flag is that this was the 'Fighting Man' personal standard of Harold.[66] Or is this the gonfanon given to Harold by William two years before at Bonneville-sur-Touques, which has lost a disk and gained a tail?

Five tails may denote kingship, potential in William and factual in Harold.

Appendix I. The West Tower of St Michael at the Northgate, Oxford

David Parsons

The text on which this appendix is based was originally drafted in the mid 1970s, in response to the archaeological discoveries made around the church in 1972–73.[67] The investigations made it clear that the nave of the church, which is a later medieval addition to the Anglo-Saxon tower, stands directly on the line of the pre-Conquest rampart, so that it was not possible to imagine a conventional church in this position until the town wall was moved to the north at a date which is uncertain, but may be c.1100.[68] The tower was therefore interpreted by me as a free-standing structure associated with the defences and forming part of a gatehouse arrangement. Ecclesiastical use of an upper floor as a gate chapel was not excluded, but the tower was regarded as an essentially secular structure and the existence of a church in the Anglo-Saxon period discounted.

This position must be modified, however, in view of the clear evidence of Domesday Book that the priests of St Michael's owned property in the city. This implies a collegiate foundation by 1086, which must have been provided with a church at a date when the original line of the Anglo-Saxon rampart was still functioning as the town defence at this point. Various suggestions have been put forward as to where this church might have been located. The upper part of the reconstruction diagram in the excavation report suggests a position on Ship Street with the church built into the tail of the rampart and entirely separate from the tower.[69] A more recent interpretation by the Oxford Archaeological Unit shows the church taking the place of the rampart behind a postulated section of masonry wall adjacent to the gateway, with the tower added only after the deflection of the wall to the north.[70] Given that a blocked opening was discovered in the south wall of the tower at first-floor level, it is not unreasonable to suggest a building, possibly the church, to the south of the tower, with a connexion between the two at gallery level or leading from the tower into the

66 *Gesta Guillelmi* 224 and *Carmen* 24/5, possibly derived from the Cerne Giant hillfigure as suggested by E.M.C. Barraclough, 'The Flags of the Bayeux Tapestry', *Armi Antichi* i, 1969, 117–24 especially 120.

67 Durham *et al.* (note 20 above), 14–18, 33–35.

68 Durham *et al.*, 33.

69 Durham *et al.*, 33, Fig. 6A.

70 Hassall, 'Buried City' (note 20 above), 22 fig. C.

roofspace of the adjoining building. There are various objections to this particular interpretation, one of which is that as drawn it takes no account of the eccentrically-placed blocked door in the west wall of the tower, a point of some significance in the understanding of the uses that may be suggested for the tower. There is also an assumption, which I do not share, that openings in the north wall of the tower make it unsuitable for a defensive role and require it to be protected on that flank by the re-aligned city north wall.

A further possibility is suggested by this last interpretation, namely that the church itself formed part of the Anglo-Saxon defences at this point, with the tower already in existence and doubling as the west tower of the church and the gate tower of the town. This suggestion receives some support from the results of archaeological work carried out at Repton (Derbyshire) in recent years. The line of the Viking defences has been established, and the termination of the ditch to the east of the chancel shows that the church building was incorporated as part of the defensive system.[71]

There are thus several different interpretations which can be put forward for the sequence of events at the north gate of Oxford and for the status of the buildings, actual or postulated:

(i) the tower was part of the north defences of the town in the Anglo-Saxon period and not attached to the church of St Michael; the deflection of the wall line, perhaps after the Norman Conquest, enabled a new church to be built to the east of the tower;

(ii) The Anglo-Saxon church was towerless and stood inside the north gate; in the late eleventh century the line of the wall was moved to the north, and it incorporated a gate tower attached to the north side of the church; the church was subsequently replaced by a building attached to the east side of the tower;

(iii) an Anglo-Saxon church with west tower formed the town defences at this point, taking the place of the rampart attested further to the east; the tower simultaneously acted as part of the gateway structure.

All these propositions merit discussion, but in the context of the present paper it seems appropriate to follow the argument of the original draft of this Appendix, which examined in more detail the first of the three possibilities. This was by no means the first attempt to interpret the tower of St Michael's as a gate-tower: in discussions and at conferences archaeologists and historians have been wont to speculate about a possible function for the tower in connexion with the Anglo-Saxon gateway. If the tower is regarded as flanking the actual entrance, with the gates hung on the line of the north wall of the tower, there are no problems of interpretation. However, attempts to see the tower as part of the entrance itself have foundered on the lack of a doorway at ground level which could have given access to the interior of the town. The rubble fabric of the lower part of the south wall of the tower has been rebuilt at some stage, and there is no apparent evidence for a former door. There are however some slight hints

71 M. Biddle and B. Kjølbye-Biddle, 'Repton and the Vikings', *Antiquity* lxvi, 1992, 36–51, esp. fig. 2.

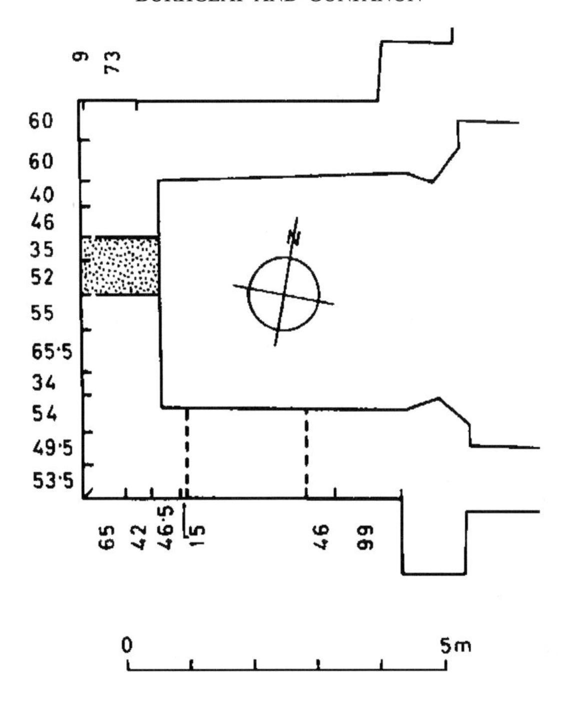

Figure 16. Measured diagram of plinth at St Michael by the Northgate Oxford

that a door once existed in the appropriate position. A plinth-like course of squared stones at the base of the tower fabric begins on the north side close to the north-west quoin, returns along the west face and continues along the south face for a short distance, after which it is hidden by modern paving surrounding the church porch. By inspection from above, however, it is possible to identify the continuation of this feature into the angle between the tower and the south-west buttress of the nave. On the west and north the stones project only about 2.5 cm from the face of the tower. They hardly constitute a plinth in the true sense of the term, and seem mostly not to be original. Fisher dismisses the feature as modern, drawing attention to the fact that it crosses the blocking of the west doorway, which he rightly says 'a plinth would not do'.[72] Figure 16 shows diagrammatically the arrangement of the stones, and it is clear that the two stones covering the blocking of the west door respect the jambs of the opening; it is therefore possible that the 'plinth' predates the blocking of the doorway, which appears to have been carried out in the eighteenth century. The two stones concerned could have been inserted with the blocking material as a cosmetic effect. Be that as it may, there appears to be a gap in the line of 'plinth' stones on the south elevation measuring 1.86 metres, which would be consistent with a doorway in this position still in use at the time that the 'plinth' was inserted. The stone immediately to the west of this gap is also anomalous, mea-

72 Fisher (note 14 above), 233.

suring only about 15 cm, whereas most of the stones are between 34 and 73 cm in length. This may indicate that a small space between the stone on its immediate left and feature to its right had to be filled. If there had been no doorway here, one would have expected a much longer stone in this position.

The suggestion of a doorway in this position has a further attraction. Excavation evidence has shown that the eastern frontage of Cornmarket Street in the Anglo-Saxon period was more than seven metres behind the present line. A pedestrian walking up this side of the street would have been heading directly towards the postulated entrance to the tower. It is wise, however, to have some reservations about this evidence. Not only is the face of the plinth not visible on the south side, but is also unclear how much original walling existed here when it was fitted. Canon Martin has recorded a substantial rebuilding of the south-west quoin earlier this century, but the extent of this reconstruction is not clear from the recent stone-by-stone survey of the interior walls.[73] It appears from Martin's account that the plinth may not have been added to the tower until the demolition of the adjoining shop on the north side about the beginning of this century. A plan of the church in the parish records shows the parish bakehouse in this position apparently in the early eighteenth century, and its west wall aligned with the west front of the tower.[74] The 'plinth' could not have been constructed with this building in situ. If not twentieth-century in date, it must be pre-eighteenth.

Accepting provisionally, then, that there may have been an Anglo-Saxon south door, the ground-floor arrangements of the tower seem ideal for part of a gateway structure. There was presumably a large gate across Cornmarket Street abutting the west wall of the tower and giving access to vehicles and animals. When the gate was closed, the tower would afford pedestrian access by means of the original west door and the postulated south door. The dog-leg route through the tower could be seen as a version of the traditional defensive device attested for many periods and types of structure. The nature of the west door itself enhances such a suggestion. Its two most obvious characteristics are its very small size and displacement north of the axial line of the tower. These characteristics argue equally against the door's having originally been the entrance to a church and for its suitability as part of a defensive structure. In particular, its position north of the centre line of the tower leaves a good stretch of tower wall available on the town side of the opening (just over 3 m) for the abutment of the presumably wooden gate structure.

The interpretation of the tower as an essentially secular structure does not preclude the use of part of it for religious purposes. The association of churches and chapels with town gateways is well established, at least from the time of Gregory of Tours. In Oxford itself there were further examples at the Southgate (another St Michael's), the Eastgate (Trinity chapel), at Smithgate (Lady chapel) and if the eastern defences of the Anglo-Saxon town followed the line currently proposed, the church of St Mary the Virgin may be the successor of a pre-

73 R.R. Martin, *The church and parish of St Michael at the Northgate, Oxford: a history*, Oxford 1967.

74 T.G. Hassall, personal communication 21 December 1976.

Conquest church associated with the original Eastgate. Elsewhere there are examples of churches, some of them Anglo-Saxon in origin, on or close to town gateways: St Mary at Cricklade, St Martin at Wareham, several St Botolphs at gates to the City of London, and in the later medieval period at Canterbury and at Winchester, where the chapel still exists over Kingsgate. The phenomenon of gate chapels is an under-researched topic, but it is clear at a superficial level that an ecclesiastical role for part of St Michael's tower would not be out of the ordinary. The dedication, if original, may have applied to the tower itself: St Michael, the protector of souls, was often associated with physical or symbolic defence.[75]

[75] The original draft went on to consider St Michael's tower in the context of Anglo-Saxon turriform churches, a discussion which appears in M. Audouy *et al.*, 'The tower of All Saints' Church, Earl's Barton, Northamptonshire: its construction and context', *Archaeological Journal* 152, 1995, 73–94.

Appendix II. The Gonfanons of the Bayeux Tapestry

Column 1 of the table below, p. 90 is the serial number used elsewhere in the text for identification. The masthead 'tails' (M) are not numbered.
Column 2 gives the nearest word of the inscription, with a slash (/) as near as possible to where the gonfanon occurs. Where there are long breaks in the inscription (during the battle for example) the last preceding word is given.
Column 3 gives the scene number as written on the backing linen and reproduced on the *dépliant* sold at Bayeux.
Column 4 gives the plate number in Stenton's edition and
Column 5 gives the plate number in Wilson's edition (note 1 above, p. 69)

The usual style of gonfanon is a rectangular flag (divided vertically) with three tapering 'tails' at the fly flown just below the lancehead on a slender lance held by a rider at the point of balance, or by a pedestrian at shoulder level.
Column 6 shows whether the lance is held

vertical (V), horizontal (H) or sloped forward (A), with the butt in the stirrup (S) or on the ground (G)

in the left (L) or right (R) hand, near the butt (U) or lies on the ground (F) and whether the flag's field has a border (B) or is a wyvern (W) and gives the number of crosses (C) and disks (D). The number of 'tails' (T) is specified, unless it is the usual three, and a final P means that the flag is supported on a stout pole, not a thin javelin.

Brackets surround doubtful items dealt with in the text.

Column 7 consists of notes. Although some of the colours of Stothard's engraving are wayward, the only significant differences noted are between Montfaucon's engraver and subsequent photographers.

Table of gonfanons in the Bayeux Tapestry

Column 1	**2**	**3**	**4**	**5**	**6**	**7**
I	EXERCIT/VS	16	21	18	VSRC	
II	VER/TIT	18	24	21	AR	
III	CONTRA/	19	26	23	VGB	
IV	DI/NANTES	19	26	23	VGB	
V	/ET	19	26	23	HLRB	Montfaucon D
VI	CV/NAN	20	26	23	HR	
VII	CLA/VES	20	26	24	ARB	
VIII	HAROL/DO	21	27	24	VGLBD2T4	Also Wilson page (22)
M	ANGLI/CA	34	36	33		
IX	MAGN/O	37	42	39	AR(U)	
M	NAVIGIO;/	38	42	40		
M	MARE/	38	42	40		
X	VENIT/	38	43	42	A(G)L	Sternpost dwarf
M	PEVENSAE;/	38	44	42		
M		38	44	42		Also Stenton VIII
XI	VERV/NT	40	46	44	AR(U)P	
XII	H/ESTINGA	40	46	44	AR(U)P	
XIII	/VT	40	46	45	VSR	
XIV	IV/SSIT	45	50	49	VGLBC	
XV	H/ESTENGA	45	51	49	VGLBD4	D4 as negative C?
XVI	WILLELMO/	46	51	50	VGLBCT4P	
XVII	MILITE/S	47	53	51	VGLBD	
XVIII	C/ONTRA	48	55	53	ARBCT5P	
XIX	HAROL/DVM	48	55	53	ARBT9(U)P	Oval, short fringes
XX	DISSET/	49	57	55	V(G)R	Rider pointing?
XXI	DVX/	50	59	57	V(S)R	Montfaucon D
XXII	SV/IS	50	59	57	AR	
XXIII	VI/RILITER	51	60	58	HR	
XXIV	SAPIENTER:/	51	61	59	VSRD3	
XXV	PRELIVM:/	51	61	60	ARD3	
XXVI	EXERCITV/	51	62	61	HRD3(U)	
XXVII		51	63	61	VG	
XXVIII		51	63	62	VGLRBDT5P	
XXIX	/REGIS	52	65	65	FBT4	Triangle, tasselled square lower fringe. Also Stenton XI
XXX	CI/VS	55	69	68	V(S)LBCD4+4	Montfaucon no shaft, no E
XXXI	HIC/	57	71	71	FW	
XXXII	/HARO	57	71	71	VGRWP	

4

The Origins of the Honour of Richmond and its Castles

Lawrence Butler

This paper examines the lands granted by William the Conqueror to count Alan in north-west Yorkshire: these formed the Honour of Richmond and were one of the most important fiefs in Norman England. Count Alan's other holdings lay in Lincolnshire and eastern England, principally Cambridgeshire (fig. 1). Together they were assessed for the service of a notional 180 knights, 60 of them due from the county of Richmond.

The first part of this examination considers the feudal conditions which influenced the establishment and consolidation of the Honour of Richmond between 1071 and 1200, while the second part considers the location of the castles and the circumstances of their creation. Taken together these aspects enable one to explore the predictive nature of tenurial and geomorphological factors in order to understand the origins of twelfth-century castles, whether earthwork or stonebuilt.

The Territory

The Honour of Richmond in Yorkshire was principally formed from the lands of earl Edwin confiscated soon after 1069.[1] These lands were the greater part of north-west Yorkshire or the western half of the North Riding; earl Edwin's other land-holdings in Northallerton and in Askham Bryan were not included in the Honour of Richmond. Northallerton was soon granted to William of St Calais, bishop of Durham, while Askham near York (though held first by count Alan) went to the Bryan family from about 1100 or 1120.[2] The Richmond territory comprised three main land divisions: the hundreds of Gilling, of Hang and of Hallikeld (fig. 2). The first two are easily defined, because Gilling and Hang correspond to medieval civil hundreds and ecclesiastical deaneries.

Gilling Hundred or 'Gillingshire' was mainly the land between the Tees and the Swale. The Tees was the northern border, with that river separating Richmondshire from the lands of the bishop of Durham; the western border was

1 C.W. Clay, ed., *Early Yorkshire Charters IV: The Honour of Richmond I*, 94–5.

2 Along with these major holdings Alan also took over the client relationships within these lands, occasionally still held by their Saxon or Danish owners: Aldred at Kirkby (Fleetham) and Melmerby, Gospatric at Colburn and Thoresby, and Bjornulfr at Thoralby. Outside the honour of Richmond count Alan occupied lands previously held by the two earls Morcar (Stillington, Clifton, Huntington and Terrington) and Godwine (Acaster Selby).

Figure 1. Map of England showing lands of count Alan

the Pennine watershed with Westmorland; its southern border was initially the watershed between the Ure and the Swale until the boundary descended to the Swale which formed the frontier until its confluence with the Wiske. The river Wiske formed the eastern boundary as far north as Great Smeaton parish where a Roman road between Hornby and Appleton Wiske provided the boundary until the Staindale Beck flowed down to the Tees at Sockburn. Gilling Hundred was divided into an eastern and a western portion. The north-south boundary ran along the Gilling Beck and then northwards along the Roman road which crossed the Tees between Cliffe and Piercebridge. The village of Gilling was close to the boundary and if the Scots Dike marks an earlier boundary within the hundred, then the village had an even more pivotal position. There is strong evidence that Gilling was a former monastery and the village layout within a circular enclosure is reminiscent of Celtic monasteries (such as Llanynys, Kells or Duleek). Gilling was the manorial centre that Richmond, only two miles (3 km) south, supplanted, just as it was the parishes of Gilling hundred that became the nucleus of Richmond deanery.

The second hundred was Hang or 'Hangshire'. Its northern boundary was the Swale where it defined Gilling Hundred; its western boundary was the Pennine watershed with Dent and Sedbergh in the West Riding; its southern border was the watershed with the Wharfe, and further east with the Nidd, until the Ure formed the boundary south of Swinton in Masham and north of Grewelthorpe; its eastern border used a variety of small streams and low ridges to reach the river Swale; it had no prominent natural features along its line. The hundred meeting place on Hang Bank was centrally located on an elevated bank in Finghall parish midway between Constable Burton and Thornton Steward. The north-south boundary between the east and west divisions of the hundred ran close to and east of Hang Bank, but it followed a sinuous course along township boundaries. The later deanery was named after Catterick, a town on its northern border with an earthwork castle, rather than from Middleham or Bedale, both of which were market towns more centrally placed than Catterick.

The third hundred was Hallikeld, comprising the parishes lying between the Ure and the Swale until their confluence was reached at Ellenthorpe. Along that stretch of the Ure closest to Ripon the lands of the archbishop of York extended east of the river in Sharow, Hewick, Givendale and Skelton; Hutton Conyers was given to the bishop of Durham and formed part of Allertonshire.[3] Of the seven parishes in Richmondshire the five northern ones (including Pickhill) were in Catterick deanery from the early twelfth century but the two southernmost

3 It is possible that Hallikeld was originally all the land between the Swale and the Ure, and that the 'civil' hundred preceded the Liberty of Ripon held by the archbishop of York. Other parts of Hallikeld hundred were held in 1086 by Gospatric, by Robert earl of Mortain and by the king. A small part of count Alan's lands lay adjacent in Birdforth wapentake: these were the townships of Howe, Baldersby, Assenby [Asebi], and Rainton (M.L. Faull and M. Stinson, *Domesday Book: Yorkshire* (1986), II, SN CtA 44). In the Domesday text and in the Summary they are in count Alan's lands within Hallikeld wapentake (Text $ 140–161; Summary $ 39–44), though these four townships all in Topcliffe parish were disputed by the Percies, who held Topcliffe and Dishforth. A mid 14th-century register of the archdeacons of Richmond (now lost) claimed that these townships were within the jurisdiction of the archdeacons, presumably because they were within the Honour in the early 12th century when the archdeaconry boundaries were created.

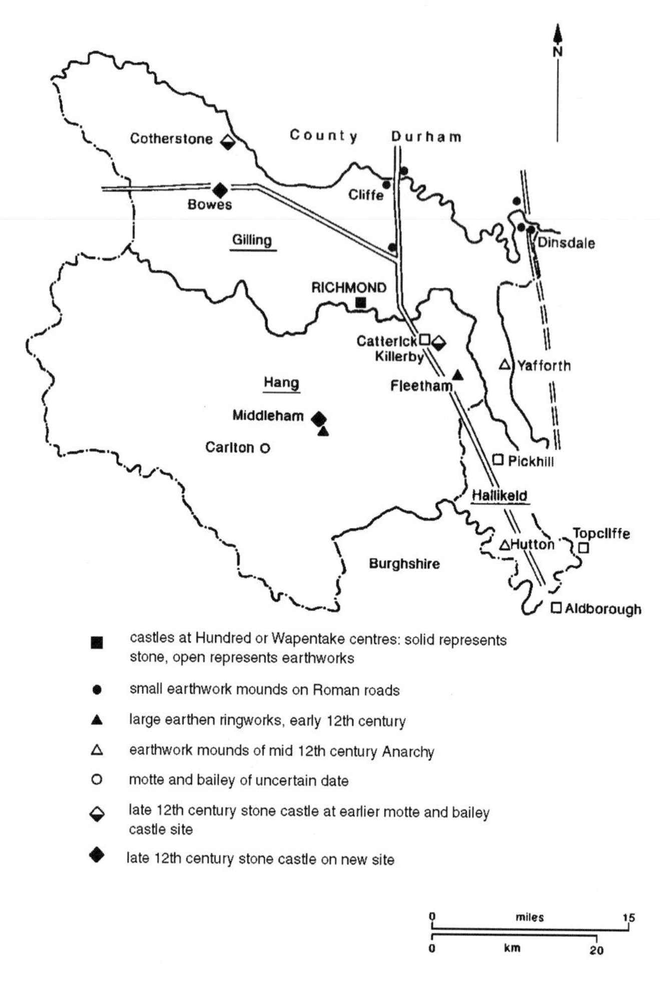

Figure 2. Map of Richmondshire showing distribution of castles

(Kirkby Hill and Cundall) were in Boroughbridge deanery. The hundred meeting place was near the Hallikeld spring in Hutton Conyers township.

The boundaries just described gave the lords of Richmond a substantial territory (37 miles east-west by 27 miles: 60 × 45 km) between the Tees and the Ure, stretching from the bleak high Pennines to the fertile Vale of York and the Great North Road. Their seat of government was a newly founded castle and town; the Norman-French name 'Richemont' indicates the intrusive nature of this defence.[4]

4 Clay (V, 62–3, 83) equates the 'Neutone' in Easby with the unnamed Richmond, but Faull and Stinson 1986 (II, notes to 6N19 and 6N23) prefer the identification of the Domesday 'Hindrelag' as the future Richmond so named because of its castle and consider Newton to be in Scorton township.

The Feudal Lordship

It is clear that in creating the Honour as a necessary military buffer zone using the Tees as the border with a semi-independent northern Northumbria, William the Conqueror was taking both a major estate (that of earl Edwin), together with its internal client relationships within the manors of Gilling and Catterick to weld it into a single feudal entity. Although a few of the pre-Conquest land-owners continued to occupy their lands and halls, such as Bjornulfr at Thoralby, Gospatric at Colburn and Thoresby, and Aldred at Melmerby and Kirkby (Fleetham), the majority of the larger landowners had their territory transferred to a single incomer, such as Bodin who took over all Thorfinnr's lands.

The succession of counts of Breton lineage to the honour of Richmond has been discussed by Clay and by Kapelle.[5] The size of the honour and its strategic position near the Scottish border made it a desirable prize to keep intact, even when passing through the female line. Those parts of the honour in midland and eastern England had less strategic importance and were more prone to subdivision and transferance. The lordship was held together by a series of sub-infeudations and a web of military service[6] including castle guard. The basic pattern, established within the first generation after the Conquest, was gradually modified by the division of knight's fees among heiresses but it remained a potent influence in subsequent centuries. It is this tenurial pattern which now needs to be examined to discern whether its early history can assist our understanding of the processes of castle foundation.

In the Register of the Honour of Richmond (B.L., MS Cotton, Faustina B, vii f. 85v) is a coloured drawing of Richmond castle viewed from the north-east (fig. 3). At eight points on the walls banners rise above the buildings or shields are hung on the curtain wall. The next eight lines of text identify the places on the walls where specified landholders had to perform their castle guard (table I). As Clay's discussion[7] makes clear, this mid fifteenth-century compilation, which appears to record the military situation in the last decade of the twelfth century, contains various inconsistencies and omissions. However what is more pertinent to this discussion is that it was then thought that 'castle guard' was a physical presence attached to a specific stretch of walling or a gateway, and that this duty had descended with a particular group of knights' fees, or with the senior land-holder in an estate when it was later divided by inheritance. This

5 Clay, IV, 84–93; more generally see W.E. Kapelle, *The Norman Conquest of the North: the region and its transformation 1000–1135* (London 1979).

6 J.C. Holt, 'The introduction of knight service in England', *Anglo-Norman Studies* VI (1983), 89–106. N.J.G. Pounds, *The Medieval Castle in England and Wales: a social and political history* (Cambridge 1990), 40–42. However his map of fees in Richmondshire shows holdings of varying origin and status.

7 Clay, V, 359–360; C. Peers, *Richmond Castle Official Guide* (1934), 6–8; Pounds 1990, 48–9. The original version of this list might have contained six names, one for each two-month spell of duty. The fifth name (Ranulf son of Henry) might originally have been Robert de Musters who served for February and March.

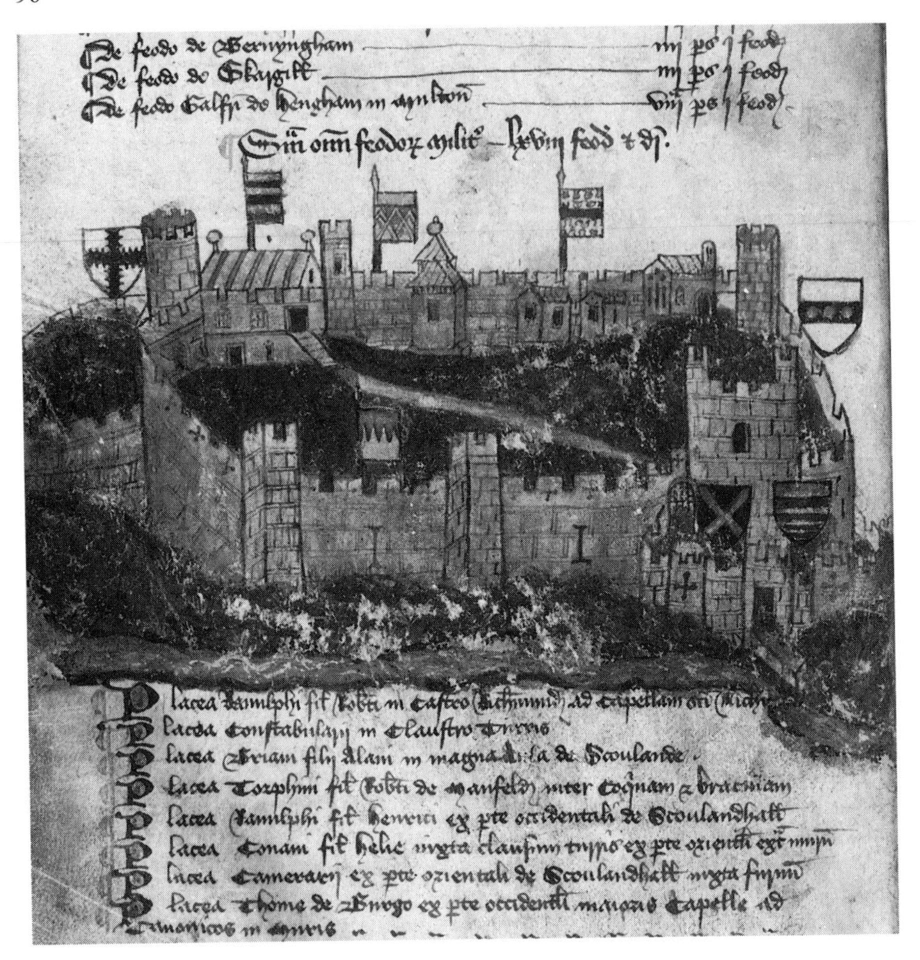

Figure 3. Richmond Castle: manuscript drawing showing where castle guard was thought to be performed, from Cott. Faust. BVII f. 85v (1010611). By permission of the British Library.

idea of a physical aspect to a military duty may parallel the order of seating for the Knights of the Round Table at Winchester Castle or of the Garter Knights in their stalls at Windsor Castle with their banners fixed overhead. Applied to the late twelfth century it is an anachronism.

The surviving twelfth-century and early thirteenth-century lists of knights' fees[8] make it clear that castle guard was not physically linked to a specific part of the castle but was a duty allocated on a two-monthly basis where the provider supplied his required number of knights to garrison the whole castle. The annual total from 1130 onwards was approximately 180 knights (i.e. 30 knights for each two-month stint). The total required from the entire Honour seems to vary from decade to decade: the minimum is 174 when a specified month for castle

8 Clay, V, 10–16.

guard is noted and 175 when the duty is commuted for a cash payment; the maximum is 187¼ on the earliest list.[9] From Yorkshire the total was 60, later raised to 68½ knights by a new enfeoffment in the late twelfth century,[10] though the minimum number is 62⅔ because of uncertainties in the calculations caused mainly by four knights fees held by Gilbert of Ghent who did not perform castle guard for them.

Table I

Name (1188–94)	*Place of service*
Ranulph son of Robert	chapel of St Nicholas [Ribald's]
The Constable	inclosure of the keep [or the barbican]
Brian son of Alan	in the Great Hall of Scolland
Torfin son of Robert of Manfield	betw. kitchen and brewhouse [Steward's]
Ranulph son of Henry	on the west side of Scolland's Hall
Conan son of Ellis	by inclosure of the keep on west side
The Chamberlain	on east side of Scolland's Hall by oven
Thomas de Burgh	on west side of greater chapel of canons

The Individual Holdings

Since the Honour remained intact for more than three centuries, it is best to examine the component parts to determine who provided castle guard and when it was due. It is clear that the service for Yorkshire (nearly one-third of the total throughout the Honour) was mainly supplied by four men: the earl's brother Ribald and the three household officials of steward, constable and chamberlain.

Ribald's holding of 15 knights centred on Middleham and passed unbroken through six generations until 1270 when the co-heiress Mary conveyed her one-third to the Nevilles. This is the best example of a large compact holding remaining intact for two centuries. Six knights' fees were located in Yorkshire.

The Steward's holding (15 knights) was initially occupied by Wimar and then by his sons Roger and Warner. Wimar's territory in Yorkshire contained three elements: that which he held as tenant of count Alan in 1086 (Aske in Easby, Harmby in Spennithorne, Leyburn in Wensley), that which he acquired from Gospatric in 15 townships and that which he received from count Alan and his brother Bodin in 9 townships. Some other lands were gained before Wimar's death in 1130; the lands were then divided with his elder son Roger receiving Thornton Steward and owing the service of 15 knights; his younger son Warner received Ellerton-on-Swale. The elder line ran through four generations, latterly called 'de Thornton', before passing to an heiress in about 1284. The younger line ended at Wimar son of Warner, whose daughter Beatrice failed to produce offspring by her husband Hugh Malebis (died *c.*1230). The steward's post

9 Clay, IV, 2 and Table II on pp. 11–12.
10 Clay, IV, 4–5 and Table III on pp. 13–15.

passed from Wimar to Scolland in about 1130, but reverted to Ralph the grandson of Wimar and then to Warner son of Wimar, but after 1158 the post passed out of the family of Wimar. Despite the later changes it is evident that the Steward's fee provided the nucleus or potential for a castle-defended holding at Thornton Steward.

The Constable's fee (13 knights, all in Yorkshire) was initially occupied by Enisant Musard, but by 1130 it was divided between Roald the constable and Richard de Rollos. The two portions were re-united by Roald's grandson after 1204. The Christian names Roald and Alan were used alternately through five generations though in the late 13th century they assumed the surname 'de Burton' (from Constable Burton) or 'de Richmond' (from their post at Richmond). Their entire holding in Constable Burton was sold in 1320/21 to Geoffrey le Scrope of Masham. The constable's holding had been distributed throughout all five wapentake divisions of the Honour but with the largest holdings at Constable Burton, Croft and Brompton-on-Swale. Any one of these three could have provided the location for a castle, though for much of the twelfth century Brompton was held by the de Rollos branch whose main interests lay in Normandy. I'Anson[11] considered that Pickhill was likely to be Roald's castle and this suggestion will be examined later.

The Chamberlain's fee (11 knights, later 11½) was initially held by Odo, but although he was succeeded in this office and fee by his son Robert in about 1130, the latter surrendered the office in 1158 and became a monk at Ely. The fee passed to his sons, first George and then to Nigel, but on Nigel's death in or before 1191 the lands were split between five co-heirs. The majority of the lands lay in Lincolnshire and Cambridgeshire; the Richmond holding (2½ knights) lay mainly at Eppleby in Gilling and Kirkby Fleetham.

The fourth hereditary office was that of the Butler (2 knights). Three successive holders named Alan held one knight's fee at Barden in Hauxwell and a second fee in Cambridgeshire throughout the twelfth century. During the thirteenth century the Yorkshire fee became fragmented. This fee seems to possess too small an income to support castle building.

The five holdings discussed above represent 56 knights' fees out of an original total of 180 (32 in Yorkshire out of 60 in Richmond). Although they total only one-third of the fees in the entire Honour, they consist of more than one-half of the fees in Richmondshire. It is clear that the tenure of the office was not necessarily attached to a specific group of lands, as when Scolland succeeded to the post of Steward, nor did a particular group of lands ensure appointment to a hereditary office once the chain of succession had been broken, as with the post of Chamberlain. There were a number of other household officials (Marshall, Lardiner, Dispenser, Usher, Forester) and administrative officers (Justice, Sheriff) but none held their post initially as a hereditary fief and from none of them were knights fees due in respect of land held by virtue of that office. On two occasions the man chosen to act as sheriff in Rich-

11 W. I'Anson, 'The castles of the North Riding', *Yorkshire Archaeological Journal* 22 (1912–13), 303–99, esp. 372–74. This article deals only with the earthwork castles; the stone castles were to be in a second article which was never completed.

mond was already a prominent land-holder and did not acquire further lands to reward him for holding that post.

The remaining fees within the entire honour of Richmond were by 1130 held by fifty-four different tenants. The holdings ranged in size from the eight knights owed by Geoffrey de Musters and by Geoffrey de Furnals to the quarter of a knight's fee owed by Philip of Cheshunt and by Roger son of Teigni. Only the nine landowners rendering the service of 5 or more knights could be regarded as substantial (table II). However their holdings were not confined to Richmondshire but were spread throughout the eastern counties of Lincolnshire, Cambridgeshire, Norfolk and Suffolk. Only Scolland, with the service of 5 knights due from Bedale, Wath, North and South Cowton, and Newton Morrell, emerges as a prominent landowner reliant on his eminence solely upon his Yorkshire holdings. The fee passed to Scolland's son Brian and then through four generations alternately called Alan and Brian. The death of the last Brian in 1306 caused the Bedale or Fitzalan holding of 5 knights (by then increased to 7) to be divided between two daughters. It may represent a genuine tradition that in 1190 Brian son of Alan renders his service in Scolland's Hall, named after his great-grandfather (see table I).

For Yorkshire the critical size seems to be 2½ knight's fees; only a fee of this size gave the political strength to contemplate castle building or to launch successfully on marriage alliances and local office holding. Ribald at Middleham (6 knights in Yorkshire), Wimar the Steward (9½), Roald the Constable (13) and Odo the Chamberlain (2½) were the major landowners in the entire Honour and three of them were major owners in Yorkshire. They were joined by Scolland (5), Robert de Musters, Hardwin de Scalers, Acaris son of Bardulf (3), Conan son of Ellis and Roger Lascelles (2½).[12]

Table II. Major land-holders in the honour of Richmond
(5 knight's fees or more)

Name in 1130	*Total fee*	*Fee in Yorkshire*
Ribald	15	6
Wimar the Steward	15	9.5
Roald the Constable	13	13
Odo the Chamberlain	11	2.5
Alan the Butler	2	1
[Intermediate Total	[56]	[32]
Robert Musters	8	3
Robert de Furnals	8	1
William de la Mare	7	1
Valognes	7	0.5
Scolland	5	5

12 There was also the estate of Gilbert de Gand (of Ghent) in Swaledale assessed at 4 knights' fees; it was of late 12th-century creation. Two fees: Sutton and de Burgh, were both of 2 knights' fees arising from their Richmond lands. The remaining Richmondshire fees were very small.

Name in 1130	*Total fee*	*Fee in Yorkshire*
Roger de Lascelles	5	2
Conan son of Ellis	5	2.5
Alan son of Eudo de Mumby	5	1
Egglestone	5	1
[Total of Fee]	110	49.5
National number of knights' fees	180	60

The Middle Rank Landholders

Having already discussed the fees of the major landowners, it is now appropriate to consider the holdings of the five landowners of middle rank. The first is the Musters fee of 3 knights, based principally at Kirklington with adjacent townships in Bedale, Burneston and Pickhill parishes. From the Domesday tenant Robert de Musters it passed through nine generations until in about 1370 Elizabeth de Musters carried the land to John de Wandesford in which family it remained until this century.

The second is the Scalers fee of 3 knights, based on Carlton in Stanwick, Stapleton in Stanwick and Croft, and Great Smeaton. It was held at Domesday by Hardwin de Scalers, but by the early twelfth century the Yorkshire lands had been divided into three and were gradually lost to the Scalers family. The part in Stapleton was gained by the Stapleton family.

The fee held by Bodin, half-brother of count Alan, at the Domesday Survey was mainly in Patrick Brompton, Kirkby Ravensworth, Scorton and Aiskew. This estate passed to his brother Bardulf and so to the latter's son Acaris, later founder of Jervaulx abbey.[13] Acaris and his descendants held these lands and an extensive tract in upper Teesdale by service of 3¹/₆ knights. In 1200 Henry son of Hervey son of Acaris was granted licence to enclose and strengthen his house of Cotherstone ('Cudereston'), the ruins of which still survive above the Tees. During the 14th century this family, later known as Fitzhugh of Ravensworth, transferred their main seat to Ravensworth.[14]

The fee held in 1180 by Conan son of Ellis rendered 2½ knights' service for East Cowton (1 fee), Ainderby Myers and Holtby in Hornby (1 fee) and Hutton Hang in Finghall and East Brompton in Patrick Brompton (half a fee). The previous owners Landric and his son Wigan were direct ancestors of Conan; the family regarded Hornby as their main residence. On the death of Conan in about 1220 the lands were divided between his three aunts and never subsequently re-united.

The Lascelles fee originated in Picot de Lascels holding Kirkby Wiske,

13 The foundation of local monasteries can also be seen as an expression of social status just as much as of religious piety. Founders were count Alan: St Mary's in York; Wimar the steward: St Martin's in Richmond; Roald the constable: St Agatha's, Easby; Ranulph of Middleham (from Ribald): Coverham. The poorer houses of Eggleston, Ellerton and Marrick were founded by knights with smaller resources.

14 P.F. Ryder, 'Ravensworth Castle', *Yorkshire Archaeological Journal* 51 (1979), 81–100, suggests (p. 100) a twelfth-century origin, and notes (p. 81) a visit here by King John in 1201.

Maunby, Scruton and Thrintoft in Ainderby Steeple at Domesday and his son Roger rendering 2½ knights' fees for this holding. The names Picot and Roger alternate through six generations until on the death of Roger IV in about 1300 the property was divided between his four daughters. Kirkby Wiske formed a compact holding on the eastern border of Richmondshire.

No other fee has the potential for the foundation of a castle by reason of its size or wealth. It is likely, therefore, that all the castles in Richmondshire are the product of three factors: they may be built directly by the count, as at Richmond, or they may be built on his desmesne lands by the king, as at Bowes, or they may be erected by his principal vassals to defend his territories or to enhance their status. In the latter category are the ten major land-holdings whose lords had the economic and social potential for castle building; these fees will need to be examined for this purpose.

The Siting of the Castles

At the time of the Conquest there would have been an immediate need to hold the new territory by securing the centres of administration. There would have been a parallel need to control lines of communication at river crossings, especially north to south routes. Three castles could be products of this period: the stone circuit at Richmond, replacing the earl's hall at Gilling, thereby securing the Swale crossing and an entry to Gillingshire; Catterick with a motte and bailey 'Palet Hill' north of the church to secure the hundred of Hang and additionally to control the Roman road crossing the Swale; and Pickhill, 100 m west of a minster church, to guard the hundred of Hallikeld. Further south there are castles at Aldborough (Stutfold Hill) to secure 'Burgshire' and the Ure crossing, at Hunsingore to secure the Nidd crossing, and at Tadcaster to secure the crossing of the Wharfe.

Within the honour of Richmond one might expect an earthwork castle near Milby on the north bank of the Ure opposite Aldborough, but there is now no visible evidence. Low mounds do occur at Cliffe and Low Dinsdale (Howe Hill and Castle Hill) on the south bank of the Tees, close to the site of the Roman road crossings, and similar mounds are visible at Piercebridge and at Hall Tower Hill, Middleton St. George on the north bank of the Tees. There is also the low mound near Violet Grange, Scotch Corner on high ground at the angle of two Roman roads, one going north to Piercebridge and Corbridge, the other heading west through Bowes across Stainmoor towards Carlisle. All these mounds seem to be potential castle sites until proved otherwise.[15]

In the half-century after the Conquest one could anticipate a period of consolidation by the major land-holders with castles built by Ribald, Odo, Roald, Wimar and Scolland. For four out of these five men there is good evidence for this. William's Hill, a prominent ringwork castle 200 m south of Middleham, seems to be the initial centre of Ribald's holding. Killerby, a strongly defended

[15] As J.C.A. Dankwerts argues within the Netherlands (Paper given at the Medieval Europe 1992 Conference in York, September 1992).

motte and bailey beside the Swale south of Catterick, could be attributed to Scolland, while I'Anson has suggested that Pickhill, another steep ringwork, was founded by Enisand Musard or Roald as the Constable's castle.[16] For Odo the Chamberlain there is good evidence at Fleetham where a lightly-defended earthwork enclosure still survives. For Wimar the Steward there is no evidence of a castle or hall at Thornton Steward though the present Hall stands on a commanding bluff overlooking the valley of the Ure.

For the five middle-rank landowners there is only one certain castle site: Cotherstone on the territory of Acaris. Just as William's Hill may have been started by Ribald, brother of count Alan, so also Cotherstone might well have been fortified by Bodin or Bardulf, half-brothers of count Alan. At this level there is far less correlation of castle to territory, or else the earthworks were much slighter and have not been recognised.

The third type of earthwork castle is the less predictable product of the anarchy of Stephen's reign, fuelled by the aggression of Alan the Black, count of Richmond, towards the bishopric of Durham; he placed the motte on Howe Hill, Yafforth to threaten Northallerton and constructed the ringwork castle at Hutton Conyers on the bishop's land to overawe the archbishop's tenants east of the Ure and to control Ripon.[17]

The circumstances surrounding the construction of Bowes castle on the count's desmesne lands are less certain; it may have been started by Conan, but is more likely to have been a royal castle built by Henry II between 1165 and 1181, being erected to control the Roman road over Stainmoor against Scottish raiding instigated by William the Lion. The building of a stone keep which used the earthworks of the Roman fort as its bailey was supervised by the count's tenants Torfin son of Robert, Osbert son of Fulk and Stephen of Barningham.[18]

No date or purpose has been assigned to the small steep motte and bailey at Carlton in Coverdale, but it was probably an outpost of Middleham either thrown up during the anarchy of Stephen's reign or intended as an advance warning post while Middleham was under construction and the threat of Scottish raids was still high. The two main danger periods were 1138 and 1174 when the Scots raided into Yorkshire and burnt some castles.

The final stage is the replacing of the earthwork castles by structures built in stone. Richmond had been constructed of stone from the time of its foundation, but the new work at Middleham seems to date from 1180 or 1190, the new work at Cotherstone is recorded in a licence to crenellate in 1200 and the new castle at Killerby[19] was provided in the 13th century. Yafforth was apparently abandoned, as presumably was Catterick, but the earthwork castle at Pickhill, like its neighbour Topcliffe,[20] continued in use into the thirteenth century.

This survey has shown the mixture of motives, the variety of structures and

16 I'Anson, as *note 11*, 372–4.

17 The reference to Hutton is John of Hexham in *Symeon of Durham* (Rolls Series 75: ii, 306); also quoted in Clay, IV, 90. The reference to Yafforth is in April 1198 and the attribution to count Alan III is circumstantial; it could have been built by William de la Mare later in the twelfth century.

18 Bowes: see Clay, V, 139–40; H.M. Colvin, *History of the King's Works*, II, 574.

19 I'Anson, as *note 11*, 320.

20 I'Anson, as *note 11*, 393–6.

the difficulty in making predictions about where castles are likely to be situated. Reliance upon the accidental discoveries from aerial survey and from groundlevel investigation may prove to be too haphazard to ensure success. However, by approaching the problem both from a geographical and a strategic viewpoint as well as from a tenurial assessment, it is likely that greater progress can be made.

5

Timber Castles – A Reassessment

Robert Higham

The vast majority of us will at some stage in our lives have heard of, read of, seen in book, magazine or on television something referred to as a 'castle'. A smaller, but still very large number of us will have seen such a place for ourselves, either in passing or on a visit. It is probably castles, together with great churches and monasteries, which most readily evoke an image of the Middle Ages in popular imagination. This in itself is not unreasonable, since these were certainly very impressive parts of the medieval landscape in both their size and their building technology. But how true a reflection of that landscape are the castles which attract large numbers of visitors, which are illustrated in most publications as well as on postcards, calendars, tea-towels and the rest? These castles impinge upon our view of the past, as well as upon our view of our contemporary surroundings, for one simple reason: they were built of stone, whose durable quality provides something to look at centuries later, even if extensively ruined.

Yet those who have studied medieval castles in greater depth will know that such castles were not the only ones to have existed. Our landscape also contains large numbers of castle sites represented only by earthworks on which there are no buildings surviving above ground at all. They take many forms, a common one being the motte and bailey in which a large mound of earth and/or rock dominates a defended courtyard. These earthworks carried the same mixture of defensive and residential structures that are found in stone castles, but with an important difference: they were built of timber, clay-clad timber, cob, wattle and daub, shingles and thatch. The total decay of these materials above ground leaves traces which are recoverable only through meticulous excavation. To uncover this information in a useful quantity takes long and painstaking work. The author has for many years been involved in the excavation of a motte and bailey castle at Hen Domen (Montgomery, Powys).[1] This has revealed a complex sequence of buildings stretching from the late eleventh to the thirteenth centuries. The contrast between the open, attractive character of the earthworks and the crowded and oppressive nature of the site as built and occupied is enormous. The complexity of the site has also another dimension, for while as a

Acknowledgment: I am indebted to my colleague Philip Barker for our continuing discussion of this topic, and to many others for advice which will be acknowledged in the volume referred to.

1 P.A. Barker, R.A. Higham, *Hen Domen, Montgomery: a timber castle on the English-Welsh border* (Roy. Arch. Inst. monograph series, London 1982).

Figure 1. The medieval castle – the popular image (Caernarvon). (Author)

monument it is *one* castle, in medieval times it had several social identities which arose from the changing pattern of its ownership and occupation. Initial perusal of the evidence published for other comparable sites confirmed this impression gained from Hen Domen: timber castles have a far more interesting structural and social history than is generally appreciated. Their importance was clearly stated by those writers who put castle studies on a modern footing at the beginning of the present century. Nevertheless, they receive little more than brief acknowledgement in the majority of books, whose authors have been concerned above all to describe the development of stone castles. To fill this gap in the literature a book devoted to timber castles is currently being prepared.[2] The main themes of this study are outlined here.

The Historical Evidence

Since the detailed structural evidence of timber castles can be studied only through excavation, discussion of the subject tends to have an archaeological bias. It is also true that there is an historical dimension to timber castles. There are certainly fewer documentary materials than exist for the study of stone castles. Nevertheless a surprising amount of information can be gleaned from a wide array of sources. Where stone and timber castles differ in this respect, however, is in the coverage of written sources *vis-à-vis* the total archaeological evidence. Whereas the identity of all but a few stone castles is known from documents, there are large numbers of earthworks, sites of former timber castles, which are completely unknown to history. Some were established at an early period, when documentary sources for medieval life in general were less full.

2 P.A. Barker, R.A. Higham, *Timber Castles* (London 1992).

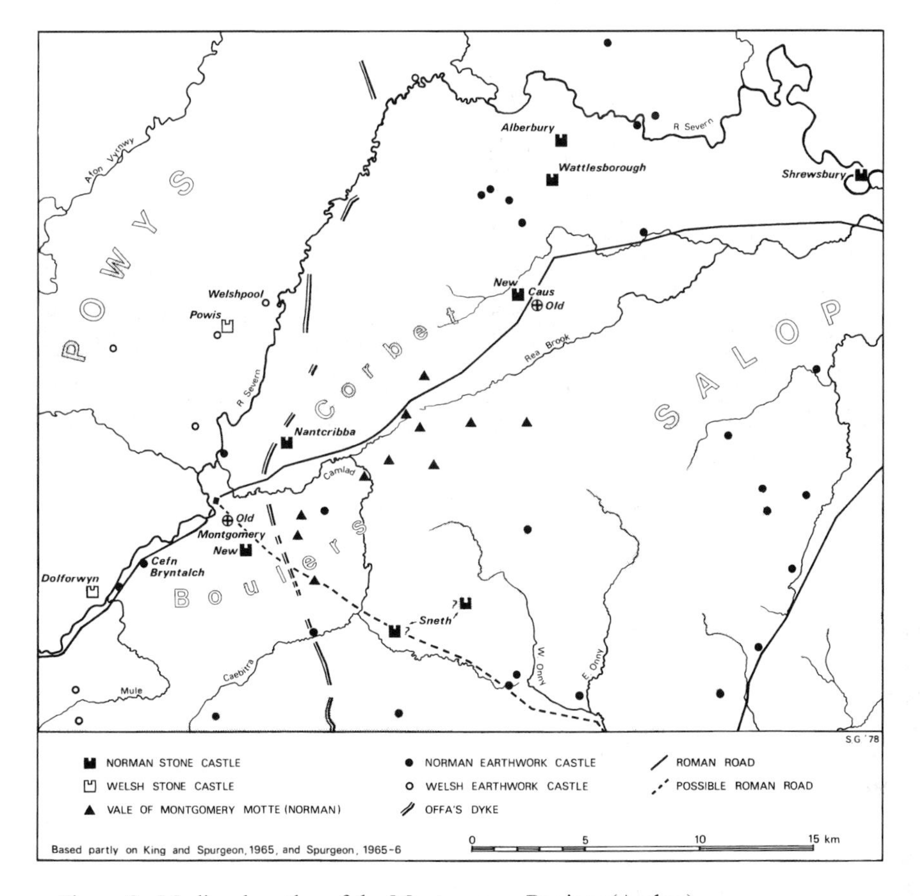

Figure 2. Medieval castles of the Montgomery Region. (Author)

Others were built by families whose activities were not recorded by contemporary writers because they had little or no impact on local or national affairs. Others still had a very brief existence, built and occupied in time of war and having little social or institutional life. It follows that the precise dating of many timber castle sites poses severe difficulty.

Allowing for such difficulties, the framework of timber castle dating is nevertheless clear enough. In France they were in use by the tenth century, perhaps earlier, and by the late twelfth century were widespread in most parts of western Europe. It is commonly assumed that timber castles were only significant at an early date. This is quite untrue. There is plenty of documentary evidence to demonstrate their use in the thirteenth and early fourteenth centuries, both in the continuing occupation of old sites and the establishment of new ones. In addition, many timber castles were gradually rebuilt in stone, having a mixed character for part of their lives. Even in so-called 'stone castles' there was much more timber than often supposed. Not only was timber an ingredient of all stone buildings, in floors, roofs et cetera, it was also used for complete residential buildings as well as for defensive structures. Large numbers of stone castles had outer defences of timber in the thirteenth and fourteenth centuries and timber

Figure 3. Now crowned by a nineteenth-century rebuild of a fourteenth-century shell-keep, the motte at Durham carried an elaborate timber tower in the early twelfth century which was described in detail by Laurence, prior of Durham, c.1150. (Author)

galleries projecting from their stone wall-tops. Even some major timber structures survived to this date: the timber motte tower at Shrewsbury eventually collapsed *c.*1270.

Some documentary references to timber castles also reveal something about their structural character, though large numbers do not. Many of the well-known components of stone castles had their timber counterparts. We hear of palisades, of gateways, of bridges, of perimeter towers and of domestic buildings. But what struck contemporaries most were the great towers, which in stone castles we would call 'keeps', which rose from their mottes and provided both the main residence and the ultimate defence of the castle. Some of these, as described by contemporary chroniclers, were complex and ornate buildings. In England, for example, the episcopal castle at Durham had a magnificent motte-tower of timber in the early twelfth century. Such descriptions are, however, few in number, and for a more detailed structural view of timber castles other sources must be used.

The Problems of Pictorial Evidence

Closest in character to the documentary sources are sources with pictorial evidence for timber castles. Though few in number they are of great interest. They include the famous embroidery known as the Bayeux Tapestry, stone sculpture, wood-carving, manuscript illustration and painting. Whereas the cumulative evidence of documentary references and of surviving earthworks will allow some generalisation to be made, the pictorial sources are so individualistic that great care must be exercised in their interpretation. The best way to illustrate this briefly is by reference to one particular example.

Figure 4. The construction of Hastings castle as depicted on the Bayeux Tapestry

The Bayeux Tapestry, in its depiction of the Norman conquest of England and the events which led up to it, provides illustrations of various castles in northern France and of Hastings in southern England. The scene illustrating the construction of Hastings is well-known, commonly used as evidence in the debate on both the chronology and physical form of English castle origins. At first sight, this evidence is simple enough: workmen are throwing soil upwards to form a motte on top of which stands a timber palisade. But in fact there are fundamental problems. First, are we viewing the building operations in proper sequence? The fact that the motte surface is already capped with a continuous deposit when the main layers themselves (lying horizontal, an unusual pattern though known from some excavations) are still being thrown up raises doubts here. Perhaps the designer 'telescoped' successive events. Equally, the outer surface may simply be an artistic device with no structural significance at all – a major consideration for the use of any pictorial source. The same problem of 'telescoping' applies to the structure on the motte top. Are we viewing what was eventually put there, or what was already there – was the motte being thrown up around it? Both types of construction are plausible and known from excavated examples. A century later, the Norman poet Wace wrote that Hastings castle had been of prefabricated timber construction, transported with duke William's fleet from Normandy. Though this tradition has sometimes been discredited because of its late date, it deserves more attention. By the twelfth century such practice was quite common, and it could have had earlier origins (at Hen Domen excavated evidence has demonstrated some prefabrication in the castle erected in the 1070s). If Hastings was built in this way it would make good practical sense to erect the structure and pile the motte around it. But here another difficulty presents itself, for the Tapestry shows not a tower rising from the motte, which we would expect, but a palisade. Here there is a strong contrast with its depiction of castles in northern France, whose mottes carry tall buildings. The second major problem lies in the date of the Tapestry's production, which was a decade after 1066. Since it was produced in southern England, it should be reliable in its evidence. Yet the designer may have been portraying what he was familiar with in Norman England of the 1070s, rather than what actually took place in 1066 at Hastings. The Tapestry undoubtedly gives us an informative depiction of castle-building, but does it necessarily apply to Hastings in particular? This we can never know. Excavation here produced no structural timber evidence of eleventh century date. Indeed the existing motte at Hastings may not even date from the conquest at all, since part of the site was destroyed by coastal erosion centuries ago.

Related Timber Structures

Given the extensive reconstruction in stone of so many timber castles and the organic nature of the building materials concerned it is hardly surprising that no timber castle, or even part of one, survives intact. There are, however, survivals of timber, or partly timber buildings within stone castles. At Leicester, the timber arcades of an aisled hall of very high quality survive in fragmentary form from the mid-twelfth century. At Tamworth (Staffs), an early fifteenth century timber-framed hall stands within the twelfth century shell keep. At Stokesay (Shropshire), the timber storey which projects from the north tower, though now owing much to seventeenth century reconstruction, was contemporary in its original form with the late thirteenth century stonework immediately below. From numerous excavations pieces of waterlogged timber have been recovered. These sometimes show evidence of carpentry techniques. At der Husterknupp (Rhineland) uprights from domestic buildings had been chamfered where they emerged from their post-holes. At Hen Domen the base of a 12ft-wide motte bridge survived *in situ*, and from the bailey ditch came parts of the base-plate of a free standing palisade made of jointed upright planks.

From other types of medieval timber building some of the character of timber castles may be indirectly inferred. The development of framed domestic buildings, which survive in great numbers in town and country from the fourteenth and fifteenth centuries, overlapped with the period when timber castles were still in use. From earlier times, other structures may be helpful, such as the twelfth century timber aisled barn of the Knights Templar at Cressing (Essex). The thirteenth century monastic barn at Great Coxwell (Berks) may also convey something of the right atmosphere, for although its external walls are of stone, the upper parts of its aisle posts and its open roof are of timber. The stave-built timber churches of Norway are another useful parallel. Their high achievement in decorative detail by the thirteenth century is a reminder that timber castles need not always have been plain. Indeed the castles depicted in the Bayeux Tapestry have some decorative carving. Builders of stone castles certainly paid

Figure 5. Stokesay, Shropshire. The lower part of the north tower is of mid-thirteenth century date. The upper part, built in the 1290s, carried a projecting timber storey some of which survives in the existing fabric. (Author)

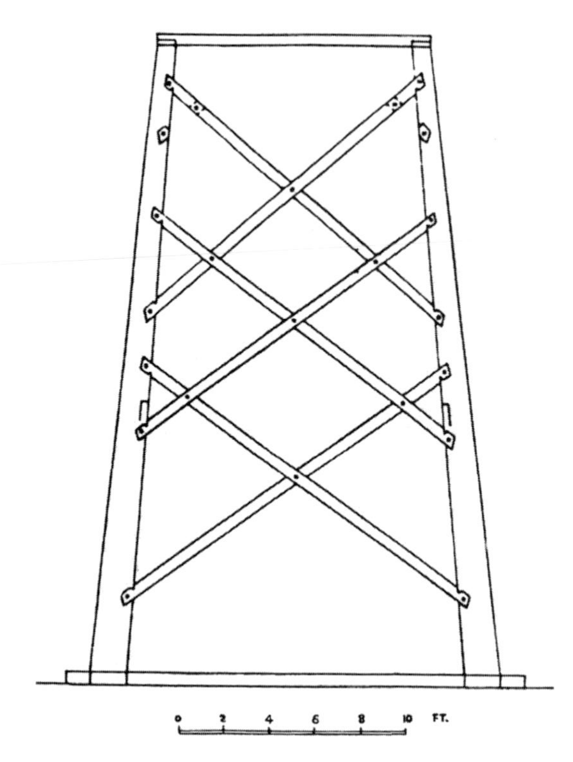

Figure 6. The timber belfry at Brookland, Kent. Standing on a 15-foot square base and framed with diagonal members and notched-lap joints, this timber tower was originally nearly 30 feet high and probably had a projecting roofed platform. (By courtesy of K. Gravett)

attention to detail, and timber castles owned by kings, bishops and rich nobles need not have been less well treated.

Perhaps the structures which most closely relate to the timber castles we know from documentary and pictorial sources, as well as from excavation, are the belfries (sometimes detached) such as those in Essex, Kent, on the Welsh border and elsewhere. Several have been dated by their carpentry techniques and/or scientific dating to the twelfth or thirteenth centuries in their original form. Brookland (Kent), Navestock (Essex) and Pembridge (Hereford) are well-known examples and there are several more. The cross-braced construction of these belfries is reminiscent of an early twelfth century stone-carving of a castle at Modena, northern Italy. That the surviving examples are belfries is perhaps no coincidence, for the word 'belfry' originally meant a timber tower used in siege warfare. Towers of this type could have a wide application – on or in mottes, on bailey perimeters, and in sieges. Perhaps the *bretasches*, to which reference in the twelfth and thirteenth centuries is common, were not dissimilar. These were often of prefabricated construction, to which towers built in this way would easily lend themselves.

Archaeology and the Timber Castle

The archaeological evidence for timber castles takes broadly two forms. From excavations comes structural evidence in fascinating detail. But for every excavated site there are countless others whose earthworks remain unexplored. From

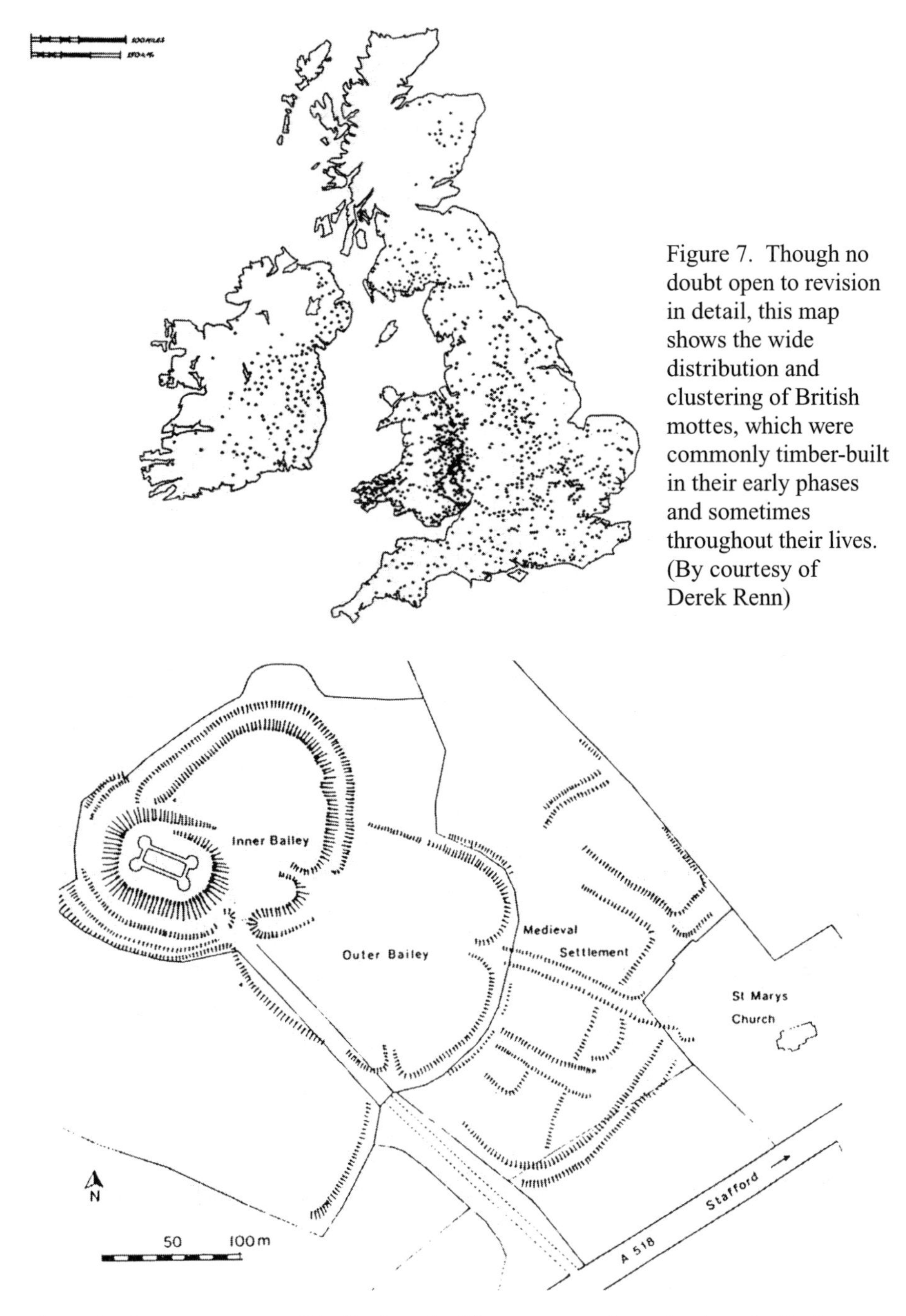

Figure 7. Though no doubt open to revision in detail, this map shows the wide distribution and clustering of British mottes, which were commonly timber-built in their early phases and sometimes throughout their lives. (By courtesy of Derek Renn)

Figure 8. A recent survey of Stafford castle. The motte was later developed with the building of a fourteenth-century stone keep, whose remains were incorporated in a Gothick keep of c.1800. But the dominant features of the site are its earthworks – the enormous motte, the inner and outer baileys as well as the hollow ways and house platforms of the attached village. The overall view of a site, which a full survey provides, reveals not only the details of its plan but also its relationship with the surrounding settlement pattern. (By courtesy of E. C. Hill and Stafford Borough Council)

these, deductions of a more general nature must be made. The most obvious lesson to be learned is the enormous quantity and wide distribution of the evidence in the field. It extends from Ireland in the west, from Scotland and Denmark in the north, eastwards into Germany, and southwards through France into Italy. It is impossible to offer precise numbers of sites. While many of them are the characteristically medieval mottes (with or without baileys), others are enclosures of varying shape and size (sometimes called ringworks) which are not always easily distinguished from sites of earlier date. In any case, estimates of numbers are meaningless historically, since many sites have already been destroyed and since excavation sometimes reveals that earthworks contain stone, not timber structures. It is the overall quantity which matters – and there are several thousand. Also of interest are variations in distribution density: political and cultural frontiers are sometimes thickly studded with these (and other) castles, for example the Welsh Marches or the Rhineland. There is no doubt whatever that timber castles were an enormously important feature of the medieval landscape. In the eleventh and twelfth centuries they must have outnumbered stone castles by a considerable margin. And although some timber castles fell out of use during the twelfth century, many continued in occupation alongside increasingly important military architecture in stone. It is a weakness of the archaeological study of castles that emphasis falls on improvement, innovation and development. It is easy to forget that for every up-to-date site in the landscape of castles there were many more of a less sophisticated nature, relicts of an earlier style of castle design. And for many of the less rich among the landowning class such sites continued to be of value.

Fieldwork on the earthwork sites of timber castles has a number of applications. First, it is only by detailed survey, on the ground and from air photographs, that the precise character of a site can be demonstrated. Field record sometimes hints at the location of buried features and at the relative chronology of different parts of a site – not all the earthworks may be contemporary. Field survey may also reveal the relationship of a castle site to an adjacent settlement, as is the case at Stafford. Today, steadily improving standards of survey, practised notably by the various Royal Commissions on Historical Monuments in Great Britain, have produced a much more reliable body of field evidence than was available to earlier students of castle studies. Comparative use of detailed site surveys, backed up by further personal observation, underlies attempts to make sense of the enormous quantity of field evidence through classification. Mottes have been categorized according to shape and height, and their position *vis-à-vis* their baileys. Enclosure or ringwork sites have been categorized according to their size and the profile of their defences. Such classification certainly demonstrates the character of the evidence and the various ways in which earthwork forms could be employed. But there is a limit to what can be achieved in this way. It does not follow that superficially similar sites are of the same date. Given the long period of time during which timber castles were appearing and disappearing, there is a danger of drawing together in categories sites which may have little to connect them historically. Field survey also illustrates how varied in detail the sites are. Their individuality is further emphasised when the results of excavation are taken into account. A general weakness of study

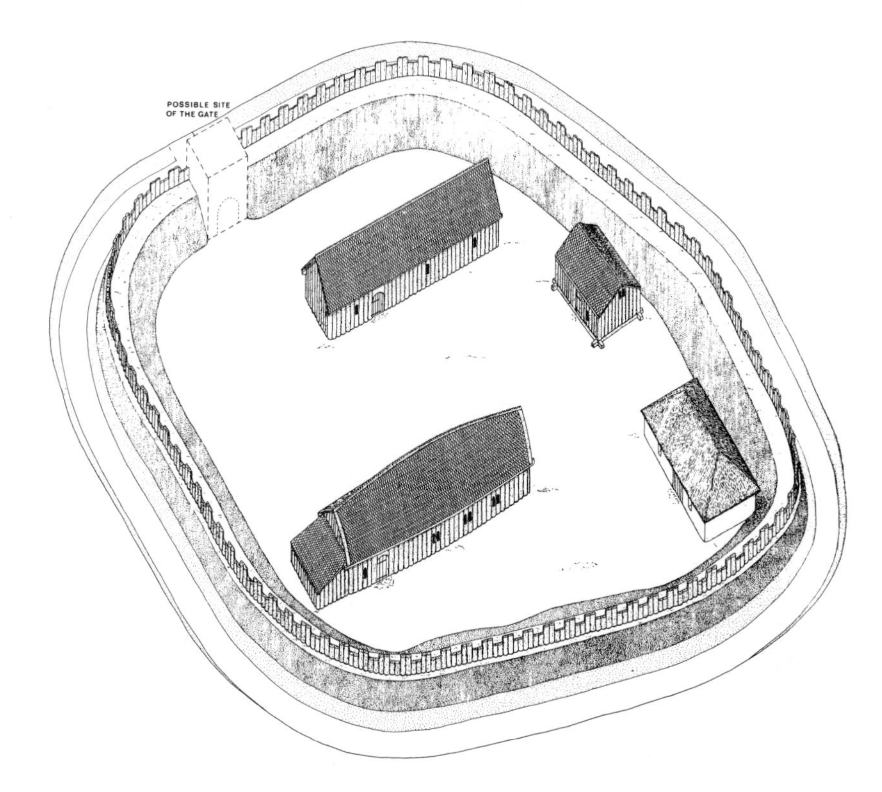

Figure 9. Goltho, Lincolnshire: a reconstruction of the defences and buildings c.850 AD. Goltho is one of a number of places where excavation has revealed earlier phases of sites where mottes were not primary features. (By courtesy of G. Beresford)

through survey alone is that the field monuments survive in a form which mainly reflects their final development. Only excavation can reveal the potentially complex sequence of occupation lying beneath, which has sometimes involved drastic alterations to the site.

The Structural Development of Timber Castles

Excavation has, without any doubt, transformed our understanding of timber castles. There was virtually no excavated evidence available to Mrs Ella Armitage and others who put British castle studies on a firm footing at the beginning of the twentieth century. Indeed, most of the excavations on timber castle sites have taken place in the last forty years. There have been numerous explorations, though few conducted on a large scale. One of the most striking results is the discovery of whole phases of sites which were otherwise invisible. At der Husterknupp (Rhineland), Mirville (Normandy) and Goltho (Lincs, England), sites which had mottes by the late eleventh century had originally been very different. Starting as defended enclosures they were transformed by

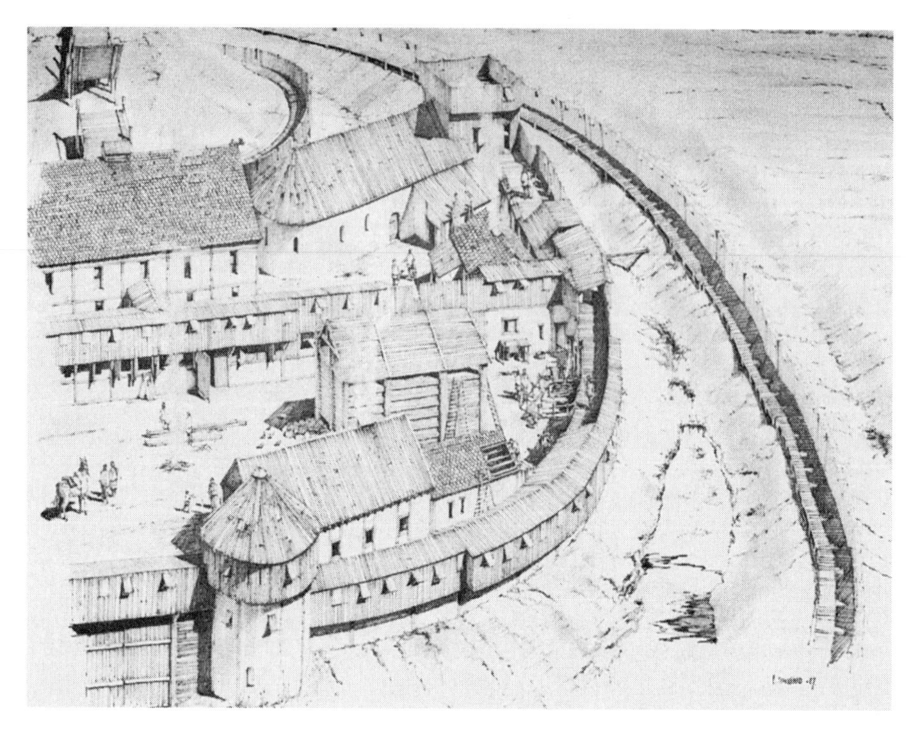

Figure 10. The medieval castle – an alternative image. Reconstruction of the northern half of the bailey, c.1150, at Hen Domen, Montgomery (Powys). This drawing and the excavated evidence upon which it is based are discussed fully in *Current Archaeology* X, No. 4 (September 1988), pp. 137–142. (Drawing by P. Scholefield)

successive generations of occupants. Drastic changes have also been observed at other sites. At Neroche (Somerset) a pre-conquest enclosure was redesigned by the Normans and only in the twelfth century was a motte built at one end of the site. In Ireland, where there was a long-established tradition of rath construction before the Normans arrived, there are similar complexities. In the late twelfth century some existing sites were filled in and raised into mottes. This occurred at Castleskreen, Baliynarry and Rathmullan (all in Co Down). Recent excavations have also suggested that some Irish sites were very similar to mottes even before the Norman invasion took place. Information from such sites raises very basic questions about the origins of castles.

From excavation we can also see how sites occupied for long periods were subject to periodic rebuilding and redesign. At Launceston (Cornwall) and Sandal (Yorkshire) timber castles were gradually transformed into stone in the twelfth century. Much evidence about timber castles, extensively disturbed by subsequent activity, must underlie many stone castles. At Hen Domen there was an almost continuous process of repair and rebuilding in the bailey between the late eleventh and the thirteenth centuries, but this was exclusively of timber. The major phases of reconstruction were very different in character from each other. A hypothetical visitor to the site would have seen very contrasting views *c.*1080, *c.*1150 and *c.*1230. The earliest castle was simple and massive, its bailey dominated by a great hall in front of the bridge leading to the motte, and a granary some yards away. The twelfth century castle was crowded with buildings of all sorts – the atmosphere within must have been very claustrophobic. The latest castle was far less densely built-up, occupation contracting towards the motte. These contrasts reflect the changing social history of the site. At its foundation it was an instrument of Norman conquest in Wales. At its end it was subordinate to a new castle of stone built a mile (1.6km) away at Montgomery by Henry III. In between it had been the main residence and administrative centre of a small Marcher lordship. Not even the most sophisticated field survey of the site could have even hinted at its complexity.

As well as overall views of structural development, excavation also reveals individual buildings of great interest. Many excavators have dissected mottes, or at least parts of mottes. Abinger (Surrey) became well-known for its rectangular timber tower and its surrounding palisade built on top of the motte. At South Mimms (Middlesex), a timber tower had a motte thrown up around it, and the motte itself was revetted in timber. At Lismahon (Co Down), a house on dry-stone footings had a slender, timber tower at one end and a surrounding palisade. These varying examples illustrate the individuality of motte structures, which must reflect one aspect of their history. But is it the whole story? Evidence of towers within mottes might only survive at their very bases, so that excavation of only their upper portions might be quite misleading. Timberwork on the outer faces of eroded mottes might be equally elusive. A fully-framed tower standing on a motte might leave virtually no evidence in the ground at all. The use of such structures might explain the apparently empty tops of some excavated mottes. Despite numerous excavations we have hardly begun to understand one of the most common classes of medieval field monument. Only total excavation can reveal the full story of a motte's development, and for various reasons this is normally an impossible task.

The excavation of the baileys which accompanied mottes, and of the interiors of enclosure castles, has produced a similarly varied picture. Ramparts, examined for example at Hen Domen, Therfield (Herts), Lydford (Devon), Launceston (Cornwall) and Ludgershall (Wilts) could be piled around their palisade timbers, revetted at front and/or back, or have their palisades dug into their tops. Domestic buildings occur in all shapes and sizes. In the twelfth century phase at Hen Domen there were two halls, a chapel, a granary, water cistern, a small house and workshop, and other small rooms tucked into the back of the defences. There was also a structural division across the middle of the bailey, creating an extra line of defence and also a social distinction between 'upper' and 'lower' halves. Other sites have also produced domestic ranges, or parts of them, with halls and ancillary buildings, for example Sandal (Yorkshire), Barnard Castle (Co Durham) and Llantrithyd and Rumney (both in Glamorgan). In contrast at Launceston (Cornwall) and Lydford (Devon) the late eleventh century plans contained rows of small buildings, perhaps quarters for an army of conquest rather than high-quality accommodation.

Generally, however, timber castles seem to have contained buildings of similar form and function to those surviving in stone castles. This reminds us that we should not view timber castles as a separate 'type' of castle, but rather as a variation on a theme. Castle designers aimed to meet similar requirements of defence and residence with whatever building technology and materials were at their disposal. Timber might be chosen because no suitable stone was available, or because the builder could not afford to buy stone, or because speed of erection was essential, or because only short-term use for the site was envisaged. The structures referred to briefly above were built in many ways. Some had ground-fast individual posts, others had posts built in trenches, others had walls laid on horizontal base-plates, and others were set on dry-stone footings. Some used much timber, others employed much wattle and daub. Some made extensive use of clay, so that the timbers were hardly visible. In their use of such practices the designers of castles were part of a very long tradition of European building technique. Timber building stretched back into prehistory and was still flourishing in the seventeenth century (later in some areas). Adapted for the most part to providing domestic accommodation, timber building had also been regularly exploited for defensive needs. Prehistoric hillforts, Roman camps, Celtic strongholds, early town defences – all had employed timber and earthwork technology. And the tradition extended far beyond western Europe into the Slav lands of the east. Timber castles were firmly rooted in the culture of the northern world. Their general reassessment is long overdue.

6

Orderic Vitalis on Castles

Marjorie Chibnall

Church and castle were the two predominant influences in the life of Orderic Vitalis.[1] His early boyhood was spent in and by the church of St Peter, just outside the gates of Shrewsbury, where he watched the foundation and first stages of building of a great Benedictine abbey. Just across the river, on a hill dominating the town, rose Roger of Montgomery's new castle, where his father served in the chapel. He may have had little contact with the knights of the garrison; presumably, since he arrived in Normandy at the age of ten speaking no French, he watched their comings and goings in silence, conversing only (outside his family) with the English priests who taught him and the better educated Norman clerks who had made an effort to master the English tongue. But even though he went to Saint-Evroult as an oblate monk and made his home among monks, there was no danger that he would be blind to the realities of Norman power, or to the importance of castles in preserving the measure of peace that made monastic life possible. Besides that, the Norman lords, however brutal and worldly, looked to the church both as a status symbol and a source of spiritual comfort. He wrote later of the knights of Maule, where Saint-Evroult had a priory beside the castle: 'These knights frequent the cloister with the monks, and often discuss practical as well as speculative matters with them; may it continue a school for the living and a refuge for the dying.'[2] So even as a monk he was constantly in the company of knights to the end of his life.

Saint-Evroult was situated on the frontier of Normandy, in a region studded with castles.[3] Even William the Conqueror and his son Henry I, who brought most of the castles in the heart of Normandy under their control, waged a constant struggle to prevent castles such as Ivry, Saint-Céneri or even L'Aigle falling into the hands of great families with interests in the Ile de France, Mortagne or Le Perche. And the powerful lords of Bellême, with their numerous castles (at one time thirty-four according to Orderic's figures), bestrode the frontier and used their strongholds as a formidable power base.[4] It was a region where lords of medium power might owe dual homage, establish themselves in

1 For his early life see M. Chibnall, *The World of Orderic Vitalis*, Oxford 1984, 3–16.

2 *The Ecclesiastical History of Orderic Vitalis*, ed. M. Chibnall, 6 vols, OMT, Oxford 1969–80, iii, 207.

3 Cf. map, *World of Orderic*, 19.

4 For the lords of Bellême see, most recently, Kathleen Thompson, 'Family influence to the south of Normandy in the eleventh century: the lordship of Bellême', *JMH* xi, 1985, 215–26, and works there cited. For Norman castles in general, J. Yver, 'Les châteaux forts en Normandie jusqu'au milieu du xiie siècle', *BSAN* liii, 1955–56, 28–115.

castles with the licence of only one of their lords, and secure a quasi-hereditary right with little reference to the duke of Normandy. Under the weak duke, Robert Curthose, and the absentee Stephen, ducal power was dissipated and castles were treated as part of the family patrimony. Orderic lamented how Curthose had impoverished himself by giving away his inheritance; he even parted with Ivry, the almost impregnable fortress built by his ancestor Aubrée, and granted Brionne, *oppidum munitissimum*, in the very heart of the duchy, to Roger of Beaumont, who had held it only as a royal castellan under William the Conqueror.[5] For the most part he surveyed the struggle for control of the castles from the point of view of the king/duke; but his respect for the patrons of his abbey, who included the lords of Saint-Céneri, gave him some sympathy with the patrimonial ambitions of the frontier families. The lords of Bellême, bitter rivals of his patrons the Giroie and Grandmesnil as well as a threat to the ducal authority, were seen at all times as the enemies of peace and order.

It is Orderic who has given us the unforgettable picture of how Robert of Bellême at the gates of Brionne heard the news of the death of the Conqueror.[6] Wheeling round his horse he galloped straight to Alençon, drove out the unsuspecting king's men from the garrison to replace them with his own knights, and went on to do the same in his other castles. Other magnates followed his example, 'et sic proceres Neustriae de munitionibus suis omnes regis custodes expulerunt'. Orderic stated the facts simply and dramatically; by doing so he made plain to later readers the sudden overthrow of the Conqueror's attempt to impose public order through control of the castles of the duchy.[7] He was no military strategist or legal theorist; but he was aware of the impact of castles on daily life. At every stage in his history he described the fate of castles, which were by turn instruments of public order or dens of brigands, elements in conquest and defence, homes, administrative centres and fortifications. In this way he has made himself in a very real sense one of the earliest in the long line of historians of Norman castles, among whom most recently Allen Brown is one of the most distinguished.[8] Although he took for granted much that was familiar to him but not to us, it is often possible to deduce his assumptions, or to give body to his statements by using archaeological or charter evidence.

He has less to say than some of his contemporaries about the design and structure of castles. There is nothing in his writing comparable to the detailed account by Lambert of Ardres of the great house that Arnold, lord of Ardres, built in his castle; an account which includes a description of all the rooms used for family life.[9] There is nothing even on the scale of William of Poitiers's assessment of the castle of Brionne in 1047: 'This castle, both by the nature of its site and its construction, seemed impregnable. For in addition to other fortifi-

5 Orderic iv, 114. Aubrée was the wife of Duke Richard I's half-brother, Ralph of Ivry.

6 Orderic iv, 112–14.

7 Cf. Yver, 'Châteaux forts', 64: 'C'est toute une politique d'ordre public qui se trouvait remise en question'.

8 See, for example, R. A. Brown, H. M. Colvin, A. J. Taylor, *The History of the King's Works*, London 1963; R. A. Brown, *English Castles*, 3rd edn, London 1976, *Castles from the Air*, Cambridge 1988, as well as numerous papers.

9 Brown, *English Castles*, 36; *Lamberti Ardensis historia comitum Ghisnensium, MGH SS* xxiv, 624.

cations required by the conditions of war, it has a stone hall which serves as a keep for the combattants.'[10] But, unlike some secular clerks, Orderic was not a domestic chaplain whose life lay inside the castles and fortified dwellings of the nobility. Occasionally, however, his narrative reveals incidentally the existence of a hall, the use of wood or stone in construction, or a detail of the fortifications. That the castle of Brionne had a hall roofed with wooden shingles appears from his description of the siege and capture of the castle by Robert Curthose in 1090. In a time of severe drought the attackers heated the metal tips of their missiles in a smith's furnace, and shot them onto the roof of the great hall of the castle, 'so that the red-hot iron of the arrows and darts showered down and was riveted into the dry and crumbly wood of the old shingles', and a great fire broke out, forcing the small garrison to surrender. 'So', commented Orderic, 'between the ninth hour and sunset Duke Robert captured Brionne, which his father William, even with the help of Henry, king of France, had scarcely been able to subdue in three years.'[11] Although Orderic is less specific, wood must also have been used in the construction of the keep of the great castle of Bellême, which finally fell to the forces of Henry I in 1113, after they had entered the town by a stratagem. 'As the defenders of the citadel continued to resist, the place was set on fire, and the noble castle, which Robert had mightily fortified and greatly enriched long ago, was burnt to the ground.'[12] Wood was the chief material for the construction of many early, hastily built castles; and its use continued in more permanent fortifications.[13] Even when the principal material was stone, intra-mural timbers were freely used in the construction of Norman castles from before the Conquest throughout the twelfth century.[14]

Orderic explicitly mentions stone chiefly in describing the newly erected or fortified houses built by rising families in their arrogance and might. Richard Basset, one of Henry I's justices, 'swollen with the wealth of England', used that wealth to build lavishly in his modest Norman patrimony of Montreuil-en-Houlme, where he constructed a very well-fortified castle of ashlar blocks.[15] Reynald of Bailleul, another *parvenu* lord, built himself a small castle or fortified house (*lapideam domum*) at Le Renouard; but after becoming involved in rebellion he was forced to surrender it to Henry I and watch it being set on fire and burnt to the ground.[16] This use of stone defences contrasts with the earthwork defences of the eleventh-century lords which had sprung up in the disor-

10 *Gesta Guillelmi*, 18: 'Opera hoc cum loci natura, tam opere inexpugnabile videbatur. Nam praeter alia firmamenta, quae moliri consuevit belli necessitudo, aulam habet lapideam arcis usum pugnantibus praebentem'. See also Brown, *English Castles*, 30.

11 Orderic iv, 209–11.

12 Orderic vi, 182–3.

13 Cf. Ella S. Armitage, *The Early Norman Castles of the British Isles*, London 1912, 208–9.

14 R. Wilcox, 'Timber reinforcement in medieval castles', *Château-Gaillard* v, 1972, 193–202, cites evidence ranging from the timber in the curtain wall of Richmond castle, built within 20 years of the Conquest, to the double tiers of timber running through the walls of the tower of Bridgnorth (*c.*1170) on each floor.

15 Orderic vi, 468.

16 Orderic vi, 214–16.

ders of the eleventh century, as M. Fixot has shown in the Cinglais.[17] In the reign of Henry I the aspirations of the rising lords were greater; but so was the power of the king to hold them in check. A similar change was appearing in France. One of the patrons of Saint-Evroult, Ansold of Maule, surrounded his house with a defensive wall of stone, but his son Peter's defiance of King Louis VI led to the demolition of both the house and its defences.[18]

Stone must also have been taken for granted by Orderic in such buildings as the castle of Ivry, constructed by the same architect as the great tower of Pithiviers;[19] but his vocabulary is often not precise enough to be a reliable guide to the nature of the buildings he describes. And frequently he wrote about castles that he himself had never seen or, at best, had viewed only from the outside.

He did, however, know the men who manned them.[20] From the lords of castles, but above all from the knights of the household troops, he learnt of the use made of castles in peace and war, the various modes of attack and defence, the military conventions governing resistance and surrender, and the odium incurred by those who flouted them. For information on such topics he is almost unrivalled among his contemporaries. From the monastic side too he absorbed the ethical code preached to knights in an effort to curb the brutalities of war, and superimposed this on his accounts of individual engagements in and around castles. This made him at times unreliable on motive: unwillingness to attack on a great religious feast-day may have been alleged in order to make moral capital out of an unsuccessful enterprise.[21] But it did not invalidate his account of the actual course of fighting, or the military means by which attackers forced their way into a castle. And his occasional indications of the peace-time uses of castles are entirely free from any moral undertones.

As Allen Brown has emphasised, castles were the places of residence for their lords' families.[22] Orderic gives occasional glimpses of this aspect of castle life: Robert of Saint-Céneri and his wife by the fireside in winter;[23] Gilbert of L'Aigle visiting the lady Duda at Moulins-la-Marche on his way home from Sainte-Scholasse; Robert of Candos, castellan of Gisors, pausing to discuss domestic matters with his pious wife Isabel before setting out to take part in a lawsuit; Isabel of Tosny listening to her young son and a group of other knights relating their dreams as they took their ease in the hall of the castle of Conches.[24] In addition to being the home of the castellan, royal castles were centres of administration and finance, and sometimes treasure-stores. When Orderic wrote of Robert of Bellême being summoned in 1112 to render account

17 M. Fixot, 'Les fortifications de terre et la naissance de la féodalité dans le Cinglais', *Château-Gaillard* iii, 1966, 61–6.

18 Orderic iii, 206.

19 Orderic iv, 290.

20 *World of Orderic*, 68–70, 210–12.

21 Cf. the failure to capture Mayet, Orderic v, 258–60.

22 Brown, *English Castles*, 14–15 and *passim*.

23 Orderic ii, 78–81; this is not entirely a peaceful domestic scene, as Robert's wife Adelaide was a kinswoman of Duke William, against whom Robert had rebelled, and she is alleged to have brought about his death by inducing him to eat two poisoned apples in play.

24 Orderic iv, 200–1; vi, 342–4; iv, 218 and p. xxiv.

for Argentan, Exmes and Falaise 'ut regis vicecomes et officialis' he gave what may well be an early indication of regular exchequer supervision of the accounts of *vicomtes* based in the castles.[25] Since his diocesan bishop was John of Lisieux, a leading *curialis*, who organised the Norman exchequer about this time, his information is likely to be reliable.[26] It was widely known that royal castles were repositories of treasure. Orderic relates how Henry I's first action after his brother William Rufus had been killed was to gallop at top speed to Winchester castle, where the royal treasure was kept.[27] His last injunctions on his death-bed included a command to his son, Robert earl of Gloucester, to take charge of his treasure at Falaise and distribute wages and largess to the members of his household and his stipendiary knights.[28]

Castles in war occupy many pages of the *Ecclesiastical History*. To Orderic and his contemporaries in Normandy the importance of castles for both attack and defence was almost axiomatic. His account of William the Conqueror's first campaigns in England after 1066 is punctuated by the building of castles; and we owe to him the well-known statement that 'the fortifications called castles by the Normans were scarcely known in the English provinces, and so the English – in spite of their courage and warlike spirit – could put up only a weak resistance'.[29] The information comes in a part of his history based on the lost chapters of the *Gesta Normannorum ducum* of William of Poitiers, who accompanied the Conqueror to England; it has, therefore, the authority of an eye-witness. It emphasises the common viewpoint of the Norman chroniclers.

Orderic saw royal castle-building as a normal process in conquest and the suppression of rebellion. Henry I began to build a castle at Old Rouen during the rebellion of 1119, 'to attack his enemies, but he left it unfinished when they made peace with him'.[30] In hostile country, castles could be used as bases for destruction and foraging designed to force opponents into submission. Rebels too, holding out against the king, sent out raiding parties for up to ten miles round their fortresses and terrorised their neighbours. During the disturbances in Bray in 1119 Hugh of Gournay and his partisans, eighteen castellans in all, carried out nightly raids around their castles.[31]

Defensively castles occur in Orderic's narrative as bases for royal or comital garrisons capable of protecting the region. Helias, count of Maine, fortified Dangeul against Robert of Bellême and placed his own retainers in the castle to defend the settlers on his lands from the ravages of the tyrant.[32] During the rebellion of 1124, once King Henry had captured the castles of Pont-Audemer and Montfort-sur-Risle with the lands dependent on them, he decided to suspend campaigning for the winter. 'He placed his household troops under chosen

[25] Orderic vi, 178; cf. Yver, 'Châteaux forts', 82 n. 80.
[26] Orderic vi, 142–5; C. H. Haskins, *Norman Institutions*, Harvard Historical Studies, Cambridge, Mass. 1925, 87–90, with corrections by J. Le Patourel, *The Norman Empire*, Oxford 1976, 223–8.
[27] Orderic v, 290.
[28] Orderic vi, 448.
[29] Orderic ii, 218.
[30] Orderic vi, 282.
[31] Orderic vi, 192–4.
[32] Orderic v, 232.

leaders in his castles and charged them to protect the country people against raiders.' Ralph of Bayeux was at Évreux, Henry of La Pommeraye at Pont-Autou and Odo Borleng at Bernay. They discharged their duties so well that, when news reached Bernay of a rebel force led by Waleran of Meulan and Amaury of Montfort plundering the country and mutilating the peasants, the household troops were able to intercept and defeat the rebels in battle at Bourgthéroulde.[33] Fortified *bourgs*, newly built and privileged around the castles, also played a part in the defensive network created by Henry I. Orderic's passing reference to the disorders after the king's death and the burning of the new *bourg* at Exmes 'which King Henry had recently enlarged', indicates that Exmes, like Verneuil, Nonancourt and Pontorsin, had its new *bourg* around the castle.[34]

Since there was little room even in the permanent castles known by Orderic for more occupants than the resident family of the lord or royal castellan and the enlarged military garrison in time of war, he has more to say about churches as places of refuge for the peasantry. These were stone buildings with a right (not always respected) to be regarded as places of sanctuary. So it was the church of Carentan and not any castle that Henry I found crammed full of the humble possessions of the peasantry when order broke down in 1105. And on the same occasion Serlo, bishop of Sées, was reported as saying: 'The church has become the refuge of the masses, although even the church is not wholly safe. This very year Robert of Bellême burnt the church of Tournay in my own diocese and killed forty-five men and women in it.'[35]

For the sieges and the conduct of war in which castles played so large a part the *Ecclesiastical History* is a mine of information. At any threat of rebellion or attack castles were put on a war footing. Garrisons were strengthened, ramparts repaired, ditches dug, palisades erected and supplies of weapons and food collected and stored.[36] Attackers harnessed their resources in the same way. The most dramatic account of such preparations is in the imagined exchange of threats and challenges between William Rufus and Helias of Maine, when Helias refused to renounce his claim to Le Mans. 'See to it' says the king, 'that you thoroughly repair the crumbling ramparts of your castles; send at once for masons and stone-cutters and repair the old breaches in the neglected walls. I will bring a hundred thousand lances against you. I will have carts laden with bolts and arrows drawn there by oxen, but I myself with many troops of armed men will be at your gates ahead of them, even as the shouting oxherds hurry them along.'[37]

Strong castles, adequately garrisoned and amply supplied with stores of food and weapons, could withstand a very long siege. Orderic describes the various

33 Orderic vi, 346–52.

34 Orderic vi, 462; cf. Yver, 'Châteaux forts', 98.

35 Orderic vi, 60–2.

36 See, for example, Orderic iv, 220, 156; vi, 278. During disturbances in Wales Robert of Rhuddlan and other knights 'munitiones suas fossis et hominibus et alimentis hominum et equorum abundanter instruehant'; Orderic iv, 124. When in 1106 William of Mortain was provisioning his castle at Tinchebray to withstand a siege he had the green corn cut down as fodder for his horses; Orderic vi, 84.

37 Orderic v, 230–3.

tactics that could be used by attackers. To avoid committing large numbers of men to a lengthy siege, attacking forces built temporary siege-castles, in which small troops of knights could keep watch and prevent supplies being brought in. William the Conqueror adopted this method early in his reign when besieging Domfront and Arques;[38] much later he had siege-towers built to contain the impregnable fortress of Sainte-Suzanne.[39] Sometimes the besieged could be tempted outside their walls to engage in jousting or more general skirmishing with the besiegers;[40] there was then a chance of forcing a way through the gates as the defenders withdrew and letting in the attackers, as happened at Bellême in 1113.[41]

Improved siege weapons made direct assault possible, even against strongly fortified castles. Much as he hated and feared Robert of Bellême, Orderic admired the ingenuity and engineering skill he showed in devising movable siege-towers, to be manned with knights and wheeled up to the walls. He heard of the use of such engines of war at Jerusalem as well as much nearer home. The siege of Courcy was so near that his remarkably graphic account must have come from eye-witnesses.[42] It took place in the course of a bitter feud between Robert of Bellême and Hugh of Grandmesnil. Hugh and Richard of Courcy, bound together in a family alliance, took up arms against Robert and provided their castles with weapons, food and garrison knights. Robert, assisted by Duke Robert Curthose, attacked Courcy, which had been reinforced so hastily that there had been no time to build a new oven and the besieged had to bake their bread in an oven outside the gates. Skirmishes took place frequently around the oven, and the men of Courcy had to buy their bread with their blood. Even so, Robert of Bellême could not starve them out and he constructed a wooden siege-tower filled with weapons against the castle. This device also proved ineffective, as the men of Courcy burnt it down. The details about the oven are remarkable, and imply that the castle was a very recent fortification for military purposes only. Normally an oven would have been constructed in an early phase of building as, for example, excavations at the fortified residence of Le Plessis-Grimoult have shown.[43]

Robert of Bellême's engineering skill was more effective when he assisted the king of France and duke of Normandy to reduce the castle of Bréval in 1092. Orderic describes how he 'built machines which were wheeled against the enemy's castle, hurling great stones at the fortress and its garrison'. These were evidently siege-towers with catapults placed on top, such as Robert Guiscard had used at the siege of Durazzo in 1081, though Orderic did not know this and wrongly credited Robert of Bellême with the invention.[44] The defenders were

38 *Gesta Guillelmi*, 36–8, 58.
39 Orderic iv, 48–53.
40 Orderic vi, 78–81, 204, 230–1.
41 Orderic vi, 182.
42 Orderic iv, 230–5, 288; such a tower was called a *berfredum*.
43 E. Zadora-Rio, 'L'enceinte fortifiée du Plessis-Grimoult, résidence seigneuriale du xie siècle', *Château-Gaillard* v, 1972, 227–39.
44 Orderic iv, 288; for William of Apulia's account of the siege of Durazzo see *La Geste de Robert Guiscard*, ed. Marguerite Mathieu, Palermo 1961, 218, vv. 248–51.

compelled to surrender by the force of the attack. Fire was another weapon which could reduce a stubborn garrison to submission, as the fate of Brionne and the temporary castle built in the abbey of Saint-Pierre-sur-Dive showed.[45] Sometimes when a town was burnt the stone-built castle survived, as at Breteuil and Évreux.[46]

Not all sieges were continued until the garrison was battered into submission or the besiegers were forced to withdraw. Orderic tells us a great deal about the conventions which governed surrender, provided the conflict had not reached a point of such bitterness that no restraints were respected. As he noted in describing the siege of Courcy, when Robert Curthose came to assist Robert of Bellême he 'spared his own barons and did not press the besieged too closely'. Hugh of Grandmesnil showed a similar respect for feudal obligations when he begged the duke to withdraw for a day, since he wished to be able to engage Robert of Bellême in combat and would not fight against the lord to whom he had done homage.[47] On many occasions a truce was agreed for a few days so that a garrison might send to their lord for help, on the understanding that they would surrender if he could not come at once to relieve them. The situation had to be desperate for a garrison to take this course; Orderic alleged that the garrison of Vignats, besieged by Robert Curthose, hoped to be attacked strongly so that they could surrender honourably.[48] A temporary truce was successfully sought by Robert of Bellême's garrison knights in Arundel castle, and since Robert could give them no help they surrendered to the king and were rewarded by him.[49] King Henry's own men, Roger and John of St John, likewise surrendered Alençon to the Angevins in 1118 when, in spite of their urgent pleas, the king failed to send any help.[50] The most courteous exchange of civilities occurred between the household troops of William Rufus holding the citadel of Le Mans and Helias of Maine, when the news of the king's death reached them. They obtained a truce in order to apply to Duke Robert Curthose and the newly crowned King Henry, because they no longer knew for whom they were holding the castle. When both lords had replied that they were too much occupied with other affairs to take any action in Maine, the garrison of 200 knights surrendered to Count Helias, and he escorted there honourably from the city, protecting them from the wrath of the citizens whose houses they had burnt during the war, and took them into his service.[51] Terms of surrender might allow the besieged to leave with their arms and horses; but rebels could count themselves fortunate if they were granted such terms. When Odo of Bayeux and his supporters surrendered Rochester they asked in vain for the additional concession that the trumpets should not sound as the men rode out, 'as is customary', Orderic explains, 'when an enemy is defeated and a stronghold taken by force'.[52] Knights who

45 Orderic iv, 209–11; vi, 80–2.
46 Orderic vi, 228–31, 524.
47 Orderic iv, 232–4.
48 Orderic vi, 22.
49 Orderic vi, 20–2.
50 Orderic vi, 194–6.
51 Orderic v, 302–6.
52 Orderic iv, 132–4.

had been spared in this way were, however, under an obligation not to take up arms against the lord who had accepted their honourable surrender. No mercy could be expected a second time. Luke of La Barre was pardoned by Henry I after the surrender of the castle of Pont-Audemer, and allowed to leave freely with his horses and arms. When he joined rebel forces against the king a second time, even though he was fighting for his own lord, no pardon was given and he was condemned to be blinded.[53]

In bitter fighting conventions were not always respected. While Henry I's rebel daughter Juliana, the wife of Eustace of Breteuil, was defending the castle of Breteuil she violated a truce with her father, who came for a parley, by shooting a bolt from a cross-bow at him. She missed, and Henry was powerful enough to punish her for her presumption.[54] A similar attempt was made on the life of William Rufus during a truce while he was besieging Mayet, and Rufus took vengeance indirectly by ravaging the country round about; his men cut down fruit-trees, tore up vines and smashed fences and walls.[55] The missile which failed to hit Rufus was a stone, not a bolt; however crossbowmen, whose bolts had sufficient penetrating power to inflict a mortal wound on a knight in full armour, were regarded with particular distrust. Incidents of the kind described by Orderic must have contributed to the attempts of church councils from the Second Lateran Council of 1139 onwards to restrict their use in fighting between Christians.[56]

Some rulers felt that knightly codes did not apply when they were attacking infidels. Orderic relates how, when King Alfonso the Battler of Aragon was besieging Fraga, he obstinately refused to listen to any offers of surrender from the citizens and vowed to capture the city by storm and slay them all. The result was the total destruction of his own army by a relieving force summoned by the desperate citizens.[57] Orderic's attitude to Alfonso's action is ambivalent; while condemning his pride he could not accept as, just the destruction of a Christian army. But he was prepared to acknowledge sadly that a harsh judgement could be just, if the rules had been kept. When King Stephen captured Shrewsbury castle after a month-long siege, during which the defenders had contemptuously refused his offers of peace, he showed his anger by having ninety-four of them put to death.[58] Orderic tacitly accepted that the king was within his rights.

Some aspects of castle warfare violated both conventions and law. Orderic spoke for many of his contemporaries when he denounced the castle building that caused oppression to peasants and monks. The rapid construction of mottes and ramparts often involved forced labour; Robert of Bellême's castle building in the region of Saint-Evroult led to abuses and hardships Orderic himself had

53 Orderic vi, 342, 352–5.

54 Orderic vi, 212–15; see also vi, 76, for the killing of Geoffrey Martel by a crossbowman during a parley.

55 Orderic v, 258–61.

56 Canon 29; 'Artem autem mortiferam et Deo odibilem ballasteriorum et sagittariorum adversus Christianos et catholicos exerceri de caetero sub anathemate prohibemus' (J. D. Mansi, *Sacrorum Conciliorum nova et amplissima Collectio*, Florence & Venice 1776 ff., xxi, 553).

57 Orderic vi, 412–16.

58 Orderic vi, 520–2.

witnessed. The tenants of his own abbey were forced to labour both in building castles and in demolishing new castles captured from Robert's enemies; in the end the abbot had no choice but to raise a tallage – a form of protection money – on his estates, so that his peasants could be left in peace.[59] Worst of all was the practice in times of particular disorder described as building castles in monasteries and churches.

Orderic's examples come from years of rebellion or border warfare around Normandy. During the disturbances early in Robert Curthose's rule William of Breteuil lost his great castle of Ivry to his own vassal, Ascelin Goel. He began a siege in an attempt to recover it, and placed knights in the nearby abbey of Ivry which, with its stone buildings, was a convenient ready-made siege work. Orderic implies that some additional fortification took place: 'munitionem in cenobio monachorum construxerat'. It did not serve its purpose; Ascelin Goel brought up a strong force of men, attacked the monastery 'which was then a den of thieves', burnt the church and other buildings and captured ten knights.[60] If that was the whole defending force, the new fortifications may have been modest. Some years later, during King Henry's final campaign in 1106 to wrest Normandy from his brother, a much more serious occupation of an abbey took place. Robert, a simoniacal abbot of Saint-Pierre-sur-Dive who supported Curthose, 'converted the abbey into a fortress, assembled a troop of knights, and so turned the temple of God into a den of thieves'. His force of knights was a hundred and forty strong; when King Henry attacked he set fire to the castle and monastery (*castrum et cœnobtum*) and burnt them down. Many knights who had taken refuge in the tower of the church were burnt with it.[61] Here Orderic's language suggests that a castle of some kind was built within the abbey enclosure. Presumably it was made of wood, since the occupation lasted only three months, but the knights made use also of the stone tower of the church.

When *c.*1116 Louis VI occupied the cell of the monks of Saint-Ouen-de-Rouen at Gasny, he fortified it so substantially that Henry I was compelled to build two siege-castles to invest the French garrison. As at Saint-Pierre-sur-Dive, though Orderic's language is conventionally arid once again he is more concerned to denounce the establishment of a den of thieves in the house of God than to describe the nature of the fortifications, he implies more substantial buildings than those in William of Breteuil's siege works at Ivry.[62] His other reference to a castle in a church was a false rumour. Henry I was persuaded to turn back from going to invest L'Aigle by a story that Hugh of Gournay and Stephen

59 Orderic iv, 300. William Ruftrs used forced labour to build his siege castle, 'Malveisin', to invest Robert Mowbray in Bamburgh (Orderic iv, 282). Henry Beauclerc also raised forced levies and compelled the men of La Trinité-de-Caen to help with his castle works in the Cotentin during the years of disturbance after the death of William the Conqueror: 'Comes Henricus pedagium accepit de Chetelhulmo et de omni Constantino et super hoc facit operari homines Sancte Trinitatis de eadem villa et patria ad castella suorum hominium' (Haskins, *Norman Institutions*, 63); but Orderic says nothing of this.

60 Orderic iv, 286–8.

61 Orderic vi, 72 n. 2, 74, 80–2.

62 Orderic vi, 184–6: 'in cella moriachorum castrum munitat'. See also A. Le Prévost, *Mémoires et notes pour servir à l'histoire du département de l'Eure*, ed. L. Delisle et L. Passy, 3 vols, Évreux 1862–9, ii, 162–8.

of Albemarle were attempting to build a castle in the monastery of La Trinité-du-Mont at Rouen and to betray the city to William Clito and the French.[63] The rumour was unfounded, but it was plausible; Orderic, perhaps unconsciously, here makes clear that Henry's peace-keeping extended to the protection of the church from the danger of local *avoués* or their kind.[64] Outside the confines of Normandy, or even within the duchy during the rule of a weak duke, such men could appropriate church buildings for their military advantage, just as they could demand slave labour for building their more permanent castles, and extort money from monastic houses as the price of peace. Orderic died too soon to know about the use of churches as siege works and adulterine castles in England during Stephen's reign, of which William of Malmesbury and the author of the *Gesta Stephani* tell us so much.[65] Had he been able to cite the examples of Wallingford, Lincoln, Bampton and Cirencester amongst others it would have helped to highlight his picture of Henry I as peacemaker and protector of the church; a role in which the proper use of castles was an important element. He had a particularly strong conviction of the right of the king to control even the castles of his vassals in times of danger; he took the king's right of entry so much for granted that we learn only incidentally that the knights expelled by Louis VI from the archbishop of Rouen's castle at Andely in 1119 were actually Henry I's household troops.[66]

How far can a military historian trust and interpret Orderic's descriptions of the building of castles and their use in war? There is an obvious difficulty in his vocabulary. Many of the terms used are general and literary rather than specific, and he used some of them interchangeably for castles, fortified towns and sometimes fortified houses. *Castrum* arid *castellum* were charter terms for castles and sometimes for other fortifications.[67] These terms and *municipium*, *praesidium* and *oppidum* were also to be found in eleventh-century chronicles for fortifications of various kinds. *Arx* and *turris* were slightly more specific. Orderic most frequently used them of keeps or citadels, as at Rouen, Ivry, Le Mans or Pithiviers, and sometimes stone buildings are implied.[68] The technical terms motte (*mota*) and donjon (*dangio*) occur more rarely. Apart from the *mota* or La Motte Gautier-de-Clinchamps, perhaps already a proper name, the term occurs only for the motte in Ballon, said to dominate the town.[69] *Dangio* was always used for a royal keep; there was a *dangio regis* at Évreux and another at

63 Orderic vi, 198–200.

64 See, J. Yver, 'Autour de l'absence d'avouerie en Normandie', *BSAN* lvii, 1965, 205–10.

65 *Gesta Stephani*, ed. K. R. Potter, revised R. H. C. Davis, OMT, Oxford 1976, 61–2, 91–2; William of Malmesbury, *Historia Novella*, ed. K. R. Potter, NMT, London 1955, 42, 48; D. F. Renn, *Norman Castles in Britain*, 2nd edn, 1973, 49–50.

66 Orderic vi, 216–19. This was the right claimed in the Norman *Consuetudines et iusticie*: 'et nulli licuit in Normannia fortitudinem castelli sin vetare domino Normannie si ipse earn in manu suo voluit habere'. Haskins, *Norman Institutions*, 282.

67 Fauroux, nos 63, 91, 93, 117, 159A, 214, 225 (*castrum*); 49, 56, 58, 114, 140, 214, 224 (castellum). No. 76, a charter of Edward the Confessor ratified by Robert the Magnificent, includes a grant of English lands and *castella* to Le Mont-Saint-Michel arid must, if genuine, mean *burhs* rather than castles, which did not exist in England at such an early date.

68 For references see *Index verborum* in Orderic i.

69 Orderic v, 234, 242.

Gisors, and when Henry I restored Alençon, Almenèches, Vignats and other castles to William Talvas he kept the *dangiones* in his own hands and placed his garrisons in them.[70] Although some writers used the word *agger* for a motte,[71] Orderic rarely if ever used it in any sense other than a rampart of some kind. Certainly when he described how the horses of the Norman knights pursuing the English after the victory at Hastings fell headlong over an *antiquum aggerem* concealed by long grass he must have meant an ancient earthwork.[72] And in his account of fighting at the palisade of the siege-castle of Vatteville, and again at the gate of Aalst, a rampart seems the most likely meaning.[73] There is, however, a predominantly literary rather than a technical flavour to his language. Castles are reinforced 'muris et vallis zetisque'; towns and castles are fortified 'muris et vallis et propugnaculis', or 'muris ac propugnaculis'.[74] The intention is to describe a strong fortification, not to provide a military blue-print.

Literary influences intrude in another way; there is sometimes a touch of legend or *chanson* in his descriptions of the capture of castles. There is a remarkable contrast between the capture of Saint-Céneri by Robert of Bellême in 1090, and that of Lincoln by Ranulf, earl of Chester, and William of Roumare in 1141, as described by Orderic. At the time of the capture of Saint-Céneri its lord, Robert Giroie, was fighting with young Henry Beauclerc, then established in Domfront, against Henry's brothers Robert Curthose and William Rufus, assisted by Robert of Bellême. Robert Giroie was returning home from an expedition against the forces of Bellême when, in Orderic's words:

> a rumour suddenly sprang up that he had been killed. At once there was general alarm, and a fearful uproar broke out in the castle. The garrison were beside themselves, and lost their nerve and judgement. Pain of Mondoubleau, Robert of Montfort, and other defenders of the castle defected and, as some say, in order to win favour with Robert of Bellême left the castle undefended. Robert Giroie's wife, Radegunde, turned pale at the terrible news and resolved to wait with her followers in the castle for confirmation of it, but one woman was powerless to defend the right against determined men. Then, as they were leaving the castle in disorder, Robert of Bellême got wind of the matter and was on the spot at once. He found the fortress undefended, entered without resistance, and sacked the place . . . As the troops rushed into the castle they found cauldrons full of meat cooking over the fire, tables covered with cloths, and dishes of food with bread set out upon them.[75]

This account has the ring of authenticity. The family of Giroie were founders and patrons of Saint-Evroult, and they had established a priory by their castle of Saint-Céneri. Orderic could have heard the story at the time from fellow-monks

[70] Orderic vi, 148, 342, 224: 'Alencionem et Almanisces atque Vinacium aliaque castra ei concessit praeter dangiones quos propriis excubitoribus assignauit'.
[71] For examples see Brown, *English Castles*, 39.
[72] Orderic ii, 176.
[73] Orderic vi, 346, 376.
[74] Orderic iii, 36, 108; iv, 156.
[75] Orderic iv, 292–5.

or from the patrons themselves; it is a convincing tale of panic spreading through a small garrison in a region of divided allegiance.

The story of the fall of Lincoln castle in 1141 is told in a different style:

> Ranulf, earl of Chester, and William of Roumare rebelled against King Stephen and captured the castle which he held at Lincoln by a trick. They cunningly found a time when the household troops of the garrison were widely dispersed, and then soot their wives ahead to the castle under the pretext of a friendly visit. While the two countesses were passing the time there, laughing and talking with the wife of the knight who ought to have been defending the castle, the earl of Chester arrived, unarmed and without his cloak, am though to escort his wife home, and three knights followed him without arousing any suspicion. Once inside the castle they suddenly snatched crossbows and weapons which lay to hand and violently expelled the king's guards. Then William of Roumare burst in with a force of armed knights, according to a pre-arranged plan, and in this way the two brothers took control of the castle and the whole city.[76]

It has been thought strange that of all contemporaries only Orderic, so far away in Normandy, knew just how Lincoln fell. But there is no proof that it actually fell that way; indeed Orderic was far enough from the scene for the story to have passed through several versions in the hands of *jongleurs* before it reached him. Castle garrisons were small, and whenever some of the knights were out foraging for food the castle was vulnerable. It was desirable to find a plausible excuse if a castellan had allowed himself to be caught unawares.

The story seems all the more improbable if we compare it with the account of the continuator of Hermann of Tourani of how the king's tower in Noyon fell to the bishop of Noyon in the early eleventh century,[77] The castellan installed by the king was said to be so oppressive that the bishop and townspeople resolved to destroy the tower. When the castellan and his garrison were out, and only his wife and servants were left behind, the bishop secured entry by a trick. He told the castellan's wife that he had a piece of precious silk to make a chasuble, which only she had the skill to cut and sew, and persuaded her to let him bring it in. Meanwhile his household troops and the citizens were gathering outside; they burst in and were able to enter and destroy the tower while the bishop, posing as the lady's deliverer from an unprincipled rebellion, led her away in safety.

The chronicler has here used, as Orderic used, one of the commonplaces of contemporary literature: a stratagem for gaining entrance to a fortress, with a side-glance at the popular literary theme of the vanity and weakness of women.[78] Such themes were part of the fictional element that crept into history

[76] Orderic vi. 538–41

[77] Hermann of Tourani, *Liber de restauratione Sancti Martini, MGH SS* xiv, 319–20; discussed in Olivier Guyotjeannin, *'Episcopus et Comes'; Affirmation et déclin de la seigneurie épiscopale au Nord du Royaume de France*, Geneva/Paris 1987, 45–7.

[78] Stith Thompson, *Motif Index of Folk-Literature* iv, 3rd edn, Copenhagen 1957; cited Guyotjeannin, 46 n. 237.

at every level, like the fables decorating the borders of the Bayeux Tapestry.[79] Even an honest historian, gathering material from the oral accounts of household knights or townspeople, often heard it already contaminated by this fictional element. But genuine information comes through all these accounts; castles fell as often through shortage of manpower as from the battering of siege engines.

Monks saw themselves as soldiers of God, engaged in spiritual warfare. Monasteries were their castles.[80] The arguments which Orderic attributed to his father in persuading Roger of Montgomery to found an abbey at Shrewsbury may be entirely imaginary; but they may incorporate ideas he had learnt at his father's knee. His theme was the need to found a monastic castle, where a garrison of monks could devote their lives to ceaseless conflict against Satan for Earl Roger's soul.[81] It would have been a suitable way to impress a commander of knights who had just built a secular castle. But whether or not this was a boyhood memory, the analogy was a monastic commonplace, popular in sermons and moral treatises designed for knights and the sons of knights who became monks. When Orderic outlined the achievements of William the Conqueror in an imaginary death-bed speech he balanced an account of his victories in battle with an enumeration of the abbeys – seventeen of monks and six of nuns – which he claimed to have founded as duke: the 'fortresses by which Normandy is guarded, in which men learn to fight against devils and the sins of the flesh'.[82] The balance was important; the secular castles played an essential part in preserving peace, and Orderic was perceptive both of their military and their symbolic importance. In Jean Yver's seminal study of castles in Normandy up to the middle of the twelfth century references to Orderic occur in forty per cent of the footnotes.[83] It is a measure of the importance of Orderic's work to contemporary historians of feudal society, in which castles were 'a characteristic institution'.[84]

79 Discussed most recently by H. E. J. Cowdrey, 'Towards an interpretation of the Bayeux Tapestry', *ANS* x, 1988, 49–65.

80 Anselm of Bec frequently used military analogies; for a spiritual castle see *Memorials of St Anselm*, ed. R. W. Southern and F. S. Schmitt, British Academy: *Auctores Britannici Medii Aevi* i, 1969, 66–7.

81 Orderic iv, 142–6.

82 Orderic iv, 90–4.

83 Yver, 'Châteaux forts'.

84 Brown, *English Castles*, 15.

7

Royal Castle-Building in England, 1154–1216[1]

R. Allen Brown

The study of English castles in the past has been largely confined to architectural or archaeological description. No broad institutional and political study has been attempted, though the evidence is available and the subject important. Recently, however, one aspect of the subject, castle-building, has engaged considerable attention for the period of Edward I's Welsh operations. In a masterly paper Professor Edwards has dealt with the construction of the eight Edwardian castles in Wales,[2] whilst in a recent number of *EHR*, Mr A. J. Taylor published his account of Master James of St George, the chief master-mason employed by the king in that work.[3] The object of the present paper is to show the extent and nature of royal castle-building in England between 1154 and 1216. The period has an historical unity in the establishment, development, and initial break-down of the Angevin system of government, and during these years an extensive programme of castle-building and maintenance was a significant, though largely neglected, feature of Angevin policy. The method of treatment will be, *mutatis mutandis*, that adopted by Professor Edwards, in the hope that such facts and figures as are available may be usefully compared with those now established for the Edwardian castles. At the same time the fact that we are dealing with building widespread over the whole kingdom, the nature of that building itself and the comparative lack of detail in the available evidence,[4] all necessitate a more general treatment than that undertaken by Professor Edwards; while in addition to any discussion of cost, time, labour, and the organization of Angevin building, the subject poses the more fundamental questions, where was this building undertaken? and why was it found necessary?

1 I wish to thank Mr H. M. Colvin who, since this paper was written, has been over the same ground, and has often saved me from error, especially in the appended Tables.

2 J. G. Edwards, 'Edward I's Castle-building in Wales' (Sir John Rhys Memorial Lecture 1944), *PBA*, vol. xxxiv. The eight castles are those of Aberystwyth, Beaumaris, Builth, Carnarvon, Conway, Flint, Harlech, and Rhuddlan.

3 A. J. Taylor, 'Master James of St. George', *ante*, vol. lxv. For the medieval building industry in general, see D. Knoop and G. P. Jones, *The Medieval Mason* (Manchester, 1933) and L. F. Salzman, *Building in England down to 1540* (Oxford, 1952).

4 Few 'rolls of particulars' (cf. Edwards, *op. cit.* pp. 16–17) have been found for the building expenditure of this period. On the Pipe Rolls themselves separate building accounts are very rare. Castle-building expenditure is normally charged as one among the miscellaneous items credited to the sheriff or other accountant – often in the bare form, 'Et in operatione castelli de *x*, *y* li.' Sometimes more detail is given, e.g. *P.R. 4 John*, p. 78. The best example of a separate building account in this period is that for Château-Gaillard, *Mag. Rot. Scacc. Norm.* ed. Stapleton, ii. 309–10; cf. *P.R. 5 Richard I*, pp. 131–2: *P.R. 2 Richard I*, pp. 1–4.

The evidence available is chiefly the evidence of expenditure. The Pipe Rolls, by far the most important source of information, survive in more or less uninterrupted series throughout the whole period,[5] and to them in John's reign are added the Close Rolls[6] and the two surviving *Misae* Rolls.[7] It is important to note at the outset that the expenditure recorded by these sources cannot be complete. The Pipe Rolls themselves were never intended to be a record of all royal finance, and their deficiencies in this respect need no emphasis here. Nor can the more numerous records of John's reign provide comprehensive figures. On the other hand, the Close and *Misae* Rolls add little to the information of the Pipe Rolls. There are surprisingly few writs of *Liberate* ordering expenditure from the Treasury upon building,[8] and though the *Misae* Rolls contain considerable castle-building expenditure not recorded elsewhere, the scale of this expenditure is much lower than the expenditure upon the Pipe Rolls.[9] In short, a collation of the financial records of the period indicates that the Pipe Rolls do record by far the greater part of royal expenditure upon castle-building, and accordingly that figures based upon their evidence, as ours must principally be, will afford something more than a rough guide to the extent and distribution of that building.

The extent and nature of castle-building and maintenance by the first three Angevin kings are best shown if the available figures are set out in tabular form. Of the two tables[10] appended to this paper, the first shows the recorded expenditure in a series of annual totals, and in addition lists the principal castles upon which that money was spent in any given year. The second table shows total expenditures on individual castles in each of the three reigns. Throughout, the figures are taken from the Pipe Rolls in the first instance, and any additional expenditure from other sources is separately added. These tables show at once that this is a period of great building activity. They reveal a large-scale and practically continuous building programme covering every quarter of the kingdom. In the whole period the grand total of expenditure amounts to nearly £46,000, representing an average of some £780 per annum.[11] This expenditure is dis-

5 *Pipe Roll I Henry II* (1154–5) survives only in the transcripts in the *Red Book of the Exchequer.* Thereafter the series is complete to Easter 1215 except for 15 John (1212–13).

6 The Close Rolls (ed. T. D. Hardy, *RLC*, Rec. Com.) begin in 6 John (1204–5) and are preceded by *Liberate* Rolls for 2, 3, and 5 John (ed. T. D. Hardy in *Rotuli de Liberate* . . . etc., Rec. Com.). There are no Close Rolls for 10–13 John.

7 11 John (1209–10) and 14 John (1212–13), respectively printed in *Rotuli de Liberate ac de misis et Prestitis*, ed. T. D. Hardy (Rec. Com.) and *Docts. illustr. of English History*, ed. H. Cole (Rec. Com.). The *Prestita* Rolls are little concerned with building expenditure.

8 The occasional entry of receipts from the Treasury (e.g. *P.R. 30 Henry II*, p. 150) – and more rarely from the Chamber (e.g. *P.R. 6 John*, p. 186) – upon the Pipe Rolls is exceptional and results from an attempt to provide a different kind of account from the normal Pipe Roll arrangement, an account, that is, drawing together all receipts for and disbursements upon one particular object, as opposed to the setting down of miscellaneous expenditure charged against a particular local revenue. Cf. n. 4, above.

9 Thus the total from the *Misae* Roll of 11 John is some £252 0*s*. 0*d*. and that from the Pipe Roll of 11 John £1314 17*s*. 5½*d*. The total from *Misae* Roll 14 John is some £476 0*s*. 0*d*. and that from Pipe Roll 14 John just over £2200 0*s*. 0*d*.

10 See below.

11 Reckoned from the Pipe Roll evidence alone. The average is reckoned on the basis of 58½ recorded Exchequer years, since the Pipe Roll of 17 John covers roughly only half the financial year. In what

bursed on some 130 castles. In many years, particularly in the period of the rebellion of the Young King, in the later years of Henry's reign, and in the later years of John's reign, the annual total is well over £1000.[12] In 1172–3 and again in 1211–12 the total is over £2000. In 1210–11 it is almost £3000, and in 1189–90 almost £4000. On certain individual castles enormous sums were spent. At Dover the grand total from the Pipe Rolls between 1155 and 1215 is little under £8000,[13] at the Tower of London just under £4000,[14] at Scarborough some £3000,[15] at Windsor some £1800,[16] and at Winchester some £1600.[17]

Comparing the three reigns we see that Henry II's reputation as a great builder[18] is amply justified. After the first few years of his reign, in which the small scale of recorded expenditure may be due to a narrower scope than usual in the contents of the Pipe Rolls, he commenced almost literally to dig himself in. Thenceforward the annual totals reach and maintain a high level. The thirty-three Pipe Rolls of the reign record a total expenditure of rather less than £21,500, an average of about £650 for each recorded year. Of the ninety castles benefiting from this expenditure, thirty each had over £100 spent upon them – an arbitrary figure which may serve to distinguish between positive building and mere maintenance. On each of six castles, Dover, Newcastle-on-Tyne, Nottingham, Orford, Winchester, and Windsor, over £1000 were spent, and amongst these Nottingham received some £1800, and Dover the vast sum of just over £6400 during the reign.[19] In Richard's reign, after the troubled period of the king's absence on Crusade and his imprisonment, the level of expenditure falls considerably.[20] Doubtless this fall chiefly reflects the increasing concentration of the king's government on the war in France, and that it indicates no lack of interest or skill in castle-building by Richard personally is sufficiently proved by his monumental work at Château-Gaillard in Normandy. The heaviest expenditure of the whole period is found in John's reign, and John's building operations by this test were even more extensive than those of his father. The total figure for the reign from the Pipe Rolls alone is over £17,000, providing an average expenditure of over £1000 for each recorded year (15½). This total was disbursed in all upon ninety-five castles, twenty-six of which each received over

follows all figures quoted are taken from the Pipe Rolls alone unless otherwise stated. Reference to the tables will show such additional expenditure as is known.

12 Because the Pipe Rolls are our principal source, chronological periods in the text are reckoned in Exchequer years (Michaelmas to Michaelmas).

13 £7648 2*s*. 5½*d*. To this further heavy sums, totalling some £600, may be added from the Close and *Misae* Rolls of John's reign. See Table B.

14 £3977 8*s*. 0*d*.

15 £2996 11*s*. 9*d*.

16 £1830 19*s*. 1½*d*.

17 £1618 10*s*. 0*d*.

18 Cf. Round, *Introductions* to *P.R.s 23 Henry II* (pp. xxiij–iv) and *28 Henry II* (p. xxiv). Cf. Torigny (Rolls Series), *Chrons. Stephen, Henry, etc*., iv. 209–10 quoted by Round.

19 £1816 0*s*. 3*d*. and £6440 7*s*. 0½*d*. respectively, cf. Table B.

20 The one great annual total of almost £4000 for 1189–90 falls within Longchamp's period of power. Of this exceptional total some three-quarters were spent on the Tower of London. That Longchamp himself was responsible for this great work at the Tower is suggested not only by the incidence of the expenditure in the Pipe Rolls, but also by the fact that the chancellor had the custody of it and is reported by the chroniclers to have caused work to be done there. It was in the Tower that Longchamp shut himself in the final crisis in 1191 (cf. *Gesta*, Rolls Series, ii. 101, 106, 212–13).

£100. Of these twenty-six, nine – Corfe,[21] Hanley, Harestan (in Horsley, Derbs.), Kenilworth, Knaresborough, Lancaster, Odiham, Scarborough, and probably Norham – each received over £500. Upon each of the four castles of Kenilworth, Knaresborough, Odiham and Scarborough John spent over £1000, and the total figure for Scarborough is over £2000.[22] These figures, taken from the Pipe Rolls and owing nothing to the new record sources of the reign, may to that extent be fairly compared with those of John's two predecessors. No doubt the increased level of expenditure is due in part to the rising prices of this whole period. To some extent also inherited castles were a liability as well as an asset, though here it must be noted that many of John's largest works, at Corfe, Hanley, Hareston, Knaresborough, Lancaster and elsewhere, were undertaken at places which had received little attention from his father. Even at Dover, upon which Henry had spent so much, we can scarcely regard John's additional outlay of some £1000 as representing merely the necessary maintenance of an existing fabric. At least it is fair to say that John rivalled his father as a castle-builder, and this building, which has hitherto received insufficient attention, is the more remarkable in that he was the heir to Henry's military works.

To consider briefly the geographical distribution of the castle-building of the period, we may divide the kingdom into four regions: the three 'frontier' districts of the south-east coast and the northern and western marches, and the interior. The castles of the south-east coastal district, which served as a defence against possible invasion, as a protection of essential communications, and as bases for continental expeditions, received considerable attention. This area indeed claimed the greatest English building operation of the period, the rebuilding of the great fortress at Dover, which absorbed nearly £7000 between 1179 and 1191. Most of this work was accomplished during Henry's reign. Although this expenditure at Dover is quite without parallel, building and maintenance were also carried out at other castles in the south-east. During Henry's reign sums of over £428 were spent upon Chilham, over £339 upon Arundel, over £150 upon Rochester (which already possessed its great tower keep) and over £100 upon Canterbury. Under Richard, besides some £725 spent upon Dover, over £175 were spent upon Canterbury, and over £160 upon Southampton castle, which guarded the principal port for the Norman passage. In John's reign some £132 were spent upon Rochester, £347 upon Southampton (much of it, perhaps significantly, after the loss of Normandy), and at Dover still further extensive work was carried out at very heavy cost.

In the north, upon castles which must be presumed to have stood at least in part for defence or offence against the Scot, Henry II again led the way. The major operations of his reign begin with works at Scarborough[23] and at Wark, upon which fortresses he spent in the course of the reign some £682 and £382

21 The total expenditure by John at Corfe is brought up to well over £1000 when the expenditure recorded on the *Misae* and Close Rolls is added to that of the Pipe Rolls. Cf. Table B. At Dover also the Pipe Roll total is just under £500, but the grand total well over £1000.

22 £2291 3*s*. 4*d*.

23 Cf. William of Newburgh (Rolls Series), *Chrons. Stephen, Henry II, etc*., i. p. 104. The castle Henry had acquired from the earl of Yorkshire.

respectively. In addition, he spent over £1144 upon Newcastle-on-Tyne, much of it upon the *turris* or square keep which still stands, some £616 upon the similar tower at Bowes in the Honor of Richmond, and some £138 upon Richmond castle itself when in Crown hands. Under Richard there was no considerable expenditure upon northern castles, save some £247 upon York, mostly in the early years of the reign, which probably finds an immediate cause in the damage suffered by that castle in the anti-Jewish riots in 1190.[24] Under John expenditure upon castles in the north was strikingly heavy, especially upon Knaresborough, Scarborough, Lancaster, and Norham. But since this building was almost certainly due not only to considerations of Scottish relations, but also as much if not more to considerations of internal security, it is more appropriately dealt with in detail in another place.[25]

For the Welsh Marches a more easily defined group of castles enables us to be more explicit in the matter of proportional expenditure.[26] In Henry's reign some £1400[27] was spent upon Welsh castles, or about one-fifteenth of the total for the kingdom of some £21,500: under Richard some £458,[28] or again about one-fifteenth of the total of some £7146, and under John some £1700,[29] about one-tenth of the total of some £17,000. The principal castles at which work was carried out are the base castles of Bristol, Gloucester, Worcester, Hereford, St. Briavel's, Shrewsbury, and Bridgenorth, and to these John's new castle of Hanley in Worcestershire should presumably be added. The largest expenditures are those of Henry II at Bridgenorth (*c.* £320) and Gloucester (*c.* £230), and of John at Hanley (*c.* £710).[30] But there are no great expenditures here like those upon Dover, Newcastle, Orford or Scarborough, and so far as the figures are reliable it appears that the building and repair of Marcher castles in this period were not a severe burden upon the Exchequer.[31]

When every allowance has been made for building expenditure upon frontier castles, a great part, probably the major part, of the overall expenditure remains devoted to castles of the interior. Up and down the land there was a continuous expenditure upon the building, strengthening and repair of castles which could have had little or no connexion with defence or attack against an external enemy. Henry's expenditure upon Nottingham, Windsor and Winchester, Longchamp's expenditure upon the Tower, or John's expenditure upon Odiham, Kenilworth, Corfe and Harestan[32] are only outstanding examples of a general

24 *Gesta* (Rolls Series), ii. 107; Hoveden (Rolls Series), iii. 33–4; cf. *P.R. 2 Richard I*, pp. 58, 75.

25 See below.

26 In the following calculations the base castles of Bristol, Chester, Gloucester, Hereford, Shrewsbury, and Worcester have been included, as well as the more exposed castles of the interior.

27 £1434 1*s.* 8*d.*

28 £458 19*s.* 4½*d.*

29 This total, £1715 17*s.* 11½*d.* taken from the Pipe Rolls alone, includes the £644 0*s.* 5*d.* spent upon Hanley castle in Worcestershire. Upon Hanley the *Misae* Rolls record a further £66 13*s.* 4*d.*, bringing the figure for this castle to £710 13*s.* 9*d.* Cf. Table B.

30 Cf. n. 4 above.

31 It is possible that the available figures for the Welsh Marches are less complete than those for other less disturbed regions. On the whole, however, this low royal expenditure reflects the very high proportion of baronial castles in this heavily fortified district.

32 In Horsley, Derbyshire.

feature of the period. It is here, therefore, that the military side of Angevin government is perhaps most clearly apparent. Expenditure upon castle-building, it is true, is not wholly military. Royal castles played their part in the normal central administration of the kingdom, as provincial treasuries[33] or as prisons, and as the official residences of sheriffs and bailiffs were often the centres of local government. They also served frequently as royal residences, for the king's itinerary was based upon them no less than upon his civil lodgings. Some of the more favoured castles of the interior, Windsor, Winchester, and Nottingham, throughout the period, and Corfe in John's reign, were visited as frequently as such favourite civil residences as Woodstock or Clarendon.[34] In consequence, upon the residential parts of such favoured castles, in particular, considerable sums were spent during the period.[35] But these secondary functions of the castle, administrative or residential, themselves largely resulted from its military strength, and it is in practice extremely difficult to distinguish architecturally between the one rôle and the other. The keep itself might serve both as a strongpoint and a residence, or be regarded as a place suitable for the safe-custody of prisoners or treasure. So far as we are able to compute it, expenditure upon specifically residential or administrative buildings within the castle seldom amounts to more than a fraction of the whole, and certainly both from written and archaeological evidence there is no reason to suppose that the non-military functions of the castle at this period detracted from its efficiency as a fortress.[36] The political implications of this extensive castle-building in the interior therefore deserve consideration.

The political significance of castle-building is clearly shown by the fluctuation of building expenditure in relation to immediate political events. Thus expenditure upon frontier castles is visibly higher at times of external threat. The seriousness of the war in south Wales in the last years of Henry's reign is reflected by the increased expenditure in those years upon the castles of the

[33] Cf. J. E. A. Jolige, 'The Chamber and the Castle Treasuries under King John', in *Studies in Medieval History presented to F. M. Powicke*, pp. 117–42.

[34] Throughout this period extensive building was carried out at these civil residences, the *domus Regis* of the records, e.g. *P.R. 23 Henry II*, p. 57, 'Et in operatione domorum regis de Clipeston' et vivariorum cc et x li'; cf. *ibid.* pp. 11, 12, 16, 26, 57, 100–3, 192.

[35] Cf. Round, *Introduction* to *P.R. 33 Henry II*, p. xxxix.

[36] The practical difficulty of distinguishing architecturally between the military and non-military functions of the castle is increased by the nature of the evidence, which seldom provides detailed descriptions of the work in hand. The following rough test, however, is of significance. Throughout this period the term *domus (Regis) in castello* is used to describe the miscellaneous buildings within the castle, not only such 'domestic' apartments as hall and chambers, but also the chapel, kitchens, storehouses, stables and other buildings of general utility. Yet if in the cases of Winchester, Windsor, and Nottingham, castles particularly favoured as residences, we add up all expenditure upon the *domus in castello* as well as that specifically stated to be upon domestic or administrative apartments, in the reign of Henry II, when such expenditure is in each case exceptionally heavy, the total amounts to only some third of the whole expenditure upon those castles in that period. The same test at John's favoured castle at Corfe in his reign provides the same result. Nor does the military efficiency of these castles appear to have been impaired. Nottingham and Windsor were of sufficient importance to be objects of contention between Count John and the Government of Richard's absence. The latter successfully withstood the siege of Prince Louis in 1216. (See Wendover in Matthew Paris, *Chron. Maj.* Rolls Series, ii. 664–5.) We have also a contemporary description of the strength of Nottingham for 1194 (William of Newburgh, Rolls Series, i. 407), 'Est autem idem castellum natura et manu ita munitum ut sola inedia, si defensores idoneos habeat, expugnabile videatur'.

affected area. The tables show considerable attention to Kenefig, Gloucester, and Llantilio (White Castle, Mon.) in 1185, and to Llantilio again in 1186, while the Pipe Roll of 1185 itself shows an expenditure upon Welsh castles heavier than for any other year of Henry's reign.[37] Similarly, in the years of Richard's absence and captivity, when the Government was faced with the imminent prospect of invasion from the continent, the lists show a marked attention to south-eastern castles, Canterbury, Southampton, Pevensey, Rochester, and Chilham,[38] which disappears after 1194 only to reappear with the appreciable expenditure upon Southampton and Rochester following the loss of Normandy.[39] Fluctuation of this kind is not confined to frontier areas. The tables show that the heaviest annual expenditures for the whole kingdom under Henry II fall in the years immediately preceding the rebellion of 1173–4, and this expenditure is disbursed upon a very large number of castles in all districts.[40] Similarly the contrast between the overall figures for the period of Richard's absence and the much reduced expenditure in the years of comparative security following his return is clearly apparent, and again the difference is certainly not due only to work upon frontier castles. Under John, also, the annual totals mount steadily towards the end of the reign and reach their recorded apex[41] in the period preceding and including the political crisis of 1212. Much of this fluctuation is likely to be caused by *ad hoc* repairs and maintenance to bring the necessary fortresses into an adequate state of defence, but we may also follow the relationship of building expenditure and immediate political developments further, into the more long-term processes of major building works. At least one example may be quoted of an entirely new fortress raised in response to a local political situation. It is tolerably certain from the context of events and the geographical position of the castle that Henry's new work at Orford was built to check the dangerous power of Hugh Bigod in Suffolk in general and to contain his castle at Framlingham in particular. At the beginning of our period, though Earl Hugh had the three strong castles of Bungay, Framlingham, and Walton, there were no royal castles in Suffolk until Henry obtained Eye and Haganet (Haughley) by escheat. After confiscating Walton in 1157, Henry began to build a new castle at Orford in 1166, while the earl strengthened his castle at Bungay by the addition of a square stone-keep. Orford was completed by the outbreak of the rebellion in 1173. In that rebellion Earl Hugh played a leading part. His defeat was followed by the confiscation of his remaining castles at Bungay and Framlingham and the demolition of the latter, if not of both.[42] Thus in twenty years the military and political situation in Suffolk, expressed in terms of

37 Distributed, in addition to the three castles mentioned above, upon Chepstow, Cardiff, Neath, Shrewsbury, Bristol, and 'Novus Burgus' (*P.R. 31 Henry II*, pp. 5–10, 127, 155). For Novus Burgus Round suggested Newton Nottage; Newport, Mon., is a more likely identification.

38 See Table A for 1191–92, 1192–93, 1193–94.

39 *Ibid.* 1203–4 and 1205–6 respectively.

40 The contrast between these figures and those which precede and follow is the more remarkable when it is noticed that the heavy annual totals at the end of the reign are chiefly due to the construction of the single castle of Dover.

41 It must be noted that the Pipe Roll of 15 John is missing.

42 The Pipe Rolls show the demolition of Framlingham and also of the previously confiscated Walton (*P.R. 21 Henry II*, p. 108; *P.R. 22 Henry II*, p. 60). They make no mention of Bungay. The *Gesta s.a.*

castles, had been entirely reversed.[43] It is also at this point that we may note the outstanding expenditure upon northern castles, representing major building operations, under King John.[44] Expenditure in the north is high throughout the reign,[45] but becomes most striking in the later years. In 1210–11 the northern total from the Pipe Roll is well over £1300 out of a total for the whole kingdom of some £2892, and in 1211–12 £1396 16*s*. 5½*d*. out of a total of just over £2200. In the later years of the reign especially, very great sums were lavished upon the castles of Scarborough, Knaresborough, Lancaster, and Norham. Upon both Scarborough and Knaresborough John spent, indeed, total sums greater than upon any other castle during his reign.[46] Any consideration of the causes of castle-building in the northern half of the kingdom must take Scottish relations into account. Even so, this scale of fortification provides a hard factual confirmation of the chroniclers' general assertions of northern leadership in the baronial opposition to King John.

Angevin castle-building in England during this period, seen against the disorders of Stephen's reign, represents the latent military power of a strong centralized government, no less necessary to its success than its other assets of economic superiority and administrative efficiency. Committed to the keeping of trusted officials, often the centres of local government, at all times an impressive display of regal power, and ready in time of emergency to be rapidly stocked and garrisoned to encourage and enforce the loyalty of surrounding districts, the royal castles were, in the expressive phrase of a contemporary writer, 'the bones of the kingdom'.[47] But in addition to such a positive interpretation, this castle-building is capable, as it were, of a more negative rendering.

It must be seen not only against the background of past disorders, but also against the background of the rebellion of 1173–4, the rumblings of discontent and disorder in 1199, the political crisis of 1212 and the final civil war of 1215. If, on the one hand, the building and maintenance of castles, by its tangible results and resources it implies, is a measure of a medieval Government's strength, it may also at times serve as an indication of insecurity, and it is difficult to dissociate the heavy building expenditure of King John at least from the mounting political tension of his reign.[48]

One general feature of Angevin building in this period is at once apparent. By far the greater part is devoted not to the raising of new castles, but to the improvement of those already existing. Into this category of operation fall not

1176 lists Bungay as destroyed with Framlingham but 'Bungeia' seems to be a later addition (Rolls Series, i. 127).

43 For details of these events see 'Framlingham Castle and Bigod 1154–1216' by the present writer in *Proc. Suffolk Arch. Inst*., vol. xxv, pt. 2.

44 See above.

45 E.g. *c*. £500 out of a total for the kingdom of *c*. £770 in 1199–1200; *c*. £280 out of *c*. £860 in 1203–4 (Pipe Roll figures). Northern castles have been reckoned here as those north of a line drawn laterally across the kingdom from the most westerly point of the Wash. The castles of the northern Welsh marches have, however, been excluded.

46 See Table B (Pipe Roll figures).

47 William of Newburgh, Rolls Series, i. 331.

48 Cf. Sidney Painter, *The Reign of King John* (Baltimore, 1949), p. 265, where part of this expenditure is noted and its significance observed.

only the continuous small-scale works of maintenance and repair during these years, but also the majority of the greater works, at Newcastle-on-Tyne, Nottingham, Scarborough, Windsor, and Winchester under Henry II, the Tower under Longchamp, and Corfe, Harestan, Kenilworth, Knaresborough, Lancaster, Norham, and Scarborough under John. Even Henry's great undertaking at Dover was in reality the rebuilding of a previously existing fortress. New castles in the sense of entirely new structures on a site hitherto unfortified, Orford[49] and Bowes[50] in Henry's reign, St Michael's Mount under Richard,[51] Odiham and Hanley,[52] and probably Sauvey,[53] in the reign of John, are rare and exceptional. The great majority of English castles were founded in an earlier age. The twelfth century as a whole saw probably a reduction rather than an increase in their overall number. It was the improvement of existing fortresses in accordance with advancing techniques in military architecture that principally occupied the attention of the Crown in this period. Moreover, this feature of the building of 1154–1216 we may expect to be continued in the centuries which follow and the building of new castles in the strict sense to be increasingly confined to the acquisition of new territory – precisely the cause which raised the Edwardian castles in Wales. The typical castle, like the typical cathedral, is the composite product of the expanding needs and skills of successive generations. The Edwar-

49 For Orford see Redstone, *Proc. Suffolk Inst. Arch*. x. 205 and *ibid.* xxv. 127; cf. elsewhere in this article, and Table B.

50 For Bowes see G. T. Clark, *Medieval Military Architecture in England* (1884), i. 259 and *Yorks. Arch. and Topog. Journ*. vii. On archaeological grounds the tower is held to be the work of both Conan le Petit and Henry II (*ibid.* xxii. 413). Cf. Hamilton Thompson, *Military Architecture in England* (Wakefield, 1975), p. 312; cf. Table B below.

51 At St Michael's Mount the site was first fortified by Henry de Pomeroy during Richard's absence and later taken over by the Crown. See Charles Oman, *Castles* (London, 1926), pp. 118–19; Hoveden, Rolls Series, iii. 237–8, 249; *P.R. 6 John*, p. 40; *Rot. Litt. Pat*. p. 41*b*.

52 For Odiham see *V.C.H. Hamps*. iv. 88 *sqq*., cf. p. 366 below and Table B. For Hanley see *V.C.H. Worcs*. iv. 93–4, cf. p. 366 below and Table B. At Odiham most, and at Hanley all, of the recorded building expenditure is described as 'in operatione *domorum* Regis' (e.g. *P.R. 10 John*, p. 61; *P.R. 12 John*, pp. 169–70 ; *Rot. Litt. Claus.* i. 86; *Rot Misae 11 John*, pp. 121, 128–9). Yet Odiham is described as a castle in contemporary official records, was used as a castle and its remains are those of a castle (*RLC* i. 142, 266*b*; *RLP* pp. 156*b*, 178; *Cal. Chart. Rolls*, i. 209; Wendover in Matthew Paris, *Chron. Maj*. Rolls Series, ii. 655; *V.C.H. ut supra*). At Hanley no remains exist save the line of the moat (*V.C.H. ut supra*) but the building is described as a castle on contemporary and near-contemporary records and played some part in the civil war (*RLC* i. 211*b*; *RLP* p. 162; *Rot. Hund.* ii. 283, 285*b*). The most likely explanation of the anomaly is the ambiguity of the word *domus*, used in this period for such civil residences as Clipston or Woodstock (cf. above n. 1), for the 'houses in the castle' (cf. above n. 3); and at times as a synonym for the castle itself (e.g. *RLP* 188*b*, Wolvesy). *Castrum* or *castellum*, on the other hand, are seldom if ever consciously applied by official sources to buildings not heavily fortified. Both Odiham and Hanley are treated here for practical purposes as castles. We may note, however, that the distinction between the castle and the civil residence was not always clear in this period and the fortified manor house not unknown.

53 No mention of the castle of Sauvey (Leics.) has been found before 1211, in which year the Pipe Roll records the very large sum of £442 13*s*. 1*d*. spent 'in operatione castri et viuarii de Sauueie et domorum in castro' (entered upon Hugh de Neville's account for Marlborough and other manors for three years; see *P.R. 13 John*, p. 84). No further building expenditure is known, but Sauvey is subsequently mentioned continually as a royal castle (e.g. *RLP* pp. 135*b*, 149, 167; *RLC*. i. 286, etc.). King John about this time acquired by exchange the forest of Sauvey from Reginald de Welleford (*ibid.* p. 149n), and it is probable that he then built the castle, which from recorded expenditure at least seems to have been a minor one. The *V.C.H. Leics*. (i. 249) reproduces a plan of the surviving earthworks at Sauvey, but entirely misinterprets them.

dian castles in Wales were exceptional in being new castles in the strict sense, raised in one concentrated operation, and this fact must be remembered if the estimates of their cost and the labour which produced them now made available are to be used as 'standards of reference' for other castles elsewhere.[54]

There is little doubt that in the history of military architecture the heavy building expenditure and continuous works of the Crown between 1154 and 1216 represent in great part the transition of the castle from the 'motte-and-bailey' stronghold of earthwork and timber to the familiar fortress of stone – a transition which, though by no means confined to this period, was largely concentrated within it.[55] Though the architectural development of the castle is not here our concern, we may notice the main features of the contemporary stone fortress, keep, walled bailey, and the miscellaneous buildings within the bailey, as they are revealed by occasional details in the records and surviving archaeological evidence. The keep, whether shell or tower, dominates the whole, and outstanding examples of the latter, the classic feature of the twelfth-century castle, are Henry's great square tower keeps at Dover[56] and Newcastle[57] and the same king's polygonal tower keep at Orford.[58] No great English examples are known for John's reign, but a writ of August 1204,[59] authorizing the Justiciar of Ireland to raise a new castle at Dublin, shows that the keep was then still regarded as the principal defence of the fortress and the focal point of its design. Part of the text of this writ, indeed, is an interesting exposition of both the process and motives of castle-building: 'uobis mandamus quod ibidem castellum fieri faciatis in loco competenti ubi melius esse uideritis ad urbem justiciandam et si opus fuerit defendendam quam fortissimum poteritis, cum bonis fossatis et fortibus muris, turrim autem primum faciatis ubi postea competencius castellum et baluum et alia procinctoria fieri possint'. We hear also of the fosse at Tickhill[60] and at Corfe,[61] and of the bailey walls at Gloucester[62] and at Windsor.[63] At Dover the stone wall of Henry's (now inner) bailey already incorporated mural towers,[64] a development which was later to revolutionize the whole design of the castle by rendering the keep unnecessary. At Worcester in 1204 the old wooden gateway of the castle was replaced by one

54 Cf. Edwards, *loc. cit.* p. 65. At Builth and at Carnarvon earlier castles had existed. With the probable exception of the earthworks at Builth, however, they were not incorporated in the Edwardian structures which remain essentially fortresses built *de novo* in one operation.

55 Cf. Hamilton Thompson, *op. cit.* p. 89. Examples of stone fortification can be found from the earliest days of the English castle, notably in the great keeps of the Tower of London and Colchester, but they are exceptional.

56 See Clark, *op. cit.* ii. 16–24 for a detailed but misdated archaeological description; cf. T. Blashill, *Journ. BAA* xl; cf. e.g. *P.R. 28 Henry II*, pp. 150–55; *P.R. 30 Henry II*, p. 144.

57 See e.g. Sidney Toy, *The Castles of Great Britain* (London, 1953), pp. 96–9. Cf. e.g. *P.R. 19 Henry II*, p. 110; *P.R. 21 Henry II*, pp. 183–4.

58 E.g. Hamilton Thompson, *op. cit.* pp. 165–6. For a list of keeps both shell and tower, attributed to Henry II from the evidence of the Pipe Rolls, see Mrs Armitage, *Early Norman Castles of the British Isles* (London, 1912), p. 366.

59 *RLC* i. 6*b*.

60 *Rot. Mis. 11 John*, p. 116.

61 *RLC* i. 178*b*.

62 *P.R. 3 John*, p. 40; cf. *Rot. Lib.* p. 12.

63 E.g. *P.R. 18 Henry II*, p. 16; *P.R. 19 Henry II*, p. 68.

64 See e.g. *Castles from the Air* (Country Life, ed. Douglas Simpson); no. 57.

of stone.[65] Expenditure upon the miscellaneous buildings within the bailey,[66] the *domur in castello*, is, as we have seen,[67] continuous and considerable. Sometimes on the records specific mention occurs of the purchase and transport of the stone for which the demand must have been so great. Squared stone is brought to Windsor in 1166,[68] and three hundred *lapides excisi* purchased for the same castle in 1172.[69] Ten cart-loads of lime are carried to Marlborough in 1194,[70] and stone is required for York in 1204[71] and for Exeter in 1208.[72] At the same time simpler and older (and also cheaper) forms of fortification survive and are continued. Launceston appears to have remained an undeveloped 'motte-and-bailey' castle of earthworks and timber throughout the period.[73] Palisades are mentioned at Norwich[74] and at Newcastle-under-Lyme[75] and are employed for the outer defences of the new castle at Orford.[76] John in 1204 provided for the repair of *castrorum nostrorum ligneorum* in Shropshire.[77] In time of war, also, the ancient sites of abandoned but almost indestructible 'motte-and-bailey' castles might be brought into use again, as Mowbray refortified Kinardferry in the island of Axholme in 1173,[78] or new strongholds of bank and ditch be hastily thrown up, as the rebels raised their *munitiunculas* in 1215.[79]

The general nature of Angevin building between 1154 and 1216, namely the improvement of existing fortification, makes it impossible to provide any estimates of the cost of the contemporary castle or the time taken to build it save in the exceptional cases of those castles built *de novo*. The estimates in those few cases are worth setting down for their own interest and for comparison with those available for the Edwardian castles a century later. Building costs are also useful as a rough guide to comparative strength, while any contemporary figures for the cost of the completed new castle are valuable for measuring the importance of those works at existing castles which are the principal feature of this period.

Of the six new castles mentioned above we have no record of the work at St Michael's Mount, and Henry II's expenditure at Bowes represents only the completion and not the entire building of the tower.[80] For Sauvey we have only the

65 *Rot. Lib.* p. 93; cf. *P.R. 6 John*, p. 88.
66 Or within the keep also in the case of shell keeps. Cf. *Castles from the Air (ut supra)*, no. 102, Restormel.
67 Above n. 3.
68 *P.R. 12 Henry II*, p. 116.
69 *P.R. 18 Henry II*, p. 141.
70 *P.R. 6 Richard I*, p. 211.
71 *RLC* i. 4*b*.
72 *P.R. 10 John*, p. 63.
73 Cf. Mrs Armitage, *op. cit.* p. 164. The castle came to the Crown on the death of Earl Reginald of Cornwall in 1175 (*Complete Peerage, G.E.C.* iii. 429; cf. *P.R. 22 Henry II*, pp. 151, 152–3).
74 *P.R, 19 Henry II*, p. 117.
75 *P.R. 2 Richard I*, p. 15.
76 *P.R. 19 Henry II*, p. 116.
77 *RLC* i. 17.
78 Diceto (Rolls Series), i. 379.
79 Coventry (Rolls Series), ii. 222.
80 Cf. n. 3.

recorded expenditure of some £400 on the Pipe Roll of 1211. To the remainder, Orford, Odiham, and Hanley, Dover may for practical purposes be added, for it is clear that the great work undertaken by Henry and completed in Richard's reign, consisting of the present keep and the walls of the inner bailey, comprised the complete rebuilding of the castles.[81] Here at Dover it is clear from the figures printed in Table B that the work was carried out between 1180 and 1191, with the greatest concentration of effort in the years 1184–6. If for purposes of calculation we assume that the Pipe Roll of any given Michaelmas records the cost of building in the season immediately preceding, then the rebuilding of Dover occupied some twelve seasons.[82] The total recorded cost of this operation from the Pipe Rolls amounts to £6589 9*s.* 5½*d.*, or in round figures some £7000.[83] In the recorded expenditure upon building in England during the period there is no parallel to this figure, and we may safely assume that the new fortress at Dover, the key of the kingdom,[84] was exceptional in its military strength. At Orford the work occupied the years 1166–73, or some eight seasons. Its completion, perhaps hastened by the outbreak of rebellion, is presumably marked by the construction in the latter year of the 'great fosse round the castle of Orford with palisades and brattices'.[85] The total recorded cost from the Pipe Rolls (1166–73) amounts to £1413 9*s.* 2*d.* From its existing remains, and perhaps also from the fact that it does not seem to have been attacked by Hugh Bigod and his allies in 1173–4, it appears that the contemporary strength of Orford was considerable. It is interesting to compare this Orford figure with the Pipe Roll figure (1207–12) of just under £1100[86] for John's new castle of Odiham, completed in some six seasons. Again, by Matthew Paris's account of the siege of 1216,[87] Odiham was a castle of considerable contemporary strength. Hanley, apparently a lesser castle, was completed in the same six seasons, 1207–12, at a cost from the Pipe Rolls of £644 0*s.* 5*d.*[88] These figures are certainly incomplete, and as a measure of building time we have for the most part only the curve of expenditure as shown by an annual record. However, from them it would seem that though a fortress of the first order might cost more than £7000, a medium castle of reasonable strength might be built for less than £2000.

To set beside the few recorded instances of the building of new castles in England we have one example of a contemporary continental castle for which

81 See especially T. Blashill, *Journ. BAA* xl. 373–8. This excellent account, though based almost entirely upon archaeological evidence alone, is completely supported and confirmed by the recorded evidence. Cf. also Clark, *op. cit.* ii. 13.

82 Though no direct evidence has been found, it may be assumed that building was largely confined to the summer months and that the (summer) season rather than the year is the true measure of building time in this period as it is under Edward I. Cf. Edwards, *loc. cit.* pp. 18–19.

83 This total includes direct expenditure from the Treasury exceptionally recorded on the Pipe Rolls (e.g. *P.R. 30 Henry II*, p. 150; cf. above p. 133, n. 4). The rebuilding of Dover did not prevent further heavy expenditure there by John (cf. Table B). Accounts of the siege of Dover in 1216 afford some indication of its contemporary strength. (cf. Blashill, *loc. cit.* p. 375).

84 'Clavis enim Anglia: est', Matthew Paris, *Chron. Maj.* (Rolls Series), iii. 28.

85 'Et in operatione j magni fossati circa castellum de Oreford cum hericiis et breteschiis, et in operatione pontis lapidei de eodem castello lviij li. et ij s. et viij d', *P.R. 19 Henry II*, p. 116.

86 £1099 4*s.* 9*d.* This figure is not accurate in respect of 1210 (see Table B). The *Misae* Roll of 11 John (p. 115) records a further £41. See Table B.

87 *Loc. cit.* ii. 655.

88 A further £100 is recorded on the *Misae* Roll of 11 John. See Table B.

the building account has survived. Richard's beloved Château-Gaillard on the Seine is generally held to be among the finest examples of late twelfth-century military architecture in the West.[89] Its cost, therefore, if known, setting aside the variable factors of the nature of the site, the availability of raw materials and the like, would be of value as a ceiling price for the contemporary castle. The account, which survives on the Norman Exchequer Roll for 1198, has every appearance of being reasonably completed[90] but unfortunately it covers the entire defensive system of Andeli. Detailed though it is we cannot separate expenditure upon the castle of Château-Gaillard itself from that upon the rest of the works.[91] The total figure amounts to some 45,000 *li*. Angevin, the equivalent in English money of rather less than £11,500.[92] Of this total the castle on the Rock, the crown of the whole position, would absorb the greater part, perhaps some £7000–£8000. Château-Gaillard was obviously an undertaking exceptional in its magnitude, and no contemporary castle can rival the speed with which it was completed,[93] but it is interesting to find that of English castles built at this time Dover, though Dover alone, can rival it in cost and perhaps therefore in strength.

The cost of Edward I's castles in Wales soars far above the general level of our period, and the speed with which they were in the main constructed, not singly but three and four at a time, can be compared only to the urgency with which Richard carried through his work at Andeli, built like them to meet an immediate military threat.[94] In part the high level of Edward's expenditure by

89 For descriptions of the building of Château-Gaillard see Kate Norgate, *England under the Angevin Kings* (London, 1887), ii. 377–81; F. M. Powicke, *The Loss of Normandy 1189–1204* (Manchester 1904), pp. 285 *sqq*., and the authorities there cited.

90 It is a separate building account (cf. above, n. 4), rendered by the officials concerned and distinct and separate from the normal accounts of bailiwicks: it brings together receipts from diverse sources including the central treasury and the Chamber: it is made up also for the two years in which the work appears to have been carried out. See *Mag. Rot. Scacc. Norm*. ed. Stapleton (Soc. Antiquaries, London 1840–4), ii. 309–10; the account is conveniently printed by Powicke, *op. cit*. pp. 303–5.

91 These included, *inter alia*, a separate fortress upon the island of Andeli (e.g. 'In operatione . . . castri de Insula et domorum Regis de Insula', *Mag. Rot. Scacc. Norm*. ii. 309) and a new fortified town on the river bank beneath the Rock, now Petit-Andeli.

92 Reckoned at 4 li. Angevin to £1.

93 Cf. William of Newburgh (Rolls Series), *Chrons. Stephen, Henry II*, etc., ii. 500.

94 Professor Edwards's estimates of time and cost for the Edwardian castles may be set out, though in bare summary only, in the following table. Estimates of time are taken from pp. 19–52 and the figures from pp. 61–3 and his Tables. A = castle; B = castle with fortified town.

		Period	*Recorded cost*				*Estimated cost*
			£.	*s.*	*d.*		
A	Builth	1277–82 = 6 seasons	1,666	9	5¼		
	Harlech	1283–9 = 7 seasons	8,184	10	9	(1285–92)	£ 9,000
			111,289	0	9	(1295–8)	£13,000
	Beaumaris	1295–1323	1,547	12	11¾	(1309–23)	
B	Aberystwyth	1277–89	13,888	0	11½		£ 7,000
	Flint	1277–81= 4½ seasons	7,021	13	7¾	(1277–86)	
	Rhuddlan	1277–81 = 4½ seasons	9,505	15	9¼	(1277–85)	
	Conway	1283–7 = 5 seasons	13,689	15	6½	(1283–92)	£19,000
			12,285	18	7¼	(1284–1301)	£16,000
	Carnarvon	1283–1323	3,497	14	11½	(1304–23)	

twelfth-century standards, £80,000 in twenty-five years upon eight castles,[95] must be set against the rising prices in the thirteenth century. Also the available figures for this expenditure, though incomplete, are likely to be less so than those for 1154–1216. Again, five of these castles, including the two greatest, were combined with fortified towns. Even so the great cost of Conway, Carnarvon, and Beaumaris is clearly the price of the change in the whole conception and design of the castle in the thirteenth century. As their grandiose remains amply testify, no English castle of our period could rival the strength of these triumphs of Edwardian engineering. Yet it remains interesting to observe that the cost of Dover, and on the continent of Château-Gaillard, mount well into the middle levels of Edward's expenditure. It is also clear from the figures and estimates of both periods that those English castles already existing, and in many cases already strong, in 1154, upon which Henry and his sons spent sums of £1000, £2000 and more[96] – the Tower of London (£3977 8*s*. 0*d*.), Scarborough (£2906 11*s*. 9*d*.), Nottingham (*c*. £2000), Windsor (£1830 19*s*. 1½*d*.), Winchester (£1618 10*s*. 0*d*.), Newcastle-on-Tyne (£1144 5*s*. 6*d*.),[97] Corfe (£1405 6*s*. 10*d*. from all sources)[98] and Kenilworth (£1115 3*s*. 11½*d*.)[98] – must have been placed in the first rank of contemporary fortresses.

The lack of detail in the available evidence for 1154–1216 prevents us from knowing the amount of labour employed upon castle-building and the cost of that labour. Professor Edwards has discussed this aspect of the Edwardian castles in great detail,[99] and on *a priori* grounds it seems safe to apply one of his conclusions to our period, namely, that wages account for some two-thirds of building costs.[100] Similarly, on the analogy of the striking figures for the Edwardian castles,[101] it is clear that the labour demand for such a work as Dover, or for such a year as 1211 when major operations were going forward concurrently at seven castles in the north and midlands alone,[102] must have been very great. That very large forces of (presumably) unskilled or semi-skilled labour were available and could be mobilized by the central government in the early thirteenth century is strikingly shown by a remarkable series of writs issued by John in July 1212 in preparation for his abortive Welsh expedition of that summer.[103] These mandates, sent out to a large number of counties and honours in all quarters of the realm, summoned to Chester 5500 *secures*[104] and 2130 *fossatores*, a

95 Edwards, *loc. cit.* pp. 62, 65.

96 The figures which follow, unless otherwise stated, are taken from the Pipe Rolls alone and are the totals for the whole period 1254–1216.

97 This expenditure all falls in the reign of Henry II.

98 This expenditure all falls in the reign of John.

99 *Op. cit.* pp. 53–61.

100 *Ibid.* p. 58 and n. 3.

101 *Ibid.* pp. 57–9. E.g. *c.* 2200–2700 employed at Conway, Carnarvon and Harlech in the three seasons 1285–6–7; *c.* 4000 at the same three castles in the seasons of 1283–4; *c.* 3500 at Carnarvon and Beaumaris in the season of 1295.

102 At Lancaster, Scarborough, Norham, Tynemouth, Knaresborough, Kenilworth, and Sauvey. Cf. Table A.

103 *RLC* i. 131 (dated 10 July 1212).

104 *Secures* presumably equals 'axe-men'. John, however, was particularly anxious to have men with a knowledge of carpentry – 'et quod plures inter eos sint qui se de carpentaria bene sciant intromittere' (*ibid.*).

total force of 7630 workmen. But we have no direct evidence to show how these provincial semi-skilled labour resources were applied to castle-building, or the precise numbers employed. What the records do reveal, however, is a comparatively small number of specialized individual craftsmen, continuously employed by the Crown and moving from one operation to another. From them also we may learn something of the types and grades of craftsmen who took part in Angevin military building.

The most important members of this specialized group are certain *ingeniatores*, who appear, by their title, activity, remuneration and status, to have occupied the top rank of their profession. Amongst these the first whose activities are at all extensively recorded is the well-known Alnoth the Engineer.[105] He first appears on the Pipe Roll of 1158 in receipt of £10 12*s*. 11*d*. for the custody of the royal palace of Westminster, which he retained to the end of his career.[106] Throughout Henry's reign he was continually employed on royal building. His activities were generally confined to London, sometimes at the Tower[107] and elsewhere, but most frequently at Westminster, so that Round's description of him as 'Henry's master of the works at Westminster' is justified.[108] He was occasionally concerned with building outside the capital, at Windsor,[109] for example, and at Woodstock,[110] and in 1175 journeyed into Suffolk with his carpenters and masons to demolish the Bigod castle of Framlingham.[111] Alnoth the Engineer appears for the last time on the records in 1190,[112] after an active career of more than thirty years. Another engineer employed by Henry II, to whom Round drew attention,[113] was Maurice Ingeniator, who was paid regularly at Dover, at the rate of 8*d*. and later 1*s*. a day, during the rebuilding of the castle.[114] A certain 'Mauricius *Cementarius*' also appears at Newcastle in 1175[115] during the opera-

105 Cf. Round, Introductions to *P.R.s 22 Henry II*, p. xxiij and *28 Henry II*, p. xxv; C. T. Clay, 'The Keepership of the Old Palace of Westminster', *ante*, vol. lix; A. L. Poole, *Domesday Book to Magna Carta* (Oxford, 1951), p. 260, n. 3, &c.

106 *P.R. 4 Henry II*, p. 113; (London account) 'Et in liberatione Ailnothi ingeniatoris qui custodit domos Regis x li. et xijs. et xjd.' The last payment occurs in 1189 (*P.R. 1 Richard I*, p. 224). For his custody of Westminster see C. T. Clay, *ut supra*.

107 *P.R. 20 Henry II*, pp. 8, 9; *P.R. 24 Henry II*, p. 128.

108 Introduction to *P.R. 28 Henry II*, p. xxv; cf. the too generous tribute of Poole, *loc. cit.* For Alnoth at Westminster, see e.g. *P.R. 15 Henry II*, p. 170, &c.

109 E.g. *P.R. 14 Henry II*, p. 1, 'Et in operatione domorum Regis do Windr' . . . per uisum Alnothi Ingeniatoris'. Building was almost invariably carried 'by the view' of law-worthy men. The essential function of the viewers was fiscal; at the Exchequer they swore that the accountant had spent the sum for which he claimed allowance in the manner in which he asserted. (*Dialogus*, Nelson, pp. 89–90; *Mem. Roll, 1 John*, P.R. Soc., new ser. 21, p. 68; cf. *Rot. Lib.* p. 28.) They should not be confused with the engineers and craftsmen occupied with the building itself (cf. Poole *loc. cit.*). It is clear from their callings sometimes given on the records that no technical knowledge was necessary (e.g. *P.R. 30 Henry II*, p. 95, a doctor and a parson; *P.R. 8 John*, p. 226, a cook). Occasionally, though no doubt conveniently, the work was viewed by a building technician as in the case of Alnoth cited, when it is reasonable to assume that such viewers supervised or were concerned in the work.

110 E.g. *P.R. 26 Henry II*, pp. 77. 123; cf. *P.R. 23 Henry II*, pp. 26, 192.

111 *P.R. 21 Henry II*, p. 108; cf. *P.R. 22 Henry II*, p. 60. He was also concerned with the destruction of the former Bigod castle of Walton, *ibid.*

112 *P.R. 2 Richard I*, p. 118.

113 Introduction to *P.R. 28 Henry II*, p. xxv.

114 *P.R. 28 Henry II*, p. 150; *P.R. 30 Henry II*, p. 144; *P.R. 31 Henry II*, p. 224; *P.R. 32 Henry II*, p. 186; *P.R. 33 Henry II*, p. 205.

115 *P.R. 21 Henry II*, p. 184.

tions there, and it seems very probable that this Maurice employed on Henry's new tower keep at Newcastle is the 'engineer' of the same name later employed on the greater work at Dover.

Probably more important a man, by the test of his recorded activities, than either Alnoth or Maurice, is a certain Master Elyas of Oxford, who has so far received little attention. He first appears as 'Elyas the Stonemason (*cementarius*) of Oxford', on the Oxfordshire account of 1187, in receipt of 50 marcs for work upon the king's houses in Oxford, presumably Beaumont.[116] In 1188 he received 30*s*. and 5*d*. (1*d*. per day) 'pro custodia domorum regis de Oxineforda',[117] and thus became like Alnoth the keeper of a royal palace. In the same year, in addition to payment for work at Beaumont he also received 100*s*. 'ad se sustentandum in seruitio Regis'.[118] The office of keeper of Beaumont and this annual grant he retained until 1200 and 1201 respectively,[119] at which time he was approaching the end of his career. At the beginning of the reign of Richard I some confusion appears in Elyas's affairs. On the Pipe Roll of 1190 he is paid, still as Elyas the Stonemason, for his custody of Beaumont for only half the financial year, and there is no record of his annual stipend.[120] On the Oxfordshire account of the following year neither payment is entered, though £10 is paid to 'Elyas the Carpenter' (*carpentarius*) on the Winchester account.[121] In 1192, however, the annual stipend and the custodian's salary, together with half a year's arrears in either case, are entered on the Oxfordshire account, but again to Elyas the Carpenter.[122] There seems no reasonable doubt that Elyas the Carpenter and Elyas the Stonemason are one and the same person. The arrears of 1191 do something to span the gap in the series of payments. It is unlikely that the same office and emoluments would be enjoyed by two men of the same not common name in so short a space of time. Further, in the years that follow we hear of Elyas the Carpenter,[123] Elyas of Oxford,[124] (Master) Elyas the Engineer,[125] and also on one further occasion of Elyas the Stonemason.[126] If the unity of Elyas be assumed, it is in the reign of Richard I that he is found to be most active. While Oxford remained his base, he was continually employed on building works throughout southern England. In 1192 he was in charge of the carpenters and others at work at Porchester castle.[127] In 1194 he brought up Richard's siege engines from London to the siege of Nottingham castle.[128] In

116 *P.R. 33 Henry II*, p. 45.
117 *P.R. 34 Henry II*, p. 149.
118 *Ibid.* p. 150.
119 *P.R. 2 John*, p. 21; cf. *ibid.* p. 26, 'Galfridus [*recte* Walterus] Buistard r.c. de x *m.* pro habendis domibus Regis de Oxon' in custodia cum liberatione assisa', and cf. *Rot. Chart.* p. 54. On *Pipe Roll 3 John* (p. 205) the last recorded payment of Elyas's annual 100*s*. stipend is entered for half the year only.
120 *P.R. 2 Richard I*, p. 10.
121 *P.R. 3 Richard I*, pp. 91, 99.
122 *P.R. 4 Richard I*, pp. 267–8.
123 E.g. above. Cf. *P.R. 6 Richard I*, pp. 88, 176.
124 E.g. *P.R. 7 Richard I*, p. 113.
125 E.g. *ibid.* p. 2; *P.R. 10 Richard I*, p. 167.
126 *P.R. 2 John*, p. 21.
127 *P.R. 4 Richard I*, p. 294.
128 *P.R. 6 Richard I*, p. 176.

1195 he was at work upon Rochester, Hastings, and Pevensey, in addition to working at Westminster palace[129] and supervising the repairs at Oxford castle and at Beaumont.[130] It is in this year also that he is first referred to as Master Elyas the Engineer.[131] In 1196 he is mentioned again at Hastings and Pevensey and as supervising work at Oxford castle and Beaumont.[132] In 1197 he was at the civil residence of Freemantle (Hants.), at Oxford, and at Marlborough,[133] in 1198 at Westminster,[134] and in 1199 at the Tower of London.[135] In 1200, however, the custody of Beaumont passed to Walter Buistard,[136] and the Pipe Roll of 1201 records the last instalment of his annual stipend.[137] The active career of Master Elyas of Oxford, nevertheless, continued into John's reign, for in 1200 he was at work at Oxford, the Tower of London, Porchester, and the royal hunting lodges in the New Forest.[138] The last discovered reference to him occurs on the Pipe Roll of 1203 where he is again paid for work at the Tower.[139]

In the remaining years of the period, though miscellaneous references are found to other engineers, to William Baard, or Baiard, *Ingeniator* at Nottingham in 1205,[140] to Fortinus *Ingeniator* at Colchester in 1204,[141] or to Master Albert *Ingeniator* who was paid (for work?) at Ramsey Abbey in 1207,[142] none of them by the test of their recorded activities appear to have attained the importance of Master Elyas or Alnoth. The more numerous records of John's reign, however, do show a small group of lesser men, master craftsmen and craftsmen, also regularly or frequently employed by the Crown in building operations. Thus a certain Master Nicholas the Carpenter, or Nicholas de Andeli,[143] appears continuously on the central records between 1207 and 1215. He was paid for work at the king's houses at Finmere in 1207 and at Gloucester in the same year.[144] In 1210 he was in charge of carpenters working at Knepp Castle in Sussex in the spring, and later he was among the carpenters and other artificers accompanying King John on his Irish expedition.[145] In 1212 he appears with two carpenters under him on his way to work at Cambridge Castle.[146] He was also employed at times on the construction of siege engines, as for example at Knepp Castle in

129 *P.R. 7 Richard I*, pp. 2, 113, 240.
130 *Ibid.* p. 142.
131 *P.R. 7 Richard I*, p. 2.
132 *C.R. 8 Richard I*, pp. 20, 70, 81.
133 *P.R. 9 Richard I*, pp. 17, 34, 216.
134 *P.R. 10 Richard I*, p. 167.
135 *P.R. 1 John*, p. 129.
136 Cf. above n. 9.
137 *P.R. 3 John*, p. 205.
138 *P.R. 2 John*, pp. 21, 149, 191.
139 *P.R. 5 John*, p. 9.
140 *P.R. 7 John*, p. 221. For the considerable building expenditure at Nottingham in this year see Table B.
141 *P.R. 6 John*, p. 46.
142 *P.R. 9 John*, p. 111. Cf. *RLC* i. 76, 95*b*, 290.
143 (Master) Nicholas of Andeli was certainly a carpenter (e.g. *RLC* i. 80; *P.R. 17 John*, *Rot.* 1, *mem.* i) and it appears safe to identify him with the Master Nicholas the Carpenter of, e.g., *RLC* i. 97.
144 *Ibid.* pp. 80, 97.
145 *Rot. Misae 11 John*, p. 155; *Rot. Prest. 12 John* (ed. Hardy, *Rot. de Lib* . . . &c.), pp. 195, 196, 206, 226.
146 *Rot. Misae 14 John*, p. 232.

1212,[147] at Nottingham in 1214,[148] and at Knaresborough in 1215.[149] In November 1215, he received a grant of land from the king and was then specifically described as a king's carpenter, 'Magister Nicholaus Carpentarius domini Regis'.[150] A second category of master-craftsmen is represented by Master Pinellus the miner (*minator*) who is found with his miners at work upon the vaults at Dover Castle in 1205,[151] at Corfe in 1207,[152] and is paid with his men for further unspecified work on the Nottinghamshire and Derbyshire account of the Pipe Roll of 1214.[153] He too, with a company of miners went with the king to Ireland in 1210.[154] Again, Master Osbert *petrarius* was at Gloucester in 1207,[155] is mentioned in the early months of 1210 with three men under him on his way first to London and then to Corfe,[156] and later in the same year took part in the Irish expedition.[157] This Master Osbert *petrarius* is presumably to be identified also with the Osbert *quareator* who with four *guareatores* under him worked upon the fosse at Knaresborough in 1208.[158] In addition to these master craftsmen, a small number of ordinary craftsmen working under them are also mentioned by name upon the central records and are found at one building operation after another. Thus Hugh de Barentin, a carpenter, was working under Master Nicholas the Carpenter at Finmere and at Gloucester in 1207,[159] was in Master Nicholas's company of five carpenters in Ireland in 1210,[160] and was engaged in the making of siege engines, again under Master Nicholas, at Knaresborough Castle in 1215.[161] A certain Falkes de Bardonville was at Gloucester under Master Osbert *petrarius* in 1207, at Knaresborough among the *quareatores* under Osbert *quareator* in 1208, served in the Irish expedition in the same Master Osbert's company of *petrarii* in 1210, and in 1214 was among the small company of *petrarii* at work on the fosse at Corfe – this time apparently under a Master Albert.[162] Similarly, Peter the Poitevin is found with Master Osbert's *quareatores* at Knaresborough in 1208, with his company of *petrarii* in Ireland, and also among the *petrarii* at Corfe in 1214.[163]

The central records thus refer to engineers, to *cementarii* or stonemasons,

147 *Ibid.* p. 233.
148 *P.R. 16 John*, *Rot.* 15, *mem.* j.
149 *P.R. 17 John*, *Rot.* 1, *mem.* j.
150 *RLC* i. 239.
151 *Ibid.* p. 42.
152 *Ibid.* p. 78.
153 *P.R. 16 John*, *Rot.* 15, *mem.* j.
154 *Rot. Prest. 12 John* (*loc. cit.*), pp. 195, 196, 206, 226–7.
155 *RLC* i. 97. He appears simply as Osbert *petrarius*, but is distinguished from the ordinary craftsmen by being listed with other masters present, including Master Nicholas the Carpenter, paid at a higher rate. See below.
156 *Rot. Misae 11 John*, pp. 146, 155. Here, as in the Irish references below (n. 15), he is specifically 'Magister Osbertus (petrarius)'.
157 *Rot. Prest. 12 John*, pp. 195, 196, 206, 209, 226.
158 *RLC* i. 107; *P.R. 10 John*, p. 50; cf. below p. 134, n. 6.
159 *RLC* i. 80, 97.
160 *Rot. Prest. 12 John*, p. 195; cf. pp. 196, 226.
161 *P.R. 17 John, Rot.* 1, *mem.* j.
162 *RLC* i. 97, 107, 178*b*; *Rot. Prest. 12 John*, p. 195; cf. pp. 196, 206, 226.
163 *RLC* i, 107, 178*b*: *Rot. Prest. 12 John*, *ut supra*.

petrarii and *quareatores*, the cutters of stone and quarry-men,[164] to *carpentarii*, and to *minatores* and *fossatores*, who work upon the moat, vaults or foundations of the castle, or upon mines and siege works. In addition, we have the *secures* or axe-men of 1212,[165] the pick-men who were employed in demolition in 1214,[166] and the detailed Château-Gaillard account adds to the list 'talliatores petre ad muros faciendos' and *reatores* or lime-workers, over and above its references to wood-men, smiths and the porters of timber and stone.[167] Most of these men were employed on field campaigns as well as on building works,[168] and the engineers and carpenters were also engaged on the construction and operation of engines of war.[169] In several cases, as with Master Nicholas of Andeli and Peter the Poitevin, the names of these craftsmen on the English records suggest a foreign origin. In remuneration, the engineers received the most liberal maintenance as befitted their status. Master Elyas of Oxford had his annual 'gift' of 100*s*. and his wages of 1*d*. a day as custodian of Beaumont in addition to any payment for work done. Alnoth had the custody of Westminster palace, to which pertained the high salary of 7*d*. a day, and appears to have possessed land in Westminster.[170] Grants of land were made by the king to Master Albert and to Master Urric.[171] Maurice received 8*d*. a day at Dover in 1182 and thereafter 1*s*. The wages of the master craftsmen and craftsmen employed on royal building are at fairly uniform rates, though here also grants of land are found to favoured individuals.[172] The masters received generally 6*d*. a day,[173] while of the ordinary craftsmen the carpenters and *petrarii* received 4*d*. a day, the stone-masons, quarrymen and miners 3*d*.[174] These wages, current under John,[175] show a tendency to rise towards the end of the reign.[176] The evidence for the building organization of the period thus reveals a considerable degree of specialization, but its most interesting and complimentary feature is the centralization which it

164 The distinction between *petrarii* and *quareatores* is not clear. Master Osbert, Falkes de Bardonville and Peter the Poitevin all appear under both designations (above). On the other hand the *petrarius* received generally 4*d*. and the *quareator* 3*d*. a day (see below). But cf. Round, *King's Serjeants*, p. 16.

165 *RLC* i. 131 (see above).

166 Et in expensis Stephani de Oxenef' et duorum magistrorum piccatorum cum ix aliis ad prosternendum castrum de Mealton et pro Roberto Cord 'xj li et ijs. et viijd.' *P.R. 16 John*, *Rot.* 8, *mem*. j.

167 See the account in Powicke, *op. cit.* pp. 303–5.

168 The *Prestita* Roll of 12 John is especially interesting in showing a corps of master craftsmen and their small companies with John in Ireland in 1210.

169 Master Urric, the well-known engineer of Richard and John seems to have been concerned exclusively with campaigns in the field and the royal siege train in particular. Cf. *Rot. Lib.*, p. 14.

170 C. T. Clay, *ante*, lix. 7.

171 *RLC* i. 76, 95*b*, 290.

172 E.g. to Master Nicholas the Carpenter (*ibid.* p. 239), to Hugh de Barentin, carpenter (*ibid.* p. 277*b*).

173 E.g. *P.R. 9 John*, p. 54; *RLC* i. 42, 80, 97, 107, 178*b*.

174 E.g. *ibid.* p. 80, carpenters 4*d*.; p. 178*b*, miners 3*d*., *petrarii* 4*d*.; p. 107, *quareatores* 3*d*.; p. 78, miners 3*d*.; *P.R. 9 John*, p. 54; *cementarii* 3*d*. No clear evidence for the wage rate of *fossatores* has been found.

175 It is important to note that the rates quoted here, save some of the engineers', are taken from John's reign, and are probably higher than those current under his two predecessors.

176 Thus on the Pipe Roll of 17 John (*i.e.* Easter 1215) Master Nicholas of Andeli received 9*d*. a day and three ordinary carpenters 6*d*. each. (*Rot.* 1, *mem*. j.) In February 1215 Master Richard de Arches, carpenter, received 7½*d*. a day for work at Oxford Castle. (*RLC* i. 188.)

implies. The appearance of the small group of specialized craftsmen by name upon the records, their uniform and high rates of pay, together with occasional specific references to them as king's men,[177] and above all the movement of the same individuals and groups of individuals from one work to another, all point to the existence of something like a small central engineering department.[178] There can be little doubt that the task of this small corps of specialists was to direct and supervise the labour of the larger numbers of less skilled provincial workmen which castle-building demanded, but for which in this period there is no direct or detailed evidence on the central records.

One further aspect of the centralized organization of Angevin castle-building deserves mention. The more numerous records of John's reign reveal a close relationship between the royal itinerary and the programme of building, and both by this and by more direct evidence indicate the personal control of castle-building by the king.[179] At times the wording of writs itself bears witness to such personal direction. Thus on 15 February 1206 John, having just left Knaresborough, wrote to Brian de Insula, the constable, 'Mandamus uobis quod reparari faciatis domos et castellum de Cnarreburg' sicut providimus et sicut uobis diximus.'[180] Again, the appearance of considerable expenditure on the household rolls is indicative of the direct concern of the king, or his immediate officials, and these payments are often made out at, or close to, the operation in question.[181] The same relation between the royal itinerary and castle-building is shown by the writs enrolled on the Close Rolls. The writs of *Computate* in particular, ordering allowance to be made at the Exchequer for work undertaken or to be undertaken, could scarcely have been made out if the king or responsible officials had not been aware of the progress of the operation or of the intended operation. In fact, the dating clauses of these writs show them to have been issued in not a few cases when the king was again either at, or close to, the place in question.[182] Finally, in view of the other evidence it is unlikely to be entirely coincidental that castle-building expenditure on any given Pipe Roll is frequently found to be at places visited by the king in that year.[183] The royal itiner-

[177] E.g. 'Magister Nicholaus Carpentarius domini Regis' (*RLC* i. 239). 'Magister Ricardus de Arches Carpentarius noster' (i.e. Regis, *ibid.* p. 188), 'minatores nostri et petrarii' (*ibid.* p. 178*b*), cf. the 'Guarderobi carpentarii' of the *Prestita Roll 12 John* (p. 195).

[178] For a discussion of the medieval 'Office of Works', chiefly at a later date, but with references to some of the personnel here mentioned, see J. H. Harvey in *Journ. BAA* 3, vi (1941).

[179] At times the connexion between the itinerary and building is of a different sort, a preparation for the king's coming, e.g. *P.R. 6 Richard I*, p. 88 (Oxfordshire), 'Et pro domibus Regis . . . reficiendis contra adventum Regis xlijs. et vjd.'.

[180] *RLC* i. 65*b*. The writ is dated at Richmond. John had been at Knaresborough on 13 and 14 February. Cf. *ibid.* and Hardy's *Itinerary*.

[181] E.g. *Rot. Misae 11 John*, p. 118; *Rot. Misae 14 John*, pp. 2–35.

[182] E.g. *RLC* i. 16b; Marlborough and Ludgershall: king at Marlborough. *Ibid.* p. 286; Windsor: king there. *Ibid.* p. 26*b*; Guildford: king there on previous day. *Ibid.* p. 92*b*; Devizes: king there. *Ibid.* p. 185*b*; Winchester: king there.

[183] Thus on the Pipe Roll of 7 John (1204–5) expenditure upon Scarborough, York, and Knaresborough is entered pp. 39, 41, 53: John was in the north in February and March 1205, and at York on 6, 7, 8 March (*Itinerary*). Expenditure on Windsor is entered pp. 76, 77: John was at Windsor many times during the financial year (*ibid.*). On p. 113 expenditure upon Canterbury is recorded: John was at Canterbury in July 1205 (*ibid.*). On p. 146 work upon Oxford is recorded: John was at Oxford in March 1205 (*ibid.*).

ary, indeed, was largely based upon the royal castles and residences along the way, and it is worth noting that in consequence the king must have acquired first-hand knowledge of the principal fortresses of his realm.

The evidence pointing to the personal control of fortification by the Crown is available for the most part only for King John. On *a priori* grounds it is unlikely that the great builder Henry II, or the soldiering Richard, builder of Château-Gaillard, when in the kingdom, were less interested in the matter of castle-building. In one respect, indeed, it is perhaps fortunate that the evidence is available for John rather than for his two predecessors. As a soldier John must inevitably suffer by comparison with his brilliant brother.

Yet the great activity in military building during his reign, his own interest in and control of this building, and the conduct of his campaigns themselves, at least in the British Isles, all suggest a revision of the older estimate of John's military ability. In the civil war, in particular, his siege of Rochester was one of the greatest contemporary operations of its kind in England, and after its successful conclusion, the Barnwell annalist tells us, few cared to put their trust in castles.[184] After the fall of Rochester, indeed, castles in the king's path were surrendered with the minimum of resistance.[185] The probability is that John had a good knowledge of fortification and considerable skill as a castle-breaker and in the late twelfth and early thirteenth centuries the conduct of warfare turned largely upon the castle.

Finally, concerning the financial administration of Angevin military building little remains to be said. The building and maintenance of castles forms the largest regular item of royal expenditure in the years 1154–1216. But though we sometimes find that exceptional building activity coincides not only with periods of political unrest, but also, as we should expect, with periods of governmental affluence as in the years of the Interdict, there is no sign that the continuous heavy outlay was an embarrassment to the central Government. For the rest, by far the greater part of the expenditure was charged upon local revenues, usually upon those of the county in which the castle itself was situate. In those few cases where the castle concerned formed part of a separate fiscal unit accounting independently on the Pipe Rolls, as in the case of escheated honours or small territorial *castellarie* as those of Windsor, Marlborough or Orford, the expenditure was charged in the first instance upon the account of that unit, and if it was too great thus to be met in full overflowed onto the account of the local shire or some other adjacent unit.[186] There are few occasions when expenditure is charged upon an account for a district not close to the castle.[187] We have seen

184 'Pauci erant qui munitionibus se crederent' (Coventry, Rolls Series, ii. 227).

185 Cf. Wendover in Matthew Paris, Rolls Series, ii. 636–7, 642. In East Anglia, for example, in the early months of 1216, John took with great rapidity Earl Roger Bigod's newly rebuilt and strong castle of Framlingham in Suffolk, and in Essex the two great fortresses of Colchester and Castle Hedingham.

186 Thus very heavy expenditure upon Orford in 1167 is charged not only upon the farm of the town of Orford itself, but also upon the farms of the joint counties of Norfolk and Suffolk and of the honour of Eye (*P.R. 13 Henry II*, pp. 18, 33–5). In this instance the arrangement was particularly convenient since the same Oger Dapifer had all three farms (cf. n. 4 above).

187 Such examples are both exceptional and easily understandable. The carriage of stone across Oxfordshire for building at Windsor in 1166 is naturally charged on the Oxfordshire account (*P.R.*

that there are also few occasions when building is financed direct from the Treasury, and that though the itinerant Chamber was active in financing castle-building, as in other matters close to the king's interests, this Chamber expenditure is on a scale much lower than the normal expenditure charged upon local revenues.[188]

The actual extent and distribution of Angevin castle-building and maintenance between 1154 and 1216 is best seen in the Tables appended, upon which the text can be little more than a commentary. Over the whole period the achievement is impressive and important, and should not be obscured by the striking figures for the eight Edwardian castles in Wales a century later. The fortification of these years was a continuous work in every quarter of the kingdom, involving the regular outlay of great sums of royal treasure. It included the raising of new and major fortresses, but consisted for the most part of the strengthening and maintenance of well over one hundred existing castles. Nor need we look only to the records for evidence of this activity. Though the building of Henry II and his sons was much of it piecemeal, and though their work was often in succeeding centuries to be altered, demolished or ruined, yet much of it survives, and in no more impressive form than the great tower keeps at Dover, Orford, Newcastle, Scarborough, Peveril and elsewhere, which, during most of this period, were still the ultimate strength of the English castle.

Table A. Annual Expenditure 1155–1215

In this table royal expenditure upon the building and repair of castles is set down in a series of annual totals, arranged in exchequer years (Michaelmas to Michaelmas). All sums of £20 and over spent upon individual castles in each year are separately listed. The figure of £20 is arbitrary, chosen to distinguish between work on any considerable scale and mere maintenance. The table is of necessity based primarily upon the Pipe Rolls. In John's reign any additional expenditure from the Close Rolls and *Misae* Rolls is accordingly set down separately to facilitate comparison. The two surviving *Misae* Rolls, unlike the Close Rolls, provide precise figures of expenditure which are set down in the Additional Expenditure. The bare name of a castle in that column signifies that the Close Rolls indicate expenditure. there, to which there is no reference on the

12 Henry II, p. 116, cf. p. 130.) Lead used at Winchester in 1172 is charged on the Notts. and Derbs. account because it was obtained in those counties, probably at the mines of the Peak (*P.R. 18 Henry II*, p.7). Building at Odiham in 1208 is charged upon the Windsor account because John fitz Hugh the accountant was in charge of Odiham and the work there. *P.R. 10 John*, p. 61; cf. *RLC* i. 86, 89*b*, 93*b*, and *P.R. 11 John*, p. 171. Cf. n. 3 above.

188 See above. Moreover, while the only means of estimating its expenditure are the two *Misae* Rolls of John's reign, it is generally held that the Chamber was more active under John than under his predecessors (e.g. Lady Stenton, Introduction to *P.R. 10 John*, p. xxi). For the most recent survey of the activity of the Chamber under Henry II see J. E. A. Jolliffe, 'The *Camera Regis* under Henry II', *ante*, lxviii.

Pipe Rolls, but provide no figures. Those few additional figures which Close Rolls do provide, as in writs of *Liberate*, are given.

For the Exchequer year 1212–13 no Pipe Roll survives, but some attempt has been made to fill the gap by using the evidence, of the *Misae* Roll of 14 John and the Close Rolls alone. After Michaelmas 1214 the evidence becomes unsatisfactory for our purposes. The Pipe Roll of 17 John is made up for the most part only to Easter 1215 and contains very little expenditure. Nor can it be assumed that such expenditure as it does contain is a true measure for half that important year. It is included in the table here largely for the interest that attaches to the heavy expenditure at Kenilworth which it reveals. Apart from this roll, the only other evidence available for the last two years of John's reign is that of the Close Rolls, which is quite unsatisfactory for the purpose of compiling a table of figures. It has not been thought worthwhile to add this evidence here, and it may suffice to say that the months before Magna Carta especially show a continued attention to castles in royal control, though much of the work has the appearance of *ad hoc* preparation against the coming civil war.

The tables show royal expenditure upon castles at the time in Crown hands, and not expenditure upon ' royal' castles only.[189] The chronological basis of the tables is of necessity the date of recorded expenditure, which may not always coincide with the date of that expenditure itself. At the best, the Pipe Rolls can only date by the year, but in some cases they contain accounts for two or more years, or for a past year. In these cases all the expenditure charged on such accounts is given under the year of the Pipe Roll, but attention is drawn to the discrepancy by a footnote. Expenditure charged upon the remainder of a former account (*de veteri firma*) is similarly included under the year of the Pipe Roll, but such cases are not noted. An asterisk against any total indicates that it is incomplete by reason of some known fault or ambiguity in the record. Such deficiencies are, however, small and insignificant unless otherwise indicated in a footnote.[190] That the figures given, even in those few later years for which we have Pipe, *Misae*, and Close Rolls, cannot by the nature of the sources be complete, needs no further emphasis. Finally, though every precaution has been taken, it is unlikely that no errors have been committed in such an intolerable deal of arithmetic. Perhaps the greatest danger in compiling statistics of this sort over a long period is likely to be errors of omission. If such have been committed, then on this score as well as by a policy of excluding doubtful evidence and by the deficiencies of the available sources, the figures given below certainly do not exaggerate the building activity, and its cost, in the years 1155–1216.

[189] E.g. expenditure upon Bramber in Sussex in 1210 is included, though the castle only came into Crown hands with the fall of William de Braose. In general castles escheated, permanently like the Peak, or temporarily like Norham (see 1210–11), are included in the tables.

[190] Thus in addition to gaps in the records, entries of composite expenditure sometimes occur; e.g. 'Et in emendatione castelli de Norhant' et domorum Regis de Selveston' x m' (*P.R. 5 John*, p. 176). Such cases involving only small totals are excluded. More important cases are noted in a footnote.

(i) Henry II

Pipe Rolls	£	*s.*	*d.*		£	*s.*	*d.*
1155–6[191]	25	1	3½				
1156–7	25	5	8				
1157–8	59	13	4	Wark	21	8	11
				Worcester	20	0	0
1158–9	291	12	2½	Gloucester	20	0	0
				Scarborough	134	9	4
				Wark	103	14	3
1159–60	468	10	9	Berkhamstead	63	16	3
				Chester	122	7	0
				Llandovery	41	0	0
				Scarborough	94	3	4
				Wark	141	1	4
1160–1	258	4	2*	Oswestry	20	0	0
				Scarborough	107	6	8
				Wark	116	0	1
1161–2	160	15	1	Berkhamstead	34	0	0
				Scarborough	90	0	0
1162–3	83	11	8	Scarborough	77	5	0
1163–4	129	1	4½	Eye	32	10	7½
				Scarborough	86	11	4
1164–5	24	8	9				
1165–6	746	9	11	Orford	663	9	8
				Windsor	73	6	2
1166–7[192]	483	13	1	Bridgenorth	37	4	4
				Orford	323	0	0
				Windsor	76	1	3
1167–8	576	11	4	Bamburgh	30	0	0
				Dover	60	6	8
				Newcastle-on-Tyne	120	19	4
				Orford	120	0	1
				Scarborough	57	1	3
				Windsor	153	0	8
1168–9[193]	422	8	6	Bridgenorth[193]	143	17	5
				Dover	37	5	10
				Orford	134	17	0
				Tower[194]	25	0	0
				Winchester	36	6	0
				Windsor	19	4	10

191 *Pipe Roll 1 Henry II* (i 154–5) survives only in incomplete transcripts contained in the *Red Book of the Exchequer* (Rolls Series, ed. Hubert Hall).

192 Including £7 8*s*. 0*d*. upon Oswestry entered on an account of the Fitz Alan lands for two years (*P.R. 13 Henry II*, p. 72).

193 Including £89 10*s*. 1*d*. upon Bridgenorth entered on an account of the Honour of the Constable for two years (*P.R. 15 Henry II*, p. 110).

194 Here and hereafter the Tower of London.

Pipe Rolls	£	*s.*	*d.*		£	*s.*	*d.*
1169–70[195]	481	7	1*	Dover	34	7	0
				Exeter	87	17	3
				Orford	75	9	9
				Winchester	72	6	0*
				Windsor	190	12	9
1170–1	1137	18	7	Bowes	101	0	0
				Bridgenorth	20	16	4
				Chilham	100	0	0
				Dover	126	2	5
				Hertford	60	5	0
				Nottingham	440	0	0
				Orford	30	0	0
				Salisbury	24	4	10
				Winchester	134	19	8
				Windsor	54	6	8
1171–2[196]	1337	9	0	Bowes	224	0	0
				Bridgenorth	25	2	2
				Chilham	154	8	0
				Hertford	75	0	0
				Newcastle-on-Tyne	185	6	0
				Nottingham	229	3	10
				Richmond	51	11	3
				Tower	21	0	0
				Winchester	264	13	10
1172–3	2155	16	0	Berkhamstead	60	1	4
				Bolsover and Peak	90	0	3
				Bowes	100	0	0
				Bridgenorth	25	0	0
				Cambridge	31	0	0
				Canterbury	73	1	4
				Chilham	167	5	4
				Colchester	50	0	0
				Dover	162	4	1
				Eye	20	18	4
				Gloucester	44	0	0
				Hastings	47	2	9
				Hertford	52	8	0
				Newcastle-on-Tyne	254	0	8
				Norwich	20	4	8
				Nottingham	140	0	0
				Orford	58	2	8
				Oxford	69	0	0

195 Including £2 13*s*. 4*d*. upon Oswestry, entered on an account of the Fitz Alan lands for two years (*P.R. 16 Henry II*, p. i, 34).

196 Including £18 upon Berkhamstead 'de pluribus annis' (*P.R. 18 Henry II*, p. 46).

Pipe Rolls	£	s.	d.		£	s.	d.
				Rayleigh	25	19	5
				Rochester	111	16	2
				Salisbury	25	18	4
				Tower	60	0	0
				Wallingford	47	11	5
				Winchester	148	14	9
				Windsor	178	2	6
				Worcester	35	14	8
1173–4[197]	754	12	11*	Bowes[197]	44	16	6
				Dover	74	0	1
1173–4	754	12	11*	Canterbury	24	6	0
				Gloucester	37	0	0
				Guildford	26	13	4
				Hastings	23	8	8
				Huntingdon	21	9	7
				Malmesbury	20	0	0
				Northampton	32	17	0
				Salisbury	27	5	5
				Winchester	45	6	8
				Windsor	168	9	0
1174–5[198]	616	19	1	Newcastle-on-Tyne	187	15	4
				Norwich	20	15	0
				Nottingham	46	0	0
				Richmond	30	6	8
				Winchester	102	19	4
				Windsor	160	0	0
1175–6	664	15	10	Marlborough30	7	10	
				Newcastle-on-Tyne	144	15	4
				Norwich	40	2	2
				Peak	135	0	0
				Salisbury	33	1	5
				Wallingford	23	10	0
				Winchester	86	11	5
				Windsor	162	4	6
1176–7	537	12	3	Exeter	86	16	1
				Hereford	26	13	4
				Newcastle-on-Tyne	141	12	11
				Northampton	58	17	3
				Peak	49	0	0
				Salisbury	61	1	1

197 Including £44 16*s.* 6*d.* upon Bowes entered on an account of the Honour of Earl Conan for two years (*P.R. 20 Henry II*, p. 49).

198 Including £19 18*s.* 8*d.* upon Eye entered on an account of that Honour for two years; £9 10*s.* 2*d.* upon Scarborough and Topcliff on an account of Yorks. for two years; and a total of £20 0*s.* 11*d.* on an account of Kent for the previous year (*P.R. 21 Henry II*, pp. 126, 165, 209–12).

Pipe Rolls	£	*s.*	*d.*		£	*s.*	*d.*
				Winchester	51	7	0
				Windsor	62	4	7
1177–8	513	3	2*	Newcastle-on-Tyne	97	0	1
				Northampton	23	13	4
				Nottingham	115	0	0
				Salisbury	66	0	0
				Tower	41	11	7*
				Winchester	27	8	6
				Windsor	60	0	0
1178–9[199]	410	14	8	Arundel	29	8	1
				Marlborough	30	9	4
				Tickhill	63	12	5
				Tower	25	6	8
				Wallingford	63	15	11
				Winchester	91	11	3
				Windsor	35	0	0
1179–80	658	14	9	Berkhamstead	30	4	7
				Bowes	117	13	8
				Dover	260	0	5
				Exeter	34	16	0
				Nottingham	25	9	5
				Tickhill	60	0	0
				Winchester	94	8	6
1180–1	462	9	9	Arundel	32	2	10
				Carmarthen	93	6	8
				Dover	231	14	3
				Nottingham	43	2	0
1181–2	1487	2	8	Arundel	145	2	5
				Chester	30	0	0
				Dover	815	6	4
				Hastings	95	9	4
				Northampton	64	1	1
				Nottingham	220	12	8
				Winchester	22	1	1
1182–3	917	2	5	Arundel	73	7	10
				Colchester	30	4	6
				Dover	491	3	4
				Hastings	20	0	0
				Hereford	33	9	0
				Northampton	43	9	2
				Pickering	20	13	4
				Orford	20	0	0
				Richmond	31	12	4

199 Including; £5 7*s.* 3*d.* upon Carisbrooke entered on an account of the Isle of Wight for four and a quarter years (*P.R. 25 Henry II*, p. 109).

Pipe Rolls	£	s.	d.		£	s.	d.
1183–4	978	16	6*	Arundel	24	12	3
				Dover	784	5	7
				Kenilworth	26	9	9
				Nottingham	84	2	1
1184–5	1844	4	11½*	Dover	1329	1	5½
				Gloucester	52	8	0
				Kenfig	30	19	6½
				Llantilio	43	6	8
				Nottingham	327	17	7
1185–6	1462	0	11½*	Dover	1164	3	3
				Llantilio	85	9	4
				Nottingham	105	19	6
				Peak[200]	25	10	0
				Pickering	23	10	0
1186–7	978	9	10	Bowes	23	0	0
				Carlisle	42	4	7
				Dorchester	23	6	6
				Dover	681	2	0
				Salisbury	38	0	0
				Skenfrith	43	17	7
				Windsor	23	9	5
1187–8	307	3	9	Dover	185	9	4

(ii) Richard I

Pipe Rolls	£	s.	d.		£	s.	d.
1188–9[201]	168	4	3	Dover	50	0	0
				Salisbury	44	18	6
				Tower	33	6	8
1189–90	3945	9	4*	Cambridge	41	0	0
				Dover	568	3	0
				Kenilworth	46	7	0
				Mountsorrel	24	0	0
				Newcastle-under-Lyme	22	6	8
				Rochester	30	0	0
				Tower	2881	1	10
				Wallingford	36	1	8
				Winchester	47	6	0
				York	190	7	4
1190–1	667	11	8*	Gloucester	61	16	0
				Guildford	35	6	5
				Hertford	36	10	0
				Oxford	103	19	0
				Tower	121	10	2

200 *P.R. 32 Henry II*, p. 108, cf. *P.R. 33 Henry II*, p. 171 and *P.R. 34 Henry II*, p. 200.

201 Henry died on 6 July T 189, e.g. *Gesta* (Rolls Series), ii, 71, so that the greater part of the expenditure on the roll of 1 Richard I in effect belongs to his reign.

Pipe Rolls	£	*s.*	*d.*		£	*s.*	*d.*
				Winchester	73	0	10
				Windsor	33	14	5½
				York	28	13	9
1191–2	464	8	10	Canterbury	98	12	5
				Chilham	20	7	0
				Colchester	23	6	8
				Gloucester	20	0	0
				Northampton	43	16	8
				Oxford	75	3	5
				Rochester	20	0	0
				Southampton	46	15	0
				Tower	35	0	0
1192–3[202]	738	11	5*	Canterbury	69	3	0
				Bridgenorth	32	8	5
				Gloucester	20	7	11
				Hereford[202]	46	1	9
				Lincoln	82	16	4
				Northampton	42	16	3
				Oxford	110	8	8
				Pevensey	30	15	3
				Southampton	68	4	6
				Tower	103	11	6
				York	27	6	0
1193–4	294	12	1*	Carreghofa	20	0	0
				Nottingham	22	16	11
				Pevensey	31	1	3
				Southampton	24	6	6
				Tower	31	10	0
				Wallingford	50	0	0
				Windsor	37	2	3*
1194–5[203]	285	3	2	Carreghofa	24	0	0
				Cymaron	20	0	0
				Nottingham	23	12	8
1194–5	285	3	2	Tower	35	12	0
				Windsor	33	12	7
1195–6[204]	318	7	3*	Dover	76	3	0
				Tickhill	26	19	8
				Tower	73	10	0
1196–7	147	19	0*	Tower	24	0	0
1197–8	115	13	2*	Winchester	39	17	2

202 The expenditure on Hereford given here, plus £4 15*s.* 8*d.* on Skenfrith, is enrolled on accounts of Herefordshire covering three years, 1180–3 (*P.R. 5 Richard I*, pp. 86–92).

203 Includes £5 upon Exeter entered on a Devon account for three-quarters of the previous year 1193–4 (*P.R. 7 Richard I*, p. 125).

204 Including £10 upon Hastings entered on an account of the Exchange for two years (*P.R. 8 Richard I*, p. 20).

(iii) John

Pipe Rolls	£	s.	d.		Additional Expenditure [RLC = Close Rolls. vol. i RM = *Misae* Rolls] £	s.	d.
1198–9[205]	307	5	6	Gloucester	26	13	4
				Hertford	25	0	0
				Tower	21	10	0
				Worcester	20	3	0
1199–1200[206]	772	8	11*	Dorchester	20	0	0
				Gloucester	20	19	0
				Grimsby	80	0	0
				Harestan[207]	298	10	2
				Launceston	20	0	0
				Lincoln	20	0	0
				Tower	69	10	0
				York	37	12	7
1200–1	559	17	6*	Harestan	246	0	0
				Salisbury	29	6	8
1201–2	840	1	11	Carlisle	47	0	0
				Corfe	276	0	1
				Dunster	20	0	6
				Exeter	40	17	8
				Harestan	140	0	0
				Hereford	39	17	4
				Newcastle-under-Lyme	23	0	0
				Southampton	25	16	0
1202–3[208]	786	4	0*	Bamburgh	60	2	5
				Carlisle	61	10	9
				Corfe	246	10	4
				Exeter	19	16	10
				Harestan	22	12	2
				Hereford	75	18	8
1202–3	786	4	0	Lancaster	28	0	0
				Porchester[209]	24	3	5
				Scarborough	33	0	0
				Southampton	20	0	0
				Tower	30	0	0
				Worcester	20	12	10

205 Richard died 6 April 1199 (e.g. Hoveden, Rolls Series, iv, 84), so that some half of the expenditure entered on this roll of 1 John in effect belongs to his reign.

206 Including £5 6*s*. 8*d*. upon Wallingford on an account of the Honour of Wallingford for the previous year (*P.R. 2 John*, p. 35).

207 In Horsley, Derbyshire.

208 Including £24 3*s*. 5*d*. upon Porchester and £8 12*s*. 4*d*. upon Marlborough entered on an account of Hugh de Neville for two years plus (*P.R. 5 John*, p. 161).

209 Including £24 3*s*. 5*d*. upon Porchester and £8 12*s*. 4*d*. upon Marlborough entered on an account of Hugh de Neville for two years plus (*P.R. 5 John*, p. 161).

Pipe Rolls	£	s.	d.		£	s.	d.	Additional Expenditure
1203–4[210]	862	13	2	Carlisle	116	4	1	
				Corfe	230	12	0	
				Dover	33	6	8	
				Newcastle-under-Lyme	37	0	0	
				Nottingham	21	0	1	
				Southampton	122	0	0	
				Tickhill[210]	79	12	0	
				Tower	30	11	2	
				Worcester	25	15	0	
1204–5	1107	3	3*	Bridgenorth	30	0	0	
				Bristol	20	0	0*	RLC Carlisle
				Ellesmere	24	0	0	RLC Dover
				Exeter	26	19	3	RLC Mountsorrel
				Knaresborough	238	3	0	RLC Porchester?[211]
				Newcastle-under-Lyme	54	6	9	
				Nottingham	171	6	5	
				Norwich	85	0	0	
				Peak	33	19	7	
				Scarborough	161	12	0	
				Tickhill	88	3	4	
1205–6	729	1	6*	Kenilworth	22	0	0	
				Knaresborough	84	5	3	
				Northampton	77	12	0	
				Nottingham	63	18	6	
				Rochester	115	0	5	
				Salisbury	44	0	7	
				Scarborough	68	15	5	
				Tickhill	83	10	10	
				Winchester	29	9	8	
1206–7	704	18	9½*	Corfe[212]	72	14	2	
				Devizes	25	6	8	
				Knaresborough	96	19	7	
				Ludgershall	20	10	2	
				Newcastle-under-Lyme	40	0	0	

210 Including £18 9*s.* upon Tickhill charged upon an account of Tickhill for 1198, and 26*s.* 2*d.* upon Winchester entered upon a Winchester account for three years, 1201–4 (*P.R. 6 John*, pp. 47, 131).

211 In May 1205 Stephanus Anglicus *artifex* was sent to Porchester castle, there to be paid and maintained (*RLC* i, 31*b*, *bis*).

212 Payment £39 7*s.* 6*d.*) of miners and masons for unspecified work is entered on the Pipe Roll on the Dorset and Somerset account (*P.R. 9 John*, p. 54). Cf. *RLC* i, 78 which shows these men were to work at Corfe. On the same Pipe Roll (p. 14) an unspecified payment of £100 is made to Thomas fitz Adam, *RLC* i, 83 stipulates that 100 marcs of this money is for work at Corfe. These two examples illustrate how the Close Roll evidence at times interprets ambiguous Pipe Roll entries.

Pipe Rolls	£	s.	d.		£	s.	d.	Additional Expenditure				
1206–7	704	18	9½*	Nottingham	30	7	9					
				Odiham	39	0	1					
				Peak	21	6	10					
				Rockingham	71	16	3					
				Tickhill	43	16	2					
				Windsor	39	9	1					
1207–8[213]	1406	5	7½	Dover,[213] Rochester	89	9	4					
				Exeter	53	11	1					
				Hastings	26	13	4					
				Knaresborough	420	7	5		Chichester			
				Northampton	47	19	8	RLC	Mountsorrel			
				Odiham	287	14	2		Exeter			
				Salisbury	63	18	6					
				Scarborough	68	8	2					
				Sherborne	71	11	10					
				Southampton[213]	157	19	0½					
				Winchester	20	0	0					
				Windsor	25	19	5					
1208–9[214]	1314	17	5½	Dover	60	0	0					
				Hanley	138	7	0		Cadbury	26	13	4
				Harestan/Bolsover	134	0	5		Corfe	50	0	0*
				Hastings	31	6	8	RM[215]	Devizes	21	0	0
				Knaresborough	298	13	1½		Hanley	100	0	0
				Northampton	109	9	3		Odiham	41	0	0
				Odiham	386	10	10		Tickhill	13	6	8
				Pickering	44	18	3½		TOTAL	252	0	0
				Windsor	28	19	3					
1209–10	1616	4	11½	Bramber	95	6	1					
(plus *c.* £300?)[216]				Dover	35	8	5					
				Hanley	274	2	8					
				Hertford	55	15	9	RM[217]	Corfe			
				Lancaster	352	3	1		Knepp Castle			
				Odiham[216]	*c.* 300	0	0?					
				Orford	20	0	0					

213 Including £157 19*s.* 0½*d.* upon Southampton and £12 16*s.* upon Dover entered on William de Wrotham's account of tin mines for two years (*P.R. 10 John*, p. 171).

214 Including £10 upon Shropshire castles entered on the Salop account for two years; £10 upon Newcastle-under-Lyme entered upon the Staffs. account for two years; and £4 upon Southampton entered upon the account of Southampton town for two years (*P.R. 11 John*, pp. 146, 149, 177).

215 The *Misae* Roll of 11 John is made up for the regnal year 1209–10. The expenditure set out is taken from that part of it coinciding with the Pipe Roll of 11 John, i.e. up to 29 September 1209 only.

216 *Pipe Roll 12 John* (pp. 121–2) has the following composite entry on the Windsor account of John fitz Hugh: 'Et in operatione castri et domorum de Odiham et Wudestoche et in custo posito in equis R. per plura loca. scilicet in equis ix li. et xixs. et vjd. et ob. cccc et lij li. et vs.' The expenditure upon the civil residence at Woodstock does not concern us here. In view of the expenditure at that castle in the last two years, *c.* £300 out of the total of £442 5*s.* 5½*d.* upon Odiham and Woodstock seems a safe estimate for Odiham this year.

217 The *Misae* Roll of 11 John, under March 1210, records small payments to *petrarii* and carpenters going to Corfe and Knepp Castle respectively, but gives no indication of the cost of the work itself (pp. 155–6).

Pipe Rolls	£	*s.*	*d.*		£	*s.*	*d.*	Additional Expenditure
				Scarborough	620	0	1	
				Swansea	33	6	8	
				Winchester	32	10	4	
1210–11[218]	2892	18	3½	Corfe	50	13	4	
				Kenilworth	464	6	3½	
				Knaresborough	119	18	8	
				Lancaster	180	18	0	
				Ludgershall[218]	37	16	0	
				Marlborough[218]	72	5	6	
				Norham[218]/ Tweedmouth[218]	372	13	11	
				Peak	43	5	4	
				Rockingham[218]	126	18	6	
				St. Briavels[218]	291	12	3	
				Sauvey (Leics.)[218]	442	13	1	
				Scarborough	542	6	0	
1211–12[219]	2201	1	3*	Bamburgh	117	8	4	
				Bridgenorth	20	0	0	
				Hanley	231	10	9	
				Kenilworth	224	17	8	
				Knaresborough	31	13	4	
				Newcastle-on-Tyne	133	18	11	
				Norham	273	3	2½	RM[220] Nottingham
				Peak	24	5	8	£66 13*s.* 4*d.*
				Odiham	72	3	2	
				Scarborough	780	6	8	
				Tower	109	7	6½	
				Windsor	29	10	9½	
1212–13	No Pipe Roll							RM Corfe £210 1*s.* 11*d.*
								Dover 200 0*s.* 0*d.*
								Canterbury
								Corfe (£200)
								Dover (3100 *plus*)
								Guildford
								RLC Hereford
								Northampton
								Rochester
								Tickhill
								Tower

218 *P.R. 13 John* contains an account of the bishopric of Durham for over three years, incorporating expenditure of £372 13*s.* 11*d.* upon Norham and Tweedmouth and £13 3*s.* 3½*d.* upon Durham; also an account of Hugh de Neville for Marlborough for three years incorporating £986 14*s.* 8*d.* upon Ludgershall, Marlborough, Porchester, Rockingham, Saint Briavels, and Sauvey (pp. 35–41, 83–4). That some of this expenditure of Hugh de Neville belongs as early as 1208 is indicated by a writ of *computate* in his favour dated 22 January 1208 (*RLC* i, 100*b*), of whose content only a fraction is allowed him in the Pipe Roll of that year (*P.R. 10 John*, p. 202).

219 Including £78 6*s.* 0*d.* upon Shropshire castles entered on an account of Shropshire for three years (*Rot.* 10, *mem.* ij).

220 From the *Misae* Roll of 14 John up to 29 September 1212.

Pipe Rolls	£	s.	d.		£	s.	d.		Additional Expenditure
1213–14[221]	632	8	5	Dover	302	0	0	RLS	Bramber
				Hertford	22	5	8		Corfe £53 6*s*. 8*d*. *plus*)
				Shrewsbury	21	0	0		Dover (£200 *plus*)
				Tower	122	15	8		Knepp Castle
				Winchester	26	10	4		Nottingham (£66 13*s*. 4*d*. *plus*)
									Tower (£15)
1214–Easter 1215[222]	502	1	7	Kenilworth	402	0	0		
				Lancaster[222]	33	18	4½		

Table B. Expenditure on Individual Castles 1154–1216

The following table sets out the principal expenditures upon individual castles during the period. Each of the three reigns is treated separately, and within this division the annual expenditure on each castle is given, together with the total. Years of nil expenditure are not listed. A minimum total of £100 in each reign is taken as a qualification for inclusion in the lists, in order that only those castles where some appreciable work was done may appear. For the rest the arrangement follows the principles adopted in Table A. The figures and totals are taken from the Pipe Rolls in the first instance and the Exchequer year is the chronological basis of the table. Any additional expenditure in John's reign from other sources and not recorded by the Pipe Rolls is separately set down. Where figures of this additional expenditure are available they are set down at the foot of each individual table and added to the Pipe Roll total (Table i) to form Table ii. Where no figures are avail able the fact of this additional expenditure is noted in a footnote. Discrepancies in the chronology of the Pipe Roll accounts are noted as in Table A and the significance of an asterisk remains the same.

It should be noted again that no Pipe Roll of 15 John (1212–13) is extant, and that the Pipe Roll of 17 John is for the most part only made up for half the Exchequer year and that the expenditure it contains is probably incomplete.[223]

221 Including £21 upon Shropshire castles entered on an account of Shropshire for two years (*P.R. 16 John, Rot.* 11, *mem.* ij), and £28 3*s*. 4*d*. upon Windsor and Odiham on John fitz Hugh's account for two years (*ibid.* Rot. 11 *d*., *mem*. j).

222 *Pipe Roll 17 John* is made up for the most part from Michaelmas 1214 to Easter 1215, i.e. for half the Exchequer year. In some respects, however, it is a composite or miscellaneous roll, for it contains an account of the Exchange of London for 2 Henry III (twelve weeks only), an account of the scutage of the Honour of Bologne for the same year, and a Hampshire account for half the Exchequer year 18 John (i.e. October 1215 to Easter 1216). Of those accounts on which building expenditure is charged, however, all are for half the year 17 John, save that for Lancashire which is for the two full years 16 and 17 John (i.e. October 1213 to October 1215). Cf. the introductory remarks to this Table.

223 See n. 222 above.

(i) Henry II

Arundel	£	s.	d.
1170–1	10	0	0
1178–9	29	8	1
1179–80	9	19	5
1180–81	32	2	10
1181–2	145	2	5
1182–3	73	7	10
1183–4	24	12	3
1186–7	12	18	10
1187–8	2	1	0
Total	339	12	8

Berkhamstead	£	s.	d.
1155–6	3	3	0
1157–8	12	0	0
1158–9	14	0	0
1159–60	63	16	3
1161–2	34	0	0
1169–70	5	0	0
1171–2[224]	18	0	0
1172–3	60	1	4
1176–80[225]	30	4	7
1180–1	5	8	6
1182–3	4	0	9
1184–5	0	14	6
1185–6	1	5	7
Total	251	14	6

Bowes	£	s.	d.
1170–1	101	0	0
1171–2	224	0	0
1172–3	100	0	0
1173–4	44	16	6
1179–80	117	13	8
1186–7	23	0	0
1187–8	6	0	0
Total	616	10	2

Bolsover and the Peak	£	s.	d.
1172–3	90	0	3
1173–4	26	0	0
1174–5 (Peak only)	4	17	0
1175–6 (Peak only)	135	0	0
1176–7 (Peak only)	49	0	0
1185–6 (Peak only)	25	10	0
Total	330	7	3

Bridgenorth	£	s.	d.
1166–7	37	4	4
1167–8	14	5	6
1168–9[226]	143	17	5
1169–70	2	5	9
1170–1	20	16	4
1171–2	25	2	2
1172–3	25	0	0
1173–4	18	5	8
1181–2	6	18	8
1182–3	10	7	3
1183–4	7	1	2
1184–5	3	11	11
1185–6	3	1	0
1186–7	1	12	8
Total	319	9	10

Canterbury	£	s.	d.
1172–3	73	1	4
1173–4	24	6	0
1174–5[227]	5	11	7
Total	102	18	11

Chester	£	s.	d.
1159–60	122	7	0
1181–2	30	0	0
1182–3	10	16	5
Total	163	3	5

224 Expenditure 'de pluribus annis' (*P.R. 18 Henry III*, p. 46).
225 Of this total £23 is stated to be due to work 'de tribus annis preteritis' (*P.R. 26 Henry II*, p. 8).
226 Including £89 10*s*. 1*d*. charged upon a two years' account (*P.R. 15 Henry II*, p. 110).
227 Charged on a Kent account for the previous year (*P.R. 21 Henry II*, p. 211).

Chilham	£	s.	d.
1170–1	100	0	0
1171–2	154	8	0
1172–3	167	5	4
1174–5[228]	7	0	0
Total	428	13	4

Dover	£	s.	d.
1164–5	0	8	4
1167–8	60	6	8
1168–9	37	5	10
1169–70	34	7	0
1170–I	126	2	5
1172–3	162	4	1
1173–4	74	0	1
1174–5	3	6	8
1179–80	260	0	5
1180–1	231	14	3
1181–2	815	6	4
1182–3	491	3	4
1183–4	784	5	7
1184–5	1329	1	51
1185–6	1164	3	3
1186–7	681	2	0
1187–8	185	9	4
Total A	6440	7	0½
Total B = 1180–1188	5942	5	11½
Total C	6589	9	5½

= Total for estimated period rebuilding 1180–91, cf. Dover table for Richard I.

Exeter	£	s.	d.
1169–70	87	17	3
1170–1	6	2	0
1171–2	18	8	2
1172–3	6	13	3
1176–7	86	16	1
1179–80	34	16	0
1180–1	14	1	3
1181–2	17	0	9
1182–3	15	8	10
1186–7	15	4	6
Total	302	8	1

Eye	£	s.	d.
1163–4	32	10	71
1164–5	6	0	0
1266–7	8	15	6
1172–3	20	18	4
1174–5[229]	19	18	8
1177–8	0	19	8
1178–9	3	6	8
1179–80	1	5	0
1181–2	1	0	0
1182–3	1	7	0
1185–6	0	14	7½
1186–7	2	5	8
Total	99	1	9

Gloucester	£	s.	d.
1157–8	0	8	0
1158–9	20	0	0
1163–4	4	9	5
1171–2	17	13	5
1172–3	44	0	0
1173–4	37	0	0
1177–8	15	13	0
1180–1	9	12	0
1181–2	8	3	2
1182–3	4	10	0
I 184–5	52	8	0
1187–8	16	14	0
Total	230	11	0

Hastings	£	s.	d.
1160–1	3	6	8
1170–1	3	3	4
1171–2	19	1	0
1172–3	47	2	9
1173–4	23	8	0
1181–2	95	9	4
1182–3	20	0	0
Total	211	11	1

Hereford	£	s.	d.
1164–5	0	7	0
1168–9	1	12	6
1172–3	3	6	0
1173–4	15	3	9

228 Charged on the account of n. 4 above.

229 Charged upon an account of the Honour of Eye for two years (*P.R. 21 Henry II*, p. 126).

Hereford	£	s.	d.
1176–7	26	13	4
1177–8	15	0	0
1178–9	18	0	0
1181–2	1	6	6
1182–3	33	9	0
1186–7	1	0	0
1187–8	0	13	4
Total	116	11	5

Hertford	£	s.	d.
1170–1	60	5	0
1171–2	75	0	0
1172–3	52	8	0
1173–4	3	7	10
1181–2	5	0	0
1183–4	1	0	0
Total	197	0	10

Newcastle-on-Tyne	£	s.	d.
1167–8	120	19	4
1171–2	185	6	0
1172–3	254	0	8
1173–4	12	15	10
1174–5	187	15	4
1175–6	144	15	4
1176–7	141	12	11
1177–8	97	0	1
Total	1144	5	6

Northampton	£	s.	d.
1173–4	32	17	0
1176–7	58	17	3
1177–8	23	13	4
1178–9	12	0	0
1181–2	64	1	1
1182–3	43	9	2
Total	234	17	10

Norwich	£	s.	d.
1160–1	6	13	4
1172–3	20	4	8
1173–4	11	18	0
1174–5	20	15	0
1175–6	40	2	0
1183–4	4	17	9
1187–8	2	2	0
Total	106	12	9

Nottingham	£	s.	d.
1162–3	1	6	8
1170–1	440	0	0
1171–2	229	3	10
1172–3	140	0	0
1173–4	17	18	8
1174–5	46	0	0
1177–8	115	0	0
1179–80	25	9	5
1180–1	43	2	0
1181–2	220	12	8
1182–3	13	14	0
1183–4	84	2	1
1184–5	327	17	7
1185–6	105	19	6
1186–7	3	4	10
1187–8	2	9	0
Total	1816	0	3

Orford	£	s.	d.
1165–6	663	9	8
1166–7	323	0	0
1167–8	120	0	1
1168–9	134	17	0
1169–70	75	9	9
1170–1	30	0	0
1171–2	8	10	0
1172–3	58	2	8
1173–4	11	19	4
1180–1	15	0	0
1182–3	20	0	0
1187–8	10	12	2
Total A	1471	0	8
Total B	1413	9	2

for estimated period building, 1166–1173

Richmond	£	s.	d.
1171–2	51	11	3
1174–5	30	6	0
1182–3	31	12	4
1185–6	13	0	0
1186–7	11	11	0
Total	138	0	7

Rochester	£	s.	d.
1166–7	2	13	4
1170–1	16	0	0
1172–3	111	16	2

Rochester	£	s.	d.
1174–5	15	0	0
1181–2	5	0	0
Total	150	9	6

Salisbury	£	s.	d.
1170–1	24	4	10
1171–2	0	13	4
1172–3	25	18	4
1173–4	27	5	5
1175–6	33	1	5
1176–7	61	1	1
1177–8	66	0	0
1178–9	17	4	1
1181–2	9	1	0
1182–3	6	0	0
1184–5	9	2	1
1186–7	38	0	0
1187–8	1	7	0
Total	318	18	7

Scarborough	£	s.	d.
1157–8	4	0	0
1158–9	134	9	4
1159–60	94	3	4
1160–1	107	6	8
1161–2	90	0	0
1162–3	77	5	0
1163–4	86	11	4
1167–8	57	1	3
1168–9	13	11	0
1174–5[230]	2	0	0
1187–8	16	7	4
Total	682	15	5

Tickhill	£	s.	d.
1178–9	63	12	5
1179–80	60	0	0
1181–2	19	4	0
Total	142	16	5

Tower of London	£	s.	d.
1166–7[231]			
1168–9	25	0	0
1171–2	21	0	0
1172–3	60	0	0
1173–4	6	13	4 *
1174–5[232]	7	9	4
1175–6	9	3	4
1177–8	41	11	7 *
1178–9	25	6	8
1180–1	4	1	4
1181–2	0	3	9
1182–3	0	1	9
1183–4	0	12	8
1185–6	3	7	6
Total	204	11	3

Wallingford	£	s.	d.
1172–3	47	11	5
1173–4	12	7	0
1175–6	23	10	0
1178–9	63	15	11
1182–3	7	1	0
Total	154	5	4

Wark	£	s.	d.
1157–8	21	8	11
1158–9	103	14	3
1159–60	141	1	4
1160–1	116	0	1
Total	382	4	7

Winchester	£	s.	d.
1155–6	14	10	8
1156–7	14	1	0
1158–9	6	9	0
1159–60	1	7	6
1161–2	0	2	0
1167–8	6	19	4
1168–9	36	6	0
1169–70	72	6	0
1170–1	134	19	8
1171–2	264	13	0
1172–3	148	14	9
1173–4	45	6	8
1174–5	102	19	4

230 Entered upon a two years' account (*P.R. 21 Henry II*, p. 165).

231 *c.* £30? The relevant entry on the *Pipe Roll 13 Henry II* (p. 1) reads: 'Et in operatione domorum turris Lundon', et domorum Regis de Westm' scilicet Noue Aule et camerarum Regine lxiiij li.'

232 Entered upon a Kent account for the previous year (*P.R. 21 Henry II*, p. 209).

Winchester	£	*s.*	*d.*
1175–6	86	11	5
1176–7	51	7	0
1177–8	27	8	6
1178–9	91	11	3
1179–80	94	8	6
1181–2	12	0	0
1182–3	2	10	10
1183–4	2	5	0
1185–6	5	8	9
1186–7	0	14	0
Total	1233	9	2

Windsor	£	*s.*	*d.*
1161–2	13	19	8
1163–4	1	10	0
1165–6	73	6	2
1166–7	76	1	3
1167–8	153	0	8

Windsor	£	*s.*	*d.*
1168–9	19	4	10
1169–70	190	12	0
1170–1	54	6	8
1171–2	17	11	4
1172–3	178	2	6
1173–4	168	9	0
1174–5	160	0	0
1175–6	162	4	6
1176–7	62	4	7
1177–8	60	0	0
1178–9	35	0	0
1180–1	2	18	6
1181–2	2	17	0
1182–3	8	18	6
1183–4	5	12	2
1186–7	23	9	5
1187–8	6	1	5
Total	1475	10	2

(ii) Richard I

Canterbury	£	*s.*	*d.*
1191–2	98	12	5
1192–3	69	3	0
1195–6	2	0	0
1196–7	2	0	0
1197–8	3	10	0
Total	175	5	5

Dover[233]	£	*s.*	*d.*
1188–9	50	0	6
1189–90	568	3	0
1190–1	29	0	0
1193–4	2	0	0
1195–6	76	3	0
Total	725	6	6

Lincoln	£	*s.*	*d.*
1189–90	13	6	8
1192–3	82	16	4
1196–7	5	0	0
Total	101	3	0

Northampton	£	*s.*	*d.*
1189–90	4	16	3
1190–1	19	0	0
1191–2	43	16	8
1192–3	42	16	3
1193–4	13	16	8
1196–7	3	6	8
Total	127	12	6

Oxford	£	*s.*	*d.*
1189–90	0	13	4
1190–1	103	19	0
1191–2	75	3	5
1192–3	110	18	8
1194–5	12	2	0
1195–6	2	0	0
Total	304	16	51*

Southampton	£	*s.*	*d.*
1188–9	6	1	0
1189–90	7	11	8
1190–1	8	19	6
1191–2	46	15	0

233 For the total figures for the rebuilding of Dover between 1179 and 1191, cf. the figures for Henry II above.

234 This total may be incomplete because expenditure ‘in operatione domorum Regis’ has been excluded. At Oxford the *domus Regis* may refer either to Beaumont or to the houses in the castle.

Southampton	£	s.	d.
1192–3	68	4	6
1193–4	24	6	6
1195–6	0	5	2
1197–8	1	0	0
Total	163	3	4

Tower of London	£	s.	d.
1188–9	33	6	8
1189–90	2881	1	10
1190–1	121	10	2
1191–2	35	0	0
1192–3	103	11	6
1193–4	31	10	0
1194–5	35	12	0
1195–6	73	10	0
1196–7	24	0	0
Total	3339	2	2

Wallingford	£	s.	d.
1189–90	36	1	8
1193–4	30	0	0
1194–5	10	7	7
1195–6	7	5	2
1196–7	4	11	3
1197–8	1	4	0
Total	109	9	8

Winchester	£	s.	d.
1189–90	47	6	0
1190–1	73	0	10
1191–2	2	0	0
1192–3	17	1	7
1193–4	8	14	7
1194–5	5	7	5
1195–6	5	0	0
1196–7	4	13	0 *
1197–8	39	17	2
Total	203	0	7 *

Windsor	£	s.	d.
1188–9	2	14	9
1190–1	33	14	51
1193–4	37	2	3 *
1194–5	33	12	7
1195–6	10	10	0
1196–7	6	13	4
1197–8	5	0	0
Total	129	7	41 *

York	£	s.	d.
1189–90	190	7	4
1190–1	28	13	9
1191–2	0	8	0
1192–3	27	6	0
1193–4	0	13	4
Total	247	8	5

(iii) John

Carlisle	£	s.	d.
1198–9	1	14	7
1200–1[235]			
1201–2	47	0	0
1202–3	61	10	9
1203–4	116	4	1
Total	226	9	51 *

Corfe	£	s.	d.
1199–1200	5	18	4
1200–1	5	0	0
1201–2	276	0	1
1202–3	246	10	4
1203–4	230	12	0
1206–7	72	14	2
1209–10	2	0	0
1210–11	50	13	4
1214–15	2	10	0
Total (i)	891	18	3
Plus (*Misae* Rolls, 11, 14 John)	260	1	11 *
Plus (Close Rolls 1213)	253	6	8
Total (ii)	1405	6	10[236]

235 For 1200–1 cf. *P.R. 3 John*, p. 253, where the sum of £27 14*s*. is allowed to the sheriff for work on the castles in his custody. The sheriff was William de Stuteville, who had also the counties of Yorkshire and Westmorland. Further work is indicated at Carlisle in 1205, cf. *RLC* i, 27.

236 Further work for which no figures are available is indicated at Corfe in and after 1214 (*RLC* 168, 178*b*).

Dover	£	*s.*	*d.*
1199–1200	8	19	10
1200–1	18	0	0 *
1202–3	11	18	0
1203–4	33	6	8
1207–8[237]	12	16	0 *
1208–9	60	0	0
1209–10	35	8	5
1211–12*			
1213–14	302	0	0
Total (i)	482	8	11 *
Plus	200	0	0
(*Misae* Roll 14 John)			
Plus	400	0	0
(Close Rolls 1213–14)			
Total (ii)	1082	8	114 *

Hanley (Worcs.)	£	*s.*	*d.*
1206–8[239]			
1208–9	138	7	0
1209–10[239]	274	2	8
1211–12	231	10	9
Total (i)	644	0	5
Plus	100	0	0
(*Misae* Roll 11 John)			
Total (ii)	744	0	5

Harestan (in Horsley, Derbys.)	£	*s.*	*d.*
1199–1200	298	10	2
1200–1	246	0	0
1201–2	140	0	0
1202–3	22	12	2
1205–6	5	0	0
1206–7	2	1	0
1208–9[240]			
1210–11	4	5	2
1213–14	5	0	11
1214–15	2	10	0
Total	725	19	5

Kenilworth	£	*s.*	*d.*
1200–1	2	0	0
1205–6	22	0	0
1210–11	464	6	31
1211–12	224	17	8
1214–15	402	0	0
Total	1115	3	1 ½

Knaresborough	£	*s.*	*d.*
7204–5	238	3	0
1205–6	84	5	3
1206–7	96	19	7
1207–8	420	7	5
1208–9	298	13	0 ½
1210–11	119	18	8
1211–12	31	13	4
1213–14	4	18	0
Total	1294	18	41

Lancaster	£	*s.*	*d.*
1198–9	18	6	8
1199–1200	4	8	6
1201–2*			
1202–3	28	0	6
1203–4	1	2	6
1204–5	1	9	6
1205–6	5	0	0
1206–7	5	0	0
1207–8	5	0	0
1209–10	352	3	1
1210–11	180	18	0
1214–15[241]	33	18	41
Total	635	7	11 *

237 Entered on an account for two years (*P.R. 10 John*, p. 171).

238 For further work at Dover in 1205 not recorded elsewhere, see *RLC* i, 42 *bis*, 51*b*; for further references to the work of 1213–14, cf. *ibid.* pp. 204, 206, 207, 208*b*, 210.

239 Of the total on the roll of 1209–10, £70 16*s.* 0*d.* is stated to be 'de anno ix et x' (*P.R. 12 John*, pp. 169–70).

240 *Pipe Roll 11 John* (p. 112) bears a composite charge of £134 0*s.* 5*d.* spent upon the two castles of Harestan and Bolsover. The part of this sum spent upon Harestan if known would perhaps bring the recorded total for this castle for John's reign up to some £800.

241 Though, in general, *Pipe Roll 17 John* is made up for only half the fiscal year (Michaelmas-Easter) this expenditure is charged on an account of Lancaster for the two full years 16 and 17 John (1213–15).

Marlborough	£	s.	d.
1198–9	5	0	8
1199–1200	43	16	7*
1201–2	18	16	2
1202–3[242]	8	12	4
1204–5	17	18	11
1206–7[243]	28	12	21
1210–11[244]	72	5	6
Total	195	2	41

Newcastle-on-Tyne	£	s.	d.
1198–9	18	19	9
1199–1200	5	0	0
1202–3	7	7	9
1203–4[245]*			
1204–5	0	15	0
1205–6	1	6	0
1206–7	3	15	9
1207–8[245]*			
1209–10[245]*			
1210–11[245]*			
1211–12	135	18	11
Total	171	3	2*

Norham	£	s.	d.
1210–11[246]*			
1211–12	273	3	2½
Total	= *c.* £500?		

Northampton	£	s.	d.
1198–9	1	6	8
1199–1200	3	6	8
1200–1	6	13	4*
1201–2	8	13	4
1202–3*			
1203–4	4	4	0*
1205–6	77	12	0
1206–7	17	5	2
1207–8	47	19	8
1208–9	109	9	3
1209–10	1	17	5
1210–11	5	0	0
1211–12	3	15	1
1213–14	3	13	10
1214–15	2	15	2*
Total	293	2	7

Nottingham	£	s.	d.
2198–9	18	7	11
1199–1200	5	18	0
1200–1	3	14	3
1201–2	2	9	7
1202–3	2	17	1
1203–4	21	0	1
1204–5	171	6	5
1205–6	63	18	6
1206–7	30	7	9
Total (i)	319	19	7
Plus (*Misae* Roll 14 John)	66	13	4
Plus (Close Rolls 1213–14)	66	13	4
Total (ii)	453	6	3

Odiham	£	s.	d.
1206–7	39	0	1
1207–8	287	14	2
1208–9	386	10	10
1209–10[249]	*c.* 300?	0	0
1210–11	13	16	6
1211–12	72	3	2
1213–142	14	0	9
Total (i)	1113	5	6
Plus (*Misae* Roll 11 John)	4	0	0
Total (ii)	1154	5	6

242 Entered on a two-year account of Hugh de Neville (*P.R. 5 John*, p. 161).
243 Expenditure stated to be 'de duobus annis' (*P.R. 9 John*, p. 209).
244 Entered on an account of Marlborough for three years (*P.R. 13 John*, pp. 83–4).
245 £33 4*s.* 3*d.* upon castles in the sheriff of Northumberland's custody (i.e. Newcastle, Bamburgh? *P. R. 6 John*, p. 41), £1 5*s.* 4*d.*; £1 5*s.* 0*d.*, £3 3*s.* 5*d.* respectively upon Newcastle and Bamburgh (*P.R. 10 John*, p. 52; *P.R. 12 John*, p. 107; *P.R. 13 John*, p. 206).
246 £372 13*s.* 11*d* on the castles of Norham and Weedmouth, charged on an account of the bishopric of Durham for over three years (*P.R. 13 John*, p. 38).
247 Additional expenditure at Northampton is indicated in 1213 (*RLC* i, 137) and in 1215 (*ibid.* p. 195).
248 Further additional expenditure is indicated at Nottingham in 1214 (*RLC* i, 169*b*).
249 £442 5*s.* 5½*d.* upon Odiham and Woodstock (*P.R. 12 John*, pp. 121–2); cf. n. 4, p. 133 above.

Peak	£	s.	d.
1198–9	3	1	0
1199–1200	5	0	0
1201–2	12	9	1
1202–3	1	16	6
1203–4	1	7	0
1204–5	33	19	7
1206–7	21	6	10
1208–93	5	0	0
1210–11	43	5	4
1211–12	24	5	8
1214–15	2	10	0
Total	154	1	0

Rochester	£	s.	d.
1199–1200	10	0	0
1200–1*			
1201–2	5	0	0
1202–3	2	0	0
1205–6	115	0	5
1207–84*			
1213–14*			
Total	132	0	5

St Briavel's	£	s.	d.
1202–3	5	0	0
1210–11[253]	291	12	3
Total	296	11	3

Sauvey (Leics.)			
1210–11[254]	442	13	1

Scarborough	£	s.	d.
1198–9	2	15	0
1201–2	14	0	0
1202–3	33	0	0
1204–5	161	12	0
1205–6	68	15	5
1206–7[255]			
1207–8	68	8	2
1209–10	620	0	1
1210–11	542	6	0
1211–12	780	6	8
Total	2291	3	4*

Sherborne	£	s.	d.
1200–1	10	0	0
1201–2	1	13	4
1203–4	5	0	0
1205–6	5	0	0
1206–7	4	7	7
1207–8	71	11	10
1208–9	6	17	6
1209–10[256]*			
1214–15	2	10	0
Total	117	0	3

Southampton	£	s.	d.
1200–1	3	15	6
1201–2	25	16	0
1202–3	20	0	0
1203–4	122	0	0
1206–7	1	0	0
1207–8[257]	157	19	0½
1208–9[258]	4	0	0
1209–10	1	0	0
1210–11	2	5	0
1213–14	6	0	0
1214–15	3	6	8
Total	347	2	21

Tickhill	£	s.	d.
1200–1	4	18	4
1201–2	1	2	0
1202–3	1	19	9

250 Entered on an account of John fytz Hugh for two years (*P.R. 16 John*, *Rot.* 11 *d. mem.* j).
251 Entered on a Notts. and Derbs. account for the previous year (1207–8) (*P.R. 11 John*, p. 109).
252 £76 13*s.* 4*d.* for timber for Rochester and Dover castles (*P.R. 10 John*, p. 97).
253 Charged upon Hugh de Neville's account of Marlborough for three years (*P.R. 13 John*, p. 84).
254 Charged upon the same three-year account of n. 5 above.
255 In spite of the expenditure of the preceding and following years the amount involved is only some £4. A composite charge of £8 15*s.* 6*d.* for the castles of Scarborough and Pickering is made on the Yorkshire account (*P.R. 9 John*, p. 79)
256 Further work at Sherborne in the summer of 1215 is indicated by the unprinted membrane 1 of Close Roll 16 John.
257 Charged upon an account of William de Wrotham for two years (*P.R. 10 John*, p. 171).
258 Charged upon an account of Southampton for two years (*P.R. 11 John*, p. 172).

Tickhill	£	s.	d.
1203–4[259]	79	12	0
1204–5	88	3	4
1205–6	83	10	10
1206–7	43	16	2
1209–10	4	15	3
1210–11	5	0	0
1213–14	2	10	0
Total (i)	315	7	8
Plus	13	6	8
(*Misae* Roll 11 John)			
Total (ii)	328	14	44

Tower of London	£	s.	d.
1198–9	21	0	0
1199–1200	69	10	0
1202–3	30	0	0
1203–4	30	11	2
1205–6	15	9	0
1207–8	5	0	0
1210–11	17	11	2½
1211–12	109	7	6½
1213–14	122	15	8
1214–15	12	0	0
Total (i)	433	14	71
Plus	15	0	0
(Close Roll 1213)			
Plus	26	13	4
(Close Roll 1214)			
Total (ii)	475	7	11

Winchester	£	s.	d.
1198–9	16	0	0
1199–1200*			
1201–2	7	17	1
1202–3	9	17	3
1203–4[262]	15	3	1
1204–5	17	0	3
1205–6	29	9	8
1206–7	5	12	3
1207–8	20	0	0
1209–10	32	10	4
1210–11	2	0	0
1213–14	26	10	4
Total (i)	182	0	3
Plus	66	13	4
(Close Roll 1215)			
Total (ii)	248	13	7[263]

Windsor	£	s.	d.
1198–9	3	1	3
1199–1200	3	4	4
1200–1	10	0	0
1201–2	0	12	6
1202–3	5	8	2
1203–4	4	0	71
1204–5	19	7	I
1205–6	16	17	6
1206–7	39	9	1
1207–8	25	19	5
1208–9	8	19	3
1209–10	16	7	7
1210–11	9	I	5
1211–12	29	10	91
1213–14[264]	14	2	7
Total	226	1	7

Worcester	£	s.	d.
1199–9	20	3	0
1199–1200	1	15	0
1200–1	12	6	8
2201–2	7	7	5
1202–3	20	12	10
1203–4	25	15	0
1204–5	2	3	4

259 Of this total, £18 9*s*. 0*d*. is charged upon an old account (by Robert de Vipont) of Tickhill for 1198 (*P.R. 6 John*, p. 47).

260 Further work at Tickhill is indicated in 1213 (*RLC* i, 144).

261 That the quite considerable work at the Tower in the preceding and following years was continued in the fiscal year 1212–13 for which no Pipe Roll is extant, is indicated by *RLC* i, 1276, 143*b*, 153. Further work was also done there in 1214–15 (*ibid.* 175*b*, 191)

262 Including 26*s*. 2*d*. charged on a Winchester account for three years (*P.R. 6 John*, p. 131).

263 Further work is indicated at Winchester in 1215–16 (*RLC* i, 185*b*, 199, 226, 227, 268*b*).

264 Entered on a Windsor account of John fitz Hugh for two years (*P.R. 16 John*, *Rot.* 11 *d.*, *mem.* j).

1205–6	5	0	0	1209–10	5	0	0
1206–7	4	17	5	1211–12	5	0	0
1207–8	2	12	5	1213–14	4	2	0
1208–9	15	0	11	Total	131	15	21

PostScript
Since this paper was sent to the printers, Mr H. M. Colvin has drawn my attention to the entry of further relevant castle-building expenditure on the Pipe Roll of 9 Henry III, namely £97 19*s*. 1*d*.* and, probably, £2 7*s*. 11*d*. upon Bolsover, £3 15*s*. 0*d*. upon the Peak and a further 10 marks upon Knaresborough, all incurred by Brian de Insula in the last two years of John's reign (*Rot. 9d., mem.* ij): and an unspecified portion of 1000 marks spent by Geoffrey de Neville in 1216 upon Scarborough and Pickering.

8

The Castles of the Anarchy

Charles Coulson

The study of castles in the reign and wars of King Stephen has been bedevilled by a tendency to treat all fortifications of the period as a single category. The shortcomings of such an approach become apparent if castles are considered instead with a threefold structural classification in mind. First, there were the castles which were regularly founded, mostly soon after the Conquest, and which were active residentially and administratively; some may have been defensively refurbished, as Sir Frank Stenton suggests; these form the vast majority. Secondly, there were the castles which in the ordinary course of any nineteen years of twelfth-century tenurial and economic development would have been created or modernized by the largely autonomous mechanisms of growth and seignorial ambition. Thirdly, there were the notorious castles built in direct furtherance of usurpation; these, because new, must be grouped with the siegeworks and campaign works which were intentionally ephemeral.[1]

These categories serve to highlight the central question of the role of the castle in the anarchy. Even when instruments of violence (and its most noticed and durable symptom), castles were the result, not the cause, of local disturbances. Castle-building, as one of the consequences of the suspension of the juridical protection of property rights, might also measure the extent of disturbance. This line of enquiry, however, would require combining the narrative and other sources with the most exhaustive archaeological survey, and is not possible in this chapter. Here no more can be done than apply our categories in the investigation of what was seen to be the most crucial abnormality of Stephen's reign; that large numbers of new or revived castles allegedly came into existence without royal licence. The 'adulterine castles' are so prominent, both in the chronicles and in modern accounts, that they figure in Norman Pounds's recent and admirable survey as the root of all the evils of the reign.[2]

If castle-building was really licensed prior to 1135, so that applicants who

For reading this chapter in draft and for bibliographical help, I am grateful to Richard Eales. The assistance of Derek Renn with the archaeology and illustrations has been invaluable, and I have greatly benefited from affirmative discussion with Marjorie Chibnall, my former teacher, on rendability in Normandy; Tom Bisson, on castle-customs in early Catalonia; Lewis Warren, on royal 'castle-policy'; and for the opportunity to read chapter 8 of David Crouch, *The Image of Aristocracy*, in advance of publication (now published as *The Image of the Aristocracy in Britain, 1000–1300* [London, 1992]). To the courteous persistence of the editor Edmund King, particular acknowledgement is due.

1 Royal castles and warfare are beyond the scope of this discussion. The basics are well adumbrated by Stenton, *First Century*, 193–5, 200–5, 223–7, 235–56.

2 N. J. G. Pounds, *The Medieval Castle in England and Wales* (Cambridge, 1990), 26–33.

were refused permission did not build; and if licensing was resumed after 1154 and could be shown to have become again a means of 'control', whereby only 'strategically useful' castles in loyal hands came into being, or were kept in a 'militarily effective' condition; then the intervening period would reveal a breakdown of royal power in this respect also.[3] 'Adulterine castles' notoriously afflicted the anarchy. But they are also reported of other disturbances: during Duke William's minority until *c.*1047; then, after his death in 1087, they are reported most emphatically until Robert Curthose departed on Crusade in 1096, a period punctuated by his and William Rufus's declaration of the Conqueror's laws in 1091; and we hear of adulterine castles again, from Robert's return late in 1100 until the subjugation of the duchy after Tinchebrai in 1106. In England, Henry I's opportunistic seizure of the throne, and the ensuing insecurity which ended only with William Clito's death in 1128, still caused no such troubles – but compare the complaints of churchmen at his and his partisans' activities in the Cotentin. He did move decisively in 1102 to break the English power of Robert of Belléme, but only Bridgnorth (not Tickhill or Arundel) was a new castle, and even that cannot be regarded as built in defiance of royal law. Only on Henry I's death did 'adulterine castles' apparently reappear, both in England and (up to *c.*1137) in Normandy.[4] The supposed general outbreak in England should ideally be distinguished from local incidents during phases of hostilities, but the evidence is wanting. Sufficiently close archaeological dating of the few excavated sites is impossible. Documentary corroboration is rare. Inferences, ostensibly from topography or structural type, tend to reflect historical doctrine. Stenton is ambivalent. While not doubting that 'innumerable castles' arose during Stephen's reign, he is also sure that the large numbers of earthwork castles were 'the natural results of the feudal organization of Anglo-Norman society'. This, and his opinion that careful and lengthy construction was foreign to wartime creations (few of which featured significantly in the conflict), is deservedly respected.

Investigation must start with the Angevin accusation in 1153–4 that Stephen was so lacking in kingly qualities that he allowed a variously guessed but large number of castles to appear. Robert of Torigny, in his account of the peace settlement, says the total of new *castella* to be 'overthrown' exceeded 1,115, a figure of mesmerizing precision. Among later chroniclers, William of Newburgh wrote of 'those new castles which in the days of Henry I had in no way existed', which Henry II's heroic advent caused 'to melt away like wax before the flame' (as lodgements of brigands naturally would when order was restored). Gervase of Canterbury ascribed to Henry II an order that anonymous 'very nasty, little fortlets' should disappear throughout England. William of Newburgh, with alluring royalism, tells us that 'a few of the new castles which

3 Royal 'castle-policy' is treated in my *Castles and Crenellating . . . 1200–1578* (in progress); the historiography in 'Freedom to Crenellate by Licence: An Historiographical Revision', *Nottingham Medieval Studies* 38 (1994), 86–137.

4 Examples of complaints at new castles or castle-works, rarely 'adulterine' but habitually since assumed to be'unlicensed', are: *William of Jumièges*, ed. J. Marx (Paris, 1914), 115–16, 123; *William of Poitiers*, ed. R. Foreville (Paris, 1952), 14–20; Haskins, *Norman Institutions*, 38, 64, 86, 289; *GS* 104–5.

were conveniently located' were retained to be held by 'peaceful men for the strengthening of the kingdom'. This last passage contains a useful hint that a castle's novelty was not decisive, and that discretion and partisanship were exercised. Nothing solid on numbers exists, nor is to be expected.[5] A fossilized trace of the idea that the Conqueror and his sons jealously restricted castle-building, so that a great many of the thousand or more castles structurally attributable to before 1189 must have been anarchic, is occasionally still encountered, despite Stenton. Robert of Torigny has thus escaped the routine scepticism applied to medieval military statistics. Estimates of numbers have been revised by Richard Eales, proposing a post-Conquest proliferation followed by a slow decline, possibly stemmed temporarily or even mildly reversed under Stephen, then resumed more steeply as obsolescence, physical decay, tenurial change, and the cost of rebuilding in masonry contracted the social range of castle-ownership. First Stephanic mentions of castles listed by John Beeler total ninety. David King counted 110 but considered only twenty-seven of all kinds stated to be new.[6]

As Stenton emphasizes, *firmare* frequently meant refortification, indeed often only munitioning, like *infortiare*. Structures tend constantly to be over-stressed and manning neglected. After all, an 'incastellated' church and a 'house held as a castle' were just buildings filled with armed men. What to moderns is *the* castle to contemporaries was only *a* castle. It was a structure with features of fortification, both utilitarian and symbolic, ranging from a kit of prefabricated timber *bretasching* to equip an earthwork, via a bewildering variety of buildings, up to a major honorial *caput* or a walled town like the ancient hill-fort of Old Sarum. All these were 'castles', though not consistently so described, as many terms were in literary vogue. Most regrettably no medieval equivalent existed of the Victorian engineer's distinction between 'permanent fortification' and 'fieldwork', which weaker forces always relied on. Thus the empress and her partisans met their 1141 crisis and the king's release: 'she built castles over the country wherever she might to best advantage; some to hold back the king's men more effectively, others for the defence of her own people', which caused 'grievous oppression to the people, a general devastation of the realm, and the seeds of discord on every hand'. Forts are mentioned at Woodstock, at Radcot near Oxford among the Thames marshes, and also within Cirencester. In this last reference ecclesiastical castro-phobia reinforces the chronicler's political sympathies, this castle being 'next the holy church of the religious like another Dagon before the ark of the Lord'. The *Gesta Stephani* held the empress responsible for much castle-building by her supporters, and blamed Robert of Gloucester especially for imposing the labours of

5 WN i. 94,102; GC i.160; *RT* 177, 183. Not all the manuscripts of *RT* have the figure 1,115; one has 126 new castles.

6 R. Eales, 'Royal Power and Castles in Norman England', in C. Harper-Bill and R. Harvey (eds.), *Ideals and practice of Medieval Knighthood* 3 (Woodbridge, 1990), 55–63, and *passim*: J. Beeler, *Warfare in England 1066–1189* (New York, 1966), 397–422, 430–4 (with references); D. J. C. King, *Castellarium Anglicanum* (New York, 1983), pp. xxxi–xxxii. Renn (*Norman Castles*, gazetteer) notes about forty possible Stephanic foundations, including about fifteen siegeworks. A possible siege-castle has now been found by Exeter (1136?): *Fortress* 18 (1993), p. i.

castleworks.[7] Cirencester was later razed by Stephen; and he also took down the famous castle built upon and in the old stone tower of Bampton church, near Oxford, and another in 1149 at Wheldrake near York by the citizens[8] procurement.' Stephen, perhaps more than Henry II, was the great destroyer of illicit fortlets.[9]

The siege- and campaign-castles were seemingly the least obnoxious of fortifications, being ephemeral army fieldworks not entailing long-term arrogated lordly rights, nor prises of food and money. But siege-castles are elusive. Wallingford had a cluster, among them probably Crowmarsh Giffard and Brightwell; but judging a site by its slight construction or incomplete state or by its location, without documents to refine archaeological possibilities, is hazardous. Earl Robert's recorded castle nearby, identified with Faringdon, built in 1144 and destroyed by Stephen the next year, shows how suggestion can become false certainty in citation. Castles of all kinds were strong only when stocked and heavily manned – insubstantial wartime works especially so. Although depredations by the 'castle-men' are prominent in clerical condemnation, they were but one of the numerous disasters of war. Conditions requiring self-defence and an environment of seignorial competition, both distantly akin to the scramble of the Conquest decade, explain Thomas of Cockney's slight earthwork thrown up around his estate church, which Stenton notes, and doubtless many others also.[10]

The contemporary indictment of Stephen for permitting new castle-building is a specious and propagandist circular argument, rubbing in his failure to defeat the Angevins and to establish his dynasty; but the accusation that he allowed *unlicensed* castles is a modern invention. Certainly, irregular fortlets were a traditional proof of governmental incapacity and even illegitimacy, alleged as late as the Dunstable meeting of January 1154, when it was alleged that Stephen had disarmed those of his supporters with undue partiality. (Henry of Huntingdon's comment implies that few such castles remained at this date, and fewer still for Henry II to disarm.) There is no foundation for the modern charge that he allowed to lapse the royal prerogative to license castles (and hypothetically to stop unlicensed ones).[11] The historiography is complex. The prerogative is asserted as a peculiar royal right by the compiler *c.*1115 of the *Leges Henrici Primi*,[12] but it has a much longer continental pedigree. Scholars have read it into clause four of the *Consuetudines et justicie* (1091),[13] even though the whole declaration was an interim peace-keeping measure, which exempted from interfer-

7 *GS* 138–9 (comment in Stenton, *First Century*, 203), 150–1 (comment in Davis, *Stephen*, 73–4; and cf. 15–16, 105, 115–17, 119). Works, not castellation *per se*, were the grievance.

8 *GS* 140–1; SD ii. 323–4.

9 S. Painter (*Feudalism and Liberty* (Baltimore, 1961), 127) notes a minimum of twenty-one demolitions under Henry 11.

10 King, *Castellarium Anglicanum*, *sub* Berkshire; Davis, *Stephen*, 88–90; J. Kenyon, *Medieval Fortifications* (Leicester, 1990), 10, 24, 38, 141 (with excavation report references). Renn (*Norman Castles*, 189) shows the discrepancy between the archaeology at Faringdon and the sources.

11 R. A. Brown, 'A List of Castles 1154 to 1216', *EHR*, 74 (1959), 250 (and *passim* 249–80); and *English Castles* (London, 1976), 82, 215.

12 *Leges Henrici Primi*, ed. L. J. Downer (Oxford, 1972), 108, 116.

13 Haskins, *Norman Institutions*, 277–84.

ence (baronial as well as ducal) just the sort of *munitiunculum* castigated in 1153–4. The *Consuetudines*, moreover, forbade absolutely brigand occupation (*fortitudo*) of natural lairs (*et in rupe vel in insula*) typical of outbreaks, of lawlessness. (The Isle of Ely from Hereward's time until after the 1320s is a barometer of the state of the peace.) In 1091 there is no mention of that constant clerical grievance – the armed conversion of churches – nor in the chronicles for 1153–4, although cases recorded had been quite numerous.[14] The emphasis given to 'unlicensed' castles would be unbalanced even were they what Orderic Vitalis in another context twice, but modern writers constantly, call 'adulterine'. Whereas the *Consuetudines* say nothing about licensing, clause four is quite clear on rendability – the duke's right to take over castles for his own use when he needed them.[15]

It is instructive to read some of the *conventiones* of Stephen's reign with French custom in mind. In the most famous of them the earls of Chester and Leicester not only agreed to refrain from fortifying castles on the sensitive marches of Leicestershire, but mutually undertook to ensure that no-one else did. Neither the removal of the possibility of enforceable royal arbitration nor pervasive anarchy determined the castle-clauses of this celebrated treaty.[16] Bilaterally agreed zones where no new fortification (or refortification) was to be undertaken by the principals or their men; tolerance for contentious castles (here Whitwick), or arrangements to disarm castles (here Ravenstone); and careful provisions for the munitioning or the further strengthening of intrusive or crucial fortresses: these are all familiar elements of French practice. Similar arrangements on a larger scale occur in the successive Anglo-French treaties of 1194, 1195–6, and 1200, covering the borders of Normandy and the provinces to the south.

Other aspects of the Chester–Leicester agreement become clearer when read in the light of French custom. Chester, in granting, or accepting, Leicester possession of Mountsorrel castle, with its appurtenant *burgus* or *villa*, affirmed his continuing lordship in the conventional fashion by reserving refuge-rights there for himself and his retinue. The purpose is 'to make war on whomsoever he wished' (*ad guerreandum quencunque voluerit*), and the entitlement *ut de feudo*

14 E.g. Bampton, Bridlington, Cirencester, Coventry, Hereford, Lincoln, Malmesbury, Ramsey, Reading, Wallingford, Wherwell, Wilton, and perhaps Hailes and Selby: Renn, *Norman Castles*, 49, 100, 117, 144, 160, 161–2, 199, 205, 226–7, 272, 289, 291, 307–8, 338, 344, 347. Roger of Salisbury intruded Malmesbury castle into the Abbey precinct, but in 1118: *ibid.* 239.

15 On jurability, whereby security was given that the fortress would not be injurious to the lord of the fief (here, Ravenstone may be reprieved by Chester but must not be hostile to Leicester in any eventuality), see C. L. H. Coulson, 'Fortress-Policy in Capetian Tradition and Angevin Practice', *ANS*, 6 (1983), 13–38; 'Rendability and Castellation in Medieval France', *Château-Gaillard*, 6 (Caen, 1972), 59–67; 'Castellation in the County of Champagne', *Château-Gaillard*, 9–10 (Caen, 1982), 347–64. These customs have particularly early records in Catalonia and in Provence: D. Herlihy (ed.), *The History of Feudalism* (London, 1970), 99–102, 228–9 (1058 *bis*, 1115, mistranslated); C. Brunel, *Les Plus Anciennes Chartes en langue provençale* (Paris, 1926), nos. 2 (*c.*1034), 8,10 (*c.*1103), etc. Coulson, 'The French Matrix of the Castle-Provisions of the Chester–Leicester Conventio', *ANS*, 17 (1995), 65–86.

16 For the texts, see Stenton, *First Century*, 250–6. See further Davis, *Stephen*, 108–10, 162–3; King, 'Mountsorrel and its Region in King Stephen's Reign', *Huntington Library Quarterly*, 44 (1980),1–10; Renn, *Norman Castles*, 53 map F.

meo; so Leicester, despite the scrupulous respect for mutual interest which dominates the pact, could have no control over, or compensation for, Chester's use of the castle. The lord's right was paramount, and conventionally it was expressed as though in contemplation of war. Refuge was a component of basic readability, which might extend not only to putting in troops on demand by messenger, but to requiring the vassal to vacate his castle first to symbolize complete takeover of control. The occasions, if not the lord's mere will, were war and the lord's necessity. Both are present here. Chester, for warring against whomsoever he wished, had right of entry in company to the *burgus* and castle-baileys of Mountsorrel, but *si necesse fuerit comiti Rannulfo* he must personally be admitted in *dominico castro* – presumably Leicester's own *donjon* or whatever inner ward existed on this heavily damaged hill-top site. This restricted the lord's right, but is an early feature in circumstances of strict reciprocity. If Chester entered unaccompanied, Leicester was bound by feudal etiquette (*portabit ei fidem*), subject as throughout to the king's liege lordship. Both parties relied on established castle-customs to define a long-term relationship. Stenton's 'uneasy state of half-suspended hostilities' between the earls, and the 'new feudal order' he believes had 'arisen in reaction from the anarchy of previous years', were probably less uneasy, novel, or impermanent in intention than he supposes.

Stephen regarded his obligations under readability much less scrupulously than did the two earls in the preceding agreement. In council at Winchester in 1139 rendability was raised as a means of trying the subordination of the bishops. Archbishop Hugh of Rouen voiced the commonplace, according to William of Malmesbury, that 'as it is a time of suspicion all the chief men, in accordance with the custom of other peoples, ought to put all the keys of their fortifications (*munitionum*; i.e. give symbolic entry) at the disposal of the king who has to strive for the peace of all'. Demanding castles in pledge was standard form, and was acceptable if 'reasonable', but it was not reasonable to make this demand with the intention of depriving their owners. Temporary use only was the superior's right. Arresting Roger of Salisbury (with Sherborne castle, Malmesbury, and Devizes), Alexander of Lincoln (with Newark, Sleaford, and Banbury all of his own building), and later Nigel of Ely, gained Stephen their castles but serious repercussions as well. Taking Geoffrey de Mandeville in 1143 at the St Albans court gained at least Pleshey and Saffron Walden, but Henry of Huntingdon thought it dishonourably done. At Northampton in 1146 Stephen once more broke the rules, extorting Lincoln castle from Ranulf of Chester.[17]

By Henry II's standards, Stephen did well; nor did he fall short of Anglo-Norman practice regarding new castles. Even by the exemplary test of the *Leges Henrici Primi* he must be exonerated. They reserved to the king, in a spirit of Carolingian nostalgia, judgement of *castellatio sine licentia*, but in another clause it is *castellatio trium scannorum*, which meant that, even theoretically, earthworks nearly three times the size of those exempted from interfer-

[17] Davis, *Stephen*, 29–30, 32–3, 78–9, 92–3; WM, *HN* 32–3. With Devizes (1140) and Berkeley (1145) for special causes the method failed (Davis, *Stephen*, 42, 90–1).

ence in 1091 were excluded from the king's ban, along with all works of masonry. The *scabulum* of the *Consuetudines* is undoubtedly the *scannum* of the *Leges Henrici Primi*.[18] Three casts of earth or relays of earth-moving, even stages of scaffolding, would cover all but the greatest castles. Suggestions by Liebermann and Ella Armitage, recently endorsed by L. J. Downer, that the phrase meant triple embankments would make exemption virtually total. Wartime forts were not of this order, whether fieldworks or the competitive entrenchments of minor lordlings, defending their positions or exploiting the weakness of royal and magnatial authority to enhance them.

The 'adulterine' castle must be looked for elsewhere. As a polemical term it may have been invented by Abbot Suger of Saint-Denis or by Orderic himself, writing about Normandy after 1087. In his exhaustive trawl of the French chronicles, Robert Aubenas found it used solely by Orderic and by Suger (varied by *castrum sceleratum*) in denouncing the new castles of Robert of Bellême and other great Norman lords. Orderic used also *adulterina municipia* and Aubenas notes the peculiarly English fashion, citing Stubbs's *Constitutional History*, to which much is due. It was an integral part of a long castrophobic ecclesiastical *genre* exemplified *c*.1025 by Fulbert of Chartres's invective against Count Theobald for failing to stop the vicomte of Châteaudun building two castles as scourges, 'one from the east the other from the west', to strike down upon the cathedral city. For incastellated churches, conversion into *spelunce latronum* (after Matt. 21: 13) was the stock phrase.[19] Peace of God provisions, monastic castle-free *banlieues*, and conciliar anathemas all have a common parentage. The concern in Stephen's reign with castleworks builds on these ideas. 'Undue works of castles' were forbidden in 1148 at the Council of Reims. Ecclesiastics had blamed William I for 'oppressing poor men' in this way, and the *Gesta* arraigned the empress but particularly Robert of Gloucester for it. Levying *tenserie*, to sustain chiefly the old and recognized castles, was another grievance, as was forcible provisioning from church lands particularly, even when the king did it.[20] In 1153–4 two traditions merged. The pusillanimity of the house of Blois, exemplified by Stephen's father at Antioch, blended with the fashion for branding rulers, like Robert Curthose, as incompetent (and even illegitimate) for allowing intrusive castles. The combination has condemned Stephen to posterity.

The term *adulterinus* is dear to the British. Hamilton Thompson translated it as 'counterfeit' or 'spurious', which sprang from the notion that 'adulterine castles' were misbegotten, not the genuine article. The 1217 reissue of Magna

18 As noted by Pounds, *Medieval Castle*, 305 n. 17. E. Armitage (*Early Norman Castles of the British Isles* (London, 1912), 378 n. 1) has caused some confusion.

19 E.g. M. Chibnall, 'Orderic Vitalis on Castles', in C. Harper-Bill, C. Holdsworth, and J. L. Nelson (eds), *Studies Presented to R. Allen Brown* (Woodbridge, 1989), 52 (cf. 56 on 'spiritual castles'); R. Aubenas, 'Les Châteaux-forts des Xe et XIe siècles', *Revue historique de droit français et étranger*, 4:17 (1938), 548–86 (at 567 n. 4); H. d'Arbois de Jubainville, *Histoire . . . de Champagne*, 1 (Paris, 1859), 275–8.

20 The passage from Robert of Torigny is translated in Davis, *Stephen*, 119; *ASC*, *s.a.* 1137; William of Newburgh couples castles and tyranny (WN i. 69–70). D. C. Douglas, *William the Conqueror* (London, 1964), 373; Count Henry in the Cotentin (1087–1100) likewise, in person and by proxy: Haskins, *Norman Institutions*, 63.

Figure 1. South Mimms, Middlesex: keep and motte (B.K. Davison, J. Dimond, and Frederick Warne Ltd)

Carta, itself a pacification document, has the only authoritative definition. Its final provision (47) explains that *castella adulterina*, to be razed in principle, were 'those castles which were constructed or rebuilt from the beginning of the war waged between the Lord King John our father and his barons of England'.[21] The rule was most exactly, if selectively, applied. There is still nothing about licensing, but the feeling was that the castle was an attribute of established lordship, not one intruded by upstarts while the rule of law was suspended. Possessions 'invaded' and new castles built in 1154 concerned Robert of Torigny equally, although neither figures in the official text of the Winchester accord. The notorious 'tyrannies of the castle-men' were not this sort of usurpation, but partly the exacting of the old Anglo-Saxon *burhbot* services, to a degree unknown since the Conquest era.

Despite this evidence, there is frequent reference to the Norman kings' supposed 'control of private castles'.[22] Richard Eales has emphasized the impact of the multitude of castles rapidly established after 1066, endowing their lords with customary rights and precedent, upon existing law. Only a small proportion of the 'castles of the Conquest', in J. H. Round's phrase,[23] could have been ordained. The demands of the Norman settlement, producing a range of marcher-type franchises, would have entrenched and extended seignorial liberties. Any consultation would have been chiefly by the great, who by continen-

21 W. Stubbs, *Select Charters*, 9th edn (Oxford, 1913), 344; cf. A. H. Thompson, *Military Architecture in England* (Oxford, 1912), 56 n. 3, 89 n. 1.

22 Painter asserted that 'the charters which were granted to Geoffrey de Mandeville . . . prove conclusively that a specific license from the crown was required for castle-building' (*Feudalism and Liberty*, 141), despite his candour about some of the difficulties, not least the lack of evidence.

23 *Archaeologia*, 58 (1902), 313–40.

tal precedent already had the right. The implanting o£ the great majority of lesser castles, along with claim-staking disputes, would fall to the magnates' courts. Eynsford castle in Kent, an early and lowly stone castle, doubtless came into being in this way under the archbishops' aegis. The vassal's castle enhanced his lord's position, whether formally rendable or not. Little encouragement was needed by William I for his tenants to build castles. Their self-interest sufficed[24] William fitz Osbern's and Odo of Bayeux's authority to found castles was in the common spirit of the enterprise. Aubenas argued cogently that castles were built by delegation of official authority. He firmly refuted views expressed by Flach, Luchaire, Calmette, and many others (deriving ultimately from the work and fraternity of Eudes de Mézeray,1610–83) that France 'bristled with feudal castles', so that any 'adventurer' could become count or baron in no time by building one. Jean Yver concurred, but had the ducal honour much at heart, finding no place in Normandy for the *châtellenie indepéndente* despite the great franchises, nor for the *avoué* whom ecclesiastics so disliked. Both scholars championed the legitimacy of the new feudal order. What they and Marcel Garaud have demonstrated for tenth- and early eleventh-century France is highly relevant for the anarchy. Unfortunately it is the *anarchie féodale* school which has been drawn upon, which in France is never far from the surface. Garaud went so far as to put back the view that plus d'un millier de châteaux forts . . . hérissaient . . . le sol de la France' into the remote Gallo-Roman period.[25]

By the end of the eleventh century perhaps as many as a thousand castles had fixed the feudal map of England. New castles, not refortifications, affected holders of vested rights. The supply was ample for normal purposes, but earth and timber castles perished quickly from rot, wind, and erosion. Frequent repairs and alterations are the pattern shown by the meticulously excavated castle of Old Montgomery at Hen Domen. Ditches had to be re-cut, timber revetments and palisading replaced. Most vulnerable were the wooden towers shown by the Bayeux Tapestry crowning the mottes of Bayeux, Dinan, Dol, Rennes, and Hastings, the type verified by excavation. Only the large foundation-posts found at Abinger and at South Mimms (see Fig. 1), speculatively attributed to the anarchy, would be difficult to reinstate.[26] Whether mere sentry-box look-outs on stilts, or structures as grand as Lambert of Ardres's famous multi-chambered tower, such castles were almost as easily rebuilt as destroyed. Wooden structures of earth-fast posts, established for the fifteen or so years until the first major repair, were automatically and lawfully rebuilt (compare mills, weirs, deer-leaps, barns – all seignorial furniture, variously lucrative and prestigious). Painter justly commented, 'if it were to be even reasonably effective, royal regulation of castle-building could not be confined to

24 Pounds (*Medieval Castle*, 30, 305 nn. 23, 24) cites FW ii. 34. His quotation from William of Poitiers refers only to putting 'energetic custodians into castles' (ii. 35).

25 J. Yver, 'Les Châteaux-forts en Normandie jusqu'au milieu du XIIe siècle', *Bulletin de la société des antiquaires de Normandie*, 53 (1955–6), 28–115; 'Autour de l'absence d'avouerie en Normandie', *ibid.* 57 (1963–4), 189–283; M. Garaud, 'La Construction des châteaux et les destinées de la *Vicaria* et du *Vicarius* carolingiens en Poitou', *Revue historique de droit*, 4:31 (1953), 54–78 (at 58).

26 Kenyon, *Medieval Fortifications* (Leicester, 1990), 10, 13–17, 22, 35–7, 83–5, 98–101, etc. R. Higham and P. Barker (*Timber Castles* (1992)), now surveys the issues.

controlling the creation of new strongholds on sites never before used'; but *idée fixe* then compelled him to assert that castles became dangerous only after the Settlement and Scandinavian threat were past, when 'the kin could . . . begin to enforce his right to control new construction'.[27]

That licensing implemented some politico-strategic Norman castle-plan is as imaginative as supposing that the omission of castle-builders to seek this, like other privileges, contributed to the disorders of the anarchy. Even oral pacts as important as is implied would have been solemnly made and attested, surviving significantly in the record. The few documents, while not properly licences and due to extraneous motives, do offer some illumination. An agreement between Henry I and William de Corbeil, archbishop of Canterbury, dated 1127, allowed him and his successors to build a *turris* or *munitio* within the royal castle of Rochester. The archbishops enjoyed little security as custodians and had to have the new keep in full proprietorship for the expense to be justified. In 1088 Rufus had bargained with Bishop Gundulf of Rochester to wall the bailey in stone after Odo's revolt. It cost him £60 in discharge of a debt of £100. Henry's deal was sharper, since his great-grandson not only resumed the custody but got the great donjon-palace as well for no more than a brush with the Church. William of Corbeil may have hoped to strengthen his hold on the custody, as well as on his vassal the bishop, whose cathedral the great tower overawes. King Henry's terse *et concedo ut in eodem castello municionem vel turrim quam voluerint sibi faciant et in perpetuum habeant et custodiant* is outweighed by provisions for the complications of castle-guard which did not involve the tower.[28]

The impression that the fortifying was a subsidiary issue is stronger still in the series of privileges gained by Bishop Alexander of Lincoln to endow his fine new castle of Newark on Trent in the early 1130s. To dignify this strongly walled, palatial, and very conspicuous masonry fortress, he was allowed to divert the king's highway (otherwise *stretbreche* by the *Leges*); to erect a bank or causeway to dam up his fishponds; to build a bridge 'at the castle', subject to not diminishing the king's revenues in Lincoln nearby or at Nottingham upstream; to hold a fair 'at the castle'; and to do a third of his knight service by castle-guard at Newark. This last concession Stephen confirmed early in his reign, allowing the bishop to transfer there his Dover service also.[29] The only routine assistance Alexander lacked, which, being on the Trent, he probably did not need, was with the getting and transporting of materials. It is not surprising that lay nobles envied the superior castles of Roger of Salisbury and his clan.[30] Henry I's chamberlain, Geoffrey de Clinton at Kenilworth, had less help over his new castle with its large moats or fishponds and adjacent monastery; but this castle or Brandon could hardly have come into existence without tacit royal

27 Painter, *Feudalism and Liberty*, 141.

28 *RRAN* ii, p. clxxxviii, nos. 1475, 1606; R. W. Southern, 'The Place of Henry I in English History', *PBA*, 48 (1962), 161 n. 2.

29 *RRAN* ii, nos. 1660, 1661, 1770, 1791; iii, no. 465.

30 WM *HN* 25–6; Newark was 'a magnificent castle of very ornate construction' (HH 266). See Renn, *Norman Castles*, 100, 111, 163–4, 173, 187–8, 242, 308–10, 312–13, 319, 349, for plans and succinct descriptions of Banbury, Bishop's Waltham, Devizes, Downton, Farnham, Merdon, Sherborne, Sleaford, Taunton, Wolvesey (on which also M. W. Thompson in *Fortress*, 12 (1992), 18–22).

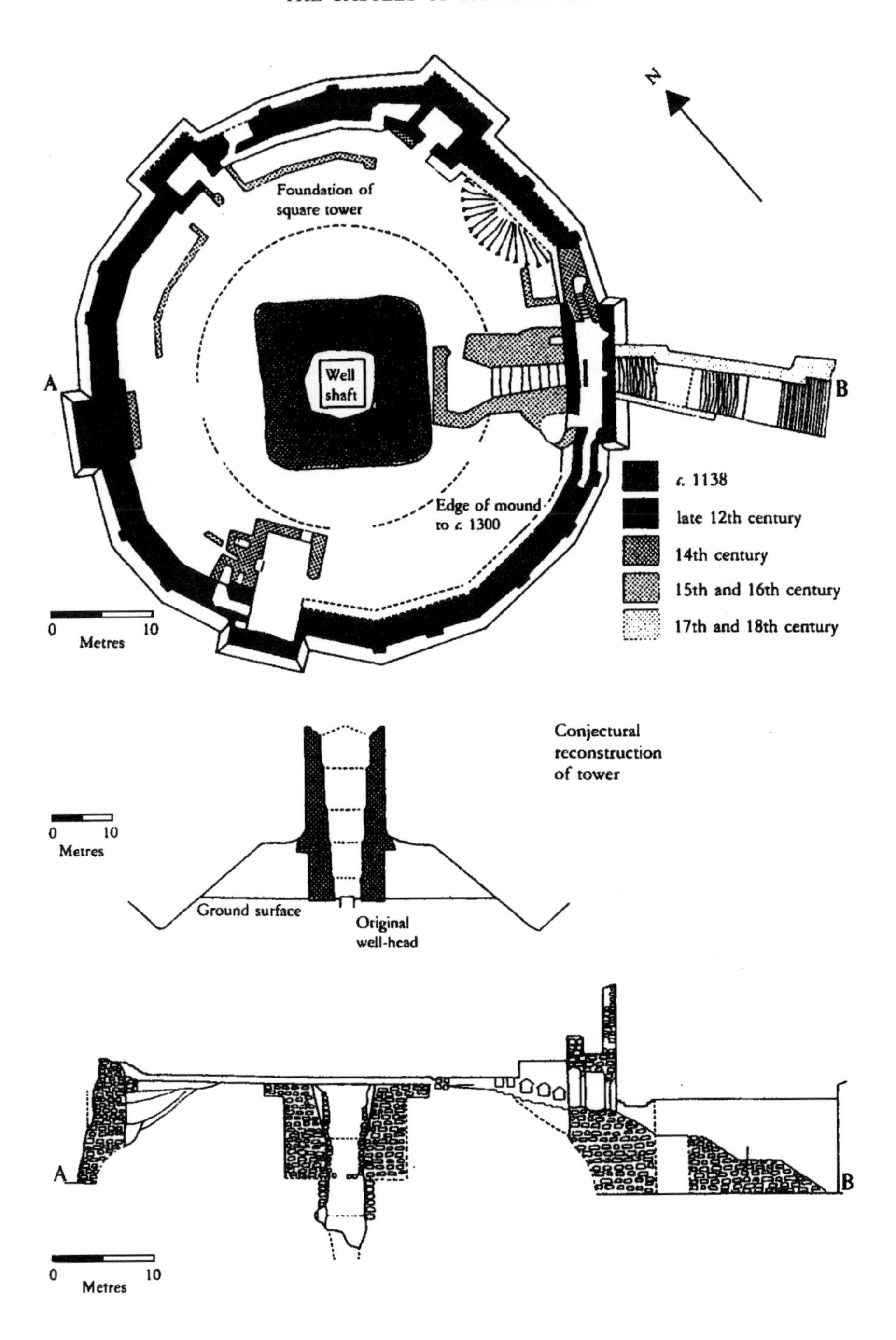

Figure 2. Farnham, Surrey: keep and motte (J. M. Kenyon, Fiona Gale; reproduced by kind permission of the Society for Medieval Archaeology)

support, not least because of its close encroachment upon Warwick. The king's licence might legalize various novelties (markets, tolls, mills, parks, chantries) if circumstances permitted. It might even overbear objectors; but, while a form of law operated, existing rights called for circumspect evasion.

The bishop of Lincoln, builder also of Sleaford and Banbury castles, insured his gains from loss of favour and from the challenge at law to which royal charter gave little immunity, but can have expected no dispute over building castles upon his own soil and lordship. The same insouciance must be inferred in Roger of Salisbury's attitude to his new or rebuilt castles at Devizes and Sherborne; and in Henry of Winchester's to his at Downton, Farnham, Merdon, Taunton, Bishop's Waltham, and Wolvesey. When in 1155 he secretly sent his treasure out of England and discreetly followed it, and the new king in revenge for his mother's and his own humiliations razed his castles, including probably the magnificent enmotted stone tower revealed by excavation at Farnham (see Fig. 2), the rationalization that they were all 'adulterine' would have astounded him. It is equally inapt of ancient Mandeville Pleshey or Saffron Walden, dismantled in 1158. Bishop Nigel may have had doubts about his masonry rebuild at Ely, probably of the small and old motte near the cathedral, but if so they were due to the hostility of the monks and of Saint Etheldreda, to whose intervention the monks credited its disappearance following capture by Stephen and in 1143 by Geoffrey de Mandeville.[31] This so-called *munitio fermissima* can have been one of the least deserving of the grandiloquent language habitually used of castles by chroniclers, in eulogy and in anathema alike.

The stone castles of this first twelfth-century 'great rebuilding' are much undervalued, and impossible to list with confidence, but were an aesthetic and technical leap forward, whether represented by William of Corbeil's *egregia turris* at Rochester; by the moated enclosure castle at Kenilworth; by Robert of Gloucester's great tower-keep rediscovered at Bristol, where Stephen was held prisoner; or by the de Veres' beautiful ashlar tower-palace at Castle Hedingham, with its lofty and well-lit galleried hall, thrown into one stately apartment by carrying the cross-wall on a wide arch (see Fig. 3). Closets, chambers, latrines, and fireplaces are lavishly provided, but, as with towers as late as Orford (1165–73) and Dover (1180–90). Hedingham contains no archery loops or even dual-purpose windows. That Geoffrey de Mandeville in 1141 may have had to be content with the extemporized fort at South Mimms near St Albans, and with other less distinguished earthworks, shows his straits. The vertically planked-up motte, with its central stone-footed timber tower with tunnel access to the basement, possibly built by him, was perhaps as powerful a symbol of the lordship he sought to gain as time and resources allowed. Masonry construction was phased over several years, with slow-setting lime-mortar wall masses. It was costly and required free movement of skilled craftsmen and materials, both scarce in many regions.

About this time, in Norfolk, the late eleventh-century great mansion within

[31] Brown ('Castles 1154 to 1216', 250 n. 1, 251 n. 2) had doubts; Southern, 'Place of Henry I', 137–40, 162; King, *Castellarium Anglicanum, sub.* Cambridgeshire, Lincolnshire, Oxfordshire, Warwickshire, etc.; Kenyon, *Medieval Fortifications*, 41–3.

Figure 3. Castle Hedingham, Essex, interior of the great hall. The castle was a favourite residence of Stephen's queen Matilda, and was the place where she died in 1152.

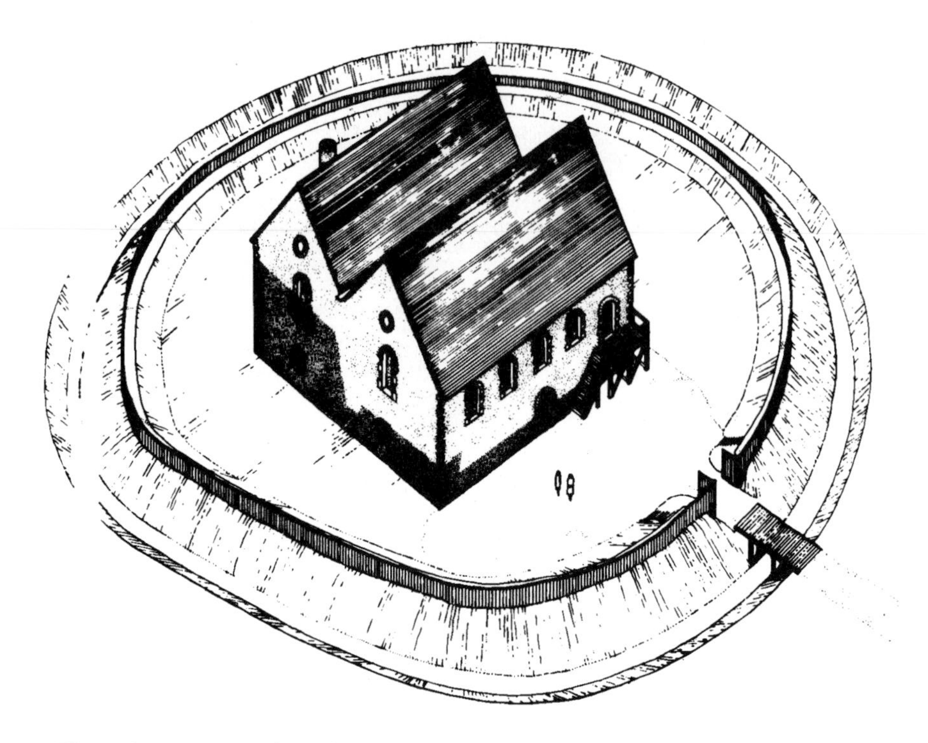

Figure 4. Reconstruction of Castle Acre, Norfolk, in the late eleventh century (R. Warmington, English Heritage Photographic Library)

the large embanked motte or upper ward at Castle Acre may have been converted into a tall rectangular tower by sacrificing about half the original area and thickening and heightening the rest (see Figs 4 and 5).[32] Even major adaptation was slow and expensive, and aesthetics not military determinism deserve respect here as elsewhere. What a great lay magnate with a taste as ambitious as that of Bishop Roger at his opulent Sherborne might seek is shown by William d'Aubigny's 'hall-keep' at Castle Rising. Roofs recessed behind upper walls are standard (the forebuilding summit is later). The block is squat in proportion, with many large windows and excellent ashlar with enriched detail, especially to the processional stairway to the first-floor *piano nobile*. The wall-arcading is like that once at Norwich and, while moderately fire-proof, the *ambiance* is of quasi-regal state. It was good enough for Isabella of France after 1330. Although the massive encircling ramparts were probably heightened at some early period, the so-called 'keep' is worlds away from any anarchic scenario (see Fig. 6).

By 1146 the earl of Arundel had moved his other East Anglian seat from the large sub-rectangular moated castle at Old Buckenham, seemingly up to date but soon to be demolished, to the new castle at a more frequented site two miles

32 Kenyon, *Medieval Fortifications* 28, 49–51; guidebook by J. G. Coad (English Heritage, 1984).

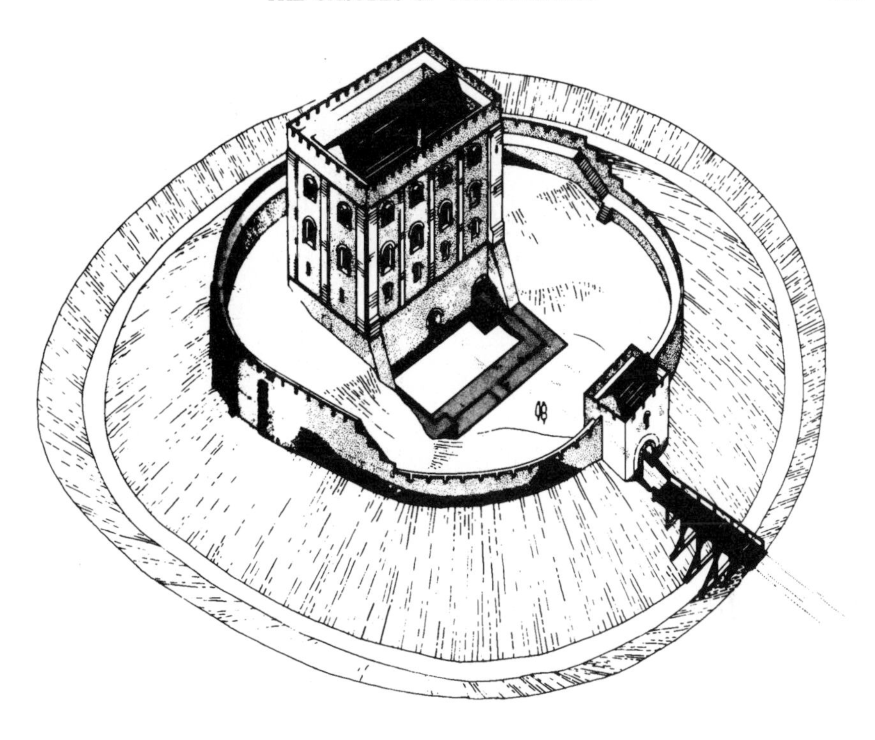

Figure 5. Reconstruction of Castle Acre, Norfolk, during Stephen's reign (W. Brouard after R. Warmington, English Heritage Photographic Library)

away.[33] An ambitious town-plantation scheme figured also at new Sleaford, at improved Devizes (1135–9), at Mountsorrel (by 1148), and effectively also at Newark-on-Trent and at Rising. Maurice Beresford's list of new towns shows no slackening of impetus, Stephen having eleven to thirteen compared with Henry I's thirteen to twenty-one.[34] A castle on its own was much less disruptive. The many new religious houses and towns entailed more adjustment of rights and tenures. New Buckenham was enhanced by a neat grid-plan *burgus*, adjoining the carefully laid-out, almost circular, moated ringwork with a vast levelled interior about seventy yards across, containing the base of a cylindrical tower about seventy feet in diameter with walls about ten feet thick and a crosswall (see Fig. 7). No lack of money, time, or care is apparent. The crude flint workmanship with sparing use of ashlar revealed by loss of the rendering is due to lack of good local stone, which may also explain the cylindrical shape. The habitual militarism about reduced vulnerability to mining and battery may certainly be disregarded.

Normal lordly castle-building, on excavated sites, is represented also by Brandon and Ascot Doilly, both smaller rectangular towers within earthwork

33 *Monasticon*, vi. 419; *Religious Houses*, 138, 150.

34 M. Beresford, *New Towns of the Middle Ages* (London, 1967), 462–3, 466–7, 504, 637–8. Land for New Buckenham itself was acquired from the bishop of Norwich on the Thetford to Norwich road.

Figure 6. Castle Rising, Norfolk: the east face of the keep seen from the gatehouse. The castle was built by Earl William d'Aubigny after his marriage to Queen Adeliza, widow of Henry I.

Figure 7. New Buckenham, Norfolk. Castle mound of c.1150 and new town of the late 12th century. Earl William d'Aubigny moved here from Old Buckenham at the end of the civil war.

enclosures, tentatively dated to the second quarter of the century.[35] Ascot, in the contentious Oxfordshire–Berkshire region, is one of several 'keeps' built up with mounded earth to the ground storey forming an enmotted tower. Its destruction has inevitably been attributed to Henry II. Brandon's 'keep' had a plinthed base ornamented by a decorative string course. New but 'early' castles tend doctrinally to be dated to Stephen's reign, but the probability is that aristocratic construction continued almost normally, and that the reign possessed a certain style of its own. When new or rebuilt castles occur in royal donations, as New Buckenham does and Gainsborough in favour of William de Roumare, analysis should precede the inferring of any licence.[36] That major rebuilding was known to the county community and thence to the king, and that confirmation of the privileges of the *caput* might be sought then, would be entirely natural.

To all this, the fieldworks of campaigns and sieges, essential to warfare, stand in some contrast. Positive identifications are few, but possibles, mostly slight ringworks or almost imperceptible mottes and enclosures, have been excavated at Bentley and Powderham (Hampshire), possibly attributable to Henry of Blois's siege of his own castle of *Lidelea*. Others considered by D. E. Renn include two near Arundel, Castle Cary, Corfe, Coventry, Cricklade, Harptree, Hereford, Lincoln (two), Ludlow, Oxford, and the Wallingford group. Seignorial and 'unofficial' works by emergent individuals, aspiring to permanency, may be represented by Peter of Goxhill's *capitalis curia* and by Cuckney. Therfield may be one, being of hasty construction and incomplete. Deddington, also excavated, was an embanked Saxon residence, later perhaps a castle of Odo of Bayeux and possibly refortified in stone by Stephen's Oxfordshire captain William de Chesney.[37] Individualism, stimulated by the relaxing of social constraints, unaccustomed – as the chroniclers in 1153–4 suggest – but scarcely unlawful, must have affected castle-building; but exactly how remains uncertain.

Geoffrey de Mandeville's charters are firmer ground. Since magnates were entitled to fortify in their own land and honour, his insecurity in Essex as earl, obliging him to make accessories of each *de facto* ruler in turn, explains his 'licences', as does their context. His titular position was confirmed by the empress 'about midsummer' 1141, with hereditary custody of the White Tower and of 'Ravenger's little castle' ('with the castle nearby' in her second charter).[38] These he might munition (*infortiare*) for her. When the citizens had expelled the Angevins from the city and from Westminster, this provision had to be more emphatic; so, by the empress's late-July charter, Geoffrey might hold the Tower, *ad firmandum et efforciandum ad voluntatem suam*. The empress also promised to make no separate accord with the Londoners, 'seeing that they are his mortal

35 Kenyon, *Medieval Fortifications*, 40–1, 43. No correlation with hostilities can be seen. Other suggested Stephanic foundations and additions are Aldingourne, Bedford, Benington, Bungay, Carisbrooke, Carlisle, Castle Cary, Christchurch, Guildford, Mileham (Renn, *Norman Castles*, 46–8 and gazetteer). David of Scots' Carlisle is elusive.

36 *RRAN* iii, no. 494 (cf. Round, *Geoffrey*, 159–60); also Bishopton, '1143' after John of Hexham: Renn, *Norman Castles*, 51, 111.

37 Kenyon, *Medieval Fortifications*, 10, 24, 31–3, 58–9; Renn, *Norman Castles*, 162–3.

38 *RRAN* iii, nos. 274, 275; Davis, *Stephen*, 55–6, 57–8, 77–82, 157–60.

enemies' (surely Geoffrey's own words). If he has to defend the Tower, she, in effect, accepts the consequences. The latent royal licensing prerogative is not invoked. She recognizes his gains, including 'his castles which he has', which 'shall stay and remain to him', with the normally superfluous 'to be munitioned at his discretion'. Saffron Walden was one such castle, with its early motte and bailey, now almost obliterated, and its large but roughly built square flint-rubble 'keep' upon and within the motte. Geoffrey can hardly have had facilities or time to build it. He had also the ancient castle of Pleshey, with its baileys and *burgus*. Any other castles he claimed, or fieldworks thrown up for his contest with Blois partisans based in East Anglia, and perhaps his 'castle on the river Lea' mentioned in late-July, might be covered; but the eloquent irregularity of it all contrasts starkly with the correct but perfunctory licence to transplant his market from Newport 'into his castle of Walden'. He too desired the enhancement of his capital complex of donjon, baileys, and *burgus* with the profits and public quality of a market. The worsened military position after the Londoners' revolt and the Angevins' flight to Oxford required Geoffrey to be confirmed in his father's and grandfather's tenures in the full panoply of established lordship, *in terris et turribus, in castellis et bailliis*. The empress undertook to make the bishop and cathedral clergy of London yield to Geoffrey the irksomely positioned castle of Stortford; and, if they refused, she would seize it and 'make it collapse and entirely fall'. The first licence to fortify two new castles follows; one retrospective, the other at a site not yet chosen by Geoffrey but still *in terra sua*, which he took as previously granted.[39] The diagnostic 'stay and remain' and 'for him to munition at his will' are reiterated, providing some colour of legality to endue his gains with permanency, while sanctioning violence with some show of propriety.

Whereas hints of hostilities in the Chester–Leicester pact, so greatly illuminated by Edmund King, are standard formulae of feudal antiquity, Geoffrey's *stet et remaneat* and the munitioning clauses are one with that disingenuous deal to eliminate Bishop's Stortford castle. A straightforward warrant to take and hold in fief, as in earlier thirteenth-century Ireland, was doubtless too blatant. Stephen could not endorse it, but based his charter closely on his rival's, her *turris Lundonie cum castello quod subtus est* becoming his *cum castello quod ei subest*; and her 'licence' being reworded as *preterea firmiter ei concessi ut possit firmare quoddam castellum ubicumque voluerit in terra sua, et quad stare possit*. Ratifying usurpation required both emphasis and caution. The castle *super Luiam* was left out, and Geoffrey's opportunities generally had shrunk. Neither he, in 1143, nor others could resist arrest and extortion of their castles

39 The *sicut ei per aliam cartam meam concessi* are nominally the empress's words. Foundations 'tentatively identified as a defensive tower and stair-turret and dated to the mid-twelfth century', discovered at Pleshey, and remains of the keep and market emplacement at Saffron Walden, may relate: F. Williams, *British Arch. Reports*, 42 (Oxford, 1977); S. R. Bassett, *Council for British Archaeology Research Report*, 45 (London, 1982). 'Ravenger's little castle' is elusive: R. A. Brown, H. M. Colvin, A. J. Taylor, *The History of the King's Works*, ii (London, 1963), 707 n. 3; G. Parnell, *Trans. London and Middlesex Arch. Soc.*, 36 (1985), 14, 23–5; and ibid. 33 (1982), 120. The 'castle on the Lea' could be Hertford, or one of two possible sites near Bow Bridge, or in Luton. His association with South Mimms is purely conjectural: Round, *Geoffrey*, 336–7 n. 7; J. Dyer *et al.*, *The Story of Luton* (Luton, 1964), 54–7, 63–4; J. P. C. Kent, *Bull of Barnet and District Local Hist. Soc.*, 15 (1968).

Figure 8. Burwell, Cambs: view of the castle site from the south-east. Built by Stephen on the edge of the fenland to control the activities of Geoffrey de Mandeville, who died here in 1144.

by Stephen's crafty breaches of the conventions of hospitality, which may have aborted castle-based revolts but generated fatal mistrust. A man of Geoffrey's stamp was forced into savage frustration. The moated sub-rectangular platform at Burwell where he was killed, built on the margin of the Fens near Cambridge, probably one of the fieldworks Stephen erected to house the troops checking his piratical operations, affords but weak witness of his name (see Fig. 8). The Peterborough chronicler's lurid passage, probably the most influential specimen of the castrophobic writing of the time, is Geoffrey's most eloquent memorial.[40]

Earl Ranulf's charter for Lincoln castle, probably of 1146 just before his own arrest, also gives no support to any practice of Anglo-Norman royal licensing of fortification. It is a specious guarantee of possession of the castle, city, and constableship, akin to the licence for the city-castle of Rochester in 1127. Both show the possessory aspects of 'fortifying' and hinge on tenure in fief of a *turris* within a royal castle held in 'perpetual' custody. It appears Ranulf obtained it to revive his claim by his late mother, Countess Lucy, to the castellanship, using the feudal leverage of his Norman lands lost in the Angevin conquest; and, since Stephen cherished Lincoln, to secure the eventual reversion of the castle and lands of Tickhill. Stephen's concessions were of expediency, as Ranulf surely knew. No resultant construction is likely, nor is any now visible or known from excavation. The charter, surviving only in a summary of 1325, provides for Ranulf, pending receipt of Tickhill, to munition (*firmare* basically 'to establish'), and have *dominium*, over and above his custody, of one of the two tower-crowned mottes (*unam de turribus suis*). This motte, for its symbolism and other reasons, was probably the *motte-maîtresse* of *c*.1068, now distractingly known as the Lucy Tower. Stephen's loyal city, which he lost his liberty in February 1141 trying to regain, Ranulf was to hand over, with the *turris*, in return for his lands in Normandy 'with all his castles'.[41]

Stiff local competition came from Bishop Alexander's aggrandisement of the complex of cathedral, palace, and precinct close by. In 1133 the bishop had annexed the city's East Gate and tower by royal licence. Further expansion was authorized in 1155–8, mainly by taking land from the city and breaching its ancient walls to extrude the intended eastern arm.[42] The castle must already have suffered some eclipse. Ranulf had seized it by a trick in 1140, which Stephen initially condoned and then tried to reverse. Although he had recognized Ranulf's title to 'the constableship of the castle of Lincoln and of Lincolnshire by hereditary right', the security of having, in full right as heir, *turris sua quam mater sua firmauit* was a natural demand. Although the Lucy Tower has since the eighteenth century at least been the 'shell-keep' upon the principal motte, and the name existed in 1225, excavation of the substructure of the smaller south-eastern mound has shown that this is the addition. Beneath the

40 Quoted Davis, *Stephen*, 80. Burwell and other comparable local sites have been investigated: T. C. Lethbridge, *Proc. Cambridge Antiquarian Soc.*, 36 (1936), 121–33; A. E. Brown, C. C. Taylor, ibid. 67, 97–9 and ibid. 68, 62–5. I have to thank Derek Renn for references in this and the preceding note.

41 *RRAN* iii, no. 178; Davis, *Stephen*, 46–50, 88–94, 161–5; Renn, *Norman Castles*, 226–7.

42 *RRAN* ii, no. 1784; *Calendar of the Charter Rolls* 4 (1912), 106–12; C. L. H. Coulson, 'Hierarchism in Conventual Crenellation', *Medieval Archaeology*, 26 (1982), 69–100 (at 75).

early nineteenth-century observatory, a rectangular masonry core infilled with mortared boulders was discovered, around which the earth had been heaped, making a foundation of the type at Farnham and Ascot Doilly. Upon it, finer twelfth-century and later masonry indicated a fashionable enmotted stone tower, which the excavator attributed to Ranulf, in the belief that the charter was permission to build a new tower.[43] Lucy might have had the base erected before she died *c.*1136, and perhaps a timber superstructure. Her son could have added to it, but work by either is unlikely on the Conqueror's motte, where the munitioning of temporary ownership is Ranulf's likely 'fortification'. At Rochester the archbishops after William of Corbeil long kept their 'great tower' and their custody, but Ranulf by his arrest shortly afterwards lost both his mother's tower and all his rights in Lincoln castle.

One pseudo-licence, for Berkeley in 1153, remains for discussion. As a castle-pact the Berkeley charter is significant, even though it does not incorporate any licence to fortify, despite the Regesta headline and index.[44] Duke Henry did not actually 'grant the Manor of Bitton and £100 of land in Berkeley with permission to build a castle there', but rather promised 'to fortify a castle at Berkeley to Robert fitz Harding's requirements'.[45] Henry had just landed at Wareham and bought the adherence at Bristol of the *parvenu* heir-by-marriage to this small but crucial motte-and-bailey castle on the road to Gloucester. The structural improvements show how much he valued both, and suggest that Robert was quite demanding. Some of the early Berkeley documents have been tampered with, but this one rings true,[46] being a guarantee by the leading Angevins of active support in return for Robert's homage. Had the conflict with King Stephen lasted longer, further similar pacts might have arranged a series of defensive outposts to Bristol and the empress's redoubt of the south-west. As it is, the good quality plinthed revetment encasing the scarped motte, embellished with three semi-cylindrical turrets and, not much later, by a forebuilding and ramped ceremonial stairway approximating to the increasingly fashionable tower-keep, testify to fitz Harding's adroit opportunism. Henry II, whom the 'feudal-anarchy' school has praised for striving with conscientious altruism against all 'private castles', may have anticipated his reign by building one himself.

Fieldworks once abandoned quickly perished, leaving faint traces, unlike the concrete, brick, and metal debris of modern war. Little can have been left for Henry II to clear up. His destructions recorded as paid for differed entirely in target and in motive. Henry of Winchester's castles were slighted, and those of his nephew William of Boulogne were seized. Punishment was the common

43 N. Reynolds, 'Investigations in the Observatory Tower, Lincoln Castle', *Medieval Archaeology*, 19 (1975), 201–5.

44 *RRAN* iii, no. 309.

45 As noted by Renn, *Norman Castles*, 107–8, and King, *Castellarium Anglicanum, sub* Gloucestershire.

46 On the authenticity of these charters, see further E. King (ed.), *The Anarchy of King Stephen's Reign* (Oxford, 1994), Ch. 9 n. 58.

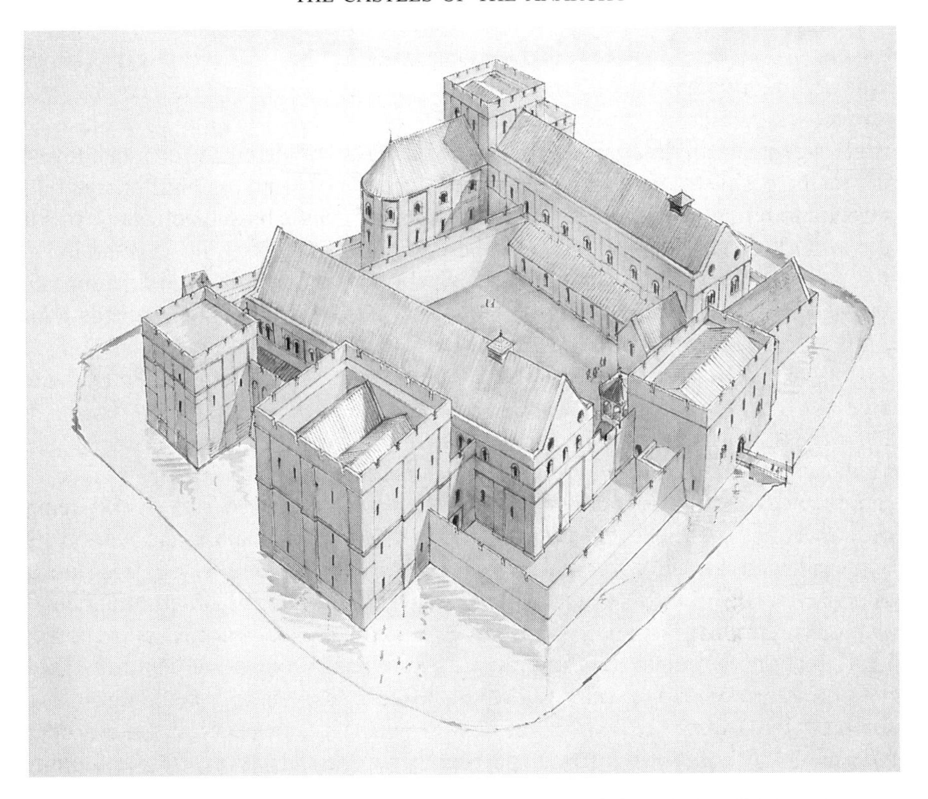

Figure 9. Wolvesey Palace, Winchester, Hants (M. Biddle and T. Ball, English Heritage Photographic Library)

denominator.[47] Castle-polemic has scored a famous victory for the churchmen over the 'castle-men'. Clerical self-interest and royalism have since triumphed. Expectations of licences to fortify after 1154 are in reality still less fulfilled than during the anarchy or before it, for Henry II issued none which can be substantiated; nor did Richard I. They begin with one by John (*c.*1194) as count of Mortain, for the walling of the house of a partisan at Haddon. His series of licences as king, aborted in 1204, begins with Wheldrake near York (1199), perhaps the Stephanic castle.[48] The citizens seem to have outbid the grantee, Richard Malebisse. The grant is not enrolled and Howden says it was promptly revoked, a significantly solitary reference.

That organized warfare and consequential disorder in parts of England, not castles, were the problem of the anarchy hardly requires demonstration. Keeping castles on a war-footing, whether in defence or aggressively, so that the normal skeleton estate staff was enlarged to the extent of 'garrisoning', and the lord with his 'riding household' based himself there, was exceptional and expensive.

47 Brown, 'Castles 1154 to 1216', 250–3; Pounds, *Medieval Castle*, 31; William of Newburgh's *complanare* (above, n. 3) is as exaggerated as the rest.

48 Brown ('Castles 1154 to 1216', 251 n. 10) claims a licence 1160–1180 for Pleshey; also 279 n. 8; *Historical MS Commission, Rutland MSS*, iv. 24; Howden, iv. 117.

Analysis of all references to castles in the sources might offer some hint as to how commonly this was done in contested and lawless zones. Established castles – being, at diverse levels of noble society, *inter alia* country mansions, estate offices, farmsteads, hunting lodges (with park and warren), court-houses, and gaols, with widely varying emergency capacities for defence if adequately stocked and manned – had 'permanent' status, unlike purely military fieldworks. Regular castle-building by episcopal and lay magnates continued little affected, producing noble capital-seats, no more overtly 'military' but as ostentatiously palatial and 'fortified' as before and since. Bishop Alexander's Banbury has gone, but traces of his rectangular, towered and moated Sleaford remain, logically laid out, as is Bishop Roger's Sherborne, with its central rectangular keep and small mural turrets to the curtain wall. Bishop Henry may have added a large keep to Taunton, and his Farnham must have been an impressive sight. His palatial castle of Wolvesey boasted a square dwelling tower (keep') and excellent sanitary arrangements (see Fig. 9). Systematic survey and some bold redating would greatly strengthen the 'normal' contingent and extend its social range, provided 'anarchic' expectations are neutralized. But categories of 'warlike' and 'normal' castle-building (already problematic) will remain archaeologically unsubstantiated, even were generous excavation funding available. Very many lesser gentry-seats, some at least still administratively and residentially active and needing only to be refortified, manned, and stocked, will be among the 'normal' castles. These, the vast majority, products of the Norman settlement, differ radically from the crisis-only fortifications, mostly fieldworks serving the passing needs of a campaign. They also differ significantly from any new castles, permanently intrusive in intention, which the 1153–4 comments have been taken to imply. Archaeologically the two are virtually inseparable, nor can either usually be distinguished from sub-manorial farmsteads, especially if short lived. All of these diverse forms might be 'castles', as we have seen.

It has been the argument of this chapter that, with due allowance for necessary conjecture, the better-recorded fieldwork castles matter chiefly for the military history of the anarchy, of which they were the most durable symptom. The new and 'unprecedented' castles, which the traditional view has determinedly emphasized – whether brigand lairs, which could only slightly increase the predatory potential of lawless men, or, maybe, the aspiring lordship seats of 'feudal lawlessness', carved out of the confusion by genuine acts of usurpation – should both, more objectively, be regarded as the inevitable reaction of an acquisitive noble society to the state-sponsored turmoil and governmental abdication which was the anarchy of King Stephen's reign.

9

Castle-Guard*

Sidney Painter

While the importance of the part played by castles in feudal England has long been recognized by historians, comparatively little attention has been paid to the arrangements which were made for garrisoning these fortresses. Since its appearance in 1902, J. H. Round's article in the *Archaeological Journal* has been the standard authority on the subject.[1] In a recent chapter on 'Castles and Castle-Guard' Professor Stenton brought to light some new material, but he made no significant addition to the work of Round whose general conclusions he accepted.[2] The failure of these two scholars to use the invaluable material in the Hundred Rolls makes their results far from comprehensive. Round's central thesis will not bear examination in the light of the evidence now available. The whole subject is far more complex and hence far more interesting than either Round or Professor Stenton realized. It therefore seems worth while to survey all the evidence available in print in the hope of answering the obvious questions – what were the feudal arrangements for the custody of royal and baronial castles and on what bases were the original castle-guard services commuted to money payments. In order to simplify a highly complicated subject, I shall restrict myself to the services owed by knightly tenants and omit all discussion of tenure by sergeanty.

Reasonably clear evidence of castle-guard obligations owed by tenants by knight service exists for at least forty-two English castles.[3] In the case of nine more it is not quite certain whether knight service or sergeanty was involved.[4] Of the forty-two, eleven were royal and thirty-one baronial – placing in the latter group such castles as Wallingford and Tickhill which were supported by single honors even though they were commonly in the king's hands. But while the evidence is sufficient to show the extensive existence of arrangements by which a

* This article is reprinted from *The American Historical Review*, Vol. XL, No. 3 (April, 1935), pp. 450–59.

1 J. H. Round, 'Castle Guard', *Archaeological Journal*, LIX (1902), pp. 144–59.

2 F. M. Stenton, *The First Century of English Feudalism*, 1066–1166 (Oxford, 1932), pp. 190–215. As he was dealing with the period 1066–1166, Professor Stenton was obviously under no obligation to make a complete survey of later material.

3 Aldford, Alnwick, Arundel, Banbury, Belvoir, Brecknock, Chester, Clifford, Clun, Corsham, Devizes, Dodleston, Dover, Eye, Farnham, Hastings, Kington, Lancaster, Launceston, Ledbury, Lincoln, Montgomery, Newcastle upon Tyne, Northampton, Norwich, Pevensey, Plympton, Prudhoe, Richmond, Rochester, Rockingham, Salisbury, Shrawardine, Skipsea, Skipton, Tickhill, Trematon, Wallingford, Warwick, Wem, Whitchurch, Windsor.

4 Bamburgh, Baynard, Canterbury, Framlingham, Hedingham, Knockin, Peak, Stogursey, Wigmore.

baron's tenants guarded his castle, material which might illuminate the actual mechanism of the system is extremely scanty. Only for Richmond and Hastings is full information available and because of their strategic importance these fortresses can hardly be considered as typical baronial strongholds. Usually a whole knight's fee was bound to supply a completely equipped horseman for forty days in a year. In some cases it is stated that the service was due only in time of war, while in others in seems to have been exacted every year. For fractions of fees adjustments were made either in the duration or the quality of service. Thus a half fee might owe twenty, days service instead of forty or a sergeant instead of a knight for the full period.[5] Except in the case of castles supported by very large baronies these services, even if exacted every year, could furnish only an insignificant permanent garrison. At Clun, an exposed post in the Welsh marches, the lord of Hopton owed one knight for the entire year and another for forty days. The other six and one half fees owing ward at Clun would bring the garrison up to two knights or their equivalent in sergeants for some three hundred days in the year.[6] In short, at forty days service per fee it would require nine fees to supply a single knight as a permanent garrison. The average baron must have been forced to entrust the peacetime defense of his castle to the porter, the watchman, and one or two of his household knights while his tenants were bound to supply a more adequate force in time of war.

When the strategic importance of a baronial castle made a strong permanent garrison necessary, the term of service was increased as at Richmond and Hastings. A twelfth century list of the fees owing castle-guard duty at Richmond shows that the garrison was maintained by one hundred and eighty-six knights who were divided into six groups each of which served two months. These groups varied in strength from twenty-six to forty-two knights, the larger ones serving in the summer months when the danger from Scottish raids was greatest.[7] Hastings was guarded by the sixty knights of the count of Eu's honor. They were divided into four wards each of which served for a month three times a year. Apparently in consideration of this very heavy castle-guard duty the knights were released from all service outside the rape of Hastings except at the lord's cost.[8] Thus the permanent garrisons of Richmond and Hastings averaged thirty-one and fifteen knights respectively.

In the case of certain royal castles a strong regular garrison was provided by combining the service due from a number of baronies. The best example is that of the great fortress of Dover, which was considered the key to England. Nine baronies were responsible for its custody. The largest of these, the constable's honor of Haughley, consisted of fifty-six knights' fees which were divided into thirteen groups of four or five. Each of these groups is marked *unum mensem* on a list in the *Red Book of the Exchequer*, which seems to indicate a month's service in the castle. On this basis the constable's barony alone would supply a

5 *Rotuli hundredorum* (Record Commission), II, 55–58, 64, 76–77, 81, 232, 235–36, 707–8. *Calendar of Inquisitions post Mortem* (Rolls Series), I, 279; III, 173; IV, 10. *Book of Fees* (Rolls Series), p. 740.

6 *Rot. Hund.*, II, 77. Book of Fees, p. 963. *Cal. Inq. p. Mortem*, I, 280.

7 *Calendar of Inquisitions Miscellaneous*, I, 167–68. The inquisition was made under Henry III, but the first list given, no. 519, belongs to the middle of the twelfth century.

8 *Cal. Inq. p. Mortem*, VII, 427. *Red Book of the Exchequer*, ed. Hubert Hall (Rolls Series), pp. 622–23.

permanent garrison of four or five knights, each of whom served a month of four weeks. Then five baronies varying in size from fourteen to twenty-four fees were each made to furnish an approximately equal amount of service by forcing some tenants to perform their ward two or three times a year. In this way each barony furnished about thirty-nine periods of service. Finally, enough fees were taken from three other baronies to form another group of thirty-nine service periods.[9] As each of these six groups of thirty-nine periods of ward could obviously furnish three knights to join the constable's monthly contingent, the total permanent garrison of Dover was twenty-two or twenty-three knights.

The royal castle of Norwich was cared for by a similar group of fiefs. The bishops of Norwich and Ely and the abbot of St Edmunds each owed forty knights, the barony of Rye thirty-five, the barony of Peche twenty, the barony of Wormegay probably fifteen, and the barony of Kentwell ten.[10] Unfortunately only in the case of the honor of St Edmunds is there evidence as to how the ward was actually performed. The abbot's forty knights were divided into four constabularies each of which served ninety days in the year. There is some reason for believing that originally the whole service owed by a knight was done at one stretch, and that this was later changed to allow a month of duty three times a year.[11] If the above list of baronies owing ward at Norwich is correct and if the obligations of each were proportionate to those of St Edmunds, the permanent garrison of the castle consisted of fifty knights. The Conqueror's well-known fear of Scandinavian invasions would account for this extremely generous provision for the defense of the principal stronghold of East Anglia. Henry I's release of the knights of the bishop of Ely from their service at Norwich certainly indicates that he considered the garrison more than adequate for the needs of his day.[12]

While it is perfectly clear that the same sort of arrangements provided for the custody of Lincoln, Newcastle upon Tyne, Northampton, Rochester, Rockingham, Salisbury, and Windsor, the most one can do is to identify the baronies which owed ward, and in several cases not even that is possible. Round has done this for Rochester, Rockingham, and Windsor.[13] In the case of Rockingham I suspect that the Ridel-Basset barony of fifteen fees should be added to Round's list to bring the total to the neat figure of one hundred and twenty.[14] The baronies which guarded Newcastle are listed in the *Red Book of the Exchequer*.[15] The constable's fief of La Haye certainly owed ward at Lincoln, and Professor Stenton is probably correct in assuming that at least part of the knights of the bishop of Lincoln did service there.[16] At Northampton only the Fitz Hamon and

9 *Red Book*, pp. 706–12.

10 *Cal. Inq. p. Mortem*, I, 11; II, 116; III, 222; IV, 169; VI, 50; VII, 176; VIII, 96. *Book of Fees*, pp. 1324–29. Sir William Dugdale, *Monasticon Anglicanum* (London, 1846), I, 482.

11 *Feudal Documents from the Abbey of Bury St. Edmunds*, ed. D. C. Douglas (London, 1932), pp. lxxxvi–lxxxvii, 84. *Cronica Jocelini de Brakelonda*, ed. J. G. Rokewode (Camden Society, no. 13, 1840), pp. 49–50. Compare Jocelin's account with Stephen's charter.

12 *Monasticon*, I, 482.

13 *Op. cit.*

14 *Rot. Hund.*, I, 237. *Cal. Inq. p. Mortem*, VIII, 469.

15 *Red Book*, p. 606.

16 *English Feudalism*, p. 212. *Cal. Inq. p. Mortem*, vii, 223.

Chokes baronies, each of fifteen fees, can be identified with any confidence.[17] In 1166 the earl of Salisbury and Walter Waleran admitted that they owed twenty and five knights respectively for the custody of Salisbury castle, and at least one of the bishop of Salisbury's fees did ward there. A thirteenth-century list in the Hundred Rolls which adds the abbesses of Wilton and Shaftesbury, the Dunstanville barony, and several others is rendered doubtful by an earlier statement in the same source that no fees owed ward at Salisbury castle.[18] Despite the fairly full evidence on the baronies assigned to some of these royal castles, in most cases the lack of detailed information about the system in use makes it impossible to estimate the size of the garrisons provided. If I am correct in my belief that at Windsor and Rockingham the knights owed forty days service a year,[19] the garrisons of those castles must have been eight and thirteen or fourteen respectively.

The twenty-ninth article of Magna Carta raises a most interesting question about these arrangements for the custody of the king's castles. It implies that castle-guard service was, at least in the eyes of the rebellious barons, an alternative rather than an addition to regular service in the host. In 1224 the regency acted in conformity with this principle when it released from their turn of duty at Lancaster castle certain vassals of the honor of Lancaster who had participated in the siege of Bedford.[20] There is evidence to show that this claim was not entirely new in 1215. In 1166 Earl Patrick of Salisbury stated that he owed forty knights to the king's army and twenty to the custody of Salisbury castle. Walter Waleran acknowledged twenty and five in the same categories. The earls of Salisbury seem to have made good their claim as they never paid scutage on the twenty extra fees, but the Waleran barony, despite at least one fine made with the king, usually paid on the full twenty-five fees.[21] In the inquest of 1212 Hugh de Balliol claimed to hold his barony of Bywell for five fees, although he admitted that he owed thirty knights to the ward of Newcastle. As his barony usually paid scutage on thirty fees, his claim does not seem to have been allowed.[22] The list of scutages and fines paid in lieu of military service shows that in general the kings did not admit that castle-guard duty could take the place of service in the host.[23]

Before the close of the twelfth century the king and his barons began to commute into money payments the whole or part of the castle-guard services owed by their vassals. Round was particularly interested in this process. He believed that the tenants were required to pay an amount sufficient to hire a substitute to perform their service. A study of the rates of commutation at Dover and Windsor convinced him that they were based on a wage of eight pence a day for a knight. As this was the standard pay during most of the reign of Henry II,

17 *Ibid.*, VI, 36, 90, 313; VIII, 222, 463. *Rot. Hund.*, I, 25–31.
18 *Ibid.*, II, 238, 268. *Red Book*, pp. 236, 240, 242.
19 *Cal. Inq. p. Mortem*, II, 284; VII, 324–25.
20 *Rotuli litterarum clausarum*, ed. T. D. Hardy (Record Commission), I, 606.
21 *Red Book*, pp. 58, 73, 89, 152–53, 240, 242, 482. *Pipe Roll 14 Henry II* (Pipe Roll Society, XII), 160. *Pipe Roll 2 Richard I* (*ibid.*, xxxix), 123.
22 *Pipe Roll 14 Henry II* (*ibid.*, XII), 172. *Red Book*, p. 563.
23 *Rotuli de oblatis et finibus*, ed. T. D. Hardy (Record Commission), pp. 127–73.

he concluded that the rates must have been established under that monarch. The available evidence tends to support Round's belief that the process of commuting castle-guard services into money payments began in the time of Henry II. A charter of the first year of Richard I shows that the knights of Peterborough owing ward at Rockingham castle were allowed to commute their service in time of peace. A document of 1198–1199 gives the castle-guard dues owed to Dover, Eye, Norwich, and Richmond by various Norfolk tenants. Finally a list of the wards owed to Richmond castle by the Yorkshire tenants of its honor early in the thirteenth century indicates that their service had been commuted at the rate of one half mark per fee.[24]

Unfortunately Round's reasoning is not as convincing as his result. His whole theory is based on the assumption that a knight paid whatever was needed to hire a substitute to perform his service. This he sought to establish by a study of the systems in operation at Dover and Windsor. Round concluded, and he had at least one excellent piece of evidence to support his view, that the regular period of guard service at Dover was fifteen days, and hence the ten shillings paid as commutation would hire a substitute at eight pence a day. But the evidence indicating a fifteen day period of service at Dover seems to me far too weak to stand up against the fact that the knights of the honor of Haughley were divided into thirteen groups and each group carefully labeled *unum mensem* on the *Red Book* list. Then in the same list under the ward of Crevequer are found several irregular *tenementa*. One of these paid twenty shillings in commutation of a twenty day service period performed three times a year.[25] As a full fee doing ward three times paid thirty shillings, this indicates a regular service period of thirty days. Obviously a knight could not hire an eight pence a day substitute for thirty days for ten shillings. In the case of Windsor, where the rate of commutation was twenty shillings a fee, Round's theory demands a ward of thirty days. There is no satisfactory evidence as to the period of service exacted from those who owed castle-guard at Windsor. Round's thirty day term is supported, as he admits, only by its mathematical convenience for his theory. One entry in the *Inquisitions post Mortem* strongly indicates a forty day service at Windsor.[26] Considering that of the fifteen English castles where the term of castle-guard can be definitely established thirteen show a ward of forty days, the burden of proof seems to fall on the advocates of the thirty day period. In short, while it is impossible to disprove Round's conclusions in respect to Dover and Windsor, his theory that in the case of these two castles a knight's commutation payment was sufficient to hire a substitute to perform his service appears decidedly tenuous.

The conviction that the rate of commutation did not in general suffice to replace the service becomes stronger as one examines other castle-guard dues. Unfortunately there are very few castles at which both the yearly service period

24 *Calendar of Charter Rolls, 1327–1341* (Rolls Series), p. 277. *Book of Fees*, pp. 1324–29. *Cal. Inq. Miscellaneous*, I, 168–69. The two lists given in numbers 520 and 521 are approximately contemporary with the returns dated 1210–1212 and 1211–1212 in the *Red Book*.

25 *Red Book*, pp. 706–707, 711.

26 VII, 324–25.

and the rate of commutation can be established with reasonable certainty. While it is clear that the knights of the count of Eu originally owed ninety days service per year at Hastings, the exact rate of commutation is uncertain. Fourteenth century figures for the total castle-guard payments and for the shares assigned to each of the four wards indicate a rate of one half mark per fee, while records of the obligations of individual tenants point to one of ten shillings sixpence. One is tempted to suggest that John of Brittany, who held the honor of Hastings under Edward III, reduced the rate to correspond to that charged the Yorkshire tenants of his honor of Richmond.[27] But as the pay of a knight for ninety days at eight pence comes to sixty shillings, the higher of these rates would be utterly insufficient to replace the actual service. Again Jocelin de Brakelond shows that the king received from the abbot of St. Edmunds nine shillings in commutation of the ninety days ward at Norwich owed by each of the forty fees of his *servitium debitum*.[28] Finally, if the evidence indicating a forty day service at Rockingham is to be relied on, the commutations paid there were equally insufficient. The barony of Odell paid six shillings per fee, that of Wardon five, and the abbey of Peterborough four.[29] In none of these cases did the castle-guard payments approach what was necessary in order to hire substitutes at the lowest wage suggested by Round.

A general survey of the dues exacted at other English castles tends to support this conclusion. Except for the thirty shillings paid by the fees which owed three wards a year at Dover, the highest rate was twenty shillings at Devizes and Windsor. The Northumbrian strongholds of Alnwick and Prudhoe received one mark per fee from their tenants and Rochester twelve shillings. The rate at Tickhill was ten shillings, but an extra eight pence was paid to furnish food for the watch. The baronies owing guard at Northampton and the fees of the honors of Lancaster and Richmond which lay outside Lancashire and Richmondshire paid ten shillings. At Norwich the rate varied. The fees of the bishop of Norwich and of the baronies of Kentwell, Rye, and Wormegay seem to have paid between six and seven shillings. If the extremely scanty evidence for the barony of Peche is to be trusted, its fees paid at the very meager rate of three shillings seven pence. The knights of the honor of Eye, again on rather slight evidence, appear to have paid sums ranging from one shilling eight pence to three shillings four pence per fee.[30] As all the available evidence points to thirty or forty days as the usual term of service, these rates vary from insufficient to ridiculous from the point of view of supplying funds for hiring substitutes.

One reason for this situation seems obvious. It is quite conceivable that tenants owing castle-guard refused to commute their services at the prevailing rate of pay. Expeditions to Wales, Ireland, Scotland, and France were costly and dangerous, and a knight might well be willing to secure his release by a scutage

27 *Cal. Inq. P. Mortem*, I, 75; II 134, 214–15; VII, 427; VIII, 232.
28 Jocelin de Brakelond, pp. 49–50.
29 *Cal. Inq. p. Mortem*, II, 207–208, 284; IX, 108. *Cal. Charter Rolls*, 1327–1341, p. 277.
30 *Rot. Hund.*, I, 25; II, 236. *Red Book*, pp. 716–17. Round, *op. cit.*, pp. 158–59. *Book of Fees*, pp. 1148, 1150, 1324–29. *Cal. Inq. p. Mortem*, I, 11; II, 116, 139–40, 210–21, 291; III, 222, 469; IV, 65, 169; V, 264, 316; VI, 50, 379–80; VII, 67–68, 176; VIII, 96, 222, 463.

payment of two marks that would hire a substitute for forty days. But guard duty in a castle must have been far less arduous. There was little or no danger attached to it and it involved, usually at least, a comparatively short journey. Consider, for instance, the question of the food needed during the term of service. We have ample evidence of the cash loans required to support themselves by the feudal tenants who followed King John to Ireland in 1210.[31] When, however, the knight was on castle-guard duty, he could ordinarily supply himself from his own manors. In this connection it is interesting to notice that the tenants of the honor of Richmond whose lands lay outside Yorkshire paid ten shillings per fee as against the half mark owed by the knights of Richmondshire.[32] In short I believe that the rate of commutation was the result of a bargain between the lord and his tenants. The more onerous the obligations, the more the lord could persuade his vassals to pay in commutation, but I doubt if the payments were ever sufficient to hire substitutes to perform the original service. Even at the low rates which were established the tenants seem to have been inclined to prefer performance of their castle-guard duty to payment of the commutation. Richard's charter to Peterborough and Magna Carta suggest this very strongly. While baronial dislike of John's foreign mercenaries may have had something to do with this provision of Magna Carta, I believe that the main motive was economic.

Obviously in time of peace the lord of a castle would prefer to receive money instead of service. The difficulty of enforcing the due attendance of the feudal tenants must have been enormous. The mercenary garrison made possible by the castle-guard payments might be small, but it was permanent and reliable. But in time of war a far larger force would be needed to secure the safety of the fortress. How could the lord obtain an adequate wartime garrison without imposing an intolerable burden on his exchequer? A possible solution of this problem may be found by examining the system in operation at the Wiltshire castle of Devizes. About twenty fees were assigned to the custody of this stronghold. Each full fee owed the service of a knight in the castle for forty days in time of war, and each half fee owed a sergeant for the same period. In time of peace, however, each full fee paid twenty shillings a year and each half fee ten shillings. The Hundred Rolls state that Devizes could be held for twenty-five marks in time of peace – a sum comfortably within that provided by the castle-guard payments if the latter were duly enforced.[33] Thus a combination of guard service and money payments provided Devizes with a fair sized garrison in war and a small permanent one in peace. I can find only one clear instance of a similar system elsewhere. King Richard agreed to acquit the knights of the abbey of Peterborough of the four shillings a fee which they were accustomed to render for the ward of Rockingham castle in time of peace if they chose to perform

31 *Rotuli de liberate ac de miss et praestitis*, ed. T. D. Hardy (Record Commission), pp. 174–226.

32 *Cal. Inq. p. Mortem*, II, 210–21. Although it is not quite certain that tenants supported themselves while on castle-guard duty, it seems probable that such was the general rule. In a number of cases the evidence clearly indicates that they did. Only in respect to a tenant's service at Aldford in Chester can I find the definite statement that the lord paid the expenses.

33 *Rot. Hund.*, II, 236.

their service as they had in the reign of Henry I.[34] This seems to prove that sometime after the death of the latter king the abbey had been allowed, or more probably compelled, to commute its service in peace time. The conclusion that Richard still expected the knights to perform their guard duty in time of war seems inescapable. An extensive use of this distinction between services due in peace and in war is indicated by one of the articles of inquiry in the Hundred Rolls – 'Of the castles of the lord king, that is . . . what wards are owed in time of peace and what in time of war.'[35] An arrangement such as those described above must have been ideal from the king's point of view. It furnished money for a small mercenary garrison in time of peace and yet supplied an adequate force to safeguard the castle in wartime. I should like to suggest the possibility that other early commutations of castleguard service may have been made on this same basis.

Although the sparsity of evidence makes dogmatic statements impossible and generalizations dangerous, I wish to offer a tentative summary of the history of castle-guard service. During the first century after the Conquest, feudal arrangements provided strong permanent garrisons for the seats of large baronies and royal castles which were cared for by groups of baronies. As the internal condition of the country grew more peaceful, the king and his barons found these garrisons unnecessarily large in time of peace. Meanwhile the feudal castle-guard obligations became more difficult to enforce as their necessity grew less evident. As a result, the lord of a castle was inclined to commute his tenants' services in time of peace at the highest rate that he could persuade them to pay. With this money he could hire a small, reliable mercenary garrison. This process seems to have started during the reign of Henry II. At first, however, the king and his great barons probably continued to insist that their tenants perform their service in time of war. This was true to some extent at least during the baronial wars of the mid-thirteenth century. Later, possibly at the time of the general collapse of the feudal military system, the actual performance of castle-guard duty ceased, and the commutation payments became ordinary rents.

34 *Cal. Charter Rolls*, 1327–1341, p. 277.
35 *Rot. Hund.*, II, 68.

10

Castle Guard and the Castlery of Clun

Frederick C. Suppe

Clun was the site of an important baronial castle, probably erected in the later 1090s, in western Shropshire close to the Welsh border. Sidney Painter twice drew upon evidence concerning Clun Castle when he wrote on the subject of castle guard service.[1] Both times he confined himself to thirteenth-century evidence such as the Hundred Rolls and an Inquisition *Post Mortem* from 1272. He thus ignored earlier materials which would have permitted him to examine both the circumstances under which this castle and its castle guard system were created and the manner in which the system functioned. It is my purpose to consider the full range of evidence available about Clun in order to answer these questions.

The most complete description of the feudal military obligations which provided manpower for Clun castle was compiled upon the death of John Fitz Alan (III) in 1272 and is embodied in two separate versions. The first is an Inquisition *Post Mortem* to determine and list John's holdings,[2] and the second is an enrollment on the Close Rolls of a temporary division of these holdings between a dower portion for his widow and the remainder to be administered by a crown-appointed guardian during the minority of his heir.[3] The Inquisition *Post Mortem* lists the various holdings held from the lord of Clun which comprise the castlery. It rates these lands at 10½ fiefs and notes that in wartime each fief, with the exception of that held by Sir Brian de Brompton, owes the service of a man with a corselet or mail shirt and a horse at Clun Castle for forty days. This armament is not the standard of equipment expected of a knight (*miles*) in this period, but rather that of a sergeant (*serviens*), whose military services were usually considered as equivalent to half those of a knight. The inquest goes on to state that this castle guard is worth £6 15s. each year in time of war, and that the services of each esquire (or sergeant) are worth 4½d. per day. The sum £6 15s. is equivalent to 1,620 pence. Simple calculation shows that this figure exactly represents wages of 4½d. per day for nine sergeants for a 40–day term. The Close Roll extent of Clun also states that this castle guard is worth £6 15s. in wartime

1 In 1935 Painter's article, 'Castle Guard' appeared in the *American Historical Review* 40 (1935), 450–459; it is here cited as printed in *Feudalism and Liberty*, ed. Fred A. Cazel, Jr. (Baltimore, 1961), 144–56. Painter also addressed this subject in *Studies in the History of the English Feudal Barony* (Baltimore, 1943), 45–46, 130–36.

2 *Calendar of Inquisitions Post Mortem*, Public Record Office, 12 vols (London, 1904–38), 1: 280.

3 *CR*, 1268–1272, 506–14.

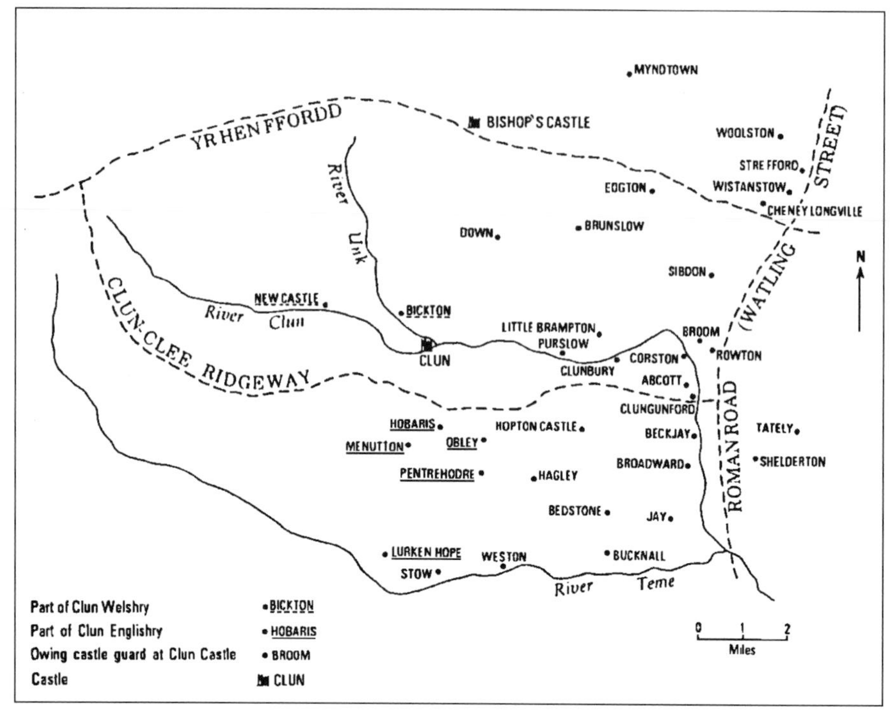

Figure 1. The Castlery of Clun

and adds that it is worth nothing in peacetime.[4] The emphasis on wartime as a condition for the rendering of this castle guard strongly suggests that in 1272 garrison duty was still a real and useful military service which had not been commuted. Commenting on this situation, Painter noted that the Hundred Rolls of 1254 listed the amounts of service owed from some of these same feudal holdings and concluded that the £6 15s. mentioned in 1272 was simply 'an evaluation of these services in terms of money'.[5]

There is some discrepancy about the total number of fiefs owing military service at Clun. As stated above, the Inquisition *Post Mortem* extent of Clun states that 9½ of the 10½ fiefs which it lists owe this service. However, the Close Roll extent assigns some of the holdings different feudal ratings, perhaps partly because it divides them into two portions to provide a dower for John Fitz Alan (III)'s widow, Isabella; and these ratings yield a total of 11 fiefs. This account says nothing about de Brompton's fief being excluded from castle guard, but allowing for this exemption still yields ten fiefs owing the guard. Both of these totals conflict with the figure of nine fiefs, each responsible for the service of one sergeant for 40 days, reached by analysis of the monetary evaluation provided in the Inquisition *Post Mortem* extent. Since the latter number presumably reflects actual wage levels and is also the smallest of the

4 The verb used here, *extenditur*, means 'is extented', i.e. is valued at in the official extent or full listing of property. It can thus be interpreted as merely assigning a monetary value without suggesting that the feudal dues involved have necessarily been commuted.

5 Painter, *Studies*, 134.

three, it is perhaps safest to assume that the wartime garrison of Clun *circa* 1272 included at least nine sergeants whose service was the responsibility of feudal tenures in the Clun district.[6]

The location of these tenures provides further grounds for presuming that the feudal service which they owed was part of a practical and functioning military defense system. All the places are in Shropshire east of Clun.[7] The castle there presumably would protect them from Welsh raids originating from the West. Also most of the tenures are within a half dozen miles of Clun. The lordship's feudal tenants could travel this fairly short distance in response to a summons to Clun Castle in a reasonable amount of time. Stenton has estimated that a rider on royal business, one presumably taking care not to exhaust his horse, could accomplish somewhat more than 20 miles per day, and that horsemen in a hurry could manage over 40 miles on a summer day.[8] One notes too that those members of the Clun castle guard scheme which were further away from the castle were located along the path of the old Roman road, which ran north and south just east of the River Clun and continued in active use throughout the Middle Ages. Easy access to this road would permit military men based in these places to respond within a few hours to a summons from Clun.There does not seem to have been a castle at Clun when Domesday Book was compiled in 1086.[9] Furthermore, there is no evidence that the group of nine fiefs which later provided castle guard was organized at this early date.[10] Picot de Say is listed in 1086 as lord of many manors which were not included in this group of nine fiefs and many of which in fact later passed out of control of the de Says and their successors, the Fitz Alans. Also, two of these nine fiefs were not held in 1086 by Picot, the lord of Clun.[11] In the case of two more fiefs, which were each comprised of scattered lands with separate names, major constituents were not held in 1086 by Picot.[12] There were thus considerable differences between the lands held in 1086 by the lord of Clun and the lands which comprised that castlery later on. Therefore the origins and development of the Clun castlery lie between 1086 and 1272. Since the castlery definitely did exist in 1272 and definitely did not in 1086, the sources providing data about the castlery and its system of mili-

6 R.W. Eyton, *Antiquities of Shropshire*, 12 vols in 6 (London, 1854–60), 11: 232 also chooses this conservative interpretation of the data.

7 See Map, 'The Castlery of Clun', infra, 125.

8 F.M. Stenton, 'The Road System of Medieval England', *Economic History Review* 7 (November 1936): 16–17; Marjorie Boyer, 'A Day's Journey in Medieval France', *Speculum* 26 (1951): 597–608, agrees with these figures on rate of travel.

9 Compare the Domesday Book term used at Clun, *curie*, with *castellum*, as used to describe Meresberie (i.e. Oswestry) and Stantune (Castle Holgate). There are several alternative methods of reference to Domesday Book. In the recent Phillimore edition of separate volumes for each county (*Domesday Book*, gen. ed. John Morris, vol. 25, *Shropshire*, eds Frank and Caroline Thorn and trans. Celia Parker [Chichester, 1986]), which uses a system of numbered chapters, sections, and entries, the appropriate references are: (Clun) 4, 20, 8; (Oswestry) 4, 1, 11; and (Castle Holgate) 4, 21, 6. The equivalent references in the more traditional Vinogradoff system are: fols 258b, 253c, and 258c.

10 See Table, 'Organization of the Castlery of Clun', infra, 128.

11 These were Languefelle (modern Cheney Longville) (Morris, *Domesday Book, Shropshire*, 4, 27, 32) and Brampton (ibid., 6, 23). The equivalent Vinogradoff references are fols 259d, 260c.

12 These were Wistanestou, Straford, and Marsh, which later combined with Sibdon (see Group 'C'); and Bucknell, which was later combined with Purslow and Myndtown (Group 'G').

tary service will be considered in reverse chronological order in order to determine at what time the system was established.

The Hundred Rolls of 1254 do not discuss the organization of the Clun castlery per se, but treat each feudal holding separately and do not mention some of the constituents of the castlery at all, probably because these lay within the hundred of Clun, which the lords of Clun had declared to be a franchise out of bounds to the royal commissioners compiling the rolls.[13] Those holdings which are listed make a total of 7⁴/₁₀ fiefs reported as owing castle guard at Clun.[14] Particularly interesting are features which the Hundred Rolls provide about two of the castlery members. The tenant of Hopton, Bradford, and Coston owed service for two fiefs. For one fief the service of one knight for forty days in wartime sufficed, but with the second fief went responsibility for providing a knight in residence at Clun the year round. One presumes that this knight was left in charge of the castle when raids and war did not threaten. The rolls also describe separately the constituents, Bucknell, Purslow, Acton, and Munede, which in 1272 were lumped together as one fief. In 1254 these constituent members were rated as fractions of a fief. The military service due from Bucknell, for example, was given as that of a sergeant with a horse for eight days, implying that Bucknell was rated as one fifth of a fief. Since each of these members was held by a different feudal subtenant under the lord of Clun in 1254, the question arises of whether these tenures sent their sergeants to Clun in series, so that when a sergeant had served the requisite number of days he was replaced by another to provide continuous service for the forty day term, or if, on the other hand, these details are a precise and bureaucratic formulation which does not exactly reflect the actual workings of the system. Perhaps the tenants of these lands were grouped together and left to make their own informal arrangements as to how they collectively were to provide the military service due from one fief. That one should not rely too heavily upon the detailed information provided in the records of local juries is strongly suggested by the fact that the Bucknell group was rated as one fief in 1272, but its constituent parts totalled ⁹/₁₀ fief in 1254 and 1½ fiefs in 1242.[15] Such numerical changes may be the result of the vagaries of memory afflicting the presumably knowledgeable local men on an inquest jury. They may also suggest the possibility that feudal ratings on this lowest level were subject to frequent change as a result of political bargains between each lord and his subtenants. Such bargains might reflect changes either in the, condition of the lands involved or in local political or personal relationships.

Continuing in reverse chronological order, we find that in 1246 the lord of Clun paid scutage for nine fiefs.[16] Since Clun itself was a barony and an independent jurisdiction outside the royal law, Clun manor was not included in these

13 Eyton, *Antiquities*, 11: 228; and George T. Clark, *Medieval Military Architecture in England* (London, 1884), 1, 408.

14 See Table, infra, 128; *Rotuli Hundredorum*, ed. W. Illingworth and J. Caley, 2 vols (London, 1812–18), 2: 76–77.

15 *Calendar of Inquisitions Post Mortem*, 1: 280; *Rotuli Hundredorum*, 2: 76–77; BF, 2: 963. In 1242 Bucknell and Purslow comprised one fief and Munede was rated as ½ fief.

16 I.J. Sanders, *English Baronies* (Oxford, 1960), 112.

nine fiefs, which must therefore represent the holdings of feudal subtenants under the lord of Clun. An inquest of 1242 concerning tenures held by military service grouped the members of the Clun castlery together under the heading 'Barony of Cloune' (*sic*) and assigned them feudal ratings which total 9½ fiefs.[17]

In 1166 Henry II ordained a major inquest to find out from his barons how many knights they had enfeoffed under them: how many of these knights' fiefs had been in existence during the life of Henry I (who died in 1135); how many were new fiefs created between 1135 and 1166; and how many notional fiefs *super dominum* each reporting baron would have to create to bring his total number of subtenant knights up to his assigned *servitum debitum* if he had not actually subinfeudated a sufficient number of knights on his lands.[18] The baronial responses to these queries collectively constitute the *Cartae Baronum*. The *carta* of Geoffrey de Vere, who was second husband to Isabel de Say, the heiress of Clun, and who held the Clun lordship in 1166 by right of that marriage, reports a total of 9¾ fiefs, seven of them dating from at least 1135 and 2¾ new fiefs created subsequent to that year.[19] Therefore, of the nine fiefs rendering castle guard at Clun in 1272, seven were established sometime between 1086 and 1135 and two were created between 1135 and 1166.[20] Six of the seven old fiefs were held in 1166 by tenants bearing the names of the manors in question.[21] Often when a man of no particular previous importance in a district was enfeoffed with a single manor or holding, the name of that place would come to be appended to his Christian name to serve as an identifying epithet. By the time the man's son inherited the manor, the placename was usually functioning as a surname.[22] That so many of the Clun castlery tenants bore the names of their holdings may suggest that they were at least the second generation to hold the lands, although this is certainly not conclusive evidence. Buttressing this interpretation, however, is the fact that two of the fiefs were partitioned among heirs by 1166. According to R.W. Eyton, Henry Fitz Hamelin and Nicholas de Sancto Laurentio shared one knight's fief at Edgeton.[23] That neither of them is named 'de Edgeton' suggests that perhaps they were husbands of two sisters who were only heiresses to some tenant at Edgeton in the previous generation. In a second case, Hugo de Bukwel (i.e. Bucknell), Adam his brother, Osbert de

17 See Table below, p. 216; BF, 2: 963.

18 For a detailed discussion of the *Cartae Baronum*, see Thomas K. Keefe, *Feudal Assessments and the Political Community under Henry II and his Sons* (Berkeley, 1983), esp. 6–8, 18–19.

19 *RBE*, 1: 274–75.

20 Refer to Table p. 216. Group H did not render castle guard service in 1272. Groups A, B, C, D, F, and G were established between 1086 and 1135. Groups E and J were established between 1135 and 1166.

21 De Opton held Hopton for two fiefs; de Chay held Jay (alias Gay); de Sibbetone held Sibdon; de Langefeld held Cheney Longville (alias Longfelle); and de Bukwel (i.e. Bucknell, de Muneta (Munede), and de Broma held members of one fief.

22 On this point see J.C. Holt, 'Feudal Society and the Family in Early Medieval England: I. The Revolution of 1066', *Transactions of the Royal Historical Society*, 5th ser. 32 (1982): 200–1; and Holt, *What's in a Name? Family Nomenclature and the Norman Conquest* (University of Reading, Stenton Lecture, 1981). I am grateful to Professor David Spear for calling this article to my attention.

23 Eyton, *Antiquities*, 11: 260.

Table: Organization of the Castlery of Clun

(see explanation of symbols and discussion opposite)

Groups of Manors		*Years* 1086	1135	1166	1242	1254	1272
'A'	Hopton						
	Shelderton						
	Broadward	P	2	2	2	2	2
	Corston						
	Tately						
	Hagley						
'B'	Jay						
	Bedstone	P	1	1	1	1	1
	Beckjay	t					
'C'	Sibdon*	P	1	1	1	1	1
	Witstanstow						
	Broom	§					
	Strefford						
'D'	Edgton						
	Brunslow	P	1	1	1	1	1
'E'	Clungunford						
	Abcott	P		1	0.5	0.5	1
	Rowton	t					
'F'	Cheney						
	Longville	§	1	1	0.5	0.5?	1
'G'	Bucknell						
	Purslow	§	1	1	1.5	0.9	1
'H'	Brompton #	§					0.5
	Weston						
'I'	Down						0.5
'J'	Weston			1?		0.5	0.5
'K'	Clunbury	P		0.75	1		1
Total knights' fiefs reported as part of Clun castlery			7	9.75	9.5	7.4	10.5

Discussion and Explanation of Table

Numbers in the columns refer to the number of knights' fiefs at which each manor or group of manors was rated – that is, the amount of feudal military service in terms of knights which it was obligated to provide in time of war. The capital letters in front of each group of manors are purely arbitrary labels assigned to make it easier to refer to each group. The grouping of manors is that which was reported in 1272. This same pattern of grouped manors occurs in all the earlier sources, with the notable exception of 1086 (*Domesday Book*), although in some instances a source does not mention some of the manors. In 1086 Picot de Say, then lord of Clun, did not hold all of the manors which later made up the castlery of Clun. Furthermore, many of the manors which he held in 1086 were not part of the castlery later on, being held by lords of other castles. In other words, the pattern of lands owing feudal allegiance to the lord of Clun in 1086 is very different from the pattern which existed during the twelfth and thirteenth centuries, when the castle guard system is known to have existed.

Symbol Explanation

P The manor in question was held in 1086 by Picot de Sai, lord of Clun in 1086.

t A tenant named in Domesday Book (probably a knight) held the manor from Picot de Sai in 1086. Lack of such a named tenant implies that the manor did not support a knight to send in defense of Clun.

§ In 1086 the manor was held by some lord other than Picot de Sai. Therefore it could not have been part of a scheme for the defense of Clun, at least not a scheme like the later castlery possessed, in which manors contributing castle guard to Clun were held by feudal tenants of the lords of Clun Castle.

* In 1086 Picot de Sai held only Sibdon; the other three manors in the group were then held by other lords. By 1135 these four manors were assembled in a group.

Although listed among the manors comprising the castlery of Clun 1272, these lands specifically did not owe castle guard at Clun Castle.

Muneta, and Tudilius de Broma jointly held one fief.[24] Here partition of Bucknell between two brothers strongly implies that it was held by their father in the previous generation. That four tenants were holding this fief in 1166, two of them brothers and two presumably not, suggests that the fief may have been in existence at least three generations, being split once among the second generation heirs and again among the third generation ones. A scenario in which the original tenant had two heirs between whom his fief was divided (the first heir had Hugo and Adam as his sons and heirs, and the second had two daughters who married Osbert and Tudilius) could explain the 1166 situation.

Although not absolutely conclusive, these interpretations of the evidence tend to suggest that the Clun castlery fiefs were created after 1086 and at least a generation or two before 1166, probably during the reign of Henry I. Information about the manor of Longuefelle (modern Cheney Longville) reinforces this thesis. Siward, the Domesday Book tenant of this manor, bequeathed it to Shrewsbury Abbey. During the reign of Henry I, the abbey gave it to Henry de Say, then lord of Clun, as part of an exchange.[25] Henry de Say had succeeded his father, Picot, after the latter's death in 1098 and was still alive in 1129–30, so the exchange presumably occurred sometime during this period. By 1166 Henry de Say's lands had passed to his granddaughter, Isabel;[26] in that year the *carta* of her husband, Geoffrey de Vere, reported that a certain 'Roger Fitz Eustace de Langefeld' held this old fief (i.e., pre-1135) as the feudal tenant.[27] If one reads this name to mean 'Roger, son of Eustace of Langefeld,' it would seem likely that Roger's father, Eustace, was the tenant of this fief as the undertenant of Henry de Say, approximately a generation before 1166, and took his name from it. Thus the evidence relating to Cheney Longville strongly suggests that this fief was incorporated in the Clun castle guard system during Henry I's reign.

Implicit in the above attempts to determine the time and circumstances of the creation of the Clun castle ward fiefs is the assumption that this was an event rather than a continuing process. Creation of the system of 'muntatorial' fiefs to garrison Oswestry Castle, also located in the Shropshire Marches, is an example of such an event.[28] While a core group of these fiefs may have been established at one particular time by Henry de Say or his son, Helias, there is evidence to show that the lords of Clun strove to make additions to the system throughout the twelfth century. A charter of Lilleshall Abbey complains that Helias de Say unjustly acquired one of the abbey's prebends and gave it to one Baldwin de Stapleton to hold for the service of one knight. This presumably was either later in Henry I's reign or during that of Stephen. This fief apparently continued to exist for some time, for the charter complains further that Baldwin's son, Philip, held it unjustly and rendered the service of one knight at Clun to Helias' daughter and heir, Isabel.[29] However, there is no record of this fief in connection with

24 *RBE*, 1: 275.
25 Eyton, *Antiquities*, 11: 369.
26 Sanders, *English Baronies*, 112.
27 *RBE*, 275.
28 For a full discussion of the system of *muntatores* at Oswestry, see Chapter 4 of my *Military Institutions on the Welsh Marches*: *Shropshire, AD 1066–1300* (Woodbridge, 1994).
29 *Monasticon*, 6: 262.

Clun Castle during the thirteenth century. Perhaps the Lilleshall monks were able to reassert their claim.

Having described the constituent parts of the Clun castle guard system and their establishment, one is next confronted with a series of questions about the functioning of this system. Did the tenants of these fiefs actually perform castle guard during the twelfth and thirteenth centuries, or did this military obligation soon change into a financial one? Did all nine castle guard tenants perform their ward simultaneously for the same forty-day period, or did they perhaps distribute their periods of service to cover the whole year? If the former was the case, was the castle manned at all during peacetime? Were these nine knights or sergeants an adequate garrison for Clun Castle?

Sidney Painter theorized that the lord of a baronial castle could schedule his military tenants to provide his castle either with a small permanent garrison establishment or with a large emergency one. In the former case only a few tenants by castle guard would be on hand in the castle at any one time and, after one group had completed its forty-day term, it would be succeeded by another. In the latter case all the tenants would be summoned to the castle when a pressing military threat appeared.[30] Painter tried to fit the thirteenth-century evidence about Clun provided by the Hundred Rolls and the Inquisition *Post Mortem* into his model of a permanent garrison scheme. He noted that in 1254 one of the Hopton fiefs owed the service of one knight in Clun Castle year round and calculated that there were 7½ more fiefs in the castlery whose service, combined with that of the resident knight, would provide the castle with a garrison of two knights for 300 days of the year.[31] Painter does not seem to have paid very close attention to the available data. In 1272 there were 9½, fiefs owing ward at Clun, not 8½. The 1254 Hundred Rolls and the 1272 inquest are also both quite insistent that the castle guard service is due in wartime only. In fact the Close Roll version of the 1272 inquest explicitly states that this service is worth £6 15s. in wartime and nothing in peace.[32] Painter's speculation that this sum was merely a valuation of the service, and not evidence that the service had been commuted, is shown to be true by a statement in the Close Roll inquest that the knights holding these fiefs owed their service at Clun in time of war at their own cost.[33] It seems quite clear that the tenants of most of these fiefs must have performed their obligation only when a Welsh raid or other military emergency threatened and they were summoned to the castle. The knight from the Hopton fief who was permanently resident at Clun would presumably have been in charge of the castle during peacetime.

A letter patent from 1233, when the Clun district was threatened by a series of major Welsh attacks, a letter which instructs the Clun feudal tenants to perform castle guard service under the direction of Baldwin de Vere, then constable of the castle, whenever he summoned them, clearly shows that this

30 Painter, *Studies*, 132.

31 Painter, 'Castle Guard', 146.

32 *Rotuli Hundredorum*, 2: 75–77; *Calendar of Inquisitions Post Mortem*, 2: 280; *CR, 1268–1272*, 506.

33 *Ibid.*, 511.

service had real military value at thirteenth-century Clun.[34] Indeed so useful were these feudal castle guards that they continued serving at Clun under royal pay after having completed their forty-day unpaid feudal obligation.[35] The mound of Clun Castle was approximately 60 yards across at its summit and nine men were apparently an insufficient garrison for a fortress of this size,[36] for in 1233, 17 sergeants were hired to supplement the feudal garrison.[37] An unfortunately damaged document shows that in the mid-1240s the sheriff of Shropshire again hired more sergeants, both mounted and infantry, to deal with Welsh attacks at Clun and Montgomery, although it is impossible to determine how many men were involved.[38]

The Pipe Rolls provide evidence of the feudal garrison of Clun being supplemented in the mid twelfth century. Because William Fitz Alan died sometime in 1160, the Pipe Roll for 1159–60 in a separate section dealing with William's lands lists wages of £7 15s. for sergeants at the castles of Clun, Ruthin, and Blancmonasterium[39] (i.e. Oswestry).[40] Under a similar heading, the 1160–61 Pipe Roll shows expenditure of £54 15s. on wages at these three castles.[41] In both 1162–63 and 1163–64, the accounts show £36 10s. spent in wages at Clun and Ruthin and £18 5s. at Oswestry.[42] One notes that adding £36 10s. and £18 5s. yields £54 15s. It seems reasonable to conclude, at least tentatively, that £18 5s. was the sum spent at each of these three castles during these full year terms. In 1164 £54 15s. was again spent for the *custodia*[43] of Oswestry, Clun, and Ruffin (*sic*) castles.[44] The sum of £18 5s. is equivalent to 365 shillings. If one accepts J.H. Round's statement that 1d. was the daily wage for a military sergeant in the mid twelfth century,[45] then 365s. would constitute wages for twelve such sergeants for a year. Thus mercenaries would seem to have constituted the year-round or 'peacetime' garrison of Clun, when this was required.

It seems most likely that the castle guard system at Clun Castle was apparently created early during the reign of Henry I, most probably in reaction to the major Welsh rising of 1094–95 and subsequent Welsh depredations in the Clun region.[46] This system ultimately consisted of at least nine fiefs which were

34 *CPR*, 1232–1247, 32.

35 Eyton, *Antiquities*, 11: 230, quoting the Pipe Roll of 1233.

36 Clark, *Medieval Military*, 404–5.

37 *Calendar of Liberate Rolls*, Public Record Office, 6 vols (London, 1917–64), 1: 232.

38 *Ibid.*, 3: 98.

39 *P.R. 6 Henry II*, 27.

40 John Beeler, *Warfare in England*, 1066–1189 (Ithaca, N.Y., 1966), 415 and 446; and C. Warren Hollister, *The Military Organization of Norman England* (Oxford, 1965) have erred in supposing *Blancmonasterium*, one of several names for Oswestry, to refer to Whitchurch, with which the Fitz Alan family had no connection. On the various names for Oswestry, see Eyton, *Antiquities*, 10: 323; and A.H.A. Hogg and D.J.C. King, 'Masonry Castles in Wales and the Marches', *Archaeologia Cambrensis* 116 (1967): 116.

41 *P.R. 7 Henry II*, 40.

42 *P.R. 8 Henry II*, 6; and *P.R. 9 Henry II*, 4.

43 This is a term which can refer to guarding a castle (see *Revised Medieval Latin Word List*, ed. R.E. Latham [London, 1965], 128).

44 *P.R. 10 Henry II*, 9.

45 J.H. Round, *The King's Sergeants and Other Officers of State* (London, 1911), 34.

46 *The Anglo-Saxon Chronicle*, eds Dorothy Whitelock, David C. Douglas, and Susie I. Tucker (London, 1961), 171; *The Chronicle of Florence of Worcester*, ed. Thomas Forester (London, 1854), 198; and

located in a fairly compact group east of Clun and whose feudal tenants were responsible for actual military service at the castle during wartime. This feudal garrison continued to serve during the twelfth and thirteenth centuries and was supplemented by mercenaries as needed.

Each British castle was built in a particular spot for particular reasons. As Warren Hollister has observed, the castle guard arrangements at these fortifications do not follow a uniform pattern, but were created in response to particular local conditions.[47] Before meaningful general comments can be made about the creation and functioning of castle guard systems in post-Conquest England, the full range of evidence for many more castles must be carefully analyzed.[48]

Polychronicon Ranulphi Higden, Monachi Cestrensis, eds J.R. Lumley and C. Babbington, R.S. 9 vols (London, 1865–86), 7: 360; *Ann. Mon.*, i, 6. A narrative of the canons of Lilleshall Abbey relates that during this period of warfare between the Welsh and Earl Hugh of Shrewsbury (1094–98), the Welsh penetrated to the district around Cheney Longville and devastated it. See Eyton, *Antiquities*, 11: 356; and *Mon. Angl.*, 7: 750, item no. 16.

47 Hollister, *Military Organization*, 145.

48 The muntatorial' system at Oswestry mentioned above, for example, was created in 1085–86 and was added to over the next several decades. Other border castles for which there is ample castle guard evidence and which I intend to examine in future work include Montgomery, Shrawardine, and Richard's Castle.

11

Charter Evidence and the Distribution of Mottes in Scotland

Grant G. Simpson and Bruce Webster

Our intention in this essay is to bring together evidence mainly from twelfth- and thirteenth-century Scottish charters and the archaeological evidence for the distribution of mottes in Scotland, and to discuss some of the implications which follow from this.

Until the twelfth century Scotland was on the fringes of European civilisation and there was hardly any trace of the type of central government which already existed, for instance, in England or Germany. There were kings of the Scots; but their authority was more akin to the sway of a 'high king' over a series of tribes. In the later eleventh and the twelfth centuries, however, a line of kings who had very close connexions with England, especially David I (1124–53), began to establish centralised authority of a more developed kind.[1] The way in which they did this was very much determined by geography. Scotland is divided by mountains into a series of coastal regions and river valleys; and the direct power of the kings was for long limited to the east-central and south-eastern regions, to Angus, Fife, Lothian and the Tweed valley. They managed during the twelfth century to extend their direct authority to the north of the ridge of mountains called the Mounth into the lands along the Moray Firth; but in the centre and in the south-west, from Atholl down to Annandale, Nithsdale and Galloway, they had to rely on various forms of more or less indirect rule. Across the Great Glen, the highlands and islands of the western seaboard remained remote from them.

This study was first published in 1972. It seems to us that a major reappraisal of the issues is not yet appropriate, and we have therefore made only minimal changes for this reprint. A few phrases in the text have been altered to improve clarity, and up-to-date references have been inserted in the notes. Three short general surveys of the topic have appeared since 1972: Duncan, *Scotland*, pp. 433–43; G. Stell, 'Mottes', in *Historical Atlas of Scotland*, ed. P. McNeill and R. Nicholson (St Andrews, 1975), pp. 28–9, and E.J. Talbot's article cited below. Two local surveys are C.J. Tabraham, 'Norman settlement in upper Clydesdale: recent archaeological fieldwork', *TDGAS*, 3rd set., liii (1978), pp. 114–28, and *idem*, 'Norman settlement in Galloway: recent fieldwork in the Stewartry', in *Studies in Scottish Antiquity*, ed. D.J. Breeze (Edinburgh, 1984), pp. 87–124. The following excavation reports are also relevant: G. Ewart, 'Excavations at Cruggleton Castle, 1978–81', *TDGAS* (1985); G. Haggarty and C.J. Tabraham, 'Excavation of a motte near Roberton, Clydesdale, 1979', *ibid.*, 3rd set., lvii (1982), pp. 51–64; H. Murray and G. Ewart, 'Two early medieval timber buildings from Castle Hill, Peebles', *PSAS*, cx (1978–80), pp. 519–27; M.E.C. Stewart and C.J. Tabraham, 'Excavations at Barton Hill, Kinnaird, Perthshire', *Scottish Archaeol. Forum*, vi (1974), pp. 58–65; and P.A. Yeoman, 'Excavations at Castlehill of Strachan, 1980–1', *PSAS*, 114 (1984), pp. 315–64.

1 For fuller details of the changes here sketched in outline see Duncan, *Scotland*, Chs 6–8; G.W.S. Barrow, *Kingship and Unity: Scotland 1000–1306* (London, 1981), Chs 2, 3; RRS, i, pp. 27–56; ii, pp. 28–67.

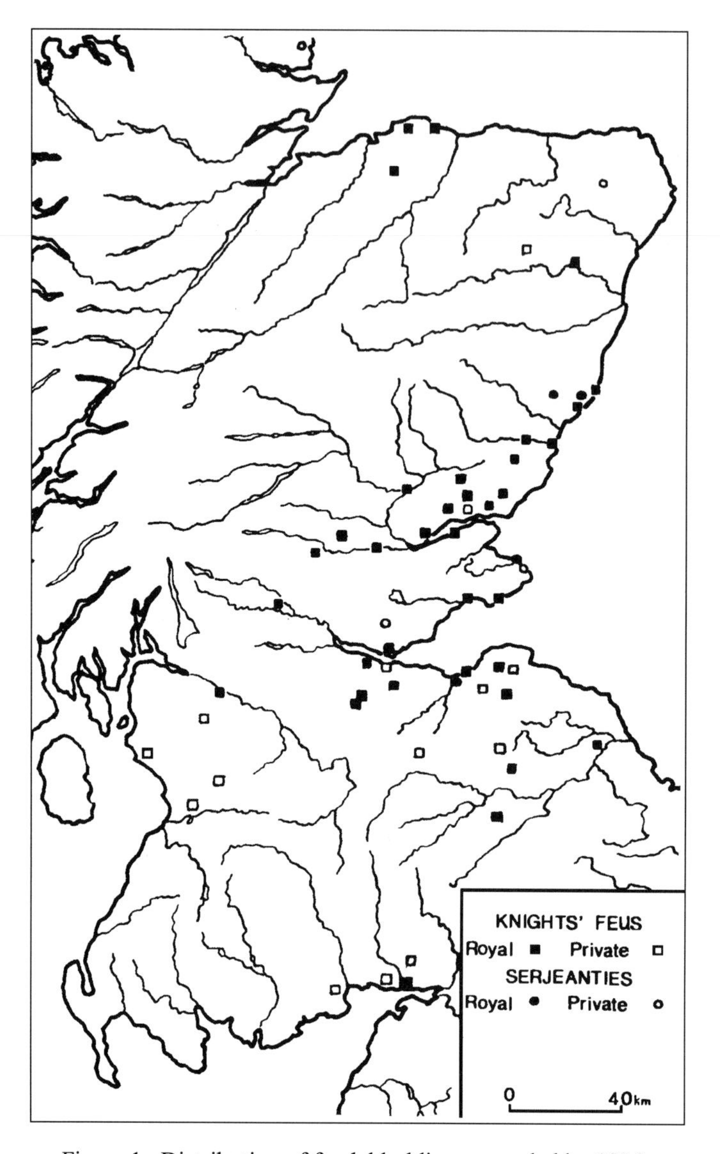

Figure 1. Distribution of feudal holdings recorded by 1214.

Royal authority just extended into Ross and there were occasional expeditions further north, but most of the far west was Celtic in culture and at this period was under the authority, direct or indirect, of the kings of Norway. There are some early castles in this western seaboard region, but they are a separate and interesting problem.[2] There are hardly any mottes in the area and we have therefore not considered it in this chapter.

2 S. Cruden, *The Scottish Castle*, revised edn (Edinburgh, 1963), pp. 38–49. See also G.G. Simpson and R.W. Munro, 'A checklist of western seaboard castles on record before 1550', *Notes and Queries of the Soc. of West Highland and Island Historical Research*, xix (1982), pp. 3–7.

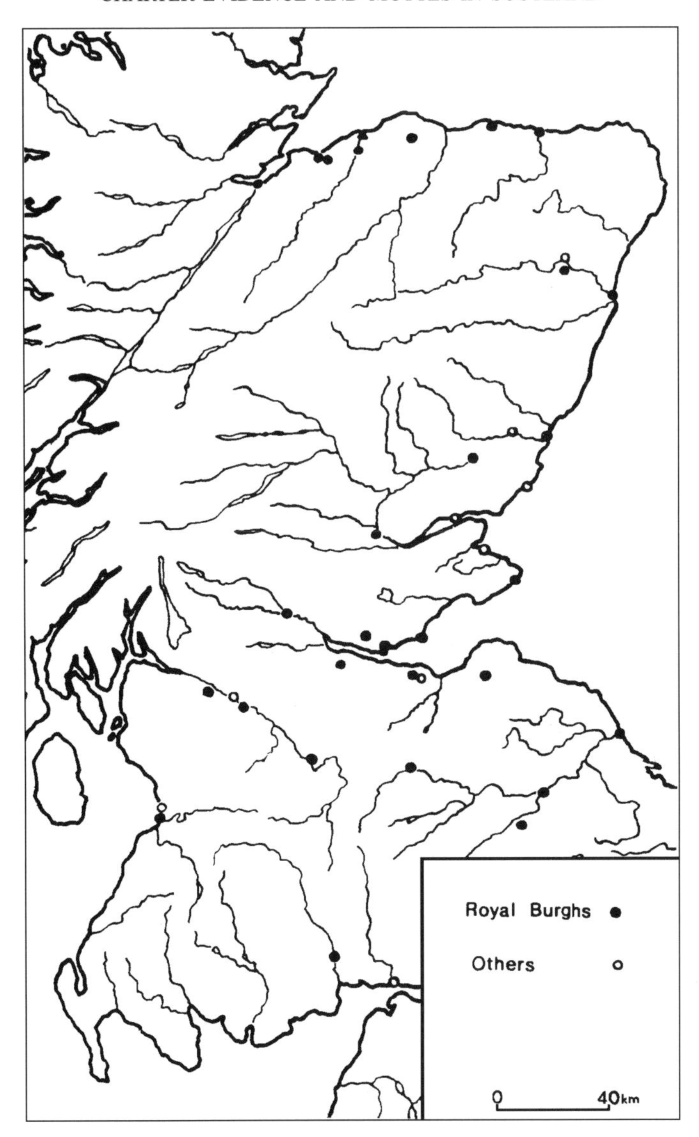

Figure 2. Distribution of burghs recorded by 1214.

In the twelfth century the kings were trying to bring the government of Scotland into line with what was then normal practice in more developed states; but Scotland was a small country, and in scale at least the closest parallels for her institutions are to be found not in the large states of England, France or Germany, but in some of the great fiefs of France, such as Normandy or Flanders. In this process the monarchs from David I onwards encouraged the settlement of barons from England and even some directly from France and Flanders.[3] Most of these settlers were established in small fiefs of one knight's

3 Barrow, *Era*, *passim*; Barrow, *Kingdom*, pp. 315–36; R.L.G. Ritchie, *The Normans in Scotland* (Edinburgh, 1954), *passim*.

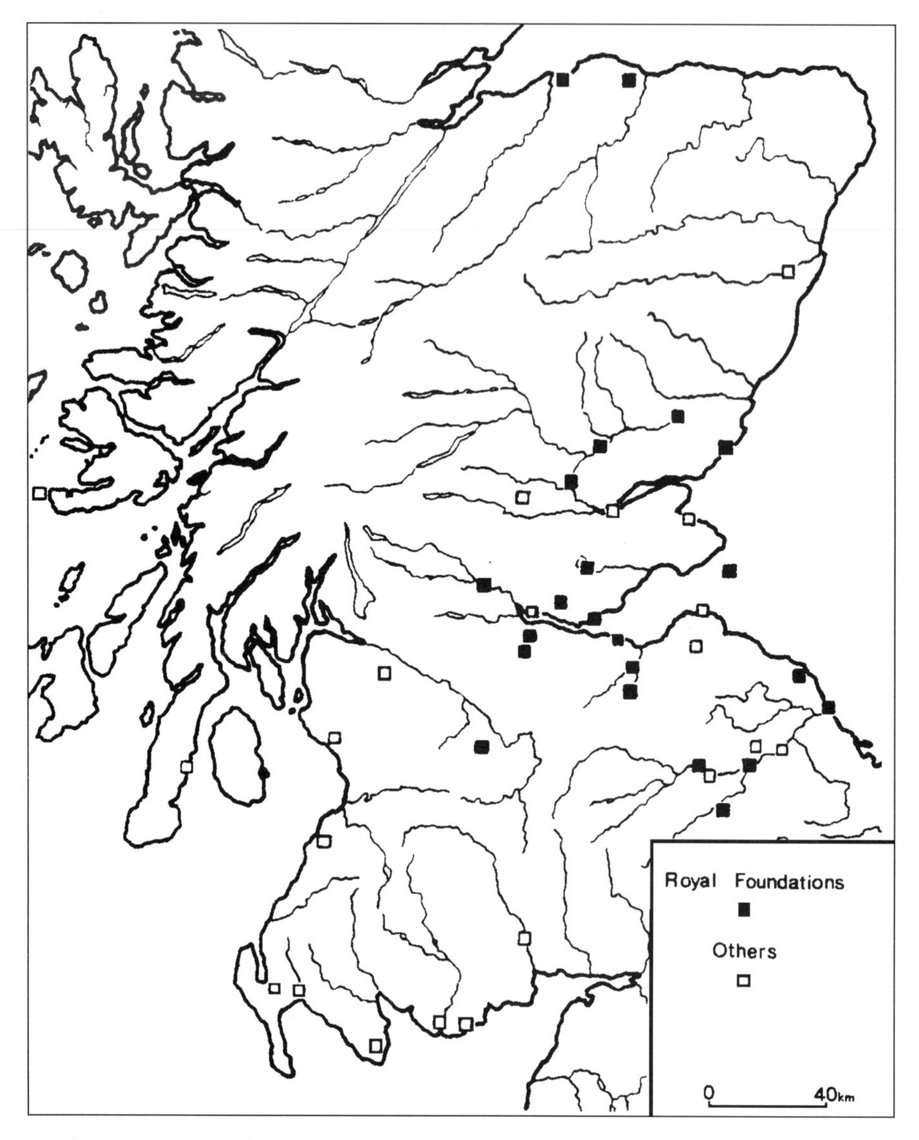

Figure 3. Distribution of monastic foundations of all kinds recorded by 1214.

feu or thereabouts, but in the areas which the king could not rule directly some great feudal estates were created. The best-known early ones are those of the Stewarts in Renfrewshire and Ayrshire, the Morvilles in Lauderdale and the Bruces in Annandale. Thus feudal land tenure was introduced; and at the same period other institutions appear: a structure of local government based on royal officials called sheriffs, the burgh as a legal concept, and a reformed ecclesiastical system which involved territorial bishoprics and regular monastic houses. Features such as feudal holdings, burghs and monasteries can be easily plotted on maps (Figs 1–3), and these maps reveal the geographical pattern of such

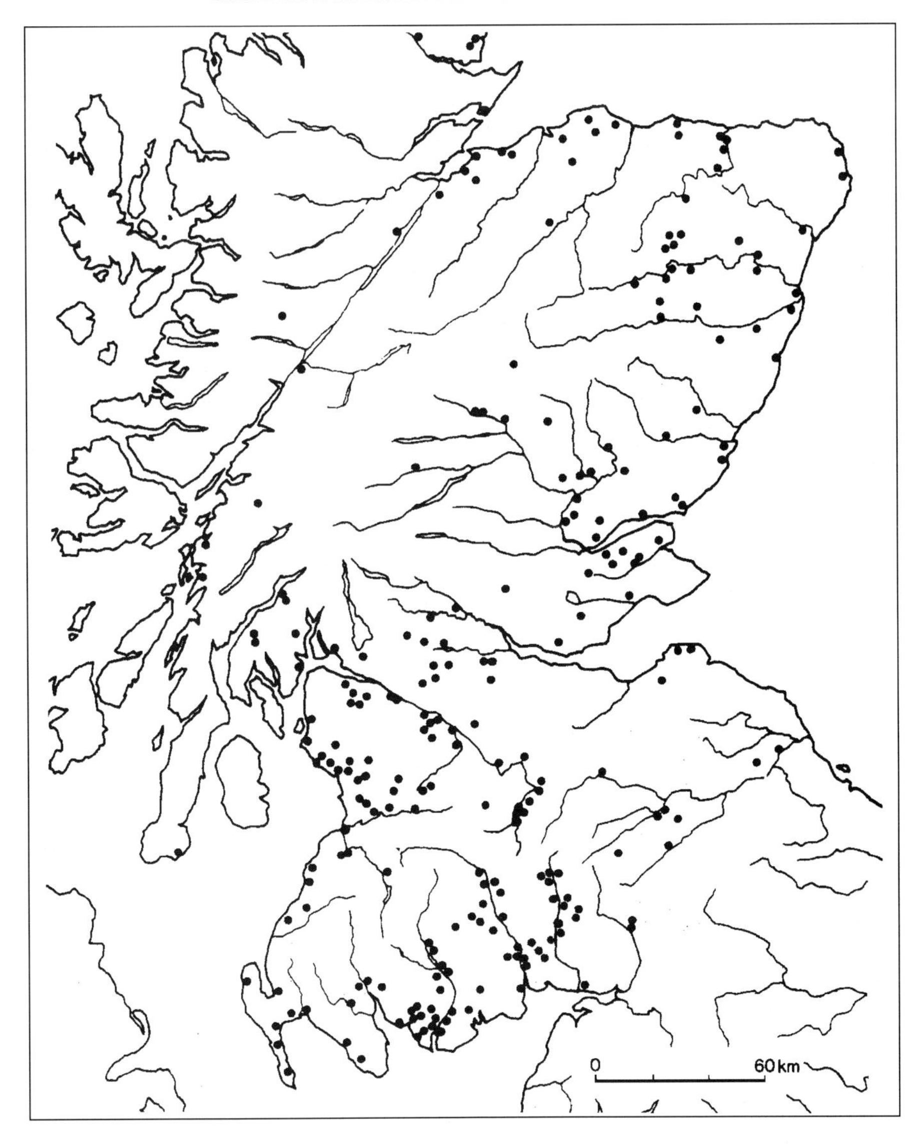

Figure 4. Distribution of mottes in Scotland.

developments.[4] As one might expect, they are concentrated particularly in the areas where royal control was at its greatest.

So far we have said nothing of the castle; and the main problem we want to discuss is how the castle fits into these processes. In Normandy, Flanders and England the castle was at the very centre of feudalisation and the development of governmental organisation. Where does it come in Scotland? It was certainly an alien import introduced by the same foreign settlers who were involved in

4 The maps are based on Barrow, *Kingdom*, pp. 311–14; G.S. Pryde, *The Burghs of Scotland* (Oxford, 1965); and Cowan (Easson), *Religious Houses*.

every other aspect of the twelfth-century revolution.[5] It has long been known that in addition to surviving stone castles Scotland has a good collection of mottes. Until 1972 the only published distribution map of these was that based on the pioneer researches made over eighty years ago by Dr David Christison.[6] His distribution was almost entirely concentrated in the south-west and was nearly blank for the rest of the country. But many mottes have been identified since 1898, and around 250 are now known: the more certain of these are shown in Fig. 4, and a provisional list appears in Appendix I, below.[7] This distribution shows a fair spread of mottes in Fife, Angus, the north-east and Moray, though there are hardly any in Lothian; but the thickest concentrations are still in Menteith, the Clyde valley and above all in Ayrshire and the lands bordering on the Solway Firth. The whole distribution is still heavy in the south-west.

This distribution is obviously different from that of the other phenomena which we have plotted; it is also very different from that of castles recorded either in charters or in chronicles. To plot the latter distribution effectively, it has been necessary to include references down to the end of the reign of Alexander II in 1249. The mention of castles in the sources is very much a matter of chance, and only by going to 1249 can one reveal a number of castles which certainly existed many decades before they are referred to in writing. The distribution of castles is shown at Fig. 5 and they are listed in Appendix II. If we compare the two maps (Figs 4 and 5) the contrast is obvious, but in a sense it is also unreal. The distribution of documentary references, like the other documentary distributions which it resembles, reflects very closely the spread of the available documents. Most of the evidence is in the form of written titles to land, and the use of such titles is itself part of the twelfth-century revolution in government. This map is plotting on the whole not so much the distribution of castles *per se* as the castles which occurred within the area of a more developed centralised government.

There is however obviously a special problem in Lothian. There are documentary records of castles at Edinburgh, Eldbotle and Dirleton,[8] and a few more occur not long after 1249; but there is only one reasonably certain motte in the area, at Castle Hill, North Berwick. At Dirleton there still exists a fine thirteenth-century castle, but the documents also refer to a *vetus castellum cum fossis suis* at Eldbotle, which is a site near the coast just over one mile to the north-west of Dirleton.[9] No motte can now be positively identified at Eldbotle, but it would clearly be worth looking for one by means of excavation or aerial

5 The first scholar to establish conclusively that the Scottish mottes were Norman was Dr George Neilson, in an article which is still of great value: 'The motes in Norman Scotland', *The Scottish Review*, xxxii (1898), pp. 209–38.

6 D. Christison, *Early Fortifications in Scotland* (Edinburgh, 1898), pp. 1–54.

7 This map is based on a list of mottes compiled by Mr Geoffrey Stell. We are greatly indebted to him for allowing us to use his material, without which our studies would have been much more difficult; and we are pleased that he has agreed to publish his list as Appendix I, below. Fig. 4 excludes those mottes (or sites of mottes) which are listed in Appendix I as 'possible' or 'doubtful', while no. 302, Langdale (Sutherland), does not appear.

8 Appendix II, nos. 26, 19, 18.

9 RCAHMS, *Inventory of East Lothian*, p. xli and no. 27.

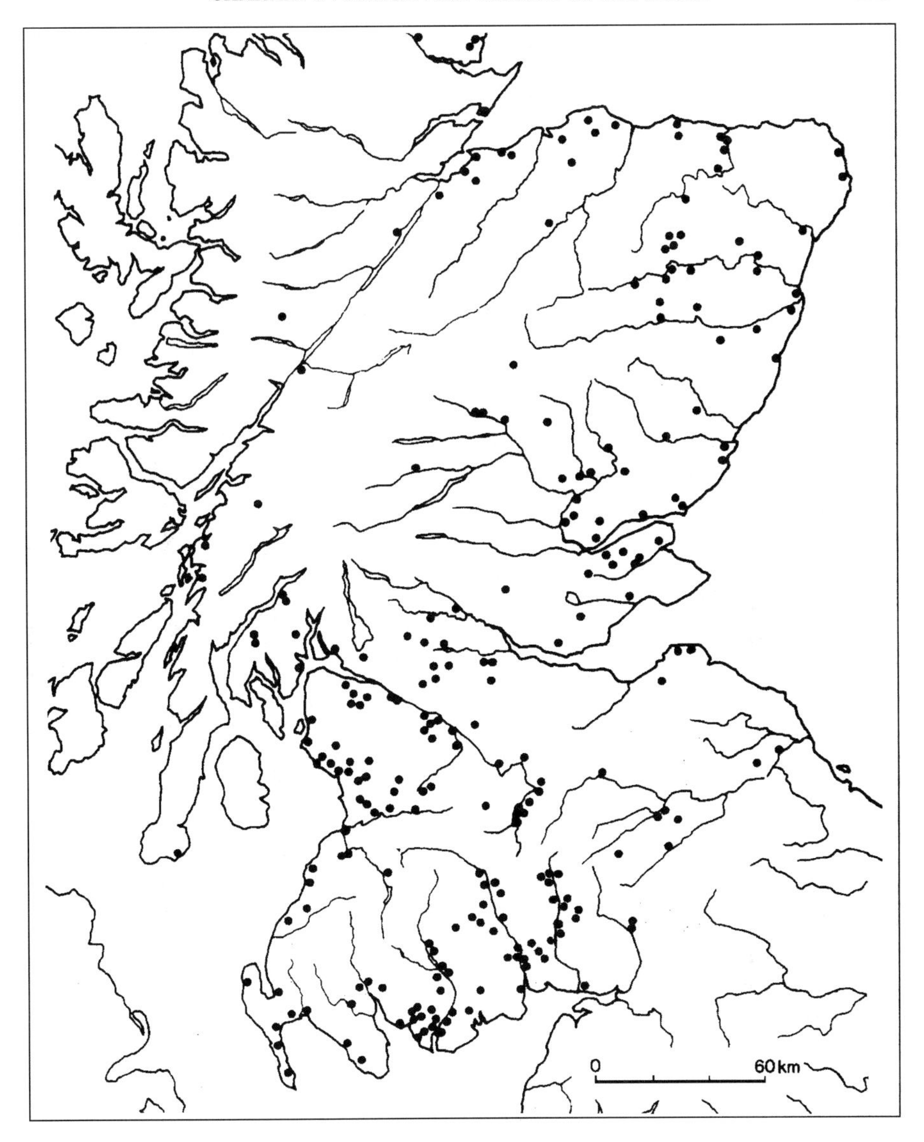

Figure 5. Distribution of castles recorded by 1249.

photography. Lothian was a relatively rich and developed region, and it is possible that mottes did exist but were superseded fairly quickly by more up-to-date structures and have therefore been lost sight of.

If the two maps are considered together, it is clear that castles are common in the regions of firm royal control: there they may be a part of the general revolution we have described. But they are even more common elsewhere. The motte is a symbol of alien authority, and these maps show how that authority extended far beyond the areas of direct royal control and also beyond the area for which written documents survive to give us a reasonable outline of what was happening. The mottes on the ground can reveal a story about which the documents may be silent. Mottes are common in Ayrshire, Annandale and Nithsdale, which were all areas where the crown depended for much of its authority on feudal control exercised by a great magnate; and mottes are also very common in Galloway, which until well into the thirteenth century was notably independent and even rebellious.

This wide distribution of mottes raises the question of exactly how the castle fits into these various patterns of rule, varying from direct royal control to very considerable independence. To consider this, it will be best to limit the discussion to three areas, each of which illustrates a different situation.

The first is the Tweed valley (Fig. 6), where royal authority was firm and castles fit into a structure of royal administration. There were sheriffs, each with a castle, at Berwick, Roxburgh, Selkirk and Peebles, and a royal castle also at Jedburgh. The situation is very like that in Flanders in the mid-eleventh century, where the count ruled through a number of castellans;[10] and it is significant that all these castles have burghs attached to them. Roxburgh has a large empty and unexcavated burgh site; the others are modern towns. At Peebles the castle site is at the confluence of two rivers, and the main street of the town leads directly to the castle: a pattern which may suggest that the town was directly dependent on the castle. At Selkirk the castle site is on the fringe of the burgh, and this might imply that the castle was a later addition. Similarly, at Hawick, which was a private castle, the well-preserved motte is on the outskirts of the town.[11] All these castles were more than just individual structures. Royal or private, they were regional centres, the keys to the administration of their areas, and they were placed at the vital points where also the centres of population developed. There are a few other castles in the region: one at Lauder was the centre of the important Morville fief, and a motte at Riddell was probably the centre of a minor but early fief, which was held about 1150 by Walter of Ryedale (Riddell).[12] But above all this was an area of administrative castles.

Our second area, in the south-west, consists of Annandale and Nithsdale (see Fig. 7). Here we still find castles which act as regional centres, but there are far more which are the centre of a single fief or holding. Annandale was a great fief belonging to an Anglo-Norman family, the Bruces. Its first *caput* was at Annan, where there is not only the castle but also a town situated at a point suitable for crossing the River Annan. The castle is at the edge of the town, directly outside the boundary wall of the burgh tenements. Later the centre of the fief moved to Lochmaben, about twelve miles away, where there was first a motte and then, close to it, an important stone castle erected in the later thirteenth century.[13] But

10 For a brief account of the Flemish system of *castellania*, which has many parallels with the Scottish *vicecomitatus*, see F.L. Ganshof, *La Flandre sous les premiers comtes*, 3rd edn (Brussels, 1949), pp. 104–6.

11 RCAHMS, *Inventories of Roxburghshire*, nos. 233, 905, *Peeblesshire*, no. 523, and *Selkirkshire*, no. 24. The whole question of the relationship of Scottish burghs to their castle sites requires investigation. On the lay-out of burghs see J.W.R. Whitehand and K. Alauddin, 'The town plans of Scotland: some preliminary considerations', *Scottish Geographical Magazine*, lxxxv (1969), pp. 109–21.

12 Lauder: Appendix II, no. 11. Riddell: *RRS*, i, no. 42.

13 RCAHMS, *Inventory of Dumfriesshire*, nos. 3, 445.

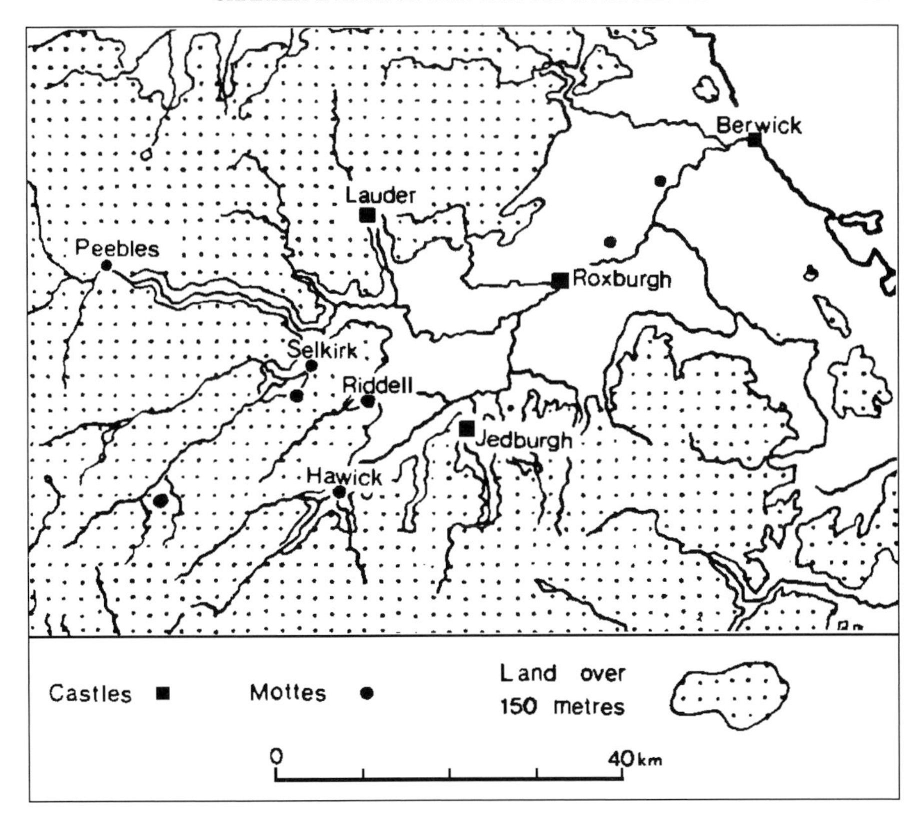

Figure 6. The Tweed valley.

the chief town remained at Annan and only a village existed at Lochmaben. The other mottes of Annandale represent the feudal holdings of the fief and are connected either with demesne lands, such as Moffat, or with sub-tenancies.[14] In Nithsdale there was a royal castle, sheriff and burgh at Dumfries.[15] The rest of Nithsdale was divided into a number of small fiefs, and the fairly thick scatter of mottes fits in with this tenurial structure. In contrast, therefore, to the administrative castles of Tweeddale, the majority of the castles of Annandale and Nithsdale belonged to individual barons of the second rank.

Galloway, on the other hand, our third area (see again Fig. 7), was an almost independent principality, ruled by its own lords. Down to 1161 its lord was Fergus, who is often called *princeps* and even *rex* of Galloway. The kings of Scotland seem to have encouraged in this area the infiltration of alien Anglo-Norman settlers, many of them from Cumberland in England, directly across the Solway Firth.[16] Between 1161 and 1185 Galloway was divided between two sons of Fergus, and in that period there appear in the few charters

14 *CDS*, i, no. 706.
15 RCAHMS, *Inventory of Dumfriesshire*, no. 128.
16 *RRS*, i, p. 13 and n. 2.

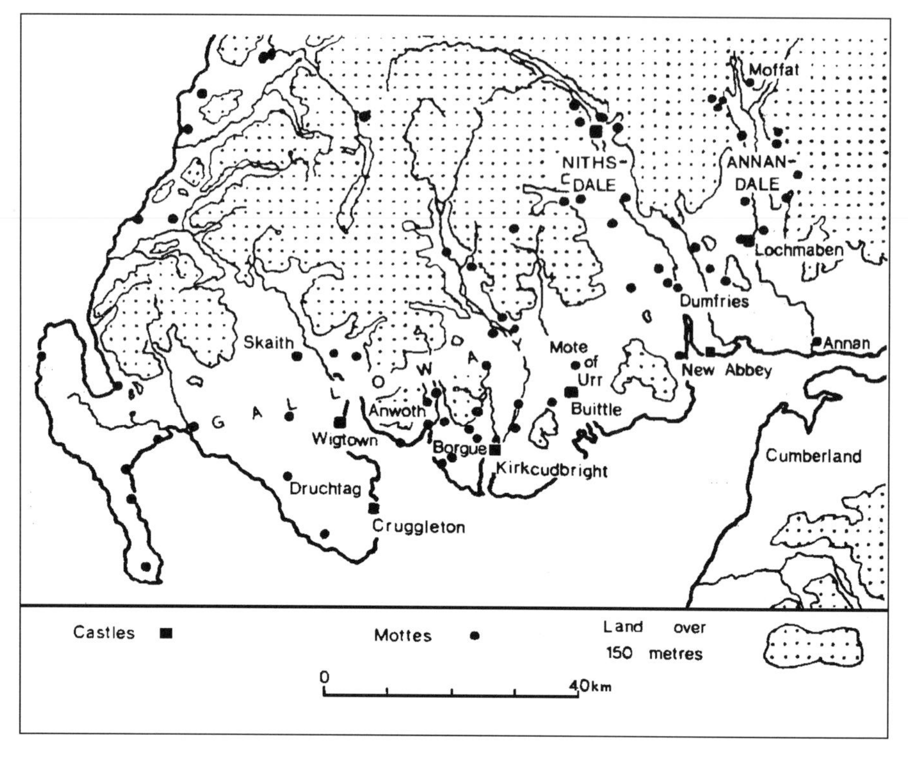

Figure 7. South-west Scotland.

which exist for the area occasional references to outsiders. Borgue was held by an important family, the Morvilles, who had ties with English Cumbria but also held extensive fiefs elsewhere in Scotland; and at Boreland of Borgue there is one of the most striking mottes in the area.[17] The lands of Urr belonged to another Anglo-Norman, Walter de Berkeley, who was chamberlain of the king of Scotland from about 1171 to about 1190; and at Urr there is a large motte with a bailey.[18] At about the same time foreigners are also recorded at two other sites, Anwoth and New Abbey, and both have mottes.[19]

The chances are that a fair number of the mottes in Galloway represent similar settlement. There was a revolt in Galloway in 1174, and an English chronicler records that the Galwegians 'at once expelled from Galloway all the bailiffs and guards whom the king of Scotland had set over them (*omnes ballivos et custodes quos rex Scotiae eis imposuerat*) and all the English whom they could seize they slew; and all the defences and castles (*munitiones et castella*) which the king of Scotland had established in their land they besieged, captured

17 Lawrie, *Charters*, no. 215; RCAHMS, *Inventory of Kirkcudbright*, no. 54; Appendix I, 190.

18 *Holm Cultram Reg.*, nos. 122–3; R. C. Reid, 'The Mote of Urr', *TDGAS*, 3rd ser., xxi (1936–8), pp. 14–17; RCAHMS, *Inventory of Kirkcudbright*, no. 489; Appendix I, no. 204.

19 *RRS*, i, p. 13, n. 2; Appendix I, nos. 181, 208.

and destroyed, and slew all whom they took within them'.[20] Clearly there were more foreigners in Galloway than the four families recorded in the charters, and it was perhaps at this time, to take two examples at random, that mottes such as the small one at Skaith and the larger one at Druchtag were built.[21]

In 1185 there was another upheaval in which one of the native line of lords of Galloway, Roland, a grandson of Fergus, seized the whole inheritance. It is recorded that he slew the most powerful men in Galloway and occupied their lands, 'and in them he built castles and very many fortresses' (*castella et munitiones quamplures*).[22] Some mottes must therefore belong to that period; and it is worth noting that according to this statement mottes were being erected by Galwegians themselves. In the thirteenth century the native line of lords ended in three heiresses, who were married to three powerful Anglo-Norman barons: a further move in the attempt to establish royal authority in the area. One of these, John de Balliol, acquired Buittle, where there are remains of an important castle.[23] Another, Roger de Quincy, earl of Winchester and Constable of Scotland, got Cruggleton, which may originally have been the site of a fort of the lords of Galloway. It is dramatically situated on a cliftop in a position unlikely to have appealed to a motte-builder. At some stage before 1292 a stone castle was built there which was still standing in the sixteenth century, although only a single arch now survives.[24] Sometime during the thirteenth century royal castles were erected at Kirkcudbright and Wigtown;[25] and it may be that by the later thirteenth century Galloway was entering a new castle-building phase and mottes were becoming a thing of the past. But that is little more than conjecture.

There is, therefore, an ample context for the Galloway mottes. Only one of them, Mote of Urr, has been seriously excavated in modern times. Unfortunately no more than an interim report has ever been published, but excavation did establish that the motte was built earlier than the thirteenth century, which is what we would expect.[26] The mottes at Borgue, Anwoth and New Abbey also have a documentary context and they should be next for excavation. For the history of the south-west of Scotland in the early Middle Ages, nothing could add so much to our understanding as a thorough programme for selective excavation of mottes in the area. But very little has yet been done, and our present aim is merely to indicate from the historical side the context into which they fit.

We have tried to show here the kind of conclusions that may emerge from the

20 Anderson, *Scottish Annals*, p. 256, translating from *Gesta Regis Henrici Secundi*, ed. W. Stubbs (Rolls Ser., 1867), i, pp. 67–8.

21 RCAHMS, *Inventory of Wigtownshire*, nos. 200, 389; Appendix I, nos. 316, 314.

22 Anderson, *Scottish Annals*, p. 288, quoting *Gesta Regis Henrici Secundi*, i, pp. 339–40.

23 RCAHMS, *Inventory of Kirkcudbright*, no. 74. On the division of Galloway see *Wigtownshire Chrs.*, pp. xxxix–xli.

24 R.C. Reid, 'Cruggleton Castle', *TDGAS*, 3rd ser., xvi (1929–30), pp. 152–60; RCAHMS, *Inventory of Wigtownshire*, no. 420.

25 RCAHMS, *Inventories of Kirkcudbright*, no. 262, and *Wigtownshire*, no. 541; Stevenson, *Documents*, i, p. 206.

26 B. Hope-Taylor, 'Excavations at Mote of Urr', *TDGAS*, 3rd ser., xxix (1950–1), pp. 167–72.

bringing together of documentary and archaeological evidence on the problems of our early castles. There are certainly many problems left. Are there really no more mottes in Lothian? If so, is there any better explanation than the one we have put forward? We have not tried to analyse the mottes into different types, and it might be that something would emerge if mottes with baileys were plotted in comparison with mottes without baileys. We have not discussed the dating of the mottes. We have tended to assume that they belong to the twelfth and perhaps also the thirteenth centuries, which seems to be the implication of the documentary evidence. But any adequate discussion of dating must wait for much more excavation. All we have tried to do is to provide a historical background against which that and other questions can in future be discussed.

Appendix I. Provisional List of Mottes in Scotland

Geoffrey Stell

This census of mottes in Scotland is based principally on field identifications made by the former Archaeology Division of the Ordnance Survey and by the Royal Commission on the Ancient and Historical Monuments of Scotland. These have been supplemented by information from other sources, and this revision has benefited especially from the work of Eric Talbot of the University of Glasgow.[1] Most of the sites noted under the counties of Berwickshire, Dumfriesshire, East Lothian, Fife, Kirkcudbright, Peeblesshire, Roxburghshire, Selkirkshire, Stirlingshire and Wigtownshire have already been published in the relevant RCAHMS *Inventories*.[2] The lists for the three south-western counties were revised, however, and other identifications were made, particularly in Ayrshire and Lanarkshire, during marginal land surveys of field monuments in 1951–5 and 1956–8.[3] In addition, since the first publication of this list in 1972, mottes and other types of medieval earthwork have been included in the classified lists of field monuments published in the RCAHMS *Archaeological Sites and Monuments Series*, No. 1 (1978)– . I am much indebted to Peter Corser for extracting and arranging all the available information that has come to light as a result of this work. Most of the other material is contained on the Ordnance Survey Archaeology Division's unpublished record cards.

The aim of the census is simply to supply a provisional list of sites as a basis for further observations and research. Doubtful cases are indicated wherever possible, but many of the identifications are of course subject to confirmation and correction. No attempt has been made to distinguish between different morte-structures or to identify other types of defensive constructions, except for the ringworks noted mainly by Mr Talbot.

The term 'motte' has been mostly omitted from the titles, but the name of the parish has been included if required for an unambiguous identification. The sites are arranged by six-figure grid references within an alphabetical order of counties, and it has proved more convenient to maintain the arrangement of the pre-1975 counties in this revision. Uncertain identifications are indicated by a four-figure grid reference or are simply marked 'unidentified'.

1 E.J. Talbot, 'Early Scottish castles of earth and timber: recent field-work and excavation', *Scottish Archaeol. Forum*, vi (1974), pp. 48–57, esp. at pp. 54–6. An attempt has been made to bring the present list up to date in the light of this and other notices of mottes, but not all have been included here. Cf., e.g., the addition suggested in Barrow, *Era*, p. 110, n. 113, the Cunnigar at Mid Calder, Midlothian, whose name and character, like that of another site in Midmar, Aberdeenshire, indicate a medieval rabbit warren or enclosure rather than a motte.

2 *Berwickshire* (1915); *Dumfriesshire* (1920); *East Lothian* (1924); *Fife* (1933); *Kirkcudbright* (1914); *Peeblesshire* (1967); *Roxburghshire* (1956); *Selkirkshire* (1957); *Stirlingshire* (1963); *Wigtownshire* (1912).

3 *Inventories of Selkirkshire*, pp. xiv–xviii, and *Stirlingshire*, p. xxv; R.W. Feachem, 'Iron Age and early medieval monuments in Galloway and Dumfriesshire', *TDGAS*, 3rd ser., xxxiii (1956), pp. 58–65.

ABERDEENSHIRE

1 Doune of Invernochty	**NJ 352129**
2 Parks of Coldstone (site)	**NJ 434054**
3 Peel of Fichlie	**NJ 459139**
4 Lesmoir Castle	**NJ 471281**
5 Kildrummy	**NJ 471169**
6 Auchindoir	**NJ 475245**
7 Cumins Craig	**NJ 478245**
8 'Castlehill', Auchindoir and Kearn parish (doubtful)	**NJ 513282**
9 Castlehill, Druminnor	**NJ 515287**
10 Huntly Castle	**NJ 532407**
11 'Roundabout', Alford parish	**NJ 555163**
12 Peel of Lumphanan	**NJ 577037**
13 Moathead, Auchterless parish (possible)	**NJ 715417**
14 Earthwork, Chapel of Garioch parish	**NJ 724262**
15 Bass of Inverurie	**NJ 782206**
16 Castle Hill, Kintore (probable)	**NJ 794163**
17 Dalforky Castle (doubtful)	**NJ 807336**
18 Pitfoddels Castle (probable)	**NJ 910030**
19 Tillydrone (probable)	**NJ 936089**
20 Earl's Hill, Ellon (probable)	**NJ 957304**
21 Moat Hill, Cruden parish (possible)	**NK 062368**
22 Castle Hill, Rattray	**NK 086574**
23 Inverugie	**NK 102487**
24 Gardybien, Glenmuick (probable)	**NO 444990**

ANGUS

25 Easter Peel, Lintrathen	**NO 264540**
26 Castleton of Eassie	**NO 333466**
27 Court Hillock, Kirriemuir (doubtful)	**NO 380542**
28 Kirriemuir Hill (possible)	**NO 392546**
29 Invergowrie	**NO 395307**
30 Castle Hill, Inshewan	**NO 445572**
31 Forfar (possible)	**NO 457505**
32 Old Downie, Monifieth	**NO 519365**
33 Barry	**NO 533347**
34 Gallowshill (possible)	**NO 573492**
35 Castle Hillock, Edzell	**NO 584688**
36 Brechin Castle (possible)	**NO 597599**
37 Glenskinno (possible)	**NO 681608**
38 Maryton Law	**NO 682556**
39 Redcastle, Inverkeilor	**NO 689510**
40 Montrose (possible)	**NO 717573**

ARGYLL

41 Ard Luing (possible)	**NM 737066**
42 Staing Mhor	**NM 814081**

43 Rera	**NM 831207**
44 Carnasserie (ringwork)	**NM 838009**
45 Dùn Mor, Bonawe	**NN 012325**
46 Strachur (Strachur House)	**NN 093016**
47 Strachur (Ballemenoch)	**NN 103999**
48 Strachur (Strachurmore Farm)	**NN 108008**
49 Otter Ferry (Ballimore)	**NN 922833**
50 Macharioch	**NR 726094**
51 Glendaruel, Achanelid (dun or rectangular motte?)	**NS 005878**
52 Glendaruel	**NS 006874**
53 Dunoon, Castle Crawford	**NS 179787**
AYRSHIRE	
54 Judge Mound, Skelmorlie Mains (possible)	**NS 199663**
55 Dowhill	**NS 203029**
56 Castle Knowe, Hunterston	**NS 203508**
57 Green Hill, Halkshill, Largs	**NS 207593**
58 Kelburne Park, Fairlie (possible motte or dun)	**NS 212562**
59 Shanter Knowe	**NS 219074**
60 Montfode Mount	**NS 227438**
61 Knockrivoch Mount	**NS 254451**
62 Auldmuir (possible)	**NS 264499**
63 Dunduff (ringwork)	**NS 272164**
64 Castlehill	**NS 283432**
65 Court Hill, Dalry (site)	**NS 292495**
66 Mote Knowe, Monkwood (possible)	**NS 298002**
67 Kidsneuk, Bogside, Irvine (site)	**NS 309409**
68 Ayr Castle (site)	**NS 335222**
69 Alloway (ringwork)	**NS 339180**
70 Chapel Hill, Chapelton	**NS 344442**
71 Lawthorn Mount	**NS 345406**
72 Woodlands (probable)	**NS 346136**
73 Court Hill, Beith (possible)	**NS 361540**
74 Lindston, Dalrymple parish (possible moated homestead)	**NS 372168**
75 Carmel Bank, Kilmaurs parish	**NS 387380**
76 Symington (possible)	**NS 38 31**
77 Helenton, Symington parish	**NS 393311**
78 Witch Knowe, Coylton parish (possible)	**NS 399199**
79 Greenhill, Kilmaurs parish	**NS 401392**
80 Barnweill Castle (probable)	**NS 407301**
81 Law Mount, Stewarton	**NS 411448**
82 Castle Hill, Riccarton parish (possible)	**NS 417359**
83 Tarbolton	**NS 432274**
84 Dalmellington	**NS 482058**
85 Castlehill Farm	**NS 483388**
86 Witch Knowe, Hillbank Wood, Ochiltree parish (possible)	**NS 502217**
87 Castle Hill, Alton	**NS 503388**

88 Judge's Hill, Loudon parish (possible)	**NS 519386**
89 East Newton, Newmilns	**NS 519385**
90 Castle Hill, Burflat Burn, Loudon parish (possible)	**NS 546378**
91 Borland Castle, Old Cumnock parish (possible)	**NS 585174**
92 Castle Hill, Sorn parish	**NS 588263**
93 Main Castle, Galston parish	**NS 612346**
94 Carleton	**NX 134895**
95 Doune Knoll (possible)	**NX 185971**
96 Dinvin, Girvan	**NX 200932**
97 Mote Wood, Camregan (possible)	**NX 221994**
98 Mote Knowe, Colmonell parish (possible)	**NX 232818**

BANFFSHIRE

99 Ha'Hillock, Deskford	**NJ 509628**
100 Castle Hill, Cullen	**NJ 509670**
101 Kinnairdy Castle, Marnoch parish (doubtful)	**NJ 609498**
102 Craig o'Boyne Castle (possible)	**NJ 616661**
103 Castlehill Farm, Marnoch parish (site)	**NJ 644513**
104 Mount Carmel, Banff parish	**NJ 679626**
105 Ha'Hillock, Alvah parish	**NJ 689584**
106 Banff Castle (probable)	**NJ 689641**

BERWICKSHIRE

107 The Chesters (possible ringwork)	**NT 740474**
108 Bunkle Castle (ringwork)	**NT 805596**
109 The Mount, Castlelaw, Coldstream	**NT 814418**
110 Fair Field, Ladykirk (probable)	**NT 893477**

CAITHNESS

111 Ring of Castlehill (ringwork)	**ND 282618**

DUMFRIESSHIRE

112 Druidhill Burn, Penpont	**NS 810015**
113 Ballaggan	**NS 835014**
114 Enoch Castle	**NS 872027**
115 Garpol Water, Moffat	**NT 051040**
116 Auchencass	**NT 063035**
117 Coats Hill	**NT 072042**
118 Auldton, Moffat	**NT 094058**
119 Ingleston, lower motte, Glencairn	**NX 799899**
120 Maxwelton	**NX 817896**
121 Moatland	**NX 865857**
122 Morton Castle	**NX 891992**
123 Dinning, Closeburn	**NX 893902**
124 Benthead, Closeburn	**NX 922958**
125 Lochside, Lincluden	**NX 958774**
126 Castle Dykes, Dumfries (medieval castle earthworks)	**NX 975747**

127 Dumfries (possible)	**NX 973764**
128 Tinwald	**NY 003815**
129 Torthorwald Castle	**NY 034783**
130 Rockhall	**NY 054767**
131 Castle Hill, Lochmaben	**NY 082822**
132 Lochwood	**NY 085968**
133 Spedlins Tower	**NY 097876**
134 Applegarth	**NY 104843**
135 Castle Knowe, Saughtrees	**NY 125950**
136 Wamphray Place, Newton	**NY 132969**
137 Castlemilk (possible)	**NY 150775**
138 Hutton	**NY 164894**
139 Gillesbie Tower	**NY 172920**
140 Annan	**NY 192666**
141 Barntalloch, Langholm	**NY 352878**
142 Wauchope Castle, Hallcrofts	**NY 355842**
DUNBARTONSHIRE	
143 Faslane (site)	**NS 249901**
144 Shandon (possible)	**NS 257878**
145 Balloch Castle	**NS 388826**
146 Catter Law	**NS 472871**
147 Peel of Kirkintilloch	**NS 651740**
EAST LOTHIAN	
148 Gladsmuir (site)	**NT 46 73 (unidentified)**
149 Tarbet Castle, Fidra Island (site)	**NT 515867**
150 Castle Hill, North Berwick	**NT 560801**
151 Eldbotle (site)	**NT 505857**
FIFE	
152 Court Knowe, Gornogrove	**NO 205103**
153 Inchrye	**NO 272165**
154 Agabatha Castle (site)	**NO 284127**
155 Collessie (possible)	**NO 293134**
156 Parbroath Farm	**NO 324178**
157 Maiden Castle, Dunipace Hill, Markinch	**NO 349015**
158 Moat Hill, Cupar (site)	**NO 372148**
159 Castle Hill, Cupar (site)	**NO 37 14 (unidentified)**
160 Newton (possible)	**NO 403246**
161 Leuchars Castle	**NO 454219**
162 Perdieus Mount, Dunfermline (site)	**NT 091867**
163 Lochore Castle	**NT 175958**
164 Hillside, Aberdour parish (possible)	**NT 193855**

INVERNESS-SHIRE

165 Erchless, Cnoc an Tighe Mhoir (possible)	**NH 410410**
166 Urquhart Castle	**NH 530286**
167 Wester Lovat, Beauly (possible)	**NH 540460**
168 Holm House (probable)	**NH 653420**
169 Petty (possible)	**NH 736497**
170 Old Petty	**NH 738498**
171 Ruthven in Badenoch (possible)	**NH 765997**
172 Cromal Mount, Ardersier	**NH 782555**
173 Old House of Keppoch	**NN 271808**

KINCARDINESHIRE

174 Castle Hill, Strachan	**NO 657921**
175 Green Castle (possible ringwork)	**NO 668765**
176 Castle Hill, Durris	**NO 780968**
177 Dunnottar	**NO 882839**

KIRKCUDBRIGHTSHIRE

178 Minnigaff	**NX 410664**
179 Machars Hill	**NX 470653**
180 Kirkclaugh	**NX 534522**
181 Boreland or Green Tower	**NX 585550**
182 Woodend, Anwoth	**NX 585566**
183 Polchree Farm, Anwoth (possible)	**NX 592584**
184 Polchree	**NX 594584**
185 Roberton	**NX 604486**
186 Moat Park, Cally	**NX 606556,**
187 Barmagachan, near Borgue	**NX 613494**
188 Palace Yard (ringwork)	**NX 613543**
189 Dalry	**NX 618813**
190 Boreland of Borgue	**NX 646517**
191 Balmaclellan	**NX 653794**
192 Trostrie	**NX 656574**
193 Culcraigie (possible)	**NX 657575**
194 Twynholm	**NX 659539**
195 Little Duchrae	**NX 664696**
196 Dunnance	**NX 674637**
197 Castle Dykes, Kirkcudbright	**NX 677509**
198 Boreland of Parton	**NX 694709**
199 Kirkland, Parton	**NX 696697**
200 Culdoach	**NX 706537**
201 Kirkcormack	**NX 717574**
202 Lochrinnie	**NX 728871**
203 Ingleston, Kelton parish	**NX 775580**
204 Urr	**NX 815647**
205 Cullochan Castle	**NX 921754**
206 Lincluden	**NX 967779**

207 Troqueer	**NX 974748**
208 Ingleston, New Abbey parish	**NX 982651**

LANARKSHIRE

209 Castle Hill, East Kilbride parish (possible)	**NS 589563**
210 Bishop's Palace, Glasgow (ringwork)	**NS 601655**
211 Carmunnock (ringwork)	**NS 613578**
212 Cawder House	**NS 613724**
213 Castle Hill, East Kilbride parish (possible)	**NS 612557**
214 Castlemilk (possible)	**NS 613598**
215 Rutherglen	**NS 623617**
216 Mains, East Kilbride	**NS 627558**
217 Laigh Mains, East Kilbride parish (possible)	**NS 627561**
218 Greenlees	**NS 638585**
219 Peelhill	**NS 643367**
220 The Tor, Torrance	**NS 649526**
221 Drumsargad Castle, Cambuslang (site)	**NS 665597**
222 Hamilton, Low Parks	**NS 727566**
223 Darngaber Castle	**NS 729500**
224 Cot Castle (possible)	**NS 739456**
225 Millfield, Cambusnethan parish	**NS 795573**
226 Ladle Knowe, Douglas	**NS 826294**
227 Castle Qua (ringwork)	**NS 873449**
228 Lanark	**NS 879433**
229 Abington	**NS 933250**
230 Moat Farm, Roberton	**NS 940270**
231 Castledykes	**NS 942287**
232 Bower of Wandel	**NS 951287**
233 Crawford Castle or Tower Lindsay (possible)	**NS 954213**
234 Couthalley Castle (possible)	**NS 971481**
235 Carnwath	**NS 974466**
236 Loanheadmill	**NS 992310**
237 Wolfclyde	**NT 019363**
238 Biggar	**NT 039377**

MIDLOTHIAN

239 Crichton (ringwork)	**NT 384618**

MORAY

240 Grant's Fort	**NJ 053316**
241 Kilbuiach	**NJ 097603**
242 Tor Chastle	**NJ 130526**
243 Duffus Castle	**NJ 189672**
244 Elgin Castle	**NJ 212628**
245 Knight's Hillock, Urquhart parish	**NJ 283651**

NAIRNSHIRE

246 Cantraydoune	**NH 789461**
247 Nairn Castle (site)	**NH 885566**
248 Auldearn, Doocot Hill	**NH 917556**
249 Hillend (possible)	**NH 932547**

PEEBLESSHIRE

250 Peebles	**NT 249403**

PERTHSHIRE

251 Tom-na-Curtaig, Kerrowmore	**NN 589467**
252 Tom na Chisaig, Callander parish (possible)	**NN 627079**
253 Carnbane Castle, Fortingall parish (doubtful)	**NN 677479**
254 Coney Hill, near Comrie	**NN 776224**
255 Tom an Tigh Moir, Blair Atholl parish	**NN 807654**
256 Struan	**NN 812653**
257 Aldclune, Blair Atholl	**NN 895643**
258 Glendevon (site)	**NN 904047**
259 Kindrogan	**NO 055638**
260 Castle Hill, Clunie	**NO 111440**
261 Motte, Scone parish (probable)	**NO 126295**
262 Cairn Beddie, St Martin's parish (site)	**NO 150308**
263 Castle Hill, Cargill	**NO 158374**
264 Blairgowrie (site)	**NO 179455**
265 Rattray	**NO 209453**
266 Law Knowe, Errol (probable)	**NO 232224**
267 Barton Hill, Kinnaird	**NO 244287**
268 Blair Drummond	**NS 724986**

RENFREWSHIRE

269 Pennytersal	**NS 337712**
270 Motte, Kilmacolm parish (site)	**NS 352661**
271 South Denniston (probable)	**NS 358683**
272 Castlehead, Paisley (ringwork)	**NS 381635**
273 Castle Hill, Ranfurly	**NS 384651**
274 Houston House	**NS 411671**
275 Castlehill, Renfrew (site)	**NS 509679**
276 Elderslie, 'The King's Inch', Renfrew (site)	**NS 514675**
277 Crookston (ringwork)	**NS 525627**
278 Pollok (ringwork)	**NS 555626**
279 Crosslees, Eaglesham (possible)	**NS 558536**
280 Camphill (ringwork)	**NS 577621**

ROSS AND CROMARTY

281 Dunscaith Castle	**NH 807690**

ROXBURGHSHIRE

282 Hawick	**NT 499140**
283 Riddell	**NT 520248**
284 Ruletownhead (possible)	**NT 617128**
285 Smailholm (ringwork)	**NT 640346**

SELKIRKSHIRE

286 Phenzhopehaugh	**NT 318127**
287 Howden	**NT 458268**
288 Selkirk	**NT 470281**

STIRLINGSHIRE

289 Woodend	**NS 555887**
290 Keir of Cashlie, Drymen (possible)	**NS 556929**
291 Craigmaddie (ringwork)	**NS 575765**
292 Fintry	**NS 611866**
293 Keir Knowe of Drum	**NS 636953**
294 Maiden Castle, Garmore	**NS 643784**
295 Sir John de Graham's Castle	**NS 681858**
296 Balcastle Motte, Kilsyth	**NS 701781**
297 Colzium, Kilsyth (possible)	**NS 734782**
298 Bonnybridge (Mote of Seabegs)	**NS 824798**
299 Slamannan	**NS 856734**
300 Watling Lodge (site)	**NS 862798**

SUTHERLAND

301 Borgie (possible)	**NC 670587**
302 Langdale	**NC 698449**
303 Invershin	**NH 572963**
304 Proncy	**NH 772926**
305 Skelbo Castle	**NH 792952**

WIGTOWNSHIRE

306 Castle Ban, near Mains of Airies	**NW 966678**
307 Culhorn, Inch parish (possible)	**NX 078594**
308 Innermessan	**NX 084634**
309 Balgreggan	**NX 096505**
310 Ardwell	**NX 107455**
311 High Drummore	**NX 130359**
312 Droughdool	**NX 148569**
313 Motte, Old Luce parish (probable)	**NX 194573**
314 Druchtag	**NX 349467**
315 Boreland	**NX 355584**
316 Skaith	**NX 382662**
317 Castle (site) near Appleby, Glasserton parish	**NX 401409**

Appendix II. Preliminary List of Scottish Castles Recorded in Documents or Chronicles down to 1249

This list is based on a survey of standard sources, but does not claim to be comprehensive. It records only places which are specifically described by the words *castrum*, *castellum*, or, occasionally, *oppidum*. Various other words of less specific meaning may also denote a fortified site or structure. For example, manerium can mean a 'manor-house', and the *manerium* of Leuchars, Fife (*St Andrews Liber*, pp. 397–8, datable 1280 × 1297) is a motte (Appendix I, no. 161). The word *curia* can mean a house as well as a court, as it does in an unusually descriptive reference to a house at Lamberton, Berwickshire, perhaps of the reign of Alexander II (J. Raine, *The History and Antiquities of North Durham* [London, 1852], app., no. 649). An aula such as that at Congalton, East Lothian, probably *c.*1224 (*Dryb. Lib.*, no. 24), may represent what in architectural terms would be called a 'hall-house'.

	Date	Source
ANGUS		
1 Forfar	before 1197	*St Andrews Liber*, p. 354
2 Montrose	1165 × 1214	*RRS*, ii, no. 556
ARGYLL		
3 Cairnaburgh (More)	1249	Anderson, *Early Sources*, ii, p. 556; Duncan, Scotland, p. 551
4 Dunaverty	1248	*CDS*, i, no. 1865; Duncan, *Scotland*, p. 550
AYRSHIRE		
5 Ayr	1197	*Melrose Liber*, i, no. 103
6 Greenan	1175 × 1199	*Ibid.*, no. 34
7 Irvine	1184	*Gesta Regis Henrici Secundi* (Rolls Ser., 1867), i, pp. 312–13
8 Unidentified site probably in Carrick	1175 × 1199	*Melrose Liber*, i, no. 31
BANFFSHIRE		
9 Boharm	before 1242	*Moray Reg.*, nos. 23, 64
BERWICKSHIRE		
10 Berwick	1173	*Gesta Regis Henrici Secundi*, i, p. 47
11 Lauder	1173	*ibid.*
BUTE		
12 Rothesay	1231	Anderson, *Early Sources*, ii, p. 476
CLACKMANNANSHIRE		
13 Clackmannan	*c.*1248 × 1264	SRO RH 6/54

	Date	Source
DUMFRIESSHIRE		
14 Annan	*c.*1124	Lawrie, *Charters*, no. 54
15 Dumfries	1175 × 1187	*Glasgow Reg.*, i, no. 50
16 Lochmaben	1173	*Gesta Regis Henrici Secundi*, i, p. 47
DUNBARTONSHIRE		
17 Dumbarton	1222	J. Irving, *History of Dumbartonshire* (Dumbarton, 1917–24), ii, p. 287
EAST LOTHIAN		
18 Dirleton	after Sept. 1219	*Dryb. Lib.*, no. 37
19 Eldbotle	probably late William I	*Ibid.*, no. 104
FIFE		
20 Crail	1153 × 1165	*RRS*, i, no. 289
21 Culross	1217	SRO Supplementary Register House Charters, *s.d.*
22 Lindores	1249	*Lind. Cart.*, no. 62
INVERNESS-SHIRE		
23 Inverness	1197	*Melrose Liber*, i, no. 103
KINCARDINESHIRE		
24 Inverbervie	1232 × 1237	*Lind. Cart.*, no. 18
LANARKSHIRE		
25 East Kilbride	1175 × 1190	*Glasgow Reg.*, i, no. 55; cf. *RRS*, ii, no. 249
MIDLOTHIAN		
26 Edinburgh	*c.*1127	Lawrie, *Charters*, no. 72
MORAY		
27 Duffus	1203 × 1222	*Moray Reg.*, no. 211
28 Elgin	1160	*RRS*, i, no. 175
NAIRNSHIRE		
29 Auldearn	1185	*Liber Insule Missarum* (Bannatyne Club, 1847), no. 2
30 Nairn	1215 × 1222	*Moray Reg.*, no. 25
PEEBLESSHIRE		
31 Peebles	1152 × 1153	*RRS*, i, no. 104

	Date	Source
PERTHSHIRE		
32 Alyth	1196 × 1199	*Ibid.*, ii, no. 410
33 Cargill	1189 × 1199	SRO Maitland Thomson Photographs, no. 6
34 Perth	1157 × 1160	*RRS*, i, no. 157
RENFREWSHIRE		
35 Renfrew	1163 × 1165	*Ibid.*, no. 254
ROSS and CROMARTY		
36 Dunskeath	1179	Anderson, *Early Sources*, ii, p. 301
37 Redcastle (Eddyrdor)	1179	Ibid.
ROXBURGHSHIRE		
38 Jedburgh	1147 × 1150	Lawrie, *Charters*, no. 189
39 Roxburgh	*c.*1128	*Ibid.*, no. 83
SELKIRKSHIRE		
40 Selkirk	*c.*1120	*Ibid.*, no. 35
STIRLINGSHIRE		
41 Stirling	1107 × 1124	*Ibid.*, no. 182

12

Fluctuating Frontiers: Normanno-Welsh Castle Warfare c.1075 to 1240

John R. Kenyon

Introduction[1] (fig. 1)

Within a few years of the Norman Conquest of England in 1066, William I had established three of his most powerful supporters on the border with Wales, no doubt because of threats from the west, which had included attacks on the important centres of Shrewsbury and Hereford in 1067–69. We find William fitz Osbern, earl of Hereford, in south-east Wales building the great castle of Chepstow from about 1067, as well as others to the north. In the centre of the Welsh March the Conqueror established Roger of Montgomery as earl of Shrewsbury, whilst in the north-east there was Hugh of Avranches based at Chester.

The earliest deep and successful penetration by the Normans into Wales was in the north of the country, led by Hugh of Chester and his cousin Robert of Rhuddlan. Here the Chester-based Normans moved west to establish strongholds at Rhuddlan around 1073/78, at Degannwy by around 1078, and further west by 1093 at Caernarfon, Bangor and Aberlleiniog, and also south into the hinterland in Meirionydd at Tomen-y-mur. Further south, from their bases at Montgomery and Shrewsbury on the central Welsh March, the Normans raided deep into Dyfed and Ceredigion in 1073 and 1074, but it was only after the death of Rhys ap Tewdwr in 1093 that they established what were envisaged as permanent bases at Pembroke, Cardigan, with Carmarthen (Rhyd-y-gors) established for William Rufus by sea from the south.

In simple terms, as far as castles are concerned, the two centuries from the late eleventh century to the time of the Edwardian conquest of Wales from 1277 saw both Anglo-Norman and Welsh successes and disasters, both sides building castles as well as capturing them, with several of the Norman strongholds falling

[1] This paper covers the period from the first recorded Welsh attack on a Norman castle, Rhuddlan around 1075/80, to the death of Llywelyn ab Iorwerth (Llywelyn the Great) who died in 1240. The precise date of the attack on Rhuddlan is uncertain, depending upon whether Robert of Rhuddlan died in 1088 or (more likely) in 1093. On this problem see M. Chibnall (ed. and trans.), *The Ecclesiastical History of Orderic Vitalis. IV. Books VII and VIII* (Oxford, 1973), xxxiv–xxxviii. I am extremely grateful to Richard Avent, Professor Rees Davies, Jeremy Knight, Derek Renn and Jack Spurgeon for their comments on the original text for the lecture given at Abergavenny, and for allowing me to include many of the suggestions made. Thanks also to Fiona Gale for preparing figure 1, and to the National Monuments Record for Wales (R.C.A.H.M.W.) for providing figures 2–4.

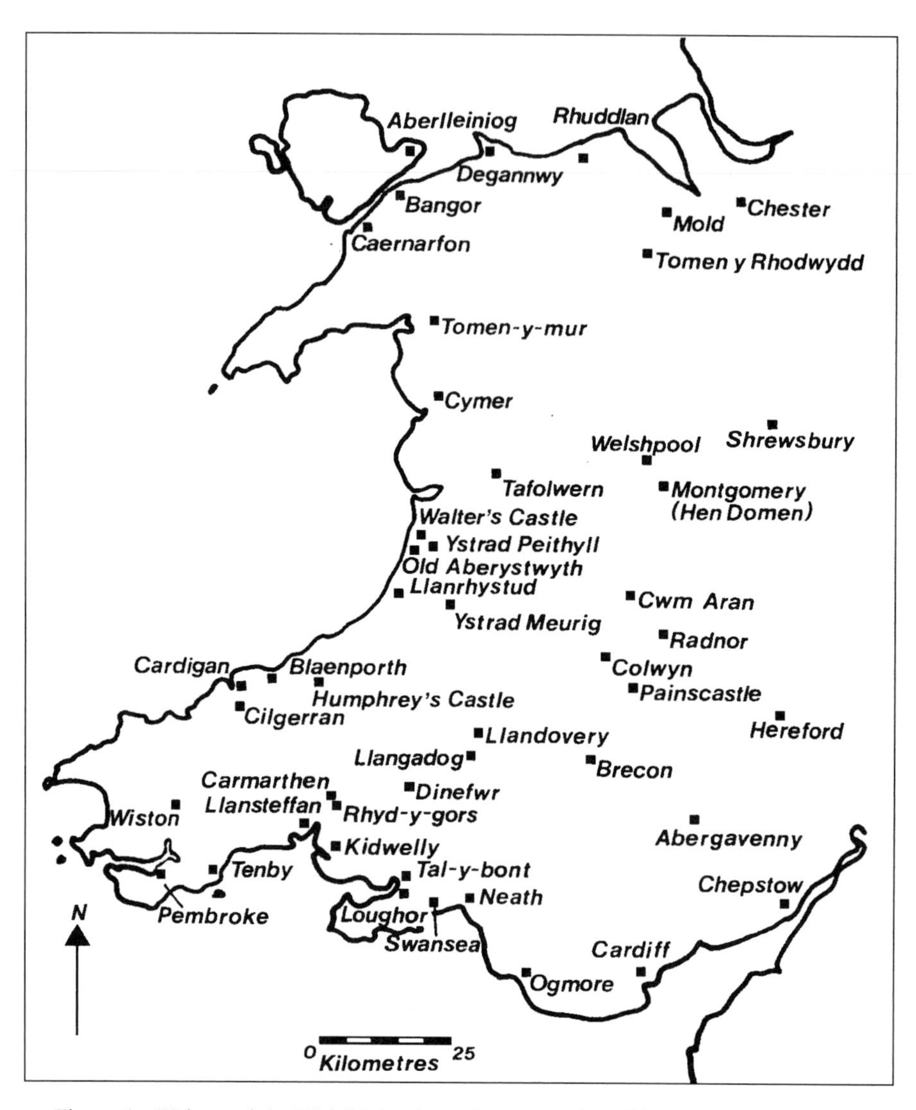

Figure 1. Wales and the Welsh Marches: places mentioned in the text. (Drawing: Fiona Gale)

into Welsh hands for a number of years. In fact anyone who reads the Welsh Latin chronicles such as the *Annales Cambriae* and the *Cronica de Wallia* and the later, fuller, translations of such documents into Welsh, known to modern scholars as the *Brut y Tywysogyon* and the *Brenhinedd y Saesson*, cannot help but come to an initial impression that one should not put one's trust in castles, so often were they taken, retaken or even slighted and never to be used again. However, in using these sources the student has to bear in mind that they may not be reliable as to the pattern of warfare throughout Wales; for example, for the period *c.* 1106–20 the *Brut* is largely concerned with the dynasty of Powys, being compiled within its borders, possibly at Llanbadarn.[2]

Those interested in European siege warfare have many contemporary accounts to capture their attention, several of which are mentioned in Bradbury's book *The Medieval Siege*. One thinks of the attacks on Le Puiset, chronicled for us by Abbot Suger, Château Gaillard captured by Philip Augustus in 1204, and closer to home the sieges of Rochester in 1215 and Bedford in 1224.[3] Nor should we forget the chronicles of the anarchy during the reign of Stephen (1135–54), namely the *Gesta Stephani* for accounts of sieges such as Exeter and Wallingford and William of Malmesbury's *Historia Novella*.[4] Details of siege warfare in the Welsh chronicles cannot hope to match the accounts I have just cited; nevertheless, those that do are of interest in that they illuminate the techniques and weaponry used by both sides in this frontier society. Therefore, I have taken the opportunity to examine the evidence for castle warfare in the land which the Anglo-Norman kings of England took two centuries to subjugate.

Chronology

The first records that we have of an attack on a castle in Wales come in the *Historia Gruffydd ap Cynan*.[5] In *c.* 1075/80 we learn of the attack on Robert's castle of Rhuddlan which resulted in the burning and temporary capture of the bailey, and the death of several of the Norman defenders. However, the tower on its motte, to which the rest of the garrison retreated, clearly held firm, emphasizing the value of these motte castles, even against 'a great host'.[6] In 1094, Gruffudd laid siege to Castell Aberlleiniog on Anglesey, and in spite of fierce Norman resistance, the defenders using bows, slings and mangonels, the Welsh were ultimately successful, and we are informed that the steward who held the castle and 124 Norman soldiers were killed.[7] In the same year, one of Welsh resurgence, the *Brut*[8] records that the castles of Gwynedd were destroyed, as were those in the south-west, except for two, namely Carmarthen (Rhyd-y-gors) and Pembroke, the latter being a stronghold which the Welsh never took. The capture in the following year (1095) of the first castle of Montgomery (Hen

2 I am indebted to Professor Rees Davies for this point.

3 J. Bradbury, *The Medieval Siege* (Woodbridge, 1992). Suger's account of the Le Puiset siege is now available in an English translation: *The Deeds of Louis the Fat* (Washington, 1992).

4 For an account of castles in Stephen's reign see C. Coulson, 'The castles of the anarchy', in E. King (ed.), *The Anarchy of King Stephen's Reign* (Oxford, 1994), 67–92.

5 *The History of Gruffydd ap Cynan*, translated, with introduction and notes, by A. Jones (Manchester, 1910). See also D.S. Evans (ed.), *Historia Gruffudd vab Kenan* (Cardiff, 1977) and D.S. Evans, *A Mediaeval Prince of Wales: the Life of Gruffudd ap Cynan* (Llanerch, 1990).

6 *Gruffydd*, 117.

7 *Gruffydd*, 137, 139.

8 *Brut y Tvwysogyon or the Chronicle of the Princes. Peniarth Ms. 20 Version*, translated by T. Jones (Cardiff, 1952), 19. *Brut y Tvwysogyon or the Chronicle of the Princes. Red Book of Hergest Version*, translated by T. Jones (2nd edn, Cardiff, 1973), 33, 35; *Brenhinedd y Saesson or the Kings of the Saxons*, translated by T. Jones (Cardiff, 1971), 87. Hereafter these three sources are referred to as *Brut* (*Peniarth*), *Brut* (*RBH*) and *Brenhinedd*.

Figure 2. 'Old Aberystwyth' (Tan-y-castell), Cardiganshire. Crown copyright: Royal Commission on the Ancient and Historical Monuments of Wales

Domen) is unfortunately not recorded in the Welsh annals, only in the *Anglo-Saxon Chronicle*.[9] In 1096 the Normans abandoned Carmarthen without a struggle, with Pembroke and some isolated castles in Brycheiniog holding out, in spite of the Welsh plundering of their hinterlands.[10]

Apart from the Welsh under Owain ap Cadwgan ap Bleddyn of Powys gaining access to Cenarth Bychan (? Cilgerran) in 1109, little occurs in the chronicles as far as castles are concerned until the year 1116, apart from Cadwgan ap Bleddyn being slain in 1111 as he was building a castle at Welshpool. 1116 was a year that was recorded as 'irksome and hateful to everyone' due to the maraudings of an army of 'hotheaded youths'.[11] In many cases the attacks were simply the destruction of the outer defences of a castle ; this was the case at Swansea, Carmarthen, the subject of a night attack, and Llandovery. At Blaenporth, the castle of Gilbert fitz Richard, it was the tower they concentrated on, but once again this core of the castle was not taken, although many of its defenders were slain. The Welsh had more success, however, at Ystrad Peithyll, the castle of Gilbert fitz Richard's steward, Ralf, for this was besieged, taken and burnt. This Ralf had more luck in the defence of 'Old Aberystwyth' (fig. 2), with attacks on the Welsh in the field and the use of a ruse leading to a Norman success.

9 D. Whitelock (ed.), *The Anglo-Saxon Chronicle* (London, 1961), 173.

10 *Brut* (*Peniarth*), 20; *Brut* (*RBH*), 35, 37; *Brenhinedd*, 87, 89.

11 *Brut* (*Peniarth*), 40–46; *Brut* (*RBH*), 87–101; *Brenhinedd*, 127–37. Professor Rees Davies has emphasized to me (pers. comm.) that the account of the Normanno-Welsh struggle in Ceredigion seen through native eyes is one of the finest sources for Norman warfare, and one rarely considered.

Professor Rees Davies has reminded us in his seminal work on medieval Wales that, besides Edward I (1272–1307), no other king of England played a greater role in the control and occupation of Wales and the creation of the Welsh March than Henry I (1100–35).[12] Following the death of King Henry the Welsh rose up in a series of revolts which saw field armies defeated and many castles captured, often with great ease, as at Walter's and Ystrad Meurig in 1136 and Wiston in 1147.[13] In some cases the Welsh held on to the castles taken and rebuilt them, for example Carmarthen in 1150.[14] The ebb and flow of both Norman and Welsh fortunes is shown by the chronicles recording castles burnt, taken or even occupied. Occasionally even a native Welsh castle was taken by another Welsh lord such as the incident that occurred in 1157 when Iorwerth Goch ap Maredudd of the Powys dynasty burnt Owain Gwynedd's castle in Iâl, Tomen y Rhodwydd.[15] In 1162 Hywel ab Ieuaf, a member of the minor dynasty of Arwstli, took the same Owain's castle of Tafolwem, but in this instance Owain moved to even the score with devastating results, and repaired the castle.[16] In fact from the time of the accession of Henry II in 1154 to the ascendancy of Llywelyn ab Iorwerth from 1212 the chronicles record over sixty instances of castles being taken or just attacked, and this figure is an underestimate for the records often state that all the castles in a particular area were attacked. For example, in 1158 and 1159 it is recorded that the castles of Ceredigion and Dyfed castles were burnt,[17] this flurry of activity resulting from a brief period of Norman recovery in 1158, when Roger de Clare rebuilt six castles, including Llanrhystud (fig. 3); further south the Normans also re-occupied Carmarthen.

In many cases castle warfare in Wales in the second half of the 12th century and the opening decade of the 13th century witnessed the Welsh recovery of areas of Wales under such strong leaders as Owain Gwynedd (d. 1170) and the Lord Rhys (d. 1197), who respectively dominated the political scene in north and south Wales, while the Normans were secure only in the extreme south-east and south-west corners of Wales, and in other small pockets. The next phase in Norman (or English)-Welsh relations in which the siege and capture of castles played a significant part was the period from 1212 to 1218, when Llywelyn ab Iorwerth was consolidating his position as prince of north Wales and much of the south, after having almost suffered complete defeat at the hands of King John in 1211–12. By 1213 Anglo-Norman castles in Gwynedd had been taken, including Degannwy and Rhuddlan.[18] In the south the year 1215 was particularly disastrous for the Normans, as they were driven from many castles, including Kidwelly, Loughor and Talybont, and more notably the royal castles of Carmarthen and Cardigan.[19] These last two remained in the custody of Llywelyn

12 Davies, *op. cit.* in note 1, 40.

13 *Brut (Peniarth)*, 51, 55–56 ; *Brut (RBH)*, 115, 125.

14 *Brut (Peniarth)*, 57; *Brut (RBH)*, 129; *Brenhinedd*, 155.

15 *Brut (Peniarth)*, 60; *Brut (RBH)*, 137; *Brenhinedd*, 159.

16 *Brut (Peniarth)*, 62; *Brut (RBH)*, 143; *Brenhinedd*, 155.

17 *Brut (Peniarth)*, 60–61; *Brut (RBH)*, 139, 141; *Brenhinedd*, 161.

18 *Brut (Peniarth)*, 88; *Brut (RBH)*, 199; *Brenhinedd*, 209.

19 *Brut (Peniarth)*, 90–91; *Brut (RBH)*, 203, 205; *Brenhinedd*, 213, 215.

Figure 3. Llanrhystud (Caer Penrhos), Cardiganshire. Crown copyright: Royal Commission on the Ancient and Historical Monuments of Wales

by the terms of the truce of Worcester in 1218, although they were regained by conquest in 1223. In the campaign in south Wales in 1231 again we find Cardigan falling to the Welsh, together with other castles such as Neath, Brecon and Radnor,[20] and two years later, in 1233, attacks were launched on several other Anglo-Norman strongholds[21] with notable successes. Castles in Brycheiniog were burnt, as was Abergavenny, although in some cases fortresses managed to hold out, notably Brecon and Cardiff.

Such is a summary of the chronology of the main event in which castles played an important role. But what evidence do we have of the actual techniques used by both sides in siege warfare, both in terms of defence and offence? Again the chronicles, notable the *Brut y Tywysogyon*, are the sources of information.

Siege Techniques and Weaponry

We learn nothing from the first account of a Welsh assault on a castle, the burning of the bailey of Rhuddlan recorded in the *Historia Gruffydd ap Cynan*, but in 1094 the same chronicle describing the siege and capture of Aberlleiniog

20 *Brut (Peniarth)*, 102; *Brut (RBH)*, 229, 231; *Brenhinedd*, 229.

21 *Brut (Peniarth)*, 102–3; *Brut (RBH)*, 231, 233; *Brenhinedd*, 229.

provides us with some information on the weaponry used by the Norman defenders, for arrows and quarrels were fired at the Welsh, implying the use of long- and crossbows, together with slings and mangonels.[22] This last weapon is well known as an example of artillery, but we cannot be certain about whether the slings were hand-held or a type of artillery; I would suggest the latter.

It is not until 1146 that we are given some detail about siege techniques.[23] In that year Cadell ap Gruffudd, having taken Dinefwr and Carmarthen, besieged and captured Llansteffan after a 'severe struggle'. Within a few days, and to the surprise of the Welsh, the Normans and Flemings tried to retake the castle which had been left in the hands of the young Maredudd ap Gruffudd. The Normans raised scaling ladders against the walls, but once they had reached the embrasures the ladders and those on them were hurled down into the ditch, and the attempt on the castle proved a failure. It is worth noting that the chronicle states that the Normans attempted their escalade upon realizing just how small the garrison was, as if they would not have made the attempt otherwise. However, this may be simply a way of emphasizing the heroism of the young Maredudd on the part of the chronicler – 'And thus did he a boy defeat many men proven in arms and battles.' The Normans could have done with the type of ladder used at the capture of Cilgerran by the Lord Rhys in 1165.[24] We are told that Rhys did not gain the castle through 'strength' but through an idea implemented by one of his men, Cedifor ap Dinawol. He had devised ladders with hooks on the ends which once planted against the castle walls would have been difficult, or even impossible, to dislodge, especially with men climbing up them.

In 1167 a combined force of Welsh from the north and the south are recorded in the *Brut* as having besieged Rhuddlan for three months, before finally destroying it.[25] Unfortunately we are not told more, such as how the Normans resisted for so long and whether the Welsh simply tried to starve out the garrison. However, in that variant translation of the *Brut*, the *Brenhinedd y Saesson*, it is stated that the Welsh first took Rhuddlan, and then occupied and rebuilt it during the said three months, before finally abandoning it and returning whence they came.[26] This seems a more reasonable story than that in the *Brut*.

The Welsh attack on Abergavenny about 1182 is not recorded in the main Welsh annals, only by Gerald of Wales. However, Gerald does give us a good account of the attack, with the Welsh using scaling ladders to take the bailey and capture the constable of the castle, his wife and most of the garrison. The effectiveness of the Welsh archers is borne out by the comment that two of the Norman garrison escaped over the motte bridge into the main tower, the arrows shot at them actually penetrating the oak doorway of the keep.[27]

Although the annals make the comment in the entry on the attack on 'Old Aberystwyth' in 1116 that the Welsh paused 'thinking to make engines to shoot

22 *Gruffydd*, 137, 139.

23 *Brut* (*Peniarth*), 54; *Brut* (*RBH*), 121, 123; *Brenhinedd*, 151.

24 *Brut* (*Peniarth*), 71, fn. 1.

25 *Brut* (*Peniarth*), 65; *Brut* (*RBH*), 149.

26 *Brenhinedd*, 169, 171.

27 Gerald of Wales, *The Journey through Wales and The Description of Wales*, translated by L. Thorpe (Harmondsworth, 1978), 111, 113.

Figure 4. Painscastle, Radnorshire. Crown copyright: Royal Commission on the Ancient and Historical Monuments of Wales

at the castle and deliberating in what way they could breach the castle', it is not until 1193 that we learn about the heavy weaponry employed by the Welsh in an attack on a castle.[28] On Christmas Eve of that year Maelgwn ap Rhys of Deuheubarth and his 'war-band' breached the castle of Ystrad Meurig by using slings and catapults. Then, in 1196, the chronicle records an attack on Trallwng, i.e. Welshpool, which provides us with the most vivid account of castle warfare between the Normans and the Welsh. Shortly before the Welshpool siege, however, the Lord Rhys, in his last campaign before his death in the following year, had swept through south Wales, taking Norman castles at Colwyn and Radnor, and then the key stronghold of Painscastle (fig. 4), where he employed catapults and engines.[29] Judging by the success of the campaign and distances covered it would seem unlikely that Rhys's army was encumbered with artillery, however small and light, and this seems to be confirmed by the entry in the *Brenhinedd y Saesson* stating that once at Painscastle the Welsh 'fashioned engines for a siege of the castle'.

For the siege of Gwenwynwyn's castle of Trallwng or Pole (Welshpool) in 1196 by Hubert Walter, justiciar of England, it is necessary to consult both the

28 *Brut* (*Peniarth*), 75; *Brut* (*RBH*), 175; *Brenhinedd*, 189, 191. In the previous year (1192) the Welsh had conducted an unsuccessful ten-week siege of Swansea, almost capturing the castle. Artillery is not mentioned, and one of the reasons for the Welsh failure was the disagreements between the Welsh leaders. See T.B. Pugh (ed.), *Glamorgan County History. 3. The Middle Ages* (Cardiff, 1971), 218.

29 *Brut* (*RBH*), 177; *Brenhinedd*, 193.

Brut y Tywysogyon and the *Brenhinedd y Saesson* in order to obtain a complete picture of the events.[30] The *Brenhinedd* states that the Normans besieged the castle 'with all the diverse methods of siege. But it availed them naught; for as they raised engines to the top of the castle in order to come inside, when they came to the embrasures they were thrown to the bottom of the ditch so that they broke their necks, others being drowned.' The chronicle then goes on to say that, nevertheless, the castle then surrendered. The Normans were clearly using some form of siege-tower or towers, but the other versions of the *Brut y Tywysogyon* make no mention of this tactic. However, the *Brut* (*Peniarth*) does inform us as to the method by which the castle of Pool was eventually taken. 'And after laboriously laying siege to it with various kinds of catapults and slings, at last, when through a marvellous device sappers had been sent into the earth and had tunnelled under the castle, they forced the garrison to surrender the castle.' The Red Book of Hergest version includes the line that the sappers made 'hidden passages underground'. The success of Hubert Walter at Welshpool was to prove shortlived. Later in the same year Gwenwynwyn retook the castle.

Painscastle features again two years later, in 1198, when Gwenwynwyn besieged the castle for three weeks without recourse to catapults or slings/mangonels. The impression from the chronicles is that the 'Saxons' were amazed that someone would try to take a castle without using siege artillery, but it seems that Gwenwynwyn was successful, although shortly after the Welsh were defeated in the field. Gwenwynwyn was later to use artillery to subdue the castles of Llandovery and Llangadog in 1203, although it is only the *Brut* (*Peniarth*) that actually goes into detail (catapults and slings).[31]

In 1213 Rhys Ieuanc ap Gruffudd, grandson of the Lord Rhys, appealed successfully for English assistance to gain his patrimony from Rhys Fychan, and a combined force laid siege to the castle of Dinefwr.[32] 'Engines and contrivances' were placed about the castle, and then with ladders the castle walls were scaled and the bulk of the castle was taken at the first assault. However, one tower, or 'the tower' as one chronicle has it (*Brut* (*Peniarth*)), held out, the garrison having retreated inside it, and they defended it with 'missiles and stones and other engines'. Meanwhile outside 'archers and crossbow-men were shooting missiles, and sappers digging, and armed knights making unbearable assaults', and soon even the tower surrendered.

It is unfortunate that we learn little of the siege techniques of Llywelyn ab Iorwerth (d. 1240) during the devastating campaigns in south Wales in 1215 when so many castles fell to him. The chronicles have little to say about his siege techniques until the entries for 1231, when the town of Cardigan was put to the sword and flames, followed soon after by a successful attack on the castle with engines which enabled the Welsh to breach the walls.[33] Two years later Llywelyn ab Iorwerth found that his engines of war did not always ensure success. He attacked the town of Brecon, which he burnt, and besieged the

30 *Brut* (*Peniarth*), 75; *Brut* (*RBH*), 177; *Brenhinedd*, 193.
31 *Brut* (*Peniarth*), 79.
32 *Brut* (*Peniarth*), 87; *Brut* (*RBH*), 197; *Brenhinedd*, 209.
33 *Brut* (*Peniarth*), 102; *Brut* (*RBH*), 231.

castle for a month, deploying catapults and engines, but to no avail, and Llywelyn was obliged to abandon the siege, and returned north, destroying Shropshire strongholds en route.[34]

Unfortunately, there is no documentary evidence for the use of siege castles in the campaigns outlined above, but it is worth mentioning that in 1991 Cadw: Welsh Historic Monuments scheduled an earthwork close to Castell Cwm Aran in Radnorshire, with the suggestion that the mound may have been a siege castle. The castle itself was rebuilt in 1144 (first mentioned), 1179 and 1195, so there may have been several occasions when the castle was besieged by the Welsh, although none is recorded.

Finally, it must be remembered that guile and treachery are frequently cited as the reasons for the loss of a castle, rather than effective siege techniques, for example at Tenby in 1153 and Ystrad Meurig in 1195.[35]

The Surrender

The chronicles give details of the fate of various castle garrisons. Usually they were put to the sword, or they fled, leaving many dead behind; for example the capture of Humphrey's Castle in 1158 where the Welsh 'slew the bravest knights and the garrison of the castle outright', and retired with much booty, including horses and armour.[36] However, this was not always the case. In 1146 Mold in north Wales fell to the Welsh, a castle 'which had frequently been besieged without success', and those of the garrison who had not been killed were taken prisoner.[37] More rarely, castles were simply abandoned before the arrival of a hostile force, as at Carmarthen (Rhyd-y-gors) in 1096, where the Normans fled without a struggle.[38] Similarly, in 1116, William de Londres, for fear of an imminent attack by Gruffudd ap Rhys, 'left his castle [Ogmore] and all his cattle and all his precious wealth'.[39]

In 1196, at the two sieges of Welshpool, described above, the garrison in both cases agreed to surrender on the condition that they could march away free, together with their arms and armour. In September 1210 Rhys Fychan, with Norman help, was able to capture Llandovery. The garrison, we are told, despaired of any assistance reaching it, and thus surrendered the castle on the condition that their lives were spared, and that they could leave with their possessions.[40] Three years later Rhys Fychan lost the castle to Rhys Ieuanc and his English-Welsh army in spite of it having been fortified with men, food, munitions and engines, and once again the garrison surrendered in return for their lives 'and their members safe'.[41]

34 *Brut* (*Peniarth*), 102–3; *Brut* (*RBH*), 231.
35 *Brut* (*Peniarth*), 58, 75; *Brut* (*RBH*), 131, 175; *Brenhinedd*, 157, 191.
36 *Brut* (*RBH*), 139.
37 *Brut* (*Peniarth*), 55; *Brut* (*RBH*), 125; *Brenhinedd*, 151.
38 *Brut* (*Peniarth*), 20; *Brut* (*RBH*), 35; *Brenhinedd*, 87.
39 *Brut* (*Peniarth*), 41; *Brut* (*RBH*), 89, 91; *Brenhinedd*, 129.
40 *Brut* (*Peniarth*), 84; *Brut* (*RBH*), 189.
41 *Brut* (*Peniarth*), 88; *Brut* (*RBH*), 199.

The siege of Dinefwr in 1213, mentioned above,[42] resulted in slightly different surrender negotiations from the examples cited so far. It will be recalled that the defenders had been forced to retreat into one tower. It was from here that they agreed to surrender on the condition that no force arrive to relieve them by noon the following day, handing over three hostages as a safeguard upon the garrison keeping to the terms. Once again the terms allowed for the garrison to march out free men with their clothes, weapons and members safe. This leniency seems to be common in castle warfare involving Welsh dynastic rivalries. In contrast, in 1215 when Llywelyn ab Iorwerth swept through south Wales, the garrison of Hugh de Meules's castle of Talybont was determined to resist the Welsh, and as a result the men were either burnt to death or put to the sword.[43]

Conclusion

The closing paragraphs of Gerald of Wales's *Description of Wales*, a work written in the late 12th century, explain much of the Welsh success at keeping the kings of England at bay for so long. Gerald also noted that it was from the English and Normans that the Welsh learnt the use of arms and how to fight on horse. The Welsh approach to warfare, with the avoidance of major fixed battles, the use of ambuscade and guerrilla warfare and at certain times very effective Welsh leadership, led to the Anglo-Norman conquest of Wales being a protracted affair, culminating in the campaigns of King Edward I of 1277 and 1282–83 against Llywelyn ap Gruffudd, the grandson of Llywelyn ab Iorwerth.[44] The Welsh were not slow to imitate the Normans in the construction of castles, the earliest known extant example being at Cymer, founded in 1116. Whether they imitated the Normans with regard to siege weaponry is impossible to say; information on this aspect for the period before the arrival of the Normans is non-existent, unfortunately. It should also be remembered that the Welsh chronicles in their earliest extant form are mainly 13th/14th-century copies or translations, with continuations into the later Middle Ages, with the *Historia Gruffydd ap Cynan* being a late 12th- or early 13th-century translation into Welsh of a Latin document now lost. Thus, one cannot be certain whether the terms for the various items of siege artillery used in the texts are 13th/14th-century literary conventions for this weaponry or genuine records of what was actually used. However, the detailed descriptions of many of the events to be found in the Welsh annals would suggest that the historian should on the whole accept the information as recorded, especially as some of the accounts bear all the hall-marks of first-hand observation.

42 See note 32.

43 *Brut* (*Peniarth*), 90; *Brut* (*RBH*), 203.

44 For a short description of Welsh military tactics see K. Williams-Jones (ed.), *The Merioneth Lay Subsidy Roll 1292–93* (Cardiff, 1976), CXXII–CXXIV.

13

Hibernia Pacata et Castellata

Thomas McNeill

Gerald the Welshman entitled Chapter 38 of his 'Expugnatio Hibernica' (written by 1190): 'How the Irish people are to be conquered'.[1] In it he gives his prescription for military success; using light horsemen and archers for the campaigns and, with the battles won, building castles. The country east of the Shannon 'should be secured and protected by the construction of many castles . . . For it is far, far better to link together slowly at first castles set in suitable places and proceed to build them gradually, than to build many far apart and in all sorts of places, unable to help each other in a systematic way or in times of necessity.' He continues in his next chapter by stressing the need for control of the unreliable and treacherous Irish to be based on force: 'A sensible man should secure his position in time of peace, and make preparations to counter the dangers of war, with which he is always threatened, by building castles and enlarging the forest roads. For this hostile race is always plotting some kind of treachery under cover of peace.' This view of a grand strategy for the conquest of Ireland as a whole, and of the role of castles both as part of the means of conquest, and to hold down the conquered lands, is reflected throughout his account of the invasion, and has greatly influenced all historians of medieval Ireland, down to the present day.

The incursion of the English into Ireland began in 1169, just a little over a century after the Battle of Hastings. The men who then succeeded in seizing control of most of the island of Ireland during the following 80 years came from a world where castles had been a prominent feature of life for the last three generations. Their use of castles in Ireland should therefore be more interesting than simply as part of the history or archaeology of Ireland; it can act as a guide to what men from England, Wales or Flanders in the later 12th century saw as the purpose of castle building. From studying the patterns of their occurrence and physical appearance, we may be able to shed light on the questions: who built castles and why? In particular, I wish to ask whether men seem to have followed Gerald's grand strategic design, with castles being built to house garrisons who would hold down the local population by force.

It is important to note the speed at which the country was seized. The 1170s saw the establishment of lordships in Leinster, Meath, Ulster and Cork. Thereafter there was a hiatus, but the 1190s opened with the granting of the two

1 A.B. Scott and F.X. Martin (eds): *Expugnatio Hibernica, the conquest of Ireland, by Giraldus Cambrensis*, Dublin, 1978.

lordships of Oriel, and the expansion of the royal lands of Waterford, and closed with the founding of the lordships of Tipperary and Limerick (fig. 1). The east and south of the island were thus occupied within thirty years, but in a variety of individual lordships, not a single conquest. Nor was the history of each lordship unbroken: Leinster was held in the King's hands from the death of Richard fitz Gilbert in 1176 to its grant in 1189 to William Marshal, while Meath was also held by the King between 1186 and 1194.

Ireland in the later 12th century had men who worked in a tradition of stone construction at least three hundred years old; fine Romanesque stone cutting went back at least fifty years, and the ability to plan and build a Cistercian abbey only a little less. None of this tradition had been applied to castle building in stone, however. If the local masons could be recruited, they would have been able to organise the resources of stone, lime, timber, etc., and to cut and lay the stones, but they would have been at a loss when faced with planning a keep. Nor should we imagine that there was anything like a surplus of skilled building labour in Ireland after the English came; apart from anything else, church building went on unabated throughout the period, by Irish and English lords. This meant that only men with extensive resources and contacts, who could bring in specialists from outside, would have been able to build their castles in stone. The pressure to build in earth and timber was very strong.

In Ireland this meant overwhelmingly the construction of mottes. Of the sites called castles in contemporary documents, where there is something physically present it is almost always a motte, or a building at least partly of mortared stone. The principal exceptions are the four or six (two are doubtfully identified) enclosures built to accommodate armies during campaigns. A list has been produced recently of 'ringworks', along with the suggestion that many more will be found, especially in areas where mottes are relatively sparsely distributed.[2] This possibility of using such structures to fill in distributions, and so make them blandly conform to a uniform pattern, could only be possible if we could meet two conditions. The first is that a reasonable number of sites where something called a castle is recorded in a contemporary document, or which are known to have been the site of knight's fees or similar estates, should prove also to be the sites of ringworks which could thus be identified as castles. The second condition is that we should have a physical definition of such sites, which would allow us to recognise them in the field. The countryside of Ireland has thousands of small circular enclosures which would be accepted in many other countries as ringworks, but which date to the first millennium A.D., i.e. the ringforts or raths. These can even be raised, and thus difficult to distinguish from mottes without excavation. It means that it is necessary when one attempts to list mottes that a definition of what is accepted as a motte be given: the problem is reinforced with so-called ringworks.[3] The list referred to above includes a

2 T.B. Barry: *The Archaeology of Medieval Ireland*, London, 1987, pp. 45–54.

3 T.E. McNeill: 'Ulster mottes, a checklist', in *Ulster Journal of Archaeology*, 38, 1975, 49. The sites of Deer Park Farms (Co. Antrim) and Big Glebe (Co. Londonderry) which were listed here as probable mottes have since been shown by excavation to date from before the 12th century. See also the report on the excavations at Rathmullan, Co. Down – C.J. Lynn: *Ulster Journal of Archaeology*, 44 and 45, 1981–1982, 65–171, and especially the discussion on mottes and mounds on pp. 148–151.

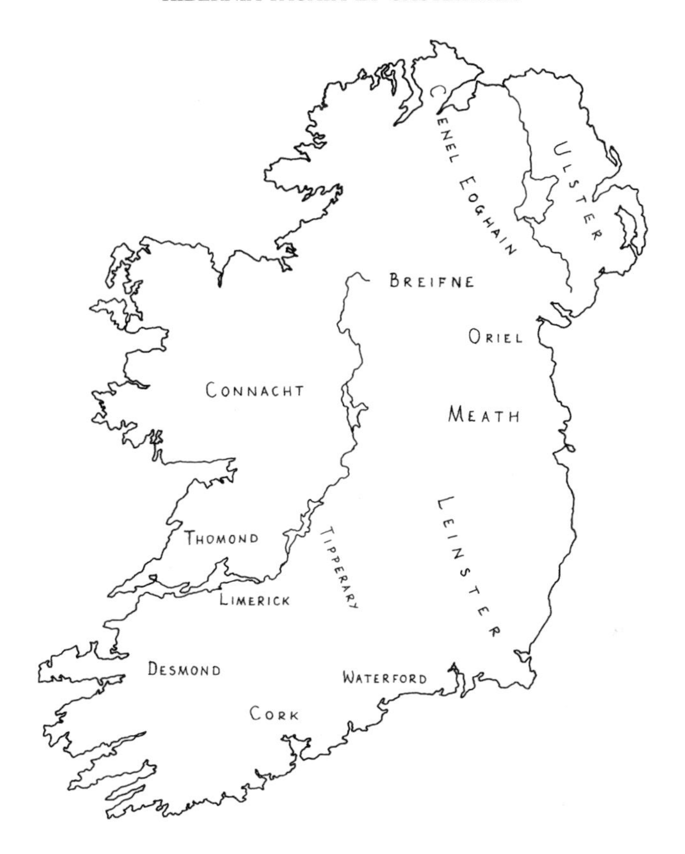

Figure 1. The location of lordships of late 12th century Ireland, mentioned in the text.

very heterogenous set of sites, and until the two conditions outlined here have been met by careful work, the sport of hunting the ringwork should be suspended in Ireland. Early castles in Ireland were usually mottes, with some stone buildings for the major magnates' centres, and a handful of enclosures put up by armies in the course of a campaign.

We have come a long way in our knowlege of the mottes of Ireland in the last ten years, since Glasscock's overtly preliminary list of 1975.[4] This was based on systematic fieldwork, and measurement, in only seven or eight counties: we now have nineteen, giving us a total of *c.*300 sites.[5] The situation is in fact better than

4 R.B. Glasscock: 'Mottes in Ireland', in *Château-Gaillard*, VII, 1975, pp. 95–110.

5 T.E. McNeill: 'Ulster Mottes, a checklist', in *Ulster Journal of Archaeology*, 38, 1975, pp. 49–56. B. Lacy: *Archaeology Survey of Co. Donegal*, Donegal, 1983. A.L. Brindley: *Archaeology Inventory of Co. Monaghan*, Dublin, 1985. V.M. Buckley: *Archaeological Inventory of Co. Louth*, Dublin, 1986. M.J. Moore: *Archaeological Inventory of Co. Meath*, Dublin, 1987. G. Cunningham: *The Anglo-Norman advance into the South-west Midlands of Ireland*, Roscrea, 1987. In addition, D. Power (Cork) and P. Gosling (Galway) have generously helped me with information based on their county surveys. Material for Leinster I collected in the summer of 1987, kindly supported by a grant from the Royal Irish Academy; I hope to publish an article on it soon.

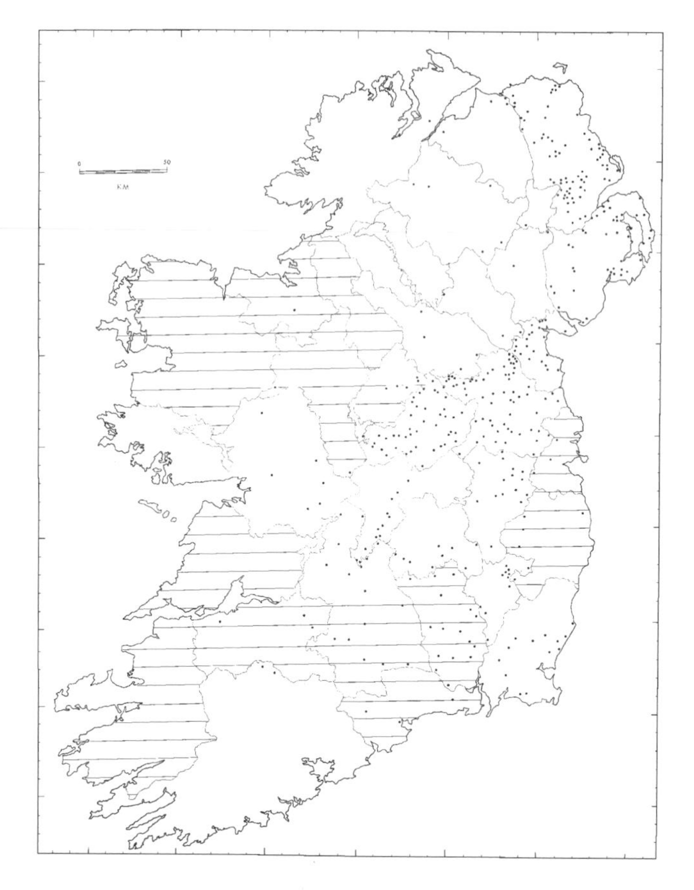

Figure 2. Map of mottes in Ireland: the hatched areas are those not yet covered by field work in Autumn, 1988.

these figures appear, because there is every reason to think that half the unsurveyed counties contain very few, or no, mottes: we need to survey the four eastern Munster counties besides Cork and northern Tipperary. When the whole island is surveyed, I would expect there to be perhaps a little over 350 mottes found. We are now talking about mottes in Ireland on the basis of field survey of approximately an 85% sample.

It needs to be stressed that our knowlege is based only on field survey. The north of Ireland, through the work of Waterman and Jope, saw the excavation of mottes as early as most regions of Europe, in the early 1950s. This has not been followed up, however, and there has only been excavation of any sort (including merely cleaning up the section of a partially destroyed site) at some fourteen mottes in the whole of Ireland; eight of these are in Co. Down, and one each in the neighbouring Cos Antrim and Armagh, with only four outside the north-east. On field work evidence, these mottes can be classified according to size. In this height has been found to be the most useful criterion; diameters being evenly distributed. We can divide the mottes up into three groups: High (over 7 metres), Medium (over 5 and up to 7 metres) and Low (5 metres and under). As regards dating, mottes were undoubtedly constructed at important castles up to 1215,[6] and presumably some years later. They appear no longer to have been built at all after 1240 or 1250.[7]

In broad terms of distribution, we can see a contrast at once between the high density of numbers of mottes in the lordships of Meath, Oriel and Ulster, as opposed to the lower densities of the lordships of Leinster and Munster (fig. 2). Mottes are also unevenly distributed between the lordships according to their heights (fig. 3). The preponderance of low mottes in Ulster is such that it is clear on a straightforward histogram and the median of the heights in Ulster, at 4.55 metres, is a metre lower than the median of any other lordship. The comparison between Leinster on the one hand, and Meath and Oriel on the other is slightly different; the medians of their heights is similar, at 6.25 metres for Leinster, 5.4 metres for Meath and 6.0 metres for Oriel. However, there is a difference visible in the upper and lower quartiles of the heights. In Leinster the upper limit of the lower quartile is 5.0 metres in Meath the figure is 3.5 metres; in Oriel it is 4.5 metres. The figures of the lower limits of the upper quartiles are: Leinster, 7.5 metres; Meath, 7.0 metres; Oriel, 7.5 metres. The difference that these figures show is not in how many high mottes there are in each lordship but in the number and proportion of low ones. The greater numbers and density of mottes in the lordships of Meath and Ulster is produced by a proliferation of low mottes in particular. Conversely, mottes are fewer in Leinster because there are fewer low ones.

If we look at our information on the structure of land holding in the three main lordships of the east of Ireland (the earliest established), Leinster, Meath and Ulster, we can compare this with the patterns of mottes (fig. 4). In Leinster there are few sites associated with holdings of less than a full knight's fee; there are also few sites at places which are not mentioned in contemporary documents, principally the feodaries generated by the division of the lordship in 1247.[8] In Meath and Ulster we have no such feodaries, but we can reconstruct the land holding from other sources. In both these lordships, but perhaps especially in Ulster, mottes are to be found at sites occupied by men further down the social scale. This social pattern correlates with the distribution of heights of mottes. High mottes are associated with high status in all three lordships studied; it can hardly be surprising that men with greater resources built larger castles. In Meath and Ulster, the greater numbers of mottes are produced because more men of lower status are building mottes than in Leinster, as well as on the higher status holdings.

Mottes in Ireland are noticeable for the relative rarity of baileys accompanying them; fewer than 30% of extant mottes have baileys present. This figure is only a crude average, of course: in the border areas of Meath, Oriel and Ulster,

6 G.H. Orpen: 'Motes and Norman castles in Ireland', in *English Historical Review*, XXI, 1906, 426; XXII, 1907, 452–55.

7 There are only three or four mottes associated with the conquest of Connacht in the 1230s; North Antrim, occupied between 1227 and 1242, has a full complement of mottes.

8 E.H. St J. Brooks: *Knight's Fees in Counties Wexford, Carlow and Kilkenny*, Dublin, 1950. A.J. Otway-Ruthven: 'Knight's Fees in Kildare, Leix and Offaly', in *Journal of the Royal Society of Antiquaries of Ireland*, XCI, 1961, pp. 161–81.

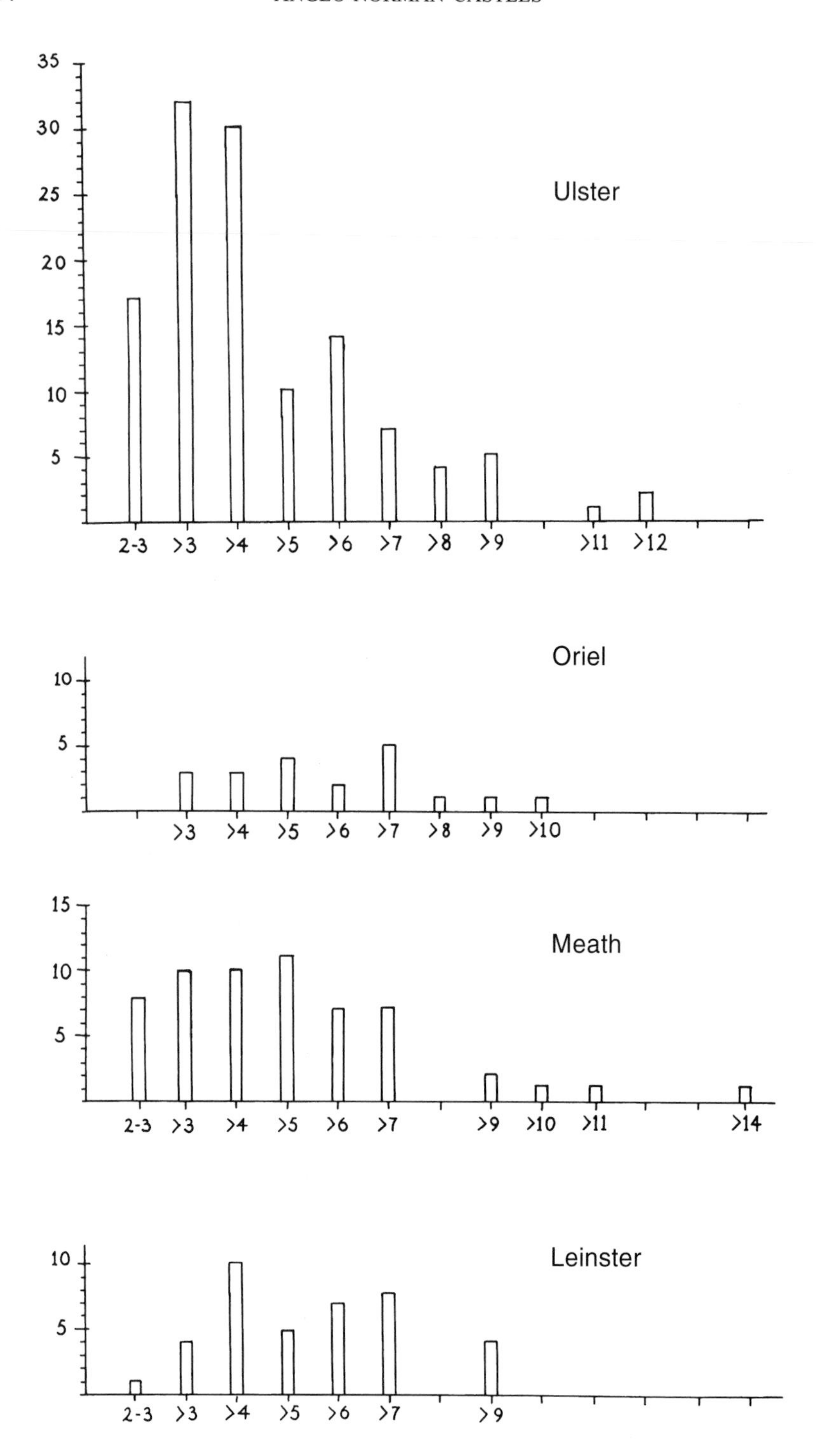

Figure 3. Histograms of the heights of mottes in the lordships of Ulster, Oriel, Meath and Leinster.

Leinster

	Known No.	Mottes			Baileys	Others	
		High	Medium	Low		Ring	'Piper's'
Earl's Demesne	13	1			1		
> 1 Fee	27	6	3/4	3/4	2	1	
1 Fee	22	3	2/3	2	2	1	
½ Fee	31	1	?1	1	1		
< ½ Fee	55	1	?1	1			
Non-military			?1				
Undocumented		2	4/5	2	2	2	1

Meath

	Known No.	Mottes			Baileys
		High	Medium	Low	
Earl's capita	7	4			3
Barons' capita	9	2	3		2
Earl's sub-fee	18	2		3	1
Barons' sub-fee	23		4	3	3
Undocumented		5	8	26	17

Ulster

		Known No.	Mottes			Baileys
			High	Medium	Low	
Earl	Capita	15	5	2		4
Earl	Demesne parcels	77		1	4	
Earl	Free tenants	54	1	1	5	2
Barons	1 Knight's fee	12	2	2	1	?1
Barons	½ Fee	2		1		
Barons	< ½ Fee	5			1	1
	Undocumented		12	17	63	20

Figure 4. Patterns of landholding and mottes in the lordships of Leinster, Meath and Ulster.

the figure rises considerably, to over 50%, while it drops correspondingly elsewhere. In the absence of excavation, it is difficult to argue exactly what this scarcity of baileys meant to the functioning of the castles in Ireland. Even if there were attached yards enclosured by timber palisades, rather than by a bank and ditch as well, these must have been significantly less well defended than the baileys of England and Wales, from where the lords had come. In other words, the mottes of Ireland seem to have offered less protection than the castles of their builders' homelands. Nor are baileys associated particularly with the upper strata socially of castle builders, as we might expect. Their association primarily with the borders implies a military function, apparently eschewed by many builders in the rest of the lordships.

This proliferation of mottes, built by the lesser land holders, is not distributed evenly geographically within the lordships. In Ulster and Meath the mottes proliferated along the frontiers. In Ulster we can see it at its strongest in the strategically vulnerable area at the north-east corner of Lough Neagh. It is particularly clear in the case of Meath where the boundary of the lordship is still reflected in the boundaries of the county and diocese: not only are there almost no mottes beyond the line, but there is a clear zone of higher density along the line than in the hinterland behind it. This frontier line is continued up along the western border of the lordships of Oriel (fig. 5). In both frontiers, the number of mottes with baileys increases as noted above, which may be because the mottes in these areas were intended to be used as bases for groups of foot-soldiers stationed there in times of war to counteract raiding.

Two further points need to be made about these frontier lines. The first is that they are not inherent in the original setting up of the lordships themselves. The Meath and Oriel borders may be based on topography, the boundary between the plain of Meath and the drumlin country to the north and west. The border of the lordship of Ulster was based roughly on pre-existing sub-divisions of the Kingdom of Ulaid, which John de Courcy conquered:[9] it was an insubstantial basis, however, and the line could and did change in time. These are frontiers which evolved during the early life of the lordships concerned, but were not part of the original creation of them: none of the major Irish lordships had their origins in charters giving lands with demarcated boundaries. The second point is that, in the case of the Meath/Oriel frontier line, it continues along the borders of at least three separate lordships: Meath, established in the 1170s, and the Pipard and De Verdon lordships in Oriel, established in the 1190s; there were also royal lands in Oriel, and De Verdon granted the eastern half of his lordship to Hugh II de Lacy.[10] None of the lords concerned had many demesne holdings along the borders, and the sites themselves, apart from the relatively large number of baileys, have no distinguishing physical characteristics, unlike those of the Vale of Montgomery in Wales.[11] The same lord might hold lands on

9 T.E. McNeill: *Anglo-Norman Ulster*, Edinburgh, 1980.

10 A.J. Otway-Ruthven: 'The Partition of the De Verdon lands in Ireland', in *Proceedings of the Royal Irish Academy*, LXVI (C), 1967, 403–405.

11 D.J.C. King and C.J. Spurgeon: 'The mottes in the Vale of Montgomery', in *Archaeologia Cambrensis*, 119, 1970, pp. 83–118.

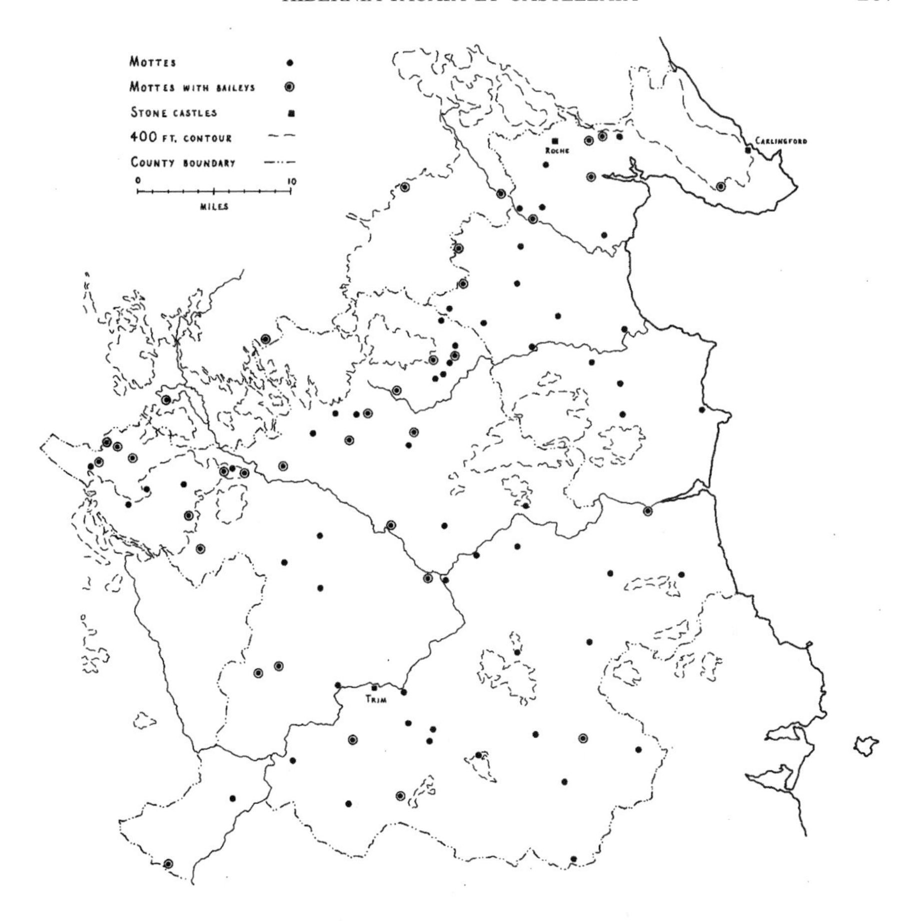

Figure 5. Mottes in the lordships of Meath and Oriel, now represented by the counties of Meath and Louth.

which mottes were densely distributed and land on which they were sparse: Hugh II de Lacy's lands of eastern Oriel have one motte and one stone castle, but the lands which he seized in northern Ulster are well provided with mottes. There is every indication that this pattern of distribution was not directed by the lords but followed from the decisions of their tenants: in the borders of Meath, Oriel and Ulster, the lesser tenants considered that they needed mottes, while in Leinster, and probably Munster, they did not consider that they did. The distribution of mottes in these lordships points to them as being built not as part of the setting up of the lordship, but as part of a later development.

Finally, it appears to be only in these border areas that we can note the evidence of stone fortifications, presumably added later to mottes. Even in these parts, only some 10% seem, on the basis of field survey, to show evidence of such a development. In Ireland mottes seem to provide the basis for a later history of continuous fortification of a castle site surprisingly rarely. The great majority would appear to have been left to rot after their construction and the initial period of their occupation. As far as can be ascertained from field survey evidence, there were less than half the number of castles in Ireland in 1300 than there had been in 1200.

Not all the early castles were mottes, however. We have a number of stone castles in Ireland which pre-date 1200, and so belong to the first generation of the conquest. Of these we can select four which are the most securely dated and best preserved to serve as exemplars for the rest. The most martial in appearance is Carrickfergus, probably started within a year of John de Courcy's arrival in Ulster, whose massive keep still dominates the town.[12] It is a curious keep, however, for it includes neither chapel nor hall; the two most public and ceremonial parts of the castle were excluded from its strong point which seems to have been reserved for John's private accommodation alone. The gate was weak, in itself and in its siting in dead ground from the keep, and the curtain is weakened by the windows of the hall and a second building, probably the chapel. In 1185 Theobald Walter was granted the lands of Ormond, and before his death in 1205 had built the first three stories of the keep at Nenagh.[13] Again it seems to have been built to provide for Theobald's accommodation rather than to house the key parts of a castle in a single block; it almost certainly excluded the hall which must have been sited in the courtyard. This was certainly the case with the castle of Geoffrey de Marisco at Adare in Co. Limerick.[14] Whether the tower in what is now the inner courtyard is early or not is a moot point, but unimportant here; whether it was or not, the undoubtedly early hall, built within a decade after Geoffrey's occupation of the lordship, was put in a relatively undefended position in the outer ward. The great De Lacy castle at Trim is dominated by its keep, a unique structure with its four projecting subsidiary towers.[15] Work was halted midway through its construction, perhaps because of Hugh I de Lacy's death in 1186, but it seems to have been completed before 1220. In the first phase it seems to have housed a rather makeshift hall in the eastern half of the main block, at entry level. As it was completed however, this room cannot have continued to serve as a hall, and the whole building culminated in a splendid chamber at third floor level. The hall had by then probably been moved to the northern side of the castle enclosure, where there is a row of fine windows in the curtain. Nor was the keep well defended. The possibilities of the projecting towers providing flanking fire are totally ignored, and there is not even a loop to cover the entrance to the building, although a mural passage runs in just the right place to provide one.

These castles are not impressive military structures. They appear to be designed to impress the visitor, by providing grand private accommodation away from the public parts of the castle, and they are prepared to leave expensive

12 T.E. McNeill: *Carrickfergus Castle*, Belfast, 1981.

13 D.F. Gleeson and H.G. Leask: 'The Castle and manor of Nenagh', in *Journal of the Royal Society of Antiquaries of Ireland*, LXVI, 1936, pp. 247–69.

14 H.G. Leask: *Irish Castles*, Dundalk, 1937, pp. 34–35.

15 *Ibid*., pp. 31–34. P.D. Sweetman: 'Archaeological excavations at Trim castle', in *Proceedings of the Royal Irish Academy*, LXXVIII (C), 1978, pp. 127–98. There has never been a full description or analysis of Trim. The dating of the structure given here differs from the accounts of both Leask and Sweetman somewhat.

buildings like the hall exposed to early attacks. The Irish never did become good at siege warfare, for it ran counter to their whole way of organising life and war, and this might be the reason for the military weakness of many castles in Ireland later. This will not work as an explanation in this early period, however. This first generation of English lords were neither anthropologists, nor equipped with knowlege of the future: they could not predict how warfare in Ireland would develop and their lack of provision for future conflict is striking.

There are in fact two instances of castles being built as part of a strategic scheme, both from the years following King John's visit to Ireland in 1210.[16] The first involved a settlement of the area of the middle Shannon river, where the provinces of Meath and Connacht meet. In 1210 the Justiciar, Henry de Gray, started the process by founding the castle and bridge of Athlone, commanding the key river crossing. In the same year he concluded an agreement with the king of Connacht, Cathal Crovderg O'Connor, which lasted until the latter's death in 1224. In 1212 disaffected junior members of the O'Melaghlin dynasty of Westmeath led successful raids on English settlements in the area. They defeated English forces twice, but were defeated in 1213 by a combination of the local Irish kings, notably Murtough O'Brien of Thomond and Donnell O'Melaghlin, the recognised tanaiste of Melaghlin Beg, king of West Meath. Later in that year the new Justiciar, Henry of London, erected a motte and bailey at Roscrea, followed by one at Clonmacnois, and repaired the castles of Birr, Durrow and Kinnity. The result was to produce peace in the region.

The second case of strategic castle building took place in 1212, when John de Gray tried to control the south-western borders of what is now called Ulster by founding the castles of Clones in Co. Monaghan and Narrow Water, Co, Fermanagh, in conjunction with a castle at Belturbet, Co. Cavan. He was trying to push the northern border of western Meath some thirty or forty kilometres beyond its existing line. The result was that the English armies were defeated and the castles were burned within the year by a confederation of the kings of the region, led by Aedh O'Neill, king of Cenel Eoghain. This ending gives one of the keys to the difference between the two stories. In west Meath, the Justiciars were acting with the overt support of the Irish kings around the region, particularly the kings of Conacht and Thomond, beyond the Shannon. In Ulster, they were faced by the hostility of the most powerful Irish king of the period, the king of Cenel Eoghain.

We are now in a position to try to answer the questions posed at the beginning of this article. Firstly, how far does Gerald's analysis of the position of the English in Ireland appear to have been believed and his solution followed? The answer must, on the evidence reviewed here, be not much, if at all. The establishment of individual lordships appears to have been spasmodic, initiated in some cases in circumstances beyond English control: an invitation to intervene, as in Ulster in January 1177, or the death of an Irish king, as in Oriel in 1189–90. Here the other more or less contemporary English narrative of events,

16 G.H. Orpen: *Ireland under the Normans*, vol. II, Oxford, 1911, chapter XXII.

the so-called *Song of Dermot and the Earl*,[17] probably gives a picture nearer to the actual course of events in its unsophisticated (not to say boring) account of a series of individual fights and land grants with no connecting theme. The same is true for Gerald's solution. Clearly the role of castles varied from lordship to lordship, according to local circumstances, without any strategic direction. Here again it is interesting to note that the *Song* mentions castles far less than does Gerald and lays very little stress on them.

Who built castles and why? These two questions are totally interlocked. The first conclusion that we can draw is that the prime purpose of the majority of our castles does not seem to have been for military defence. The stone castles have other priorities, notably providing a glamorous setting for the new lord of the area to live in. It is difficult to see why the holders of half a fee in Leinster did not need castles for defence if the holders of a full fee did; would attackers really be so discriminating? It cannot be a question of resources, for the lesser tenants of Meath and Ulster could afford mottes, and Ulster in particular is poorer land. We must also remember that most castles appear to have been abandoned not long after their construction.

When castles did proliferate it was only along the borders of Meath, Oriel and Ulster. They seem to be designed to provide a zone some eight kilometres deep where there were many strong points to protect the individual holders of land and their families, interspersed with ones equipped with baileys. These I have suggested might be to accommodate the bands of soldiers thirty or forty strong, hired to protect a district in time of war, that we find in the 1212 Pipe Roll.[18] These men could not prevent raids, particularly in the Irish countryside with its many small hills and woods, ideally suited to conceal a party of fifty or a hundred raiders. They could, however, intercept them on their way back, laden with plunder and tired from their rape and pillage, or else discouraged and wounded by defeat.

Here we must recall the general distribution of mottes in Ireland. Only the three lordships already named seem to have been impelled to produce this system: Leinster certainly and the lordships of Munster probably, did not feel the need. The difference must lie beyond their borders. The three 'military' lordships faced the kingdoms of Breifne and Argialla, behind which lay Cenel Eoghain; all had been pressing south and east in the preceding century, against the weaker kingdoms of Meath and Ulaid. Unlike Cenel Eoghain, the kings of Connacht, Thomond and Desmond, in west Munster and west of the Shannon, had consistently negotiated with the English, even if they fought as well. A modus vivendi was possible between them and the English, whose lordships of Leinster and Munster were established in areas where these kings had competed with each other in the past rather than exercised real control, and did not menace the heartland of their power. The south-western kings were simply not the threat

17 G.H. Orpen: *The Song of Dermot and the Earl*, Oxford, 1892. A new edition of this work is being prepared by Dr E. Mullally and Prof. F.X. Martin, and I am very grateful to Dr Mullally for discussion and access to her text.

18 O. Dames and D.B. Quinn (eds): 'The Irish Pipe Roll of 14 John', in *Ulster Journal of Archaeology*, 4, 1941.

to the English that the northern kings were, and so they did not evoke the same response.

This leads to our final point. The military role of castles in the first fifty years of the English presence in Ireland was not aimed at counteracting the threat of rebellion from within the lordships, which Gerald of Wales stressed so much, but rather at meeting raids from outside. The fighting that the occupation of a lordship required was over quite soon, and on this evidence, the lords do not seem to have expected it to be renewed. The establishing of a lordship meant the seizing of land from the native kings and aristocracy. Building a castle proclaimed the success of the seizure rather than making the seizure possible. Only later did exterior threats develop in certain lordships, which required the intensification of fortification along the border. The men who built castles were primarily showing off the fact that they had the wealth and status that permitted them to build a castle, rather than providing themselves with refuges to be held against local rebellions. The occupation of Ireland was much quicker than that of Wales, and I think that the Welsh model is not helpful here, any more than back-projections of more recent hostilities, erected into a natural law of hostility between the English and the Irish. Castles in 12th century Ireland were the product of lordship, not the means of establishing it because that lordship was not opposed by the whole population.

14

Orford Castle, Nostalgia and Sophisticated Living

T. A. Heslop

Medieval architecture, considered specifically as architecture, has been unevenly treated by its historians. The vast majority of the literature is devoted to churches, for the most part large cathedral or monastic churches. The implication that other types of building either do not survive or are not architecture is patently false since there are many of them, and not a few manifest a degree of complexity in design and detail equal to a major ecclesiastical building. In particular there has been no strong tradition among architectural historians for discussing the planning, iconography and aesthetics of eleventh- and twelfth-century secular structures. Perhaps this is because they fit uneasily within the style categories of Romanesque and Gothic, which were largely devised and developed through the analysis of ecclesiastical buildings.[1]

In general the scholars who discuss castles or houses are distinct from those who write about churches: they are political and military historians or archaeologists, rather than art historians. In part this has come about because of the nature of the material. Castles, for example, are more often ruinous than

Acknowledgements. Many people have helped in various ways in the preparation of this paper. In particular I would like to thank my father, who first held the other end of the tape measure, and Richard Halsey, who supplied me with plans of the keep. Peter Kidson, Eric Fernie, Roger Stalley and David Thomson contributed suggestions at various points for which I am very grateful. However, my deepest gratitude is to Don Johnson who worked in difficult circumstances to provide the figures which do so much to clarify the points being made. Don's death, shortly after finishing work on the drawings for this paper, is a great loss. Those who knew him will remember his infinite courtesy and generosity, but many more have benefited from his kindness and care. Over the last fifteen years he produced exemplary illustrations for many publications by faculty and research students in the School of Art History and Music at the University of East Anglia. Those were his gifts to us; this paper is my contribution to his memory.

1 A book on Romanesque architecture may well have over 95 percent of its text devoted to ecclesiastical building, as for example the volume of that name by H. E. Kubach (London, 1979), and the same point could be made about Henri Focillon's much older *The Art of the West in the Middle Ages: I Romanesque Art* (Oxford, 1969, first published in French in 1938), a work largely devoted to buildings and their decoration. Similar discrimination afflicts many books on Gothic architecture such as Jean Bony's recent *French Gothic Architecture of the 12th and 13th centuries* (Berkeley, Los Angeles and London, 1983). These are just sample instances of a widespread reluctance to admit non-ecclesiastical building within the confines of 'style conscious' architecture at this period. By contrast, it would be hard to conceive of books on Renaissance architecture omitting palaces. To find any sustained discussion of a castle or domestic building it is generally necessary to turn to the articles, books, even whole journals devoted to these subjects. There are exceptions to this segregationist approach: among writers imbued with the 'Antiquarian' tradition (a good example would be T. S. R. Boase, *English Art 1100–1216* (Oxford, 1953), and among those concerned with the socio-economic side of medieval building, particularly trade organization and the supply of materials. But writers such as L. F. Salzman, and Knoop and Jones have little call to concern themselves with individual architectural designs.

churches and require archaeological exposition. And they seem more closely connected than churches with the world of power politics and thus attract historians who see them as tools or vehicles of policy. For this very reason it has been their military and strategic aspects which have attracted attention rather than the architectural.[2] But there are various other factors which help to explain the segregated study of sacred and secular buildings. Whether one is a student of medieval art and architecture or not, it is most likely that the mental image that one has of 'high' culture in the eleventh and twelfth centuries, or even over a wider chronological span, is of churchmen, perhaps monks in particular, tending the gardens of intellectual and artistic endeavour in the uncongenial surroundings of a rough, even brutal, environment where the soldiery lived and died by the sword and the peasantry in poverty and oppression. Now is not the moment to examine where this caricature comes from, or how much truth there is in it. What does matter for present purposes is to point out that the antithesis which equates the ecclesiastical with 'high' culture and the secular world with 'low' culture, or even no culture, has had a serious effect on our understanding of the Middle Ages as a whole; and that the ways in which art and architecture have been studied have both been conditioned by and helped to reinforce this notional sacred/secular divide. The attitude is not unique to art historians. The widely influential French scholar Georges Duby can lapse into a statement such as 'some of the money that the great [lords] had formerly spent on their own pleasure and on sumptuous living was channelled towards the religious establishment – that is, towards culture'.[3] Clearly 'culture', without a qualifier, is identified in his mind with the Church. It is surprising that one whose approach to the past has been as anthropological as Duby's should use culture in such a restricted sense, and perhaps particularly strange in writing of the twelfth century (as Duby was in this case) when cultural self-consciousness in general became an increasingly powerful determinant of social behaviour.

The element of self-consciousness is important in this period because, for the first time since Antiquity, a substantial number of people became aware of what would now be called 'alternative life-styles'. This happened both as a result of an internal generation of alternatives and because of increasing contact through travel and commerce with foreign practices. Thus, for example, someone wishing to enter a monastery could choose between about half a dozen different orders that had burgeoned in Europe, whereas for most of the eleventh century there had been effectively only one. Looking outwards, texts in Arabic and the

2 In particular the late R. A. Brown in various work over the last four decades. For a recent review of the current standing of various aspects of the subject, archaeological and historical, see the article by R. Eales, 'Royal Power and Castles in Norman England', in *The Ideals and Practice of Medieval Knighthood*, III, ed. C. Harper-Bill (Woodbridge, 1990), pp. 49–78. Brown's comment in 'Framlingham Castle and Bigod 1154–1216', *Proceedings of the Suffolk Institute of Archaeology*, 25 (1952), pp. 127–48, that 'English medieval castles have been largely neglected by historians from every point of view, save the architectural', may have seemed true from his perspective then but is impossible to justify now.

3 In R. L. Benson and G. Constable, eds, *Renaissance and Renewal in the Twelfth Century* (Oxford, 1982), p. 255. He also offers more muted expressions of the same attitude, e.g. on p. 257, 'This culture was largely a reflection of the knowledge and forms of expression which were being "reborn" in the creative centres of the church.'

techniques and styles of Moslem architecture significantly altered the course of developments in the Christian West. They offered new paradigms and new data to come to terms with. In this situation, generally achieved by the mid-twelfth century, it was scarcely possible just to 'partake of a culture', one could place it relative to others and negotiate its position by self-conscious development or by assimilation. The relevance of these introductory remarks will, I hope, become clear when we examine the particular case of Orford Castle.

In choosing the keep at Orford for architectural analysis, I have picked a building which suits my purpose, but also one which retains its internal arrangements almost intact and has the advantage of being the first well-documented castle in England; we know how much it cost and when it was built, and it is not hard to guess why it was built when and where it was.[4] Before coming on to Orford specifically, though, it is necessary to say something about the designation 'castle' and what this is supposed to mean, since any notion that castles constitute a homogeneous building type is erroneous. The things we call castles have mixed origins and several functions and the result is a striking degree of formal variety.

The Designation 'Castle'

In recent decades, largely as a result of the powerful advocacy of Allen Brown, everyone 'knows' that castles are a foreign import into Britain around the time of the Norman Conquest.[5] Since this has now become part of the definition (i.e. we use the word castle to mean a type of building which was introduced by the Normans) it would seem to be pointless to look for any Anglo-Saxon antecedents. However, we still know very little about the dwellings of the late pre-Conquest military aristocracy, so that it is premature to say that there are no formal connections of any kind across the century from 1000 to 1100 and beyond; in one respect, the first-floor hall with exterior staircase, there probably are links, as we shall see. However, one aspect of late eleventh-century castles, the so-called motte and bailey, is very precisely a Norman import. There is no evidence that castle mottes (i.e. substantial conical mounds of earth to support a tower) were built in Britain other than as a direct result of Norman military colonization. This kind of fortification predominates in the decades following 1066 when territorial control was of crucial importance to the invaders. It is dangerous to speak of a 'typical' anything, but these castles really are fairly uniform. A

4 The documentation on Orford is set out in H. M. Colvin, ed., *The History of the King's Works* II (London, 1963), pp. 769–70. Of the total expenditure of £1,413 9s. 2d., £986 9s. 8d. was spent in the financial years 1165–66 and 1166–67; presumably this is when nearly all the building materials were purchased and building begun. In the next three years, to 1170, outgoings averaged just over £100, probably spent on wages. See also V. B. Redstone, 'Orford and its Castle', *Proceedings of the Suffolk Institute of Archaeology*, 10 (1900), pp. 205–30, and C. H. Hartshorne, 'Observations on Orford Castle', *Archaeologia*, 29 (read 1840), pp. 60–69.

5 Perhaps the most extreme expression of the links between the Normans and castles was made through the intermediary of yet another problematic term, feudalism, by R. A. Brown in his *Origins of English Feudalism* (London and New York, 1973), passim.

wall, usually of timber, surrounds a relatively level area of ground. At some point abutting this perimeter is a mound, surrounded by a ditch and surmounted by a fence enclosing a tower, often also of wood in the first instance. The tower on the mound provided a place of final refuge during an attack, whereas the pallisade enclosed storage, stabling and domestic buildings.[6] Such defensive complexes could apparently be built very quickly (the chronicler Orderic Vitalis implies that York was finished in eight days) and were sometimes erected during a military campaign. All that really distinguished them from a domestic enclosure, of hall or farm or group of homesteads, was the mound and its tower.

This kind of castle was and is widespread, but even early on one finds variations. Buildings that we regard as castles need have little to do with the motte and bailey design. At Richmond in Yorkshire, there is no mound, and for over half a century there was no tower. In the late eleventh century the long, triangular perimeter wall had a gate at one corner and an elegant first-floor hall at another.[7] At Castle Acre in Norfolk, also in the late eleventh century, there was a low earthwork surmounted not by a tower, but by what may be regarded as two semi-detached, parallel, first-floor halls, which their excavator has dubbed 'a country house'. The large entrance and substantial window openings on the ground floor suggest that defence was not the primary concern in the planning of this block. The two halls were differentiated in their fittings. That to the rear had a mural fireplace but no independent access, so that it probably functioned as a private chamber, while the room at the front had no fire (unless there was provision for a central hearth) but could be reached directly from outside by means of exterior steps; in other words it was more suitable as a communal hall. There is good evidence that major halls in Anglo-Saxon England could be raised to first-floor level and have access from an exterior stair. According to the Bayeux Tapestry, Harold dines in just such a building at his manor at Bosham in Sussex, immediately before his ill-fated trip across the Channel. Other than their use of stone as a building material, there may be little to separate the post-Conquest halls at Richmond and Acre from their aristocratic Anglo-Saxon predecessors. It is hard to see why the Norman version of the raised hall within an enclosure merits the designation 'castle' while their prototypes do not.[8]

6 Eales, 'Royal Power and Castles . . .', esp. pp. 50–54.

7 Bibliography on the English castles mentioned in this paper may be found in D. Renn, *Norman Castles in Britain* (2nd edn, London, 1973) and D. J. C. King, *Castellarium Anglicanum*, 2 vols (New York, 1983). More recent bibliography or that which relates particularly to my arguments will be cited independently.

8 On Castle Acre see J. G. Coad and A. D. F. Streeten, 'Excavations at Castle Acre Castle, Norfolk, 1972–7: Country House and Castle of the Norman Earls of Surrey', *Archaeological Journal*, 139 (1982), pp. 138–301. Harold's first-floor hall at Bosham is shown in D. M. Wilson, *The Bayeux Tapestry* (London, 1985), pls 3–4; there is an earlier literary reference to an upper hall in the 'miracle' of St Dunstan at Calne. The building type, complete with exterior staircase, was quite probably of continental origin, as for example seen in the reconstruction of the Emperor Henry III's palace as Goslar and its antecedents, see A. Labbé, *L'Architecture des Palais et des Jardins dans les Chansons de Geste* (Paris and Geneva, 1987), pp. 475–79 and pl. 33. *Ibid.* pp. 500–1 suggests that Bosham might be a Torhalle. Archaeological exploration of late Anglo-Saxon aristocratic sites is still in its infancy. The most helpful for those who support the idea that substantial enclosures were at least an occasional option is Goltho: see G. Beresford, 'Goltho Manor, Lincolnshire: the buildings and their surrounding defences c.850–1150', *Anglo-Norman Studies* IV, ed. R. A. Brown (Woodbridge, 1981),

Like the examples just cited, the Tower of London was also begun within a generation of the Norman Conquest.[9] This famous and influential monument may be regarded as a much grander version of the scheme found in the 'country house' at Castle Acre. Its grandeur comes from its size and from a further duplication; there are three storeys instead of two, and the upper level is of double height. Furthermore, on the main floor, in addition to chamber and hall, there is a substantial galleried chapel incorporated to one side. As at Castle Acre only the innermost room on the upper level had a mural fireplace, and at the Tower it also had access to latrines. Many of the characteristics of the Tower, or *arx palatium* (fortress palace) as William FitzStephen was to call it about a hundred years after it was started, were adopted by other great keeps. The twelfth-century keeps in Norfolk at Norwich and Castle Rising are clear developments of the type, and arguably the same term, fortress palace, can be used for them. In my reading of these structures, the keep is the palace and the fortress element is almost entirely concentrated in the enclosing wall, its banks and ditches.[10]

One development apparent in the keeps of Rising and Norwich is that there are more rooms per storey than in the Tower of London, and that consequently the public spaces are not as large in proportion to the whole. The way found in these two buildings to provide discrete rooms, by sectioning off parts of the interior, was only one of the options. Another was to make chambers in the thickness of the wall. This is the principle adopted at Castle Hedingham in Essex and at Scarborough in Yorkshire, the best preserved keep built by Henry II prior to Orford. It is often supposed that wall thickness in castle keeps is to do with increased strength which may be needed to resist a battering from siege engines.[11] What such an explanation does not account for is the hollowing out of the walls by passages and chambers which, of course, weakens them again. The solution found at Orford, providing rooms in towers which project from a central core, was yet another alternative, and incidentally one that needs to be accounted for since it is an idea which is at least very uncommon if not unknown up to about 1160. But before dealing with that structure in any detail it will be as well to outline when and why it was built and consider a few of the things that have been said about it in the past.

pp. 13–36. In the post-Conquest period both Richmond and Castle Acre belonged to major Norman barons.

9 See R. A. Brown, 'Some observations on the Tower of London', *Archaeological Journal* 136 (1979), pp. 99–108, for a reconstruction of the Tower's original state.

10 A substantial report on the keep at Norwich has been prepared by Paul Drury. It is to be hoped that it will shortly be published. I would like to thank Sue Margeson and Barbara Green at the Castle Museum, Norwich for showing me the typescript.

11 It is not clear that contemporary siege engines were very effective. Jordan Fantosme's *Chronique de la Guerre entre les Angloi et les Ecossois*, in which Orford first 'saw action', includes a single attempt to use such machinery, at the siege of Wark (lines 1191–284), 'Hear, lords, of the stonebow how it went on/ The first stone which it ever cast at them/ The stone was scarcely parted from the sling When it knocked one of their [own] knights to the ground . . ./ Much must he hate the engineer who contrived that for them'. See *Chronicles of the Reigns of Stephen, Henry II, and Richard I*, ed. R. Howlett, Rolls series, 4 vols (London, 1884–89), iii, 202–377.

The Need for a Castle at Orford

At the beginning of Henry II's reign in 1154, the balance of power in East Anglia was precarious. Earl Hugh Bigod held a series of castles in north Suffolk and south Norfolk. Bigod's loyalty to the crown was notoriously unreliable and during the reign of King Stephen, William of Blois, the king's son, had been given castles in Norfolk partly in an attempt to keep Bigod in check. The rivalry between these magnates threatened instability after the death of Stephen, and in 1157 King Henry decided that confiscating the castles of both parties, Bigod and William, was the best way to remove the potential for disruption. William apparently surrendered with good grace; but Bigod was furious and remained so for the rest of his days. Perhaps in an attempt to appease Bigod, Henry returned to him two of his castles, Framlingham and Bungay, in 1165, but only on the payment of a huge fine of £1,000. It was in 1165 that Orford Castle was begun, and it has partly to be seen in the context of the king's well-founded mistrust of Earl Bigod.[12]

The choice of Orford as the site of a new castle was determined by a number of factors. It had recently come into the king's hands (returned from chancellor Becket upon his becoming Archbishop of Canterbury) and although probably only a small community at the time it had obvious potential for development as a port on the increasingly prosperous east coast – a matter of obvious importance for the revenues it would yield. It was indeed to become a place of some consequence by medieval standards, featuring in an early thirteenth-century romance version of the life of St Edmund by Denis Pyramus as a name to conjure with ('silently the ships came to a port which the people called Orefort, then a great city of ancient renown') and being named on one of Matthew Paris's maps of England. The 'auxilium' it paid in 1177, at £10, was three-quarters that of Scarborough, Grimsby, Yarmouth, and Ipswich.[13] As a port it also formed a useful bridgehead for loyalist forces arriving by boat and equally it would deter enemy forces from using Orford as a landing place. Communications were good and it could be supplied from the sea if it was besieged. In brief, these are the likely economic and military circumstances and thinking behind the building of Orford Castle, but while these considerations account for a castle being built they do not explain why it took the particular form it did.

It is unfortunate that the curtain wall which surrounded the keep has disappeared (the last part collapsed in the 1840s), though its line can be very approxi-

[12] R. A. Brown, 'Framlingham Castle and Bigod', see note 3 above.

[13] The earliest evidence of commercial activity at Orford comes from 1102. For this and other references see M. Beresford, *New Towns of the Middle Ages: town plantation in England, Wales and Gascony* (London, 1967), p. 489. C. Stephenson, *Borough and Town, a study of Urban origins in England*, Medieval Academy of America, monograph 7 (Cambridge Mass., 1933), p. 165 discusses the growth of new towns and the east coast ports and gives the comparative taxations in his Appendix iv. Orford first appears in 19 Henry II paying an assise of 20 marks – directly comparable with Yarmouth's. However Yarmouth had already paid an 'auxilium' in 2 Henry II and it is not clear whether the absence of Orford in this year was because it was part of the feudum of Eye or because it was too insignificant, or both. By 1187 its tallage, at 31 + marks, was more than Ipswich (surprisingly low at 24 marks) but less than Yarmouth's (38 + marks).

mately traced in the remaining earthworks. Wall and keep were apparently more or less concentric. Early seventeenth-century topographical drawings suggest that there were at least four towers at intervals along the wall, though the drawings are divided about the nature of the wall between the towers: was it curved or straight? An alternative is that the sections between the towers were faceted. This outer defence has gone largely undiscussed in the literature, and it will remain unwise to say much about it until there has been some excavation. However, it is likely, given what we know of Henry II's other castles, that any major defensive provisions were concentrated in the perimeter wall – that is, in the first line of defence. Where such things as archery loops survive at all from this period, they are at the extremities rather than in the enclosed buildings.[14]

Because of the collapse of the outer walls of Orford attention has focused upon the keep, which commentators have tended to consider primarily as representing a technical military advance over earlier, square towers (Fig. 1). To quote Allen Brown:

> From a military point of view, the one inherent weakness in the enormous strength of the square tower keep lay in its very shape, the stones of its sharp angles could be worked away by attackers wielding pick and bore, while the same dangerous courners were blind spots more or less incapable of being covered [he means by fire power], save from directly above, by the defenders inside the square and sheer tower. The answer to the problem was to be the cylindrical tower keep. But as precursor of the round tower itself, we have several instances of keeps which are transitional – polygonal keeps of many sides and therefore no sharp angles to invite attack, the most interesting of these is Orford.[15]

There are several difficulties with such an analysis. The first is that although the core of Orford's keep is polygonal, its three large clasping towers mean that instead of its having four corners, as a square keep would have, it has six and thus offers more potential for 'picking and boring'. Although each outer corner comes notionally within the line of fire of one of its neighbours, in practical terms it was not so since a defender would need to be peering over a merlon at the outermost corner to see even a fraction of the main flank of the next tower. There are other large areas of the wall which are effectively invisible from inside the building. The faceting of the keep means that there are four inside corners which are well hidden from view except from directly above (Figs 2, 5), and there is anyway a lack of substantial windows or loops in the lateral walls. Thus the statement that Orford represents an advance in planning because it has 'three large rectangular turrets . . . from which flanking fire could be directed to

14 The use of openings specially designed as archery loops is still very restricted during Henry II's reign, though clear examples are to be found at his castle at Chinon on the Loire where they appear in the wall flanking the main gate of the Chateau de Milieu (the Tour de l'Horloge) and in the mural tower at the opposite end of the site (the Tour du Moulin). The earliest topographical view of Orford Castle, from around 1600, does not indicate the presence of loops in the mural towers. Reproductions of this early watercolour can be found in Colvin, *King's Works*, II, P. 47A, and (on a larger scale and in colour) in the recent English Heritage guidebook by Derek Renn, *Framlingham and Orford Castles* (London, 1988), p. 33.

15 R. A. Brown, *English Castles* (London, revised edn 1962), p. 52.

Figure 1. Orford Castle keep, from the west.

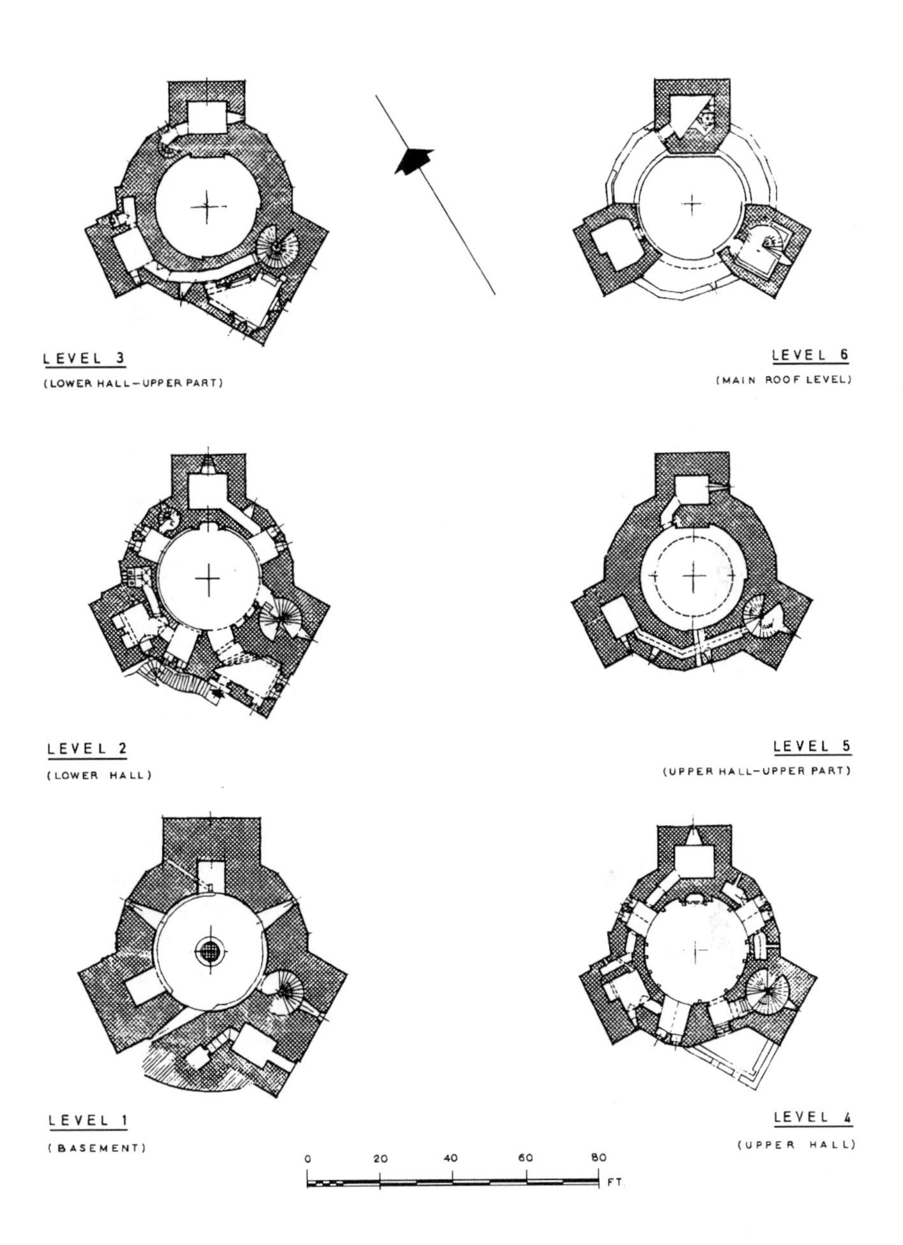

Figure 2. Orford Castle keep, plans of the different levels.

command the whole face of the main tower'[16] is simply not true. Indeed, it is not until the late twelfth century that the occurrence of towers with archery loops flanking straight walls made raking fire a serious defensive proposition.[17] At Orford, as in so many other keeps of the twelfth century, the physical evidence suggests that the form was not primarily devised with military requirements in mind.

The Provision of Rooms in the Keep

The best way to convey the character of the accommodation at Orford (Fig. 2) is probably initially in the language of an estate agent. A generous front vestibule leads to a spacious (30 ft diameter) reception room lit by three double windows in large recesses. On the wall facing the door as you enter is a substantial fireplace. Adjoining the main space to one side are a kitchen with sink and two cooking hearths and, leading off its own corridor, a double latrine. Across the other side of the circular reception room is a private chamber with its own entrance corridor. It is surmounted by a mezzanine chamber, again with its own access staircase and with a urinal on the landing. The building's main staircase leads at mezzanine level to the chapel (over the porch) and thence by a corridor to a private chamber with *en suite* facility and storage space. Returning to the main stair; at the next level is an even loftier 30 ft diameter hall with even larger windows, and again with a fireplace (Fig. 3). There is ample closet space, a chamber, what has been regarded as another kitchen, with a single flue and a sink set in the floor (as though to facilitate the disposing of water from a tub which was too heavy to be lifted),[18] and a latrine.

From this point onwards, the description necessarily becomes more complex. On the next mezzanine is a chamber with access from a wooden walkway which has now disappeared, but which originally ran round the inside of the main wall above the hall ceiling (Fig. 2, level 5). It is not otherwise differentiated from the other chambers that have been mentioned already. At this level also is to be found a room lined in its lower parts with ashlar and usually labelled 'cistern' on modern plans. It is indeed likely that this was for storing rainwater from the roof, and it is even possible that there was a system of pipes to provide 'gravity fed' water to the rooms beneath.[19] On the roof are two more spacious rooms, one with a large oven. The basement of the building contains a well and capacious storage space.

16 B. H. St J. O'Neill, *Castles* (London, 1954), p. 14.

17 P. Curnow, 'Some Developments in Military Architecture c. 1200: Le Coudray-Salbart', *Proceedings of the Battle Conference*, II (1979), ed. R. A. Brown, pp. 42–62.

18 The type of fireplace is distinct from that in the kitchen on the first floor (which is like the double fireplaces in some contemporary monastic kitchens) and it seems that it had some other function. However it is the position of the sink which most clearly suggests that the room was intended to have a particular function, one which required low level drainage.

19 At Henry II's most expensive castle project, Dover, the keep was provided with piped water: E. MacPherson and E. G. J. Amos, 'The Norman waterworks in the keep at Dover', *Archaeological Journal*, 86 (1929), pp. 253–55. Dover was probably not begun until the 1180s but it is quite possible that the provision of running water in a keep was known by the 1160s.

Figure 3. Orford Castle keep, the upper hall.

The layout of the accommodation and amenities is very cleverly thought through. Four of the private chambers are in a single tower (the easternmost) and have windows which face, more or less, the rising sun. The wall separating this tower from central circular space forms the back of the main fireplaces and thus acts as an integral night-storage heater running up the block. The only other private chamber, the one with the *en suite* latrine, is between the kitchen and the heated room above, and here the flues run up the outer wall, doubtless with the same effect of keeping the room warm. The concentration of drainage is to the north of this block. Each of the four latrines is provided with its own shute running to the base of the wall. These soil-pipes prevent unsightly stains on the exterior and concentrate the refuse so that it can be cleared up more easily. The water from the two sinks is kept clear of the wall by gutters projecting some 14 inches.

The main, ashlar-lined staircase has treads that are 5 ft 6 in. wide, that is to say, the total width of the stairwell is about 12 ft (the newel is about 1 ft wide). There is clearly no concern here with the narrowness that might inhibit the circulation of invading forces. Complementing this grandeur, the doorways into the main circular rooms are of equivalent width to the main staircase, as is the entrance corridor to the second-floor hall. As well as generous provision for circulation, a great deal of care has been taken to create discrete spaces that can be closed off from each other. Each chamber had its own door (smaller than the main doors), placed at the beginning of its entrance corridor or stair. The kitchen and the room on the main floor above it had a door each and so too did the latrines. Some notion of privacy may have been one reason for doors,[20] but

20 There are relatively few references in contemporary literature to a notion of privacy which involves

draught and smell exclusion were certainly others. Doors on the stairs may well have been to cut down draughts, and the door to the *en suite* loo must also have had this purpose, as well, probably, as containing any malodorousness. It is noteworthy that the small windows in this and the other latrines had no shutters and were thus permanent vents, whereas chamber windows are rebated and traces of hinges remain in some of them. Chambers were thus draught-proofed, but a problem arose with a chamber which had an adjoining latrine: the solution was yet another door. While it is of course true that a closed door will slow down an assailant, it is also obvious that if that is its main aim you are likely to provide draw bars or some other heavy bolting device. There are no traces of any except at the main entrance and at the entrance to the second-floor hall.

My argument is, then, that the disposition of the rooms, their access, and the provision of amenities, all suggest that the designer(s) and patron(s) were concerned with building a convenient and comfortable as well as a grand dwelling.

The Geometry of the Layout

In the last three decades much work has been done which shows that the proportional relationship between the side of a square and its diagonal, i.e. 1 to root 2, or 1:1.4142, underlies much of church planning in the Middle Ages, perhaps particularly in England. It is also a determining ratio at Orford. To give one example for the moment, the height of the third string course (measured from the lowest one) is 57 ft 7 in. This multiplied by root 2 is 81 ft 5 in. which is the height of the towers to the coping stones on the merlons (Fig. 1). The use of root 2 at Orford demonstrates that ecclesiastical structures did not have a monopoly on the use of this proportion. This is significant in that it suggests that any aesthetic harmony which might have been considered inherent in the system was not reserved for architecture designed 'in the service of God'. Secular building of the twelfth century too was allowed to partake of the same kind of geometric perfection. Thus, the identification of root 2 in this building has an importance beyond that of simply understanding how particular dimensions in the plan and elevation were arrived at.[21]

To understand the planning of the towers we need to turn to another, more subtle piece of geometry. The widths of the towers just above the batter on the basement storey are 21 ft 2½ in., 21 ft 2 in. and 21 ft 6 in. 21 ft 2½ in. is half the length of the side of an equilateral triangle placed within a circle of 49 ft in diameter, which is to within about three inches the diameter of Orford's keep

withdrawing to a separate room, and many of these stem from the segregation of the sexes, for example when a woman changes her clothes or goes to bed.

21 The measurements here are derived from the large-scale cross-section drawings based on a photogrammetic survey conducted for English Heritage. On the use of root 2 in ecclesiastical architecture see Kidson, 'Systems of Measurement and Proportion in Early Medieval Architecture', 2 vols (unpublished Ph.D. thesis, London, 1956) and various works by Eric Fernie, for example 'The Ground Plan of Norwich Cathedral and the Square Root of Two', *Journal of the British Archaeological Association*, 129 (1976), pp. 78–86 and 'Reconstructing Edward's Abbey at Westminister', in *Romanesque and Gothic, essays for George Zarnecki*, ed. Neil Stratford (Woodbridge, 1987), pp. 63–67 at 64–65.

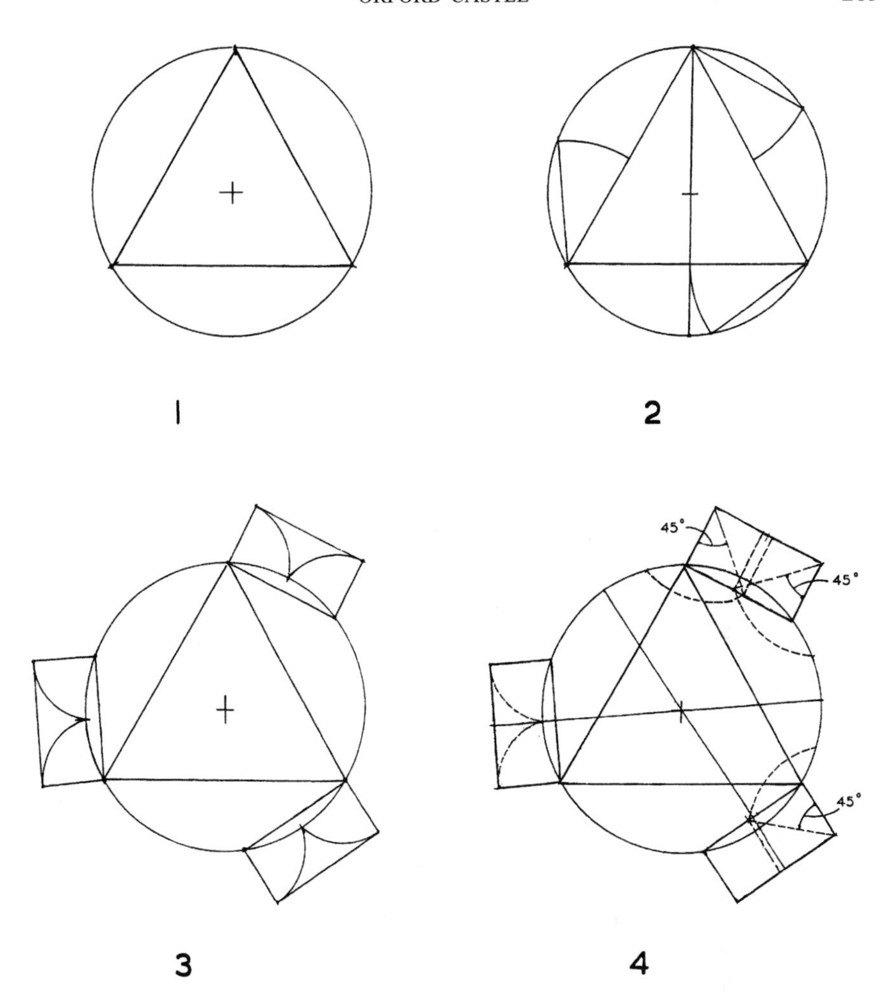

Figure 4. Orford Castle keep, diagrams showing the geometrical basis of the plan.

(Fig. 4: 1–2).[22] It need come as no surprise that an equilateral triangle is involved here since the three clasping towers are placed at 120 degree intervals around the circumference. At first it might seem merely a curiosity that they should have chosen this length for the width of the towers rather than 24 ft 6 in., which is the radius of the circle. However, on closer examination quite pertinent justifications for it will appear.

A line which is half the length of the side of an equilateral triangle within a circle, when used as a chord for the circle, will subtend at its centre an angle of just under 51 degrees 20 minutes. This angle multiplied by seven gives 359

22 It has not been possible to measure directly the wall thickness at the top of basement level, which I have calculated trigonometrically. This can be done at two points and produces figures of 10 ft 8 in. and 10 ft 9 in. When added to the 27 ft 10 in. of the interior the total is 49 ft 3 in., but there is some margin for error in the calculation.

degrees and 10 minutes, that is, less than one degree short of a full circle, an error of a quarter of one per cent. In other words, for most practical purposes this construction is a way of dividing a circle into seven. This principle (based on root 3) is indeed the method used in the fifteenth-century mason Mathes Roriczer's *Geometria Deutsch* for producing a regular heptagon.[23] It is clear from this later context that the construction was regarded as useful to architects. But why bother to use it at Orford? There are three possible explanations: it was practical, it was symbolic, and it was self-evidently clever. Quite probably all of these mattered and we should bear them in mind as alternatives (though not necessarily mutually excluding ones) as we examine further details of the scheme.

Having produced widths for each tower equivalent to a seventh of the circumference, each of these arcs was divided in half again. The chord at the perimeter of the circle which results is about 10 ft 10½ in. (Fig. 4: 3). That length is in turn used to define the depth of the clasping towers which, in the three places where they can be measured, range from 10 ft 10 in. to 11 ft 1 in.[24] There is one other oddity about the plan of Orford which derives directly from this construction. It is the irregular division of the main wall between each pair of towers into four facets. Once a decision had been taken to have four facets, one might expect that the length would simply be divided in half and then in half again. This did not happen. In fact the length of the facets nearest to the towers varies quite widely from 6 ft 5¼ in. to 6 ft 10½ in. (Fig. 5). The discrepancy is unexpected in a building as accurate as Orford and suggests that this was not in fact how the point of division was arrived at. An alternative method of positioning the arris yields much more consistent results. Measuring from the outer corner of the adjacent towers to the first arris gives the lengths 15 ft 5½ in. twice and 15 ft 6½ in. once (at the other three corners the points are obscured). These measurements are the result of multiplying 10 ft 11 in.–11 ft by root 2, and it seems that the placing of the arris was, as it were, a back formation from the extremities of the keep and based upon the depth of projection of the clasping towers (Fig. 4: 4). This is the point, then, at which what may be called the root 2 system and the circle and root 3 system of Orford are brought together and as such it is symbolic of the linking of the two geometrical principles in use there.

It would be difficult to argue that a detail such as this served any practical purpose. It was complexity for the sake of its cleverness. There were, however, common-sense considerations at work in the planning. As noted above, the diameter of the plan is about 49 ft. If one starts with an approximation for Pi (the relation of the circumference of a circle to its diameter) of 22 over 7, the arithmetical calculations for Orford become very easy if the designer was working in foot units corresponding to those that we use today. Dividing 49 by 7 and multiplying by 22 gives a circumference of 154. As the base of each tower was determined as one seventh of the circle, the length of the arc occupied by each tower is 22 ft. It means in effect that one can divide the circle into seven by

23 L. R. Shelby, *Gothic Design Techniques: the fifteenth-century design booklets of Mathes Roriczer and Hans Schmuttermayer* (Carbondale, 1977), p. 119. I am grateful to Peter Kidson for pointing me in this direction.

24 It may well be significant that the 11 ft deep tower is also the widest, as though each tower's depth was derived from its own baseline.

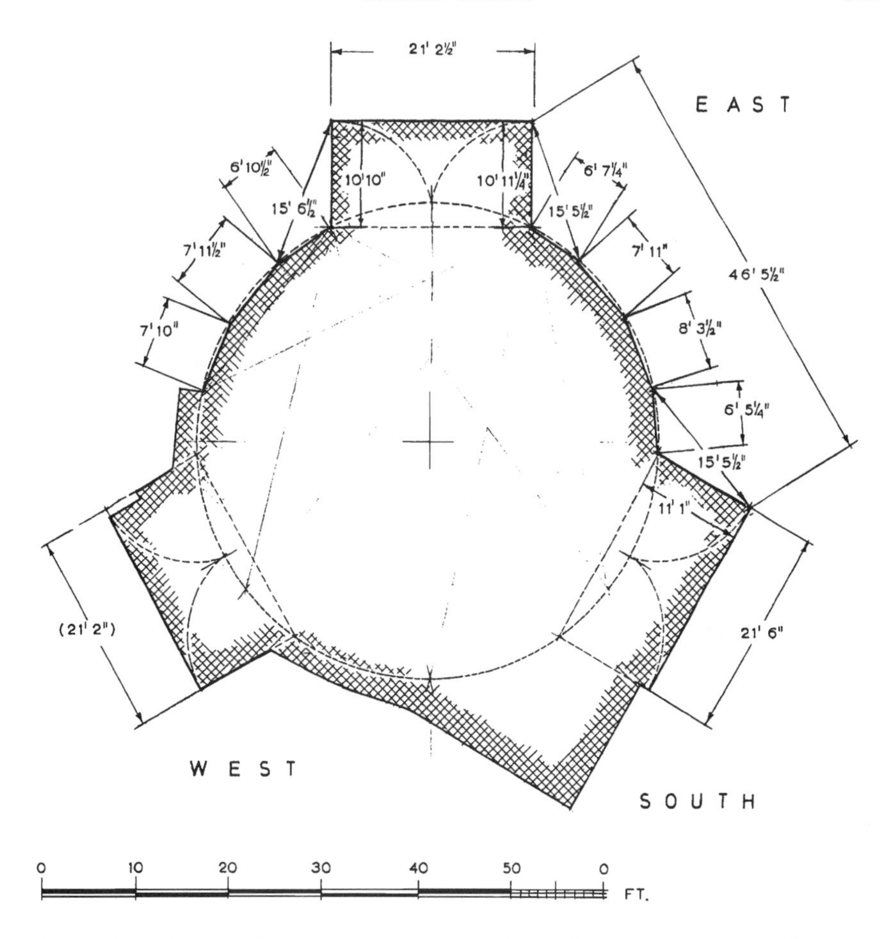

Figure 5. Orford Castle keep, measurements taken at basement level immediately above the lowest string course.

one or both of two means, by the root 3 principle outlined above, or by measuring around the circumference in set units which have been calculated beforehand. Twenty-two feet and multiples and divisions of it recur in English building from at least the seventh century to the twelfth. One reason seems to be its arithmetical relationship to the rod or perch of 16 ft 6 in.[25] But from the point of view of Orford, or any building based upon a circle, its great advantage would have been the ease of calculating with it in round numbers if one had an approximation to Pi which was 22 over 7. This may well be the practical element within the choice of dimensions at Orford. It made possible a degree of forward planning in round numbers.[26]

25 E. Fernie, 'Anglo-Saxon Lengths: the "Northern" System, the Perch and the Foot', *Archaeological Journal*, 142 (1985), pp. 246–54 for divisions of the perch. See also the support given for the use of foot units by Jean Bony, 'The Stonework Planning of the First Durham Master', in *Medieval Architecture and its Intellectual Context, studies in honour of Peter Kidson*, eds E. Fernie and P. Crossley (London and Ronceverte, 1990), pp. 19–34, at 31–32 and note 15.

26 Knowledge of the formula 22 over 7 for the relationship of the circumference of a circle to its diame-

The Iconography of the Building and the Cultural Context

In general the designers of Orford have striven for elegant simplicity. There are no mouldings of any complexity, and of the twelve carved capitals, nine are concentrated in the chapel. There they surmount half or quadrant shafts, which are the only columnar-derived supports within the building as it now stands, and the only ones there ever were. The other three capitals, to the right of the entrance to the first-floor hall, look as though they were designed to take half-shafts, but these were never supplied either as semi-cylindrical monoliths or coursed in to the masonry of the wall (Fig. 6). In other words, the half capitals must always have been employed as corbels. One may infer that in this building there is an association between columns and an ecclesiastical function. This is not particularly surprising and not a unique instance. In the Tower of London, for example, it is only the chapel that has columns and capitals, the other rooms, as at Orford, utilize square piers without capitals for both blind arcades and principal openings. In the mid 1160s, at the height of the controversy between King Henry and Archbishop Thomas Becket, it is perhaps even less surprising that this distinction should be drawn in a royal building.

The suggestion that the architectural detail of Orford is for the most part deliberately distinguished from contemporary church building is borne out elsewhere. With the exception of those in the entrance vestibule, the larger windows throughout the building are square-headed under an arch and tympanum. Such a design is quite unlike that normally found in Romanesque churches, where windows almost invariably have semi-circular heads, but it is not uncommon in other castles.[27] A similar distinction may be drawn between doorways: virtually all Romanesque church doorways are round-headed whereas those at Orford are gabled (Figs 1 and 6).

To my eye, the doorways are reminiscent of classical pedimented entrances, and the designer may well have chosen such details because they alluded to the massive buildings of Antiquity with their connotations of the heroic exploits of ancient history and myth. The popular romantic fiction of the second half of the twelfth century was, of course, set in the era of King Arthur whom some, following what little real historical evidence there was, chose to place at the end of the Roman period, but whom Chretien de Troyes made contemporary with, for example, a Greek emperor called Alexander. Since the efforts of Geoffrey of Monmouth in the late 1130s, Britain had had a mythic origin akin to that of

ter can be found in a few sources earlier than Orford. Three of these are printed by N. Bubnov, ed., *Gerberti Opera Mathematica* (Berlin 1899, reprinted Hildesheim 1963), p. 356 (also pp. 346, 354) from *Geometria incerti auctoris* probably of the early eleventh century; p. 546 from the treatise of Epaphroditus and Vitruvius Rufus architectus, perhaps of the sixth century; and p. 304 from the *Epistola Adelboldi ad Silvestrum II papam* of 999–1003. The first and last of these texts were certainly circulating in England during the twelfth century. See also *Practical Geometry in the High Middle Ages: Artis cuiuslibet Conummatio and the Pratike de Geometrie*, ed. with trans. and commentary by S. K. Victor (Philadelphia, 1979), p. 173, n. 64.

27 E.g. Newark Castle, built by Alexander, bishop of Lincoln. The feature occurs in 'castles' of all dates, (e.g. Langeais, on the Loire, c. 1000) because it was common in Roman city walls and gates.

Table of Measurements from Orford Castle

	Actual	Calculated on a circle of diameter 49 Feet
Width of towers:		
East	21 ft 2½ in.	(on the basis of dividing the circle into seven, using the square root of three) 21 ft 2½ in.
South	21 ft 6 in.	
West	(21 ft 2 in.)	
Depth of towers:		
East (N face)	10 ft 10 in.	(on the basis of dividing the circle into fourteen, using the square root of three) 10 ft 10½ in.
East (S face)	10 ft 11¼ in.	
South (E face)	11 ft 1 in.	
Diagonals from projecting corners to first intervening facet:		
East tower to N	15 ft 6½ in.	(on the basis the point was arrived at by multiplying 10 ft 10½ in. by the square root of two) 15 ft 4¾ in.
East tower to S	15 ft 5½ in.	
South tower to E	15 ft 5½ in.	
Facets between East and South towers, from E to S:		
	6 ft 7¼ in.	(The circumference of a circle 49 ft in diameter is 153 ft 11¼ in. One-third of four-sevenths of that circumference is) 29 ft 4 in.
	7 ft 11 in.	
	8 ft 3½	
	6 ft 5¼ in.	
	29 ft 3 in.	
From the S corner of the East tower to the E corner of the South tower:		
	46 ft 5½ in.	46 ft 4½ in.

Since the actual measurements and the ideal geometry correspond so very closely we may conclude:
(a) that Orford was designed on a 49 ft diameter circle
(b) that the building was laid out with remarkable accuracy.

Figure 6. Orford Castle keep, detail of the doorway from the vestibule into the lower hall.

Rome. According to this 'history', Brutus, who founded and gave his name to Britain, was a Trojan and the great-grandson of Aeneas. This may be one reason that some features of Orford were meant to call to mind the glories of the ancient Mediterranean.

The idea of setting a lintelled window under a semi-circular arch is paralleled in Late Antique fortifications, for example in the Theodosian walls (the land walls) of Constantinople: the builders of Orford must have regarded this element in their design as quite important since it caused them to seek out monoliths of greater length than those needed for the rest of the keep. The same monument could also have provided some of the enthusiasm for polygonal exteriors, since many of the mural towers of Constantinople are 5-, 6-, 7- or 8-sided. It has been argued for another English royal castle, at Caernarvon, that the Theodosian walls were the iconographic inspiration, and the arguments, of Arnold Taylor, seem entirely convincing.[28] But Caernarvon is well over a century later than Orford, and we need to demonstrate a twelfth-century context for this kind of exotic classicism.

According to a Byzantine source of the very beginning of the thirteenth century, Nikolaos Mesarites, the Emperor John II Comnenos (1118–43) built a great circular hall with apsidal projections adjacent to and at the west end of the Chrysotriklinos in Constantinople. This building, apparently a throne room, was nicknamed 'the cone' after the shape of the roof. It was internally domed, with

28 In Colvin, *King's Works* I (1963), pp. 369–71.

semi-domed spaces leading off it, and is said to have been designed by a Persian.[29] This assertion may simply have been true, but there is an additional possible explanation for it. One of the great, legendary domed 'imperial' structures which would have coloured the thinking of an informed twelfth-century Greek was the throne of Chosroes, emperor of Persia, who had been defeated by the Byzantine emperor Herachus.[30] It is clear enough from Nikolaos Mesarites' text that such a prototype (the other alternative is the Golden House of Nero as described by Suetoníus) lay behind his description and perhaps also behind John Comnenos' building.[31] Secular halls with apsed projections had long been known in Constantinople. They appeared in two forms: the polylobed and the triconch. Both types had associations either with the emperor himself or with his most important advisers.[32] They carried the connotations of high rank and great wealth. What matters for our purposes though is not so much local consumption in Constantinople, but evidence of Western responses. It appears in a number of forms.

In a French poem roughly contemporary with the building of Orford, the *Pèlerinage de Charlemagne*, the great hall in the palace at Constantinople where King Hugh (sic) receives the Frankish emperor and his knights, is described as circular and has other features of the domed hall described by Nikolaos (for example figurative imagery on the interior).[33] In this burlesque romance Charlemagne's visit has been occasioned by comments from his wife about his inferiority to the eastern emperor; he goes to Constantinople where he sees real splendour. Unfortunately, the *Pèlerinage* is not dated. One of its editors, Paul Aebischer, thought the language could be placed anywhere between 1060 and 1175. Attempts have been made to use historical evidence to determine when it was composed, seeing for example a satire on Louis VII and Eleanor of Aquitaine.[34] That would scarcely fit the facts since Eleanor and Louis had been to Constantinople together. If a particular king was being satirized, it is more likely to have been Eleanor's second husband, Henry II of England, who had never been anywhere exotic. But these speculations are necessarily inconclusive.

Other contemporary western sources reveal an awareness of the oriental tradition of centralized palace architecture, for example the *Eracle* of Gautier of Arras. The story is based on that of the Emperor Herachus, and this of course affords the opportunity to mention the throne of Chosroes.[35] Gautier seems to have dedicated his work simultaneously to three people, the count of Hainault, the count of Blois and the countess of Champagne. The latter was Eleanor of

[29] C. Mango, *The Art of the Byzantine Empire 312–1452* (Englewood Cliffs, 1972), pp. 228–29.

[30] H. P. L'Orange, *Studies on the iconography of Cosmic Kingship* (Oslo, 1953), pp. 19–27 and passim.

[31] O. Grabar, 'From Dome of Heaven to Pleasure Dome', *Journal of the Society of Architectural Historians*, 49 (1990), pp. 15–21.

[32] I. Lavin, 'The House of the Lord', *Art Bulletin*, 44 (1962), pp. 1–28.

[33] *Le Voyage de Charlemagne à Jérusalem et à Constantinople*, ed. P. Aebischer (Geneva, 1965), pp. 52–53. On the whole subject of palace architecture in twelfth-century romance literature see most recently the work of Alain Labbé, cited at note 8 above.

[34] T. Heinermann, 'Zeit and Sinn der Karlsreise', *Zeitschrift für romanische Philologie*, 56 (1930), p. 550ff.

[35] P. Frankl, *The Gothic, literary sources and interpretations through eight centuries* (Princeton, 1960), p. 167. The most recent edition of the poem is Gautier d'Arras, *Eracle*, ed. Guy Raynaud de Lage (Paris, 1976).

Aquitaine's daughter Mary, and the count of Blois was married to her other daughter by Louis VII, Alice. If literature of this kind was being produced for and circulated in the courts of northern Europe it would of course help to create just the kind of context for the exotic we are seeking. It is probably not accidental that the third quarter of the twelfth century saw the creation in France of several elaborate keeps with projecting spaces radiating from a vaulted central hall. Two of the best known are Etampes and Provins, the latter built for the count and countess of Champagne.[36] But why might the form appeal to Henry II, a king not usually noted for fashionable concerns?

In 1163 the most important of all exotic Christian kings, the three Magi, had been translated to Cologne for Frederick Barbarossa. This was part of a political public relations exercise to emphasise the direct relationship between the godhead and earthly rulers which did not depend on the good offices of the papacy. The contemporary, mythic links of the Magi with the land of the priest-king Prester John, where a Christian king ruled the church, would obviously also have been attractive to Henry II during the Becket controversy. If centralized orientalizing palace architecture was readily associated with notions of all-powerful rulers, it becomes less difficult to understand why it was specifically in the mid 1160s that Henry II might have become interested in it.[37]

But, apart from its circular hall and radiating window niches, what has Orford really to do with the centralized palace? In this context, it is important to note that the roof over the upper hall at Orford was conical. The exact form of the ceiling beneath it is lost to us but a number of its features can be determined simply by logic. The thirteen corbels supporting the principal rafters are angled at the back in such a way as to give us the overall pitch of the roof. There must have been a walkway on the haunches of the angled timbers to give access from the main staircase to the mezzanine chamber behind the chimney. The obvious way to provide for this would be by placing a plank floor on struts between the main wall and the principal rafters. However, this structure would put pressure on the rafters causing them to bend inwards. A straightforward way of preventing this would be to insert braces from a point close to the junction of the rafter and the strut. The angle at which these braces would have been placed is a matter of surmise, but if they were too near the horizontal they would tend to sag, and if too vertical would not perform their bracing function properly. The accompanying drawing indicates an acceptable compromise (Fig. 7). It is easy

36 Their fame is due in large part to their inclusion by E. Viollet-le-Duc in his *Military Architecture*, trans. M. Macdermott (London, 1879). More recently see Ch.-L. Salch, *Les Plus Beaux Chateaux Forts en France* (Strasbourg, 1978), pp. 98–101 (Etampes) and 213–16 (the so-called Tour de César at Provins).

37 The connections between Prester John, the Magi and Barbarossa have been convincingly outlined by B. Hamilton, 'Prester John and the Three Kings of Cologne', in *Studies in Medieval History presented to R. H. C. Davis*, eds H. Mayr-Harting and R. I. Moore (London and Ronceverte, 1985), pp. 177–91. The land of Prester John was often seen as the place where the apostle Thomas had preached and where he had built a palace for the king. Descriptions of the functions of the rooms in this mythic palace circulated throughout the middle ages (Lavin, 'The House of the Lord') in the legend of the saint and would have provided further stimulus for a high degree of comfort and functional specificity. On the palace of Prester John, see L'Orange, *Studies on the iconography of Cosmic Kingship*, pp. 18–19.

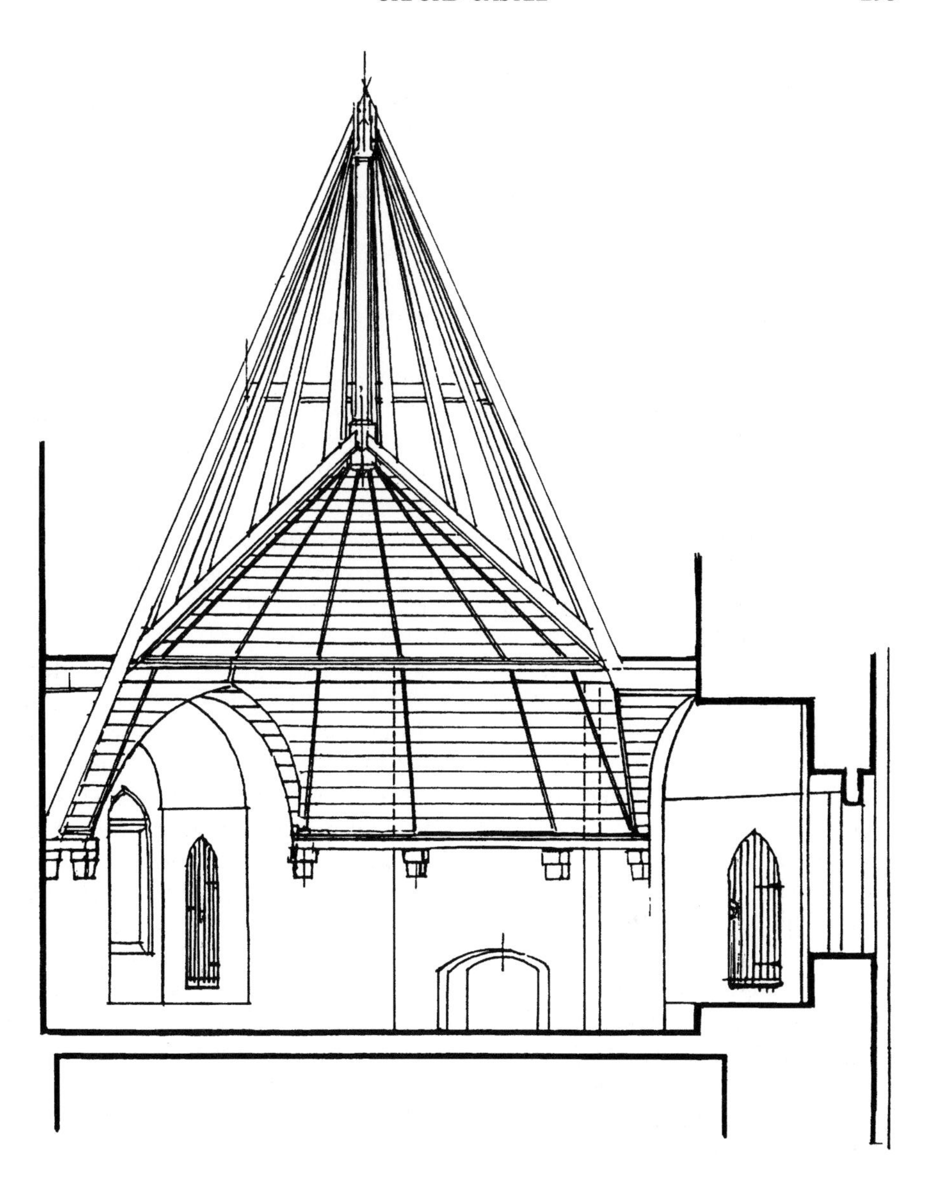

Figure 7. Orford Castle keep, suggested reconstruction of the ceiling of the upper hall.

to see that a plank ceiling nailed onto the underside of the main timber framework would have created a domed effect. From the point of view of the iconography of medieval architecture, and what constituted similarity between buildings, it may be that the keep at Orford was an acceptable approximation to an eastern tradition for circular halls. In building the keep at Orford, Henry II or his ministers were participating in a genre of palace architecture of ancient origin which had recently been made fashionable again and which may, in addition, have had useful propaganda value for them.

It remains an open question how far either the government or the architect were aware of all the possible resonances of their structure, for example in number symbolism. Were the three deep window recesses at Orford intended to recall the apses of a triconch? Equally, the use of the number seven could have been significant. We have seen that there was a practical, arithmetical reason which would justify a division of the circle into sevenths (though six would have been easier), but the number seven was important within the context of a domed royal buildings because just as the dome represented the arc of heaven, seven stood for the number of the planets and the days of the week. It was part of the iconography of cosmic kingship.[38] The choice of the thirteen corbels also raises questions. Because of the wide and deep window bays, three pairs of these corbels are set well apart. In other places four are bunched more closely together. But thirteen is the number of Christ and the Apostles, and hence of many other groups – for example, Charlemagne and his twelve knights who went to Constantinople![39]

If we do not like this line of argument we have to find another explanation for the eccentricity and sophistication of Orford. Perhaps, as hinted earlier, it was to do with self-evident cleverness on the part of the designer. In his *Eneit*, written between 1184 and 1188, Heinrich von Valdeke gives the name *Geometras* to the master builder of Camilla's tomb ('der wîse man Geometras der des werkes meister was').[40] Camilla's tomb is itself described as a centralized building, and it is likely that in the author's mind there was an association between sophisticated geometry and architectural planning in Antiquity. Clearly such ideas were in the air in the second half of the twelfth century, and it is typical of the age that they should be validated by evoking the achievements of ancient history and legend. One could never prove that such associations were in the minds of the builders of Orford, but consciously or unconsciously they are unlikely to have been entirely ignorant of them. For want of any positive historical statement to

38 Ibid., pp. 10, 18–19 and passim; and Grabar, 'From Dome of Heaven . . .', especially p. 18, for the poem of c. 1200–20 on an Azerbaijani Palace built by Shida, 'A master in the work of drawing too, and in surveying famed geometer . . . I'll make a seven domed house . . . for the seven days of every week and the seven planets . . .'.

39 It is probable that there were three shorter rafters in addition to the thirteen for which corbels are provided (Figs 3, 7). If wooden arches were sprung from the corbels either side of the large window niches, a large rafter might then have risen from each of the three apices to the point of the roof. The arches could have been planked on the underside towards the windows, and the remainder of the 'domed' plank ceiling could then have been brought down to corbel level.

40 Cited by Paul Frankl, *The Gothic* . . ., p. 172. See Heinrich von Veldeke, *Eneasroman*, ed. and trans. D. Kartschoke (Stuttgart, 1986), at p. 528. Kartschoke, pp. 852–56, considers that the text was begun in the early 1180s.

support these ideas (and that would be far too much to hope for) one can do no more than indicate that Orford may have been as 'iconographically' resonant as any contemporary ecclesiastical structure.

Conclusions

It may seem that I am on the verge of defeating my own argument. If Orford Castle goes out of its way to use a different vocabulary of forms from contemporary churches and partakes of a specifically secular genre of design, then perhaps castles and churches ought in fact to be considered separately? There is certainly an element of truth in the observation that each building type is governed by conventions that are special to itself, and that these will not be helpfully illuminated by being placed in the context of a generalized architectural history. However, it is equally true that in terms of the messages it conveys, any structure takes meanings from the things it does not do as much as from the things it does. It is surely the very fact that the vocabulary of a castle such as Orford is different from that of a contemporary church, such as the one being built 200 yards away across the top of the town during the same years, which helps to give the castle its symbolic status as representative of the other face of society. Modern students have perhaps been overpersuaded by what may have been a deliberate differentiation made by twelfth-century designers between sacred and secular buildings. As a result they have tended to go to the extreme of putting churches into the category architecture and castles into one which may perhaps be conveyed to a modern audience by the term engineering occasioned by strategic necessity.

One of my aims has been to seek ways of integrating castles into a pre-existing 'history of medieval architecture'. I have made things difficult for myself by taking a monographic approach and highlighting the individuality of one building; it has been made to seem 'special' and thereby has effectively been segregated not only from churches but from many other castles. However, reintegration does not present insuperable difficulties. All stone buildings in twelfth-century England, whether ecclesiastical or secular, were individual commissions by patrons with specific requirements and a finite budget. Each building needs to be treated on its own merits as well as finding a place within a wider context. It does no harm to an historical perspective if the objects within it are clearly seen as individual.

My second aim has been to stress the domestic and symbolic sophistication of castle keep design. Orford was primarily intended as the Suffolk base of the principal local royal officer, the sheriff of Norfolk and Suffolk.[41] It also had

[41] Two of the three royal servants responsible for overseeing expenditure on Orford, Bartholomew de Glanville and Wimar the Chaplain, subsequently became sheriffs, and therefore would have resided at the castle. The third member of the team, Robert de Valeines, was closely related to the Glanvilles by marriage. The remarkable success of this extended family in gaining important royal posts has been explored by R. Mortimer, 'The family of Ranulf de Glanville', *Bulletin of the Institute of Historical Research*, 54 (1981), pp. 1–16.

potential as a staging post for the king himself or members of his household in transit up and down the coast. What he and his administration were interested in was a symbol of royal authority befitting royal servants, and in its trappings that is precisely what Orford was. As a symbol visible for miles down the coast and from the sea it made and still makes a very brave show. To regard it as 'transitional' between the 'old' square keeps and the 'new' round ones is a mistake at a number of levels. For one thing, at a date later than Orford Henry II built the great square keeps of Newcastle and Dover. For another, Orford is a distinctive building type possessing features not usually found in either square or round keeps, most notably the centrifugal arrangement of the accommodation in projecting towers built for the purpose. In that respect Orford is the precursor of a keep such as Trim, north-west of Dublin, which is however based on a square not a circle.[42] But most fundamentally, the whole concept of a transition depends on historical hindsight and employs a Darwinian evolutionary model which is at best a dubious construct when applied to history. The explanation that is needed is one that works for the particularities of the moment.

A building such as Orford speaks eloquently of the aspirations of a small but powerful group of men within the government. Their romantic role-models were likely to be the heroes of antiquity or of Arthurian legend but their day-to-day existence was that of civil servants and administrators. As has remained the case ever since, important officers of state, whether at the heart of the kingdom, in the provinces or the colonies, require an appropriate degree of palatial splendour and comfort to reinforce their authority. It has been said that the sentiment of nostalgia was a principal element in castle design, and this is surely true of institutional building in general. Certainly, once the military necessity which produced the stockade castles of late eleventh-century England had passed and been succeeded by more settled times, and, concomitantly, by the first great era of the historical 'novel', it was likely that bare essentials would be supplemented by nostalgic dream. The design of stone castles for much of the twelfth century is about finding an image which expresses an ideal but which also provides appropriate accommodation. In those senses the problems confronting the designer of Orford were as architectural as those which faced a cathedral builder, and his ingenuity in solving them was as elegant in its subtlety and logic as it was precise in its execution.

42 On Trim see now T. E. McNeill, 'The Great Towers of Early Irish Castles', *Anglo-Norman Studies* XII, ed. M. Chibnall (Woodbridge, 1990), pp. 99–117 at 104–9.

15

The Great Tower at Hedingham Castle: a Reassessment

Philip Dixon and Pamela Marshall

The 'keep' at Hedingham is one of the best preserved and least altered Romanesque *donjons* in Britain. In consequence it is frequently referred to in print, being included, at least as a photograph or drawing, by most authors who write about castles. Despite all this attention, the modern accounts appear to derive their information from the description of the Royal Commission on Historical Monuments for England (RCHM) in its *Essex* volume, a publication which was produced comparatively early in the Commission's history, and which contains some important misconceptions. In this paper we present evidence that the Hedingham great tower has been mistakenly interpreted as a four-storey building when, in its original form, it had only three storeys, and we examine the implications of this in terms of its function.

Date of the Top Floor

The problem is the existence of the top storey. As long ago as 1912, Hamilton Thompson, in a brief description of the building, identified a top floor above the main hall as containing 'private bedrooms' with wooden partitions.[1] This interpretation was followed by the surveyors of the RCHM in 1916, whose account remains the fullest treatment of the building.[2] Almost all subsequent writers, relying on the published descriptions and plans, have repeated this analysis without adding significantly to it.[3] In his most recent paper on the development of great towers,[4] Dr Michael Thompson, who also considers it a four-storeyed building,[5] draws attention to the great tower as one of two examples in which 'the loss of a walled-off inner chamber could be compensated for by placing it

1 *Military Architecture in England during the Middle Ages* (London, 1912), pp. 145–6. Similar accounts had been given by W. St John Hope in *Archaeological Journal* 64 (1907), pp. 79–82 and by A.H. Harvey, *The Castles and Walled Towns of England* (London, 1911), pp. 74–6.

2 RCHM, *The County of Essex* I (1916), pp. 51–8.

3 For example R. Allen Brown, *English Medieval Castles* (London, 1953), pp. 44–5 republishes the RCHM drawing; in the 1976 edition (pp. 69, 74, 82 and 209) he adds the possible attribution to Aubrey de Vere III [*c.*1141 *sic*]. Douglas Simpson, *Castles of England and Wales* (1969), pp. 58–61 gives a similar account to RCHM. M.W. Thompson, *The Rise of the Castle* (1991), p. 77: very similar to the *Fortress* paper.

4 *Fortress* 14 (December 1992).

5 In his *Rise of the Castle* (Cambridge, 1992), p. 64, Hedingham is credited (perhaps through simple error) with five storeys.

Figure 1. The great tower at Hedingham. Entrance front. (All illustrations by courtesy of the authors)

above and so increasing the height of the tower. This is no doubt the simple explanation for the tall keeps at Rochester and Hedingham, and no ingenious functional differences between squat and tall towers need be invoked.' As an important element in this proposed new framework for the development of towers, Hedingham clearly merits further consideration, since these explanations based on the likely room usage have ignored several important features of the building.

The room on the top floor at Hedingham is in fact a late insertion, perhaps of the fifteenth or sixteenth century. Evidence for this is clearest at the north-western corner, where the stair turret projects into the uppermost room. Here one can see a clear roof crease marking the lower face of the rafters of a pyramidal roof on both inner faces of the turret. Below the roof creases the

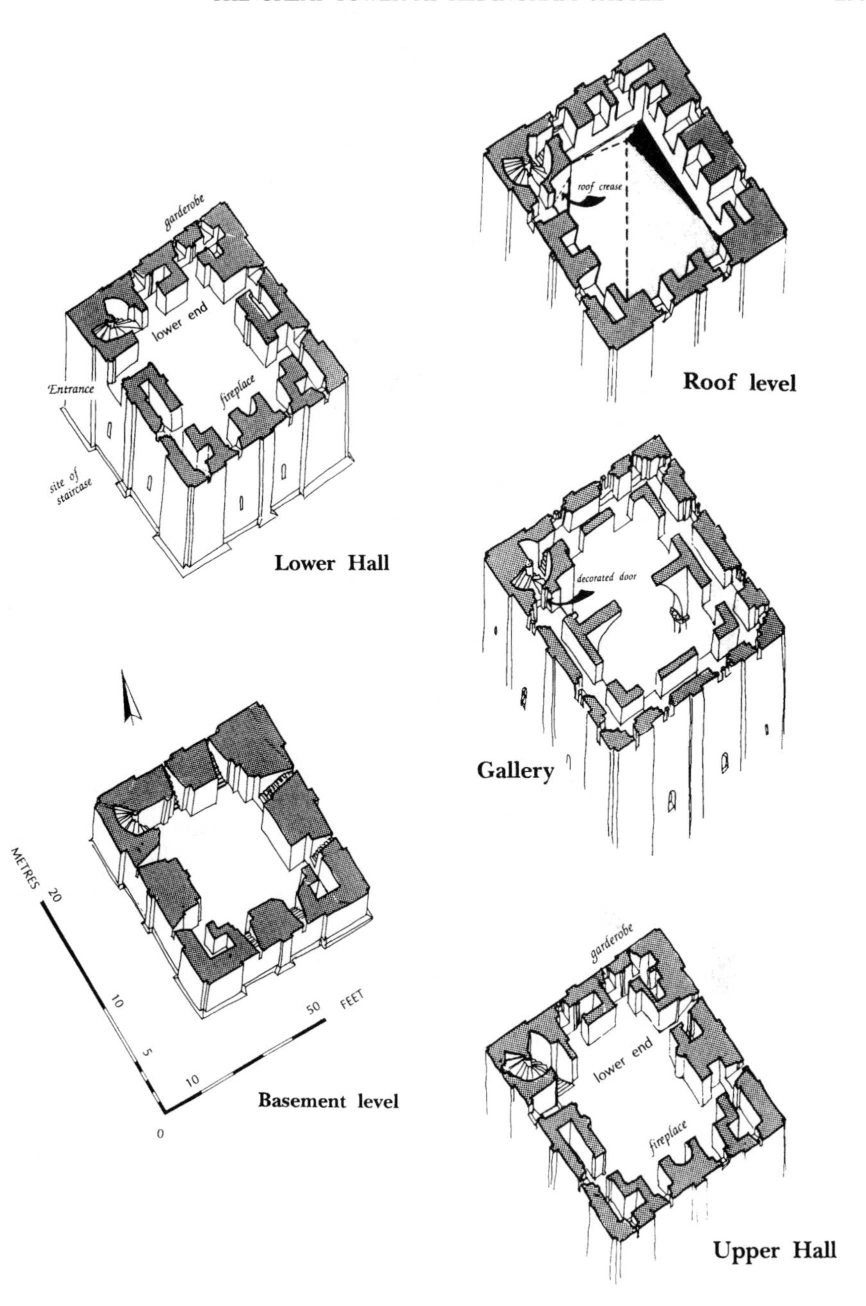

Figure 2. Sections of the tower at various levels.

Figure 3. Original roof crease on staircase turret.

masonry is largely in ashlar, and the angle has been formed into a quirked edge roll. Above the creases the walling is in the rough small rubble which characterises the inner faces of the top room, and only the quoins are in ashlar, without the edge roll. This treatment of a projection visible below a timber roof corresponds with that in the forebuilding at Castle Rising (of about 1138),[6] where the line. of the original roof, complete with a quirked edge roll and in this case a cushion capital, may be seen in the chamber added to the top of the structure.

Further evidence for the placing of the original roof at Hedingham is now visible around the walls of the uppermost room. The present top floor lies about 75cms (2ft 5½ins) below the bottoms of the window embrasures. The floor is itself modern, a replacement after the fire of *c.*1920. Its previous higher position is shown in the RCHM report (p. 54), at the level of the embrasures. The existence of the earlier floor at this higher level presumably explains the failure of the Commission's surveyors to notice that the ledge on which this floor rested is not a scarcement ledge for floor joists, but a gutter ledge for the base of a roof. It is notable that this ledge is not horizontal: from the eastward facing side of the stair turret it slopes down 40cm (16ins) to the north-east corner, where a drain discharges through the north wall. From the southfacing side of the stair turret the ledge drops 10cms (4ins) to the south-west corner, and continues falling a further 20cms (8ins) to the south-east corner, where another drain discharges

6 R. Allen Brown, *Castle Rising: Official Handbook*, HMSO (Norwich, 1978), p. 36, p. 55.

Figure 4. Interior of upper hall from the north.

through the east wall. The ledge on the east side falls from the centre to the drains at either end. The position of this ledge, and the roof creases on the stair turret, show that the original roof was a pyramid, its centre resting on the great arch above the second-floor room, and its sides and gutters on the ledges immediately above the boards of the present upper floor.[7] The existence of this roof explains the double entrance from the staircase at this level: without two separate approaches to the roof, the projection of the staircase turret would have made movement around the leads awkward. The writers of earlier accounts may further have been misled into considering the roof area to have been a room by the apparent presence of what seems to be a series of mural chambers at this level. These 'chambers', however, are somewhat different from the mural cells of the floors below, since they are simple open arched recesses in the walls, without any provision for closure. Since they correspond exactly with the position of the cells and the fireplace arch of the floor below, it seems most likely that they were intended to act as an open relieving arcade, to spread the load of the superincumbant masonry.

7 For a roof of similar design see T. McNeill, *Carrickfergus Castle* (Belfast, 1981).

The Function of the Building

We must therefore discount this upper floor from any consideration of the original arrangement of the accommodation in the great tower of Hedingham. This calls for a complete re-examination of the function of the building, for we are apparently left with no more than two large and grand rooms and a basement, but with no sleeping accommodation (nor, for that matter, kitchen, services or oratory). The second-floor room was undoubtedly a public reception room and not a private chamber. Originally open to the roof, it is the grandest apartment in the tower, spanned by perhaps the largest Romanesque arch in the country. It cannot have functioned as a private withdrawing chamber, particularly since it is overlooked by a mural gallery on all four sides, whose access is direct from the main staircase, with no provision for even a door between stair and gallery. Five mural cells are arranged off the hall, none of them large enough to act as chambers: each is only a little more than a metre in breadth. The lower hall similarly cannot have been in any sense a private chamber, since it has direct access from the outside and originally all traffic upstairs passed through its lower end, and its mural cells are not chambers, since they are no longer than those of the floor above.

A great tower with no obvious accommodation is a problem which requires explanation. Some clues may be obtained by a closer examination of the structure itself. The basement is extremely plain, and contains no domestic elements at all: its purpose was perhaps solely for storage. The external door to the *donjon* opens directly at first-floor level into the lower hall. This was a single large room spanned by a plain arch to support the floor above: the decision, by avoiding the use of a cross wall here, not to introduce an inner chamber emphasises the public function of the room. However, it displays some social orientation, with its doors and garderobe at its northern end, and a fireplace, decorated with zig-zag ornament, flanked by tall window embrasures, at its southern end. At present a door from the side of the entrance passageway gives on to the stair. Originally, however, access lay through the first-floor room, via a door now blocked in the north-western corner, allowing the occupants of this room control of circulation to the higher level. This upper room, though its plan is almost identical to that of the floor below, is very much grander, and before the insertion of the third floor was nearly twice as high (about 10m [33ft] to the apex) as the lower hall. Its arch is moulded, and its windows decorated with zig-zag ornament similar to that of the fireplace. Its entrance displays an oddity, since the door to the upper hall from the staircase has been contrived over 2m (6ft 6ins) below the level of the floor, necessitating a long straight stair, presumably always of timber, to enter the room itself.

The staircase continues up to a clerestory gallery which looks down into the upper hall, and was brightly lit by a series of two-light windows, the largest in the *donjon*. Access to this gallery is direct, to the western arm through a richly moulded arch with no provision for a door; a similar arch, moulded simply only on its inner, eastern side, joins the northern arm of the gallery to the staircase by a short flight of steps. The variation in the decorative scheme suggests that cir-

Figure 5. Dummy window at roof level.

Figure 6. Window of gallery.

Figure 7. Window of upper hall.

culation around the gallery was intended to be anticlockwise, beginning on a level with the decorated door, and finishing with the moulded side of the door at the head of the steps. The staircase continues upwards to the two entrances to the leads, and then to the battlements and turrets.

The forebuilding is clearly secondary, masking a loop from the basement and butting roughly against the masonry of the *donjon*. The roof crease of an earlier lean-to stair, and the inverted 'V' of a straight flight at right angles to the wall, can still be traced in the *donjon* wall: both seem to have been cut into the structure, and it therefore seems possible that the original approach was no more than a straight, unroofed, set of steps up to the elaborate entrance doorway. It is worth noting that this doorway is set quite low – no more than 3.8m (12ft 6in) above the present ground level – too low for good defence, but entirely suitable to make an impressive entrance at the head of a broad open flight of steps.

Conclusion

In summary, then, the great tower at Hedingham appears to consist of an elaborate, raised but perhaps undefended, entrance, a heated lower hall of some quality, an upper hall of considerable splendour (entered by an odd arrangement of stairs) and a well lit gallery giving views down into the upper hall and outwards into the countryside. It is very difficult to avoid the conclusion that this

Figure 8. Close up of entrance.

great tower, 'evidently a costly work providing comfortable accommodation for a man of high rank while appropriately celebrating his dignity',[8] was constructed not to provide accommodation, but simply to produce a pair of grand reception rooms, the upper superior in status to the lower.

When the great tower at Hedingham was built is uncertain. The form of zig-zag would fit a date in the second quarter of the twelfth century, the shape of the volutes on the capitals the same date or a little later. The most elaborate and unusual decoration, that on the door to the gallery, somewhat resembles that of two piers at the east end of Malmesbury Abbey, which may be of Bishop

8 C. Platt, *The Castle in Medieval England and Wales* (London, 1982), pp. 25–6.

Roger's build, before 1139. On stylistic grounds, then, a date between *c.*1125 and *c.*1160 is likely. Recent writers, however, have tended more precisely to attribute the building to Aubrey de Vere II or his son Aubrey III, and give a date for the construction of *c.*1140. The analysis of the building above adds a possible confirmation of this date. The de Veres grew in power from the Conquest onwards: the first Aubrey de Vere (*c.*1040–?1112) was a major lord in Essex and surrounding counties. His son Aubrey II (*c.*1090–1141) was Henry I's chamberlain by 1112 and was Lord Great Chamberlain in 1133. His son, Aubrey III (*c.*1110–1194), continued the family's rise, and was created 1st earl of Oxford by the Empress Matilda after July 1142.[9] Allen Brown suggested that the great tower at Hedingham may have been built to mark this event.[10] We would support this view, and consider that the design of the new tower shows that it was built for the new earl's ceremonial receptions comparable to the royal crown wearing. The construction of a palace to house a single event of this sort has recently been suggested for Lincoln.[11] In the case of Hedingham, the tower, in the centre of their old castle, would be a more permanent reminder of the family's enhanced status. In these ceremonies the upper hall was presumably intended for the earl, whose chair by the fireplace would come slowly and impressively into view as the visitor ascended the straight steps contrived at the end of the hall. The lower hall, with its similar but less imposing arrangements, may have been intended for a comital official, or a junior member of the family. The mural chambers, so small as to be useful only as closets, would then provide storage for the paraphernalia of the ceremonies.

That so costly a work should be constructed for show alone may seem a considerable eccentricity to the modern mind. Yet by far the most elaborately ostentatious of the windows in the *donjon* are those at fourth-floor level, which originally gave only on to the gutters. Examination of these openings shows that they were neither glazed nor fitted with shutters: reasonable enough, since there was no room behind them. They must have been designed solely to be seen from the outside, and were possibly the only openings on the tower which could be viewed above the curtain wall by people from the surrounding countryside.

Our discussion of the original form of the *donjon* at Hedingham has revealed an unsuspected purpose for the building. We offer this contribution to the study of great towers as a warning that, though classification and typologies are essential, it is first necessary to be sure of the exact nature of the structures that are so classified.

9 J. Barrow, 'A twelfth-century bishop and literary patron: William de Vere', *Viator* (1990), pp. 175–189.

10 R.A. Brown, *English Castles* (London, 1976), p. 69.

11 The small royal palace known as St Mary's Guildhall, Lincoln, was almost certainly built to house Henry II on the occasion of his crown wearing in Lincoln at Christmas 1157: D. Stocker, *St Mary's Guildhall, Lincoln* (London, 1991), pp. 38–9.

16

Hall and Chamber: English Domestic Planning 1000–1250

John Blair

The study of domestic planning in medieval England has been dominated by two scholars whose formative works were published in the 1950s and 1960s: the late Margaret Wood, and Patrick Faulkner. Interpretations of individual buildings are heavily influenced by the models of development which they proposed, and by one model above all: that the main component of a normal twelfth-century manor-house was a stone-built block containing a *first-floor hall* raised over a basement, and that this was a direct alternative to the open *ground-floor hall* of earlier and later houses. Thus Faulkner wrote in 1958:

> The earliest form of dwelling house of a purely domestic character that remains and which forms a basic type already developed in the late 12th century is the Upper Hall house. Essentially, this form of plan is arranged on two floors each of which is provided with a greater and lesser chamber. The residence within these limits appears to be self-contained. . . . Covering somewhat the same period as the upper hall house but with a tendency to a later average date is a second fundamental plan form that may be called the end hall type. The most striking characteristic of this form is the domination by a ground floor hall of both plan and elevation. This type of house shows a development through the period from the late 12th century, when it first appears, to the 14th century. . . . Its basic form is that of a structurally independent hall with a domestic block attached to one end. The type is perhaps of greater importance than the upper hall type, as from it stems the main stream of subsequent English domestic planning.[1]

Thirty years ago, this was a reasonable conclusion from the available architectural evidence. Numerous manor-houses have been excavated since then, and it is the archaeologist rather than the architectural historian who has come to realize that things are not quite so simple as they once seemed.[2] Furthermore, scrutiny of contemporary documents shows the terminology evolved by modern

Acknowledgements. For their comments on an earlier draft the author is extremely grateful to Sarah Blair, Edward Impey, Gwyn Meirion-Jones, Derek Renn and John Steane.

1 Faulkner 1958, 151, 163–4. Cf. Wood 1965, 16–34, for a detailed discussion of surviving examples which assumes the 'first-floor hall' hypothesis.

2 Thus the excavators of Wharram Percy are now careful to describe their two-storey stone house as a *camera* rather than a first-floor hall: J.C. Thorn in Hurst (ed.) 1979, chapter V. Cf. the uneasy comment by Beresford 1974, 105: 'It is at times difficult to distinguish the archaeological remains of a *camera* from those of a first-floor hall.'

architectural historians to be anachronistic and misleading in some crucial respects. It is time to make explicit the simple message which has implicitly been emerging from recent work: that the 'first-floor hall' model is inappropriate to normal manorial buildings in England between the eleventh and thirteenth centuries, because the storeyed stone buildings usually called first-floor halls are in fact chamber-blocks which were once accompanied by detached ground-floor halls of the normal kind. Thus the lineal descendant of the so-called 'first-floor hall' was not the open hall, but the solar wing.

This is not to deny the existence of halls at first-floor level in specific places and contexts. The ubiquity of the storeyed house in many parts of France from the thirteenth century onwards is clear. In Normandy, as Edward Impey shows (see his essay in *Manorial Domestic Buildings in England and Northern France*, ed. G. Meirian-Jones and M. Jones (London, 1993)), the ground-floor aisled hall was probably common until superseded by the storeyed house in the thirteenth century. In England the ancient tradition of the ground-floor hall proved more resilient, but some buildings reflect French practice. The halls of the great Anglo-Norman keeps functioned exactly like normal ground-floor halls but were raised at an upper level, while in some other castles (notably Castle Acre and Eynsford)[3] the main component was a massive two-storey block which must have contained the hall on its first floor. The word *aula* was occasionally used for exceptional storeyed buildings, notably the 'new hall' by the precinct gate at Canterbury Cathedral Priory.[4] Urban houses, despite their obvious similarity to manorial *camerae*, developed special forms which may have included raised halls analogous to the *grandes salles* of French town-houses.[5] But these are byways from the main course of development in rural England, which was directed by the almost universal survival of the ground-floor hall.

The first aim of this paper is to clear the ground by redefining normal arrangements in English royal, manorial and episcopal houses: abnormalities, including genuine first-floor halls, can then be better understood. Also reconsidered, in the light of the new model, are two innovations between the mid-twelfth and mid-thirteenth centuries which brought into being the stereotyped late medieval English house: the development of the services and cross-passage at the lower end of the open hall, and the attachment to its upper end of the previously free-standing chamber-block.

3 Coad and Streeten 1982; Rigold 1971.

4 This building is shown on the famous 'waterworks' plan of the 1150s, where it is unambiguously captioned *aula nova*. One top-rank late thirteenth-century English house which seems closer to contemporary French planning is Acton Burnell Castle, where the hall with its chambers and services is raised over a ground floor containing offices and a 'lower hall': West 1981, 85–92. This should be contrasted with the grand fourteenth- and fifteenth-century houses in which the hall has a low undercroft, such as St David's, Kenilworth and South Wingfield, for these merely exhibit a new elaboration of the ground-floor hall.

5 A clear but very special case is Chester, where the height of the 'rows' above street-level produced almost inevitably a standard house-plan including a raised hall: Brown, Howes and Turner 1986. I am grateful to Mr Turner for clarifying some points.

Aula cum camera: The Documentary Evidence

By 1100 there was already a literary convention of defining any substantial residence in terms of two main components: one communal, public and official, used for activities such as the holding of courts and the eating of formal meals, and the other private and residential: in Latin *aula* and *camera* (or *thalamus*), in Old English *heall* and *bur*, in modern English *hall* and *chamber*. We may begin with King Alfred. In his paraphrase of St Augustine's soliloquies, Alfred describes the descending order of accommodation at any royal palace: 'some men are in the chamber, some in the hall, some on the threshing-floor, some in prison' (*sume on bure, sume on healle, sume on odene, sume on carcerne*).[6] Alfred's biographer Asser praises him for his 'royal halls and chambers (*de aulis et* cambris *regalibus*) marvellously constructed of stone and wood', and in other contexts we encounter Alfred sitting talking to Asser 'in the royal chamber' (*in regia cambra*), and issuing a judgement while washing his hands 'in the chamber (*bur*) at Wardour'.[7]

A number of excavated late Anglo-Saxon manor-houses had private apartments detached from the hall.[8] A particularly clear case is the early eleventh-century phase at Goltho (Lincolnshire), where the hall and bower were juxtaposed but not actually touching (fig. 1).[9]

No rural example hitherto known from archaeology has been shown to have had an upper floor. But in 978 the Anglo-Saxon Chronicle describes the collapse of a timber floor under the weight of the royal council, assembled in the king's house at Calne in what the Latin version calls a *solarium*,[10] while the Bayeux Tapestry (which also depicts open halls) shows Harold's feast at Bosham and King Edward's death occurring in upper chambers. Texts of the late eleventh and twelfth centuries continue to juxtapose the terms hall and chamber: William II's reputed comment that his vast new hall at Westminster was 'too big for a chamber, not big enough for a hall';[11] works on the *nova aula et camera regine* at Westminster in the 1167 pipe roll;[12] St Hugh of Lincoln dining in hall and then withdrawing to his chamber with a few distinguished people (*in aula . . . finito . . . prandio, . . . sumptis vero secum viris honestioribus . . . in cameram secedebat*);[13] and numerous similar phrases.

If such sources are rather imprecise, the more specific descriptions of manor-houses in some estate surveys and leases reveal the continuance of the planning conventions displayed by late Anglo-Saxon houses such as Goltho.

6 T.A. Carnicelli (ed.), *King Alfred's Version of St. Augustine's Soliloquies* (Cambridge, Mass., 1969), 77.

7 *Asser's Life of Alfred*, ed. W.H. Stevenson (Oxford, 1904), chs 91, 88; Keynes 1992, 73.

8 Beresford 1987, 52–4.

9 *Ibid.* 74–81.

10 *The Anglo-Saxon Chronicle*, trans. G.N. Garmonsway (London, 1953), 123.

11 Colvin (ed.) 1963, 1, 45.

12 *Pipe Roll 13 Henry II*, 1.

13 Adam of Eynsham, *Magna Vita Sancti Hugonis*, v. 17 (ed. D.L. Douie and H. Farmer, 2 vols, 1961–62, 11, 202).

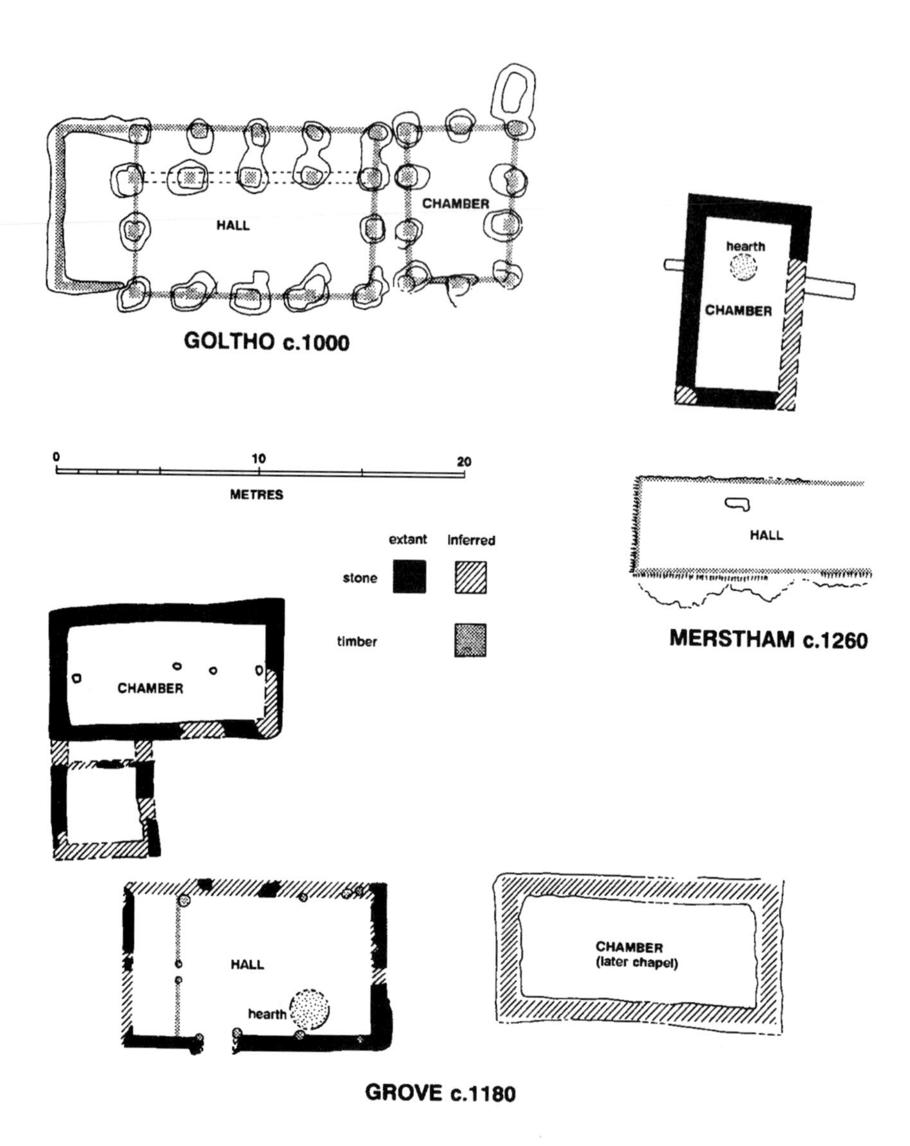

Figure 1. Three simple houses with free-standing halls and chambers: Goltho (after Beresford 1987); Grove (Based on site archive by permission of Mrs E. Baker); Alsted, Merstham (after Ketteringham 1976).

The following six examples have been chosen as particularly clear illustrations of the norms suggested by others:[14]

Horstead, Norfolk, 1106 × 1130: A house with a bower (*domum i cum buro*), a kitchen.[15]

Ardleigh, Essex, 1141: A good hall and chamber (*halla et camera*); a tresance (*trisanta*); a pentice (*appenditium*) against the hall on the south; a privy next to the chamber and another in the courtyard; a kitchen.[16]

Kensworth, Hertfordshire, 1152: A hall (*halla*) 35 feet long, 30 feet wide and 22 feet high (11 below the beams (*sub trabibus*) and 11 above); a chamber (*thalamus*) 22 feet long, 16 feet wide and 18 feet high (9 below the beams and 9 above); a house (*domus*) between the hall and the chamber, 12 feet long, 17 [*sic*] feet wide and 17 feet high (10 below the beams and 7 above).[17]

Thorp, Essex, c. 1160: A hall (*aula*); a chamber (*camera*); a tresance (*tresantia*), two privies; a kitchen.[18]

Oxford, c. 1195: A great house (*domus magna*) of stone, a cellar with solar above (*cellarium cum solario desuper*) of stone, a tiled privy, a chamber (*thalamus*) of stone, a house (*domus*) of stone and earth.[19]

Cuxham, Oxfordshire: In the later thirteenth century an existing building was known as the 'great chamber' or 'lord's chamber' (*magna camera, camera domini*). It was stone-built, and reached by wooden steps; a new timber hall was built up against it in 1331–2.[20]

These descriptions suggest four general conclusions. First, there is no indication that any of the halls was a storeyed building. The hall at Kensworth in 1152, 30 feet wide and 11 feet high from floor to tie-beam, was clearly open and almost certainly aisled. Secondly, the chambers at the early to mid-twelfth-century rural manors were also apparently single-storey buildings, and sound like later versions of the tenth- and eleventh-century bowers known from excavation; the Horstead survey actually uses the word *burum*. Thirdly, there were often ancillary buildings called 'houses', 'pentices' and 'tresances'; although *domus* can sometimes mean 'hall' (as at Horstead), the *domus* at Kensworth was evidently a connecting passage of some kind between the hall and the chamber. The impression is one of disparate buildings which might be linked by covered ways.[21] Fourthly, the group at Oxford in the 1190s, which stands for numerous urban

14 The following summaries list only the domestic buildings mentioned, not the agricultural ones.

15 *Charters and Custumals of the Abbey of Holy Trinity Caen*, ed. M. Chibnall (London, 1982), 36.

16 *The Domesday of St. Paul's*, ed. W.H. Hale (Camden Soc., old ser., 69, 1858), 136.

17 *Ibid.* 129.

18 *Ibid.* 132.

19 *The Cartulary of Oseney Abbey*, ed. H.E. Salter, II (Oxford Hist. Soc., 90, 1929), 283. I owe this reference to David Sturdy.

20 Harvey 1965, 32–4.

21 Several thirteenth-century references to 'pentices', making it clear that they were external corridors, are given by Turner 1851, 181–201.

descriptions of this sort, had a *solarium* over the cellar, not an *aula*; it looks as though the *domus magna* served as a hall. The Cuxham account (admittedly a century later) describes as a *camera* a free-standing stone building which had an important room on its upper floor.

From these archival sources we may turn to a literary one, Alexander Neckam's treatise *De Utensilibus*. This was written in about the late 1190s – in other words in the supposed *floruit* of the 'first-floor hall' – and refers to an aristocratic milieu: here, if anywhere, we should find a reflection of contemporary habits in domestic planning.[22] The following components of the ideal house are described:[23]

> *Hall (corpus aule, cors le sale):* its features include a lobby (or screens-passage?) (*vestibulum, porch*), a porch (*porticus honeste*). and posts (*postes, posz*) spaced at suitable intervals.
>
> *Chamber (camera, thalamus, la chaumbre):* contains curtains, drapes, a bed and bed-clothes.
>
> *Cellar (promptuarium, celarium, celer):* contains barrels, leather wine-bottles, coffers, baskets, beer, wine, etc.
>
> *Spense (dispensa, dispensatorium):* contains cloths, towels, knives, salt-cellar, cheesebin, candlesticks, carrying-baskets etc.
>
> *Kitchen (coquina, quisine):* contains cooking equipment.

While Neckam does not state explicitly that his *camera* is on the first floor, he clearly assumes the existence of an open aisled hall. Thus the hall was certainly not above the *celarium*, which can hardly be other than the sort of cellar normally found at semi-basement level under so-called 'first-floor halls'. *De Utensilibus* reinforces the conclusions, suggested by the other written sources, that the open hall remained ubiquitous throughout this period and that the word *aula* was not normally applied to an upper room.

Royal and Manorial Houses

Can the norms of domestic planning revealed by these written sources be observed in the standing and excavated remains of aristocratic houses? The answer to this question may be sought by considering sites where the overall layout and inter-relationship of component buildings can be recovered. The best starting point is a group of royal houses which are rooted in traditional English planning (notably the practice of aligning the buildings axially, used centuries earlier in the Northumbrian palace at Yeavering), and all of which include a larger and a smaller domestic component reasonably interpreted as the hall and the chamber.

22 Wright 1857, 96–119.

23 Words in brackets are Neckam's Latin and the near-contemporary French glosses.

Biggest by far was the palace of Westminster (fig. 2), dominated by William Rufus's vast hall. Aligned on the south end of this hall was a twelfth-century building containing a large and elaborate chamber over a vaulted undercroft; by the 1260s it was known as the 'little hall', but its twelfth-century designation is unknown.[24] Although this building was substantially larger than the ordinary chamber-blocks of the period, its juxtaposition with Westminster Hall is reminiscent of the juxtapositions of chamber-blocks with open halls at other sites. In its pairing of an open and public with a storeyed and more private building, Westminster displays traditional patterns of domestic planning articulated to the special needs of the main royal palace.

The Anglo-Saxon and Norman palace at Cheddar (Somerset) is probably more typical, and thanks to Philip Rahtz's excavations its successive phases can be traced much more clearly (fig. 2). At the end of the eleventh century, an aisled hall (termed by the excavator 'East Hall I') was built axially to the east of a small late Anglo-Saxon structure ('West Hall III'), rebuilt at the same time. It seems extremely likely that the 'West Hall', from which an end dais was removed at this stage, was adapted to serve as a *camera* or *bur* associated with the new 'East Hall', henceforth the hall proper.[25] In the early thirteenth century the 'East Hall' was itself rebuilt; a long building to its east, divided on the ground floor into four compartments, can be interpreted as a chamber-block replacing the old 'West Hall' which had now disappeared.[26] In any case it is clear that throughout the twelfth and thirteenth centuries, the main domestic building was an open ground-floor hall.

A third and rather later royal house is Henry II's at Clarendon (fig. 2). Although many of the buildings on the site date from Henry III's grandiose enlargements, some idea of the late twelfth-century plan can be recovered. Dominating the site is the aisled hall of the 1180s, with the kitchen to its west. A group of buildings east of the hall can be identified as the royal apartments of Henry III's time, and they include an earlier storeyed rectangular building which is reasonably interpreted as the *camera regis* mentioned in the 1160s.[27] This building was aligned roughly on the axis of the hall.

The alien priory of Grove (Bedfordshire) originated as a royal manor-house given to the order of Fontevrault by Henry II (fig. 1).[28] At the time of this gift, in

[24] For the thirteenth-century references see Colvin (ed.) 1963, I, 491–3; Lethaby 1906, 142; Binski 1986, 15, 22, 35. There is no clear evidence that the 'little hall' was the *nova aula* mentioned in 1167 (see note 12), though this building is otherwise unknown. I am grateful to Paul Binski for discussing this problem with me.

[25] Rahtz 1979, 60–2. The present interpretation of the functions of these buildings differs from the one published, but Philip Rahtz informs me (pers. comm.) that he does not consider it incompatible with the excavated evidence.

[26] Rahtz 1979, 62–4; again this is my interpretation, not the excavator's. The position of the 'South-east Building' near the service end of the hall is at first sight an obstacle to regarding it as a chamber-block; this may not, however, have applied in the early thirteenth century, since the service rooms were almost certainly added later. The limits of the excavation leave open the possibility that other, more peripheral chamber-blocks existed.

[27] James and Robinson 1988, 4–7, 64 fig. 10, 99–103.

[28] The complex sequence of excavated buildings is currently being assessed by Mrs Evelyn Baker, to whom I am extremely grateful for, permission to cite her latest thoughts and to use the plan reproduced in figure 1. This interpretation is radically different from the summaries hitherto published.

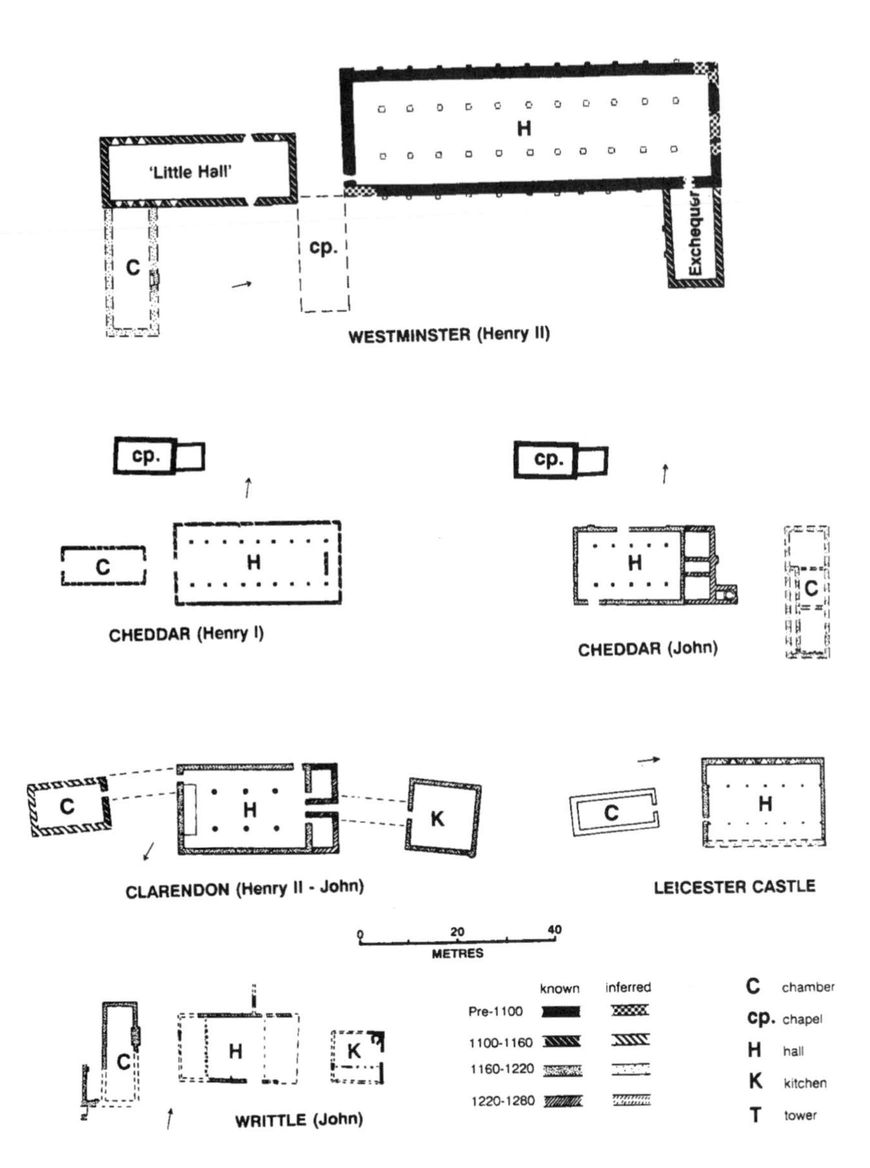

Figure 2. Royal and baronial houses on linear alignments: Westminster (after Colvin (ed.) 1963); Cheddar (after Rahtz 1979); Clarendon (after James and Robinson 1988); Writtle (after Rahtz 1969); Leicester (after Toy 1954, with further information from a survey by Edward Impey, 1992).

the 1150s, the main buildings consisted of an unaisled hall (apparently with a partitioned-off bay at its west end), to the east of which, and axially aligned on it, was a stone chamber-block later converted to a chapel. In the late twelfth century, an earlier timber structure north of the west end of the hall was rebuilt as a second chamber-block, evidently with, an upper floor supported on a row of posts.

Latest in this sequence of axially-planned royal houses is King John's hunting-lodge at Writtle (Essex) (fig. 2). The excavated early thirteenth-century buildings comprised an open hall (apparently with two internal screens), a detached kitchen to the east, and a long, narrow building (somewhat reminiscent of the early thirteenth-century compartmentalized range at Cheddar) to the west. This last stood where a chapel, a great chamber and two other chambers are recorded in 1419, and it may have been more complex in its internal arrangements than the imperfectly-surviving footings indicate.[29] It is at all events in a directly comparable position to the *camera regis* at Clarendon, at the end of the hall furthest from the kitchen.

Each of these five sites had both a hall and another major domestic building, in axial juxtaposition to each other. Although the identification of the second building as a *camera* is never (except perhaps at Clarendon) conclusive, a correlation with the written references to halls associated with *camerae* is too obvious to be resisted. The *camerae* were storeyed and solidly built at the grander sites (Westminster and Clarendon), but lighter and simpler elsewhere; this again is consistent with the conclusions already drawn from the documents.

Only a few excavations of ordinary secular manor-houses have produced coherent plans of a similar date. The house at Alsted, Merstham (Surrey) (fig. 1) comprised a small early thirteenth-century stone chamber-block alongside the platform of a timber building, and can be interpreted as a simple version of the detached hall and chamber plan.[30] Clearer to read is the moated courtyard house at Penhallam, Jacobstow (Cornwall) (fig. 5). Here the earliest recorded building is a late twelfth-century storeyed block, with a row of post-bases in the undercroft and a plinth for what was presumably a fireplace heating the great chamber above. Enlargements in the 1220s included an open hall at right-angles to this earlier block, with an enclosed stair at its 'high' end leading up to the great chamber.[31] This archaeological evidence from an ordinary manorial site tells the same story as the evidence discussed above: the two main components are the chamber-block and the open hall.

These documented and excavated sites provide a context for the beautifully preserved two-storey house at Boothby Pagnell (Lincolnshire), long celebrated

29 Rahtz 1969 (where the western building is interpreted as a chapel). I am grateful to Howard Colvin for the following description of the buildings in a survey of 1419 (Essex Record Office D/DP.M.546): 'una magna aula, et ad finem occidentalem eiusdem aule una capella bassa, et ad finem occidentalem eiusdem capelle una magna camera cum duabus aliis cameris eidem camere annexis, et ad finem orientalem eiusdem magne aule, supra panetriam et buteleriam, una camera qua dividitur in duas cameras'.

30 Ketteringham 1976, 8.

31 Beresford 1974, 90–127. Unfortunately nothing survived of the other late twelfth-century buildings which must have accompanied the chamber-block in its first phase.

Figure 3. Boothby Pagnell (Lincs.): chamber-block, c.1200 (from Turner 1851, between pp. 52–3).

as the paradigm of the 'first-floor hall' (fig. 3): they leave little room for doubt that contemporaries would have described such a building as *camera* rather than *aula*. In the light of this new model, several examples can now be recognized in twelfth-century castles, for instance Framlingham (Suffolk) and Great Chesterton (Oxfordshire).[32] The so-called 'solar tower', exemplified in a sequence of buildings between the late eleventh and mid-thirteenth centuries such as Chilham (Kent), Witney (Oxfordshire), Greenhythe (Kent) and Old Soar (Kent),[33] may be defined as a version of the chamber-block which is squatter and often has more than one storey above the basement: in essence it is a chamber-block adapted to the needs of a defensive or semi-defensive site.

Most surviving houses of the Boothby Pagnell type date from *c.* 1170–1220 rather than earlier. As is clear from the texts quoted above, many *camerae* on ordinary twelfth-century manorial sites were simple single-storey buildings. The wide diffusion of the chamber-over-basement type may be a distinctively late twelfth-century phenomenon, an elaboration of the traditional timber bower influenced by strong-houses and keeps of earlier decades and a higher social level. In Alexander Neckam's up-to-date house of the 1190s, the chamber and cellar would surely have been contained within a building such as this.

Both more adaptable and more durable, stone *camerae* have survived better than the timber open halls which would once have stood near them, and which

32 Raby and Reynolds 1989; Blair 1984.

33 Clapham 1928; Durham 1984; Gravett and Renn 1981; Wood 1950, 36–8.

Figure 4. Barnack (Northants): two-bay aisled hall, c.1200 (now demolished; from Turner 1851, between pp. 52–3).

by definition would have lacked substantial chambers. attached to either end. Small manorial halls of this type from the early to mid-thirteenth centuries are, however, being recognized in increasing numbers, as at Barnack (Northamptonshire) (fig. 4), Sandal Castle (Yorkshire), Fyfield (Essex), Temple Balsall (Warwickshire), Harwell (Berkshire) and Chalton (Hampshire).[34] The obvious reason why these, like much grander halls, seem to have such scanty private accommodation is that they were accompanied by free-standing chamber-blocks which have disappeared.

Sadly, no ordinary English manor-house with substantial and unambiguous remains of both components has yet been discovered. At Leicester Castle (fig. 2), however, a cellar axially aligned on the aisled hall has walls which are clearly older than the late medieval vaulting and may well survive from a twelfth- century chamber undercroft. Much clearer are two of the French cases discussed by Impey (1993): Beaumont-le-Richard, where the hall and chamber-block are loosely aligned as at Westminster, Cheddar and Clarendon,

[34] Turner 1851, 52–3; Michelmore 1983, 73–5 (end aisles partitioned off leaving a small service bay at one end and a still smaller space at the other); Smith 1955, figs. 1–2; Alcock 1982; Fletcher 1979 (though this house is now known to have been misidentified); Cunliffe 1969.

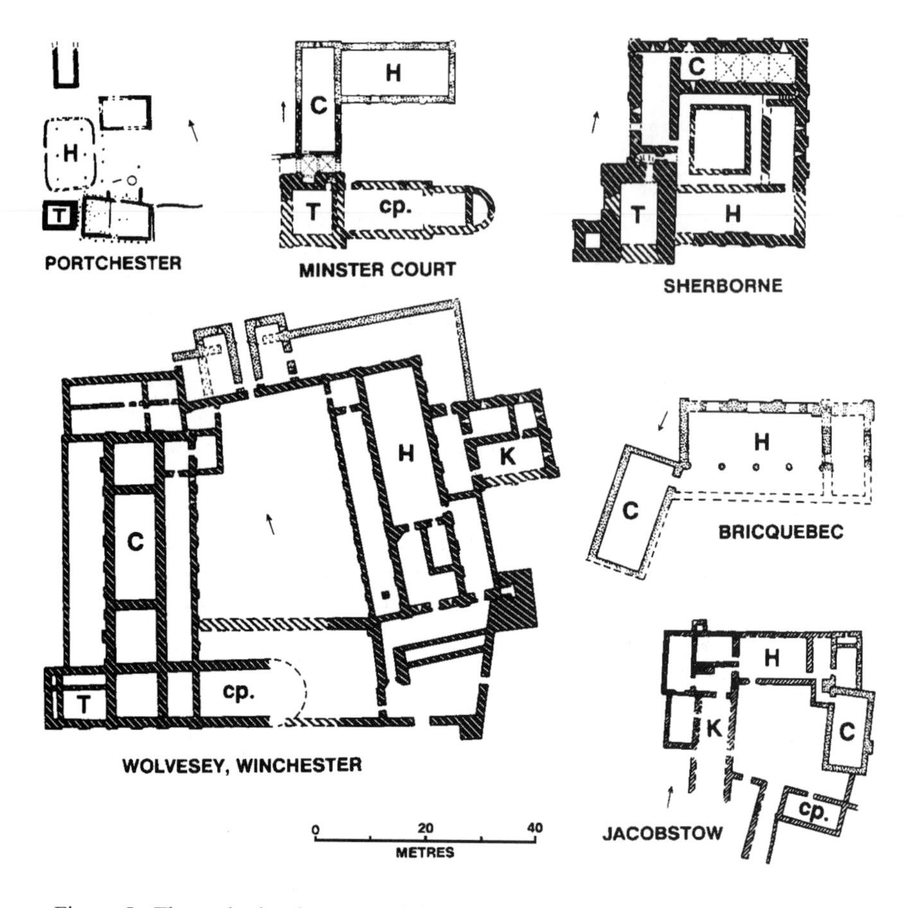

Figure 5. The early development of the courtyard house: Portchester (after Cunliffe 1976); Minster Court (after Kipps 1929, with amendments by E. Impey); Sherborne (after White 1983); Wolvesey (after Biddle 1972); Bricquebec (after chapter by E. Impey, in *Manorial Domestic Buildings in England and Northern France*, ed. G. Meirion-Jones and M. Jones [London, 1993], figs 13–18); Jacobstow (after Beresford 1974) (for key to conventions see fig. 2).

and the rather later and more developed Bricquebec (fig. 5) where they meet corner-to-corner as at Jacobstow. As well as hinting that high-status domestic planning in England and northern France may have developed along much closer lines than is. usually supposed, these buildings reveal with particular clarity the problems inherent in the traditional model. If the storeyed ranges at Beaumont and Bricquebec had stood in England, and had happened to survive in isolation, English architectural historians would unhesitatingly have classified them as 'first-floor halls'.

The royal and manorial houses derive the main features of their planning from traditional insular practice, albeit translated into grander and more modern forms. But the palaces of twelfth-century bishops form a distinct group: they are distinguished by a predilection for courtyard rather than axial layouts, they are more tightly integrated, and they are more exotic in some of their details.[35] Several have two main components, one open and the other raised over a basement, which are usually described as 'double halls'. But in fact the model of hall and chamber is as applicable to these palaces as it is to aristocratic houses of other kinds.

The two fortified houses built by Roger, bishop of Salisbury (1107–39), at Sherborne (fig. 5) and at Old Sarum Castle, are unique in their regularity and their integration.[36] The main ranges are set around square courtyards with covered walks like cloisters, and in each case there is a corner tower. Halls probably occupied the south range at Sherborne and the west range at Old Sarum; the facing ranges, in other words the north at Sherborne and the east at Old Sarum, contained large upper rooms which are surely to be interpreted as the great chambers. The only essential difference between Roger's castles and a house such as Briquebec is that they are more integrated, the hall and chamber being linked by lesser ranges to form a completely enclosed courtyard.

The same applies to Wolvesey Palace at Winchester (fig. 5), the vast fortified house of the bishops of Winchester built during the first half of the twelfth century.[37] Wolvesey is less regular than Roger's houses, but much larger. There is a gatehouse in the north range, and a chapel in the south. The other ranges contain the two main elements: on the east the open hall and its annexes, including a kitchen designed in imitation of a stone keep, and on the west a long room raised over a solid basement with smaller flanking rooms and, a corridor. Although usually called the 'west hall' this range is better interpreted as the main chamber-block.

Two smaller early twelfth-century houses of the bishops of Winchester echo features of Wolvesey. Bishop's Waltham (Hampshire) has a south-west corner tower from which a long storeyed range extends northwards; there are fragmentary remains of the south and east ranges, the latter including a chapel.[38] At Witney (Oxfordshire) the tower-lodging is at the south-east corner, but the east range again contains the chapel; there are fragments of the north range, including a gatehouse and lodgings, and later documentary evidence for a hall in the west range.[39]

These palaces of *c.*1100–40 are a highly distinctive group, drawing on traditions of ecclesiastical as well as of domestic planning. Besides the obvious resemblance of Roger's houses to monastic cloisters, the corner towers (which at least at Sherborne and Witney functioned as lodgings) recall the massive west

35 For another recent survey of this group see James 1990, 42–7.

36 RCHM 1952, 64–6 and plan; RCHM 1980, 6–11 and plan; Stalley 1971, 65–70; White 1983. Both Stalley and White interpret the grand upper room in the north range as Sherborne as a chapel, but on no more substantial evidence than that it is elaborately decorated. At Old Sarum castle, the change in levels by the height of a full storey renders ambiguous the relationship between the ranges, and it is unclear whether the main chamber was in the east range, over cellarage, or in the north range which stands on solid ground.

37 Biddle 1972, 125–31.

38 Publication of the late S.E. Rigold's excavations at Bishop's Waltham is in progress. I am grateful to Jane Geddes and John Hare for advice, though my interpretation does not necessarily agree with theirs.

39 Durham 1984.

towers characteristic of major episcopal churches, derived ultimately from the Ottonian *Westwerk*.[40] It is instructive to compare Sherborne and Old Sarum with the monastic grange of *c.*1100 at Minster Court, Thanet (fig. 5), where a hall, a lodging range and a church with a great west tower form three sides of a courtyard.[41] This arrangement is strikingly foreshadowed by a small early eleventh-century complex excavated at Portchester Castle (fig. 5), where a timber aisled hall and two domestic ranges formed three sides of a courtyard which had a stone tower at its southwest corner.[42] In the mid-eleventh century, a rich priest of Abingdon built himself a house said in the Abingdon Chronicle to resemble a monastic cloister, comprising a church with two ranges at right-angles containing the hall, kitchen and lodgings.[43] The true context of episcopal courtyard houses may be a lost group of eleventh-century establishments on the borderline between secular and monastic, perhaps including the dwellings of unreformed minster clergy and cathedral canons.[44]

From the 1170s onwards, episcopal palaces planned on a simpler and more open version of the courtyard layout appear in increasing numbers (fig. 6). The format of a large hall, a chamber-block either at right-angles or parallel, and a range closing one of the two remaining sides of the courtyard, occurs at Old Sarum (the house adjoining the cathedral, not to be confused with the castle), at Hereford, at Lincoln and at Canterbury, the chamber ranges at Canterbury and Old Sarum being reused early Norman buildings.[45] Several decades into the thirteenth century, the palace at Wells perpetuates this arrangement in its sumptuous storeyed chamber-block, linked by a chapel to the aisled hall.[46] It was doubtless in emulation of these palaces that early thirteenth-century manorial gentry started to build modest courtyard houses such as Jacobstow, which were in turn to influence manor-house planning in the late Middle Ages.

The Development of Halls and Services in the later Twelfth Century

In England the grand secular aisled hall is a feature of the later twelfth century, influenced by the architecture of great churches and, perhaps more immediately, by monastic infirmaries such as those at Canterbury and Ely. Pre-1150 aisled

40 For a recent survey of some English examples, with references, see Blair 1989, 68–70.

41 Kipps 1929.

42 Cunliffe 1976. There is no documentary evidence that the site was ecclesiastical, but the small cemetery established in the eleventh century on the site of the hall provides a strong suggestion that it was.

43 *Chronicon Monasterii de Abingdon*, 2 vols, ed. J. Stevenson (Rolls Ser., Chronicles and Memorials, 2, London 1858), I, 474: 'ecclesiam . . . fabricavit, cuius in lateribus dextrorsum et sinistrorsum claustralibus ad monachorum formam habitaculorum, cum domibus edendi, victusque coquendi, quiescendique, et ceteris conversationi virorum necessariis mirifice coaptatis'.

44 The first phase of the house by Old Sarum cathedral (fig. 6) is worth considering in the light of the last suggestion: was it originally built for the canons?

45 Note 47 below for Old Sarum; Blair 1987, 67–9; Chapman, Coppack and Drewett 1975; Rady, Tatton-Brown and Bowen 1991. The chamber-block at Canterbury was a building of Lanfranc's time, connected to the north-west corner tower of the cathedral. At Lincoln the chamber-block is known as the 'east hall', a name resulting from the same wrong premise as that of the 'west hall' at Wolvesey.

46 Wood 1965, 23–4. Once again, the storeyed range is usually conceived as an earlier hall, but is clearly a direct descendant of the main chamber-blocks in twelfth-century palaces.

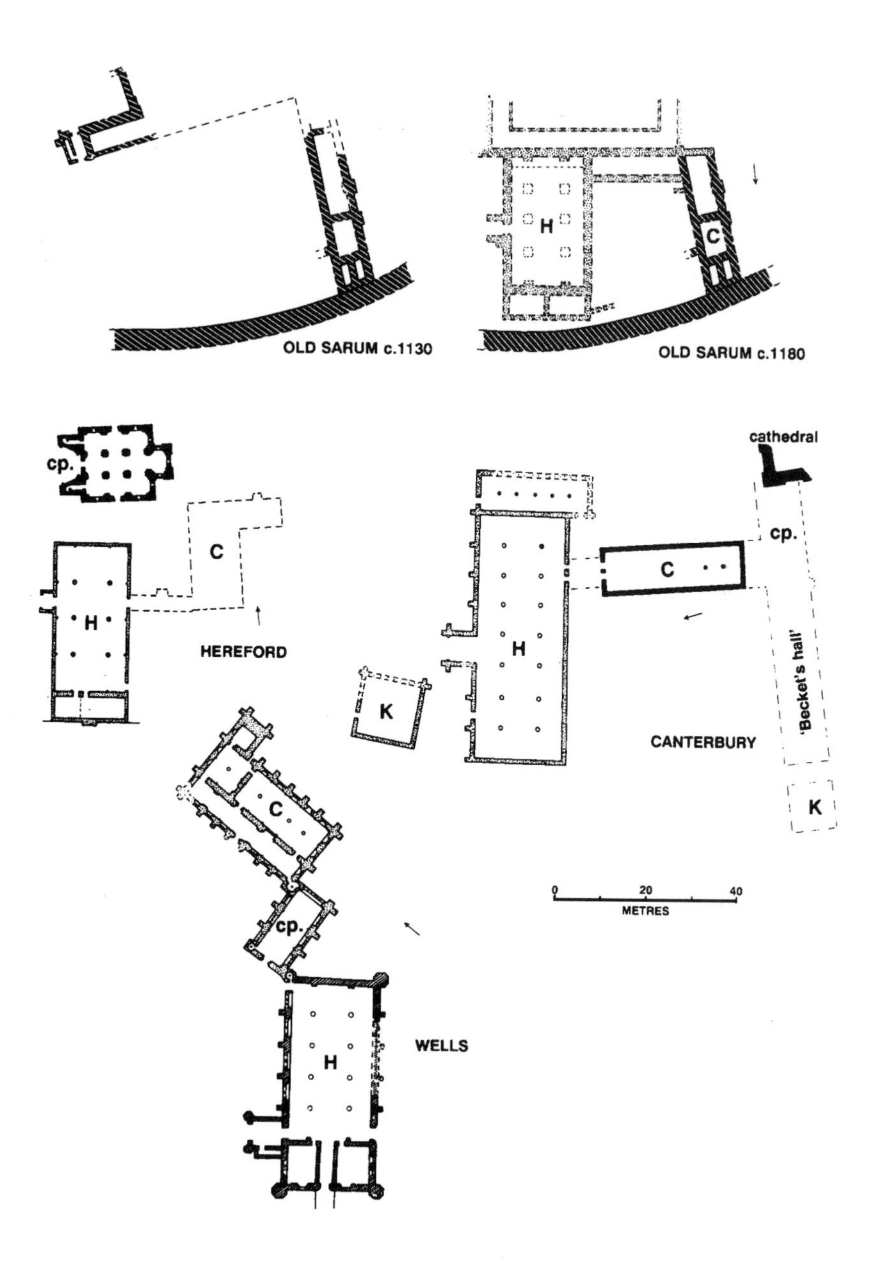

Figure 6. Bishops' palaces, mid-twelfth to mid-thirteenth centuries: Old Sarum (after Hawley 1914–15 and Hawley 1915–16, with new phasing); Hereford (after Blair 1987); Canterbury (after Rady, Tatton-Brown and Bowen 1991); Wells (after Wood 1965) (for key to conventions see fig. 2).

halls so far known in England (such as Goltho, Portchester and Cheddar 'East Hall I') are of a supra-vernacular character, modest in conception and simple in construction. A supposed early twelfth-century example on a grander scale, the hall of the house beside Old Sarum cathedral, has clearly been misdated: it overlies the east range of a courtyard apparently laid out *c.*1100, and should be ascribed to a reconstruction in *c.*1160–80 which retained the existing west range as its chamber-block (fig. 6).[47] Even the most elaborate early twelfth-century complexes, such as Sherborne and Wolvesey, had halls which were unaisled and relatively narrow, with tall side walls. This form, also exemplified on a very grand scale by the 'Echiquier' at Caen (Impey, 1993) is an Anglo-Norman aristocratic fashion which may reflect the influence of monastic refectories.

The first evidence that architecturally ambitious halls were becoming at all common dates from the third quarter of the twelfth century, with the fragmentary timber arcades at Leicester (fig. 2) and Farnham castles.[48] In the Midlands and the South, the fashion was developed in halls of the 1170s and 1180s such as Hereford bishop's palace (in timber imitating stone) (fig. 6), Clarendon palace (fig. 2) and Oakham Castle.[49] In northern England, the tradition of grand aisled halls with stone arcades has been traced through Archbishop Roger's hall of *c.*1170 at York[50] to Hugh du Puiset's halls at Durham and Bishop Auckland, and to their ecclesiastical analogue, his Galilee at Durham Cathedral.[51] The proliferation of sumptuous halls, like that of storeyed stone chamber-blocks, is less an early Norman phenomenon than a reflection of the growing personal wealth of Angevin England.

A feature of the grandest later twelfth-century halls was the. development of cellarage at the 'lower' end with subsidiary chambers above. Chronologically isolated, and startlingly precocious, is Wolvesey Palace at Winchester, where the early twelfth-century 'east hall' included a three-storey chamber-block at its south end (fig. 5). Hereford (*c.*1180) had a tall, narrow range of three storeys over a basement, in series with the hall, while a basement of similar proportions has been excavated at the end of the huge early thirteenth-century archiepiscopal hall at Canterbury (fig. 6).[52] Although these halls lacked the service doorways and screens-passage which were soon to become ubiquitous, they clearly foreshadow the developed service end.

47 Interim reports are Halesey 1913–14, Hawley 1914–15 and Hawley 1915–16; Hawley's phasing is substantially followed by RCHM 1980, 15–22. The latrine-block at the north end of the west range is contemporary with, or earlier than, the early twelfth-century curtain wall. However, Hawley's 1915 season revealed a substantial building, at right-angles to the west range but on a different alignment from the hall, which partly underlay the cloister. Hawley's diaries (now in Salisbury Museum) make it clear that his excavations were innocent of stratigraphy, and there seem to be no grounds for preferring his interpretation to the one proposed here in figure 4.

48 Alcock 1987. His dating of the Leicester arcades is perhaps too early, and the Farnham arcades are associated with high-quality masonry of *c.*1180.

49 Blair 1987, 63; James and Robinson 1988, 5–7, 90–6; Turner 1851, 28–31, Wood 1974, 47–9, and James 1990, 60–3.

50 Gerald of Wales, *De Vita Galfridi Archiepiscopi Eboracensis, in Giraldi Cambrensis Opera*, 8 vols, ed. D.S. Brewer (Rolls Ser., Chronicles and Memorials, 21, London 1873), IV, 367n: *et columnis sublimibus erectam, pariisque structures et marmore distinctam.*

51 Halsey 1980, 67. Cf. James 1990, 52.

52 Biddle 1972, 127–8; Blair 1987, 63–7; Rady, Tatton-Brown and Bowen 1991.

The distinctive elements of fully-fledged services are (i) a buttery and pantry entered through separate doorways in the end wall of the hall; (ii) a main hall entrance at the lower end of one of the side walls, at right-angles to these doorways; and (iii) a facing entrance in the opposite wall, allowing the formation of a screens-passage. There is thus a critical difference between houses of *c.*1160–80 where the entrance or porch is in the centre of the side wall (notably Old Sarum and Hereford, fig. 6),[53] and houses of *c.*1190 onwards where it is usually placed at the lower end. This change is the clearest signal of the advent of the screens-passage, the first well-attested case of which is in the 1190s at Bishop Auckland Castle.[54] Neckam's prescription of a *vestibulum* adjoining the hall porch (above) may well refer to this newest of innovations. Permutations occur, however, over several decades. As already noted, the early thirteenth-century archbishop's hall at Canterbury had a single undercroft rather than service-rooms, and accordingly still had a centrally-placed porch (fig. 6). The juxtaposition of service-doors and main entrance can also occur where there is no opposed entrance, as at Oakham in the 1180s,[55] or a century later at Stokesay (Shropshire) where the moat precludes a through-passage.

Continuing the precedent of Wolvesey and Hereford, large houses of *c.*1190–1230 normally had a subsidiary chamber above the services, reached from the hall by a timber stair such as still survives (albeit a century later) at Stokesay. Bricquebec (Impey, 1993), where the chamber over the services was entered from the hall by a grand high-level doorway, is again an important parallel, suggesting that the arrangement was well known in Anglo-Norman aristocratic society by the end of the twelfth century. At Oakham, the lower end wall of the hall retains service doorways in conjunction with a first-floor doorway approached from the north aisle. In the small manor-house at Appleton (Berkshire) the service doors (one slightly larger than the other) are flanked, on the side furthest from the main entrance, by a full-height quoined opening which probably contained a straight stair from the hall to the chamber above.[56] At Warnford (Hampshire), slightly later than Appleton but more complete, one entrance to the cross-passage survives and the other appears on a plan of 1779. Two service doorways lead to basements of unequal size; above these was a single chamber, entered from the hall through a high-level doorway.[57]

A further sophistication, the separation of the two service rooms by a passage allowing direct access from the hall to the kitchen, occurs at Clarendon, Old Sarum and Cheddar East Hall II (figs 2 and 6), but in all three cases the

53 Cf. Blair 1987, 65–7. Both halls had service doorways, but they were later at Old Sarum (note 58 below) and of unknown date at Hereford.

54 Cunningham 1990, 87–8.

55 *VCH Rutland*, 2 (1935), 8–10 (showing the original position of the entrance, moved since 1730), and references in note 49.

56 Wood 1974, 21–2 and Pl. IA; the quoined opening (identified in a new survey by J. Blair, C. Currie and E. Impey, *Oxoniensia*, 57 (1992), 100–2) is not shown on Wood's plan but can be seen indistinctly in the plate. It is unknown whether this house had a cross-passage, since the hall entrance now faces a later oriel window. A pair of service doorways very similar to those at Appleton has recently been identified by J. Blair at Maunds Farmhouse, Deddington (Oxfordshire).

57 Wood 1950, 27–9.

service-blocks are additions of unknown, probably thirteenth-century date.[58] This plan may be used *c.*1180 at Farnham Castle (Surrey) and at Oakham, though in neither case is the function of the three doorways entirely clear;[59] it survives intact in the thirteenth-century episcopal halls at Lincoln and Wells (fig. 6), and is documented in royal works at Guildford in 1244.[60]

The Integration of Halls and chamber-Blocks

It is a curious fact that although the aristocratic houses discussed above were made up of free-standing components, integrated all-timber houses are known from an early date. The late tenth-century house at Sulgrave (Northamptonshire) consisted of a long range with complex internal divisions, including a pair of opposed doorways associated with a screen.[61] The twelfth-century houses at Ellington (Huntingdonshire) and Brooklands (Surrey) each had a pair of rooms separated by a cross-passage and with a screened-off compartment in the larger room.[62] It might be argued that these are more akin to the long-house than to the late medieval hall-house. But in 1183 the tenants of Bishop Auckland (Co. Durham) were obliged to build a hunting-lodge which sounds like a fully-integrated house of a century later: *faciunt aulam episcopi in foresta, longitudinis lx pedum et latitudinis infra postes xvj pedum, cum butilleria et dispensa, et cameram et privatam; preterea faciunt capellam longitudinis xl pedum et latitudinis xv pedum.*[63] It appears that in the twelfth century, as much later, the grandest houses were often the least compact. Aspects of the planning conventions adopted from the 1180s onwards may thus have drawn on an established vernacular tradition.

In great houses the integration of the main chamber-block with the upper end of the hall lagged somewhat behind the development of services at its lower end, as is clear from the plans of palaces in figure 6: In lesser houses too, the separation of *aula* and *camera* remained common well after 1200. The thirteenth-century manor-house at Harwell had a detached chamber-block, as well as a compartment at the end of the hall called the 'wardrobe' or *extrema camera.*[64] As late as *c.*1300 the house built at Eltham (Kent) by Bishop Bek had a cellared chamber-block separated by a four-metre gap from the high end of the hall, while the hall at Nurstead (Kent) was linked to a slightly older chamber block corner-to-corner.[65] But starting probably in about the 1220s or 1230s, and

[58] James and Robinson 1988, 90–4 and fig. 23 (showing the services at Clarendon butt jointed to the late twelfth-century hall), 236; Hawley 1914–15, 234 and plan facing p. 232; Rahtz 1979, 178–86.

[59] *VCH Surrey*, 2 (1905), 600 and facing plan; Nairn and Pevsner 1971, 233. See note 55 above for Oakham, where the three doorways are not, however, arranged symmetrically.

[60] Colvin (ed.) 1963, II, 950.

[61] Davison 1977, 109–11.

[62] Tebbutt *et al.* 1971, 31–73; Rigold 1977, 55–8. Rigold perceptively notes: 'Perhaps it is better to adduce the three requirements in the 12th century leases of St. Paul's . . ., *camera* or *thalamus*, *aula* and *domus* . . ., and to find them precociously forced into a single building but thought of as separate.'

[63] *Boldon Buke*, ed. W. Greenwell (Surtees Soc., 25, 1852), 26.

[64] Fletcher 1979, 176, 187–9.

[65] Woods 1982, 218–27; Cherry 1989, 458–60.

increasingly common thereafter, are surviving or excavated houses in which the main chamber-block is attached directly to the upper end of the hall. This development, not surprisingly, is often seen in the upgrading of old houses: replacement halls were built up against the sides of existing chamber-blocks, and chamber-blocks were added to existing halls. On three quasi-monastic sites, the alien priory of Cogges (Oxfordshire) and the Templars' *camerae* at Strood (Kent) and Harefield (Middlesex), halls were built against older chamber-blocks at dates between the mid-thirteenth and early fourteenth centuries, a sequence which is also recorded in the manorial accounts for Cuxham (Oxfordshire).[66] A more integrated example (though even here the two elements may not be exactly coeval) is the manor-house at Burmington (Warwickshire), where the two-bay (or three-bay) aisled hall and the storeyed solar wing are both of the early thirteenth century.[67] At Woodstock palace in the 1230s the 'king's high chamber' was at one end of the hall, and was entered by a flight of stone steps from the courtyard.[68] After 1300, the addition of spacious chamber-blocks to existing halls became ubiquitous practice.[69]

Terminology in the first half of the thirteenth century was fluid, as it so often is at times of rapid change. Some descriptions are ambiguous to the extent that they list 'chambers' at both ends of the hall. Thus a farm at Thorpe or Egham (Surrey) in 1241 included *aula et duobus talamis eidem aule adiunctis*, while a monastic grange at Addington (Surrey) in the late thirteenth century comprised a hall with a *maior solarium* and a *minor solarium*.[70] Perhaps because the *camera* basement had always been a service room, the services in some of these earlier small integrated houses were not at the 'lower' end of the hall but under the main chamber, which increasingly is called the *solarium*. The early thirteenth-century chamber-blocks at Little Chesterford (Essex) and Hambledon (Hampshire) have service-doors in their side walls at basement level, presumably once communicating with attached halls.[71] The manor-house at Sandon (Hertfordshire) described in a text of *c.*1258, apparently built within the previous twenty years, consisted of a hall with a wardrobe (*warderoba*) at one head and a 'spense' with a solar (*spenseriam cum solario*), at the other; the 'spense' was presumably a service-room under the solar.[72]

But the pattern was about to crystallize. In 1268 the monks of Eynsham made a contract for a house to be built at Histon (Cambridgeshire). It was to contain a hall with a 'spense' (*dispensa*) at one end and a suitable chamber with a privy

66 Blair and Steane 1982, 69–84; Rigold 1965. For Cuxham see above, p. 311.

67 Cooper 1985, 27–30; Brodie 1990, 92. The likelihood of a third hall bay was suggested by a small excavation in 1993.

68 Colvin (ed.) 1963, 11, 1011. The arrangement must have been very similar to Stokesay.

69 Examples are Faccombe, Hampshire (Fairbrother 1975), Bisham, Berkshire (Fletcher and Hewett 1969), Chalgrove, Oxfordshire (excavation by the Oxford Archaeological Unit, report in progress) and Harwell, Berkshire (Fletcher 1979, 176–9).

70 PRO, CP25(i)/226/11(247); Blair 1978. The stated dimensions of the *solarii* at Addington suggest that they were cross-wings.

71 Wood 1950, 19–22, 106. Little Chesterford still has remains of a later thirteenth-century hall in this position.

72 St Paul's Cathedral inventory: Guildhall Library MS 25,324. The house had apparently not existed, at least in this form, at the time of the previous lease in 1239: MS 25,122/1220.

(*unam cameram competentem cum necessariis camere*) at the other, all of which were to be under one roof (*erunt sub eodem tecto*).[73] This defines, in essence, the classic three-part house of later medieval England: at the upper end of the hall the great chamber, perhaps over a parlour, and at the lower end the services, either with or without a lesser chamber above them. For the next three centuries, English houses at all levels but the lowest were to approximate to this type.

Bibliography

ALCOCK, N. W. 1982. 'The hall of the Knights Templars at Temple Balsall, W. Midlands', *Medieval Archaeol.*, 25, 155–8

———, 1987. 'Leicester Castle: the great hall', *Medieval Archaeol.*, 31, 73–9

BERESFORD, G. 1974. 'The medieval manor of Penhallam, Jacobstow, Cornwall', *Medieval Archaeol.*, 18, 90–145

———, 1987. *Goltho: the Development of an Early Medieval Manor c.850–1150*, HBMC(E) Archaeol. Rep., 4, London

BIDDLE, M. 1972. 'Excavations at Winchester, 1970: ninth interim report', *Antiq. J.*, 52, 93–131

BINSKI, P. 1986. *The Painted Chamber at Westminster*, Soc. Antiq. London Occ. Pap., new ser., 9, London

BLAIR, W.J. 1978. 'A late thirteenth-century survey of buildings on estates of Southwark Priory', *Antiq. J.*, 58, 353–4

———, 1984. 'Great Chesterton, Manor House', *Medieval Archaeol.*, 28, 235–6

———, 1987. 'The twelfth-century bishop's palace at Hereford', *Medieval Archaeol.*, 31, 59–72

———, 1989. 'The early church at Cumnor', *Oxoniensia*, 54, 57–70

BLAIR, W.J. and STEANE, J.M. 1982. 'Investigations at Cogges, Oxfordshire, 1978–81', *Oxoniensia*, 47, 37–125

BRODIE, A.M. 1990. 'The sculpture of Burmington Manor, Warwickshire', in *Medieval Architecture and its Intellectual Context: Studies in Honour of Peter Kidson* (eds E. Fernie and P. Crossley), 91–101, London

BROWN, A.N., HOWES, B., and TURNER, R.C. 1986. 'A medieval stone townhouse in Chester', *J. Chester Archaeol. Soc.*, 68, 143–53

CHAPMAN, H., COPPACK, G. and DREWETT, P. 1975. *Excavations at the Bishop's Palace, Lincoln, 1968–72*, Occ. Pap. Lincolnshire Hist. Archaeol., 1, Lincoln

CHERRY, M. 1989. 'Nurstead Court, Kent: a reappraisal', *Arch. Journ.*, 146, 451–64

CLAPHAM, A.W. 1928. 'An early hall at Chilham Castle, Kent', *Antiq. Journ.*, 8, 350–3.

CORD, J.G. and STREETEN, A.D.F. 1982. 'Excavations at Castle Acre Castle, Norfolk, 1972–77: country house and castle of the Norman earls of Surrey', *Arch. Journ.*, 139, 138–301

COLVIN, H.M. (ed.), 1963. *The History of the King's Works: I: The Middle Ages*, HMSO, London

COOPER, N. 1985. 'Burmington Manor, Warwickshire: the thirteenth-century building', *RCHM (England) Annual Review 1985*, London

CUNLIFFE, B.W. 1969. 'Hampshire: Chalton', *Med. Arch.*, 13, 269–71

———, 1976. *Excavations at Portchester Castle. II: Saxon*, Soc. Antiq. London Res. Rep., 33, London

[73] *The Cartulary of the Abbey of Eynsham*, 2 vols, ed. H.E. Salter (Oxford Hist. Soc., 49, 51, 1906–7, 1908), I, 260.

CUNNINGHAM, J. 1990. 'Auckland Castle: some recent discoveries', in *Medieval Architecture and its Intellectual Context: Studies in Honour of Peter Kidson* (eds E. Fernie and P. Crossley), 81–90, London

DAVISON, B.K. 1977. 'Excavations at Sulgrave, Northamptonshire, 1960–76', *Arch. Journ.*, 134, 105–14

DURHAM, B.G. 1984. *Witney Palace: Excavations at Mount House, Witney, in 1984*, Oxford Archaeological Unit, Oxford

FAIRBROTHER, J.A. 1975. 'Hampshire: Faccombe, Netherton', *Med. Arch.*, 19, 250–1

FAULKNER, P.A. 1958. 'Domestic planning from the twelfth to the fourteenth centuries', *Arch. Journ.*, 105, 150–83

FLETCHER, J.M. 1979. 'The bishop of Winchester's medieval manor-house at Harwell, Berkshire', *Arch. Journ.*, 136, 173–92

FLETCHER, J.M. and HEWETT, C.A. 1969. 'Medieval timberwork at Bisham Abbey', *Med. Arch.*, 13, 220–4

GRAVETT, K.W.E. and RENN, D.F. 1981. 'The tower of Stone Castle, Greenhythe', *Archaeol. Cantiana*, 97, 312–18

HALSEY, R. 1980. 'The Galilee chapel', in *Medieval Art and Architecture at Durham Cathedral*, Brit. Archaeol. Assoc. Conference Trans., 3 (for 1977), 59–73

HAWLEY, W. 1913–14; 1914–15; 1915–16. Interim reports on the excavations at Old Sarum Cathedral, *Proc. Soc. Antiq. London*, 26, 100–19; 27, 230–9; 28, 174–84

HARVEY, P.D.A. 1965. *A Medieval Oxfordshire Village*, Oxford

HURST, J.G. (ed.) 1979. *Wharram: a Study of Settlement on the Yorkshire Wolds*, Soc. Medieval Archaeol. Monograph Ser., 8, London

IMPEY, E. 1993. 'Seigneurial Domestic Architecture in Normandy 1050–1350', in *Manorial Domestic Buildings in England and Northern France* (eds G. Meirion-Jones and M. Jones), 82–120, London

JAMES, T.B. 1990. *The Palaces of Medieval England*, London

JAMES, T.B. and ROBINSON, A.M. 1988. *Clarendon Palace. The History and Archaeology of a Medieval Palace and Hunting-Lodge near Salisbury, Wiltshire*, Soc. Antiq. London Res. Rep., 45, London

KETTERINGHAM, L.L. 1976. *Alsted: Excavation of a Thirteenth-Fourteenth-Century Sub-Manor House*, Surrey Archaeol. Soc. Research Vol. 2, Guildford

KEYNES, S. 1992. 'The Fonthill Letter', in *Words, Texts and Manuscripts: Studies in Anglo-Saxon Culture Presented to Helmut Gneuss* (ed. M. Korhammer), 53–97, Cambridge

KIPPS, P.K. 1929. 'Minster Court, Thanet', *Arch. Journ.*, 86, 213–23

LETHABY, W.R. 1906. 'The palace of Westminster in the eleventh and twelfth centuries', *Archaeologia*, 60, 131–48

MICHELMORE, D.J.H. 1983. 'Interpretation of the buildings of the timber phase', in *Sandal Castle Excavations* 1964–1973 (eds P. Mayes and L.A.S. Butler), Wakefield Historical Publications, 73–5, Wakefield

RCHM 1952. *An Inventory of the Historical Monuments in Dorset*, 1, London

RCHM 1980. *Ancient and Historical Monuments in the City of Salisbury*, 1, London

RABY, F.J.E., and REYNOLDS, P.K.B. 1989. *Framlingham Castle*, revised reprint, English Heritage, London

RADY, J., TATTON-BROWN, T., and BOWEN, J.A. 1991. 'The Archbishop's Palace, Canterbury', *Journ. BAA.*, 144, 1–60

RAHTZ, P.A. 1969. *Excavations at King John's Hunting Lodge, Writtle, Essex*, Soc. Medieval Archaeol. Monograph Ser., 3, London

———, 1979. *The Saxon and Medieval Palaces at Cheddar*, Brit. Archaeol. Rep. Brit. Ser., 65, Oxford

RIGOLD, S.E. 1965. 'Two camerae of the military orders', *Arch. Journ.*, 122, 86–132
———, 1971. 'Eynsford Castle and its excavation', *Archaeologia Cantiana*, 86, 109–71
———, 1977. 'Discussion of the medieval buildings', in *Brooklands, Weybridge: the Excavation of an Iron Age and Medieval Site 1964–5 and 1970–71* (R. Hanworth and D.J. Tomalin), Surrey Archaeol. Soc. Research Vol. 4, Guildford
SMITH, J.T. 1955. 'Medieval aisled halls and their derivatives', *Arch. Journ.* 112, 76–94
STALLEY, R.A. 1971. 'A twelfth-century patron of architecture: a study of the buildings erected by Roger bishop of Salisbury', *Journ. BAA*, 3rd ser., 34, 62–83
TEBBUTT, C.F. et al. 1971. 'Excavation of a moated site at Ellington, Huntingdonshire', *Proc. Cambridge Antiq. Soc.*, 63, 31–73
TOY, S. 1954. *The Castles of Great Britain*, 2nd edn, London
TURNER, T.H. 1851. *Some Account of Domestic Architecture in England from the Conquest to the End of the Thirteenth Century*, Oxford
WEST, J. 1981. 'Acton Burnell Castle, Shropshire', in *Collectanea Historica: Essays in Memory of Stuart Rigold* (ed. A. Detsicas), Kent Archaeol. Soc., 85–92, Maidstone
WHITE, P. 1983. 'Sherborne Old Castle', *Arch. Journ.*, 140, 67–70
WOOD, M. 1950. *Thirteenth-Century Domestic Architecture in England: Arch. Journ.*, 105, supplement, London
———, 1965. *The English Mediaeval House*, London
———, 1974. *Norman Domestic Architecture*, Royal Archaeol. Inst., London
WOODS, H. 1982. 'Excavations at Eltham Palace, 1975–9', *Trans. London Middlesex Archaeol. Soc.*, 32, 215–65
WRIGHT, T. 1857, *A Volume of Vocabularies*, Liverpool

17

Fortress-Policy in Capetian Tradition and Angevin Practice: Aspects of the Conquest of Normandy by Philip II

Charles Coulson

The Director of the Battle conference in 1959 first established that the treatment of non-royal fortresses in Britain in the period 1154 to 1216 was sufficiently systematic and purposeful to constitute a 'castle-policy', in Professor Allen Brown's words, 'consciously directed to the augmentation of royal power, chiefly at the expense of the baronage'.[1] Taken together with the programme of royal castle-building under Henry II, Richard and John (already in 1955 analysed and financially quantified) this 'Angevin castle-policy', by a calculated campaign of seizure, confiscation, escheat and demolition, changed the ratio of royal to recorded baronial castles markedly in favour of the Crown. By the close of 1214, before the Civil War broke out, ninety-three were physically or lawfully in royal possession compared with forty-nine in 1154; in effect, 'nothing less than a drastic alteration in the balance of power'.[2] Although various documentary estimates of the number of seignorial castles in the later twelfth century have been shown by D. J. Cathcart King's recently published ground-survey to have been too low by a factor of about three, the siege-worthiness of the great majority of unrecorded sites was arguably so slight that Professor Brown's conclusion, on its own terms of reference, is not greatly affected. Whether the ratio in 1214 was two to one, or in fact ten to one, all numerical assessments are vitiated by problems of reconciling modern structural and military criteria with the original usage of *castrum* and *fortericia* and by such extraneous factors as manpower, stocking and political will; and it may be that an official presence might

1 For his tolerant supervision of the thesis upon which this paper is largely based (C. L. H. Coulson, 'Seignorial Fortresses in France in Relation to Public Policy c. 864 to c.1483', University of London Ph.D., February 1972 – hereafter Coulson 1972) and for many subsequent kindnesses my thanks are due to R. Allen Brown; and for discussion of 'rendability' over many years to H. R. Loyn, R. H. C. Davis, J. C. Holt and to the members of the Medieval and Renaissance Seminar at Eliot College, University of Kent at Canterbury.

2 R. Allen Brown, 'A List of Castles 1154–1216', *EHR* lxxiv, 1959, 249, 256 and 249–80 *passim*; 'Royal Castle-Building in England 1154–1216', *EHR* lxx, 1955, 353–98. R. Allen Brown, H. M. Colvin, A. J. Taylor, *The History of the King's Works*, London 1963, I, 64–81, II, 553–894 *passim*, 1023. Dr Brown's supplementary notes to F. M. Powicke, *The Loss of Normandy* 2nd edn (Manchester 1961 – hereafter Powicke 1961) and D. Phil. thesis ('The Place of English Castles in the Administrative and Military Organization 1154–1216 with Special Reference to the Reign of John', Oxford University 1953) and his *English Castles* (London 1976 – with revised estimates of the total of operative castles c.1200) have also been of great value and deserve special acknowledgement.

be better established by a dense network of administrative bases (even sub-fortified manors) than by a handful of major strongholds, strategically significant perhaps but sparsely scattered, their phases of active service brief and occasional, military value somewhat equivocal, and their construction, guard and repair decidedly burdensome. Territorial power obviously correlated with castle-building; but exactly how, be it psychologically or in contemplation of war, or as the celebration and guarantee of a *fait accompli* of local dominance, clearly varied in time and place. In addition, there is value in thinking of a *fortress*-policy, comprehending all kinds of fortifications and especially the walled-towns.[3]

Acknowledging this dimension of Angevin statecraft at once directs attention to seeing how public policy originally in France, and that of the Capetians subsequently, may have intervened in the world of seignorial fortresses. Comparisons with Anglo-Norman practice particularly during that part of the struggle for Normandy between John's accession and the battle of Bouvines, offer some illumination. Philip Augustus had a fortress-policy of his own, which evolved out of traditions differing hardly at all in doctrine but markedly in their implementation from the Angevin. These antecedents may repay examination.[4] Down to the treaty of Le Goulet (January 1200) Capetian practice was conditioned by the underdog situation of the Kings of France. Philip II succeeded in 1180 at the age of fifteen to an insecure throne with wide pretensions but power confined narrowly to the Île de France, the Orléannais and to Berri. The Crown had survived partly because it had appeared too weak to evoke any lethal combination of feudatories. Philip may have been a Carolid, as Sir Maurice Powicke has it,

3 Mr D. J. Cathcart King has most generously allowed me over many years use of the draft of his virtually exhaustive site-catalogue and bibliography listing about 1500 'fortified' places datable between 1052 and c.1500 (*Castellarium Anglicanum*, 2 vols, New York 1982). Ella Armitage (*Norman Castles*, London 1912) appended 'a schedule of English castles known (from documents) to date from the eleventh century' (total 84). Sidney Painter ('English Castles in the Early Middle Ages . . . ', *Feudalism and Liberty*, Baltimore 1961, 126–8, reprinting *Speculum*, x, 1935, 321–32) stressed the problem of ephemeral works and twelfth-century abandonment but was 'inclined to believe' in a peak of 500–600 in use c.1100 and 'reasonably certain' of a decline to about 200–250 'castles' by c.1200. His confidence as to criteria and terminology, and assumption that early thirteenth-century records omitted relatively few, are not supported by King, especially with subinfeudated places. Structural definitions apart, *castellum* is often used for the lordship as a whole (e.g. 1154 Saint-Clair-sur-Epte, *Monuments Historiques*, J. Tardif, Paris 1866, no. 529). On the statistical and terminological problems even of detailed fief rolls, listing at least 341 'fortresses' in a single county, see Charles Coulson, 'Castellation in the County of Champagne in the Thirteenth Century' (*Château-Gaillard*, ix–x, Caen 1982 – hereafter Coulson 1982 – 349–56, 362–3). Documentary mention usually indicates a place in use ('militarily'?) but the totals given by John Beeler (*Warfare in England 1066–1189*, New York 1966, 427–38) of 'castles built before 1189' (England 298, Wales 80) and by Brown (1959) for 1154–1216 (with Wales 327 'castles') are dwarfed by unrecorded sites (cf. Brown, 1959, 259; Beeler, 397–426) especially if those disregarded as merely manorial are included (e.g. *Bibliography of Moated Sites*, ed. H. Mytum, Moated Sites Research Group, Newcastle on Tyne 1982; on the general issues see Charles Coulson 'Hierarchism in Conventual Crenellation . . .', *Med. Arch.*, xxvi, 1982, 69–100).

4 The few *addenda* to Powicke (1961), 180–6 are required by his entire omission of rendability. The traditional French caricature of patriotic monarchs warring with usurping castle-building 'barons' (for the *genre* see the 'nobles brigands' of A. Luchaire in *Louis VI, le Gros . . .*, Paris 1890, ch. iv; Ch. Petit-Dutaillis, *Etude sur la Vie et le Règne de Louis VIII*, Paris 1894, 403) still persists (J.-F. Finó, *Forteresses de la France Médiévale*, Paris 1970, 72–3) despite R. Aubenas' important 'Les Châteaux Forts des Xe et XIe Siècles' (*Revue Historique de Droit français et étranger*, 4e série, 1938, 548–86).

intent from the outset on destroying the Angevin Empire and going on to develop ambitions to revive the power of the house of Charlemagne, but he had twenty years of uphill endeavour before he could make much progress and what distinguishes his fortress-policy is that he was the first of the Capetians to break with tradition; to discard the imperial and sub-Carolingian pretence of royal control as such over all the fortresses of his kingdom, irrespective of their tenure. He chose instead to rebuild the monarchy by consent upon the rights which feudal evolution had placed in the hands of direct lords over the fortresses of their immediate vassals. While Philip was patiently laying new foundations of power to supplement the old, Henry II continued to implement prerogatives of monopolistic and imperial type over the fortresses in his vast empire using force, fear and not a little fraud, just as John was to do with such ultimately disastrous results. The contrast with Capetian castle-policy pointedly bears out the francophile Gerald of Wales' opinion that the despotic governmental methods employed by the Norman dukes in England alienated their continental subjects and crushed their desire to resist the French: nevertheless, the castle-liberties so dear to the baronage on both sides, and likewise the public accountability for those franchises, derived from common parentage; for all that the fortress-policy of Philip II until after Bouvines was moderate and only mildly interventionist, whereas John's was ruthlessly *dirigiste* and opportunistic from first to last.[5]

How much of either was innovation can be judged only by considering the inheritance which the Angevin, Norman and other comital dynasties, along with the Capetian dukes of *Francia*, received from late Carolingian government. Powicke's proposed late-eleventh-century origin for what he called the Norman dukes' 'right of entry' to castles must be questioned; the final part of clause 4 of the 1091 *Consuetudines et Justicie* not only refers back to the mid-century but has been modelled upon contemporary rendability, namely the formerly royal and now widespread lordly right to take over temporarily at pleasure the possession or use of a vassal's fortress.[6] Sufficient direct and corroborative

5 W. L. Warren, *King John*, London 1961, 22 (map), 37, 259; Powicke (1961), 17, 105, 297–302; Ch. Petit-Dutaillis, *The Feudal Monarchy in France and England*, London 1964, 181. Brown (1959), on the 100 cases of confiscations and appropriations of baronial castles and 30 cases of demolition by the Crown, comments (pp. 257–8) 'the Angevin kings . . . seem often to have ridden rough-shod over right and precedent. . . . Not infrequently no cause is known, and we seem faced with the brute facts that the king desired certain castles and felt himself strong enough to take them.' The suggestion is then made that this 'castle-policy' was a factor in the baronial revolt of 1215, drawing attention to *Magna Carta* clause 52 and to a clinching passage in the *Brut Y Tywysogion*. Capetian comparisons amply confirm this view.

6 Text below; Powicke (1961), 180, citing C. H. Haskins, *Norman Institutions*, New York 1918, 282 cl. 4 – *nulli licuit in Normannia fortitudinem castelli sui vetare domino Normannie si ipse eam in manu sua voluit habere*. R. Allen Brown, *The Normans and the Norman Conquest*, London 1969, 239; J. H. le Patourel (*The Norman Empire*, Oxford 1976, 304–6) refers to ducal 'control' of castles but does not elaborate upon Haskins, Powicke (1961) or Jean Yver (note 8 below). Rendability awaits systematic publication but see Ch. L. H. Coulson, 'Rendability and Castellation in Medieval France', *Château-Gaillard*, vi, Caen 1972, 59–67 and Coulson 1972 for the *vetare* formula etc. Index 'Rendability'. This phrase was already conventional c.1034 (C. Brunel, *Les Plus Anciennes Chartes en Langue Provençale*, Paris 1926, 3–5, cf. 11–12, 13–14 etc.) and may be discerned in Aquitaine-Poitou c.1022–8 (pact of Hugh *Chiliarchus* ed. J. Martindale, *EHR* lxxxiv, 1969, 528–48 e.g. 546, 548) but R. Richard, 'Le Château dans la structure féodale de la France de l'est au XIIe

evidence survives to establish the monarchical provenance of fortress-control, comprising licensing and rendability, notably the very suggestive terms of many Carolingian ecclesiastical privileges of mid-ninth-century date onwards, which explicitly or tacitly acknowledge monastic and episcopal fortifying. With conventual establishments claustral jurisdictional immunities were redefined so as to accord with the alignment of the newly fortified circuits (*castra* and *castella*) leaving very little doubt but that this was done to avert being taken over as fortifications, under colour of royal warrant, by the local count or those claiming his authority. Fortress-rights, rendability chief among them, were already eluding central control and similarly Charles the Bald's famous second capitulary of Pîtres in 864, ordering the destruction of all *castella, firmitates et haias*, built *sine nostro verbo*, shows that local initiative was already participating in the defence of the lower Seine and elsewhere against the Norsemen. The doctrine of royal monopoly persisted nonetheless, insisting that all kinds of fortress, including the newly prominent and multiplying personal strongholds, popular refuges of all kinds, as well as episcopal, comital and sub-comital city-seats and other walled towns and citadels, possessed by virtue of being fortifications of a public character which vested in the local agent of imperial authority (arrogated or legitimate) whatever substance or remnant of monarchical control had survived.[7] Robert Aubenas has stressed the continuity of public authority in tenth and eleventh-century France with a wealth of examples, but he concentrated on the construction of fortresses not their use. Jean Yver developed the theme as it applies to Normandy down to the mid-twelfth century and their powerful testimony is emphatically endorsed if we trace rendability back from the feudal age to its source. Far from doing so, Yver and Aubenas entirely ignored rendability which deprived them of some of the strongest evidence against the perverse dogma that castles were contrary to public policy unless kept in the hands of the ruler. Yver quoted but did not appreciate the statement by Robert of Torigni, that Henry I had 'used the fortresses of many of his barons as though they were his own'. Like the joint declaration of 1091, this represents normal rendability not some peculiarly Norman ducal act of sovereign power. Whenever the sub-Carolingian comital rôle in the regions survived the upheaval

siècle' (*Problème des 12 Jahrhunderts*, Reichenau Vorträge 1965–7, 169–76) found no evidence of (feudal) rendability (in Burgundy) before that time. Robert Boutruche (*Seigneurie et Féodalité . . .*, Paris 1970, 38) more correctly regarded it as going back 'à la fin du XIe siècle' but cited only charters of 1182 and 1245.

7 Rendability survived best where Charlemagne's successors' rule had been strong and outside the regions disrupted by invasion, within an area probably once coextensive with Carolingian Gaul, including Catalonia, Lombardy, Provence, Lotharingia, Netherlands, Germany (Charles L. H. Coulson, 'Fortresses and Social Responsibility in Late-Carolingian France', *Zeitschrift für Archéologie des Mittelalters*, 4, 1976, 29–36). For the Edict of Pistes MGH Legum II, II 310–28 (328 cap I) cf. 302–10, 355–61; MGH I, 62–4 (739 AD); also *Recueil des Actes de Charles III . . .*, ed. Ph. Lauer, Paris 1949, nos. 2, 10, 34, 41, 67, 90, 98, 101; *Recueil des Actes de Louis IV . . .*, ed. Ph. Lauer, Paris 1914, nos. 2, 9, 14, 18; *Recueil des Actes de Lothaire et de Louis V . . .*, ed. L. Halphen. F. Lot, Paris 1908, nos. 4, 18, 21. Cf. the royal and papal immunity, dispensable only for defence and by abbatial consent, accorded to Sainte-Trinité, Péronne, in 1046 (*Catalogue des Actes d'Henri Ier . . .*, ed. F. Soehnée, Paris 1907, no. 72). For the *castellum* of Compiègne see note 12 below.

and transformations of society, the construction and use of fortresses remained the peculiar sphere of public authority.[8]

Their different circumstances caused the Anglo-Normans and the early Capetian kings to deal divergently with the Carolingian legacy of fortress-rights. Four years' disorderly rule in Normandy by Robert Curthose required the ban pronounced jointly with William Rufus upon any substantial earthwork and timber fortification, the making of any *fortitudo* on a naturally defensible site (*in rupe vel in insula*), and on the usurped creation of any castellany (*castellum*). Their forthright *nulli licuit in Normannia* applied the rule to the whole territory of the duchy, irrespective of immunity, liberty or mode of tenure. It was part of a general reassertion of the rule of law, intended to deal with the illicit and adulterine gains of violence and lawlessness and typical of such pacifications of which in England 1154 and 1217 are the most familiar.[9] The realities of Capetian power were very different. About the year 1005, the monks of Cormery by Tours, having seen their lands and rights diminished and threatened for the future by the Count of Anjou's new castles of Montbazon and Mirebeau, persuaded Fulk Nerra to guarantee them harmless and prevailed upon him to seek King Robert's corroboration. Cormery esteemed the honour and sanction, and perhaps valued the security and permanence, of a solemn charter so highly, and Fulk no doubt cynically or piously humoured them, because the royal

8 Powicke (1961) 181 and n. 10 on *aedificare*; S. Painter (1961), 17–40, and *Speculum*, xxxi, 1956, 243–57 on 'Castellans of the Plain of Poitou . . .'; R. Aubenas (1938) *passim*; Jean Yver, 'Les Châteaux Forts en Normandie jusqu'au milieu du XIIe siècle . . .', *Bulletin de la Société des Antiquaires de Normandie*, liii, 1955–6, 111, 112 *et passim* 28–115. To R. Boutruche (1970, 36) it was still axiomatic that the seignorial castle was (*de seipso*) 'un signe de l'anarchie féodale' just as it had been to W. S. McKechnie (*Magna Carta*, Glasgow 1905, 176) who supposed that 'it was the aim of every efficient ruler to abolish all fortified castles'. With *id genus omne* (likewise Boutruche, 38) he insisted that any castle without royal licence was 'adulterine' in contradiction to his text (1217 version cap 47) which precisely defined the *castra adulterina* as illegal because the product of recent wartime force. Even Yver was nervous about the baronial fortress as such while Auguste Longnon's antipathy was muted only because 'nos comtes pouvaient en temps de guerre faire occuper par leurs chevaliers certains châteaux ou maisons-fortes . . . rendables' (*Histoire des Ducs et Comtes de Champagne*, H. d'Arbois de Jubainville, vii, Paris 1869, 93). The continuity of public authority is correctively stressed by Marcel Garaud in his 'La construction des châteaux et les destinées de la *vicaria* et du *vicarius* Carolingiens en Poitou' (*Revue Historique du Droit* . . ., 4e série, 1953, 54–78) and, in a more 'feudalised' context, by J. Richard in his important paper 'Châteaux, châtelains et vassaux en Bourgogne aux XIe et XIIe siècles' (*Cahiers de Civilisation Médiévale*, iii, 1960, 433–47). Rendability in Normandy was already seignorial (as well as ducal) by the twelfth century as elsewhere (note 15 below).

9 *Castellum* and *castrum* are persistently juridical not architectural terms (unlike *munitio*, *firmitas*, *fortalicium*) meaning not just the fortified *caput* but the whole parcel of appurtenant lordly rights (note 3 above; *Rotuli Chartarum*, Record Commission 1837, 93a) whence the suggested translation of cl.4 which avoids the usual tautology and equally implausible juxtaposing of *fortitudo* in its literal and figurative senses. Attempts to apply the very precise wording to include masonry and major works (the diagnostic *turris* is absent) are conventional but questionable (A. H. Thompson, *Military Architecture in England during the Middle Ages*, Oxford 1912, 89–90; Armitage (1912), 337–8; Powicke (1961), 180; M. de Boüard, 'Les Petites Enceintes Circulaires . . .', *Château-Gaillard*, i, Caen 1964, 32; Brown (1976), 17, 49). The illegality lay in the usurpation as much as in the fortifying and imperial doctrines are no longer applied e.g. in 1088 against Robert de Mortagne, or in 1087–99 against Count Henry (*Cal. Docs France* nos. 39, 424). The maintenance and up-dating of established castles were not touched, unless by special compact as in 1144 with Humphrey de Bohun for Malmesbury and William de Albini in 1203 at Belvoir (*Regesta*, iii, no. 111; *Rotuli de Liberate ac de Misis et Praestitis* . . ., Rec. Comm. 1844, 34–5).

authority over fortresses had retained its aura while losing its material reality. Abbot Gauzelin of Saint-Bénoît-sur-Loire rejoiced at the destruction in a storm of Yèvre-le-Châtel (Loiret), and having seized the opportunity to buy out the irksome *avouerie* owned by its thunderstruck lord, tried to make both changes stick by expensively purchasing the moral backing of his royal brother. Gauzelin's biographer, André de Fleuri explains: *utque eversio castri Evere omnium saeculorum permaneret tempore, centum nonaginta quinque libras Gauzelinus abbas probatissimi argenti Regis Roberto regali proli contulit, quod et scripto corroborat.* Gauzelin also hoped to procure the endorsement 'of the bishops of the whole of Gaul' to complete a familiar cocktail of sanctions; the more naturally since the Church also exercised, by default or by right, the monarchical power to ban. As late as 1148, when the right was already feudalised like rendability, the bishops at the Council of Reims fulminated against the usurpation of clerical property associated with the 'new plague' of castle-building, among other grievances inveighing against 'undue works of castles' being imposed on their men and seeking to submit to parochial discipline the clergy serving the new chapels *in munitionibus et turribus*.[10]

As new socio-political relationships coagulated, feudal custom brought a new pluralism to bear on inherited Carolingian principles. Monarchism becomes little more than a reminiscence in the pronouncements of ecclesiastics affecting fortresses, and in the atavistic grandiloquence of early Capetian charters. Old and new elements mingle in the 'sacred ban' established by the Council of Anse in 994 in favour of Cluny Abbey. The diploma preserves many of the elements of a later Carolingian protection, *inter alia* forbidding intrusion by any *judex publicus aut exactionarius, comes quoque*, but also including the up-to-date injunction that no such intruder should *castrum facere aut aliquam firmitatem* within or near the monastic lands or burgus. The Church habitually defended her own by such means but the King's special rôle was acknowledged by obtaining his confirmation. The young Robert le Pieux, in association with Duke Henry,

10 *Thesaurus Novus Anecdotorum* . . ., E. Martène and U. Durand, iv, Paris 1717, cols 141–4. The analogy of castle licensing with chapels, mill-bans and market-bans etc. deserves attention. R. W. Southern, *The Making of the Middle Ages*, London 1953, 84–5 (map of Anjou 987–1040); *Catalogue des Actes de Robert II* . . ., ed. W. M. Newman, Paris 1937, nos. 25, 95. Late in the eleventh century the knowledgeable forgers of Saint-Denis fathered upon Robert II, as 'the successor of Dagobert, Charlemagne, Louis I and Charles III', in order to strengthen their hand against the Montmorency family, a charter confirming the monks' immunity in the conventual *castellum* (precinct; genuinely granted 898, *Recueil . . . Charles III*, no. 10) and banning (not synonymous with forbidding in the medieval era) fortifying on the Ile Saint-Denis. They relied on this forgery in 1219 successfully (*Catalogue . . . Robert II* . . ., nos. 80, 120, pp. 294–5; *Layettes du Trésor des Chartes*, i, Paris 1863, no. 1372). On the early thirteenth-century Yèvre-le-Châtel, see Finó (1970), 445–7; cf. the symbiotic not confrontational relations with a castle-based avoué at Corbie and Montier-en-Der in 1016–42 and 1027–35 (*Catalogue . . . Robert II* . . ., no. 45; *Catalogue . . . Henri Ier* . . ., no. 62, cf. note 24 below; *Catalogue des Actes des Comtes de Brienne, 950–1350*, ed. H. d'Arbois de Jubainville, Bibliothèque de l'Ecole des Chartes, xxxiii, 1872, no. 5). The clergy seem only to have anathematised (usually in much-used and unduly influentially lurid language) castle-building from which they did not benefit (e.g. near Chàlons-sur-Marne in 1048–63, note 13 below). The Touraine Peace of God decretals issued at the Council of Clermont (1095) ordered that no *nova munitio* be built in churches or churchyards. Only very indirect general condemnation of fortresses can be inferred from making the community of the *receptacula* and *munitiones* of Touraine used as bases by malefactors collectively liable to make redress (*Thesaurus Novus* . . ., iv, cols 121–4).

his uncle, and their respective magnates, put their names to a new charter which defined the Cluny *banlieue* to comprise a tract of surrounding country, about 35 miles by 20 miles, in the most fulsome style of royal majesty. The consent of Robert's nobles is acknowleged but the ban was evidently a hallowed and pious act of kingship, combining the royal attributes of protector of the Church and overseer of fortifications in one documentary celebration of regality.[11] His grandson, Philip I, continued to prefer monarchical theory to feudal reality in his protection to the canons of Compiègne dated at the ancient palace in 1092. The atavism of this charter is substantial and illuminating, particularly the statement in the preamble that the house had been *sic nobilitata et premunita* by the Emperor Charles (? II) and Pope John (? VIII) that any attempt to violate it, to construct any *munitio* or to usurp lordship in the lands of the abbey would incur the full rigour of royal justice and the Church's anathema besides. Philippe le Gros admitted that the royal wrath and eternal damnation, manifest or merely presumed, had alike been impotent; *munitiones et turris* had even been built near the abbey church, although the outrage is said to have occurred *ante tempora nostra*. The phraseology here is all of a piece. When, we are told, Philip assumed the *imperium . . . totius Francie* (in 1059) he had the encroaching tower destroyed by mining and to avert any recurrence, now in 1092, transferred to the canons the reversion of his right, namely *jus regie potestatis et dominationis*, to prohibit fortifying upon or near their properties. Such powers devolved upon the greater franchises, and even lesser ones, most often not by grant but by mere user.[12] Between 1111 and 1118 the struggles of Louis VI to eradicate the castle

11 To comment that 'Robert n'était pas un méchant homme mais c'est bien certainement un des plus nuls qui ait jamais porté la couronne' (d'Arbois de Jubainville, *Histoire . . . Champagne*, ii, Paris 1860, 278) fails to grasp that he was keeping alive an imperial tradition which he had no power to implement otherwise. *Recueil des Chartes de l'Abbaye de Cluny*, ed. P. Bernard and A. Bruel, i, Paris 1876, no. 2255, cf. iv (Paris 1888) no. 2800; *Catalogue . . . Robert II . . .*, 2–4, 18–19 (as 996–1002). The Council, by the 'pontifical authority' of the archbishops of Lyon and Vienne and nine other bishops from central eastern Gaul, accorded to Odilo (abbot 994–1049) the petition of Maieul of Cluny (died May 994) that the abbot be vested with episcopal rank (*praesulatus dignitas*) to repress the evils and *angustiae* about the *locus Cluniacensis sanctissimus* by power of anathema. Any infractor was also decreed excommunicated in advance. King Robert adduced royal precedents (giving only unspecific acknowledgement to *privilegia apostolica*) and expanded this spiritual protection of all Cluniac property into a geographical, non-feudal and non-proprietorial, castellation *banlieue* extending 35 miles from Châlon to Mâcon on the Saône, 30 miles west from Mâcon to Charolles, thence 20 miles to Mont-Saint-Vincent. This banal zone influenced castle-building in c.1147, c.1122–56, 1166, 1173, 1264, 1309–10 (*Recueil . . . Cluny*, v, Paris 1894, nos. 4131, 4244; *Les Olim ou Registres des Arrêts rendus par la Cour du Roi . . .*, ed. Beugnot, Paris 1839, i, no. 6; iii nos. 34, 69). It is unique among ecclesiastical, royal and ducal protections to Cluniac houses; the urban *banlieues* of Ponthieu afford a later parallel (note 15 below), cf. *Recueil . . . Cluny*, ii, Paris 1880, no. 980; iii, nos. 1950, 2270, 2465, 2466; iv, nos. 2949, 2976, 3389, 3632; v, nos. 3689, 3720 all dating between 955 and 1097.

12 *Recueil des Actes de Philippe Ier . . .*, ed. M. Prou, Paris 1908, no. 125, from three thirteenth-century copies whose glosses (eg. *Philippus rex de firmitatibus non edificandis in Compendio vel in vicinio Compendii absque licentia nostra*) confirm that the canons were dispensing the ban (such bans were invitations to treat, not prohibitions *d'en haut*) in normal franchisal fashion. Other late sixteenth-century glosses show this was used to stop building on the bridge and riverside by the rival town authorities. King Charles II (840–77) founded the abbey; Charles III rebuilt it and (917) exempted from all (non-royal) takeover (rendability *de facto*) the fortified precinct and outworks (*de castello autem et propugnaculis ejus et de terra exteriori inter murum et fossatum, ut nullus externus ejusdem loci quasi ad praevidendum castellum principatum accipiat et nemo ibi mansionem accipiat*

of Hugh du Puiset in the Beauce, to stop Thibaud of Blois fortifying at Allaines, and to remove the castle of Quierzy, near Laon, make better sense as acts of partisan majesty than of peace-keeping. The royal example was copied as widely as the Carolingian mantle of fortress-control had fallen. Propaganda by local potentates against castles, when their construction was still technically an official act and possessory right did not yet apply, has combined with the interested complaints of dispossessed ecclesiastical first-comers to bias our own views, but it is profoundly significant that in the proto-feudal age fortress-control, along with protection of the Church, was inherent in regalian authority; and, conversely, that fortress-tenure was conditional and precarious *ab ovo.*[13]

Such allusions to the erstwhile royal monopoly of fortress-control as survive before Philip Augustus naturally occur predominantly in ecclesiastical contexts. In this facilitating environment Capetian practice most nearly approached its

concedimus eis; Recueil . . . Charles III . . . , no. 90). Philip I's other affirmations of undisturbed tenure of fortified precincts were made to Senlis cathedral (1068; *firmitates omnium domorum canonicorum*), and to Reims Abbey *castrum* (1090; *Recueil . . . Philippe Ier . . .*, nos. 39, 102). Louis VI did likewise for the new *castellum* of Vézelai Abbey, adapting an immunity charter of Louis II (Luchaire (1890) no. 253). At Compiègne the comital *fisc* was already vested in the abbey in 917, very likely with a (small) geographical castellation *banlieue* anticipating Cluny. Philip's ban *ne aliquis possit aut presumat construere turrim aut munitionem sive domum defensabilem in toto territorio et convicinio Compendii*, 'within or without the town on the islands or beyond the river' (Oise). The abbey of Ferrières-en-Gâtinais (Loiret) undoubtedly enjoyed a similar ban (valid even against the Crown), with other extensive monopolies, granted or confirmed by Philip I and defined by Louis VI on request as operative within the abbey lordship not territorial circumscription (Luchaire (1890) no. 500, cf. feudal redefinition in 1208 of 1156 old-style castellation franchise of the see of Maguelone, notes 16, 27 below, and Corbie Abbey *banlieue*, note 24 below).

13 But Philip I, according to Suger, advised his son to keep the *turris* (and castle) of Montlhéry, near Corbeil, in his own hands for 'it has caused me untold trouble. Frankly, that tower has made me old before my time' (quoted R. Fawtier, *The Capetian Kings of France*, trans. L. Butler and R. J. Adam, London 1962, 17). Luchaire (1890) nos. 108, 117, 118, 128, 609; *Histoire . . . Champagne*, ii, 194–202, suggesting Allonnes but A. Molinier and A. Luchaire prefer Allaines (also Eure et Loir) only 1¼ miles from le Puiset. Before the *donjon* there was destroyed by fire the first time Thibaud (*per* Suger) opportunistically alleged his right to build a tower at Allaines, within the lordship but held of Louis VI in chief, offering to prove his right by judicial duel between his seneschal and the king's. Hugh du Puiset and his castle jointly were blamed for local brigandage as was Quierzy castle (Aisne), formerly royal but given by Philip I (c.1068–98) for refuge from attacks to the bishop of Noyon (*Recueil . . . Philippe Ier . . .* no. 136). Suger's almost obsessive clerical animosity towards seignorial fortresses was probably excited in this case by the territorial competition in the Beauce between lay magnates and the clergy of Saint-Père de Chartres and with the influential abbot of Saint-Denis. Compare the lurid denunciation of castle-oppression against Saint-Mard Abbey, Soissons, in 1048 (*Veterum Scriptorum . . . Amplissima Collectio*, E. Martène and U. Durand, vii, Paris 1733, 58–9); Compiègne (above, probably drafted by the canons), and in Fulbert of Chartres' (died 1028) request to Robert II to obtain action by Count Eudes over the new castle of Illiers (16 miles south-west of Chartres) and to stop the rebuilding of Gallardon castle (6 miles north-west). Fulbert protested at the very possibly justified efforts by Geoffroi de Châteaudun to restore the separate integrity of the viscounty on the death (1023) of his uncle Hugh, both viscount and archbishop of Tours (*Histoire . . . Champagne*, i, Paris 1859, 275–8; clericalist tone and argument taken directly from Nicolas Brussel, *Nouvel Examen de l'Usage Général des Fiefs en France . . .*, Paris (1727) 1750, 378, ch. 30 *passim*). Comital righteousness also imbues Geoffrey Plantagenet's solemn charter celebrating his siege and destruction of 'the entire tower and defences' of Montreuil-Bellay, near Saumur (1151; *Recueil des Actes de Henri II Roi d'Angleterre . . . concernants . . . les Affaires de France*, L. Delisle ed. E. Berger, i, Paris 1916, no. 18; cf. Sempigny, razed in 1171 by the archbishop of Reims allegedly as a brigand lair, *Histoire . . . Champagne*, iii, Paris 1861, 77–80). A good corrective is Pierre Héliot's 'Sur les Résidences Prinçières bâties en Frances du Xe au XIIe siècle', *Le Moyen Age*, série 4, 10, 1955, 27–61, 291–319 *passim*.

theory. Philip I's Compiègne declaration on the royal banning of fortification matches the Norman statement of 1091; and the latter assertion of universal ducal rendability compares closely with Louis VI's statement in 1119 that the 'Crown of France' could take over the fortresses dependent on Cluny Abbey (and by implication others), 'whenever the public defence should require'.[14] Similarly, the protection granted by Louis VII in 1156 to the abbot and monks of Villemagne in the diocese of Béziers (Hérault) continued the traditional policy of affirming ecclesiastical franchises on application, especially in Languedoc and beyond the royal demesne of the Île de France. By endorsing fortifying *carte blanche*, abbey, town and elsewhere, *viz ut possitis munire fossa et vallo et muro et turribus et munitionibus*, Louis le Jeune really did no more (but it might be crucial) than facilitate the exercise of their lordship in competition with magnates less well disposed to the Crown. Conversely, any fortifying by intruders on abbey land would be met by the royal ban fulminated by proxy; and, if no more, the royal power would not die of disuse. Having little to lose, the authority of the distant monarch could only benefit by acts done in his name. By solemnly 'assigning' to the monks in advance the *fortias* which he had authorised them to build, Louis perpetuated the doctrine that all castles, however created or held, were public works at the king's disposal. In somewhat modernised language but still conventional manner the charter then confirms the monastic immunity to lay intrusion, omitting the old threats of Divine retribution but warning infractors simply that no prescriptive right will accrue to seizures however long enjoyed. Time will not run against the abbey; in particular, any previous rendering of their fortresses (forbidden henceforth) shall be reputed null and void, *quia hec redditio regii juris esse dignoscitur.* Because, with the multiplication of fortresses and of subinfeudation, rendability was in fact percolating down through the strata of tenure and was becoming a normal attribute of immediate lordship, any such precedent had to be quashed; but the new world of feudal relationships could not be set aside simply by declaring it *de facto* and of no legal effect.[15] Four similar ecclesiastical franchises with corresponding for-

14 *Fortalicia autem, castra et munitiones, propter necessitates et deffensiones corone regni Francie publice faciendas, in manu corone Francie habebimus, abbate et conventu Cluniacensi prius requisitis. Predicta autem aliquo casu extra manum et coronam regni Francie non poterunt ad aliquam aliam personam aliquo modo transferri sive pervenire* (*Ordonnances des Rois* . . ., iii, Paris 1732, 545–8); recognised as rendability by the editor Secousse from Du Cange's 1668 treatise, 'Des fiefs jurables et rendables', appended to his edition of Joinville (reprinted ed. Petitot, *Collection Complète des Mémoires* . . ., Ire série, iii, Paris 1819, 490–527). Louis VI's charter was royally confirmed in 1270, 1294, 1314 etc. (*Chartes . . . Cluny*, v, no. 3943; vi, Paris 1903, no. 5154; and *Layettes*, i, no. 46).

15 Louis VII's text recited in 1210 confirmation *Recueil des Actes de Philippe Auguste, roi de France* (hereafter *Rec. Ph. Aug.*), iii, Paris 1966, no. 1120. It applied to all possessions *ad jus monasterii pertinentia* as enumerated, comprising a region in the north-west of Béziers diocese (Hérault); a full baronial-level castellation franchise, monopolising the right to fortify and license others, linked by the Compiègne ban with the pre-feudal Cluny-type *banlieue*; another link is the control often exercised over the environs of major towns (cf. Carolingian *pagus*) e.g. Dijon, 1153; bishop of Langres and Duke Hugh of Burgundy (*Recueil Général des Anciennes Lois Françaises* . . ., i, Paris 1822, 150–3); markets and fortifications within 6 miles of Carpentras (Vaucluse) banned 1155 by the bishop and Raymond of Toulouse (*Layettes*, i, no. 139). That *de facto* territorial urban circumscriptions were far from obsolete is suggested by ducal licensing in Gascony (Coulson 1972, appendix B 3) and the formal castellation *banlieues* of such northwestern towns as Corbie, Abbeville,

tress-rights were endorsed by Louis VII down to 1186, all in the south; namely, the bishoprics of Maguelone (1156, 1161) and Lodève (1162, 1188), and the abbacies of Sarlat (1181) and of Figeac (1186), both in Périgord. These were in no way 'des privilèges assez extraordinaires', as Leopold Delisle would have it (1856). In each case the initiative lay with the grantee and the king readily lent his authority whenever he might acquire the credit of obedience and establish some vicarious presence. The early Capetians were responding to events but they kept their powder dry, realistically eschewing the pyrotechnics and the machismo displayed by the Angevin treatment of baronial fortresses. Philip II's predecessors made such use as they were able of their meagre political and financial resources. This necessary moderation was vindicated by the contribution made by their fortress policy to the worsting of King John.[16]

It may be allowable to regard Angevin castle-policy as a programme of investment in governmental plant, designed to maximise the Crown's portfolio

Crécy-en-Ponthieu, Noyelles-sur-Mer, Waben, Marquenterre, Ponthoile, Doullens, Rue, Ergnies all confirmed 1180–1210 (*Rec. Ph. Aug.*, i, Paris 1916, nos. 10, 52; *Ordonnances des Rois . . .*, iv, Paris 1734, 53–9; *Recueil des Actes des Comtes de Ponthieu (1026–1279)*, ed. C. Brunel, Paris 1930, nos. 131, 134, 150, 152, 155, 206, 212, 298). The rendability to the Crown of the *munitiones* of the monks of Villemagne, alodial tenure notwithstanding, apparently pre-dates the feudalisation of rendability; cf. licence by Louis VII in 1174 to fortify Bourges Cathedral precinct under renewable oath to render it on demand, omitted in Louis VI's licence (1120) for Sens Cathedral close; renounced except in vacancies (1122) over the archbishop of Bourges' castle of Saint-Palais; and left, uncertain in the reservation of 'regalian rights' (1134) over the lands and fortresses of the bishops of Le Puy (*Ordonnances des Rois . . .*, xi, Paris 1769, 206–7; Luchaire (1890) nos. 295, 317, 532). Non-royal rendability was ubiquitous and is the essential complement to the present study (Coulson 1972, appendix A), however rarely found (recorded) in Angevin Normandy e.g. Robert de Neubourg's oath 'not to with-hold' his castle (Eure) from Count Waleran of Meulan's use at will (*Cal. Docs France*, no. 338) 'c.1155' but *rectius* 1141–2 (information supplied by Mr D. B. Crouch).

16 Delisle's dogmatic prejudice is most significant regarding the 1186 Figeac grant (although confirmed 1257, 1302, 1442, 1463. *Catalogue des Actes de Philippe Auguste . . .*, Paris 1856, xcvii–iii). Delaborde (*Rec. Ph. Aug.*, i, no. 167) was also worried by 'l'énormité de quelquesun des privilèges concédés' (*sic*) that despite finding no diplomatic fault he labels it 'acte suspect'. The misconception is fundamental but could hardly have survived the briefest consideration of the whole group of franchises, to go no further (*Layettes*, i, nos. 143, 167, cf. 141; *Ordonnances des Rois . . .*, xvi, Paris 1814, 226–9; *Rec. Ph. Aug.*, i, nos. 22, 242). The Figeac ban (dép. Lot) which Philip merely endorsed (*annuentes pariter . . .*) was defined by lordship and applied to forts or *bastides* and religious foundations *viz. ne quis etiam infra metas possessionum ecclesie oppida seu municipia seu habitaciones alia sive domos religiosas, sine voluntate abbatis et capituli, edificare valeat*. The sporadically archaic phraseology is still more marked in the protection to Sarlat Abbey (Dordogne, about 35 miles north-west of Figeac) . . . *juxta tenorem . . . privilegii Ludovici Regis* (prob. Louis VI) . . . *nullus judex publicus* . . . etc., enjoining the abbey tenants not to build any *turris* in Sarlat town or any *castellum* in the monks' lordships or around Sarlat *proprius quam sit hodie absque eorum licentia*. This ban was upheld against Castelréal, a *bastide* project of Henry III and Edward I of England in 1268 and 1281 (*Les Olim*, i, no. 21; ii, no. 25). Louis VII's first protection (Feb. 1155) to Bishop John of Maguelone (Hérault) modelled on Louis VI (*sanximus ut nullus comes, nullus princeps, nulla alia layca potestas . . .*) has no castellation provision, added next year for Bishop Raymond *viz. et si castrum vel aliquam munitionem per to vel per alium ibi* (in the demesnes listed) *facere volueris, liceat tibi et successoribus tuis de nostra concessione absque omni contradictione* (confirmed 1208, 1271, 1287). Power to ensure security and due recognition of superior lordship is still clearer in Louis VII's (again very atavistic) Protection to Bishop Gauzelin of Lodève (Hérault) confirming (1162) royal *licenciam faciendi . . . turres, municiones, muros, portarum tuiciones* (*munitiones* in 1188), *vallos* (*sic*) in all his alodial properties and extensive *regalia* including (judicial cognisance of) *novas forcias*, especially within church appurtenances *et jus prohibendi facere novas forcias in toto episcopatu*. Philip II renewed this with insignificant modifications in 1188 (also confirmed 1210, 1283, 1464). Lordship support was the aim not restriction of fortifying as such; indeed, the grantee's castellation was facilitated.

of fortresses: or, less plausibly, as a campaign of military preparedness on Vegetius' maxim that *qui desiderat pacem praeparet bellum*; but legality of title and acceptability were essential to political security. *Realpolitik*, nevertheless, has a seductive glamour. By such a view it matters little whether a castle was demolished preventively, punitively or purely vindictively if firm government was thereby manifested – but no vassal was likely to acquiesce. It may well be that tenurial right in fortresses lagged behind other forms of realty so that fortress-tenure had remained precarious: the hypothesis would see Henry II and his sons acting within Carolingian doctrine, with unmitigated monarchy strengthened by conquest. Such terms as 'appropriation', 'resumption' or 'seizure' of baronial castles need careful use; 'receive in pledge', or 'borrow' might often be more correct. It may be significant beyond semantics that Henry II's legislation made seisin the *prima facie* test of right whereas under rendability the castle-tenant's occupation was interruptible but not his right of tenure and restitution. In one case before the Parlement of Louis IX, proof of delivery of a fortress for war to the count of Brittany as lord established that it was an act of rendability vindicating the claimant's right to restitution, despite prolonged deprivation. That rendability was indeed the principle of Henry II's resumption of 'all the castles in England and the March' (in Normandy also says Howden) by sending custodians to take them over, after the Young King's rebellion, at the Council of Windsor in 1176, can scarcely be doubted. Ceremonies of notional royal takeover, whether by exercising right of entry, by banner-placing *in signum dominii*, by receiving keys or by other acts reasserting Henry's lordship, could soon be performed at all the castles of bishops, earls and barons, as we are told was done, without recorded charge to the Exchequer. Rendability entailed such acts of recognition as well as delivering fortifications on demand for war or other purposes. English practice tallies equally with continental doctrine in the authorising of fortifying, except that the needs of the Conquest implied general franchises and until John's accession few licences survive or seem to have been given, at least in writing. In that it was centralised and decisive, albeit comparatively elementary, Angevin castle-policy seemingly radiates statecraft. In France, however, where pragmatic feudal management with Philip Augustus displaced imperial ideology, we look somewhat hard for that reawakening of national monarchy attributed to his reign. His was certainly not a fortress-policy of Angevin type: but if the methods are less recognisable Capetian aims become no less clear, for all that control of fortresses was necessarily more subtle and much more diversified than the Angevin.[17]

[17] A social interpretation of licences to crenellate and of castle-building is outlined in my 'Structural Symbolism in Medieval Castle Architecture' (*Journ. BAA*, 132, 1979, 73–90) whose specifically religious aspects are developed in my 'Hierarchism in Conventual Crenellation . . .' (note 3 above). W. L. Warren exults conventionally at royal ruthlessness with baronial castles but also stresses the heavy political cost of Angevin behaviour (*King John*, 50, 109, 170, 175–6, 181–3; Brown 1959, 252–3 for citations *et passim*). The reign of Henry I was a 'turning point' in the development of hereditary tenure, even landed security being precarious. Henry 'took for his own use the castle of Blyth' before Michaelmas 1102 (*Regesta*, i, no. 598; R. W. Southern, 'The Place of Henry I in English History', *Proc. Brit. Acad. BA*, 48, 1962, 145; Marjorie Chibnall, 'Robert of Belleme and the Castle of Tickhill', in *Droit Privé et Institutions Régionales . . . (études historiques offertes à Jean Yver)*, Rouen 1976, 151–6). Carolingian doctrines of public utility applied as much to the pre-Conquest *burh*

The *trésor des chartes*, apparently established in the castle of the Louvre after Richard's surprise attack at Fréteval in July 1194, still contains some eighty non-royal charters which directly relate to Philip II's fortress-policy and another forty-five which illuminate the intra-seignorial fortress-politics of the reign, often in great detail. Most of these eighty are rendability charters, that is, sworn undertakings, some with mainpernors and penalty clauses, obliging particular fortresses to be delivered to Philip whenever he should require, by summons under letter patent. A few are additionally summarised among the records of royal acts in Philip's three initial Registers for extra security and ease of reference, the originals being stored in the coffers or *layettes* later in the Sainte Chapelle treasury. The peripatetic records were largely reconstituted and successive rearrangements and up-dating of the Registers provided an accessible administrative memory for exercising the Crown's feudal and other powers, fortress-rights prominent among them. The new comprehensive Register of c.1211–20, for instance, was organised under ten sections with a separate folio for the communes and another for the services due from royal fiefs. Louis IX's *Registrum Guarini* improved upon it further, having eighteen sections, the first three being entitled *Feoda*, *Civitates*, *Castella*. A copy was made for the king to take on the Seventh Crusade (1248–55), leaving the original for his mother's use as Regent. Clearly, there is much more to this administrative thrust than bureaucratic tidiness. From the *securitates* granted to Philip II (or incidentally involving him) and from the seventy or so relevant royal issues down to 1214, a threefold distinction emerges; namely, fortress-cases due to the royal appeal jurisdiction; cases brought to the king as alternative to the pope, a bishop or a great feudatory for mediation and record; and thirdly, that category of cases, initially very small, which concerned the royal demesne or the royal power directly and arose from the king's own intervention and initiative, in all probability.[18]

(C. Warren Hollister, *Anglo-Saxon Military Institutions on the Eve of the Norman Conquest*, Oxford 1962, 142–5; and, less happily on 'The Conqueror's castle-policy', 141–2; J. M. Hassall and D. Hill, 'Pont de l'Arche: Frankish Influence on the West Saxon Burh?', in *Arch. Journ.*, 127, 1970, 188–95) as to post 1052 'castles'. Under rendability length of disseisin was no bar to title provided delivery for war on demand was duly proved; the tenant of Roche Derrien (Brittany) rendered the castle in 1230–5, his heir winning restitution from Duke John in 1272 (*Les Olim*, i, 311–13, 395–6, 904; *Actes du Parlement de Paris*, ed. E. Boutaric, i, Paris 1863, nos. 1456, 1788, 1845).

18 Royal judicial arbitrations were unsystematically recorded prior to 1254 but Boutaric appended to his preface an exceptionally notable case of June–September 1180, conducted at Pierrepertuis near Vézelai, which is very pertinent here (*Actes du Parlement* . . . , i, lxxx, ccxcvii; also *Rec. Ph. Aug.*, i, no. 8). The castellar (and seignorial) rivalry in Mâcon between the bishop and Count Gerard of Vienne was resolved by upholding a charter of Louis VII exempting the cathedral from comital lordship, the corollary being that Gerard in *villa Matisconensi nullam firmitatem habere debeat preter turrim suam quam tum temporis habebat*, whereas the clergy were entitled to fortify (*firmare*) both of their city precincts at will and likewise *firmitates aedificare vel augere* at all their extramural *ville* previously having defences. In Mâcon the count was neutralised symbolically and architecturally; his (other) dwelling there *quia supra consuetum statum firmitatem eadem domui adjecerat* (evidently part of his feudal aggrandisement) was adjudged rendable at will to the king to receive a large or small number of troops (significantly, *cum ad jura feodi nostri eadem pertineret*, not by regalian right, cf. Cluny 1119, Villemagne 1156, above) on pain of demolition of the newly fortified superstructure. For the archival details quoted see A. Teulet, *Layettes*, i, v–vi; H. F. Delaborde, *Layettes*, v, Paris 1909, ij–x; *Rec. Ph. Aug.*, i, v–xl; ii, Paris 1943, vj–xiii. The rubrics to licences to fortify on the English Rôles Gascons are comparatively haphazard, cf. Champagne record-keeping e.g. the c.1172 list of direct fiefs and dependent fortresses taken on the Third Crusade by Henri *le Libéral* (*Docu-*

The medieval usage of *castrum* and *castellum* suggests that 'castle-policy' to contemporaries would have signified what 'fortress-policy' means to us, but no philological purism is needed to justify giving a major place here to the walled towns and especially those chartered by Philip Augustus. The reserves of man-power, arms and money controlled by the *villes fermées* made them as important strategically as they were financially. Significantly, nearly all of Philip II's relate directly to the struggle for Normandy in the north-west and fall within the scope of the present paper. Their juridical status gives them immense importance in any consideration of the roots and evolution of fortress-customs, reaching back to Roman times. That public character which generically belongs to fortifications is the quintessence of the Gallo-Roman and Merovingian *civitas*, no less than the Carolingian, and it clung nowhere more tenaciously than to the ancient walled cities of Gaul. The contrast is very great with the relative absence of continuity in Anglo-Saxon England where the word *castrum*, vernacularised to variants of *chester* (*Ceaster*; *Caer* in the Celtic fringe) and tagged on to corrupted remnants of Latin names, became a popular term for almost any kind of major Roman fortified site. Soldier merged with civilian in the later Roman Empire and large fortified complexes, whether military-gone-native or urban militarised, became Frankish and eventually royal, comital or episcopal administrative centres, or capitals of lesser dignity, their special status still denoted by the style *castrum* in tenth and eleventh-century France. Direct links with the Crown, or the top comital échelons, ecclesiastical or lay, enhanced and perpetuated this rank especially as the *villes fermées* were both public fortresses and jurisdictional entities.[19] When evidence becomes more available in the charters of the twelfth century, the convention is ubiquitous that the defences of towns were public property, vested in the local ruler or in the Crown, or delegated to a

ments Relatifs au Comté de Champagne . . ., A. Longnon, i, Paris 1901, xiij *et passim*; Coulson 1982 *passim*).

19 The analogy with immune religious precincts is both intimate, ancient and persistent. S. E. Rigold pointed out that in Carolingian *Francia* and across the Channel coins and seals provide complementary evidence of the styles of rulers and the formal status of towns. Of the over eighty mint-towns of Charles II, nearly all fortified, 'about half are *civitates*, representing practically every see in *Francia* proper. The next most numerous category is *castra* or *castella*, other sites fortified since Roman days. . . . Then there are the privileged religious houses . . . and the royal establishments, *palacia* and *fisci* . . .' On the early *castrum* etc. see also J. Richard, 1960, note 8 above, 433–7; S. E. Rigold, Presidential Address, *British Numismatic Journal*, 44, 1974, 101–3, 106. Jean Mesqui has recently shown that the Crécy agglomeration was collectively styled *castrum* until 1289 when town and 'castle' are first distinguished. He gives a valuable note on terminology and attributes the style *castrum* in Champagne to the *statut juridique* of the site ('Les Enceintes de Crécy-en-Brie . . .', *Mémoires, Fédération des Sociétés Historiques et Archéologiques de Paris et de L'Ile de France*, 30, 1979, 15–16, 18–19, 44 note (2), 75 note (1) etc.). The defences of Langres (*munitio civitates*) market and mint were 'delegated' to the bishop as early as 814 (*Recueil . . . Lothaire* . . ., no. 29; confirmed 887; again, adding the *comitatus* and tolls taken at the gates, in 967). Licensing of town fortification has (2nd-century) Roman precedent and Imperial symbolism became increasingly military. MacMullen comments 'everything to do with the emperor . . . was already called *castrensis* before Septimius Severus ever entered the scene' (J. Wacher, 'A Survey of Romano-British Town Defences', *Arch. Journ.*, 119, 1962, 107 notes 16, 17, map 108 etc.; R. M. Butler, 'Late Roman Town Walls in Gaul', *Arch. Journ.*, 116, 1959, 25–50; R. MacMullen, *Soldier and Civilian in the Later Roman Empire*, Harvard 1963, 169). On the Chester names a convenient summary is K. Cameron, *English Place Names*, London 1977, 35–6, 54–5, 90, 110–12, 116, 154–5, 214; varied examples in *Arch. Journ.*, 124, 1967, 65; 127, 1970, 243–4; 128, 1971, 31–2 etc.

plenary commune. Repair was commonly a first charge on general or specific revenues and cognisance of the crime of dilapidation, and the right to oversee upkeep and guard in emergencies, belonged to the public domain. References abound to deleterious encroachment by house-building which so often obstructed the circulation within the *enceinte*, encumbered or blocked the *chemin de ronde* at the summit, or even endangered the walls themselves owing to the thrust of floor joists and roof timbers. Latrines built to overhang the ditch and windows (worse still, posterns) illicitly pierced in the wall, particularly by religious establishments desiring both wall-side seclusion and private access to extra-mural gardens, continually jeopardised urban defensibility. Philip II's predecessors proclaimed their peculiar authority over all such works in walled towns in direct royal lordship as insistently as over rendability and licensing but they were too easily seduced by the revenue-potential of dispensing their ban. In 1112 Louis VI sold back to the canons of Sainte Croix the right to build onto the city wall of Orléans next to their precinct, on condition of not making any doorway through it; but in 1127 he ratified the bishop's charter permitting them to do just that. Louis VII in 1163 licensed one Vulgrin d'Étampes to support his house on the wall and gave him a charter to produce if the work was challenged by the citizens.[20]

The power latent in the walled towns had to be cultivated, which is doubtless why Philip II in confirming (1181–2) the privileges granted by his father to Bourges (c.1175) conceded permission, which Louis VII had expressly refused, for houses to be built against and upon the city wall. Philip also made over his judicial cognisance of *muri pejoratio*, thus allowing an offender to fine and make good the damage at the citizens' discretion. Civic trusteeship in law enhanced the urban franchise and also the renown of the place and of its lord, which compensated for any resultant loss of defensibility. Moreover, the traditional belief that, of all fortification, work on town defences was pre-eminently publicly beneficial, indeed pious, was no lip-service. Urban oligarchies were habitually entrusted by kings and other lords with the upkeep, guarding and improvement of their fortifications; and when this duty and privilege was withheld, not fear of wartime treachery explains it most often but resentment of encroachment upon the lord's *dominatio* or his revenues. Resident ecclesiastical lordships, under whose tutelage a borough had originated or grown up, were notably sensitive about pressure on their lien on the fortifications; but lordly status was the cause not military strategy: indeed, fortress-policy cannot be

20 Luchaire (1890) nos. 137, 392. *Monuments Historiques*, no. 583. Orléans in 1057 was not a commune or privileged to have custody of its defences so royal officials had to be asked to keep the gates open during the *vendenge* (*Catalogue . . . Henri Ier . . .*, no. 109; instances collated in Coulson 1972, Index 'Towns, Fortified'). By the customs of Hénin-Liétard (Pas-de-Calais) confirmed c.1071–1111 (Count Robert I or II of Flanders) and renewed in 1144 by Count Thierry as *avoué*, again by Philip II in 1196, *valli munitionem et firmitatem tocius ville . . . burgenses . . . absque perjurio nequeunt pejorare*. Fines for damage allocated to repairs were kept in the burgesses' hands not the lord's (*Rec. Ph. Aug.*, ii, no. 529) Louis VII seems to have accepted a fine from the townsmen of Tournon *videlicet de domibus eorum quas intra et extra et supra murum nostri castelli et in fossatis nostris edificaverant, et altius solito levaverant, et de chiminis nostris supra et intus occupatis* (i.e. both the wall-walks and circulation at ground level; *Layettes*, i, no. 75). Henry I in 1101 alienated to Eudo *Dapifer* 'the city and tower and castle and all the fortifications of Colchester' with interesting emphasis (*Regesta*, ii, no. 552).

shorn of its social dimension. A complex of compelling reasons induced lords of towns to give up, not just defer for future increment, large sums of potentially taxable borough income by virtually irrevocable allocations at source of tolls and dues to be spent on the walls, along with streets, bridges and other common utilities; and to make on application continuous or *ad hoc* grants of timber, stone and other materials in addition to money, whether in cash or in tax remissions. This important part of Philip Augustus' fortress-policy merely applied the general and inherited principle more abundantly. It was regalian only insofar as it was also seignorial.[21]

His father's confirmation as early as 1150 to the river-port and arsenal at Mantes of a comprehensive set of privileges, including full control over the town barriers, the repair, defence and funding of the fortifications, showed the way forward. To his new commune at Chaumont-en-Vexin (Oise), not far from Saint-Clair-sur-Epte, Philip gave in 1182 the same perpetual power to fortify and levy murage, terms closely followed for the new communes of Pontoise and Poissy (Seine and Oise), both probably in 1188, all three like Mantes outposts of Paris against Normandy. The customs of Mantes were much used, notably in 1204 after the fall of Château-Gaillard for the borough of Les Andelys (Sure), but the equally popular customs of Lorris (Loiret) provide only for common works, and the studied omission of the fortification clauses from some Mantes-type charters shows that this culminating privilege, apogee of bourgeois liberty and prestige, was conferred selectively and with deliberation. In the exposed north-western region of Picardy four towns received charters modelled upon that of 1195 for Saint-Quentin, or, it may be, upon Royeen-Vermandois (both Somme) dated between 1185 and 1205. The others are Chauny-sur-Oise (Aisne, 1213) and Crépy-en-Valois (Oise, 1215). Each contains a slight variant of the clause *ubicumque major et jurati villam firmare voluerint, in cujuscumque sit terra, sine forisfacto eam firmabunt*. Specified court-fines are allocated to the defences, except in the Roye charter; and since all four were authorised to purchase land compulsorily, as with the Mantes-group, their

21 Louis VII's charter was to Bourges, Dun and the people of the *castellania* and *septena* (*Rec. Ph. Aug.*, i, no. 40; *Catalogue . . . Ph. Aug.*, 270, 395–6 for alienation in 1209/10 and 1218 of a postern and a gatehouse in his new enceinte of Paris. Defence was one factor only among many). On the licence to Bourges cathedral (1174) see note 15 above. Some walled towns were rendable in set form (e.g. Périgueux, 1204, below) particularly in the south. For examples 1095–1180 see *Layettes* i, nos. 39, 49, 59, 81, 186, 207, 250; v, ed. H. F. Delaborde, Paris 1909, nos. 34, 53, 70, 72, 78. Most of these are styled 'castle' (on vernacular 'castle' names cf. J. Gardelles, *Les Châteaux du Moyen Age dans la France du Sud-Ouest . . .*, Geneva 1972, 7–12 *et passim*). The *castrum* or *castellum* of Montchauvet (Seine et Oise) founded perhaps c.1120, was a refuge for the rural populace in war and had a civilian population (*Rec. Ph. Aug.*, ii, no. 732). The lord's right of access to towns (fortress-customs distinguish entry rights to towns; lordly refuge in danger, lordly garrisoning and/or requisitioning) seldom had to be spelled out, but lordship-competition might require explicitness (e.g. 1153, Le Tremblay town, Seine et Oise, *Monuments Historiques*, no. 523; 1155, city of Vienne, Isère, in Denis de Salvaing, *De L'Usage des Fiefs et Autres Droits Seigneuriaux*, Grenoble 1731, 81). Seignorial parallels are Anseau de Gallande's charter (1193, *Layettes*, i, no. 410) to his burgesses of Tournan (Seine et Marne); the liberties included cooperative fortification and licence: abbatial licence c.1100 to Saint Sever town (Landes): licence by the count of Sancerre to the abbey to fortify la Charitésur-Loire town, 1164 in perpetuity (*Thesaurus Novus . . .*, i, Paris 1717, 277–81, 464). For the lord-townsmen conflicts at Corbie and Noyon see note 24 below.

officials evidently had power to extend their fortifications not just to maintain them.[22]

In form all eight charters by Philip II confer the fullest licence to fortify without time limit, and royal authorisation is almost as explicit and fully as effectual in the privileges of Amiens (Somme, 1190), whereby two-thirds of the 9 li. fine for wounding one of the jurats is payable *firmitati urbis et communie.* Permanent assignment of fines *ad firmitatem ville* by view of the *échevins* figures also in the charter of Péronne, adapted for Cappy (both Somme) and for the *castellum* and *villa* of Hesdin (Pas de Calais), all issued in 1207 and specifying penalties for assault (100 s), wounding with edged weapons (10 li.), and for slander and brawling (50 s). The elimination of all allusion to fortifications (clauses 3, 4, 9) from the grant to Athies near Péronne, an otherwise almost *verbatim* version, confirms the careful discrimination between fortified and open towns in the same custumal group. In the case of Athies, rivalry with Péronne, or more likely with the non-royal town (*viz. castrum* or *castellum*) of Ham-en-Vermandois close by, may well explain it, but this charter of Athies does make clear that under the Péronne customs the Crown was relinquishing a half-share in these judicial profits. Péronne was strategically crucial and Philip not only renewed the 1207 charter, itself consolidating existing privileges, but renewed it two years later (1209) and on a visit there in May 1214, shortly before Bouvines was fought to the north-east (27 July), he supplemented the fortification-fund by giving up his rights over a plot of land close to the walls which could conveniently be inundated to make cress-beds to yield it further revenue.[23] As usual, the king reserved no powers of supervision or audit, other than implied by the presence of a royal bailiff, and he evidently had such confi-

22 Issoudun in Berri (1213) is the only significant case noted of a (subinfeudated) town denied the right to fortify by Philip Augustus (*Layettes*, i, no. 1040). Luchaire (1890) no. 254, confirming Louis VI (not recited), printed *Ordonnances des Rois* . . ., xi, 197 (8); *communes necessitates ut de excubiis, de cathenis et fossatis faciendis et de omnibus ad ville munitionem et firmitatem pertinentibus communiter ab omnibus procurentur,* according to individuals' means (Mantes). Between 1 Nov. 1201 and 13 April 1202, Philip II confirmed their fiscal advantages *pro servitio quod nobis faciunt et antecessoribus nostris (sic) fecerunt videlicet quod adjuvant ad honerandum et ad exhonerandum nostras machinas infra Meduntam* (i.e. shipping siege engines on the Seine to and from Normandy). The fortification clause (7 or 8) is almost *verbatim* 1150 in the other charters (*Rec. Ph. Aug.*, i, nos. 59, 233, 234; ii, 782, Les Andelys April-October 1204. Château-Gaillard fell on 6 March). The confident extension of such a degree of military juridical autonomy to Les Andelys reflects the firm Capetian *entente* with their own communes (Powicke 1961, 279 note 169; cf. Petit-Dutaillis, *Feudal Monarchy* . . ., 195–7 on borough-policy and the Lorris customs initiated by Louis VI). The Picardy formula lacks explicit delegation of custody of the defences. Artois with part of Vermandois, including Saint-Quentin, whose comital customs were ratified 1188–1197, became royal demesne in 1183 (*Rec. Ph. Aug.*, ii, nos. 491, 540, 1295, 1389). There may well be a sub-Carolingian regalian echo in *sine* (or *absque*) *forisfacto* as also in compulsory purchase for fortification (Coulson 1972, Index).

23 Amiens: *Rec. Ph. Aug.*, i, no. 319; iii, no. 1072 at Lorris; renewed *verbatim* 1209. Amiens must have had these powers of fortification and ground-purchase long before 1471 when enumerated (*Ordonnances des Rois* . . ., xvii, Paris 1820, 401–3). Péronne: *Rec. Ph. Aug.*, iii, nos. 977, 1067, 1333 cf. 408; renewed 1209, there was an earlier charter than 1207. Cf. *Recueil* . . . *Ponthieu*, no. 197 for the peat-revenues shared between Count William and the fortifications of Montreuil in 1210; Cappy cf. Athies, 1212 (*Rec. Ph. Aug.*, iii, nos. 984, 1217, 1237); Hesdin (*Rec. Ph. Aug.*, i, 408; iii, no. 983, as to Péronne, text lost) conceded *pacem et communiam propter amorem quam erga burgenses Hesdini habere volumus, tam propter ejusdem castelli commodum.* Philip acquired the fief from the bishop of Thérouanne (Petit-Dutaillis, *Feudal Monarchy* . . ., 201). In the Hesdin charter (1192) half the redemption fines of houses penally to be razed (especially for anti-commune crimes; a Picard feature,

dence in the loyalty, fiscal probity and technical expertise of his communes in general that he was able, as also at Noyon (1181–2) and at Saint-Omer (1197), to entrust them unreservedly with their own defence. Such emergency subsidies and interventions as were resorted to both by Philip Augustus (e.g. 1209–14) and by John (e.g. 1203–4, 1215–16) might be no more than ephemeral partnerships forged in the heat of crisis, but in Philip's case his borough charters are part of a long-term fortress-policy which had consistent aims and shows a shrewd grasp of the political and feudal realities.[24]

The essential context and understanding was, of course, that the royal host would be admitted at need to use the town defences as military base, refuge and arsenal like any other fortress, in cooperation with the citizenry. Rendability and the whole gamut of fortress-customs had long since articulated these obligations in terms of direct tenure in fief, lending a new feudal vigour to ancient monarchical right whenever no immediate (and prior) lordship intervened. There was no ambiguity about the military duties of royal walled towns, but it was otherwise when the burgesses of distant Périgueux (Dordogne) chose the climax of Philip's conquest of Normandy, in May 1204 at the siege of Rouen, as the appropriate moment to submit their city to his protection. Because direct royal lordship over Périgord had hitherto been in dispute with the Angevins, the envoys'

see J. H. Round, *Feudal England*, London 1964, 416–19) were allocated half to the king and half *ad villam firmandam*. For Ham town see note 26 below.

24 The contribution to Philip's army at Bouvines of civic levies is familiar (C. W. Oman, *A History of the Art of War in the Middle Ages*, London 1924, i, 474). All kinds of 'Grants for Fortification in France' are listed, including for Ponthieu after 1283 under Edward I and ducal Gascony, in Coulson 1972 appendix C I. They are of great significance, whether perpetual and vested or *ad hoc* for one to three years mostly, as in England where a number of murage grants were obtained by mesne lords (outlined in H. L. Turner, *Town Defences in England and Wales*, London 1970, appendix etc.). Embezzlement might occur, as shown by Edward I's great enquiry of 1274–6, but grants were still made on application (*Calendar of the Patent Rolls passim; Rotuli Hundredorum* . . ., Rec. Comm. 1834, i, 105, 108, 115, 131, 314–15, 322, 327–8, 353, 372, 398–9). At Noyon and at Corbie (Somme 1182) Philip II backed the townspeople against anciently entrenched ecclesiastical lords over the crucial seignorial test of control of the fortifications. At Noyon (near Compiègne) the bishop sought his support but *patrum nostrorum inherentes vestigiis* Philip confirmed the commune accorded by Louis VII and Louis VI and declared (clause 1): *Pro quacumque commonitione quam fecerint sive pro banno, sive pro fossato vel firmatione ville, neque episcopus neque castellanus habent ibi aliquid justicie vel implacitationis*. Notably this was probably not long after the count of Flanders had sacked Noyon (Nov. 1181). The later lordship-struggle is of great interest (*Rec. Ph. Aug.*, i, no. 43; etc.). At Saint-Omer control of the fortifications was probably completed by vesting the usufruct of the ditches, as at Doullens in 1202 (*Rec. Ph. Aug.*, ii, no. 557; *Recueil . . . Ponthieu*, no. 155). The sequence of events at Corbie is of exceptional interest: Charles III, in an assembly of counts and bishops (901) renewed Charles II's grant of immunity to the abbey, and by his mother's and local count's request reserved the newly fortified precinct to the monks' control *viz . . . ut nullus judex publicus in castello propriis sumptibus ac juribus (sic) infra ipsa monasterii moenia constructo nullam ibi quasi potestative licentiam habeat discutiendi aut ordinandi aliquod aut disponendi*. By the abbot's plea and assent, we are told, Louis VI founded a joint commune comprising the clergy, knights and burgesses, which Louis VII *assecuravit et manutenuit* and Philip II confirmed (1180) adding (possibly initiating but probably modifying) the provision that *nulli firmitatem infra banlivam Corbie licebit edificare, nisi per nostram (sic) et communie licenciam* (renewed 1182 and 1225 despite unspecified objections by the abbot). In 1255 the burgesses' murage-fund was quashed; jurisdiction was regained by the abbey (1306) and violence, provoked by the abbot, ensued (1307). In 1310 the commune was dissolved for debt, all rights reverting to the abbey, except for royal use in emergencies of the town defences (i.e. rendability; *Recueil . . . Charles III*, no. 41; *Rec. Ph. Aug.*, i, nos. 10, 52; *Layettes*, ii, Paris 1866, no. 1735; *Actes du Parlement* . . ., i, i, 6; i, ii, 32, 40; *Registres du Trdsor des Chartes*, i, Paris 1958, ed. R. Fawtier, 233).

act of recognition naturally took the form of a very explicit rendability charter. The cooperation between Philip and the men of Reims against the Anglo-Imperial coalition, prompted by his lending them 4000 li. to expedite their fortification in 1209, had to be expressed differently since the archbishop was lord of Reims and consequently had the defences under his authority, symbolised and to some extent implemented by custody of the keys of the gates.[25] Rendability had preserved but feudalised the uniquely public and regalian quality of fortifications in France, fragmenting and distributing the former royal monopoly, so that a subinfeudated fortress could be rendered only to the immediate lord who became answerable for it to his vassal and might not transfer his temporary right of use to his own superior. Walled towns present a few exceptions to this rule against 'sub-rendability', the pressures on mesne lordship being particularly strong from above and below. Odo lord of Ham-en-Vermandois agreed to the 'castle' being rendable by his burgesses to the king in 1223, and the public character of the major towns facilitated Philip's intervention at Reims in 1209, and in 1193–4 to help Count Peter of Nevers obtain aid from the clergy of Auxerre (Yonne) for walling that town along the river-side. In the growing danger of May 1210, Philip combined military precaution with scrupulous feudal propriety in tactfully lending the townsmen of Châlons-sur-Marne 2000 li. to speed up their works of fortification, without prejudice to the rights of the bishop who had denied clerical liability to contribute.[26]

25 Coulson 1972, Index, 'Keys and their Symbolism'; both aspects are evident in the revolt of Najac town (Aveyron) on the death of Raymond VII (1249); at Tours in 1241 the symbolic dominates the practical (*Layettes*, ii, no. 2892; iii, no. 3947). The citizens of Reims promised repayment in two years and *quod personam vestram et omnes vestros, quotiens necesse fuerit, contra Imperium et alia regna, que vos vel regnum Francie vellent impugnare, bona fide Remis recipient et civitatem . . . defendent.* This may have aggravated the lordship rivalry alluded to in Philip's order to the burgesses to restore the keys (1211; i.e. custody of the gates and tolls) to the archbishop (cf. Duke Hugh of Burgundy's settlement of a similar conflict in Lyon in 1208: *Layettes*, i, nos. 855, 903; *Rec. Ph. Aug.*, iii, no. 1221). The Périgueux envoys bound to the king *tota communitas ville . . . in perpetuum facere fidelitatem contra omnes homines et feminas qui possunt vivere et mori; et tenemur ei et heredibus suis tradere totam villam de Petragolis integre, ad magnam vim et ad parvam, quocienscumque dominus rex noster Philippus et heredes sui inde nos requisierint.* Philip reciprocated with inalienability and protection; renewed in detail to Louis VIII on his accession (*Layettes*, i, no. 714; ii, no. 1602; *Rec. Ph. Aug.*, ii, no. 800). In 1197 Count Baldwin of Flanders and Hainault, by force and bribery, neutralised the royal lordship over Tournai by a treaty whereby the burgesses would *inter alia* neither *firmare* the town nor receive (*receptare*) any French or hostile troops. Reception in towns, under rendability, is wholly distinct from the (obsolescent) *droit de gîte* (*albergamentum*; *Thesaurus Novus . . .*, i, 664–6; cf. 1182, 1210 *Layettes*, i, nos. 309, 947).

26 *Catalogue . . . Ph. Aug.*, no. 396, non-prejudice by Peter; *Rec. Ph. Aug.*, iii, no. 1130; cf. voluntary castle-works by the clergy for Count Simon to Epernon town and Houdan castle in 1208–9 (*Catalogue des Actes de Simon et d'Amauri de Montfort*, ed. A. Molinier, Paris 1874, nos. 23, 28) and King John's exhortations to the clergy of Limoges to fortify the city (*Rotuli Litterarum Patentium*, Rec. Comm. 1835, 134a; 1215). On sub-rendability see Coulson 1972, Index. The vassal-lord nexus of rendability was unimpaired by the introduction of liege homage; nor was it much affected by the revival of monarchic universalism under Philip IV. Although corroborative undertakings directly by burgesses to the overlord do occur (Joigny *castrum*, 1220–2; Neufchâteau en Lorraine, 1252) it is towns only and rarely, e.g. the *castrum* or *castellum* of Ham, sworn rendable by Odo to the king and heirs *vel eorum certo mandato, sicut suum feodum, ad magnam vim et ad parvam, quotiens . . . fuero requisitus*, underwritten by charter of the mayor and commune (*Registres du Trésor . . .*, i, nos. 768, 794–8, 876, 1498; Coulson 1982, 349–50, 358, 361; *Layettes*, i, nos. 1583, 1584). The feudal reciprocity of rendability is fully expressed by the ex-*bailli* Philippe de Beaumanoir (c.1283, ed. A. Salmon, Paris 1970; *Coutumes de Beauvaisis*, 1662–5) very much from the vassal's standpoint,

Fortresses under individual rather than collective lordship ('castles' according to modern convention) also required and rewarded a judicious fortress-policy but the seignorial niceties were here all-important: Philip, having put the theory of the past behind him, respected them impeccably. Castle-lords as of right and duty kept their defences up to date, fortified and licensed within their baronies, and had their vassals' castles rendered to them, looking to the king (if they held in-chief) to uphold their right as a good lord should, in case of need. Philip Augustus therefore continued his predecessors' policy of endorsing ecclesiastical castellation franchises, as much in the period of initial consolidation (1181, Sarlat Abbey) as after the treaty of Le Goulet (1208, bishops of Maguelone; 1210, bishops of Lodève and monks of Villemagne). Royal *dirigisme* and initiative, nevertheless, during the decade from the fall of Rouen to the battle of Bouvines, clearly formed new patterns in the texture of seignorial castle-politics with Philip sensitively exploiting fortress-customs to strengthen his feudal and military resources and to deny advantages to his enemies. This interventionism intensified after 1214 in his dealings with King John's defeated allies in the north-west, most notably the restive Flemish communes, and is best considered not here but in the context of his fortress-policy as a whole. Feudal politics must never be under-rated. There is an obvious danger in interpolating modern strategic ways of thought.[27] In the three Anglo-French treaties which usher in John's conflict with Philip Augustus, the fortresses are concerned primarily as tenurial entities: the body of law articulated safeguards and cease-fire lines. These are conventional elements in the treaties of 1194, 1195–6 and 1200, concluded respectively on Richard's return from his Austrian captivity; then after his partial retrieval of the situation in the duchy; and finally, after the accession of his brother. All the ramifications of fortress-tenure were within the law, but in such circumstances the liberties of castellans and of communes might suffer some usually temporary infringement, particularly to get assent to bans on fortifying. Such exceptions had to be carefully defined to preserve the quasi-demilitarised border zones from all but major and calculated breach; for example and most notably, Richard's building of Château-Gaillard after 1196.[28]

whose *forteresce* the lord might requisition at any time. Good lordship enabled Philip II in June 1214, just before Bouvines, confidently to abandon his *turris* of Montreuil-sur-Mer to the commune, despite the frontier location (*Rec. Ph. Aug.*, iii, no. 1336).

27 The forthrightness of Lt Col. A. H. Burne (*The Crécy War*, London 1955, 12) about what he calls 'inherent military probability' is as rare as rigorous analysis, but see R. C. Smail (*Crusading Warfare 1097–1193*, Cambridge 1956, 1–17, 60–2, 204–44) and C. Warren Hollister (*The Military Organization of Norman England*, Oxford 1965, 161–6). Philip II's fortress-policy was no more 'anti-castle' than it was 'anti-feudal'. Diagnostic early cases, not cited elsewhere in this paper, are 1180/1, comital rights at Parai-le-Monial; 1181/2, section of town wall of Soissons removed to obviate harm to the royal castle; 1182/3, fortifying in the castellany (*firmitas* . . . cf. *castellum* . . . *castellania*) of Concressaut in coparceny; 1188, 1192 castellation-lordship arbitration, le Puy, Auvergne; 1204/5 ban continued in lands of lay abbacy of Seignelai (*Rec. Ph. Aug.*, i, nos. 17, 44, 71, 239, 425; ii, no. 852). Philip II extended or made more efficacious and up to date his father's four ecclesiastical castellation franchises giving Lodève (1188, 1210) power also to coin money; feudally re-defining Maguelone's castellation rights (1208); confirming Sarlat and Villemagne (1181, 1210) and originally recognising the castellation franchise exercised by Figeac Abbey, Lot (note 12 above; *Rec. Ph. Aug.*, i, nos. 22, 167, 242, iii, nos. 1037, 1119, 1120).

28 Rymer's *Foedera*, i, i, Rec. Comm. 1816, 64 (1194, *per* Howden); *Rec. Ph. Aug.*, ii, no. 517; *Layettes*, i, no. 431 (1196: Philip's and Richard's counterparts); *Rec. Ph. Aug.*, ii, no. 633 and *Layettes*, i, no.

At this princely and pragmatic level the differences between Capetian and Angevin practice are submerged in common methods and concern to endow with legal durability the ephemeral effects of violence. Thus the 1194 armistice made 'between Verneuil and Tillières' debarred Richard from rebuilding any of the *munitiones* razed by the French during hostilities with four exceptions, but otherwise allowed both sides to fortify or to destroy all the *fortellescie* which were in their hands on 23 July. Richard gained more when the formal peace was duly concluded in early December 1195, as embodied in reciprocal charters dated 15 January 1196. The unstable balance of power had been forcibly tilted in his favour meanwhile. Philip's counterpart calls Richard his *amicus et fidelis* and royal right might be inferred from his apparently licensing Richard and Count Raymond of Toulouse to fortify within their lands henceforth as before *tanquam de sua*, but the reality was otherwise: it is a pact between equals, pragmatic not feudal, and Philip gained in return the right to fortify Châteauneuf-sur-Cher. All three treaties avoid the term *castrum* whenever the fortress proper not the castellany is meant, in accordance with this empirical spirit. Lesser magnates than these needed no licence from the Crown to fortify, and no vassalage was invoked here or elsewhere; the clause merely differentiated Richard's and Raymond's other territories from the sensitive war zone, where *ad hoc* and contractual restrictions were temporarily in force, on either side of the new frontier situated mid-way between the fortresses of Gaillon and Vaudreuil. The king of England similarly was permitted to rebuild Châteauneuf-de-Tours, but under French supervision and he categorically agreed not to fortify within the archbishop of Rouen's manor of Les Andelys, which was explicitly neutralised in Angevin possession. This was a quite conventional way of resolving the strategic problem due in this case to the enclave or 'bulge' north and west of the river Epte. Although by May 1200 the Angevin position was much less strong, especially by John's advent, King Richard's 'Saucy Castle' was left defending the breach and the way to Rouen down the Seine, although the treaty made at Le Goulet awarded to Philip the Évrecin. All new fortifying by either party was renounced in respect of the tract of country lying between Évreux and Neubourg, safeguarded by razing the fortresses of Portes and Les Londes as was not uncommonly done to ensure the integrity of partitions and new frontiers.[29]

578 (Philip's and John's counterparts); discussed e.g. Powicke (1961) 104, 107, 170–2, 192–6, 204–6. The ubiquitous *firmare* and *inforciare* made no distinction between such drastic feudal and strategic innovations caused by Château-Gaillard; extempore works such as the emergency 'enclosing' and 'fortifying' (*firmitas*, actually ditching) Evreux c.1193–4, partly on the bishop's land (the see and countship being vacant) *propter timorem regis Gallie* by an *ad hoc communia* of citizens and local villagers (challenged c.1205 as a civil trespass by the bishop and *ultra vires* though admitted to be within ducal powers: *Amplissima Collectio*, note 13 above, i, Paris 1724, 1061–2; also *Cal. Docs France* no. 414 n d); and thirdly, between mere stocking and 'garrisoning'. For comparisons of detail see e.g. the Franco-Castilian truce of 1280; 1176 Flanders-Hainault alliance; and 1173 Lyon-Forez partition, papally confirmed 1174 but not recorded in the royal court until 1183/4 (*Foedera*, i, ii, 581; *Thesaurus Novus* . . ., i, 585–6; *Rec. Ph. Aug.*, i, no. 103).

29 Jurisdictional boundaries of all kinds and scale up to inter-state frontiers were habitually defined topographically, and castellanies by reference to the component manors or units (e.g. Powicke 1961, 197–201, map IV; R. Allen Brown on *castellarie*, *The Normans and the Norman Conquest*, 215; C. Warren Hollister (1965) 150, 153). Whereas the knightly castle-guard circumscription of Montereau c.1172 was the *castellania*, at Provins it was specially delimited (*Histoire* . . . *Champagne*, ii, nos. 62,

Although Philip II's fortress-rights served his needs as king they owed almost everything to lordship over immediate vassals, very little to overlordship and almost nothing to monarchy. Notwithstanding his few (but important) advantages after Le Goulet unavailable to the great feudatories, he relied as they did on making a feudal reality out of sub-Carolingian theory and dealt remarkably confidently with fortresses, especially after 1196, in his piecemeal conquest of Normandy. By the treaty set down in January he gained Nonancourt castle and the entire salient northwards to Pacy and probably the castle of Grossœuvre also. Had the rôles been reversed, Angevin practice would surely have kept and garrisoned both with royal troops, alienation in custody at will, for term, life or in fief being less likely, and full hereditary enfeoffment hardly conceivable: and yet Philip, undeterred by briefly losing and promptly retaking Nonancourt, soon gave both away in full feudal right respectively to Peter Mauvoisin, and to his Pantler of the Household, William Poucin. The case is only one of many. Philip clearly judged that his vital interests were amply secured by the explicit but customary conditions of rendability attached to both enfeoffments, although his grip upon the fringes of Normandy remained precarious until Richard's death; likewise with the fortresses of Ivry, on the road to Évreux and near Grossœuvre, and of Avrilli, both taken from the duchy since the death of Henry II but in 1200 rendably enfeoffed to Robert of Ivry. The king was thus enabled to requisition them as often as he wished and Robert conventionally swore that he would deliver both fortifications *quotiens et quandocumque eas ipse . . . rex . . . vellet habere*, an oath underwritten by six mainpernors including Mauvoisin.[30]

70). Lordship-competition and war swept aside bounds of this kind, substituting a patrolling radius of effective surveillance (R. C. Smail, 1956, 61–2 *et passim*; Coulson 1972, Index, 'military functions of fortresses'; 'operational bases'). Precise topography and vaguely defined marches coexist in these treaties e.g. (1194) *citra Ligerim versus Normanniam*. Because the castle-proper of Châteauneuf-de-Tours was meant (1196) it is styled *domus Castelli Novi Turonis*. Fortifying at Quitteboeuf was forbidden in 1200 since it was on the English side of the new frontier but had been allocated to Philip (Powicke 1961, 170). Radepont castle (Seine Maritime, note 33 below) was razed in 1219 so as to favour neither co-heir, truly a judgement of Solomon. Cf. the 1201 partition between the four sons by her two husbands of the Poitevin lands of Lady Agnes (*Amplissima Collectio* . . ., i, 1138; *Catalogue . . . Ph. Aug.*, no. 1886 ; *Layettes*, v, no. 131.

30 *Layettes*, i, no. 594; cf. *Catalogue . . . Ph. Aug.*, no. 632; Peter, Gui and Manasses Mauvoisin and three others pledged all their lands. Robert's charter is not present. The *castellum* of Nonancourt, close to the new (1196) border, in William the Breton's phrase *in fisci castellum jura reducit* was the entire castellany, as Powicke (1961, 199 and note) pointed out. The enfeoffment of Mauvoisin was apparently preceded by a grant to Robert of Dreux but is likely to be 1196, at the same juncture as the nearly identical charter for Grossœuvre (*Grandis Silva*, near Avrilli *viz. Aprilliacum*, Stapleton map). Delaborde, Petit-Dutaillis and Monicat follow Audoin in suggesting 1196 despite Delisle and their own '1196–1202' for both charters (*Rec. Ph. Aug.*, ii, nos. 548, 549 and notes; Léopold Delisle, *Cartulaire Normand* . . . , Paris 1852, no. 182 as c.1201). The standard French editorial gloss and calendarist's formula for rendability 'livrer . . . à toute réquisition' is employed, vouched for by the phrase *ad magnam vim et ad parvam* but their comments betray some confusion with revocable grants, ignoring also that both are expressly hereditary despite their abbreviated Register form and apparent haste. Many instances show that such a phrase as *quotiens requisierimus nobis reddet Nonencurt et totam forterieiciam* means 'Nonancourt, namely the fortress', and the habitual *quotiens* or *quocienscumque* cannot be translated as 'when'. Furthermore, both texts (but not the glosses supplied) make clear that the liege bond was personal to the vassal, just as the rendability was peculiar to the fortifications (not generally to the fief). In 1205 Nonancourt was granted under rendability with Conches castle to Robert de Courtenai and heirs who thereby *nobis . . . tenentur tradere forterecias predictorum castrorum ad guerreandum et ad magnam vim et ad parvam*. Perhaps the male heir

Absence of trust and reciprocity of good-will, by contrast, pervade King John's very characteristic treatment of Ranulph of Chester over the earl's castle of Semilly (Manche) during the crisis of 1202. John first seized Semilly for suspicion then restored the castle on receiving guarantees from the archbishop of Canterbury and the bishop of Ely that Ranulph would acquiesce in a renewed arbitrary dispossession; which was, in fact, demanded and duly obeyed, discharging the guarantors from their obligations once for all but still giving the earl no promise of restitution. John was admittedly at a disadvantage: so much depended on moral and legal rectitude, sanctioned as it may be by success in arms. These assets he was losing or had already lost. Pledging of castles on an *ad hoc* basis, in which fear of treachery was balanced by fear of lasting disseisin, could not achieve that certainty of operation and security for both vassal and lord which rendability operated by the rule-book afforded. The Angevin record was bad and John's erratic seizures, hostage-taking and vindictive expedients inflicted on loyal and waverer alike had implanted mistrust and hatred not duty and respect. Rendable fortresses could more easily be demanded as pledges of good conduct, or to abort revolt, since no suspicion on the lord's part or demonstration of good-faith on the vassal's but an unconditional duty was the motive. Although John occasionally did utilise his lordship to obtain rendability in Gascony and in his other continental dominions, and perhaps also in England, the combination of the mistrust and misfeasance peculiar to himself with the whole antifeudal and dispossessory thrust of Angevin fortress-policy was to deprive John in adversity of the support which the Capetian confidently obtained.[31] Philip lacked neither precedent nor legal precision, needing only, to

envisaged c.1196 had not materialised (*Rec. Ph. Aug.*, ii, no. 875). Robert's counterpart states other restrictions but oddly omits the rendability again recognised in 1217 by his son (*Layettes*, i, nos. 747, 1262).

31 For Semilly (Similli) see *RLP*, 7b, 28 a; *Rotuli Normannie*, Rec. Comm. 1835, 96–7; Powicke (1961) 167. That John's conduct over baronial fortresses was true to his arbitrary style overall is unsurprising but still insufficiently pondered and related to fortress-custom (e.g. S. Painter, *The Reign of King John*, Baltimore 1949, 272, 352–3, 370; J. C. Holt, *The Northerners*, Oxford 1961, 94–5, 138; Warren, *King John*, 57–9, 109, 175–6, 181, 184–7, 190, 312). John's vindictive animosity in ordering castles and houses to be razed even without military expediency reached a pitch of idiosyncracy so that such an order seems to have been among the countersigns he used during the civil war to authenticate mandates to his henchmen. Even Henry II did not go so far nor, probably, did any ruler before Louis XI and the era of the Machievellian prince (*RLP*, 33a, 46a, 58a, 98b, 99a, 112a, 124a, 135a, 137b, 138a, 148b, 184b, 186, 187a, 190a, 195b; *Rotuli Litterarum Musarum*, Rec. Comm., i, 1833, 82a, 122a, 166b, 200 a, 244b, 260a, 279a, 284, 291b; *Rot. Norm.*, 55, 59, 95, 97, 118). The case of Montrésor (Indre et Loire) is characteristic: Gerard d'Athies was to free Geoffrey de Palluau in August 1203 leaving his castle in Gerard's hands as security, but John ordered it to be razed when received, nominally as a military precaution. This seems not, in fact to have been obeyed, as was often the case in England also, but Geoffrey defected to Philip Augustus as soon as it was safe to do so (*Layettes*, i, nos. 772–5; *Lettres de Louis XI*. . ., ed. J. Vaesen, E. Charavay, iv, Paris 1890, no. 566). Of the general doctrines of rendability signs in the English records from the later twelfth century are plentiful but lack legal precision. Continental phraseology used for Trim castle, co. Meath (1254) may be scribal confusion due to Gascon preoccupations, although repeated later (1267: *Calendar of the Patent Rolls*, 1247–58, 335; 1266–72, 109). The position is still as stated by Brown in 1976 (*English Castles*, 18, 235 note 10) but the apparent borrowing of baronial castles requires case by case investigation; even instances in France of rendable requisitioning may not be obvious e.g. John's mandate, 30 Sept. 1206, to take over Fronzac castle, Gironde, *ad opus nostrum in custodia* removing any disloyal occupants, *quod plus nobis reportamus necessarium* (*Rot. Litt. Pat.*, 67b). John denounced Langton (1215) as a 'notorious and barefaced traitor to us since he did not deliver up our castle of

cope with the exceptional strains of war and competing lordship, explicit charters of rendability, with collateral guarantees on occasion, to carry Capetian fortress-policy irresistibly forward to its vindication. As Philip's direct lordship was asserted within his conquests in Normandy, and as southwards towards Saintonge the wave of politic or coerced submission spread, so his feudal right of direct lordship attracted the prescribed formal recognition from fortress-tenants. Warfare afforded just the lawful occasion and military need to activate rendability where it was latent, or to extend it where lax lordship had let the practice fall into disuse despite the familiarity of the theory.[32]

The castle of Radepont (Seine Maritime) checked Philip's army for three weeks before being surrendered in late September 1203, as the blockade of Château-Gaillard began. Ruthlessly pursued through a severe winter and into the spring and as resolutely resisted, this siege is as well known as it was exceptional and untypical even of the military rôle of castles. The king's treatment of Radepont, about ten miles north and west on the river Andelle and essential to the blockading ring against English counter-attack, is therefore of the utmost interest. In 1202 an attempt to take it had failed but when he succeeded Philip promptly alienated Radepont to Peter de Moret in hereditary liege fief together with other lands late of Brice the Chamberlain, castellan for King John of Mortain and Tinchebrai, so that the fortress itself should be rendable on demand. Powicke found only the enfeoffment by Philip in 1206 of Montbazon castle in Touraine to compare with what he called the 'special conditions of service' attached to Radepont in the autumn of 1203. In fact, their peculiarity is confined to the stipulation that succession to the fief (*castrum*) should go only to Peter's children by his then wife and, secondly, to the extreme care with

Rochester to us in our so great need'. 'Necessity' is diagnostic. The bailey was in the archbishop's perpetual custody but William de Corbeil's dominant *turris* was their property since 1127 (*Regesta*, ii, 203, 356; R. Allen Brown, *Rochester Castle Guide*, HMSO, London 1969, 10–12; Warren, *King John*, 257). If rendability was, as we have suggested, more monarchical in England the efforts to preserve the Crown lien over castles given in longer-term custody (for life, life-fief, heritable fief) gain significance since the lien of rendability was a normal seignorial property, not a royal prerogative, within the European tenurial environment.

32 The contrast is notable between Philip's and John's dealings with William de Guierche (1204–15, especially 1214) over his castle of Ségré (Normandy-Maine border). Seeking to regain his grip on Poitou, based at La Rochelle, John in March-June 1214 made various conciliatory castle-grants in terms more generous than the usual enigmatic e.g. Rochefort (*Rot. Chart.*, 196a) to be held *libere et quiete, bene et in pace* as for landed fiefs; cf. (*RLP*, 68a, November 1206) grant of Châteauneuf and three other castles in full fief to R. de Talmont elliptically *salvo jure et servitio nostro*; similarly Coutures (Gironde) to the archbishops of Bordeaux but *quamdiu . . . fideliter versus nos continuebunt* (1214: *Rot. Chart.*, 201a; also *RLP*, 112b, 118b, 119b). The lord of Ségré had apparently already promised Philip II *quod non denegabimus ei, vel mandato ejus, domum nostram de Segreio in magna vel parva necessitate* when John (23 June, just before his ignominious retreat from the siege of Roche-au-Moine, 2 July, forced by the Poitevin barons' disaffection) 'granted and confirmed' to William de Guierche in full fief the *castellum . . . cum omni castellaria*. John was reduced to persuasion of good faith by terms which impliedly renounced seizure though not rendability (the habitual *quiete et pacifice . . .* supplemented by *sine aliquo retenemento preter servicium . . .* with most explicit warranty and the bribe of Guiomarc'h's forfeited houses in Anjou (*Rot. Chart.*, 199a; *Catalogue . . . Ph. Aug.*, no. 1496 as '1214, April?'; Du Cange, 'Dissertation', note 14 above, 506). Philip II in Anjou-Touraine-Poitou undoubtedly learned from John's *débâcle* (1202–4), negotiating pragmatically to obtain rendability and other fortress facilities with agreed penalties for breach, although by Capetian precedent or by current feudal law he could have demanded, and punished, non-compliance by outright forfeiture (Coulson 1972, 130–5, 221–31; note 33 below).

which the normal implications of rendability were applied to the local circumstances. In the traditional and elliptical phraseology habitual north of the Loire, worded as a perpetual grant, Peter de Moret undertook to hand over the *fortelicia ad magnam vim et ad parvam* to Philip in person and his heirs on demand, or to his well-known envoy bringing the king's mandate by letters patent. It was not unusual (and very natural at Radepont) to provide also that Peter's custodian for the time being should take the same oath, and likewise every member of the garrison, in case Peter or his heirs should be killed, captured or put under duress by the English.[33] The castle and town of the counts of Meulan at Beaumont-le-Roger, about thirty miles to the south-west on the river Risle, shared the strategic importance of Radepont at this juncture. This chief defence of central Normandy was betrayed in May 1203 by Count Robert's son Peter, although King John had observed feudal protocol and military prudence by sending in cash and supplies *ad emendam warnisionem ad castrum nostrum (sic) de Bello Monte*; perhaps it was in part a legacy of Richard's punitive and humiliating demolition of the *turris* of Beaumont in 1194. In October 1203 after Peter's death, by a charter dated 'at Gaillard', Philip II gave the *castellum* in liege fief to Guy de la Roche *tanquam aquestum nostrum*. As at Radepont, the fortified *caput* (*castellum cum fortelicia*) was to be rendered to the king as often as asked, by mere summons, under oath renewable by Guy's heirs. There is nothing to anticipate Philip's severe (but most interesting) punishment of Guy's offence of talking to 'the traitor and thief' Walter de Mondreville, for which complicity Beaumont town and all his rights there (evidently including the fortifications) were judicially forfeited, in January 1206. Guy was banned from central Normandy across the rivers Eure and Epte, and seven of his knights were made responsible for denouncing any future suspicious behaviour. In addition, 'all his other fortresses' were to be handed over to Philip on demand, ominously and abnormally *ad faciendum voluntatem suam* which is redolent of pledging not of rendability. The implied threat of disseisin may well have stiffened a pre-existing rendability since Guy's *quotiens . . . fuero requisitus* and Philip's absolute discretion are diagnostic. And rendability, in that it affirmed lordship, was not employed punitively and even the banning of fortifying by individuals was seldom precautionary in any military sense. The tenure of a fortress in fief

33 Powicke (1961), 164–5 (including an excerpt of Philip's charter), 258 note, 275, map IV. John had fortified and garrisoned Radepont, crucial after the loss of the Norman Vexin, and financed the same at Stephen Longchamps' manor of Douville on the other bank of the Andelle (relevant fortification grants 1200–3 by John are *Rot. Norm.*, 26, 52, 74, 87, 88, 97; *Rot. Litt. Pat.*, 10b, 11a, 25a). Despite phraseology exclusive to rendability and peculiar the note to *Rec. Ph. Aug.*, ii, no. 761 infers that 'le roi a voulu tout de suite confier la place importante de Radepont à un homme sur, et les précautions qu'il prend montrent qu'on est en pleine guerre'. On this reckoning, royal garrisoning not alienation might be expected. The editors wrongly imply that Peter was custodian only and the tenure anomalous; it should be compared with Ségré (above) and Philip II's other fortress-pacts 1204–14 as well as with Montbazon (*Rec. Ph. Aug.*, ii, no. 839; *Catalogue . . . Ph. Aug.*, nos. 967, 1165; *Amplissima Collectio . . .*, i, 1099; *Layettes*, i, nos. 771, 772, 804, 805, 813, 892, 936, 954, 995, 1002, 1010, 1014). Even Radepont's military importance must not be exaggerated; under four years after Bouvines Philip readily agreed that the *forteritia* be razed and rebuilding forbidden in order to perfect an equal division of the fief between Peter de Moret's two sons (March 1219; *Amplissima Collectio . . .*, i, 1138; *Catalogue . . . Ph. Aug.*, no. 1886) cf. Portes and les Londes after Le Goulet (note 29 above).

implied and sometimes explicitly obliged repair and improvement. To remove this entitlement at the *caput*, or within the lordship at a new site, was an act of derogation of the vassal whereas by rendering his castle he signalised his feudal relationship and his lord's security.[34]

We have suggested that French fortress-customs, interwoven with the other ties of the castle-tenant to his immediate lord, very largely obviated the arbitrary expedients of Angevin practice. The continental context will supply the detailed proof. Rendability is no more than part (albeit the most expressive) of a complex of regional customs possessing a strong family resemblance throughout what was once Carolingian Gaul. Intimately and exclusively linked to direct lordship in the earliest feudal evidence (of the earlier eleventh century), fortress-customs comprise 'jurability', lordly refuge rights, protection and military support, 'razeability' or precarious existence, and also include rights of fortifying and of lordly authorisation. The recognitory procedures of banner-placing and delivery of control (*potestas* in the Languedoc); the mode and occasion of summons to render; the reciprocal duties of vassal and lord, and not least the formidable historiographical problem of the obscurity of fortress customs since the end of the Ancien Régime, all require systematic examination. What is true of thirteenth-century Champagne probably holds good for many of the provinces north of the Loire, and gives some indication of the prevalence of rendability; but its latent potentiality is no less important although much harder to quantify. In the provinces of the Provençal cultural area and throughout the south, rendability was evidently inherent in fortress-tenure to the point of being axiomatic by the thirteenth century. It is possible to speak of rendability as a contingent liability at least throughout the north, judging from declarations of general and official record ranging from the Norman *Consuetudines* to the legist Beaumanoir, and from a sample of the charter material in print; but if the customs were demonstrably ubiquitous their application was clearly less than universal. The 1091 declaration might justify assuming that a fortress held *per consuetudines Normannie* would be rendable, at least if held in chief of the

34 Powicke (1961), 101–2, 161 note, 283, 344–5; *Rec. Ph. Aug.*, ii, no. 766; *Layettes*, i, no. 799; *Catalogue . . . Ph. Aug.*, no. 968. Guy was to hold *in ea saisina in qua Petrus de Mellento illud tenebat eo die quo decessit.* The distinction between his personal liege homage for the fief and the rendability attached to the fortifications clearly emerges, the latter (in the editor's conventional modern and inadequate phrase) Guy and heirs 'devront . . . remettre au roi à toute réquisition'. Guy's counterpart, not in the *Layettes*, will have been exchanged for the cancelled royal issue in 1206 when the town (and castle proper) was quitclaimed. No fortification ban (or prohibition) was imposed but Philip II interfered with such *seignoralia* extremely rarely. Castleworks were appurtenant rights of the Norman *mota* in a hauberk fief (*Jugements de l'Echiquier de Normandie* . . ., ed. L. Delisle, Paris 1865, nos. 73, 341, 679). Security and symbolism dictated Philip's treatment of the defeated allies of Bouvines (Coulson 1972, 135–8) but the trusted partisan of Arthur of Brittany, Juhel de Mayenne, tenant in rendability of Guesclin castle (1210) was only stopped from fortifying (1211) at Bais (Mayenne) so as not to encroach upon the royal forest or lordship (*Layettes*, i, no. 936; *Rec. Ph. Aug.*, iii, no. 1177; Powicke 1961, 74, 132, 146, 176). It must be stressed that Gui de la Roche's forfeiture by due process was for treason not connected with the contingent tenurial liability of Beaumont castle to be delivered on demand 'to great force and to small' (usually coupled in the Langue d'Oîl with a corresponding promise by the lord to restore the place *cessante negotio* or similar phrase), cf. Philip II's threat to Renaud de Dammartin (August-September 1211) demanding delivery of Mortain castle on his fealty in pledge to abate suspicion. The *fortericia* was not apparently rendable (*Rec. Ph. Aug.*, iii, nos 1202–3).

duke, but when individual specification is so precise silence in the record is very telling. One instance is the enfeoffment of Argentan (Orne) in June 1204 to Henry Clément, marshal to Philip Augustus, which does however state most exactly what use he might make of the forest there. Personal proximity, or otherwise, to the king gives no help, or scarcely any guidance, even less than do bans on fortifying. Exemption from rendability was so exceedingly rarely accorded, and then temporarily, that its presumptive effect is strong. Certainly, the nature of the sources and probably also the medieval legal mentality itself make any rigidly quantitative approach to fortress-customs somewhat misjudged.[35]

What mattered to William Marshal, earl of Pembroke, in his dilemma of double lordship in May 1204, and likewise in very many critical and run-of-the-mill contingencies of fortress-tenure, was that a legal code and chivalric *vade mecum* was always available which safeguarded vassal rights and lord's interests, clear in principles and precise in detail. Philip Augustus in the worsting of King John reaped the advantages of his record of good lordship and the Marshal was only the most noteworthy beneficiary, in the matter of his three Norman castles. He received far better treatment than at John's hands. His pact with Philip in late May 1204 at Lisieux hinges upon the central principle of rendability that the use, possession and control of a fortress may be temporarily but indefinitely transferred to the lord, without impugning the tenant's right or security of restitution; conversely, the lord's right to requisition or have assurance of the neutrality of the place made to him ('jurability') implied no derogation of and required no dispeace towards the tenant (*iratus seu pacatus*, as it was phrased in the Midi). William accordingly handed over *ad presens* (since the act unqualified of itself recognised Philip's lordship) his capital fortress of Orbec (*castrum Orbec et fortericia*), south-west of Lisieux, for the king to use for warfare or not. Longueville and Meulers, William's two lordships in the north near Dieppe, were beyond the war zone so the correct course was to place their capital fortresses (*castra . . . et fortericie*) in the hands of a non-suspect third party Osbert de Rouvrai under pledge of neutrality until midsummer. After that time Philip might requisition, garrison and use them also. For this respite of homage until mid-May 1205 William paid 500 marks by instalments but secured thereby recovery of his land and his *castra . . . in eo puncto in quo ei illa tradidi* exactly according to the terms and phraseology of rendability. Until that time the Marshal would only suffer forfeiture if he failed to pay the instalments due in

35 *Rec. Ph. Aug.*, ii, no. 807; iii (1207/8), no. 986; cf. Powicke (1961), 257, 275; Coulson (1982), 362–3 *et passim*; general summary of Coulson 1972 in my 'Rendability and Castellation . . . ' (note 6 above). A study is in preparation including the historiography of rendability since 1610 (Heinrich A. Rosentall, Cologne) *via* the *feudistes* (Salvaing, c.1667, Du Cange 1668, Brussel 1727) to Auguste Longnon (1869–1901) and Charles Bémont (1906). The contrast between Capetian rectitude and Angevin harshness can be ingenuously, or chauvinistically, exaggerated (R. Fawtier, 1962, note 13 above, vii–viii, 25–6, 38, 42, 45, 47 etc.) but in fortress-policy its significance can hardly be over-emphasised. Even when determinedly exploited feudal custom was the common *modus operandi* of noble social relations. After 1216 the Angevin monarchy was obliged to work more within the consensus afforded. Whereas their castle building slackened in pace that of the Capetians (notably in the construction of feudally eloquent *donjons*) accelerated after c.1214 (Raymond Ritter, *Châteaux, Donjons et Places Fortes*, Paris 1953, 55–8; R. Allen Brown, H. M. Colvin, A. J. Taylor, *The History of the King's Works*, London 1963, i, 113–19).

June and August 1204, or otherwise broke his side of the agreement. The sum was moderate and the terms quite generous. Indeed, Philip ignored his own promise to the count of Boulogne in 1203 to give to him the lordship of Meulers when it should be captured, but personal regard for the Marshal was one factor only in procuring this favourable treatment.[36]

The Marshal castles were duly restored in 1205 as was envisaged. Since rendability took no cognisance of the innovation (and rather brief efficacity) of liege homage the legal problems of serving two masters did not affect Longueville, Meulers and Orbec which, after the elimination of John's mesne lordship, were held directly from the French Crown. In July 1219, after the Marshal's death, these tenures were provisionally renewed without cavil in favour of his widow. The Countess Isabella undertook that her custodians would swear to render the castles, supplementing her personal oath (as non-resident and multi-castle tenants were occasionally asked to do) in war or peace *ad magnam vim et ad parvam* in the usual form. When her eldest son William passed on the family's Norman lands to Richard Marshal in 1220, the rendability of the three *fortericie* was reiterated as a matter of course.

Thinking of castles in a context of national politics no less than as part of such an armed and diplomatic struggle as was fought out between 1202 and 1204 over the duchy of Normandy predisposes one to concentrate on their military rôle, but feudal protocol was just as much attached to their symbolic aspect; perhaps more so. King Philip's counterpart contract for the surrender of Rouen dated 1 June 1204, if John failed to relieve the city, specified that it meant *civitas . . . integre cum omnibus fortelicus*. All knights holding fortresses were to provide hostages individually, in addition, surely so that due recognisance of Philip's lordship should be made in respect of them and rendability be written into their enfeoffments under the new dispensation.[37]

36 The fortress-law aspects of this well known pact, made during the siege of Rouen, deserve attention (*Layettes*, i, no. 715; *Cartulaire Normand . . .*, no. 74; S. Painter, *Reign of King John*, 37–8, 213–14; Powicke (1961), 213–14, 251, 260, 262, 266, 294–7, 350; Warren, *King John*, 104–5, 184–7). W. L. Warren follows Sir Maurice Powicke in assuming that the lands primarily were made over but Philip's reversion in case of William's default governed *predicta castra*, the administrative centres and symbols of their respective lordships. Whereas William was to recover for his eventual homage *castra et terram meam* this looks like a catch-all phrase and although the form of words *castrum et fortericia*, habitually used to distinguish *caput* from fief, is not found here, clearly the castles were paramount. Philippe de Beaumanoir (c.1283) admirably expresses the chivalric mutuality which imbues the pact between Philip II and the Marshal. The aspect touching King John's personal proclivities most nearly is illustrated by *Coutumes du Beauvaisis* cap. 1662 denouncing abuse of rendability by a lord to oppress his vassal or to *pourchacier vilenie de sa fame ou de sa fille ou d'autre fame qui seroit en sa garde* (Salmon, 351).

37 *Layettes*, i, nos. 1354, 1397; *Rec. Ph. Aug.*, ii, no. 803. In 1219 at Pont de l'Arche William junior and Richard Marshal were given leave (severally) *veniendi in Franciam* but with five knights only in addition to their suites (*familia*). Rouen surrendered on midsummer's day 1204, six days before the very typical (but exceptionally detailed) truce ran out.

18

The Impact of Bouvines upon the Fortress-Policy of Philip Augustus

Charles L. H. Coulson

Castles, the whole phenomenon, are a humane study demanding, beyond the now-fashionable synthesis of 'history' and 'archaeology', a broad and humane perspective. This supreme quality, served by architectural insight, Allen Brown has long combined with a forcefully expressed vision of the central place of the castle in the feudal world. We have all learned much. Those who have been privileged to work under his inspiriting and relaxed supervision have been particularly fortunate. Fortresses were juridical and dynastic statements, as well as pieces on the political chessboard, and to treat of them accordingly *im Rahmen der politischen Geschichte*, without as well as within the bounds of *Normannitas*, is to follow where Allen has led.

We have sought elsewhere to show how Capetian traditions, derived from Carolingian theory mediated by feudal custom, equipped Philip II, during the years of precarious growth of kingship culminating in the seizure of Normandy, with wide-ranging powers over fortresses, both castles and walled towns, some immediate and others latent and potential.[1] Direct feudal rights over fortresses held in-chief had, in practice, displaced the universal control of use (rendability) and licensing of fortifying of sub-Carolingian doctrine. These fortress customs went far to meet the needs of monarchy, political as well as military, while also safeguarding the interests and goodwill of fortress-tenants, sole or corporate – in clear contrast with Angevin practice. The Capetian moved cautiously, affirming the fortress-rights of ecclesiastical franchises, acting on appeal or as arbitrator in castle-disputes, and as lord in the royal demesne, but taking no more than *dominatio*, with perhaps just a tincture of regalian prerogative, might justify. Re-activating existing feudal liens upon fortresses, making the potential actual and sometimes initiating castle-pacts contractually but in feudal format, Philip's fortress policy down to about 1202 was largely opportunistic, responding to events.[2]

The present contribution must again be restricted to the Capetian-Angevin

1 For fuller references on the issues touched on in this paper see Charles Coulson, 'Fortress Policy in Capetian Tradition and Angevin Practice: aspects of the conquest of Normandy by Philip II', *Battle* vi (*hereafter* Coulson 1983), 13–38 *passim*. My thanks are due to Richard Eales for commenting on the draft version.

2 On the administrative impact of the conquest of Normandy cf. J. W. Baldwin, 'La décennie décisive des années 1190–1203 dans le règne de Philippe Auguste', *Revue Historique* cclxvi, 1981, 311–37. Castle policy before 1214 lends little support to his thesis.

confrontation in north-western France, ignoring the English provinces south of Normandy. It seeks to complete the previous essay, by considering Philip's castle-pacts immediately before his transforming triumph at Bouvines on 27 July, 1214, and examining how far, in relation to the treatment of King John's defeated French allies, 'new' elements may have been developed. When kingship was as pragmatic as Philip's, such a question must largely turn upon the chronological perspective and definitions adopted – the fortress powers of sub-Carolingian imperial ideology were so complete that any advance in monarchical theory would be relative. In practice, however, Philip's full use of the feudal means available to him, and his disregard of the fictions current in Capetian diplomatic down to 1180, are what distinguishes his monarchy, at least until Bouvines. It is then, in his ascendancy, that further development might be expected: and fortress-practice is an acute gauge of governmental power.

In the sensitive provinces, bordering on the Empire and English-influenced Flanders, we have shown with what realism and care Philip endowed the strategic walled towns with control of their defences, with revenues and powers of fortifying, attributes which ennobled the communal franchise and at the same time assured their loyalty and gave the king military advantages. From the fall of Rouen on 24 June 1204 the conflict in the north was prepared by giving privileges to Cappy and Hesdin (1207), to Péronne (especially important; 1207, 1209, May 1214) and to Chauny-sur-Oise. The majority of Philip II's borough charters for walled towns are, in fact, related to the Angevin struggle in the north-west. They were complemented by castle-pacts typical of the other current marches of Capetian influence, particularly Touraine and northern Poitou, and well exemplify the subtle negotiated coercion which Philip employed. In July 1203 already, while at Vaudreuil, Gui de Senlis the Butler and two other lords went bail, each in 100 *livres*, that Simon de Beausart (Somme) would hand over (usually *reddere*; sometimes *tradere*) his *fortericia* on royal summons instantly *ad magnam vim et ad parvam* (i.e. to mere request as to force) however many times it should be demanded.[3] The format is normal feudal rendability (Simon apparently held Formerie castle, Oise, also rendably of the Bishop of Beauvais), but the political imperative is clear.[4] The castle (*domus*) of Malannoi in Artois,

3 *Layettes du Trésor des Chartes* i, ed. A. Teulet, Paris 1863, nos. 680–2; each notifies that *Simon de Bellosarto juravit domino meo Philippo illustri regi Francie quod reddet ei forterciam de Bellosarto ad magnam vim et ad parvam quocienscumque dominus rex eundem Simonem super hoc requisierit*, and undertakes to pay the 100 li. Paris within forty days of Simon's default upon royal summons.

4 *Recueil des Actes de Philippe Auguste* (hereafter *Rec. Ph. Aug.*) ii, eds H. Fr. Delaborde, Ch. Petit-Dutaillis, J. Monicat, Paris 1943, no. 714; *ibid.* iii, eds J. Monicat, J. Boussard, Paris 1966, no. 1137: donation of Formerie to Philip's kinsman and ally the bishop for twenty-two years (1202) until return to the due heir (who may have pledged it for payment of relief). The royal charter of 1210 notes that Simon *de Bello Sacco* has redeemed the town of Beausart and holds it in liege fief of Beauvais, adding *domum autem et fortericiam ad magnam vim et ad parvam episcopo et successoribus ejus reddere ad suam voluntatem preterquam contra nos idem Simon juravit*. Intrusion of the king's interest (inherent in the liege tie) in this limited form is notable and so is the spelling out in this instance of the normally (in the Langue d'Oïl) assumed duty to return the castle in the same condition as it was when delivered as soon as the lord's need of it was over (*et ipse episcopus eidem Simoni creantavit quod domum et fortericiam post negotium suum in eo puncto in quo eam episcopo tribuet* (a rare word in this context) *ipse Simon, Simoni reddet episcopus bona fide*). The precision was no doubt called for by the bishop's personal standing and by the unexpired term of the 1202 charter, in order to safeguard

being a fief of Lillers and the rightful heirs of Flanders, could not be made rendable to Philip but its lord was able (1209/10) to promise its support to the king and his heirs against all others. A relative guaranteed the charter under penalty and should the immediate lords sue for breach of the legal proprieties as a result of the concession to the king, Philip promised his backing.[5] The Count of Saint-Pol, also in Artois, was not bound to the Imperial coalition and was thus able to make his capital castle (*fortericia*) unequivocally rendable (1210).[6] Philip was notably tactful in trimming feudal rectitude to raison *d'état*. It was often done by granting a money-fief to create a direct bond incorporating rendability or some lesser facility. Philip also, in 1210, obtained the promise of support against the Emperor from the castle of Nogent-le-Roi to the north-east (Haute-Marne), a fief held of the county of Champagne, in dispute since the death in 1201 of Thibaud III, and so any action prejudicial to the rightful heirs was duly excluded.[7] Also on the marches of the Empire, control at will of the *castrum* of Cours-en-Bourgogne (Yonne) was secured in 1212. The castle was evidently in addition 'jurable' (i.e. *reddibilis et jurabilis*) since Geoffroi de Cours by the same charter 'swore it' in traditional form promising, namely, *quod vobis vel vestris gentibus de dicto castro malum non veniet neque dampnum*.[8]

Simon's rights to seisin under normal rendability tenure. The usage 'house and fortress' (i.e. 'the fortified dwelling', *anglice* 'castle') was habitual in Champagne. For this and nomenclature generally see C. Coulson, 'Castellation in the County of Champagne in the Thirteenth Century', *Château-Gaillard. Études de castellologie européenne* ix–x, Caen 1982 (*hereafter* Coulson 1982), 349–56.

5 *Layettes*, i, nos. 870, 871; charter by Hugh and guarantee by Renaud d'Amiens (perhaps the heir's designated guardian) pledging all his lands (but after Hugh's death, if his heir break this bond, only 400 li. Paris) effective within forty days on royal demand. Should Hugh's land come into Renaud's possession he will be directly liable. *Rec. Ph. Aug.* iii, no. 1082 (royal version) adds the promise to favour Hugh judicially should the lords of the fief *super hoc moverent ei questionem injuste*: this much Philip as overlord could do. Unusually the rendability formula is used for Hugh's promise of military aid from Malannoi (*juravi super sacrosancta . . . quod ego et heredes mei ad magnam vim et ad parvam erimus eidem et heredibus ejus fideliter in auxilium de domo mea de Malno-alneto* except against Flanders (heirs of Emperor Baldwin, 1204–5) and the Lady of Lillers (near Béthune) *si forte dominus rex adversus eos guerram haberet in capite*. The conflict in the north was clearly expected.

6 *Layettes* i, no. 914. Gaucher de Châtillon, Philip's cousin, for himself and his (immediate) heir promised *corporals fide* to deliver Saint-Pol-sur-Ternoise (Pas-de-Calais) to the king (and heirs) *quocienscumque ei opus fuerit et nos exinde requisierint*. The succinct text (known only from copies in two of Philip's registers) has an *ad hoc* character. Gaucher, in April 1213 (*Rec. Ph. Aug.* iii, no. 1291) received a life-grant of the impoverished priory of Oeuf-en-Ternois from the distant mother-house of Marmoutier (near Tours). He was to maintain and improve it. Significantly, the king ratified but did not manipulate the situation. The stipulation (in archaic language evidently derived from the Marmoutier original) that Gaucher should build there no *turris vel aliquod propugnaculum* derives from concern that monastic use was to be preserved (one monk was to be kept) and their reversion protected. Fortifying often symbolised proprietorship. For an exact analogy (1238) see *Recueil des Chartes de L'Abbaye de Cluny*, eds A. Bernard, A. Bruel, vi, Paris 1903, no. 4736.

7 *Catalogue des Actes de Philippe Auguste* ed. L. Delisle, Paris 1856 (*hereafter* Delisle 1856) nos. 1189, 1190: charters by Renier de Nogent and two guarantors pledging 1000 li. Provins. Nogent is not mentioned in the Champagne fief rolls as rendable (or jurable) to the counts, but omissions and discrepancies do occur (Coulson 1982, 363). For castle-pacts procured by granting *fiefs-rentes* see *ibid.*, 358–61. Philip's partisan stance towards Countess Blanche and the young Thibaud IV may well have facilitated this pact. Royal overlordship was clearly a factor with Malannoi but any direct intervention was again highly punctilious.

8 *Layettes* i, no. 1009. Each charter in this phase is idiosyncratic, reflecting crisis conditions rather than a settled tenurial situation. In a charter of letter-close style, with a personal address, Geoffroi *de Brena* pledges himself and all his lands, binding himself by oath *quod vobis vel certo nuntio vestro reddam castrum meum de Corz ad magnam vim et ad parvam quociens a vobis vel certo nuntio vestro*

Neutrality was sometimes almost as valuable as active help. Takeover under rendability afforded full control (*plena potestas* is the Languedocien term) whether of nominal command of a castle or the right to garrison it or to resort there with a field force.

In each of these cases, entirely typical of the large *corpus* of such charters, Philip acts very much as an ordinary great magnate did, operating the feudal levers, moving into any vacuum. A delicate balance between his persuasive pressure and competing spheres of influence adjusted the realities of castle-tenure with a calculated but minimal infringement of mesne rights. There is no attempt, on the analogy of liege homage, to institute – or revive – what may fairly be termed *arrière-rendabilité* (sub-rendability) at this stage or after 1214. Procedure was directly feudal. Marchéville (Eure-et-Loir) was a fief of Chartres and Count Thomas of Perche in 1211/12 obtained first his lord the bishop's permission before making the castle rendable to the king.[9] Even the acquisitive Philippe le Bel, a century later, could not override mesne rights and directly take over fortresses in sub-fief, although in one instance he seems to have tried.[10] Instead, special pacts with the mesne lord, safeguarding his rights, are occasionally found. As with Marchéville, they are temporary expedients only and highly exceptional, only adopted apparently when the intervening body was a compliant ecclesiastical lordship. It was also exceptional for Philip II to interfere more than incidentally with the right of the direct lord, if as usual of baronial rank, to authorise fortifying by his vassals. Like rendability this was claimed as a royal monopoly by the Carolingians, notably by Charles the Bald in 864 at Pîtres, but had since devolved to various levels of the feudal hierarchy. Case by case, Philip showed no more interest than had his predecessors – or indeed his successors, until the special conditions of warfare under Charles V – in reclaiming this long-lost royal right. Bans, which postulate licensing in dispensation, were individually motivated; of a general policy of restricting fortifying, which has received much misplaced attention, there is no sign. Rendability, however,

per vestras patentes litteras fuero requisitus. This is conventional style but adding the promise of jurability' (C. Coulson, 'Readability and Castellation in Medieval France', *Château-Gaillard* vi, 1972, 60–1) shows the emergency prevailing. Guarantors to such pacts normally incurred penalties less than the forfeiture which applied to the fortress-tenant (if the building was rendable). The reciprocal obligations and contractual nature of the feudal bond are well illustrated by such pacts (however monarchical their ultimate origins); even the warlike contracts were permanent in intention (and usually in effect) modifying the map of feudal *mouvance* to accord with the realities of power.

9 *Layettes* i, nos. 1008, 1217; Delisle 1956, no. 1293. Only the Latin calendar by Dupuy survives. In March 1217, Bishop William of Châlons, Thomas' uncle, notified this pact most curiously adapting the formula commonly used in the Languedoc to attach rendability explicitly to the buildings themselves, both present and future additions, *viz fortericia de Marchesii-villa qualis ibi est modo et qualem fecerit*. The legal precision of the South with the constant improvement of fortifications in view often phrased this as *fortesie que modo ibi sunt vel inantea erunt*.

10 The case of Béraud de Mercoeur (Puy-de-Dôme) was complex and protracted (1308–12). The documents are calendared in *Registres du Trésor des Chartes* i, ed. R. Fawtier, Paris 1958, nos. 768, 794–8, 876, 1498. Béraud refused (1308) to render his castles not held in-chief but was eventually pardoned, not having conceded the point. That Philip IV respected the (much used) ducal right to license fortifying in Gascony is seemingly demonstrated by the quashing of the royal licence for Budos (Gironde), issued (1301) while the duchy was largely in Philip's hands, *propter defectus in ea repertos*. Budos was then re-licensed by Edward I (1306) after regaining possession (*Les Olim*, ed. Beugnot, iii, Paris 1839, 91: *Rymer's Foedera*, Rec. Comm. 1816, I ii, 981.

which has received virtually none, was highly important to Philip II, as it was at every stratum of tenure in medieval France.[11]

Much was changed after the battle at Bouvines in Flanders, but much more remained the same. Having overcome the forces of the Imperial and English coalition and after thirty-four years of perilous survival, opportunistic advances and many setbacks, at long last dispelled the Angevin menace, Philip II was truly 'Augustus'. The treaties he imposed on the conquered rebel counts and communes of Ponthieu, Boulogne, Flanders and Eu might well, like the Anglo-French truces of 1194, 1195–6 and 1200, have spurned feudal niceties in the interests of *Realpolitik*. Gauged by the fortress-clauses which constitute a major part of these settlements, there is new confidence but no *hubris*. That there should be a new degree of interventionism, a penal element previously rare and even some studied derogation of contumacious vassals (all closely reflected in the fortress-terms) was probably inevitable: but there is no monarchical leap forward, no Carolingian revivalism – despite some unknightly vindictiveness to the Dammartins and Ferdinand of Flanders.[12]

The dangerous county of Boulogne and the Dammartin faction had first to be dealt with. Count Renaud had already incurred suspicion in early autumn 1211. Sometime in late August or early September he sent to the king informing him that he was in negotiation with Emperor Otto and the King of England. Philip's envoy was instructed to tell him in reply that the king had frequent intelligence of this and Renaud's other activities, which would greatly surprise the count if he knew the whole. In earnest of his good faith (more exactly, to force revolt into the open or force its abandonment) the king required Renaud on his liege homage and fealty to hand over the castle (*fortericia*) of Mortain, by the hands of his brother Simon, husband of Mary heiress of Ponthieu, the king's niece. The handing over was to be performed ceremonially by Simon *vel alium talem* at Pont-de-l'Arche on 7 or 8 September and be made to the king in person or to one of his privy council. Renaud prevaricated, offering to deliver (*reddere*) the castle personally within the week following. It was soon clear that he did not intend to take advantage of the latitude allowed by custom and Philip's moderation to draw back from the brink of open rebellion, which, by pledging Mortain, he could still have done. From Pont-de-l'Arche Philip sent another message to say he was proceeding to forcible measures and would take Renaud's fiefs and any of his fortresses which were not given up to him *en route*. The chronicler Rigord regarded Renaud as acting wrongfully in this technical respect, but Philip still afforded him a brief respite, to avert total breach, if he would only hand over the castle of Mortain, which the royal forces would meanwhile blockade to stop the munitioning which was in progress.[13] In the event, Renaud had

11 The *domes fortis* of La Houssaye-en-Brie (Seine-et-Marne) (evidently a mere *gentilhommière*) was rendable (1217–40) to the Gallande lords of Tournan by various family cadets who held it under a complex series of arrangements designed to respect and demonstrate the superior lordship of the head of the family. It is a highly interesting case (*Layettes* i, no. 1243; ii, nos. 1607, 2807, 2911 etc.).

12 Gui de la Roche, lord of Beau mont-le-Roger, was punished for suspected treason in January 1206 by making his fortresses liable to be delivered on demand to the king but *ad faciendum volunlatem suam*, which smacks more of pledging than of continuous rendability (Coulson 1983, 35–6).

13 *Rec. Ph. Aug.* iii, nos. 1202, 1203; two highly rare surviving memoranda for oral messages. Renaud

gone too far to turn back; his lands were forfeited and he thereafter and at Bouvines animated the anti-Capetian coalition.

The whole case deserves a detailed summary because it illustrates with exceptional clarity how subtly the commonplace practices and conventions governing the pledging of fortresses (and other property) to purge reasonably entertained suspicions on the part of the lord, relate to the special fortress-tenure customs of rendability. The security the lord enjoyed with a rendable fortress – deliverable on demand with no reason given, no prevarication allowable, no ill-will or misconduct, real or imagined, having been alleged – was of an altogether higher order. As the Languedoc formulae made explicit, rendering was due (at once on summons, personally by the lord or by his written order) whatever their relations, hostile or amicable (*iratz e pagatz* etc.) or, with slightly different emphasis, in the Langue d'Oïl *ad magnam vim et ad parvam*. Naturally, some ill-feeling might be present, but with pledging it was of the essence and normally had to be reasonable and just before the demand to hand over could be made.[14] Pledging diagnosed incipient breakdown of lord-vassal relations whereas under rendability fortresses (never totally unfortified places, even if *capita* of fiefs) were deliverable *pro bono dominio* (Languedoc) so that the lord could assert his lordship and, perhaps, display his banner on the *donjon* for a day and have his war-cry (*signum*) proclaimed. No hostilities were involved, nor any other 'necessity' of the lord. The formulae of the South (including Catalonia), where fortress-law had developed relatively uninterruptedly since Carolingian times, frequently spell out with legal precision what was taken for granted in the lands north of the Loire. Such symbolic rendering, moreover, was still physical – control of the actual fortifications was transferred, however notionally or briefly; it was not a ceremonial sometimes performed miles distant, as with Mortain in 1211.

After his experience with Renaud de Dammartin so great was royal suspicion of the family that, long after Bouvines and the conferment of Boulogne on Philippe *Hurepel*, the king in 1221 seized Ponthieu to stop Simon succeeding as

replied to the first that he would deliver Mortain personally during the week beginning 8 September. Philip's riposte that, on his advance on Mortain, he would 'require' *feoda vestra et fortericias et si vetite* (*vetare* is diagnostic) *fuerint nobis nos posse nostrum faciemus de illis capiendis*, demonstrates it would be an act of contempt (in the circumstances) for castles not to be given up, whether under rendability or otherwise is unclear. Philip's final offer was that if Renaud came to the king to hand over *castrum Moritolii et fortericiam* (i.e. a symbolic transfer again) for the king 'to do his will therewith', he would take counsel how Renaud might be favourably treated by the customs of France and of Normandy. He offered to send his Almoner to conduct Renaud to his presence. Rigord regarded the refusal by Renaud to deliver his *munitiones* as *contra jus et consuetudinem patriae* (quoted Ch. Du Cange, 'Des Fiefs Jurables et Rendables', his 22nd *dissértation* to his edition of Joinville's *Life of St. Louis* (1668); Coulson 1983, 20 n. 14). The whole case compares closely with King John's requiring Semilli castle from Ranulph of Chester in 1202 (*ibid.* 33).

14 In June 1249, Raymond VII of Toulouse, whose greatly weakened authority and vast apanage were shortly to pass to Alphonse de Poitiers, demanded of the vicomte de Lomagne possession of his castle of Auvillers (Tarn-et-Garonne) and all his land in pledge to purge a contempt. The terms are those of rendability and the case was argued in detail (*Layettes* iii, nos. 3778. 3780). Raymond again used veiled threats in requiring the Templars to hand over *in signum recognitionis dominii nostri* their *munitiones* in the county of Larzac (Aveyron), in August 1249, just before his final illness (*ibid.*, no. 3790). Rendability was peremptory, nonetheless, in law, irrespective of antecedent dispute (*Philippe de Beaumanoir: Coutumes de Beauvaisis* ed. A. Salmon, Paris 1970, 351–3).

count on the death of his wife's father William II. Mary was only restored and their children accepted as heirs in 1225 on severe conditions.[15] Simon remained exiled; she had to sell tracts of the county including Doullens castle and Saint-Riquier itself in lieu of relief, and also to procure oaths of over-riding loyalty to the Crown from all the communes of Ponthieu. Making all the comital fortresses rendable to the Crown at the same time certainly enabled future revolt to be nipped in the bud but it also asserted demonstratively the immediate feudal subordination of Ponthieu. Philip Augustus' fortress-policy was to be continued under his successor Louis VIII (1223–26) and also during the remarkable regency of his widow, Blanche of Castile. Her deliberate derogation in 1231 of Simon de Dammartin, when he was at last admitted to fealty as count, obliged future counts of Ponthieu to seek royal permission before they built *aliquam novam forterіciam* or refortified any old one – this in a region where lords of the rank of *haut justicier* as a class freely fortified.[16]

The measure was hitherto exceptional, and the more significant consequently, when Philip in the same way had humiliated the more ancient, prestigious and recently imperial house of Flanders. The capture at Bouvines of the unfortunate Ferdinand of Portugal (the *Ferrand enferré* mocked by the Parisian crowds in his chains) led to the submission two months later, in October 1214 of Joanna, countess also in her own right of Hainault, wholly in the Empire.[17] She pledged her own authority, first, to humble her four powerful industrial towns of Cassel, Oudenarde, Valenciennes and Ypres by undertaking to demolish their walls (*fortericie*) when, and if, the king should require it. The psychology here was more subtle than merely reducing outright the power of the formidable urban militias: rather, by making precarious the very existence of the town walls and gates, eloquent instruments of civic lordship, now dependent on grace not right, subject to a suspended sentence of demolition, the urban franchise was curtailed and the right to fortify of their own authority removed. It was a cherished privi-

15 *Recueil des Actes des Comtes de Ponthieu (1026–1279)* ed. C. Brunel, Paris 1930 (hereafter *Actes Pont.*), vi–viii. Mary of Ponthieu married Simon prior to 1211. Her mother was Philip's sister; he was Renaud's brother. *Ibid.*, no. 278 (Mary's charter); *Veterum Scriptorum . . . Amplissima Collectio*, ed. E. Martène, i, Paris 1724, 1198–9 (Louis's charter); cp. *Layettes* ii, nos. 1713, 1733. The countship derived from the *avouerie* of Saint-Riquier abbey. Mary promised (1225) *quod omnes forterіcias meas totius terre mee Pontivii . . . regi et heredibus suis reddam ego et heredes mei ad magnam vim et ad parvam quotiens et quando fuero super hoc requisita.*

16 A plea upheld by the royal Parlement in 1272 in favour of the Abbot of Saint-Riquier against the royal *baillis* there (*Les Olim* i, 917–18). Mary did, in effect, license to fortify: in April 1226 she ceded by exchange the viscounty of Montreuil to Philippe Hurepel of Boulogne with power to build a fortress there, a normal way of clinching a transfer of lordship (Ch. Petit-Dutaillis, *Etude sur la Vie et le Règne de Louis VIII*, Paris 1894, 'Catalogue des Actes . . .' no. 352). *Actes Pont.*, no. 287; also Layettes it, no. 2121 (1231). While Ponthieu was in royal hands (1223) the *castrum* of Senarpont (Somme, near Amiens) was sworn rendable (in rather *ad hoc* phraseology) to Philip II and its lord promised not to *inforciare* it without his permission (*Layettes* i, no. 1578).

17 *Layettes* i, no. 1088. Louis VIII in 1224 promised not to raze the walls of La Rochelle on its submission (*Catalogue . . . Louis VIII*, no. 144). Simon de Montfort was more severe; the walls of his assumed duchy-*caput* of Narbonne were made razeable on demand in 1218; in 1214 Daurde Baras promised to destroy two castles of his to Simon's order (*Catalogue des Actes de Simon et d'Amauri de Montfort*, ed. A. Molinier, Paris 1874, nos. 81. 152). The symbolic aspects of castellation are treated generally in Coulson, 'Structural Symbolism in Medieval Castle Architecture' (*Journ. BAA* cxxxii, 1979, 73–90); and primarily from the ecclesiastical angle in Coulson, 'Hierarchism in Conventual Crenellation' (*Med. Arch.*, 1982, 69–100).

lege, as Philip's own borough charters demonstrate. The device is to be found elsewhere. Joanna recognised this contingent liability in 1225 in acknowledging the help given her by Louis le Lion against the anti-French impostor, the *faux Baudoin*, who roused much urban support. Quite possibly, these popular demonstrations provoked the repetition; but the threat was still not put into execution. It remained a deterrent.[18]

Douai was less harshly treated. The burgesses had submitted to Philip while he was besieging Lille (*in castris apud Insulam*) in June 1213. He confirmed their customs, promised to respect their interests in negotiating with their rebel count and merely reserved to the Crown the right to build a rendable fort (*fortericia*) within the town. Their hostages he would keep until this was completed to his satisfaction.[19] Having dealt vicariously with the rebel communes of Flanders, Philip's settlement proceeded to punish Joanna directly. She agreed, secondly, apart from the *fortericie* of the four towns, that *omnes alie fortericie Flandrie in eo puncto in quo modo sunt remanebunt, neque aliquo modo inforciabuntur, neque alie forterecie poterunt fien nisi per ejusdem domini regis beneplacitum*. This is not so much a prohibition as a ban, properly speaking (as so often is the case when not so explicit), proclaiming and establishing the lordly right to be consulted and to give consent by licensing.[20] Its character is, however, exceptionally sweeping: it would appear intended to apply to the vassals of Flanders, as well as to their count, and may well reflect the exceptional conditions of the post-Bouvines pacification. Whereas the verb *inforciare* normally meant not only 'fortify' in the structural sense but munitioning or garrisoning of warlike intention, comparison with the 1231 Ponthieu settlement does suggest that works of repair and improvement to buildings were intended here. Significantly such maintenance was very rarely subject to authorisation, being an assumed corollary – occasionally, indeed, a tenurial obligation – of fortress-tenure.[21] Conversely, the absence of any rendability of comital for-

18 *Layettes* ii, no. 1707; also a bond in the sum of 10,000 *livres*. The suspended demolition of the four towns' defences is not mentioned in the 1226 treaty for Count Ferdinand's restoration and it may well have served its purpose and been allowed to lapse.

19 *Rec. Ph. Aug*, iii, no. 1304. The editor's gloss inaccurately translates the king's stipulation that *si viderimus forterciam in villa Duaci que nobis placeat et quam possimus vel velimus tenere nos eis reddemus hostagios suos cum perfecta fuerit fortericia ad gratum et voluntatem nostram*. That Philip was reserving the right to have a citadel of some kind available for royal garrisoning (outright purchase of fortresses, sometimes compulsorily, in the 14th century became quite common) is confirmed by Delisle's calendar (*Catalogue . . . Ph. Aug*, no. 1451) and may be compared with Louis VIII's similar reservations at the towns of Saint-Emilion and La Réole in 1224 (*Ordonnances des Rois de France . . .* xii, eds Vilevault and Bréquigny, Paris 1777, 316–17). Under the 1226 reseisin treaty Louis VIII was to hold for ten years the *fortericia Duaci* (apparently this citadel not the town walls) *in qua nunc est garnisio nostra*.

20 See Coulson 1982, 357–62 on comital licensing in Champagne. The conditions of the regency of Blanche of Navarre for the young count and the attempts by co-heiresses to force the county's partition caused Philip II in 1213 to require that the four chief towns of Champagne should not be fortified or strengthened, to avoid provocation. Blanche obtained the limited dispensation which she requested in 1216 to rebuild part of the *enceinte* of Provins castle (*ibid.*, 356). This shows a political judgement in some ways similar to Flanders, but Philip's refusal to hear claims on Champagne until Thibaud's majority was protective rather than strictly impartial.

21 The obligation to deliver 'the fortifications which are there now and shall be in the future' was exploited by Raymond VI of Toulouse in 1201 to make the Count of Foix have repaired damage done to the town and castle defences of Saverdun (Ariège) very probably with Raymond's own connivance

tresses, such as was imposed in 1225 on Mary of Ponthieu (since 1221 these had in any case been in royal hands), is a fact to be pondered. Some clarification is provided by the complex and elaborate arrangements for the release from prison and restoration of Count Ferdinand, agreed in April 1226.[22] The fortification-ban now received definitive shape, being restricted to the Flemish lands on the French side of the river Scheldt (*Escauz* or Escaut) and to comital works solely. The feudal irregularity (if one was really intended by the 1214 treaty) of extending royal licensing of comital works (exercised, for instance, for the castle of Ruplemonde in 1255) to their vassals, sub-tenants of France, thereby disappeared.[23] Licensing continued to be exercised by the counts as direct lords. Imperial lordship of part of Flanders, nominal though it was, is roughly recognised by making the Scheldt the boundary of royal jurisdiction. The whole treaty bears the stamp of Philip Augustus, though not his seal; a troublesome vassal had been brought firmly, albeit temporarily, to obedience through the fullest use yet of the fortress powers of the feudal monarchy. After the early death of Louis le Lion, Queen Blanche renewed the treaty in time for Ferdinand's release, as originally envisaged, at Christmas 1226.

The treatment accorded to Alice, Countess in her own right of Eu, is remarkably consistent with that meted out to those of Ponthieu and Flanders. Ralph of Exoudun, least of the continental allies, was kept true to his English loyalties until his death in 1219 by his extensive lands across the Channel. Alice then secured from Philip seisin of her diminutive maritime county in northern Normandy on terms appropriate to a widow and on the now familiar condition that, as her charter puts it, *nec ego nec heredes mei firmabimus, nec infortiabimus fortericias aliquas a puncto in quo sunt modo nisi per dominum regem.*[24] Each of these three settlements had been imposed on an heiress whose husband was a rebel, a life-tenant and, in various degrees, a foreigner or outsider.[25] Ralph of

(*Layettes* i, nos. 612, 623 cp. no. 186). Such abuses demonstrate the strength of these fortress-customs but they were clearly exceptional and a breach of propriety.

22 *Layettes* ii, nos. 1761–2 (April 1226); nos. 1895, 1908 (December renewal with guarantees of 5,000 *livres*). These terms were reiterated successively in 1237, by Joanna and Thomas of Savoy, her second husband; in 1245, by Countess Margaret of Flanders and Hainault; in 1246, by William de Dampierre, her son, as heir to Flanders; and in 1252 in anticipation of his succession by the eventual heir Gui de Dampierre (*ibid.*, nos. 2584, 3340, 3552–3, 3981). In each charter the limitation is repeated: *nos non possumus facere fortericias novas nec veteres infortiare in Flandria citra fluvium qui dicitur Eschaut nisi per dominum regem vel successores ipsius* (1237).

23 *Layettes* iii, no. 4139; notification by Countess Margaret of licence by Louis IX to (re-) fortify the castle of Ruplemonde in East Flanders and actually on the Scheldt, expressly recalling the 1226 treaty made with her late sister Countess Joanna. During the minority of Thibaud IV of Champagne, it may be noted, comital licensing (even to a major magnate such as Robert of Dreux in 1206–7, for La Fère-en-Tardenois) proceeded as normal, despite the restraint imposed in 1213.

24 *Layettes* i, nos. 133, 1360. She also gave up claims to Neufchâtel (*Driencort*) and to Mortemer, in Normandy. She gave the king security not to remarry *nisi per eum*, Philip promising not to constrain her to do so. For this she paid 15,000 marks Troyes and all the revenues of Eu were appropriated to pay off this relief-fine in three instalments. The nearby Marshall lands were also in 1219 settled on William the Marshall's widow, Countess Isabella, the castles of Longueville, Meulers (and Orbec) being continued in rendable tenure of the Grown (Coulson 1983, 37–8; F. M. Powicke, *The Loss of Normandy*, Manchester 1961, 338 and 'Stapleton map' endpaper).

25 The context of assessment of these measures should also properly include the general treatment of female fortress-tenants (in warlike circumstances and in peaceful), namely unmarried heiresses, female guardians, widows and dowagers. This evidence presents many parallels and suggests that the

Exoudun died in England, Simon de Dammartin suffered seventeen years' exile, and Ferdinand of Portugal twelve years of unusually unchivalric confinement. Family links with the Capetians, in the case of Flanders and Ponthieu, secured no alleviation. Each countess was put under the duty, demeaning for a major magnate, of seeking royal licence for *de novo* fortification which conventionally did touch the superior lord's right; at least initially, the same rule was applied to repairs and improvements, which scarcely ever did. Reasons for this probably go beyond any merely military explanation and it is certainly significant that no attempt was made to have the Counts of Flanders' castles rendable, a far more valuable assurance. The ducal rights in Normandy were expressly reserved to the Crown in the reseisin arrangements for Eu, and may have included rendability, but this is explicit only in the case of Ponthieu (1225) and probably elsewhere not practicable at that time, even for French Flanders.

The later Capetian fortress-policy, essentially that of Philip Augustus down to the crisis period after the disastrous defeat at Poitiers in 1356, had come far from its tentative beginnings. The contrast between Philip's assured mastery after 1214 and his patient and piecemeal negotiation for fortress-rights prior to the successful seizure of Normandy is very striking. Development was, however, necessarily restricted in scope. The same methods were to carry Capetian power onwards into southern Poitou and Saintonge under Louis VIII, to make a significant contribution to the triumph of Queen Blanche over the aristocratic reaction of Louis IX's minority, and to assist that enormous increase of royal territory achieved by the various initiatives of the so-called Albigensian Crusade. The vast cultural region of *Occitanie* – Provence, Catalonia, Toulouse, Foix and Aquitaine – was the homeland to which fortress-law retreated, and where it was refined and developed while the Capetian Dukes of *Francia* were learning to be Kings of France.

purely political aspects of the four cases here considered should not be over-stressed (see Coulson 1982, 363; also 'Seignorial Fortresses in France in Relation to Public Policy *c.* 864 to *c.* 1483', unpublished Ph.D. thesis, University of London, 1972, ii, index 'Fortress Customs: female tenure', for references and discussion.

19

Castles and Politics in England 1215–1224*

Richard Eales

The subject of royal castle policy, and the political importance of castles in general, tends to flit uneasily in and out of the narrative history of twelfth- and thirteenth-century England. At times of crisis like episodes of revolt and civil war the issue demands attention, and estimates must be made of the number and distribution of castles, who held them in fee or in custody, their strategic value, state of preservation and preparedness for defence. Such snapshots of the territorial *status quo ante bellum* can be used as the starting point for subsequent military events. Campaigns and sieges also provide the most crucial evidence for many archaeologists, who study castles primarily as architectural forms evolving in response to the demands of military technology. Yet these pictures can only be interpreted properly against the background of longer term changes and policies pursued through intervening years of peace. The aim here is to set the events of 1215–24 in a wider perspective of twelfth- and thirteenth-century development.

I

The period 1154–1216 has been the subject of detailed study by R. Allen Brown, which remains the most sustained attempt to relate castle policies to more general politics so far attempted for medieval England.[1] His conclusions provide a useful checklist for the subsequent period. Cumulative totals in the pipe rolls of 1155–1215 show a minimum expenditure of £46,000 on royal castles (including those temporarily in the king's hands), an average of £780 a year. The expenditure was maintained fairly consistently from decade to decade after about 1165, following a rise from lower figures in the early part of Henry II's reign, when the exchequer was auditing much smaller sums. The annual average over all of Henry's reign was £650, rising to over £1,000 under John, though much of this increase must have been accounted for by inflation in

* I should like to thank David Carpenter and Charles Coulson for reading and commenting on a draft of this paper.

1 R. A. Brown, 'Royal Castle-Building in England, 1154–1216', *EHR* lxx (1955), 354–98; idem, 'A List of Castles, 1154–1216', *EHR* lxxiv (1959), 249–80; *The History of the King's Works, Vols. I–II The Middle Ages*, ed. R. A. Brown, H. M. Colvin, A. J. Taylor (London, 1963), especially i, 51–81. The figures which follow are taken from the tables in Brown, 'Royal Castle-Building', 377–98. The pipe rolls do not of course provide a complete account of all royal expenditure.

building costs. Such sums were adequate to rebuild royal castles in stone on a large scale as well as to carry out immediate repairs: 30 castles had over £100 spent on them under Henry II and 26 under John. But many others were still substantially defended by timber and earthworks in 1215, and this must have been a matter of choice, because the concentration of resources on a few key sites was an equally clear feature of the Angevin period. Over two-thirds of the £21,000 spent by Henry II went on 7 fortresses (Dover, Newcastle, Nottingham, Orford, Scarborough, Winchester and Windsor); well over half of John's £17,000 on 9 (Corfe, Dover, Hanley, Harestan, Kenilworth, Knaresborough, Lancaster, Odiham and Scarborough). Few of these were entirely new sites, but all were transformed. Dover alone cost £6,600 between 1180 and 1191, while £2,880 for the Tower of London appears in one year's account (1189–90). There is little sign of nationwide strategic planning and castles of the interior were as liable to be strengthened as those that had a role in border defence. The Welsh March, in particular, took only a low proportion of expenditure. On the whole, it is better to explain the selection of key sites in local or regional terms. For example, it has been plausibly argued that the new castle of Orford was constructed after 1165 to oppose the power of the Bigod family in East Anglia, and in particular to out-build their nearby fortress of Framlingham.[2] Work at Rochester, Dover, Canterbury and the largely new castle of Chilham in the early 1170s might be ascribed to unsettled conditions in Kent after the *dénouement* of the Becket affair, and so on.[3]

Angevin policy towards the custody of royal castles shows a steady drift towards the installation of accountable officials in place of baronial and hereditary castellans, but the overall picture was patchy and many of the latter survived, even being reinstated on occasion after periods of disturbance.[4] The key periods for changes in the control of castles, 'ownership' as well as custody, were the early years of Henry II's reign, the mid-1170s after the suppression of the great revolt of 1173–4, and the latter part of John's reign. Brown has shown clearly how large numbers of royal castles were re-possessed, and baronial castles seized and sometimes demolished in these episodes. But he has also emphasized (and this is perhaps his central conclusion) that the process of royal aggrandisement was continuous and statistically imposing: '255 baronial and 49 royal castles in 1154, a ratio of nearly 5 to 1; 179 baronial and 93 royal castles in December 1214, a ratio of just under 2 to 1. . . . The alteration in the balance of power in terms of castles which took place in these years was almost entirely the result of direct action by the Crown at the direct expense of the baronage.'[5] To assess the real significance of these changes, though, it is necessary to look to what happened after December 1214.

Many historians have also assumed that this practical success of the Angevin

2 R. A. Brown, 'Framlingham Castle and Bigod', *Procs. of the Suffolk Institute of Archaeology* xxv (1952), 127–48.

3 R. Eales, 'Local Loyalties in Norman England: Kent in Stephen's Reign', *Anglo-Norman Studies* viii (1985), 107–8.

4 J. Beeler, *Warfare in England 1066–1189* (New York, 1966), 161–92, 283–92, 439–46, on Henry II's reign.

5 Brown, 'List', 249–58, quotation at 256–7.

kings went hand in hand with the establishment of firm customary rights over castles and castle-building. Thus J. C. Holt has argued that 'Title to castles was markedly less secure than title to land' and that among the reasons for this were 'the need to license private castle-building' and 'a prerogative right of seizure' by the Crown, both traceable back to the Norman 'Consuetudines et Justicie' of 1091.[6] According to this model, Henry II in the 1150s was destroying 'the adulterine, or unlicensed, castles of the Anarchy',[7] and reviving a royal power to control castle-building which had been acknowledged in the reigns of his predecessors. The feudal right to demand the temporary cession of a vassal's castles in time of need or as a test of loyalty, Holt's 'prerogative right of seizure', often called 'rendability' in the context of French customary laws,[8] has not been identified with such confidence in England, though there is one episode in 1176 which is otherwise hard to explain. In that year, according to both Howden and Diceto, Henry II at the Council of Windsor 'took into his own hands' all the castles of England and Normandy, ecclesiastical as well as baronial.[9] Any such assertion of right must have remained largely theoretical, and probably served as a cover from which the king could strike at individual targets in the aftermath of the 1173–4 revolt, but the mere fact that it was made is striking enough. It can be concluded that these customs of feudal jurisdiction over castles were known in Norman and Angevin England. They could indeed have been independently introduced from France at later dates – 1176 may represent one such attempt – as well as indigenously evolved since the days of William I. What must remain unlikely is that the resultant range of traditions was ever assimilated or enforced as a common body of customary law in twelfth-century England. Whatever the cumulative practical consequences of the Angevin kings' treatment of castles between 1154 and 1214, that treatment was too arbitrary and opportunistic to be regarded as a consistent policy or to establish generally accepted legal powers as a platform on which later rulers could build.

II

The course of the civil war of 1215–17 bears out a number of conclusions about the military role of castles in conditions of serious warfare, when substantial forces were in the field. It is well understood that castles could not physically block communications routes, or oppose the passage of armies larger than their own garrisons. But even a mobile army faced a cumulative danger from leaving unsubdued castles on its route of march, while a commander like Louis of France, who aspired to rule England, had to make territorial gains permanent and that meant capturing all the castles sooner or later. He was in rather the

6 J. C. Holt, 'Politics and Property in Early Medieval England', *Past and Present* lvii (1972), 25–7, quotation at 25.

7 Brown, 'List', 250. For the concept of 'adulterine' castles, see 383–5 below.

8 C. L. H. Coulson, 'Rendability and castellation in medieval France', *Château-Gaillard: Etudes de Castellologie médiévale* vi (1973), 59–67, is an introduction to this subject.

9 See discussion and references in Brown, 'List', 25–4; D. J. C. King, *Castellarium Anglicanum* (New York, 1983), i. xxiv.

same position as his father Philip in Normandy in 1203–4. The main issue at stake was the order in which he could proceed. One possibility was to aim for a knockout blow: a pitched battle if that were possible, otherwise a series of attacks on the greatest centres of enemy power, in castles and towns. The alternative was to make easier gains in less well-defended territory, so as to build up a momentum of conquest and isolate the difficult targets before risking assault. In this way Philip Augustus delayed his attack on Rouen in 1204 until he had received the submission of western Normandy, and John never seems to have contemplated an open advance on London at the end of 1215 or early in 1216. Overt military operations had to be conducted in concert with propaganda and opinion, particularly in a civil war in which many men were uncommitted and awaiting the outcome. William Marshal is said to have advised John not to hazard his kingdom on a single battle by opposing Louis's landing in Kent in May 1216.[10] Prolonged warfare was a progressive testing of loyalties as well as an attempt to gain military success by piecemeal stages.

In this process, castles had an immediate function as rallying points and as centres for the stockpiling of money and equipment, but when they came under attack the most important benefit they conferred was time, and the tying down of enemy units.[11] Prince Louis kept much of his army before Dover between July and October 1216, and again in May 1217 while the other half of his forces was being decisively defeated at Lincoln. Lincoln castle itself, under its royalist castelian Nicholaa de la Haye, had been besieged with varying seriousness by Gilbert de Gant since July or August 1216. Windsor castle also held off a baronial siege for two months in the summer of 1216 with a garrison commanded by Engelard de Cigogné, until it was lifted in September by John himself. Louis made the classic mistake of committing his forces and then not pushing his attacks to a conclusion. Whatever his reasons for abandoning the siege of Dover in October 1216 and granting the defenders an extended truce until the following Easter while he looked for easier gains elsewhere, it was a blow to the confidence of his allies and possibly a crucial error. The most famous of successful sieges was John's capture of Rochester at the outset of the civil war, in October and November 1215. But even that success, after which according to the Barnwell Annalist 'there were few who would put their trust in castles', was bought at significant cost.[12] It took almost seven weeks, and a large sum from the king's resources, if not the imaginative 60,000 marks estimated by Ralph of Coggeshall.[13] John occupied the next six months with highly successful raiding campaigns in the North and in East Anglia, during which many rebel castles

[10] Dunstable annals, in *Ann. Mon.* iii. 46. Compare the tactical judgements of W. L. Warren, *Henry II* (London, 1973), 117–37, on 1173–4; idem, *King John* (London, 1961), 113–15, on 1203–4, 269–70, on 1215–16.

[11] No attempt has been made to provide full references for all narrative examples below. Clear accounts of the civil war can be found in S. Painter, *The Reign of King John* (Baltimore, 1949); idem, William Marshal (Baltimore, 1933); Warren, *King John*; K. Norgate, *The Minority of Henry III* (London, 1912). I have also made use of an unpublished dissertation by N. A. Hooper, 'The War of 1215–1217 between King John and the Rebel Barons', for which I would like to thank the author.

[12] Barnwell annals, in *The Historical Collections of Walter of Coventry*, ed. W. Stubbs (RS, 1873), ii. 227.

were surrendered to him, but in the end he failed to suppress the baronial opposition before Louis landed with major French reinforcements in May 1216. The time factor had proved to be vital.

Financial resources were also crucial in a war in which both sides employed mercenary troops on a large scale. Insofar as they were garrisoned and had control of their immediate areas, castles were bases for collecting vital revenues, regular or irregular. The latter, under the general name of *tenseries*, often amounted to free plunder, though it could be dressed up as exceptional taxation, fines for misconduct, or the confiscation of rents and produce from enemy-held estates. The struggle for resources could also be waged negatively; assets which could not be carried off could at least be destroyed and so rendered unavailable to the enemy, as John wasted the Scots borders in January 1216. Castle garrisons had sometimes to collect their revenues in competition with their opponents. While John was in the North during the winter of 1215–16, his commanders around London detached forces to raid in East Anglia and replenish their supplies, with great success according to the chroniclers. Two lesser captains paid 450 marks of profit into the royal treasury, after one such expedition.[14] Even uncaptured castles could be weakened and deprived of some of their usefulness by these means. Towns, which always needed open markets and free access to their hinterlands, could similarly be coerced by the garrisons of surrounding castles or by raiding forces, if they were in a position to disrupt supplies. Clearly this was John's long-term plan to soften up London.

The events of 1215–17 also suggest that the military importance of minor castles was sometimes very low. During John's victorious tour of the North in December 1215 to February 1216 some fortresses of moderate strength like Castle Donnington surrendered to detached troops on request, once it was known that a royal army was operating within reach. Louis enjoyed similar success in June 1216, taking Reigate, Guildford, Farnham, Winchester, Odiham and Porchester in succession within four weeks, and once again the lesser castles surrendered in the wake of the greater ones.[15] It is also notable that at least a quarter of the 270 or so English castles known from documentary evidence at this time were not set in defence or used in the war, or at least do not appear in the sources. Many others played no significant part.[16] Even larger fortresses could not be expected to sustain serious attack for long unless they had been adequately manned and prepared. In time of war the long-term investment of castle building had to be augmented by short-term mobilization of resources of all kinds. Rochester in 1215 was held by a force variously estimated at between 95 and 140 knights with other troops in support, though it seems clear that there was no time to lay in adequate provisions. Hubert de Burgh's garrison at Dover

13 *Radulphi de Coggeshall Chronicon Anglicanum*, ed. J. Stevenson (RS, 1875), 176.

14 *Coggeshall*, 177–8; Paris, *CM* 639–41, 645–6; *RLP* 169.

15 Paris, *CM* ii. 639; *RLC* i. 251, on Castle Donnington. *Histoire des Ducs de Normandie et des Rois d Angleterre*, ed. F. Michel (Paris, 1840), 172–4, is the best account of the 1216 campaign.

16 Comparing figures given in Brown, 'List', 261–80, and Painter, *Reign of John*, 352–3 with narrative events.

in 1216 was also said to contain 140 knights.[17] Such forces bear no relation to the size of any permanent 'castle-guard' arrangements, even those which, as at Dover and Rochester, could draw on substantial feudal resources. In most cases, despite clause 29 of the Magna Carta, which provided that tenants should be allowed to do their castle services in person if they wished, obligations survived as cash payments in the early thirteenth century, and there is no evidence that the events of 1215–17 breathed life into an obsolete system.

But no castle, whatever the state of its walls and provisions, could be held unless it had a loyal castellan and the morale of the defenders was sustained. Defiance like that of Hubert de Burgh at Dover or William de Albini at Rochester was recognized as heroic but it was not dishonourable, having delayed the attacking forces for a while and appealed in vain for outside relief, to surrender upon terms. Even the immediate surrender of a weak castle might be seen as no more than a recognition of the inevitable. But many castles changed hands for other reasons. Belvoir capitulated to John in December 1215 because its lord William de Albini was a prisoner in his hands and was threatened with death. John de Lacy surrendered Pontefract to the king in January 1216 when he changed sides and pledged his loyalty, his relative Earl Ranulf of Chester interceding for him.[18] Giving up castles in such circumstances was like giving hostages (John actually provided his brother Roger on this occasion), an earnest of good intentions. Rather different were the desertions John experienced in the summer of 1216 when the tide was flowing the other way after Louis's landing in England. The earls of Warenne, Arundel and Salisbury and the count of Aumâle all went over in a concerted move at the end of June, taking their castles with them. Hugh de Neville, who was in command of the royal castle at Marlborough, shortly afterwards betrayed it to Louis, and others followed.[19]

The Angevin castle policy of the 60 years up to 1215 can be re-assessed in the light of these events. It is clear that the mere token possession of large numbers of fortresses, of varying quality and preparedness, was not a decisive asset. It was of no value to have 90, rather than 50, castles, unless one had 90 loyal commanders and the resources to hold them. The dividing line between royal and baronial castles was always blurred by disputed claims, such as that over Bristol maintained by the earl of Gloucester since it was taken by the Crown in 1175. There were also attempts, some of them successful, to establish hereditary tenure by custodians. During the open season for complaints against the Crown which followed John's acceptance of Magna Carta in 1215, such claims were brought in respect of several major royal castles: Hertford, Colchester, York, Hereford, Trowbridge and the Tower of London. The first two at least were conceded.[20] In the civil war between two rival claimants to the throne distinctions

17 *Histoire des Ducs*, 157; *Coggeshall*, 176; *Walter of Coventry*, ii. 226; Paris, *CM* ii. 621; for Rochester. *Histoire des Ducs*, 170; for Dover.

18 Paris, *CM* ii. 639; for Belvoir. *Histoire des Ducs*, 163, for John of Lacy.

19 *Histoire des Ducs*, 174–6.

20 *Earldom of Gloucester Charters*, ed. R. B. Patterson (Oxford, 1973), 3–8; *Accounts of the Constables of Bristol Castle*, ed. M. Sharp (Bristol Rec. Soc., xxxiv, 1982), xx–xxiii, 70–5; M. Altschul, *A Baronial Family in Medieval England: The Clares 1217–1314* (Baltimore, 1965), 27–8, 77, 127; Holt, 'Politics', 26–7.

were further eroded. Rochester became a *casus belli* at the outset when the constable maintained by Archbishop Stephen Langton, Reginald de Cornhill, would not surrender the castle to the king, but gave it up to baronial forces advancing from London. Yet Rochester was a royal castle, though in theory, and to a large extent in practice, in the permanent custody of the archbishop since 1127.[21] It might seem an obvious device to shift royal castles into the hands of officials, trusted *curiales* and military professionals and away from aristocratic custodians in time of crisis, but this was not a certain remedy. Among those who deserted John in the last months of his life were some of his intimates and officials like Warin fitz Gerold, chamberlain of the exchequer, John fitz Hugh and Hugh de Neville, taking their castles with them, though the royalist cause was preserved for John's son by the loyalty of many others.[22]

Angevin kings were of course aware of the potential dangers, and that is why their castle policies from the 1150s onwards were marked as much by the concentration of resources on selected key sites as by the sheer accumulation of fortresses. Some of those in royal possession had only negative value: by keeping them in his own hands the king was preventing anyone else modernizing them or making greater use of them. For the same reason at least 30 baronial castles confiscated by the Crown between 1154 and 1214 were demolished rather than retained as they stood. In time of war the same logic of finite resources applied: in January 1216 John issued instructions for Tamworth castle to be dismantled.[23] It might be suggested that John's record total of 'royal' castles in December 1214 represented a dangerous overstretching of his resources, or at least a dubious gain to set against the accumulating resentments of those from whom castles had been taken, ecclesiastics as well as laymen. Clause 52 of Magna Carta stated these grievances very clearly. Sidney Painter took as indicative of the strength of John's position at the outset in September 1215, the fact that of 209 castles 'that seem certainly to have been used during the civil war . . . John and his men held 149 castles against 60 held by his foes.' Painter then proceeds to narrate John's gains over the following six months, yet strangely fails to draw conclusions from the fact that none of this won the war for him, or saved him from the dramatic reversals that overtook him in 1216.[24] The obvious conclusion is that it was necessary for the king to have a loyal body of servants to whom royal castles could be entrusted, but also one which could be employed without alienating the greater noblemen on whose support the king also relied.

Despite everything, including the general unpopularity of the Poitevins shown all too clearly in Magna Carta, John's cause and that of his son was preserved by his and William Marshal's ability to get military commanders like Fawkes de Breauté, Engelard de Cigogné and Peter de Maulay to work reasonably well with his chief baronial supporters. Conversely, Louis's collapse from

21 *Regesta Regum Anglo-Normannorum, ii* (1100–1135), ed. C. Johnson and H. A. Cronne (Oxford, 1956), no. 1475. *King's Works*, ii. 807 summarises subsequent changes.

22 *Histoire des Ducs*, 175–6; *RLC* i. 277; *RLP* 190.

23 Brown, 'List', 261–80. *RLC* i. 244; for Tamworth, which is one example of many. See C. Coulson, 'Fortress-policy in Capetian tradition and Angevin practice. Aspects of the conquest of Normandy by Philip II', *Anglo-Norman Studies* vi (1983), 33 and n. 31, reprinted in this volume.

24 Painter, *Reign of John*, 352–3, 362–73.

what was still a very strong position in the spring of 1217, though brought about by the fortunes of battle at Lincoln, was prepared by the recurrent tensions between his English allies and the men he brought over from France. In March 1217, when Louis temporarily returned to France to seek reinforcements, his cause was deserted by William, earl of Salisbury and William Marshal the younger, who were followed by over 100 lesser men. According to Roger of Wendover, Marshal was disaffected because he had been refused custody of the royal castle of Marlborough, while Louis's French followers were busy advising him that the English were traitors and could not be trusted.[25] In this climate the sustained attempts of the regent to win back support, by a combination of individual persuasion and general pronouncements like the reissue of Magna Carta, began to make real headway.

Clearly major castles served many functions and formed crucial points around which the civil war of 1215–17 was fought. But equally clearly the fluctuations of loyalty and confidence which were crucial in determining the outcome were far too dynamic to be predicted from the initial balance of territorial power as expressed in control of castles. And even after the build up of royal finances, war preparations and access to mercenary troops which had taken place between 1208 and 1214, the ultimate dependence of royal government on the loyalty of the aristocracy had again been displayed in 1215 and its aftermath. Any royal castle policy in the subsequent period had to take these broader considerations into account.

III

The sudden, and in some ways unexpected end to the civil war in 1217, with the Treaty of Kingston and Louis's departure from England in September following rapidly on the sea battle off Sandwich in August, inevitably had the effect of freezing in place the territorial dispositions of the winning side.[26] William Marshal as regent and the papal legate Guala could only rule with and through the agency of great noblemen like Ranulf, earl of Chester and William, earl of Salisbury, and John's leading officials and military commanders headed by Hubert de Burgh and Fawkes de Breauté. From 1217 the earl of Chester held the shrievalties of Shropshire, Staffordshire and Lancashire, grouped strategically around his independently-administered earldom of Chester. De Burgh held office as sheriff in Kent, Norfolk and Suffolk, and was custodian of the royal castles of Dover, Canterbury, Rochester, Orford and Norwich. De Breauté held the shrievalties of six midland counties: Bedfordshire, Buckinghamshire, Cambridgeshire, Huntingdonshire, Northamptonshire and Oxfordshire, along with their attendant royal castles. A little lower down among the hierarchy of royalist commanders, Philip Marc at Nottingham, Engelard de Cigogné at Windsor, Peter de Maulay at Corfe, and many others, also wielded tremendous power

25 Paris, *CM* iii. 11–13.

26 On the treaty, see J. Beverley Smith, 'The Treaty of Lambeth, 1217', *EHR* xciv (1979), 562–79. Accounts of events 1217–1219 in Norgate; Painter, *William Marshal.*

within more limited areas, based on the same combination of office and custody of royal castles.[27]

Inevitably, the holding of important castles had assumed an enhanced importance during the years of civil war. John was already making increasing use of regional castle treasuries, at Corfe, Bristol, Nottingham and elsewhere, to handle war finances in the second half of his reign.[28] As conflict broke out in 1215 and the central administration ceased to operate, trusted local commanders were given more and more freedom to operate independently. Castles were set in defence and garrisons built up by custodians who were able to draw on any local revenues within reach, augmented where necessary by *tenseries* and the licensed or unlicensed seizure of rebel lands and their revenues. The civil war of 1215–17 did not see the same recrudescence of small-scale castle building as in Stephen's reign, but the sub-contracting of royal power to local military commanders, in units centred on major fortresses, served a similar purpose to the creation of new earldoms by Stephen and Matilda in the conditions of the mid-twelfth century. Writing about the counties of the far north, J. C. Holt drew a close parallel with the events of the 1170s: 'In a crisis Border government tended to dissolve and reform along different lines, especially around the great castleries of Carlisle, Bamburgh and Newcastle, and around escheats and custodies temporarily in the hands of the Crown.'[29] As in 1173–4, so in 1215–17, 'the supra-shrieval authority of royal castellans and custodians' was tolerated by the king and was sustained by whatever means were available.

The difference in 1217 was that there was no king of full age to restore control (or to put it more realistically, to arbitrate between competing claims and allow the balance of central and local authority to re-stabilize) as Henry II had done in the 1150s and 1170s. Many sheriffs and officials were reappointed to their positions by the regency government in the later part of 1217, as the civil war came to an end. Others, especially castellans, seem to have regarded their appointments by John as valid until the new king came of age, or even argued that they had taken oaths to that effect on assuming office. In the first months of the new reign, and while war still raged, the Marshal entertained some such notion; for instance, in October 1216 William de Ferrers, earl of Derby was granted the royal castle of Peak to hold until the king reached the age of fifteen.[30] Such grants almost ceased in the course of 1217, mostly because the leaders of the minority government were no longer committed to a fixed date for Henry's majority, but ideas of this kind, once current, were not easily dispelled. The minority has thus been seen as a period when there was a real danger that

27 *PRO Lists and Indexes, IX List of Sheriffs in England and Wales* (reprinted with corrections, New York, 1963), 117, 72, 67, 86, 1, 12, 92, 107.

28 J. E. A. Jolliffe, 'The Chamber and the Castle Treasuries under King John', in *Studies in Medieval History Presented to Frederick Maurice Powicke*, ed. R. W. Hunt, W. A. Pantin, R. W. Southern (Oxford, 1948), 117–42.

29 J. C. Holt, *The Northerners: A Study in the Reign of King John* (Oxford, 1961), 200–01, and 241–50 on the resultant consequences after the civil war.

30 G. J. Turner, 'The Minority of Henry III, Part I', *TRHS* new ser., xviii (1904), 280–4; Norgate, 280–6. *PR 1216–25*, 1; on Peak castle: the king's fifteenth birthday is the most plausible interpretation of 'usque in quartumdecimum annum etatis nostre completum'.

royal government and its territorial power would be fragmented. The narrative has been written by some historians as a series of small castle wars through which the minority governors averted the threat, culminating in the crisis of 1223–4 when the custody of over 30 royal castles was re-allocated by Hubert de Burgh on the king's behalf. Sir Maurice Powicke argued that during the Marshal's regency the danger was all too apparent, 'so long as half a dozen barons and military experts ruled from their strongholds nearly a score of shires in the midlands and west of England. . . . What was needed was a general resumption of castles by the crown, and a redistribution which would emphasize their dependence on the crown. The change was effected between 1221 and 1223.'[31]

The general question raised by such views is whether the threat to royal government was potentially as great as has been supposed. A full examination would have to take into account the social and economic tensions of the period, the progressive definition and implementation of Magna Carta and the readjustments consequent on the loss of further territories in France. The specific question most relevant here is whether the control of castles was such a crucial indicator of territorial power, or such a vital factor in the political outcome, as Powicke and others have assumed.

In the early years of the minority the regency government of William Marshal accepted the need to work within the balance of territorial power bequeathed to it on the conclusion of peace in 1217. The aim was certainly to rebuild royal income and set the administrative system to work again, by such measures as the general eyre of 1218–19, and to restore lands as they had been held before the civil war, in accordance with the terms of the Treaty of Kingston of September 1217. Lesser men accordingly found themselves pursued for their debts and impleaded for land to which they had a dubious or recent claim. But the powerful were handled with great caution.[32] Aware of his limited room for manoeuvre, he tried to achieve as much as possible by agreement, though in the last resort open defiance had to be suppressed in case it proved infectious. Brian de l'Isle, who had been instructed to surrender Peak castle to William de Ferrers, and had perhaps resisted the Marshal's instructions, was given Knaresborough castle instead in May 1217, and was allowed to appoint a deputy when he went on crusade the following year. Later in 1217 a dispute arose over the custody of Lincoln castle, which was claimed by William, earl of Salisbury after his appointment as sheriff of the county in May 1217. For a time he may have succeeded, but not surprisingly he was resisted by Nicholaa de la Haye who had held the castle as hereditary castellan and defended it in the civil war. In October 1217 she seems to have recovered both the castle and the county, but by the end of the year a compromise had been reached: William was confirmed in office as sheriff while Nicholaa retained the castle. At times the Marshal could achieve his ends by persuasion and his personal prestige. In June 1217 Fawkes de Breauté wrote to Hubert de Burgh to complain about the seizure of some lands

31 F. M. Powicke, *King Henry III and the Lord Edward* (Oxford, 1947), i. 55–6.

32 For recent analyses of the general political problems involved, see J. C. Holt, *Magna Carta* (Cambridge, 1965), 269–92; R. C. Stacey, *Politics, Policy and Finance under Henry III, 1216–1245* (Oxford, 1987), 1–44.

in his custody by the regent's servants, emphasizing that he was tolerating such intrusion and prepared to negotiate about it only because the Marshal was involved. At other times he was prepared to accept a temporary reverse. In February 1218 William de Forz, count of Aumale, already a potential trouble-maker, was ordered to surrender the royal castles of Rockingham and Sauvey, but no action was taken after he failed to obey.[33]

After the Marshal's death on 14 May 1219, the pressure for stronger measures in such cases increased. Already on 10 May 10 the legate Pandulf, to whom the Marshal wished to leave some kind of supervisory authority over the government, wrote to Ralph Neville, the vice-chancellor, asking on what terms the legate Guala, his predecessor, had granted the custody of castles.[34] In the autumn of 1219 the dispute over Lincoln broke out again, and Fawkes de Breauté was ordered to garrison the castle to dissuade William of Salisbury from violent action. Measures against William de Forz were stepped up: in November 1219 royal letters were sent to the men of Yorkshire, Lincolnshire and four other counties warning them that he was detaining Sauvey and Rockingham against the king's will. The younger William Marshal's custody of Marlborough and Fotheringay castles was also coming under pressure. Fotheringay was part of the lands of David, earl of Huntingdon, but on the earl's death in June 1219, his estates had been taken into the king's hands, while Marlborough was actually a royal castle.[35] A more concerted campaign against castle custodians was shaped in 1220, by agreement between the leading ecclesiastics and secular figures of the administration. In May 1220 Pope Honorius III wrote several letters to the legate Pandulf, urging that bishops and others who held royal castles should surrender them, and more specifically that no one should hold more than two royal castles.[36] On 17 May, the young Henry had been re-crowned at Westminster. According to the Dunstable annalist the barons present took an oath on the day after the ceremony that they would surrender their castles on the king's command and render account for them; also they would make war on anyone who refused to obey and had been excommunicated by the legate.[37] This symbolic act was followed by a royal progress through the Midlands, culminating in Henry's arrival at Rockingham towards the end of June. Though preparations for a siege had been begun in case of need, the personal presence of the king had the desired effect and William de Forz's garrisons submitted, both there and at Sauvey.[38] Henry then went straight on to Canterbury for a second symbolic cer-

33 *CPR 1216–25*, 1, 4, 7, 15, 64, 190; for Peak and Knaresborough. *CPR 1216–25*, 65, 117, 130; *King's Works*, ii. 705; for Lincoln. *Royal Letters*, i. 4–5; for Fawkes de Breauté. *CPR 1216–25*, 136; for Rockingham and Sauvey. Stacey, 10–22, is a useful short summary of events to the end of 1220. David Carpenter has suggested that de Breauté's letter should be re-dated to June 1219, in which case it would refer to William Marshal the younger.

34 *Royal Letters*, i. 117; if the date is emended from 1220 to 1219 as proposed by F. M. Powicke, 'The Chancery during the Minority of Henry III', *EHR* xxiii (1908), 229–31. Stacey, 15, appears to prefer Shirley's dating.

35 *CPR 1216–25*, 201; for Lincoln. *CPR 1216–25*, 257–8; *Royal Letters*, i. 56–8; for Sauvey and Rockingham. *RLC* i. 397; for Fotheringay.

36 *Royal Letters*, i. 121, 535–6.

37 Dunstable annals, in *Ann. Mon.* iii. 57.

38 Barnwell annals, in *Coventry*, ii. 244–5. *CPR 1216–25*, 238, 240; for negotiations with William de

emony, the translation of the relics of Thomas Becket on 7 July, after which Archbishop Stephen Langton, having reasserted the king's position as well as his own, departed for Rome.

From 1221 onwards Hubert de Burgh was able to increase the pressure for recovery of the royal castles as his own position strengthened. In November 1220 William Marshal finally relinquished Fotheringay castle, probably to an agent of the justiciar.[39] There followed the futile revolt of the count of Aumale in December and January 1220–1 in Lincolnshire which was crushed by an army led by the justiciar. This confirmed de Forz's loss of royal castles the previous year, and compelled him also to give up Castle Bytham, which his own vassal (and ex-rebel) William de Coleville had been trying to recover judicially since 1217. Otherwise the count was forgiven because of his faithful service to King John in the civil war, an excuse which in his case was now wearing thin.[40] In 1221 Peter de Maulay was compelled to surrender his custody of Corfe castle after being accused in the royal court at Whitsun of plotting treason. Fawkes de Breauté later, probably rightly, accused Hubert de Burgh and his allies of trumping up this charge for their own purposes.[41] Further piecemeal recoveries continued during 1222, but towards the end of 1223, following a successful campaign against Llywelyn on the Welsh March which had strengthened an alliance between Hubert de Burgh and William Marshal, the justiciar was ready for more drastic action, Since the summer of 1223 he had been in possession of papal letters declaring Henry to be of age and ordering those who had lands or custodies from the king to be prepared to surrender them. When in November he had these letters proclaimed and ordered the resumption of Gloucester and Hereford castles, the party opposed to the justiciar took this as a warning shot and began to raise arms. In the event they only accelerated change. The 'opposition' Christmas court at Leicester was outnumbered by those who rallied to the king and de Burgh; the potential rebels headed by the earl of Chester backed down and a major redistribution of castles and shrievalties followed in January and February 1224.[43] In the wave of complaints and judicial cases against the dispossessed which followed now that they were vulnerable to attack, Fawkes de

Forz, and royal proclamation of the surrender on 29 June. Fawkes de Breauté was allowed £100 for his expenses at the 'siege' of Rockingham: *RLC* i. 439.

39 After receiving four royal requests to do so between June and Nov.: *CPR 1216–25*, 236, 257, 272; *RLC* i. 429, 442. See Stacey, 21–2, on other interests in Fotheringay, which was seized by William de Forz in his subsequent rebellion.

40 Above, notes 33, 35, 38. R. V. Turner, 'William de Forz, Count of Aumale: An Early Thirteenth-Century English Baron', *Procs. of the American Philosophical Soc.* cxv (1971), 232–43, is a full account of his career through the minority. See also B. English, *The Lords of Holderness, 1086–1260* (Hull, 1979), 40–7; and the reappraisal in Stacey, 22–4. Bytham was demolished by the royal army.

41 Stacey, 24–5. Peter des Roches, bishop of Winchester (who held the custody of Winchester, Southampton and Porchester castles until Jan. 1224) was also accused. This episode begins de Breauté's *querimonia* addressed to the papal court in 1225, and preserved with the Barnwell annals in *Coventry*, ii. 259–72,

42 R. F. Walker, 'Hubert de Burgh and Wales 1218–32', *EHR* lxxvii (1972), 473–6, on the 1223 campaign. For narrative accounts of the 1223–4 crisis, see Norgate, 200–17; Powicke, *Henry III*, i. 55–60; Stacey, 27–30.

43 *PRO, List of Sheriffs. Royal Letters*, i. 508–16 (Appendix II), brings together the main changes between Nov. 1223 and Mar. 1224.

Breauté seems to have been singled out for particular attention, which drove him into his disastrous revolt in June 1224.[44] Bedford castle, in which his brother William had imprisoned a royal judge, was besieged for eight weeks in July and August. The defenders, surrendering *in extremis* were hanged at the king's personal wish. Once again, as with William de Forz in 1220 and 1221, the man who risked rebellion found no allies to join him; once again the personal presence of the king, even a king who was a minor or a figurehead, counted for a great deal. De Breauté threw himself on the king's mercy and was exiled, taking his grievances to the papal court, to which is owed the preservation in writing of his side of the story.

Like so many other things in Henry III's minority, the recovery of the royal castles can be regarded either as an evident need of royal government, or as the product of factional manoeuverings. Both of these approaches have some validity and the balance between them is hard to draw. On both political sides there were mixed motives. It was perhaps desirable that those who acted in the king's name should succeed in recovering the royal castles, but having recovered them they could only hand them on to other custodians more loyal to the justiciar and his colleagues. Even the Marshal had put his own friends and allies in positions of power, and had been expected to do so. This was a matter of degree: such use of patronage was only dangerous when it passed beyond acceptable limits. Against this background, the castellans in office in 1217 had a reasonable claim, based on past loyalty, to be regarded as the natural upholders of the new king's authority, at least until he came of age. After the Marshal's death in 1219 they also had good reason to fear that if they left office voluntarily they would be unrewarded for their past services and brought to account by men prejudiced against them. Their possession of royal castles provided a kind of security, symbolic as well as military, for their other possessions and general political position.

This emphasizes the crucial point that the recovery of royal castles in the minority cannot be seen as a discrete issue. It spilled over into other areas of politics. Castles and shrievalties were often held together, and, in 1223–4, redistributed together. But, in peace as in war, all castles were only of limited value unless they carried with them sufficient services and income to be self-supporting, and preferably profitable. Lesser men and professional administrators, who could not afford to run castles from their own resources as part of broader political ambitions, were all the more aware of this. In February 1220 Hugh de Vivonne, constable of Bristol castle refused to surrender the barton, the bundle of property and jurisdiction which went with the castle, to the earl of Gloucester until he received the alternative revenues he had been promised.[45] The cost of running a castle included in the first instance building and maintenance of the fabric, but the recurrent cost of stocking and wages were just as important, and

44 Narrative of the revolt and siege in Norgate, 223–4, 230–49, 296 9; Powicke, *Henry III*, i. 60–6; Stacey, 30–2. The castle was demolished despite the protests of its would-be hereditary castellan William de Beauchamp: *Royal Letters*, i. 236; *King's Works*, ii. 559.

45 *Royal Letters*, i. 90–1; *Accounts of the Constables of Bristol Castle*, liv–lv. There was no question of surrendering the castle itself, as stated by Stacey, 14.

rapidly escalated to enormous burdens if a castle were to be kept in any sort of war readiness.

Destruction in the civil war did create an important need for repair and rebuilding at several major fortresses.[46] At Dover the outer gate which had been undermined in 1216 was now closed up and a completely new gatetower constructed. At least £4,865 was spent between Michaelmas 1217 and Easter 1221, though as much as two-thirds of the total may have been used to sustain the garrison. Another £1,290 went on building costs between 1221 and 1225. Repairs at Lincoln also began early, in 1217 and 1218, with at least £500 spent by 1220. By 1219 work was underway at Rochester, though the major repair of the keep, which was eventually to cost over £500, was only authorized in 1226. At Windsor, Northampton, Hertford, Marlborough and other sites too, the backlog of remedial work from the civil war continued through the 1220s, though gradually giving way to more general improvements, like new mural towers at the Tower of London and a new barbican at Bristol. The Welsh March was an area of special strategic need, for Llywelyn the Great's enhanced power was also a consequence of the civil war in England. The royal campaign in 1223 headed by Hubert de Burgh resulted in the construction of a major new royal castle at Montgomery. At least £3,300 was spent between 1223 and 1228, though again this was divided between building costs and the pay of the garrison. Subsequent royal campaigns in Wales in 1228 and 1231 were also associated with new castle works.[47]

It might seem as though, within the tight financial constraints of the minority regime, resources were being concentrated upon the most important castles in accordance with strategic need. This, though, is only a partial view. The treatment of specific castles owed as much to individual influence as to overall planning. Hubert de Burgh's personal prestige was obviously identified with Dover, which he had defended against Louis's attacks, and he was well placed to lavish funds on it. Between 1217 and Easter 1221 he accounted for the works in person. Among the revenues committed were the entire renders of Kent, Norfolk and Suffolk, the counties of which de Burgh was sheriff. At Northampton, held by Fawkes de Breauté, over £300 was spent on the castle between 1217 and 1219; at Nottingham Philip Marc obtained a writ in 1219 to cover £213 which he had spent on building and repairs.[48] Such operations were arguably necessary by any definition of the needs of national defence and royal government. It was, after all, the most important castles which were most likely to have been seriously attacked and seriously defended in the civil war, and to have been entrusted to powerful custodians by John in the first place. But custodians who retained their influence and local authority after the conclusion of peace in September 1217 were the best placed to carry them through and inevitably, in the process, their own personal priorities and ambitions entered the picture. Both claimants to the disputed castles of Lincoln are found receiving allowances for work on it: William, earl of Salisbury £374 in 1217, and Nicholaa de la Haye

[46] Figures which follow are from *King's Works*, ii. 633–4, 705, 807–08.
[47] Walker, 'Hubert de Burgh', 465–94; *King's Works*, i. 111; ii. 739–40, 775–6.
[48] *King's Works*, ii. 633, for Dover; ii. 751, for Northampton; ii. 757, for Nottingham.

£130 between 1218 and 1220. How the money was spent on the ground, and by whom, is not clear.[49] Such costs had always been met from local revenues whenever possible, and in the conditions of the early minority custodians were often able to retain for local use part of the revenues for which otherwise they would have had to account at the exchequer. William de Forz appears to have paid nothing in respect of the farms of Rockingham and Sauvey between receiving them in December 1216 and surrendering them in June 1220.[50] Even on the Welsh borders, where royal castle building appears most clearly geared to national strategic needs, it was also deeply interwoven with Hubert de Burgh's own personal ambitions, all the more so as his grip on the royal administration strengthened in the 1220s. Montgomery castle, built during the royal campaign of 1223 and lavishly funded, was put in the justiciar's custody and granted to him for life in 1228. The success of that operation was largely the work of William Marshal's campaign in the west. He recovered Cardigan and Carmarthen from Llywelyn, who had held them since 1215 and had been granted their custody when he did homage to Henry III in 1218. The Marshal was then given charge of the two castles and seems to have spent heavily on restoring them, but he lost the custody in 1226, and in 1229 both were granted in perpetuity to Hubert de Burgh, to hold for the service of five knights.[51] The three linked border castles of Grosmont, Skenfrith and White Castle, first granted to de Burgh by John in 1201 and recovered by him in full fee by a decision of the royal court in 1219, were also massively rebuilt subsequently, though there is no documentary evidence to furnish precise dates.[52] Ambitious moves of this kind prepared the way for the justiciar's downfall in 1232, and already in 1228 the derisory nickname of 'Hubert's Folly' (*stultitia Huberti*) given to the abortive castle begun by the royal army invading Wales in that year was an indication of growing hostility.[53]

Work on castle fabric was accomplished by equally variable costs for stocking and wages. It is hard to generalize about 'garrisons' because the term is so ambiguous and covers such a variety of arrangements. When castles were prepared for war, costs would rise rapidly, but this could mean in effect that a lord or the king was temporarily basing part of his forces (and their supplies) in a castle, rather than furnishing a garrison for the sole purpose of defending it. When the war moved elsewhere, so would the men. When peace returned such forces were run down rapidly, even in major royal castles in the thirteenth century, to a token military presence with an attendant staff of watchmen and janitors. But castles did not serve purely military purposes, and this too is reflected in their running costs. Bristol castle in 1224–5 contained 4 knights, 3 sergeants and 13 squires, with 25 horses and a large number of servants, but Bristol was a major administrative and accounting centre with an enduring

49 *King's Works*, ii. 705.

50 *CPR 1216–25*, 240.

51 Walker, 'Hubert de Burgh', 465–94; *King's Works*, ii. 590, 600, 739–40; *CChR 1226–57*, 74, 100; *CPR 1225–32*, 186, 276.

52 *King's Works*, ii. 657–8, 837, 854; *RLC* i. 386, 398.

53 Walker, 'Hubert de Burgh', 476–91; D. Carpenter, 'The Fall of Hubert de Burgh', *Journ. British Studies* xix (1980), 1–17; Paris, *CM* iii. 159.

strategic importance in relation to Wales and Ireland. It was also a prison, in which at this time Henry III's cousin Eleanor of Brittany was kept in secure but honourable captivity.[54] The extreme case of military expense in the minority years is Dover, whose large paid garrison is known to have cost about £1,000 a year between 1221 and 1228, and is unlikely to have been on a smaller scale in previous years. Such exceptional provision could be regarded as meeting a national need at a crucial strategic point, but it also once again reflected and bolstered the power of the justiciar, who also held the royal castles of Rochester and Canterbury, to which he received life grants in 1228 after he became earl of Kent.[55] When Peter de Maulay was removed as constable of Corfe in 1221, the exchequer allowed 7,000 marks to cover his expenses there since Louis's landing in England in 1216, an indication of the running costs of another major royal castle.[56] It is no wonder that those who controlled such sums, and attendant patronage, as long as they had revenues to draw on, were reluctant to relinquish office.

Because of the cost of putting a castle in readiness for defence was so great, it was both a warning sign to others and a declaration of political intent. The royal letters of November 1219 announcing that William de Forz was holding Rockingham and Sauvey castles against the king's will accused him also of fortifying them and stocking them with grain from the surrounding countryside. In April 1220 the legate Pandulf wrote to Hubert de Burgh urging that similar measures should be taken against William Marshal in respect of the royal castle of Marlborough which he was fortifying, that is preparing for war. The legate urged that he be ordered to stop, and others banned from aiding him 'sine domini regis speciali licentia et mandato'. Evidently, rumours of this kind were in constant circulation.[57]

The recovery of royal castles in Henry III's minority was also associated with the broader political issue of royal policy towards baronial fortification. Some of the royal castellans ejected by Hubert de Burgh in the 1220s can be classified as foreign adventurers or military professionals with nowhere else to go. Even Fawkes de Breauté can be regarded in this light, though with his marriage in 1215 into the Redvers lands of the earldom of Devon he appeared to have successfully made the transition into the English aristocracy until the disaster of 1224. But others were building on an existing power base. It was the pattern of lands and loyalties he already possessed which made William de Forz's detention of royal castles so threatening. The extreme case of this is the massive territorial power of the earl of Chester, which could have made the brief wars of 1221 and 1224 infinitely more dangerous if he had moved into open rebellion instead of eventually surrendering his royal custodies. The castle of Beeston which Earl Ranulf built around 1225 blatantly defended Cheshire from England

54 *Accounts of the Constables of Bristol Castle*, xvii–xxxvi, 6.

55 *King's Works*, ii. 633; *CChR 1226–57*, 74, 27 April 1228. This grant of Dover, Rochester and Canterbury castles for life promised 1,000 marks a year from the exchequer for maintenance (and another 200 for Montgomery): 'in case of war or rebellion the king shall give him further help in money that he may be able to keep the said castles'.

56 *King's Works*, ii. 620. In 1217–18 there were still 12 knights and 112 serjeants at Devizes: *RLC*. i. 467.

57 *Royal Letters*, i. 56–8, 100–01.

rather than from Wales and was perhaps a symbolic act of defiance, but the earl had too many interests in the rest of England to fall back on a policy of local separatism, though his relations with the royal government were very distant for most of the 1220s.[58]

In such conditions, leading political figures were concerned at any reports of castles being fortified or constructed. Fawkes de Breauté received a letter from William Souder and Nicholas de Thebotot, perhaps in 1219, to tell him that Gilbert de Gant was rapidly strengthening his castle at Folkingham in Lincolnshire, and that it was said he had 'licentiam de domino rege et de comite de Salesbire' for his activities. De Breauté's concern arose from its nearness to his own castle of Oakham, which was specified in the letter, but he was also involved with the earl of Salisbury in the dispute over the custody of Lincoln castle. Folkingham was much nearer to Castle Bytham, 10 miles or so to the south-west, which William de Forz was withholding from William de Coleville between 1217 and 1221.[59] Under 10 miles north of Folkingham was Sleaford castle, which, with Newark 20 miles or so further to the north-west, belonged to the bishop of Lincoln. The bishop had turned the castles over to John at the outset of the civil war, but orders were given in June 1217, following the battle of Lincoln, that they be returned to him. William de Albini at Sleaford seems to have complied, but Robert de Gaugi at Newark ignored both this and three further letters from William Marshal in the next two months, though he was promised that all his reasonable claims would be met and he would be well provided for, perhaps by a post elsewhere. By March 1218 the Marshal was issuing orders for a force to be raised to recover the castle, but action was again postponed until finally the task was accomplished by a brief siege in July 1218. Even then the Marshal's moderation was evident: according to Wendover, de Gaugi was allowed to reach a kind of settlement with the bishop and was compensated, or repaid, for the food and stocks he had assembled within the castle. Personal considerations were not absent from this incident either. Early in 1218 the bishop of Lincoln gave William Marshal 100 marks for his own use to revive his interest in the recovery of the castle.[60] The minority government's general aim of restoring property seized during the civil war and resolving outstanding claims thus had to be pursued with close attention to the complexity of local interests in a disputed area like Lincolnshire. The recovery of castles presented certain specific problems, but their re-allocation was an important symbol of the return to normality after the civil war.

The other specific obligation taken on by the royal government in relation to

58 *Annales Cestrienses*, ed. R. C. Christie (Rec. Soc. of Lancashire and Cheshire, xiv, 1887), 52–5; R. Eales, 'Henry III and the End of the Norman Earldom of Chester', in *Thirteenth Century England I*, ed. P. R. Coss and S. D. Lloyd (Woodbridge, 1986), 101–08. It seems clear that Ranulf was also rebuilding Bolingbroke castle in Lincolnshire during the 1220s.

59 *Royal Letters*, i. xliii, 64. The editor, Shirley, misidentifies the site as Fillingham, north of Lincoln, but 'distat ab Ocham tredecim leucas ad dextram viae versus Lincolniam'. For potential interests of Salisbury, de Forz and others, see above nn. 33, 35, 40.

60 *CPR 1216–25*, 68, 71, 81, 85, 121, 164. *RLC* i. 602, for the 100 marks. Paris, *CM* iii. 33–4. G. J. Turner, 'The Minority of Henry III, Part II', *TRHS* 3rd ser., i (1907), 224–34, is still the best general account of the episode.

castles was stated in the new final clause of the 1217 reissue of Magna Carta: 'all adulterine castles [*castra adulterina*], that is those built or rebuilt since the beginning of the war between the lord John our father and his barons of England, shall be destroyed immediately'.[61] This specific and limited definition does not support the view that 'adulterine' should be equated with 'unlicensed', in the sense of contrary to a universal system of royal authorization applicable to all castles. Executive action in the following years usually corresponded closely with the Charter provision: for example, Anstey castle in Hertfordshire was ordered to be returned to the condition it was in before war broke out. It survived as a castle, and is referred to again in 1225.[62] The most detailed illustration of the issues involved comes from a letter written by Richard de Umfraville to Hubert de Burgh in 1220, replying to a royal letter querying the status of his castle at Harbottle in Northumberland. Contrary to information which had reached the king, his castle was not adulterine but had been built in the time of Henry II with the help of the whole *comitatus* of Northumberland and the bishopric of Durham. It was valuable in the defence of the Scottish border and more than nine leagues distant from the royal castle of Bamburgh: 'non sit adulterinum, cum constructum fuerit per assensum et praeceptum domini regis Henrici, ad utilitatem tam regis quam pacis regni'.[63] This is a comprehensive range of justifications for possession of a castle, possibly intended to screen the real issue, that de Umfraville had carried out adulterine (that is, wartime) improvements to it. The reference to Henry II might be read as an appeal to a specific licence or royal grant but, if so, nothing specific about it was preserved. Probably it should be seen rather as a claim of long tenure since Henry II's day. Further south, on the Tyne, de Umfraville found that his castle of Prudhoe was challenged by Philip of Oldcotes's construction of another nearby at Nafferton. He complained to the king that Nafferton was a new castle, and orders were issued for it to be demolished, though this was only done in 1221–22, after its owner's death. Philip de Oldcotes, joint-sheriff of Northumberland and keeper of the bishopric of Durham, was another of the recalcitrants of the post civil war period, who ignored numerous orders to surrender Mitford castle to Roger Bertram between September 1217 and his eventual compliance under threat of excommunication in 1220.[64]

In nearly all of these cases, though Richard de Umfraville was put to the defence of his castle at Harbottle, the onus of proof was on anyone who claimed that an existing castle was illegal or objectionable, the 'adulterine' clause forbidding wartime building from becoming permanent being the usual grounds. Evidence for a positive system of licensing, by which all castles would be required to have specific royal approval, remains very thin, though so-called 'licences to crenellate' do survive on the chancery rolls from their beginnings in John's

61 Text in Holt, *Magna Carta*, 357.

62 *RLC* i. 350; *CPR 1216–25*, 543.

63 *Royal Letters*, i. 140–1. See also Holt, *Magna Carta*, 279.

64 *RLC* i. 379, *CPR 1216–25*, 287–8, 291; B. Harbottle and P. Salway, 'Nafferton Castle, Northumberland', *Archaeologia Aeliana*, 4th ser., xxxviii (1960), 130–5. Holt, *Northerners*, 244–6, on Philip of Oldcotes's activities in these years.

reign. Ten such grants survive from before 1216: seven from 1200 and 1201, all on the charter rolls, and one each from 1202, 1203 and 1204 enrolled as letters close.[65] Nor did Henry III's minority see any proliferation of 'licences', either to establish new rights or confirm old ones. Six were issued for England and Wales between 1216 and 1231 but only one pre-dated 1227. It appears as a royal letter to Ranulf, earl of Chester in 1221, ordering him not to hinder Fulk fitzWarin from fortifying Whittington castle in Shropshire, as Fulk had 'undertaken by his charter that he would never commit any misconduct by means of the castle so as rightfully to be reputed as transgressor of his fealty'.[66] The others were grants to the burgesses of Montgomery (1227), Henry de Audley for Red Castle in Shropshire (1227), Maurice de Gant for Beverstone in Gloucestershire (1229), Hubert de Burgh for Hadleigh in Essex (1230) and Robert de Tattershall for Tattershall in Lincolnshire (1231).[67] All of these were apparently new works except Beverstone, which was allowed to 'stay and remain', perhaps a case of an adulterine castle which had gradually been rendered acceptable by the passage of time, but for which the unusual assurance of a specific grant was thought worth procuring. This exiguous evidence only goes to support the conclusion that though in practice royal intervention in baronial castles could be justified on a variety of grounds, as it had been in the twelfth century, it still did not rest on any defined legal basis and should not be regarded as a system of control.

IV

The balance of political forces in early thirteenth-century England was such that the possession and relative distribution of castles was not in itself decisive. Even in war, as the events of 1215–17 showed, castles were valuable assets only insofar as they were inherently strong, well supplied and prepared for defence, and entrusted to a loyal commander and garrison. The first of these required prior investment, usually over a prolonged period, as stone castles grew more and more elaborate. The others required a prompt response to emergency conditions and sensitivity to the political attitudes and loyalties of one's own men, as well as potential allies and enemies. Merely to acquire or build castles did not ensure security unless accomplished without creating too much local opposition while leaving adequate resources for other costs. Kings, magnates and lesser men alike had to balance the future advantages of investment in fortification against all the other long-term and short-term calls on their finances. When war broke out, castles could be sustained in a brief conflict by pillaging but over any length of time this was liable to prove counter-productive by alienating local populations and powerful neighbours. And whatever the current conclusions of military historians about the balance between technologies of attack and

65 *Rotuli Chartarum in Turri Londoniensi asservati*, ed. T. D. Hardy (London, 1837), 60, 70, 89, 103; *Rotuli de Liberate ac de Misis et Praestitis, regnante Johanne*, ed. T. D. Hardy (London, 1844), 32, 34–5, 104.

66 *RLC* i. 460. It is of course stretching a point to call this mandate a 'licence'.

67 *CChR 1226–57*, 10 ; *CPR 1225–32*, 138, 260, 417 and 422, 435.

defence in this period, no castle was ever invulnerable. Castles were held because their defenders were motivated to hold them when they came under attack in the hope of eventual gains. The prolonged sieges of Dover and Lincoln in 1216–17 only assumed the importance they did against the background of dynamic changes in political fortunes elsewhere. A king or lord who failed to provide acceptable leadership risked losing such loyalty, and many of his castles might become peacetime assets only, liable to fail him in a crisis when they were most needed.

If the value of castles appears so relative and provisional even in time of war, this is all the more true for the subsequent period of pacification. The real threat which faced the minority government in the years after 1217 was the gradual insidious alienation of royal offices, rights and incomes while they were in the hands of men who had partially escaped from central control.[68] The custody of royal castles was only part of the problem and the recovery of them was only part of the solution. It was evidently linked with the staged process through which the king came of age, in 1220, 1221 and 1223. It was linked also with the mounting pressures on royalists to disgorge most of their land seizures and other gains made during the war. In some respects the royal government actively restored order, a process reflected in the records of the *curia regis* and eyre circuits from 1218 onwards. In other respects it presided over the return of more stable conditions, ratifying local agreements shaped by ransom payments, family alliances and individual bargains of every kind. Nor was the minority government itself always united or able to follow consistent policies. At every stage the interests of individuals, officials or powerful supporters in council and country had to be taken into account.

Seen in this context the recovery of the royal castles symbolized the success of Hubert de Burgh and his allies in re-asserting royal rights on a much broader front. But the question remains: could the castles have been used to defy the justiciar after all? Such a conclusion is implicit in Powicke's view that if de Burgh and Stephen Langton had not prevailed in 1223–4, 'this development would have changed the course of history in incalculable ways. It would have made the castle the embodiment, not the instrument, of power, and given a new strength to what in fact became, in the greater part of thirteenth-century England, an old-fashioned place of business or the object of architectural experiment.'[69] The restraint and ultimate loyalty of the baronial group, especially Ranulf, earl of Chester, led them to give way when they could have made a stand. But these arguments are not really convincing. Rather, it was the case that Hubert de Burgh, with ecclesiastical support, the declaration of the king's majority, and a careful calculation of baronial allegiances, had outmanoeuvered his opponents. The testing of strength at the Christmas courts of 1223 made the point; Earl Ranulf and his allies accepted the inevitable, judging that by fortifying their castles they would only risk greater losses. Fawkes de Breauté's fatal rebellion in 1224 displayed the consequences of over-reliance on castles and

68 As recent research has generally confirmed. See the survey in Stacey, 6–12.
69 Powicke, *Henry III*, i. 51.

inadequate calculation of the other factors involved. The siege of Bedford bore out the tactical value of the castle very well, as it held up a massive royal army for almost two months, but in the meantime de Breauté's political support, instead of strengthening, withered away completely.[70]

If the political role of castles in Henry III's minority has sometimes been overstated, it has usually been underestimated for his majority rule down to 1258. Except for sporadic warfare on the Welsh March, which briefly spilled over into domestic politics in 1233–4, this was a generation of internal peace, but the investment in 'architectural experiment' was still considerable. H. M. Colvin estimated royal expenditure on castles during the whole period 1216–72 at £85,000, an average of £1,500 a year. Though much of this went on residential building in the great palace castles of Windsor (about £15,000), Winchester and the Tower of London (almost £10,000 each), the remainder was sufficient to complete the process of rebuilding in stone which had been initiated before 1216, on almost every site still thought worth fortifying. Apart from Dover, there was a growing concentration on Wales, where Degannwy castle alone cost up to £10,000, and royal power was consolidated by the acquisition of the earldom of Chester and its castles in 1237.[71] Custodial arrangements show a nice balance between loyalty and authority on the one hand, and economy on the other.[72] Probably this had been true in earlier periods too, but the process can be demonstrated more clearly from the fuller records of the thirteenth century. Individual cases must be scrutinized to see which motive was predominant: sometimes castles might be removed from the sheriff and put in the care of a powerful nobleman or *curialis* for reasons of security, sometimes this was done because such a man could relieve the king of running costs, while the castle itself was left in the hands of an underpaid deputy. Concentration on fewer sites meant that some castles were effectively alienated to save money, as Sauvey was in 1235, or demolished, as Bedford was after the 1224 siege.[73] Henry III's family policy also emerges clearly, with grants to Richard of Cornwall and Simon de Montfort culminating in the creation of Edward's great apanage in 1254. As far as royal policy towards baronial castles is concerned, the striking fact is that between 1232 and 1251 no 'licences to crenellate' appear on the chancery rolls at all. Though it is always possible that some grants were made and not enrolled, this general picture strikingly confirms that the unsystematic inheritance of royal rights over castles had yet to be systematized, even in a more legalistic age.[74] In 1258, Henry's baronial opponents were anxious to gain control of key royal castles and to safeguard themselves from the danger of

70 Above, n. 44; R. A. Brown, *English Castles* (3rd edn, London, 1976), 191–4. G. H. Fowler, 'Munitions in 1224', *Bedfordshire Hist. Rec. Soc. Trans.*, v (1920), 117–32, gives some idea of the resources employed.

71 *King's Works*, i. 110–15; ii. 624–6.

72 D. Carpenter, 'The Decline of the Curial Sheriff in England 1194–1258', *EHR* xci (1976), 1–32, esp. at 27.

73 *CPR 1232–47*, 100, grant of Sauvey to Hugh Paynel 'provided that the said Hugh will maintain the castle and buildings at his own cost'. Above, n. 44.

74 I am grateful to Dr Charles Coulson for giving me access to his unpublished handlists of royal licences to crenellate.

foreign invasion, but they advanced no complaints about royal interference with castles in general.[75]

Many of the elements which composed royal castle policy in the thirteenth century closely parallel those of the pre-1216 period. Seen in a longer perspective, the events of the crisis years 1215–24 serve to highlight the enduring forces which both shaped and set limits to the importance of castles in twelfth- and thirteenth-century England.

75 *DBM* 80–1, 102–3, 112–13.

Select Bibliography

This bibliography is by no means exhaustive, but is intended as a general guide and expands on the references given in the footnotes in the Introduction. Its focus is chiefly on material concerning castles and castle-building in western Europe in the eleventh and twelfth centuries, but for the sake of completeness contains additional sections on areas not specifically dealt with in this volume. The material here generally consists of broad survey articles rather than case studies. For comprehensive bibliographies see: J. R. Kenyon, *Castles, Town Defences, and Artillery Fortifications in Britain and Ireland: A Bibliography* vol. *i* (CBA, 1978); *ii* (CBA, 1983); *iii* (CBA, 1990) and the annual bibliographies compiled by John Kenyon and published by the Castles Studies Group. For individual sites see Guidebooks published by Cadw, English Heritage and Historic Scotland.

Gazetteer

Coventry, M., *The Castles of Scotland: A Comprehensive Reference and Gazetteer to more than 2000 Castles* 2nd edn (Edinburgh, 1997).

King, D. J. C., *Castellarium Anglicanum: An Index and Bibliography of the Castles in England, Wales and the Islands* (New York, 1983).

Mesqui, J., *Châteaux Fortes et Fortifications en France* (Paris, 1997).

Pettifer, A., *English Castles: a Guide by Counties* (Woodbridge, 1995).

———, *Welsh Castles: a Guide by Counties* (Woodbridge, 2000).

Renn, D., *Norman Castles in Britain*, 2nd edn (London, 1968).

Salch, C. L., *L'Atlas de Châteaux-Fort en France* (Strasbourg, 1977).

———, *L'Atlas des Villes et Villages Fortifiés en France* (Strasbourg, 1978).

General Surveys

Anderson, W., *Castles of Europe from Charlemagne to the Renaissance* (London, 1970).

Baylé, M., ed., *L'architecture Normande au Moyen âge*, 2 vols (Caen, 1997).

Brown, R. A., *English Castles*, 3rd edn (London, 1976).

———, *The Architecture of Castles* (London, 1984).

———, *Castles from the Air* (Cambridge, 1989).

Clark, G. T., *Medieval Military Architecture in England* (London, 1884).

Clapham, A., *Romanesque Architecture in Western Europe* (Oxford, 1936).

Colvin, H. M., Brown, R. A., and Taylor, A. J., *The History of the King's Works, The Middle Ages*. 2 vols (London, 1963).

Conant, K. J., *Carolingian and Romanesque Architecture 800–1200*, 4th edn (Harmondsworth, 1978).

Fernie, E., *The Architecture of Norman England* (Oxford, 2000).

Higham, R. and Barker, P., *Timber Castles* (London, 1992).
Johnson, M. H., *Behind the Castle Gate: From Medieval to the Renaissance* (London, 2002).
Kenyon, J., *Medieval Fortifications* (Leicester, 1990).
King, D. J. C., *The Castle in England and Wales: An Interpretative History* (London, 1988).
McNeill, T., *Castles* (London, 1992).
Mesqui, J., *Châteaux et Enceintes de la France Médiévale*, 2 vols (Paris, 1991, 1993).
Platt, C., *The Castle in Medieval England and Wales* (London, 1982).
Pounds, N. J. G., *The Medieval Castle in England and Wales* (Cambridge, 1990).
Stalley, R., *Early Medieval Architecture* (Oxford, 1999).
Thompson, A. H., *Military Architecture in England during the Middle Ages* (Oxford, 1912).
Thompson M. W., *The Rise of the Castle* (Cambridge, 1991).

Historiographical Treatments and Castle Origins

Armitage, E., *Early Norman Castles of the British Isles* (London, 1912).
Beresford, G., *Goltho: The Development of an Early Medieval Manor* (London, 1987).
Brown, R. A., 'An Historian's Approach to the Origins of the Castle in England', *Archaeological Journal* cxxvi (1969), pp. 131–148.
———, 'The Norman Conquest and the Genesis of English Castles', *Château-Gaillard* iii (1969), pp. 1–14.
Coulson, C., 'Cultural Realities and Reappraisals in English Castle-Study', *Journal of Medieval History* xxii (1996), pp. 171–207.
———, 'Peaceable Power in Norman Castles', *Anglo-Norman Studies* xxiii (2001), pp. 69–95.
Counihan, J. M., 'Mrs Ella Armitage, John Horace Round, G. T. Clark and Early Norman Castles', *Anglo-Norman Studies* viii (1986), pp. 73–87.
———, 'The Growth of Castle Studies in England and Normandy since 1850', *Anglo-Norman Studies* xi (1989), pp. 77–85.
Davison, B. K., 'The Origins of the Castle in England', *Archaeological Journal* cxxiv (1967), pp. 202–11.
———, 'Early Earthwork Castles: A New Model', *Château-Gaillard* iii (1969), pp. 37–47.
English, B., 'Towns, Mottes and Ringworks of the Conquest', *The Medieval Military Revolution*, ed. A. Ayton and J. Price (London, 1995), pp. 43–62.
Harfield, C. G., 'A Hand-list of Castles Recorded in the Domesday Book', *English Historical Review* cvi (1991), pp. 371–92.
Horsman, V., 'Eynsford Castle: a Reinterpretation of its Early History in the Light of Recent Excavations', *Archaeologia Cantiana* cv (1988), pp. 39–58.
Round, J. H., 'The Castles of the Conquest', *Archaeologia* lviii (1912), pp. 144–59.
Saunders, A. D., ed., *Five Castle Excavations: Reports on the Institute's Research Project into the Origins of the Castle in England* (London, 1978).
Stocker, D., 'The Shadow of the General's Armchair', *Archaeological Journal* cxlix (1992), pp. 415–420.
Thompson, M. W., 'The Military Interpretation of Castles', *Archaeological Journal* cli (1994), pp. 439–445.
Williams, A., 'A Bell-House and a Burh-Geat: Lordly Residences in England Before the Conquest', *Medieval Knighthood* iv, ed. C. Harper-Bill and R. Harvey (Woodbridge, 1992), pp. 221–40.

France

Aubenas, R., 'Les Châteaux-forts des Xe et XIe Siècles', *Revue Historique de Droit Francais et Entranger*, 4e ser. (1938), pp. 548–86.

Bachrach, B. S., 'Early Medieval Fortifications in the "West" of France: A Revised Technical Vocabulary', *Technology and Culture* xvi (1974), pp. 531–69.

———, 'Fortifications and Military Tactics: Fulk Nerra's Strongholds circa 1000', *Technology and Culture* xx (1979), pp. 531–49.

———, 'The Cost of Castle Building: The Case of the Tower at Langeais, 992–994', *The Medieval Castle, Romance and Reality*, ed. K. Reyerson and F. Powe (Iowa, 1984), pp. 47–62.

———, 'The Angevin Strategy of Castle-Building in the Reign of Fulk Nerra, 987–1040', *American Historical Review* lxxxviii (1983), pp. 533–60.

Barbier, P., *La France Féodal, I: Chateaux forts et Églises Fortifiées du midi de la France* (Paris, 1968).

Bates, D., *Normandy Before 1066* (Harlow, 1982).

Baudry, M. and Langeuin, P., 'Les Tours de la Basse-Cour du Château de Coucy', *Congrès Archéologique de France* cxlviii (1994), pp. 249–62.

Baylé, M. (ed.), *L'Architecture Normande au Moyen Âge*, 2 vols (Caen, 1997).

Baylé, M., 'Norman Architecture around the Year 1000: its Place in the Art of North-Western Europe', *Anglo-Norman Studies* xxii (2000), pp. 1–28.

Blary, F., 'Les Fortifications de Château de Château-Thierry des Derniers Comtes Herbertiens au Premier Duc de Bouillon (XIe–XVIe Siècle)', *Congrès Archéologique de France* cxlviii (1994), pp. 137–80.

Bur, M. (ed), *La Masion Forte au Moyen Âge* (Paris, 1986).

Chedeville, A. and Tonnere, N., *La Bretagne Féodale, Xie–XIIIe Siecle* (Rennes, 1987).

Dé Poüard, M., 'Les Petites Enceintes Circulaires D'Origine Médiévale en Normandie', *Château-Gaillard* i (1964), pp. 21–35.

Débord A. (ed.), 'Les Fortifications de terre en Europe Occidentale du Xe au XIIe Siècles', *Archéologie Médiévale* xi (1981), pp. 5–123.

Decaëns, J., 'De la Motte au Château de Pierre dans le Nord-Ouest de la France', *Manorial Buildings in England and Northern France*, ed. G. Meirion-Jones and M. Jones (Society of Antiquaries Occasional Papers Vol. 15, London, 1993), pp. 65–81.

Durand, P., 'Les Conséquences de la Datation Dendrochronologique de Donjon de Loches pour la Castellologie, Proposition de Datation', *Bulletin Monumental* clix (1996), pp. 222–8.

Fixot, M., 'Les Fortifications de Terre et la Naissance de la Féodalitie dans la Cinglais', *Château-Gaillard* iii (1969), pp. 61–6.

Gauthiez, B., 'La Ré-Occupation Plannifiée de la Cité de Rouen au Haut Moyen Ages', *Transactions of the Annual Conference of the British Archaeological Association: Medieval Art, Architecture, and Archaeology at Rouen* (Leeds, 1993).

Héliot, P., 'Sur les Residences Princières Bâties en France du 10e Siècle au 12e Siècle', *Le Moyen Age* iv (1955), pp. 27–61, 219–319.

Impey, E., 'Langeais, Indre-et-Loire. An Archaeological and Historical Study of the Early Donjon and its Environs', *Journal of the British Archaeological Association* cli (1998), pp. 43–106.

Langeuin, P. with Jollet, U., 'Le Front Sud de Donjon de Loches et ses Tours en Amande: un Jalon pour L'étude de la Fortification des Plantagenet', *Bulletin Monumental* cliv (1996), pp. 235–67.

LeKraie S. and Dustart, D., 'Les Châteaux du Cambrésis Médiéval (Xe–XlIe siècle):

début d'inventaire', *Le Château Médiéval et la Guerre dans l'Europe du Nord-Ouest: Mutations et Adaptations*, ed. A. Salamagne and R. Le Jan (Lille, 1998), pp. 35–51.
Mesqui, J., 'Les Programmes Résidentiels du Château de Coucy di XIIIe au XVIe Siècle', *Congrès Archéologique de France* cxlviii (1994), pp. 207–47.
Rolland, D., 'Le Donjon d'Ambleny', *Congrès Archéologique de France* cxlviii (1994), pp. 23–40.
Yver, J., 'Les Châteaux-forts en Normandie jusqu'au Milieu de XIIe Siècle', *Bulletin de la Société des Antiquaires de Normandie* liii (1955–6), pp. 28–115.

Ireland

Barry, T. B., *The Archaeology of Medieval Ireland* (London, 1987).
———, 'Anglo-Norman Ringwork Castles: Some Evidence', *Landscape Archaeology in Ireland*, ed. T. Reeves-Smyth and F. Hamond (British Archaeological Reports 35, Oxford, 1983), pp. 295–314.
Graham, B. J., 'The Mottes of the Norman Liberty of Meath', *Irish Midland Studies*, ed. H. Mutagh (Athlone, 1980), pp. 39–56.
———, 'Medieval Timber and Earthwork Fortifications in Western Ireland', *Medieval Archaeology* xxxii (1988), pp. 110–29.
———, 'Twelfth and Thirteenth-Century Earthwork Castles in Ireland: An Assessment', *Fortress* ix (1991), pp. 24–34.
Holland, P., 'The Anglo-Normans and their Castles in County Galway', *Galway: History and Society*, ed. G. Moran and R. Gillespie (Dublin, 1996), pp. 1–26.
———, 'The Anglo-Norman Landscape in County Galway: Land-Holding, Castles and Settlements', *Journal of the Galway Archaeological and Historical Society* xlix (1997), pp. 159–93.
Leask, H. G., *Irish Castles and Castellated Houses*, 3rd edn (Dundalk, 1977).
Manning, C., 'Dublin Castle: the Building of a Royal Castle in Ireland', *Château-Gaillard* xviii (1998), pp. 119–22.
Mc Neill, T. E., *Anglo-Norman Ulster* (Edinburgh, 1980).
———, *Castles in Ireland: Feudal Power in a Gaelic World* (London, 1997).
———, 'Early Castles in Leinster', *Journal of Irish Archaeology* v (1990), pp. 57–64.
O'Connor, K., 'Irish Earthwork Castles', *Fortress* xii (1992), pp. 3–12.
———, *The Archaeology of Medieval Rural Settlement in Ireland* (Dublin, 1998).
O'Keefe, T., *Medieval Ireland: An Archaeology* (Stroud, 2000).
Orpen, G. H., *Ireland Under the Normans*, 4 vols. (Oxford, 1911–20).
Sweetman, D., 'The Development of Trim Castle in the Light of Recent Research', *Château-Gaillard* xviii (1998), pp. 223–30.
———, *Medieval Castles of Ireland* (Woodbridge, 2000).

Scotland

Cruden, S., *The Scottish Castle*, 3rd edn (Edinburgh, 1981).
Fawcett, R., 'Castle and Church in Scotland', *Château-Gaillard* xviii (1998), pp. 87–92.
Lindsay, M., *The Castles of Scotland* (London, 1986).
MacGibbon D. and Ross T., *The Castellated and Domestic Architecture of Scotland from the Twelfth to the Eighteenth Century* (Edinburgh, 1887–92).
Phillips, G., *Scottish Castles* (Glasgow, 1987).
Tabraham, C. J., *Scottish Castles and Fortifications* (Edinburgh, 1986).

Welfare, H., Bowden, M. and Blood, K., 'Fieldwork and the Castles of the Anglo-Scottish Border', *Patterns of the Past: Essays in Landscape Archaeology for Christopher Taylor*, ed. P. Patterson, D. Field and S. Ainsworth (Oxford, 1999), pp. 53–60.
Yeoman, P. A., 'Mottes in Northeast Scotland', *Scottish Archaeological Review* v (1988), pp. 125–33.

England and Wales: Morphological Studies

Braun, H., 'Earthwork Castles', *Journal of the British Archaeological Association*, 3rd Series i (1937), pp. 128–156.
Creighton, O., 'Early Leicestershire Castles: Archaeology and Landscape History', *Transactions of the Leicestershire Archaeological and Historical Society* lxxi (1997), pp. 21–36.
———, 'Early Castles in the Medieval Landscape of Rutland', *Transactions of the Leicestershire Archaeological and Historical Society*, lxxiii (1999), pp. 19–33.
———, 'Early Castles and Rural Settlement Patterns: Insights from Yorkshire and the East Midlands', *Medieval Settlement Research Group Annual Report* xiv (1999), pp. 29–33.
Higham, R., 'Early Castles in Devon, 1066–1201', *Château-Gaillard* ix–x (1982), pp. 101–16.
Hogg, A. H. A. and King, D. J. C., 'Early Castles in Wales and the Marches', *Archaeologia Cambrensis* cxii (1963), pp. 77–124.
King D. J. C., and Alcock, L., 'Ringworks of England and Wales', *Château-Gaillard* iii (1969), pp. 90–127.
King, D. J. C., 'The Field Archaeology of Mottes in England and Wales: Eine Kurze Übersicht', *Château-Gaillard* v (1972), pp. 101–112.
King, D. J. C. and Spurgeon, J., 'Mottes in the Vale of Montgomery', *Archaeologia Cambrensis* cxiv (1965) pp. 69–86.
McNeill, T. E., and Pringle, M., 'A Map of Mottes in the British Isles', *Medieval Archaeology* xli (1997), pp. 220–23.
Renn, D. F., 'Mottes: a Classification', *Antiquity* xxxiii (1959), pp. 106–112.
Spurgeon, C. J., 'Mottes and Castle Ringworks in Wales', *Castles in Wales and the Marches: Essays in Honour of D. J. Cathcart King*, ed. J. R. Kenyon and R. Avent (Cardiff, 1987), pp. 23–49.
———, 'The Castles of Glamorgan: some Sites and Theories of General Interest', *Château-Gaillard* xiii (1987), pp. 203–26.

Significant Excavations

Alcock, L., *Dinas Powys: An Iron Age, Dark Age and Early Medieval Settlement in Glamorgan* (Cardiff, 1963).
———, 'Castle Tower Penmaen: a Norman Ring-Work in Glamorgan', *Antiquaries Journal* xlvi (1966), pp. 178–210.
Austin, D., 'Barnard Castle, Co Durham', *Château-Gaillard* ix–x (1982), pp. 293–300.
Bennett, P., Frere, S. S. and Stow, S., *Excavations at Canterbury Castle* (Canterbury Archaeological Trust, Maidstone, 1982).
Coad, J. G. and Streeton, A., 'Excavations at Castle Acre Castle, Norfolk, 1972–77', *Archaeological Journal* cxxxix (1982), pp. 138–301.
Coad, J. G., Streeton, A. D. F. and Warmington, R., 'Excavations at Castle Acre Castle,

Norfolk, 1975–1982: The Bridges, Lime Kilns, and Eastern Gatehouse', *Archaeological Journal* cxliv (1987), pp. 256–307.

Cunliffe, B., *Excavations at Porchester Castle. 3. Medieval, the Outer Bailey* (London, 1977).

Cunliffe, B. and Munby, J., *Excavations at Porchester Castle. 4. Medieval, the Inner Bailey* (London, 1985).

Curnow, P. E. and Thompson, M. W., 'Excavations at Richard's Castle, Herefordshire, 1962–1964', *Journal of the British Archaeological Association*, 3rd Series xxxii (1969), pp. 105–27.

Davison, B. K., 'Castle Neroche: An Abandoned Norman Fortress in South Somerset', *Somerset Archaeology and Natural History Society* cxvi (1971–72), pp. 16–58.

Drury, P. J., 'Aspects of the Origins and Development of Colchester Castle', *Archaeological Journal* cxxxix (1982), pp. 302–419.

Drury, P. J. *et al.*, 'The Temple of Claudius at Colchester Reconsidered', *Britannia*, xv (1984), pp. 7–50.

Ellis, P. (ed.), *Ludgershall Castle, Excavations by P. Addyman 1964–72* (Wiltshire Archaeological and Natural History Society Monograph Series ii, 2000).

Everson, P., 'What's in a Name? Goltho, "Goltho" and Bullington', *Lincolnshire History and Archaeology* xxiii (1988), pp. 92–99.

Frere, S. S., Stow, S. and Bennett, P., *Excavations of the Roman and Medieval Defences of Canterbury* (Canterbury Archaeological Trust, Maidstone, 1982).

Higham, R. A., 'Excavations at Okehampton Castle, Devon. Part 1: The Motte and Keep', *Proceedings of the Devon Archaeological Society* xxxv (1979), pp. 3–42.

Higham, R. A., Allan J. P. and Blaylock, S. R., 'Excavations at Okehampton Castle, Devon: Part 2: The Bailey', *Proceedings of the Devon Archaeological Society* xl (1982), pp. 19–151.

Higham, R. and Barker, P., *Hen Domen Montgomery: A Timber Castle on the English-Welsh Border: A Final Report* (Exeter, 2000).

Hope-Taylor, B., 'The Excavation of a Motte at Abinger Castle in Surrey', *Archaeological Journal* lvii (1950), pp. 15–43.

Kent, J. P. C., 'Excavations at the Motte and Bailey Castle of South Mimms, Hertfordshire, 1960–1967', *Barnet District Local History Society Bulletin* xv (1968).

Mahany, C., 'Excavations at Stamford Castle, 1971–76', *Château-Gaillard* viii (1977), pp. 223–45.

Mayes, P. and Butler, L., *Sandal Castle Excavations 1964–1973* (Wakefield, 1983).

Thompson, M. W., 'Excavation in Farnham Castle Keep, Surrey, England', *Château-Gaillard* ii (1967), pp. 100–5.

Royal Policy and Fortress Customs

Brown, R. A., 'Royal Castle-Building in England, 1154–1216', *English Historical Review* lxx (1955), pp. 353–98.

———, 'A List of Castles, 1154–1216', *English Historical Review* lxxiv (1959), pp. 249–80.

Coulson, C., 'Rendability and Castellation in Medieval France', *Château-Gaillard* vi (1973), pp. 59–67.

———, 'Fortresses and Social Responsibility in Late-Carolingian France', *Zeitschrift für Archäologie des Mittelalters* iv (1976), pp. 29–36.

———, 'Castellation in the County of Champagne in the Thirteenth Century', *Château-Gaillard* ix–x (1982), pp. 347–64.

———, 'The French Matrix of the Castle-Provisions of the Chester-Leicester Conventio', *Anglo-Norman Studies* xvii (1994), pp. 65–86.
———, 'The Sanctioning of Fortresses in France: "Feudal Anarchy" or Seigneurial Amity?', *Nottingham Medieval Studies* xlii (1998), pp. 38–104.
Kaeuper, R. W., *War, Justice and Public Order: England and France in the Later Middle Ages* (Oxford, 1988).

Garrisons and Castle-Guard

Ballard, A., 'Castle Guard and Barons' Houses', *English Historical Review* xxv (1910), pp. 712–15.
Hollister, C. W., *The Military Organization of Norman England* (Oxford 1965).
Lapsley, G. T., 'Some Castle Officers in the Twelfth Century', *English Historical Review* xxxiii (1918), pp. 348–59.
Moore, J., 'Anglo-Norman Garrisons', *Anglo-Norman Studies* xxii (2000), pp. 205–60.
Prestwich, M., 'The Garrisoning of English Medieval Castles', *The Normans and Their Adversaries at War: Essays in Memory of C. Warren Hollister*, ed. R. P. Abels and B. S. Bachrach (Woodbridge, 2001), pp. 185–200.
Round, J. H., 'Castle Guard', *Archaeological Journal* lix (1902), pp. 144–59.
———, 'The Staff of a Castle in the Twelfth Century', *English Historical Review* xxxv, (1920), pp. 90–7.
Stenton, F. M., *The First Century of English Feudalism 1066–1166*, 2nd edn (Oxford, 1961)
Suppe, F. C., *Military Institutions on the Welsh Marches, Shropshire, 1066–1300*, Studies in Celtic History XIV (Woodbridge, 1994).
———, 'The Persistence of Castle-Guard in the Welsh Marches and Wales: Suggestions for a Research Agenda and Methodology', *The Normans and Their Adversaries at War: Essays in Memory of C. Warren Hollister*, ed. R. P. Abels and B. S. Bachrach (Woodbridge, 2001), pp. 201–21.

Masonry Castles and Seigneurial Dwellings

Blair, J., 'Hall and Chamber: English Domestic Planning 1000–1250', *Manorial Buildings in England and Northern France*, ed. G. Meirion-Jones and M. Jones (London, Society of Antiquaries Occasional Papers vol. 15, 1993), pp. 1–21.
Curnow, P., 'Some Developments in Military Architecture *c.*1200: Le Coudray-Salbart', *Proceedings of the Battle Conference* ii (1979), pp. 42–62.
Dixon, P., 'The Donjon of Knaresborough: the Castle as Theatre', *Château-Gaillard* xiv (1990), pp. 121–39.
———, 'Design in Castle Building: The Controlling of Access to the Lord', *Château-Gaillard* xviii (1998), pp. 47–56.
Dixon, P. and Marshall, P., 'The Great Tower at Hedingham Castle: A Reassessment', *Fortress* xviii (1993), pp. 16–23.
———, 'The Great Tower in the Twelfth Century: The Case of Norham Castle', *Archaeological Journal* cl (1993), pp. 410–32.
Faulkner, P. A., 'Domestic Planning from the Twelfth to the Fourteenth Centuries', *Archaeological Journal* cxv (1958), pp. 150–83.
Fernie, E., 'Saxons, Normans and their Buildings', *Anglo-Norman Studies* xxi (1999), pp. 1–9.

Gem, R., 'Lincoln Minster: ecclesia pulchra, ecclesia fortis', *Medieval Art and Architecture at Lincoln Cathedral* (British Archaeological Association Conference Transactions for 1982), pp. 9–28.

Gravett, C., 'Kitchens and Keeps: Domestic Facilities in Norman Castles', *Royal Armouries Yearbook* iii (1998), pp. 168–75.

Grenville, J., *Medieval Housing* (Leicester, 1997).

Heslop, T. A., 'Orford Castle: Nostalgia and Sophisticated Living', *Architectural History* xxxiv (1991), pp. 36–58.

———, *Norwich Castle Keep: Romanesque Architecture and Social Context* (Norwich, 1994).

———, ' "Weeting Castle", A Twelfth-Century Hall House in Norfolk', *Architectural History* xliii (2000), pp. 42–57.

Impey, E., 'Seigneurial Domestic Architecture in Normandy, 1050–1350', *Manorial Buildings in England and Northern France*, ed. G. Meirion-Jones and M. Jones (Society of Antiquaries Occasional Papers vol. 15, London, 1993), pp. 82–120.

———, 'The Buildings on the Motte at Kilpeck Castle, Herefordshire', *Archaeologia Cambrensis* cxlvi (1997), pp. 101–8.

———, 'The Seigneurial Residence in Normandy: An Anglo-Norman Tradition?', *Medieval Archaeology* xliii (1999), pp. 45–73.

Impey, E. and Parnell, G., *The Tower of London: The Official Illustrated History* (London, 2000).

Kenyon, J. and Thompson, M., 'The Origin of the Word "keep" ', *Medieval Archaeology*, xxxviii (1994), pp. 175–76.

Leyland, M., 'The Origins and Development of Durham Castle', *Anglo-Norman Durham 1093–1193*, ed. D. Rollason, M. Harvey and M. Prestwich (Woodbridge, 1994), pp. 407–24.

Longley, D., 'The Royal Courts of the Welsh Princes of Gwynedd AD 400–1283', *Landscape and Settlement in Medieval Wales*, ed. N. Edwards (Oxford, 1997), pp. 41–54.

Marshall, P., 'The Twelfth-Century Castle at Newark', *Southwell and Nottinghamshire: Medieval Art, Architecture and Industry*, ed. J. S. Alexander (British Archaeological Association Conference Proceedings, 1998), pp. 110–25.

Murphy, K., 'The Castle and Borough of Wiston, Pembrokeshire', *Archaeologia Cambrensis* cxliv (1995), pp. 71–102.

Quiney, A., 'Hall or Chamber? That is the Question: the Use of Rooms in post-Conquest Houses', *Architectural History* xlii (1999), pp. 24–46.

Shoesmith, R. and Johnson, A. (eds), *Ludlow Castle: its History and Buildings* (Almeley, 2000).

Stocker, D. and Vince, A., 'The Early Norman Castle at Lincoln and a Re-evaluation of the Original West Tower of Lincoln Cathedral', *Medieval Archaeology* xli (1997), pp. 223–33.

Thompson, M. W., *Farnham Castle Keep, Surrey* (London, 1987).

———, 'Another "proto-keep" at Walmer, Kent', *Medieval Archaeology* xxxix (1995), pp. 174–76.

———, 'Keep or Country House', *Fortress* xii (1992), pp. 13–22.

———, 'A Suggested Dual Origin for Keeps', *Fortress* xv (1992), pp. 3–15.

———, *The Medieval Hall: The Basis of Secular Domestic Life, 600–1600 AD* (Aldershot, 1995).

White, P., 'Castle Gateways During the Reign of Henry II', *Antiquaries Journal* lxxvi (1996), pp. 241–47.

Palaces

Biddle, M., *Wolvesey: The Old Bishop's Palace, Winchester* (London, 1986).
Blair, J., 'The Twelfth-Century Bishop's Palace at Hereford', *Medieval Archaeology* xxxi (1987), pp. 59–72.
James, T. B., *The Palaces of Medieval England* (London, 1990).
Keevil, G. D., *Medieval Palaces: An Archaeology* (Stroud, 2000).
Rahtz, P., *The Saxon and Medieval Palaces at Cheddar* (BAR British Series 65, 1979).
Thompson, M. W, 'The Place of Durham among Norman Episcopal Palaces and Castles', *Anglo-Norman Durham 1093–1193*, ed. D. Rollason, M. Harvey and M. Prestwich (Woodbridge, 1994), pp. 425–36.
———, *Medieval Bishops' Houses in England and Wales* (Aldershot, 1998).

Siege Weapons, Strategy and Tactics

Bachrach, B., 'Fortifications and Military Tactics: Fulk Nerra's Strongholds circa 1000', *Technology and Culture* xx (1979), pp. 531–49.
———, 'The Angevin Strategy of Castle-Building in the Reign of Fulk Nerra, 987–1040', *American Historical Review* lxxxviii (1983), pp. 533–60.
———, 'Medieval Siege Warfare – a Reconnaissance', *Journal of Military History*, lviii (1994), pp. 119–33.
Beeler, J. H., 'Castles and Strategy in Norman and Angevin England', *Speculum* xxi (1956), pp. 581–601.
———, *Warfare in England 1066–1189* (New York, 1966).
Bradbury, J., *The Medieval Siege* (Woodbridge, 1992).
Contamine, P., *La Guerre au Moyen Âge* (Paris, 1980), trans M. Jones, *War in the Middle Ages* (Oxford 1984).
Corfis, I. A. and Wolfe, M. (eds), *The Medieval City Under Siege* (Woodbridge, 1995).
Gillingham, J., 'William the Bastard at War', *Anglo-Norman Warfare*, ed. M Strickland (Woodbridge, 1992), pp. 143–60.
———, 'Richard I and the Science of War in the Middle Ages', *Anglo-Norman Warfare*, ed. M. Strickland (Woodbridge, 1992), pp. 194–207.
Gillmor, C. M., 'The Introduction of the Traction Trebuchet into the Latin West', *Viator* xii (1981) pp. 1–8.
Goodall, J., 'Dover Castle and the Great Siege of 1216', *Château-Gaillard* xix (2000), pp. 91–102.
Gravett, C., 'Siege Warfare in Orderic Vitalis', *Royal Armouries Yearbook* v (2000), pp. 139–47.
Hill, D. R., 'Trebuchets', *Viator* iv (1973), pp. 99–114.
Hooper, N. and Bennett, M., *The Cambridge Illustrated Atlas of Warfare: The Middle Ages, 768–1487* (Cambridge, 1996).
Kenyon, J., 'Fluctuating Frontiers: Normanno-Welsh Castle Warfare *c.*1075 to 1240', *Château-Gaillard* xvii (1996), pp. 119–26.
Morillo, S., *Warfare Under the Anglo-Norman Kings, 1066–1135* (Woodbridge, 1994).
Prestwich, M., *Armies and Warfare in the Middle Ages: the English Experience* (New Haven, 1996).
Renn, D., 'Castle Fortification in England and adjoining countries from 1150 to 1250', *Le Château Médiéval et la Guerre dans l'Europe du Nord-Ouest: Mutations et Adaptations*, ed. A. Salamagne and R. Le Jan (Lille, 1998), pp. 53–60.

Speight, S., 'Castle Warfare in the *Gesta Stephani*', *Château-Gaillard* xix (2000), pp. 269–74.

Spurrell, M., 'Containing Wallingford Castle, 1146–1153', *Oxoniensia* lx (1995), pp. 257–70.

Strickland, M., 'Securing the North: Invasion and the Strategy of Defence in Twelfth-Century Anglo-Scottish Warfare', *Anglo-Norman Warfare*, ed. M. Strickland (Woodbridge, 1992), pp. 208–29.

———, *Warfare and Chivalry: The Conduct and Perception of Warfare in England and Normandy 1066–1217* (Cambridge, 1996).

Turvey, R., 'The Defences of Twelfth-Century Deheubarth and the Castle Strategy of the Lord Rhys', *Archaeologia Cambrensis* cxliv (1995), pp. 103–32.

Crusader Castles

Boase, T. S. R., *Castles and Churches of the Crusading Kingdom* (Oxford, 1967).

———, *Kingdoms and Strongholds of the Crusaders* (London, 1971).

Dean, B., *The Crusaders' Fortress of Montfort* (Jerusalem, 1982).

Deschamps, P., *Les Châteaux des Croisés en Terre Sainte*, 3 vols (Paris, 1934–73 (1977)).

Kennedy, H., *Crusader Castles* (Cambridge, 1994).

Lawrence, T. E., *Crusader Castles*, ed. R. D. Pringle (Oxford, 1988).

Marshall, C., *Warfare in the Latin East 1192–1291* (Cambridge, 1992).

Müller-Wiener., W., *Castles of the Crusaders* (London, 1966).

Pringle, R. D., *The Red Tower* (London, 1986).

———, 'Crusader Castles: the First Generation', *Fortress* i (1989), pp. 14–25.

———, 'Architecture in the Latin East, 1098–1571', in J. Riley-Smith (ed.), *The Oxford Illustrated History of the Crusades* (Oxford, 1995), pp. 160–83.

———, 'A Castle in the Sand: Mottes in the Crusader East', *Château-Gaillard* 18 (1998), pp. 187–91.

Rogers, R., *Latin Siege Warfare in the Twelfth Century* (Oxford, 1992).

Smail, R. C., *Crusading Warfare (1097–1193)*, 2nd edn, intr. C. Marshall (Cambridge 1995).

Castles as Settlements

Austin, D., 'The Castle and the Landscape', *Landscape History* vi (1984), pp. 69–81.

Barley, M. W., 'Town Defences in England and Wales after 1066', *The Plans and Topography of Medieval Towns in England and Wales*, ed. M. W. Barley (London, 1976), pp. 57–71.

Barton, K. J. and Holden, E. W., 'Excavations at Bramber Castle, Sussex, 1966–67', *Archaeological Journal* cxxxiv (1977), pp. 11–79.

Beresford, M., *New Towns of the Middle Ages: Town Plantation in England, Wales and Gascony* (repr. Stroud, 1988).

Bond, C. J., 'Anglo-Saxon and Medieval Defences', *Urban Archaeology in Britain*, ed. J. Schofield and R. Leech (London, 1987), pp. 92–116.

Everson, P., 'Delightfully Surrounded with Woods and Ponds: Field Evidence for Medieval Gardens in Britain', *There by Design: Field Archaeology in Parks and Gardens*, ed. P. Patterson (Oxford, 1998), pp. 32–38.

Everson, P., Brown, G. and Stocker, D., 'The Castle Earthworks and Landscape Context',

Ludgershall Castle, Excavations by P. Addyman 1964–72, ed. P. Ellis (Wiltshire Archaeological and Natural History Society Monograph Series, ii, 2000), pp. 97–119.

Gilchrist, R., *Gender and Archaeology: Contesting the Past* (London, 1999).

Hughes, M., 'Hampshire Castles and the Landscape', *Landscape History* xi (1989), pp. 27–60.

Hunt, J., *Lordship and Landscape: a Documentary and Archaeological Study of the Honour of Dudley c.1066–1322* (Oxford, 1997).

Landsberg, S., *The Medieval Garden* (London, 1995).

Liddiard, R., 'Castle Rising, Norfolk: A "Landscape of Lordship?" ', *Anglo-Norman Studies* xxii (2000), pp. 169–86.

———, *Landscapes of Lordship: The Castle and the Countryside in Medieval Norfolk, 1066–1200* (Oxford, 2000).

Murphy, K., 'Small Boroughs in south-west Wales: their Planning, Early Development and Defences', *Landscape and Settlement in Medieval Wales*, ed. N. Edwards (Oxford, 1997), pp. 139–56.

Palliser, D. M., 'Town Defences in Medieval England and Wales', *The Medieval Military Revolution*, ed. A. Ayton and J. Price (London, 1995), pp. 105–20.

Radford, C. A. R., 'The Later Pre-Conquest Boroughs and Their Defences', *Medieval Archaeology* xiv (1970), pp. 83–103.

Taylor, C., 'Medieval Ornamental Landscapes', *Landscapes* i (2000), pp. 38–55.

Schofield, J. and Vince, A., *Medieval Towns* (Leicester, 1994).

Thompson, M. W., 'Associated Monasteries and Castles in the Middle Ages: a Tentative List', *Archaeological Journal* cxliii (1986), pp. 305–21.

Turner, H. L., *Town Defences in England and Wales. An Architectural and Documentary Study AD 900–1500* (London, 1971).

List of Castles mentioned in the text

England and Wales

Angelsey
Aberlleiniog
Beaumaris

Bedfordshire
Bedford

Berkshire
Brightwell
Faringdon
Wallingford
Windsor

Brecknockshire
Brecon

Caernarfonshire
Bangor
Caernarfon
Conway
Degannwy

Cambridgeshire
Burwell
Cambridge

Cardiganshire
Baenporth
Cardigan
Humphrey's Castle
Llanrhystud
Tan-y-castell (Old Aberystwyth)
Ystrad Meurig
Ystrad Peithyll

Carmarthanshire
Carmarthan
Dinefwr
Kidwelly
Llandovery
Llangadog
Llansteffan

Cheshire
Beeston
Chester

Cornwall
Launceston

Cumberland
Carlisle
Cliffe

Denbighshire
Ruthin
Tomen y Rhodwydd

Derbyshire
Harestan
Peak

Devon
Exeter
Lydford

Dorset
Corfe
Sherborne

Durham
Barnard
Durham
Hylton
Low Dinsdale

Essex
Castle Hedingham
Colchester
Hadley
Knepp
Pleshey
Saffron Walden

Flintshire
Mold
Rhuddlan

Glamorgan
Cardiff
Kenefig
Llantrithyd
Loughor
Neath
Ogmore
Swansea

Gloucestershire
Berkeley
Beverstone
Bristol
Cirencester
Gloucester
Sharpness
St Briavel's

Hampshire
Bentley
Bishop's Waltham
Lidelea
Merdon
Odiham
Portchester
Powderham
Southampton
Winchester
Wolvesey

Herefordshire
Clifford
Ewias Harold
Hereford
Richard's Castle
Wigmore

Hertfordshire
Bishop's Stortford
Hertford
Therfield

Kent
Canterbury
Chilham
Dover
Eynesford
Rochester
Tonbridge

Lancashire
Lancaster

Leicestershire
Kirby Muxloe
Leicester
Mountsorrel
Oakham
Sauvey

Lincolnshire
Castle Bytham
Kinardferry
Lincoln
Sleaford
Stamford

Merioneth
Cymer
Talybont
Tomen y mur

Middlesex and London
South Mimms
Tower of London

Monmouth
Abergavenny
Chepstow
Grosmont
Rumney
Skenfrith
White Castle

Montgomery
Hen Domen
Montgomery
Tafolwern
Welshpool

Norfolk
Castle Acre
Castle Rising
New Buckenham
Norwich
Old Buckenham

Northamptonshire
Fortheringay
Northampton
Rockingham

Northumberland
Alnwick
Bamburgh
Berwick
Harbottle
Hawick
Nafferton
Newcastle-on-Tyne
Norham
Prudhoe
Wark
Warkworth

Nottinghamshire
Cuckney
Newark
Nottingham

Oxfordshire
Ascot Doilly
Banbury
Crowmarsh Giffard
Deddington
Oxford

Pembrokeshire
Cilgerran
Pembroke
Tenby
Wiston

Radnorshire
Colwyn
Painscastle
Radnor

Shropshire
Bridgnorth
Clun
Ludlow
Oswestry
Redcastle
Shrewsbury
Stokesay
Whittington

Somerset
Castle Cary
Castle Neroche
Harptree
Taunton

Staffordshire
Newcastle-under-Lyme
Stafford

Suffolk
Bungay
Eye
Framlingham
Haughley
Orford
Walton

Surrey
Abinger
Farnham
Guildford
Reigate

Sussex
Arundel
Bodiam
Bramber
Hastings
Herstmonceux
Pevensey

Yorkshire
Aldborough
Bowes
Carlton
Catterick
Cotherstone
Fleetham
Howe Hill
Hutton Conyers
Huningsore
Killerby
Knaresborough
Middleham
Pickhill
Richmond
Sandal
Scarborough
Tadcaster
Tickhill
Topcliffe
Yafforth
York
Violet Grange
William's Hill

Warwickshire
Brandon
Coventry
Kenilworth
Tamworth

Wiltshire
Cricklade
Devizes
Downton
Ludgershall
Marlborough
Malmesbury
Old Sarum
Salisbury
Trowbridge

Worcestershire
Hanley
Worcester

France

Aisne
Quierzy

Calvados
Bayeux
Le Plessis-Grimoult
Vignats

Côtes-du-Nord
Dinan

Eure
Andely
Beaumont-le-Roger
Breteuil
Brionne
Château-Gaillard
Conches
Évreux
Gaillon
Montfort-sur-Risle
Noget-le-Roi
Port-Audemer
Radepont
Portes
Ivry-la-Bataille
Vaudreuil

Ille-ete-Vilaine
Dangeul
Dol
Rennes

Indre-et-Loire
Loches
Montbazon

Loiret
Pithiviers (Yèvre-le-Châtel)

Manche
Mortain
Semilly

Maine-et-Loire
Montreuil

Mayenne
Sainte-Suzanne

Orne
Alençon
Almenèches
Bellême
Domfront
L'Aigle
Le Renouard
Montreuil-en-Houlme
Saint-Céneri

Pas-de-Calais
Ardres

Sarthe
Le Mans

Seine-et-Marne
Provins

Seine-et-Oise
Bréval
Étamps
Houdan

Seine-Maritime
Arques-la-Bataille
Mirville

Vienne
Mirebeau

Ireland

Antrim
Carrickfergus

Cavan
Belturbet

Down
Baliynarry
Castleskreen
Lismahon
Narrow Water
Rathmullan

Dublin
Dublin

Limerick
Adare

Meath
Trim

Monaghan
Clones

Offaly
Birr
Clonmacnois
Durrow
Kinnity

Tipperary
Nenagh
Roscrea

Westmeath
Althone

Rhineland

der Husterknupp

Scotland

Berwickshire
Lauder

Dumfriesshire
Dumfries
Lochmaben

East Lothian
Castle Hill, North Berwick
Direlton
Eldbotle

Kirkcudbrightshire
Buittle
Kirkcudbright

Midlothian
Edinburgh

Peeblesshire
Peebles

Roxburghshire
Jedburgh
Riddell
Roxburgh

Selkirkshire
Selkirk

Wigtownshire
Wigtown

Index

Page numbers in bold type indicate illustration or diagram